CHILTON BOOK COMPANY

REPAIR & TUNE-UP GUIDE

CHEVROLET GMC VANS 1967-86

All U.S. and Canadian models of 1/2, 3/4 and 1 ton Vans, including Cutaway, Motor Home Chassis and diesel engines

President LAWRENCE A. FORNASIERI
Vice President and General Manager JOHN P. KUSHNERICK
Editor-in-Chief KERRY A. FREEMAN, S.A.E.
Senior Editor RICHARD J. RIVELE, S.A.E.
Editor MICHAEL A. NEWSOME

CHILTON BOOK COMPANY
Radnor, Pennsylvania
19089

SAFETY NOTICE

Proper service and repair procedures are vital to the safe, reliable operation of all motor vehicles, as well as the personal safety of those performing repairs. This book outlines procedures for servicing and repairing vehicles using safe, effective methods. The procedures contain many NOTES, CAUTIONS and WARNINGS which should be followed along with standard safety procedures to eliminate the possibility of personal injury or improper service which could damage the vehicle or compromise its safety.

It is important to note that repair procedures and techniques, tools and parts for servicing motor vehicles, as well as the skill and experience of the individual performing the work vary widely. It is not possible to anticipate all of the conceivable ways or conditions under which vehicles may be serviced, or to provide cautions as to all of the possible hazards that may result. Standard and accepted safety precautions and equipment should be used during cutting, grinding, chiseling, prying, or any other process that can cause material removal or projectiles.

Some procedures require the use of tools specially designed for a specific purpose. Before substituting another tool or procedure, you must be completely satisfied that neither your personal safety, nor the performance of the vehicle will be endangered.

Although the information in this guide is based on industry sources and is as complete as possible at the time of publication, the possibility exists that the manufacturer made later changes which could not be included here. While striving for total accuracy. Chilton Book Company cannot assume responsibility for any errors, changes, or omissions that may occur in the compilation of this data.

PART NUMBERS

Part numbers listed in this reference are not recommendations by Chilton for any product by brand name. They are references that can be used with interchange manuals and aftermarket supplier catalogs to locate each brand supplier's discrete part number.

SPECIAL TOOLS

Special tools are recommended by the vehicle manufacturer to perform their specific job. Use has been kept to a minimum, but where absolutely necessary, they are referred to in the text by the part number of the tool manufacturer. These tools can be purchased, under the appropriate part number, from the Service Tool Division, Kent-Moore Corporation, 29784 Little Mack, Roseville, MI 48066-2298, or an equivalent tool can be purchased locally from a tool supplier or parts outlet. Before substituting any tool for the one recommended, read the SAFETY NOTICE at the top of this page.

ACKNOWLEDGMENTS

Chilton Book Company expresses appreciation to the Chevrolet Motor Division, General Motors Corporation, Detroit, Michigan 48202; and GMC Truck and Coach Division, General Motors Corporation, Pontiac, Michigan 48053 for their generous assistance.

Information has been selected from Chevrolet and GMC shop manuals, owner's manuals, data books, brochures, service bulletins, and technical manuals.

Copyright © 1987 by Chilton Book Company
All Rights Reserved
Published in Radnor, Pennsylvania 19089 by Chilton Book Company

Manufactured in the United States of America
34567890 654321098

Chilton's Repair & Tune-Up Guide: Chevrolet/GMC Vans 1967–86
ISBN 0-8019-7751-7 pbk.
Library of Congress Catalog Card No. 86-47773

CONTENTS

1 General Information and Maintenance

2 Tune-Up and Performance Maintenance

3 Engine and Engine Overhaul

4 Emission Controls and Fuel System

5 Chassis Electrical

6 Drive Train

7 Suspension and Steering

8 Brakes

9 Body and Trim

10 Troubleshooting

11

Quick Reference Specifications For Your Vehicle

Fill in this chart with the most commonly used specifications for your vehicle. Specifications can be found in Chapters 1 through 3 or on the tune-up decal under the hood of the vehicle.

Tune-Up

Firing Order ______________________

Spark Plugs:

Type ______________________

Gap (in.) ______________________

Torque (ft. lbs.) ______________________

Idle Speed (rpm) ______________________

Ignition Timing (°) ______________________

Vacuum or Electronic Advance (Connected/Disconnected) ______________________

Valve Clearance (in.)

Intake ______________ **Exhaust** ______________

Capacities

Engine Oil Type (API Rating) ______________________

With Filter Change (qts) ______________________

Without Filter Change (qts) ______________________

Cooling System (qts) ______________________

Manual Transmission (pts) ______________________

Type ______________________

Automatic Transmission (pts) ______________________

Type ______________________

Front Differential (pts) ______________________

Type ______________________

Rear Differential (pts) ______________________

Type ______________________

Transfer Case (pts) ______________________

Type ______________________

FREQUENTLY REPLACED PARTS

Use these spaces to record the part numbers of frequently replaced parts.

PCV VALVE	OIL FILTER	AIR FILTER	FUEL FILTER
Type	Type	Type	Type
Part No.	Part No.	Part No.	Part No.

General Information and Maintenance

1

HOW TO USE THIS BOOK

Chilton's Repair and Tune-Up Guide for Chevrolet and GMC Vans is intended to help you learn more about your van and save you money on its upkeep and operation.

The first two chapters will be the most used, since they contain maintenance procedures and tune-up information. Chapters 3–9 nine deal with the more complex systems of your van. Systems from the engine through the brakes are covered to the extent that the average do-it-yourselfer can perform seemingly difficult operations with confidence. Chapter ten is devoted to troubleshooting and diagnosis. This book will give you detailed instruction how to change your van's brake pads and shoes, replace points and plugs and do many more jobs that will save you money and help avoid expensive problems.

This book can also be used as a reference for owners who want to understand their van and/or their mechanics better.

Before undertaking any repair, read through the entire procedure. This will give you the overall view of what tools and supplies will be requircd.

When the overhaul of the defective part is not considered practical, we tell you how to remove the old part and then how to install the new or rebuilt replacement. Rebuilt parts of excellent quality are, in most cases, readily available. These generally carry a guarantee similar to that of a new part. Inasmuch as the price of a new part and the quality is often comparable, the option to purchase a rebuilt part should not be overlooked.

When working on your van, remember that whenever the left side of the van is mentioned, it refers to the driver's side. The right side always refers to the passenger's side. The same applies to front and rear. Front is always toward the front of the van and rear is always toward the rear.

Safety must always be considered the most important aspect of working on any automobile. Constantly be aware of the danger involved when working on or underneath your van and take the proper precautions. (See the section in this chapter headed "Servicing Your Vehicle Safely" and the SAFETY NOTICE on the acknowledgment page.)

TOOLS AND EQUIPMENT

Naturally, without the proper tools and equipment it is impossible to properly service your vehicle. It would be impossible to catalog each tool that you would need to perform each operation in this book. It would also be unwise for the amateur to rush out and buy an expensive set of tools on the theory that he may need one or more of them at some time.

The best approach is to proceed slowly, putting together a good set of those tools which are used most frequently. Don't be misled by the low cost of bargain tools. It is far better to spend a little more for better quality. Forged wrenches, 12 point sockets and fine tooth ratchets are far preferable to their less expensive counterparts.

Begin accumulating those tools that are used most frequently; those associated with routine maintenance and tune-up.

In addition to the normal assortment of screwdrivers and pliers you should have the following tools for routine maintenance jobs:

1. SAE (or Metric) or SAE/Metric wrenches – sockets and combination open end/box end wrenches in sizes from 1/8" (3mm) to 3/4" (19mm) and a spark plug socket (13/16" or 5/8" depending on plug type).

If possible, but various length socket drive extensions. One break in this department is that the metric sockets available in the U.S. will all fit the ratchet handles and extensions you may already have.

2. Jackstands—for support and safety.
3. Oil filter wrench.
4. Oil filter spout—for pouring oil.
5. Grease gun—for chassis lubrication.

The second list of tools is for tune-ups. While the tools here are slightly more sophisticated, they're not necessarily expensive. There are several inexpensive tach/dwell meters available that are every bit as good for the average mechanic as the expensive professional model. Just be sure that it goes to at least 1,200–1,500 rpm on the tach scale and that it works on 4, 6 or 8 cylinder engines. Tune-up equipment could include:

1. Tach-dwell meter.
2. Spark plug wrench.
3. Timing light (a DC light that works from the van's battery is best, although an AC light that plugs into 110V house current will suffice at some sacrifice in brightness).
4. Wire spark plug gauge.
5. Set of feeler blades.

Here again, be guided by your own needs. A feeler blade will set the point gap as easily as a dwell meter will read dwell, but slightly less accurately.

In addition to these basic tools, there are several other tools and gauges you may find useful. These include:

1. A compression gauge. The screw-in type is slower to use, but eliminates the possibility of a faulty reading due to escaping pressure.
2. A manifold vacuum gauge.
3. A test light.
4. An induction meter. This is used for determining whether or not there is current in a wire. These are handy for use if a wire is broken somewhere in a wiring harness.

As a final note, you will probably find a torque wrench necessary for all but the most basic work. The beam type models are perfectly adequate, although the newer click type are more precise.

NOTE: *Special tools are occasionally necessary to perform a specific job or are recommended to make a job easier. Their use has been kept to a minimum, since they are not readily available for the do-it-yourself mechanic. When a special tool is indicated, it will be referred to by a manufacturer's part number, and, where possible, an illustration of the tool will be provided so that an equivalent tool may be used. When it is possible to perform the job with more commonly available tools, it will be pointed out, but occasionally, a special tool which was designed to perform a specific function should be used. Before substituting another tool, you should be convinced that neither your safety nor the performance of the vehicle will be compromised. Some special tools are available commercially from major tool manufacturers, others can be purchased from your dealer. A list of tool manufacturers and their addresses follows:*

Service Tool Division
Kent-Moore
29784 Little Mack
Roseville, MI 48066-2298

SERVICING YOUR VEHICLE SAFELY

It is virtually impossible to anticipate all of the hazards involved with automotive maintenance and service but care and common sense will prevent most accidents.

The rules of safety for mechanics range from "don't smoke around gasoline," to "use the proper tool for the job." The trick to avoiding injuries is to develop safe work habits and take every possible precaution.

Do's

• Do keep a fire extinguisher and first aid kit within easy reach.

• Do wear safety glasses or goggles when cutting, drilling, grinding or prying.

• Do shield your eyes whenever you work around the battery. Batteries contain sulphuric acid. In case of contact with the eyes or skin, flush the area with water or a mixture of water and baking soda and get medical attention immediately.

• Do use safety stands for any undercar service. Jacks are for raising vehicles; safety stands are for making sure the vehicle stays raised until you want it to come down. Whenever the vehicle is raised, block the wheels remaining on the ground and set the parking brake.

• Do disconnect the negative battery cable when working on the electrical system. The primary ignition system can contain up to 40,000 volts.

• Do properly maintain your tools. Loose hammerheads, mushroomed punches and chisels, frayed or poorly grounded electrical cords, excessively worn screwdrivers, spread wrenches (open end), cracked sockets, slipping ratchets, or faulty droplight sockets can cause accidents and injuries.

• Do use the proper size and type of tool for the job being done.

• Do, when possible, pull on a wrench handle rather than push on it, and adjust your stance to prevent a fall.

• Do be sure that adjustable wrenches are tightly adjusted on the nut or bolt and pulled so that the face is on the side of the fixed jaw.

• Do select a wrench or socket that fits the nut or bolt. The wrench or socket should sit straight, not cocked.

• Do strike squarely with a hammer—avoid glancing blows.

• Do set the parking brake and block the drive wheels if the work requires that the engine be running.

Don'ts

• Don't run an engine in a garage or anywhere else without proper ventilation—EVER! Carbon monoxide is poisonous. It takes a long time to leave the human body and you can build up a deadly supply of it in your system by simply breathing in a little every day. Always use power vents, windows, fans or open the garage doors.

• Don't work around moving parts while wearing a necktie or other loose clothing. Short sleeves are much safer than long, loose sleeves and hard toed shoes with neoprene soles protect your toes and give a better grip on slippery surfaces. Jewelry is not safe when working around a car. Long hair should be hidden under a hat or cap.

• Don't use pockets for toolboxes. A fall or bump can drive a screwdriver deep into your body. Even a wiping cloth hanging from the back pocket can wrap around a spinning shaft or fan.

• Don't smoke when working around gasoline, cleaning solvent or other flammable material.

• Don't smoke when working around the battery. When the battery is being charged, it gives off explosive hydrogen gas.

• Don't use gasoline to wash your hands. There are excellent soaps available. Gasoline may contain lead, and lead can enter the body through a cut, accumulating in the body until you are very ill. Gasoline also removes all the natural oils from the skin so that bone dry hands will absorb oil and grease.

• Don't service the air conditioning system unless you are equipped with the necessary tools and training. The refrigerant, R-12, is extremely cold and when exposed to the air, will instantly freeze any surface it comes in contact with, including your eyes. Although the refrigerant is normally non-toxic, R-12 becomes a deadly poisonous gas in the presence of an open flame. One good whiff of the vapors from burning refrigerant can be fatal.

SERIAL NUMBER IDENTIFICATION

Vehicle

The vehicle identification number (V.I.N.) on models through 1978 is on a plate fastened to the left door frame. On 1979 and later models, the V.I.N. plate is mounted on the driver's side of the instrument panel, and is visible through the windshield. The gross vehicle weight (GVW) or maximum safe total weight of the vehicle, cargo, and passengers is usually also given on the plate through 1978.

1967–69

The first letter is the chassis type: G for van. The second letter identifies the engine: S for 6-cyl. and E for V8. The first number gives the load capacity (GVW) range: 1 for under 5,600 lbs, 2 for over 5,500 lbs. The second and third numbers are the cab to axle measurement code. The fourth and fifth numbers (letters for GMC) are a body style code. The sixth number is the last digit of the model year: 9 for 1969. The next number indicates the assembly plant. The remaining numbers are the vehicle's individual serial number.

1970–71

The first letter is the chassis type: G for van. The second letter identifies the engine: S for 6-cyl. and E for V8. The first number gives the load capacity (GVW) range: 1 for under 5,500 lbs, 2 for 5,500–8,100 lbs, and 3 for 6,700–10,000 lbs. The next number or two numbers indicates the body style: 5 for van, 26 for Custom Sportvan, and 36 for Deluxe Sportvan. The next number is the last digit of the model year: as 1 for 1971. The next letter indicates the assembly plant. The remaining numbers are the vehicle's individual serial number.

1972–80

The first letter indicates a Chevrolet (C) or GMC (T) vehicle. The second letter is the chas-

Typical vehicle identification plate

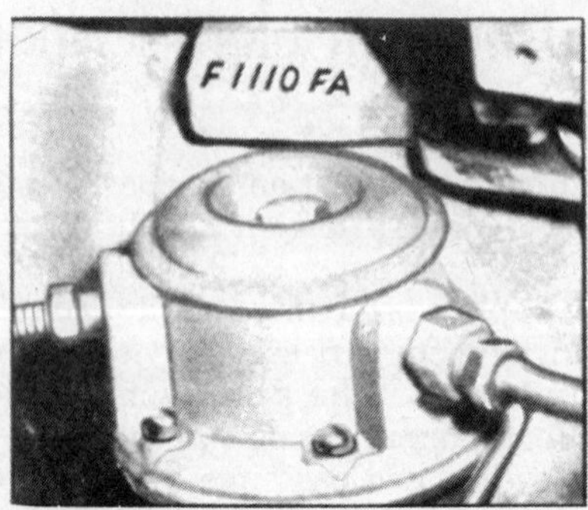

Six cylinder engine serial number

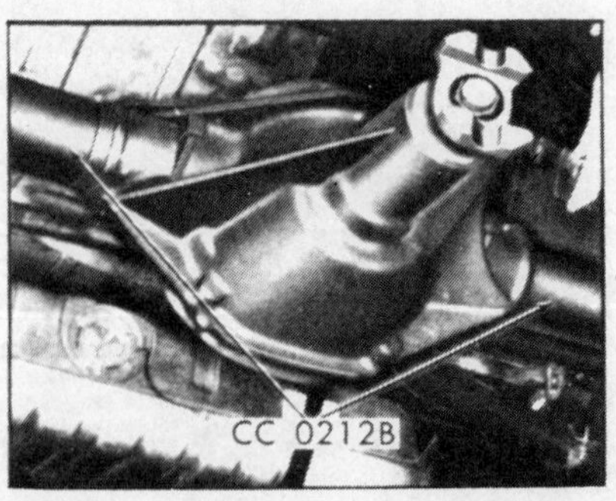

1974 and later rear axle serial number—on earlier models, it is on the bottom flange of the differential housing

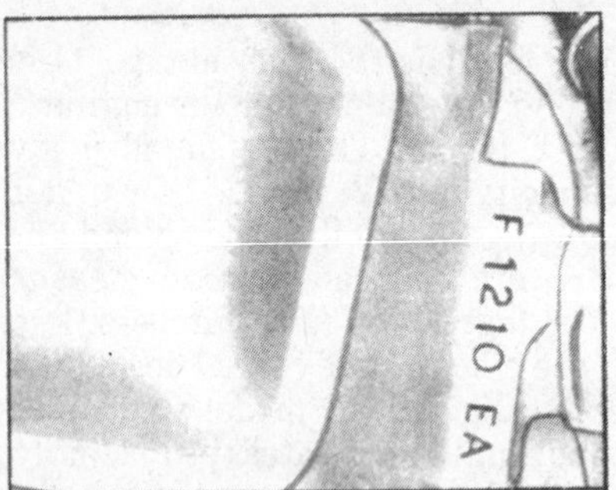

V8 engine serial number

Alternator serial number

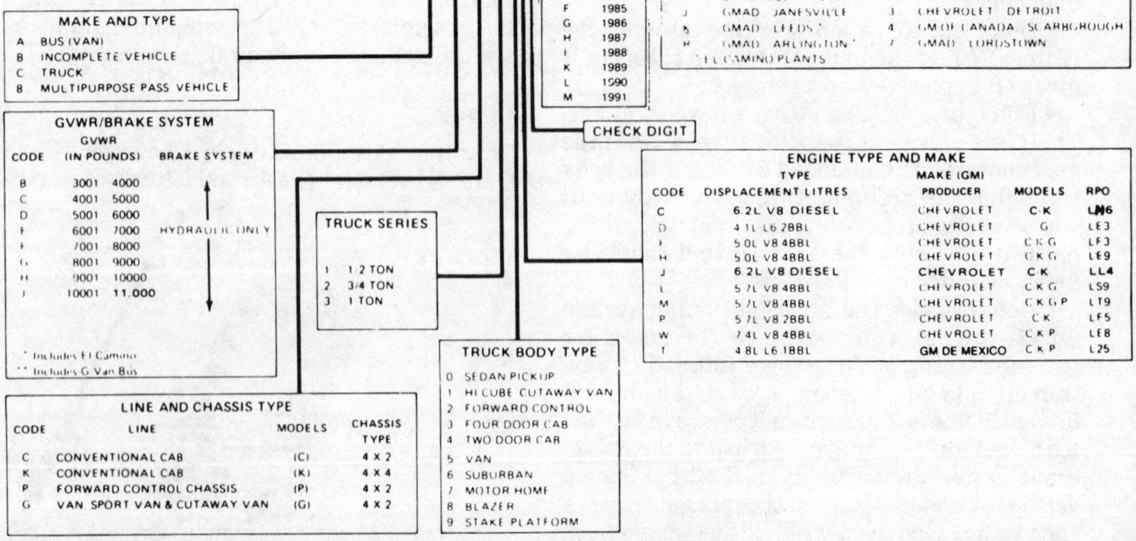

1GCEC14D9DF123456

NATION OF ORIGIN

Code	
1	USA
2	CANADA

MANUFACTURER

Code	
G	GENERAL MOTORS

MAKE AND TYPE

Code	
A	BUS (VAN)
B	INCOMPLETE VEHICLE
C	TRUCK
8	MULTIPURPOSE PASS VEHICLE

GVWR/BRAKE SYSTEM

CODE	GVWR (IN POUNDS)	BRAKE SYSTEM
B	3001 4000	HYDRAULIC ONLY
C	4001 5000	
D	5001 6000	
E	6001 7000	
F	7001 8000	
G	8001 9000	
H	9001 10000	
J	10001 11,000	

* Includes El Camino
** Includes G Van Bus

TRUCK SERIES

Code	
1	1/2 TON
2	3/4 TON
3	1 TON

LINE AND CHASSIS TYPE

CODE	LINE	MODELS	CHASSIS TYPE
C	CONVENTIONAL CAB	(C)	4 X 2
K	CONVENTIONAL CAB	(K)	4 X 4
P	FORWARD CONTROL CHASSIS	(P)	4 X 2
G	VAN, SPORT VAN & CUTAWAY VAN	(G)	4 X 2

TRUCK BODY TYPE

Code	
0	SEDAN PICKUP
1	HI CUBE CUTAWAY VAN
2	FORWARD CONTROL
3	FOUR DOOR CAB
4	TWO DOOR CAB
5	VAN
6	SUBURBAN
7	MOTOR HOME
8	BLAZER
9	STAKE PLATFORM

ENGINE TYPE AND MAKE

CODE	TYPE DISPLACEMENT LITRES	MAKE (GM) PRODUCER	MODELS	RPO
C	6.2L V8 DIESEL	CHEVROLET	C·K	LH6
D	4.1L L6 2BBL	CHEVROLET	G	LE3
F	5.0L V8 4BBL	CHEVROLET	C K G	LF3
H	5.0L V8 4BBL	CHEVROLET	C K G	LE9
J	6.2L V8 DIESEL	CHEVROLET	C·K	LL4
L	5.7L V8 4BBL	CHEVROLET	C K G	LS9
M	5.7L V8 4BBL	CHEVROLET	C K G P	LT9
P	5.7L V8 2BBL	CHEVROLET	C K	LF5
W	7.4L V8 4BBL	CHEVROLET	C K P	LE8
T	4.8L L6 1BBL	GM DE MEXICO	C K P	L25

CHECK DIGIT

MODEL YEAR

B	1981
C	1982
D	1983
E	1984
F	1985
G	1986
H	1987
J	1988
K	1989
L	1990
M	1991

ASSEMBLY PLANT

CODE	ASSEMBLY PLANT	CODE	ASSEMBLY PLANT
A	GMAD LAKEWOOD	S	GMAD ST. LOUIS
B	GMAD BALTIMORE	V	GMT & C PONTIAC
D	GMAD DORAVILLE	Z	GMAD FREMONT *
F	CHEVROLET FLINT	1	GM OF CANADA OSHAWA
J	GMAD JANESVILLE	3	CHEVROLET DETROIT
K	GMAD LEEDS *	4	GM OF CANADA SCARBOROUGH
R	GMAD ARLINGTON *	7	GMAD LORDSTOWN

* EL CAMINO PLANTS

PLANT SEQUENTIAL NUMBER

17-digit VIN, 1981 and later models

sis type: G for van. The third letter identifies the engine. For 1972, it was S for 6-cyl. and E for V8. For 1973 80, it is:

- Q – 250 six through 1975
- D – 250 six from 1976
- N – 262 4 bbl V6
- T – 292 six
- U – 305 V8
- X – 307 V8
- V – 350 2 bbl V8
- Y, L – 350 4 bbl V8
- U – 400 V8 through 1976
- R – 400 V8 from 1977

The first number gives the load capacity range: 1 for ½ ton, 2 for ¾ ton, and 3 for 1 ton. The second number is 5 for van body. The third number is the last digit of the model year: as 6 for 1976. The next letter indicates the assembly plant. The remaining numbers are the vehicle's individual serial number.

1981 and Later

Beginning in 1981 a new 17 digit code is used. The interpretation is the same as previous years except that the engine code is the eighth digit. Additional engines/codes include the 305 V8 (F and H codes); a 350 V8 (P code); a W-code 454 V8 and a Chevrolet built 379 cu. in. V8 diesel, in both C and J codes.

Engine

The engine number is located as follows:

- 6 Cylinder: On a pad on the right hand side of the cylinder block, at the rear of the distributor.

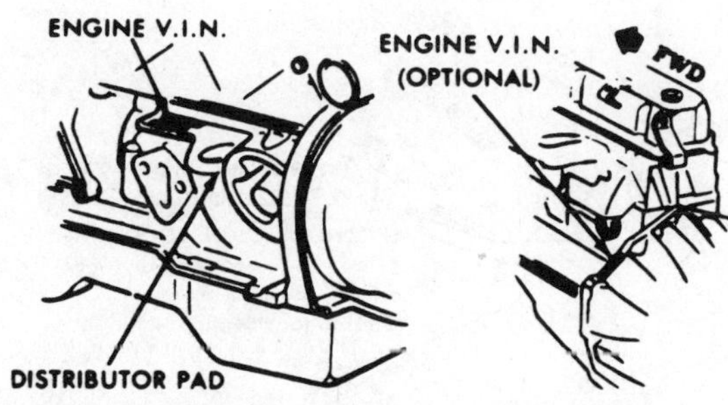

VIN location, inline sixes

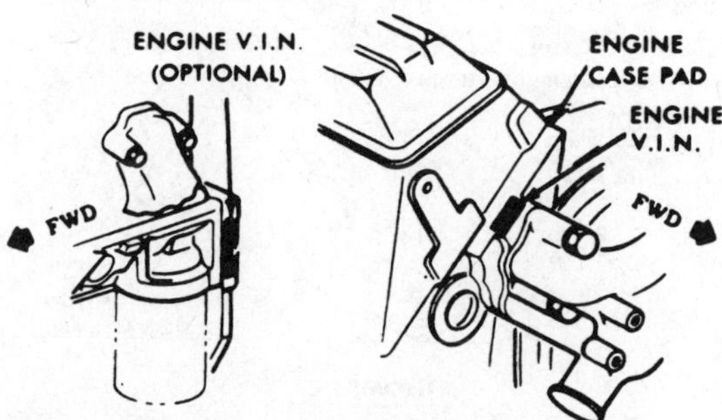

Gasoline V8 engine VIN location

379 diesel engine VIN locations

- V8: The engine number is found on a pad at the front of the right side cylinder head.

The engine number is broken down as follows:

Example – F1210TFA

- F – Manufacturing Plant. F-Flint and T-Tonawanda
- 12 – Month of Manufacture (December)
- 10 – Day of Manufacturer (Tenth)
- T – (1970 and later) Truck engine
- FA – Transmission and Engine Combination

Transmission

The Muncie or Saginaw 3-speed manual transmission serial number is located on the lower left side of the case adjacent to the rear of the cover. The 3-speed Tremec transmission has the number on the upper forward mounting flange.

The 4-speed transmission is numbered on the rear of the case, above the output shaft. The Turbo Hydra-Matic 350 serial number is on the right rear vertical surface on the fluid pan. The Turbo Hydra-Matic 400 is identified by a light blue plate attached to the right side, which is stamped with the serial number. The Powerglide transmission (through 1972 only)

Early 3- and 4-speed Saginaw serial number identification

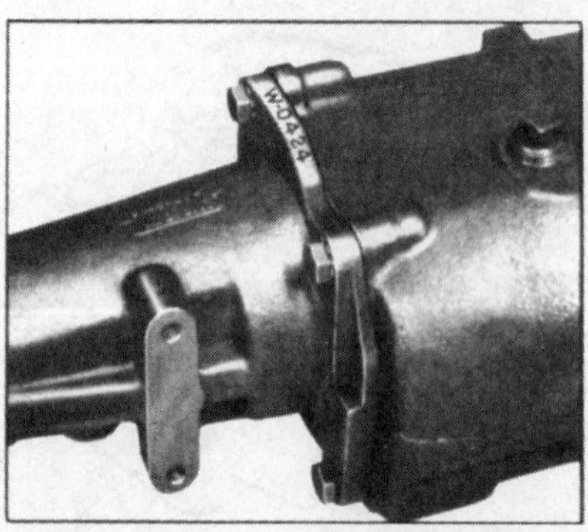

Borg-Warner transmission serial number—on the boss at the right rear of the extension housing

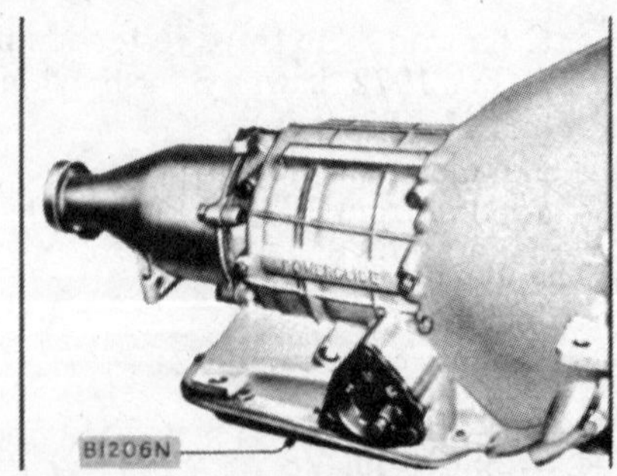

Powerglide transmission serial number

Starter motor serial number

Early Turbo Hydra-Matic serial number identification

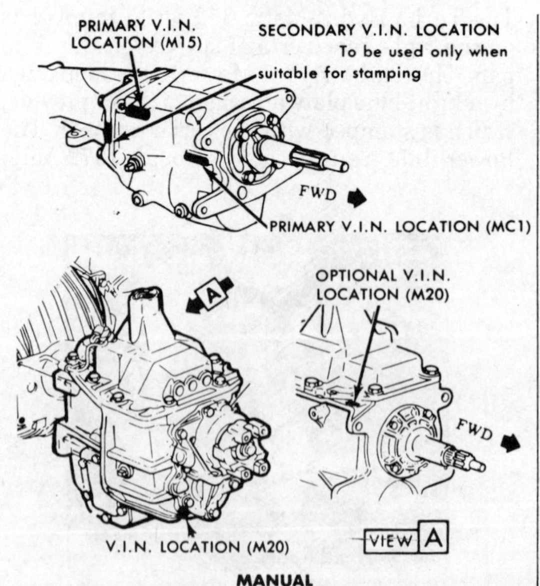

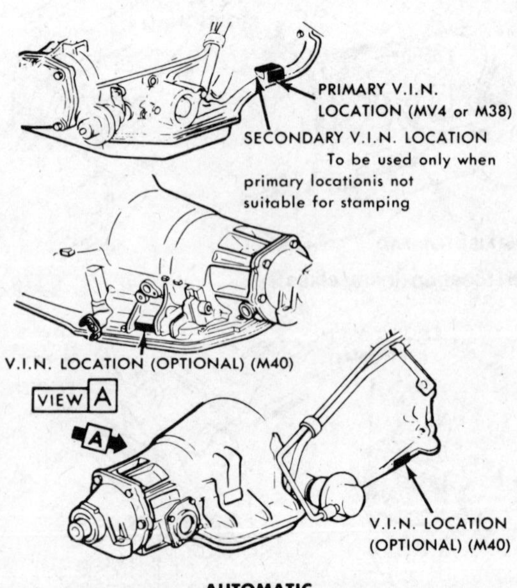

Later transmission serial number identification

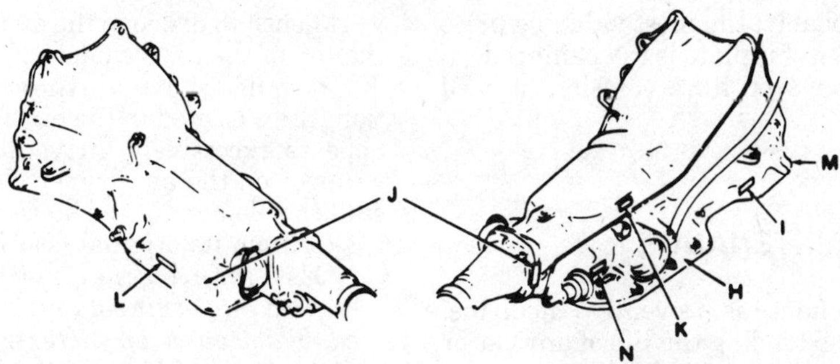

H. THM 350C stamped I.D. location
I. THM 350C VIN location
J. THM 350C optional VIN locations
K. THM 400 I.D. tag location
L. THM 400 VIN location
M. THM 700-R4 stamped I.D. location
N. THM 700-R4 VIN location

Turbo Hydra-Matic 350, 400, and 700 series I.D. locations

is stamped in the same location as the Turbo Hydra-Matic 350.

Drive Axle

The drive axle serial number is stamped on the axle shaft housing, where it connects to the differential housing, on 1974 and later models. On 1974 and earlier models the drive axle serial number is located on the bottom flange of the differential housing.

Rear axle serial number location

Service Parts Identification Plate

The service parts identification plate, commonly known as the option list, is usually located on the inside of the glove compartment door. On some vans, you may have to look for it on an inner fender panel. The plate lists the vehicle serial number, wheelbase, all regular production options (RPOs) and all special

SERVICE PARTS IDENTIFICATION

SERIAL # PAINT SE #

NOTE: THE SPECIAL EQUIPMENT LISTED BELOW HAS BEEN INSTALLED ON THIS VEHICLE. FOR PROPER IDENTIFICATION OF REPLACEMENT PARTS BE SURE TO SPECIFY THE APPLICABLE OPTION NUMBERS.

OPTION NO.	DESCRIPTION	OPTION NO.	DESCRIPTION

IMPORTANT: RETAIN THIS PLATE AS A PERMANENT RECORD

Service parts identification plate

equipment. Probably, the most valuable piece of information on this plate is the paint code, a useful item when you have occasion to need paint.

ROUTINE MAINTENANCE

Routine maintenance is preventive medicine. It is the key to extending the life of any car or truck. By getting into the habit of doing some quick and simple checks once a week, you'll be surprised how easy it is to keep your van in tiptop shape. It will also give you a greater awareness of the workings of your van.

By taking the time to check the engine oil, transmission fluid, battery and coolant level and the brake fluid regularly, you'll find yourself with a meticulously maintained van. You'll also be able to spot any developing problems (like a slow leak in the radiator) before they become expensive repairs. Try to check all the hinges and keep them well lubricated, too. Routine maintenance really does pay off.

The Maintenance Intervals chart gives the maintenance intervals recommended by the manufacturer.

Air Cleaner

REMOVAL AND INSTALLATION

Paper Element Type

Loosen the wing nut on top of the cover and remove the cover. The element should be replaced when it has become oil saturated or filled with dirt. If the filter is equipped with a foam wrapper, remove the wrapper and wash it in kerosene or similar solvent. Shake or blot dry. Saturate the wrapper in engine oil and squeeze it tightly in an absorbent towel to remove the excess oil.

Leave the wrapper moist. Clean the dirt from the filter by lightly tapping it against a workbench to dislodge the dirt particles. Wash the top of the air cleaner housing and wipe it dry. If equipped, replace the crankcase ventilation filter, located in the air filter housing if it appears excessively dirty. Replace the oiled wrapper on the air cleaner element and reinstall the element in the housing, repositioning it 180° from its original position.

NOTE: *Inverting the air cleaner cover for increased intake air volume is not recommended. This causes an increase in intake noise, faster dirt buildup in both the air cleaner element and the crankcase ventilation filter, and poor cold weather driveability.*

Oil Bath Type

To service the optional (through 1971) oil bath type air cleaner, remove the wing nut at the top and remove the cover and element. Drain all of the oil from the reservoir. Clean all of the parts and dry thoroughly, but do not use compressed air on the element.

Reinstall the reservoir and fill to the mark with SAE 50 engine oil (above freezing) or SAE 20 engine oil (below freezing). Install the element in the reservoir and replace the cover and tighten the wing nut.

Fuel Filter

REMOVAL AND INSTALLATION

Gasoline Engines

The fuel filter should be serviced at the interval given on the Maintenance Interval chart. Two types of fuel filters are used, a bronze type and a paper element type. Inline fuel filters may be used on some engines which should be changed at the same time as the filter in the carburetor body. Filter replacement should be attempted only when the engine is cold. Additionally, it is a good idea to place some absorbent rags under the fuel fittings to catch the

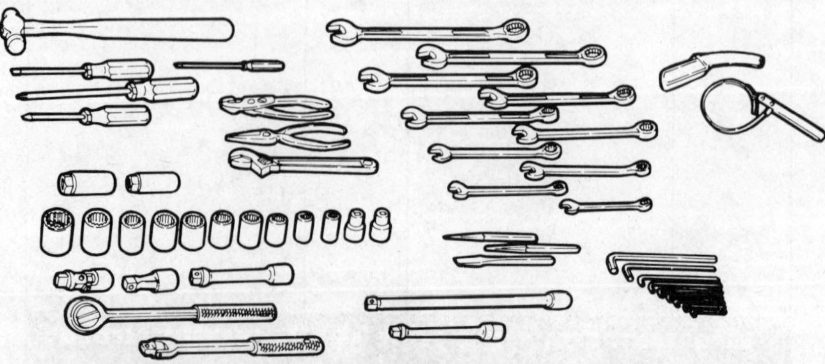

Some of the tools you'll need for routine maintenance

PAPER ELEMENT
OIL BATH

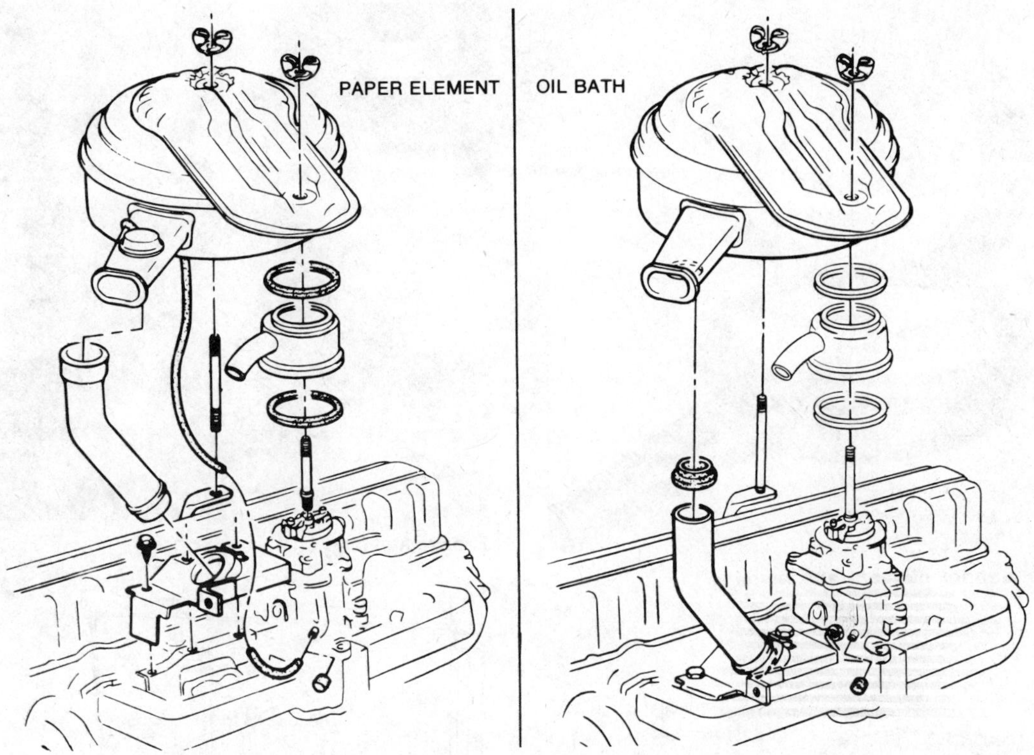

Typical six cylinder air cleaner

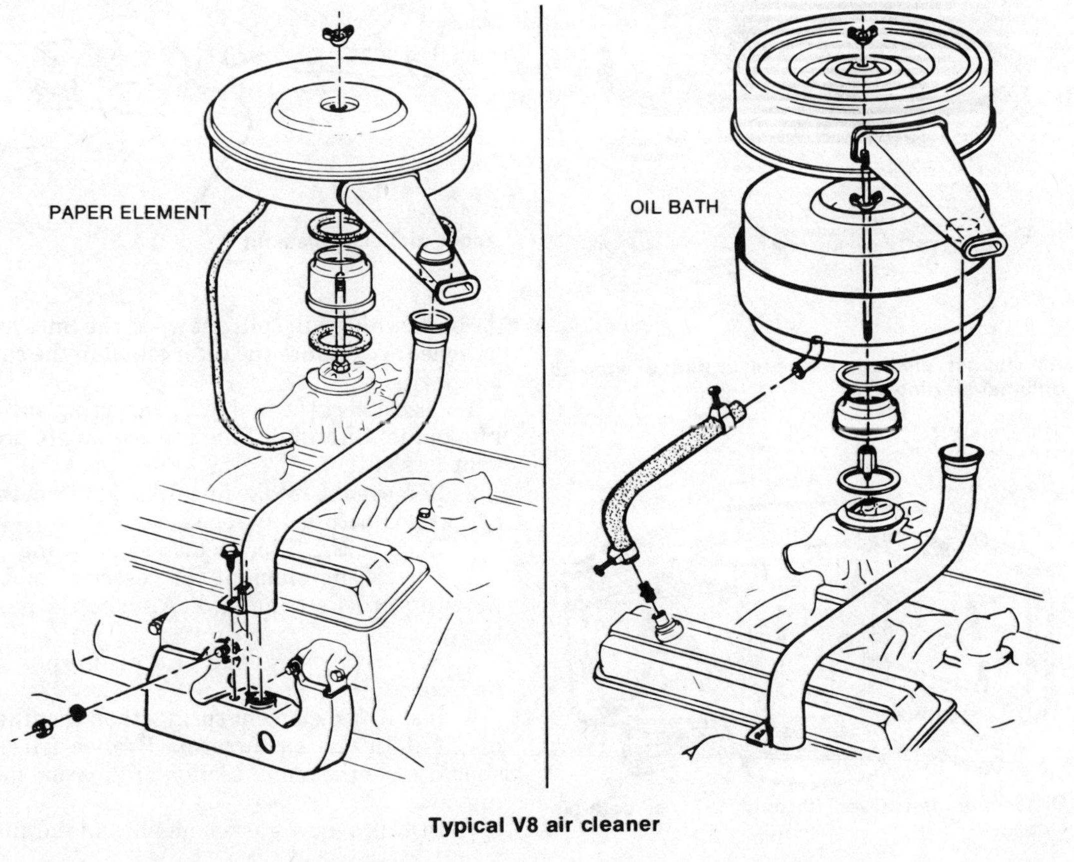

PAPER ELEMENT
OIL BATH

Typical V8 air cleaner

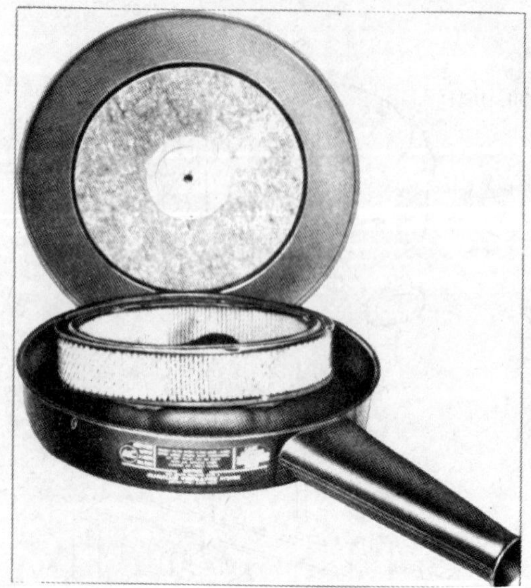

Air cleaner element and housing

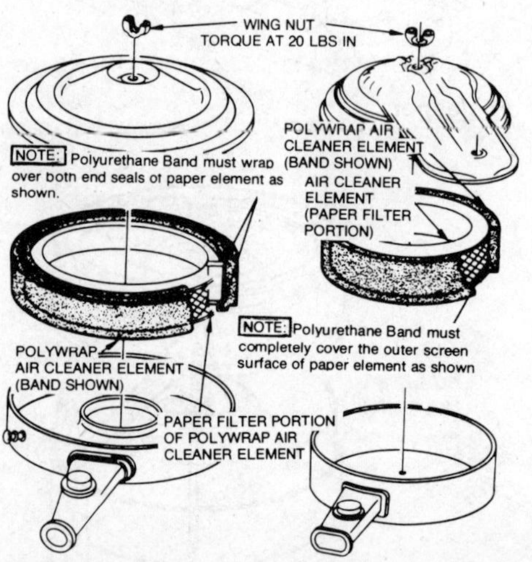

Air cleaner element with polyurethane wrap is optional starting 1972

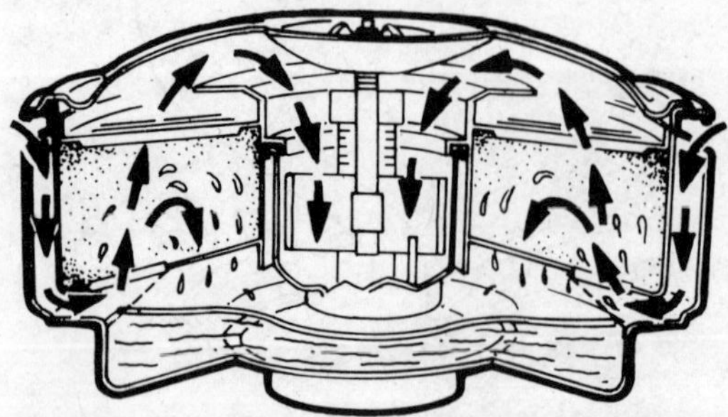

Oil level in the optional (through 1971) oil bath air cleaner

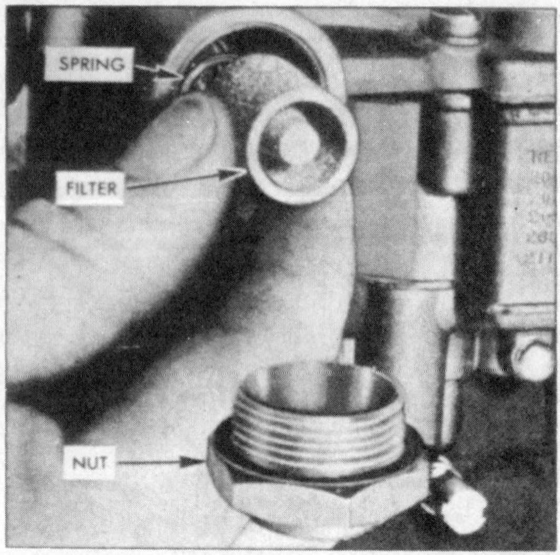

Bronze fuel filter

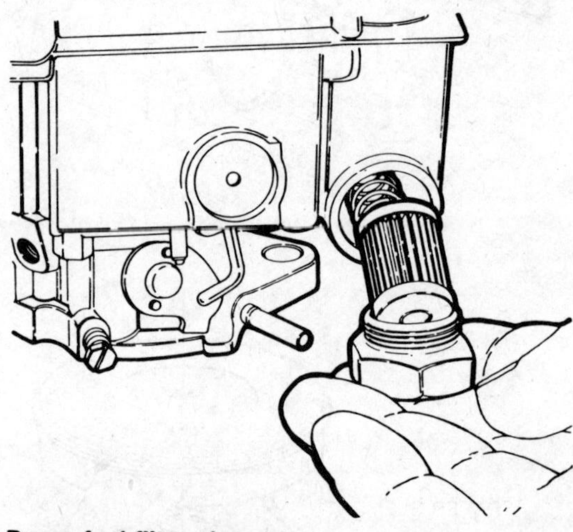

Paper fuel filter element

gasoline which will spill out when the lines are loosened. To replace the filter found in the carburetor body:

1. Disconnect the fuel line connecting at the intake fuel filter nut. Plug the opening to prevent loss of fuel.
2. Remove the intake fuel filter nut from the carburetor with a 1" wrench.
3. Remove the filter element and spring.
4. Check the element for restrictions by blowing on the cone end. Air should pass freely.
5. Clean or replace the element, as necessary.
6. Install the element spring, then the filter element in the carburetor. Bronze filters should have the small section of the cone facing out.
7. Install a new gasket on the intake fuel

nut. Install the nut in the carburetor body and tighten securely.

8. Install the fuel line and tighten the connector.

Some trucks may have an inline filter. This is a can shaped device located in the fuel line between the pump and the carburetor. It may be made of either plastic or metal. To replace the filter:

1. Place some absorbent rags under the filter. Remember, it will be full of gasoline when removed.

2. Use a pair of pliers to expand the clamp on one end of the filter, then slide the clamp down past the point to which the filter pipe extends in the rubber hose. Do the same with the other clamp.

3. Gently twist and pull the hoses free of the filter pipes. Remove and discard the old filter.

NOTE: *Most replacement filters come with new hoses that should be installed with a new filter.*

4. Install the new filter into the hoses, slide the clamps back into place, and check for leaks with the engine idling.

8–379 (6.2L) Diesel Engines

The 1983 model 379 diesels utilize two fuel filters: a primary canister type screw-on filter, located on the chassis right hand under body cross sill forward of the fuel tank, and a clip-on secondary filter mounted on the rear of the intake manifold. These filters should be serviced at the regular intervals specified in the Maintenance chart. See Diesel Fuel System in Chapter 4 for more information.

DRAINING WATER – PRIMARY FILTER

1983 Models

1. Open the petcock on the top of the filter housing.

2. Place a drain pan below the filter. Attach a length of hose to the petcock to direct the fluid down below the frame. Open the petcock on the bottom of the drain assembly.

3. After all the water has been drained, close the petcock lightly.

NOTE: *If the filter is drained completely, remove the filter and refill it with clean diesel fuel before starting engine.*

4. Close the upper petcock tightly.

5. Start the engine and let it run a bit. The engine may run roughly for a short time until the air is purged from the system.

NOTE: *If the engine continues to run roughly, check that both petcocks at the primary filter are closed tightly.*

SECONDARY FUEL FILTER REPLACEMENT

1983 Models

1. Remove the engine cover.

2. Remove the air cleaner and place a rag under the filter.

3. Unstrap the lower bail on the filter to relieve fuel pressure in the filter.

4. Unstrap the upper bail and remove the filter.

5. Before installing the new filter, insure that both filter mounting plate fittings are clear of dirt.

6. Install the new filter, snap the upper bail clamp only. Any time the secondary filter is removed or replaced, the air must be purged from the filter to prevent the engine from stalling or excessive cranking time to restart.

7. Disconnect the pink electrical wire from the injection pump to prevent the engine from starting.

8. Crank the engine (for 10 seconds max.)

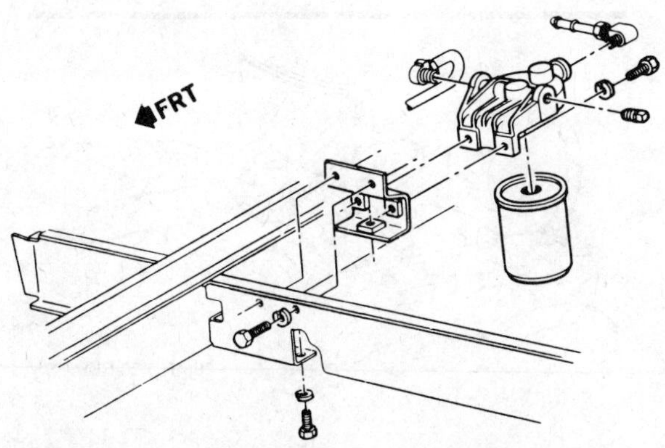

1983 model primary fuel filter, 379 (6.2L) diesel

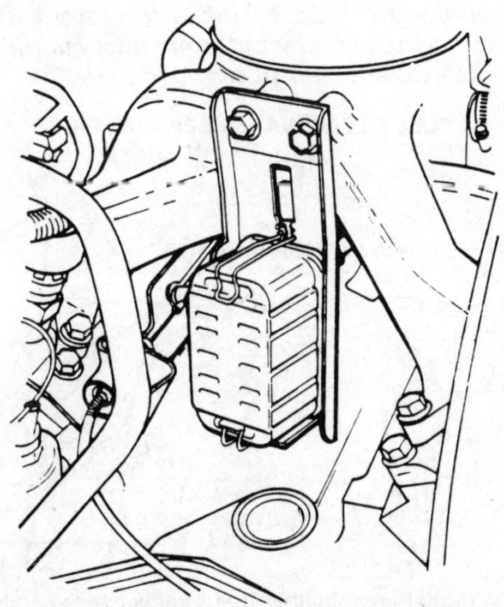
1983 model secondary fuel filter, 379 (6.2L) diesel

until the fuel is flowing at the lower fitting.

9. If the fuel is not observed for 10 seconds, wait 15 seconds and repeat Step 8.

10. When fuel is observed at the lower fitting, connect the lower bail clamp.

11. Reconnect the pink wire on the injection pump and install the air cleaner.

12. Start the engine and allow it to idle for several minutes to purge the remaining air. Check for fuel leaks.

13. Remove the rag and reinstall the engine cover.

1984–86 Models

1. Drain the fuel from the fuel filter by opening both the air bleed and the water drain valve allowing the fuel to drain out into an appropriate container.
2. Remove the fuel tank cap to release any pressure or vacuum in the tank.
3. Unstrap both bail wires with a screwdriver and remove the filter.
4. Before installing the new filter, insure that both filter mounting plate fittings are clear of dirt.
5. Install the new filter, snap into place with the bail wires.
6. Close the water drain valve and open the air bleed valve. Connect a 1/8" (3mm) I.D. hose to the air bleed port and place the other end into a suitable container.
7. Disconnect the fuel injection pump shut off solenoid wire.
8. Crank the engine for 10–15 seconds, then wait one minute for the starter motor to cool. Repeat until clear fuel is observed coming from the air bleed.

NOTE: *If the engine is to be cranked, or starting attempted with the air cleaner removed, care must be taken to prevent dirt from being pulled into the air inlet manifold which could result in engine damage.*

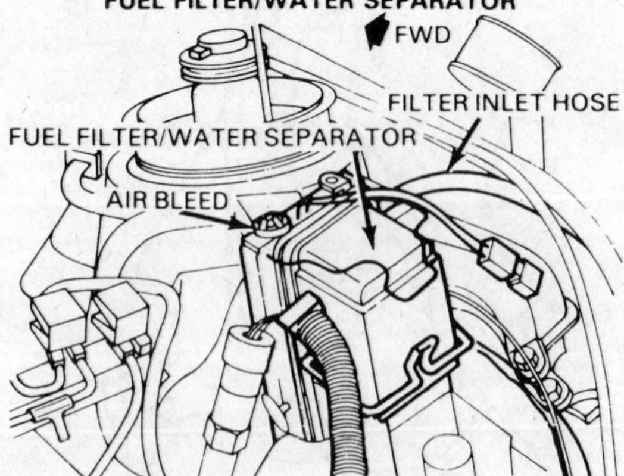

1984 model combination fuel filter/water separator, 379 (6.2L) diesel

9. Close the air bleed valve, reconnect the injection pump solenoid wire and replace the fuel tank cap.
10. Start the engine, allow it to idle for 5 minutes and check the fuel filter for leaks.

PCV Valve

REMOVAL AND INSTALLATION

The PCV valve is located on top of the valve cover or on the intake manifold. Its function is to purge the crankcase of harmful vapors through a system using engine vacuum to draw fresh air through the crankcase. It reburns crankcase vapors, rather than exhausting. Proper operation of the PCV valve depends on a sealed engine.

Engine operating conditions that would indicate a malfunctioning PCV system are rough idle, oil present in the air cleaner, oil leaks or excessive oil sludging.

The simplest check for the PCV valve is to remove it from its rubber grommet on top of the valve cover and shake it. If it rattles, it is functioning. If not, replace it. In any event, it should be replaced at the recommended interval whether it rattles or not. While you are about it, check the PCV hoses for breaks or restrictions. As necessary, the hoses should also be replaced.

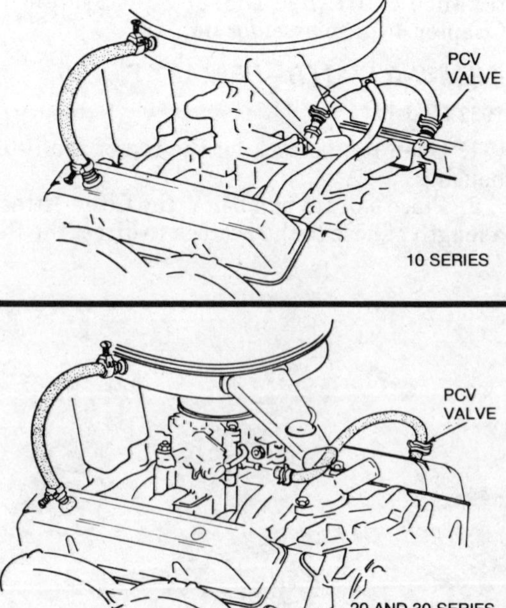

Typical PCV valve location

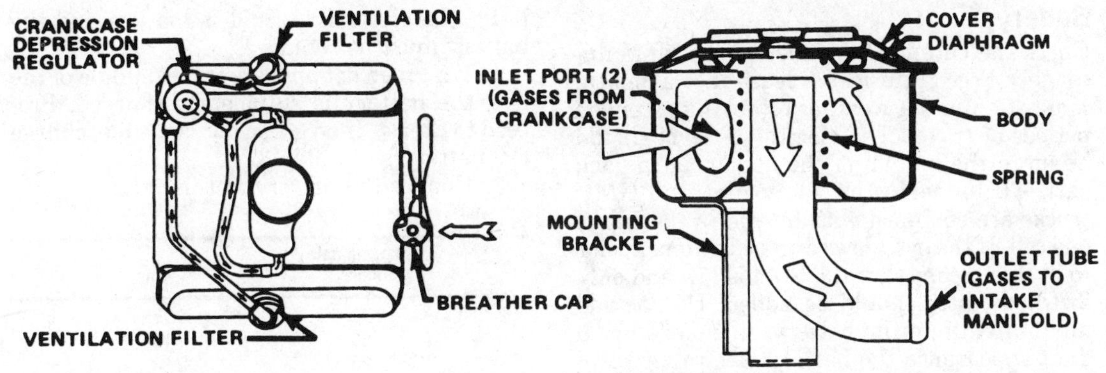

Diesel crankcase ventilation flow and depression regulator

Crankcase Depression Regulator and Flow Control Valve

SERVICING

Diesel Engines

The Crankcase Depression Regulator (CDR), found on 1982 and later diesels is designed to scavenge crankcase vapors in basically the same manner as the PVC valve on gasoline engines. The valves are located either on the left rear corner of the intake manifold (CDR). On this system there are two ventilation filters, one per valve cover.

The filter assemblies should be cleaned every 15,000 miles by simply prying them carefully from the valve covers (be aware of the grommets underneath), and washing them out in solvent. The ventilation pipes and tubes should also be cleaned. The CDR valve should also be cleaned every 30,000 miles (the cover can be removed from the CDR). Dry each valve, filter, and hose with compressed air before installation.

NOTE: *Do not attempt to test the crankcase controls on these diesels. Instead, clean the valve cover filter assembly and vent pipes and check the vent pipes. Replace the breather cap assembly every 30,000 miles. Replace all rubber fittings as required every 15,000 miles.*

Evaporative Canister

SERVICING

The only regular maintenance that need be performed on the evaporative emission canister is to regularly change the filter and check the condition of the hoses. If any hoses need replacement, use only hoses which are marked EVAP. No other type should be used. Whenever the vapor vent hose is replaced, the restrictor adjacent to the canister should also be replaced.

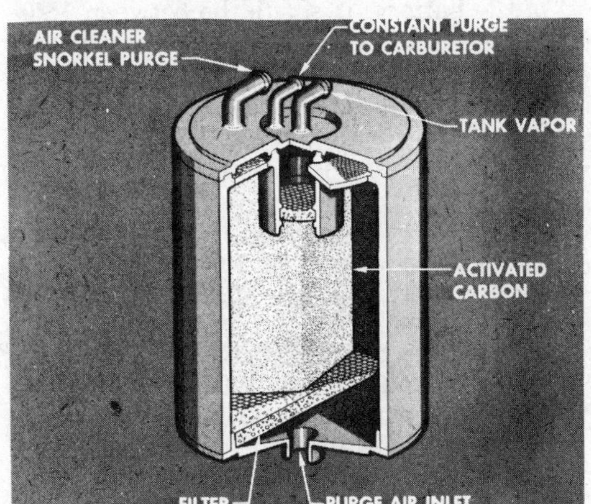

Typical evaporative canister

The evaporative emission canister is located on the left side of the engine compartment, with a filter located in its bottom. Not all vans have one.

To service the canister filter:

1. Note the installed positions of the hoses, tagging them as necessary, in case any have to be removed.
2. Loosen the clamps and remove the canister.
3. Pull the filter out and throw it away.
4. Install a new canister filter.
5. Install the canister and tighten the clamps.
6. Check the hoses.

Battery

Check the battery fluid level (except in Maintenance Free batteries) at least once a month, more often in hot weather or during extended periods of travel. The electrolyte level should be up to the bottom of the split ring in each cell. All batteries on Chevrolet and GMC trucks are equipped with an eye in the cap of one cell. If the eye glows or has an amber color to it, this means that the level is low and only distilled water should be added. Do not add anything else to the battery. If the eye has a dark appearance the battery electrolyte level is high enough. It is wise to also check each cell individually.

CAUTION: *Keep flame or sparks away from the battery. It gives off explosive hydrogen gas, while it is being charged.*

At least once a year, check the specific gravity of the battery. It should be between 1.20–1.26. Clean and tighten the clamps and apply a thin coat of petroleum jelly to the terminals. This will help to retard corrosion. The terminals can be cleaned with a staff wire brush or with an inexpensive terminal cleaner designed for this purpose.

If water is added during freezing weather, the truck should be driven several miles to allow the electrolyte and water to mix. Otherwise the battery could freeze.

If the battery becomes corroded, a solution of baking soda and water will neutralize the corrosion. This should be washed off after making sure that the caps are securely in place. Rinse the solution off with cold water.

Some batteries were equipped with a felt terminal washer. This should be saturated with engine oil approximately every 6,000 miles. This will also help to retard corrosion.

If a fast charger is used while the battery is in the truck, disconnect the battery before connecting the charger.

NOTE: *Keep flame or sparks away from the battery. It gives off explosive hydrogen gas.*

TESTING THE MAINTENANCE-FREE BATTERY

All later model trucks are equipped with maintenance-free batteries, which do not require normal attention as far as fluid level checks are concerned. However, the terminals require periodic cleaning, which should be performed at least once a year.

The sealed top battery cannot be checked for charge in the normal manner, since there is no provision for access to the electrolyte. To check the condition of the battery:

1. If the indicator eye on top of the battery is dark, the battery has enough fluid. If the eye is light, the electrolyte fluid is too low and the battery must be replaced.
2. If a green dot appears in the middle of the eye, the battery is sufficiently charged. Proceed to Step 4. If no green dot is visible, charge the battery as in Step 3.
3. Charge the battery at this rate:

Charging Rate Amps	Time
75	40 min
50	1 hr
25	2 hr
10	5 hr

CAUTION: *Do not charge the battery for more than 50 amp/hours. If the green dot appears, or if electrolyte squirts out of the vent hole, stop the charge and proceed to Step 4.*

It may be necessary to tip the battery from side to side to get the green dot to appear after charging.

4. Connect a battery load tester and a voltmeter across the battery terminals (the battery cables should be disconnected from the battery). Apply a 300 amp load to the battery for 15 seconds to remove the surface charge. Remove the load.
5. Wait 15 seconds to allow the battery to recover. Apply the appropriate test load, as specified in the following chart:

Battery	Test Load
Y85-4	130 amps
R85-5	170 amps
R87-5	210 amps
R89-5	230 amps

Apply the load for 15 seconds while reading the voltage. Disconnect the load.

6. Check the results against the following chart. If the battery voltage is at or above the specified voltage for the temperature listed, the battery is good. If the voltage falls below what's listed, the battery should be replaced.

Temperature (°F)	Minimum Voltage
70 or above	9.6
60	9.5
50	9.4
40	9.3
30	9.1
20	8.9
10	8.7
0	8.5

FILLING THE BATTERY

Batteries should be checked for proper electrolyte level at least once a month or more frequently. Keep a close eye on any cell or cells that are unusually low or seem to constantly need water – this may indicate a battery on its last legs, a leak, or a problem with the charging system.

Top up each cell to about 3/8″ (9.5mm) above the tops of the plates. Always use distilled water (available in supermarkets or auto parts stores), because most tap water contains chemicals and minerals that may slowly damage the plates of your battery.

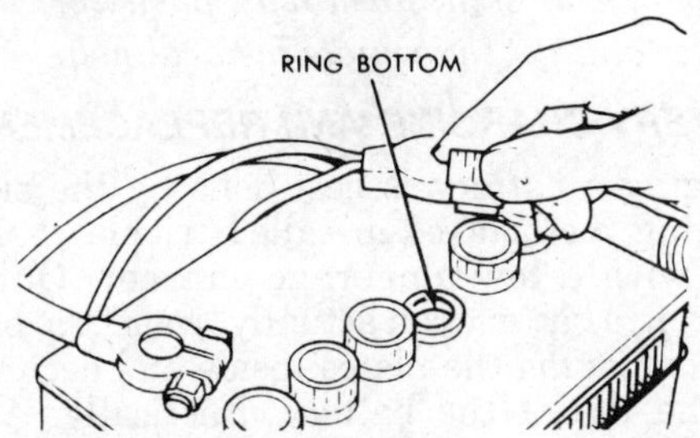

Fill each battery cell to the bottom of the split ring with distilled water

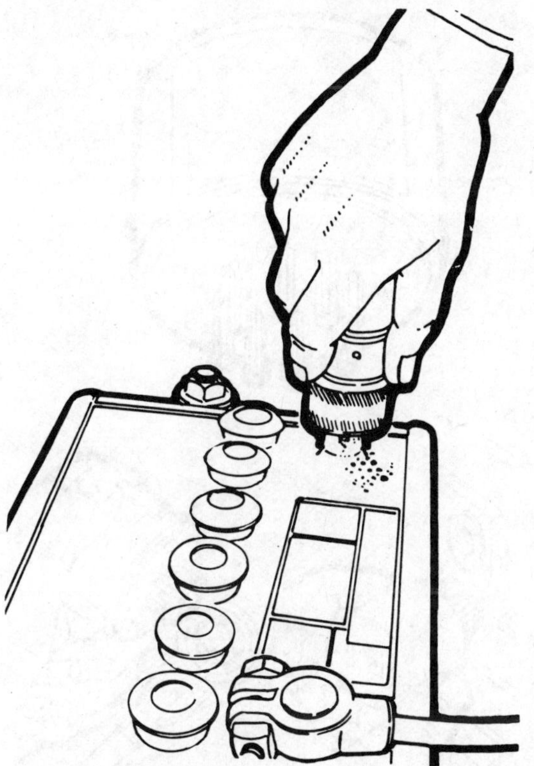

Clean the battery posts with a wire brush, or the special tool shown

CABLES AND CLAMPS

Twice a year, the battery terminal posts and the cable clamps should be cleaned. Loosen the clamp bolts (you may have to brush off any corrosion with a baking soda and water solution if they are really messy) and remove the cables, negative cable first. On batteries with posts on top, the use of a battery clamp puller is recommended. It is easy to break off a battery terminal if a clamp gets stuck without the puller.

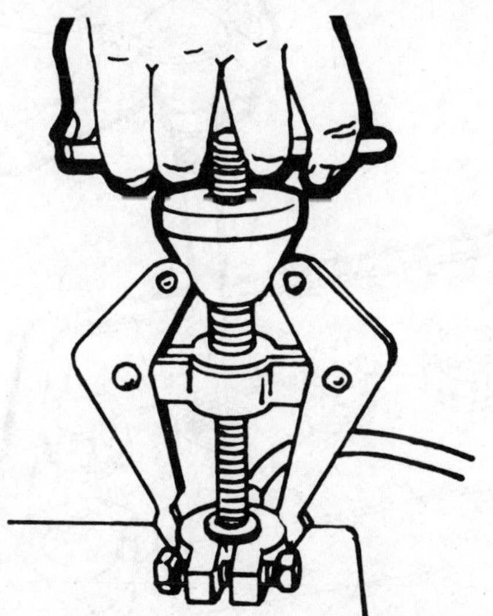

Special pullers are available to remove cable clamps

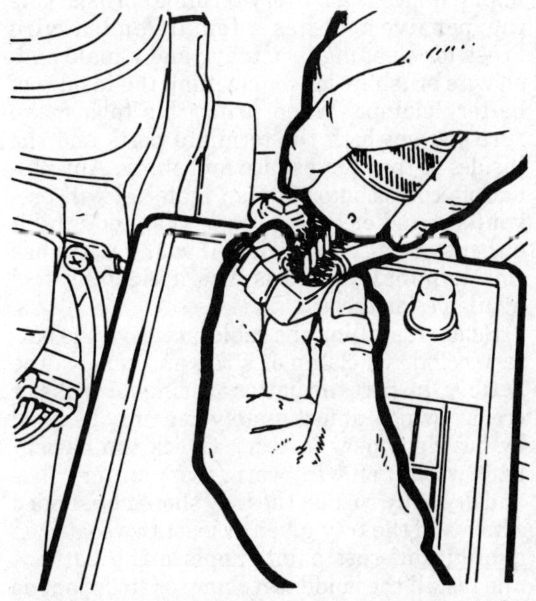

Clean the inside of the cable clamp with a wire brush

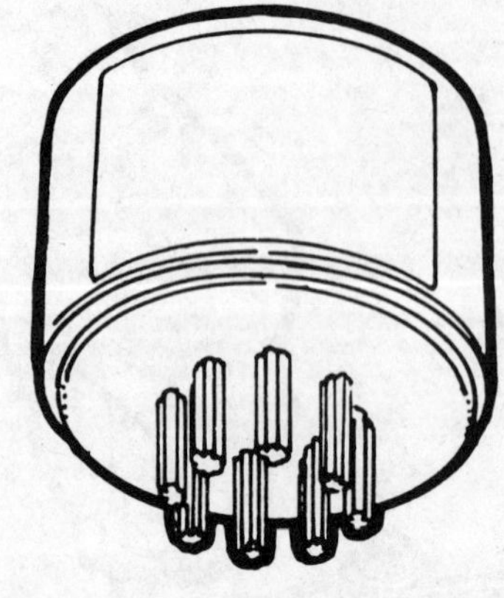

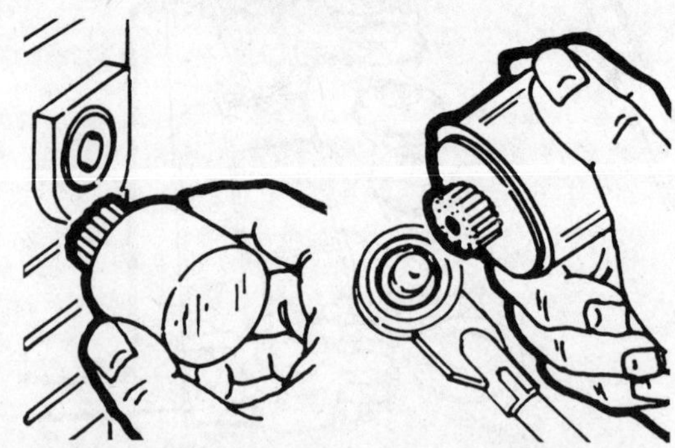

Special tools are available for cleaning the terminals and cable clamps on side terminal batteries

These pullers are inexpensive and available in most auto parts stores or auto departments. Side terminal battery cables are secured with a bolt.

The best tool for battery clamp and terminal maintenance is a battery terminal brush. This inexpensive tool has a female ended wire brush for cleaning terminals, and a male ended wire brush inside for cleaning the insides of battery clamps. When using this tool, make sure you get both the terminal posts and the insides of the clamps nice and shiny. Any oxidation, corrosion or foreign material will prevent a sound electrical connection and inhibit either starting or charging. If your battery has side terminals, there is also a cleaning tool available for these.

Before installing the cables, remove the battery holddown clamp or strap and remove the battery. Inspect the battery casing for leaks or cracks (which unfortunately can only be fixed by buying a new battery). Check the battery tray, wash it off with warm soapy water, rinse and dry. Any rust on the tray should be sanded away, and the tray given at least two coats of a quality anti-rust paint. Replace the battery, and install the holddown clamp or strap, but do not overtighten.

Reinstall your clean battery cables, negative cable last. Tighten the cables on the terminal posts snugly; do not overtighten. Wipe a thin coat of petroleum jelly or grease all over the outsides of the clamps. This will help to inhibit corrosion.

Finally, check the battery cables themselves. If the insulation of the cables is cracked or broken, or if the ends are frayed, replace the cable with a new cable of the same length or gauge.

NOTE: *Batteries give off hydrogen gas, which is explosive. DO NOT SMOKE around the battery! The battery electrolyte contains sulfuric acid. If you should splash any into your eyes or skin, flush with plenty of clear water and get immediate medical help.*

BATTERY CHARGING AND REPLACEMENT

Charging a battery is best done by the slow charging method (often called trickle charging), with a low amperage charger. Quick charging a battery can actually "cook" the battery, damaging the plates inside and decreasing the life of the battery drastically. Any charging should be done in a well ventilated area away from the possibility of sparks or flame. The cell caps (not found on maintenance-free batteries) should be unscrewed from their cells, but not removed.

If the battery must be quick charged, check the cell voltages and the color of the electrolyte a few minutes after the charge is started. If cell voltages are not uniform or if the electrolyte is

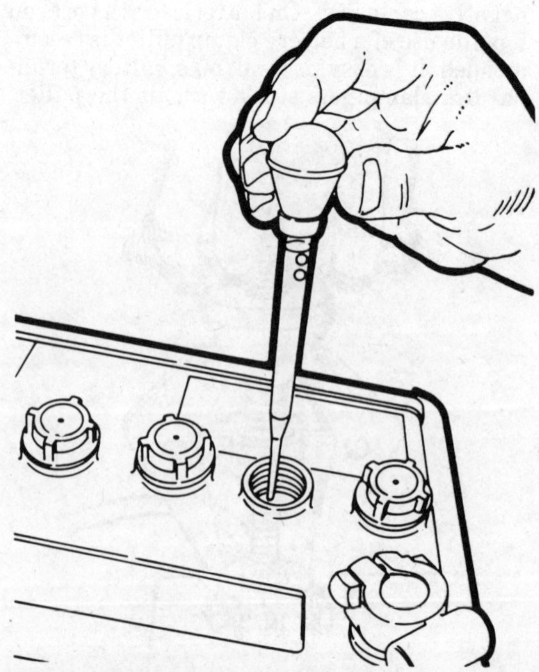

The specific gravity of the battery can be checked with a simple float-type hydrometer

Battery State of Charge at Room Temperature

Specific Gravity Reading	Charged Condition
1.260–1.280	Fully Charged
1.230–1.250	¾ Charged
1.200–1.220	½ Charged
1.170–1.190	¼ Charged
1.140–1.160	Almost no Charge
1.110–1.130	No Charge

discolored with brown sediment, stop the quick charging in favor of a trickle charge. A common indicator of an overcharged battery is the frequent need to add water to the battery.

Heat Riser

The heat riser is a thermostatically or vacuum operated valve in the exhaust manifold. Not all engines have one. It closes when the engine is warming up, to direct hot exhaust gases to the intake manifold, in order to preheat the incoming fuel/air mixture. It it sticks shut, the result will be frequent stalling during warmup, especially in cold and damp weather. If it sticks open, the result will be a rough idle after the engine is warm. There is only one heat riser on a V8. The heat riser should move freely. If it sticks, apply GM Manifold Heat Control Solvent or something similar (engine cool) to the ends of the shaft. Sometimes rapping the end of the shaft sharply with a hammer (engine hot) will break it loose. If this fails, components must be removed for further repairs.

Typical heater riser valve, six cylinder shown

Drive Belts

INSPECTION

At the interval specified in the Maintenance Intervals chart, check the water pump, alternator, power steering pump (if equipped), air conditioning compressor (if equipped) and air pump (if equipped) drive belts for proper tension. Also look for signs of wear, fraying, separation, glazing, and so on, and replace the belts as required.

BELT TENSION

Belt tension should be checked with a gauge made for the purpose. If a tension gauge is not available, tension can be checked with moderate thumb pressure applied to the belt at its longest span midway between pulleys. If the belt has a free span less than 12″ (305mm), it should deflect approximately ⅛–¼″ (3–6mm). If the span is longer than 12″ (305mm), deflection can range between ⅛″ (3mm) and ⅜″ (9.5mm).

REMOVAL, INSTALLATION AND ADJUSTMENT

1. Loosen the driven accessory's pivot and mounting bolts.

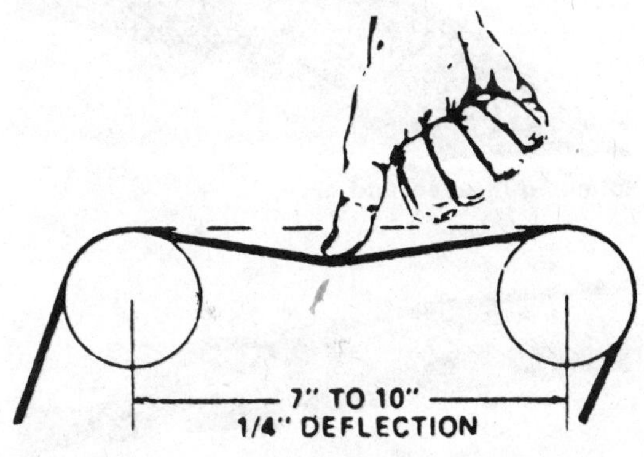

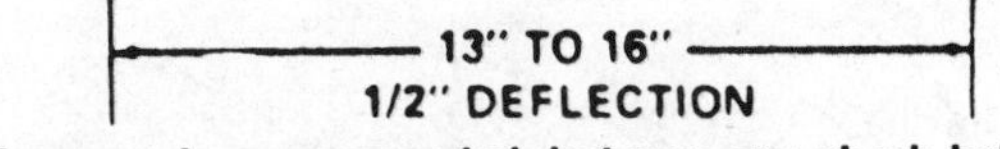

A gauge is recommended, but you can check belt tension with thumb pressure

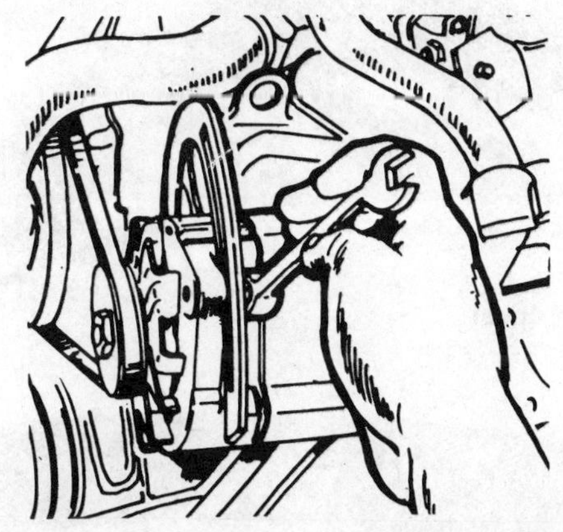

To adjust belt tension or to replace belts, first loosen the component's mounting and adjusting bolts slightly

HOW TO SPOT WORN V-BELTS

V-Belts are vital to efficient engine operation—they drive the fan, water pump and other accessories. They require little maintenance (occasional tightening) but they will not last forever. Slipping or failure of the V-belt will lead to overheating. If your V-belt looks like any of these, it should be replaced.

Cracking or weathering

This belt has deep cracks, which cause it to flex. Too much flexing leads to heat build-up and premature failure. These cracks can be caused by using the belt on a pulley that is too small. Notched belts are available for small diameter pulleys.

Softening (grease and oil)

Oil and grease on a belt can cause the belt's rubber compounds to soften and separate from the reinforcing cords that hold the belt together. The belt will first slip, then finally fail altogether.

Glazing

Glazing is caused by a belt that is slipping. A slipping belt can cause a run-down battery, erratic power steering, overheating or poor accessory performance. The more the belt slips, the more glazing will be built up on the surface of the belt. The more the belt is glazed, the more it will slip. If the glazing is light, tighten the belt.

Worn cover

The cover of this belt is worn off and is peeling away. The reinforcing cords will begin to wear and the belt will shortly break. When the belt cover wears in spots or has a rough jagged appearance, check the pulley grooves for roughness.

Separation

This belt is on the verge of breaking and leaving you stranded. The layers of the belt are separating and the reinforcing cords are exposed. It's just a matter of time before it breaks completely.

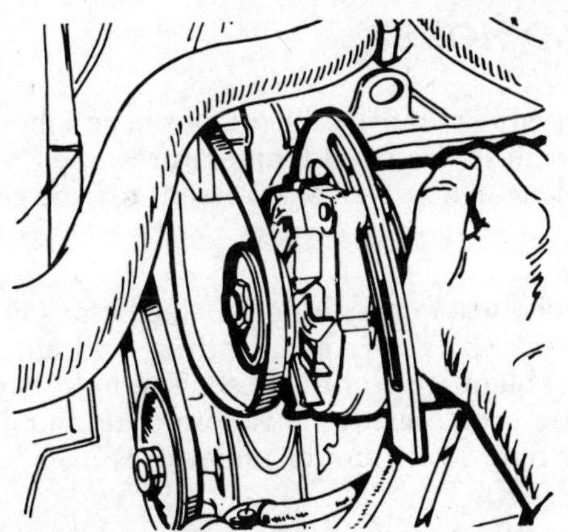

Push the component toward the engine and slip off the belt

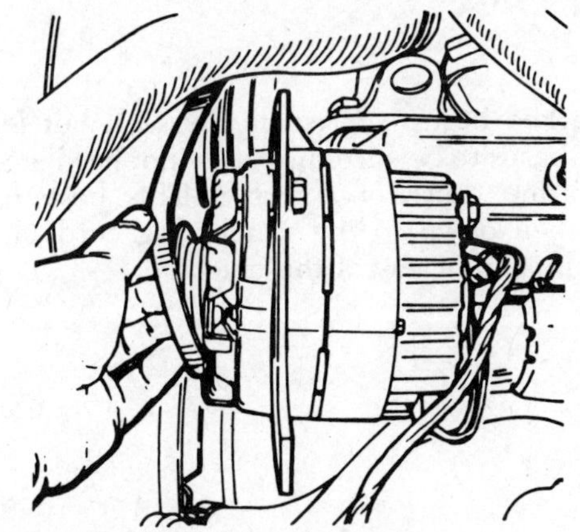

Slip the new belt over the pulley

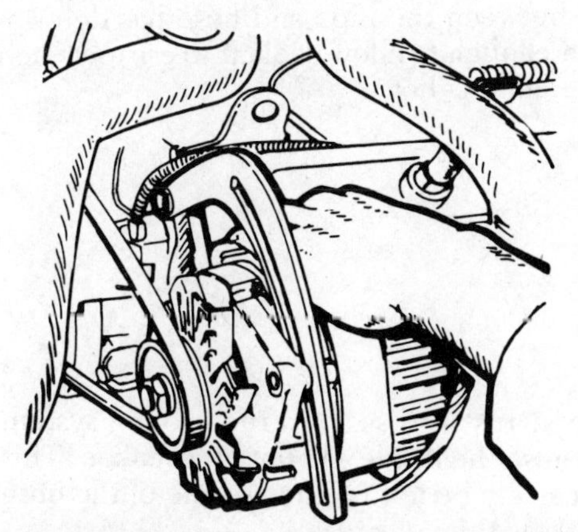

Pull outward on the component and tighten the mounting bolts

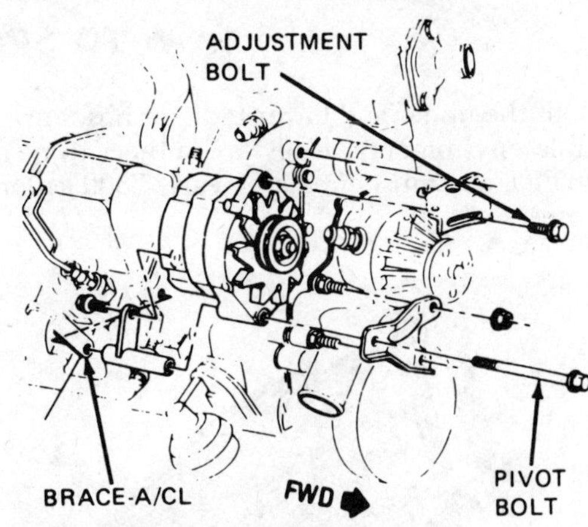

GENERATOR

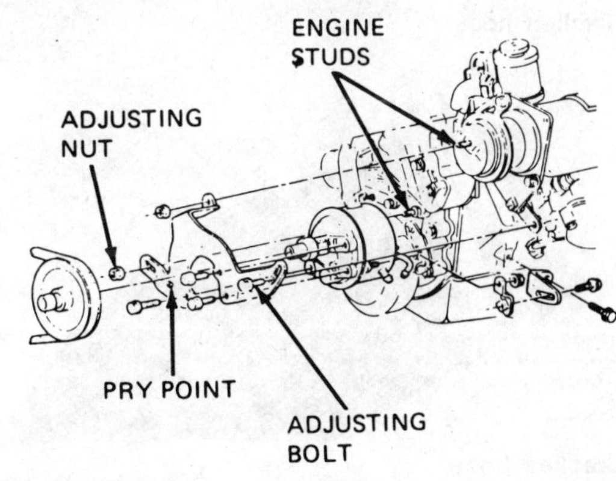

POWER STEERING

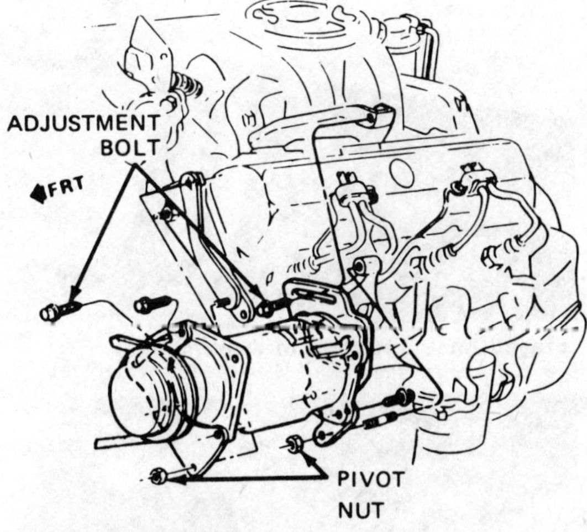

AIR CONDITIONING

379 diesel belt adjustments

2. Move the accessory toward or away from the engine until the tension is correct. You can use a wooden hammer handle, or broomstick, as a lever, but do not use anything metallic, such as a prybar.

3. Tighten the bolts and recheck the tension. If new belts have been installed, run the engine for a few minutes, then recheck and readjust as necessary.

It is better to have belts too loose than too

HOW TO SPOT BAD HOSES

Both the upper and lower radiator hoses are called upon to perform difficult jobs in an inhospitable environment. They are subject to nearly 18 psi at under hood temperatures often over 280°F., and must circulate nearly 7500 gallons of coolant an hour—3 good reasons to have good hoses.

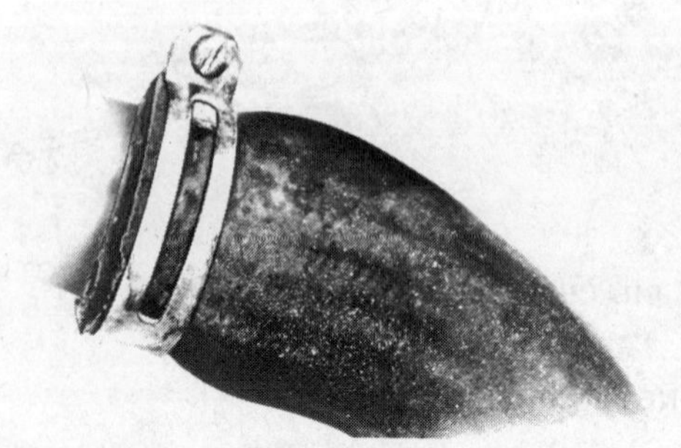

Swollen hose

A good test for any hose is to feel it for soft or spongy spots. Frequently these will appear as swollen areas of the hose. The most likely cause is oil soaking. This hose could burst at any time, when hot or under pressure.

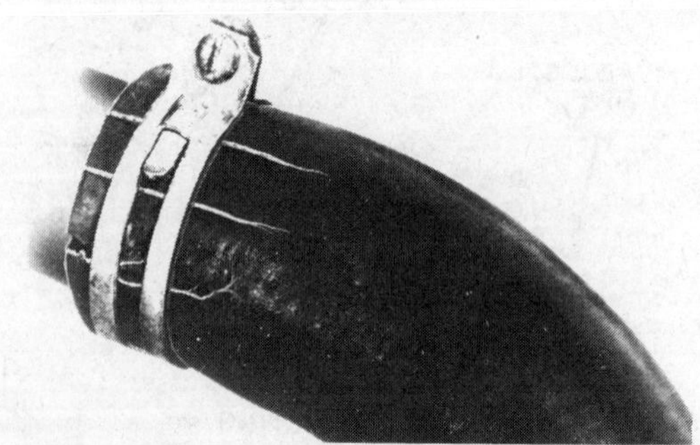

Cracked hose

Cracked hoses can usually be seen but feel the hoses to be sure they have not hardened; a prime cause of cracking. This hose has cracked down to the reinforcing cords and could split at any of the cracks.

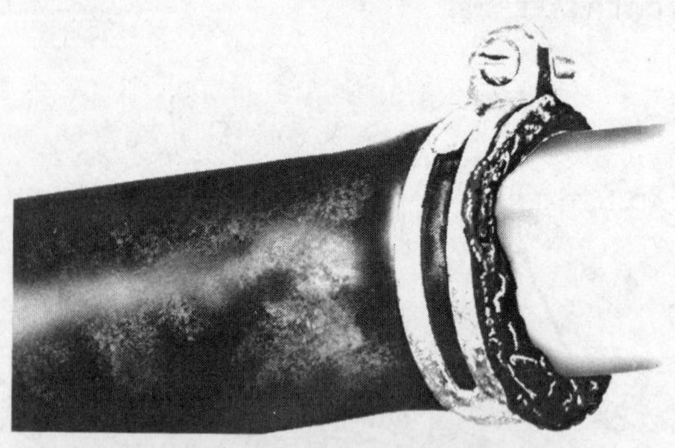

Frayed hose end (due to weak clamp)

Weakened clamps frequently are the cause of hose and cooling system failure. The connection between the pipe and hose has deteriorated enough to allow coolant to escape when the engine is hot.

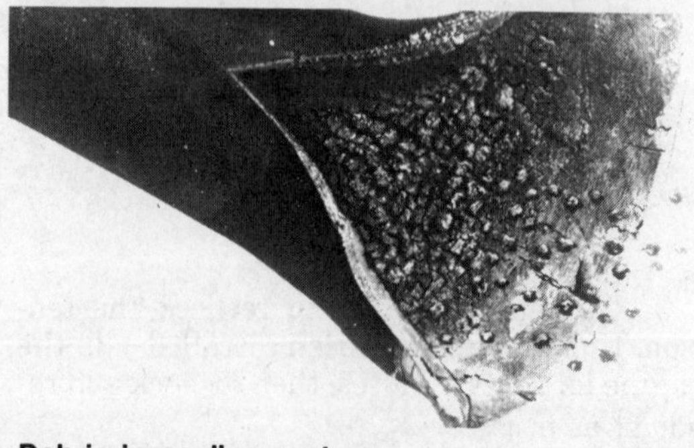

Debris in cooling system

Debris, rust and scale in the cooling system can cause the inside of a hose to weaken. This can usually be felt on the outside of the hose as soft or thinner areas.

tight, because overtight belts will lead to bearing failure, particularly in the water pump and alternator. However, loose belts place an extremely high impact load on the driven component due to the whipping action of the belt.

Hoses

REMOVAL AND INSTALLATION

1. Open the petcock located at the bottom of the radiator and drain the antifreeze into a suitable container.

   CAUTION: *When draining the coolant, keep in mind that cats and dogs are attracted by the ethylene glycol antifreeze, and are quite likely to drink any that is left in an uncovered container or in puddles on the ground. This will prove fatal in sufficient quantity. Always drain the coolant into a sealable container. Coolant should be reused unless it is contaminated or several years old.*

2. Using a flat screwdriver loosen the clamps on the hose you wish to remove.
3. Apply sufficient twisting and turning force to remove the hose.
4. Install the new hose and clamps, close the petcock and refill the radiator.

Air Conditioning System

CAUTION: *Do not attempt to charge or discharge the refrigerant system unless you are thoroughly familiar with its operation and the hazards involved. The compressed refrigerant used in the air conditioning system expands and evaporates into the atmosphere at a temperature of −21.7°F (−30°C) or less. This will freeze any surface, including your eyes, that it contacts. In addition, the refrigerant decomposes into a poisonous gas in the presence of flame.*

SYSTEM INSPECTION

The air conditioning system should be checked periodically for worn hoses, loose connections, low refrigerant, leaks, dirt and bugs. If any of these conditions exist, they must be corrected or they will reduce the efficiency of your air conditioning system.

REFRIGERANT LEVEL CHECK

Through 1977

These units have a slight glass for checking the refrigerant charge. This is on top of the receiver dehydrator, alongside the radiator.

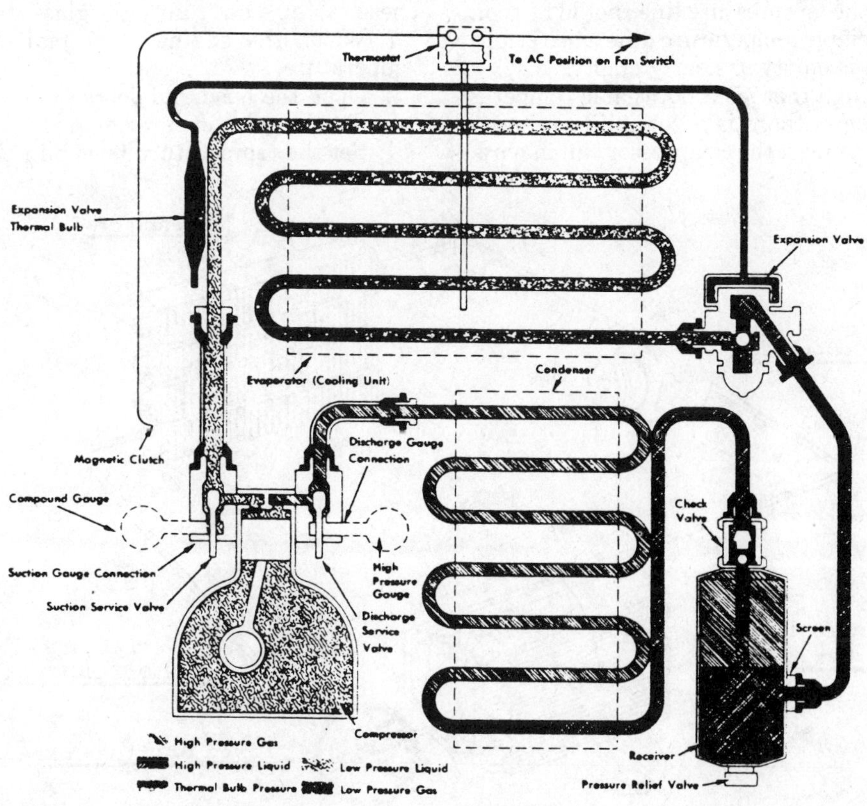

Basic air conditioning system

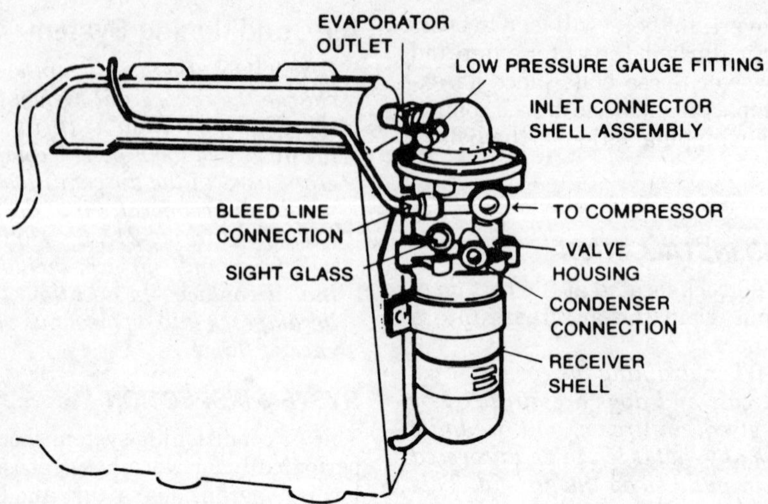

The air conditioning sight glass on most models is located near the top of the VIR unit, mounted on the left side of the radiator.

1. Start the engine and set it on fast idle.
2. Set the controls for maximum cold with the blower on high.
3. If bubbles are present in the sight glass, the system is low on charge. If no bubbles are present, the system is either fully charged or empty.
4. Feel the high or low pressure lines at the compressor. The high pressure line should be warm and the low pressure line should be cool. If no appreciable temperature difference is felt, the system is empty or nearly empty.

Even though there is a noticeable temperature difference, there is a possibility of overcharge. Disconnect the compressor clutch wire. If the refrigerant in the sight glass remains clear for more than 45 seconds before foaming and then settling away from the sight glass, an overcharge is indicated. If the refrigerant foams and then settles away from the sight glass in less than 45 seconds, it can be assumed that the system is properly charged.

1978–86

These systems have no sight glass.

1. Warm the engine to normal operating temperature.
2. Open the hood and doors.
3. Set the selector lever at A/C.
4. Set the temperature level on COLD.

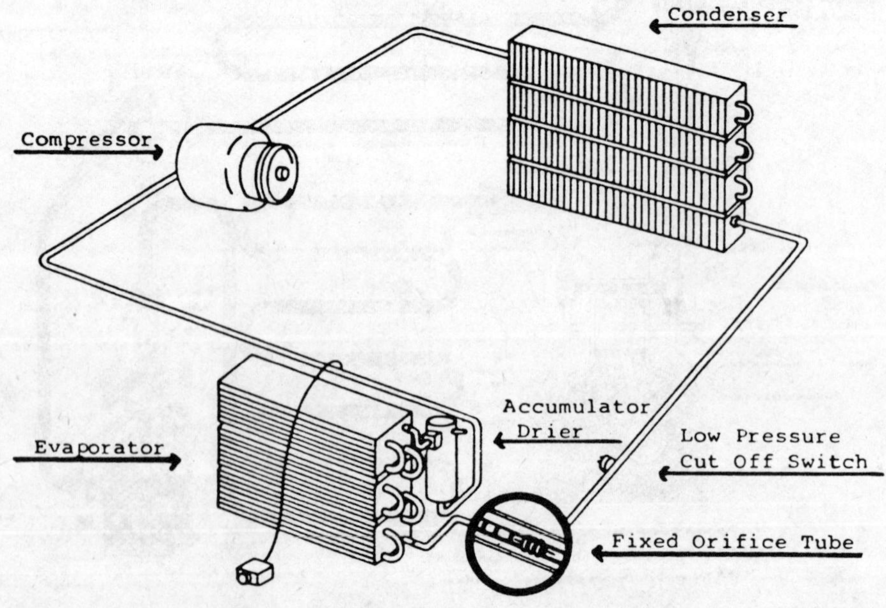

Cycling Clutch Orifice Tube (CCOT) system

5. Set the blower on HI.
6. Idle the engine at 1,000 rpm.
7. Feel the temperature of the evaporator inlet and the accumulator outlet lines with the compressor engaged.

Both lines should be cold. If the inlet pipe is colder than the outlet pipe the system is low on charge.

NOTE: *This system has an internal filter combined with the expansion tube at the evaporator inlet (the lower line). If the filter is clogged, the result will be poor cooling and occasional external icing at this point on system startup, even though system pressures will be near normal.*

GAUGE SETS

Most of the service work performed in air conditioning requires the use of two gauges, one for the high (head) pressure side of the system, the other for the low (suction).

The low side gauge records both pressure and vacuum. Vacuum readings are calibrated from 0 to no less than 60 psi.

The high side gauge measures pressure from 0 to at least 600 psi. Both gauges are threaded into a manifold that contains two hand shut off valves. Proper manipulation of these valves and the use of the attached test hoses allow the user to perform the following services:

1. Test high and low side pressures.
2. Remove air, moisture, and contaminated refrigerant.
3. Purge the system of refrigerant.
4. Charge the system with refrigerant.

The manifold valves are designed so they have no direct effect on gauge readings, but serve only to provide for, or cut off, flow of refrigerant through the manifold. During all testing and hook-up operations, the valves are kept in a closed position to avoid disturbing the refrigeration system. The valves are opened only to purge the system of refrigerant or to charge it. When purging the system, the center hose is uncapped at the lower end, and both valves are cracked open slightly. This allows refrigerant pressure to force the entire contents of the system out through the center hose. During charging, the valve on the high side of the manifold is closed, and the valve on the low side is cracked open. Under these conditions, the low pressure in the evaporator will draw refrigerant from the relatively warm refrigerant storage container into the system.

DISCHARGING THE SYSTEM

CAUTION: *Perform in a well ventilated area. The compressed refrigerant used in the air conditioning system expands and evaporates into the atmosphere at a temperature of –21.7°F (–29.8°C) or less. This will freeze any surface (including your eyes) that it contacts. In addition, the refrigerant decomposes into a poisonous gas in the presence of flame.*

1. Operate the air conditioner for at least 10 minutes.
2. Attach the gauges, shut off the engine, and the air conditioner.
3. Place a container or rag at the outlet of the center charging hose on the gauge. The refrigerant will be discharged there and this precaution will control its uncontrolled exposure.
4. Open the low side hand valve on the gauge slightly.

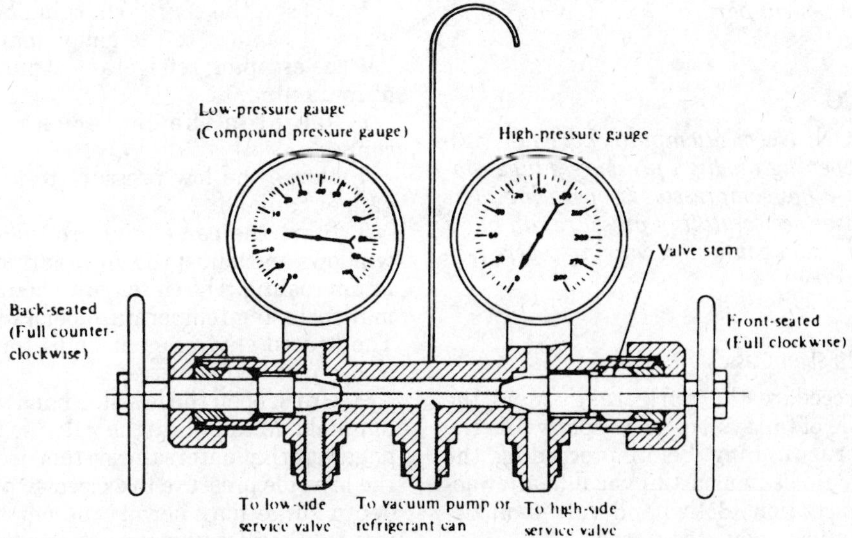

Typical manifold gauge set

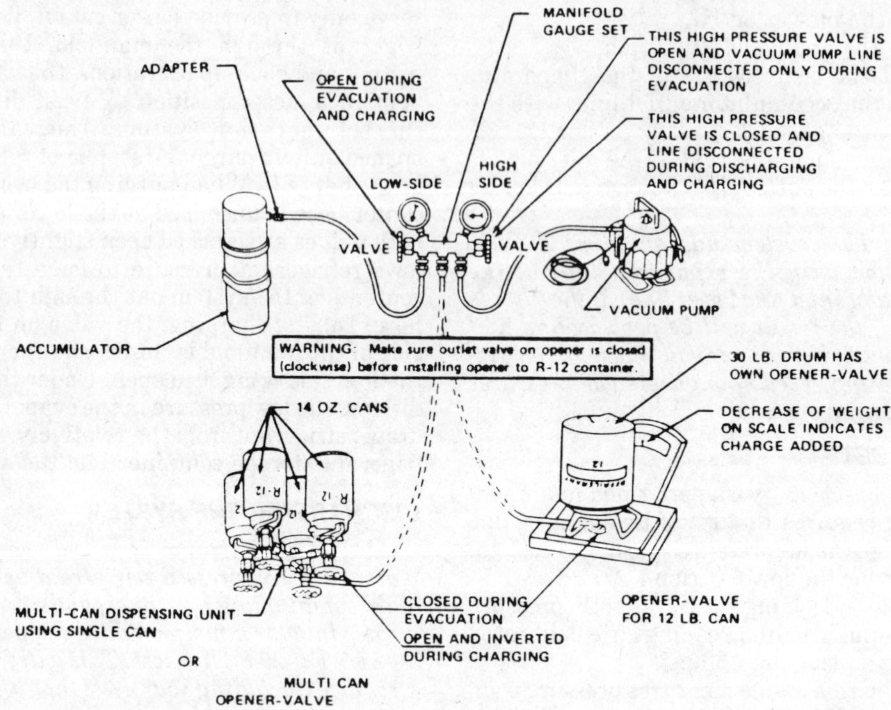

Typical gauge connections for discharge, evacuation and charging the system

5. Open the high side hand valve slightly.

NOTE: *Too rapid a purging process will be identified by the appearance of an oily foam. If this occurs, close the hand valves a little more until this condition stops.*

6. Close both hand valves on the gauge set when the pressures read 0 and all the refrigerant has left the system.

NOTE: *The system should always be discharged before attempting to remove any hoses or component parts of the air conditioning system.*

CHARGING

CAUTION: *Never attempt to charge the system by opening the high pressure gauge control while the compressor is operating. The compressor accumulating pressure can burst the refrigerant container, causing severe personal injury.*

1967–77

Systems With Sight Glass

In this procedure the refrigerant enters the suction side of the system as a vapor while the compressor is running. Before proceeding, the system should be in a partial vacuum after adequate evacuation. Both hand valves on the gauge manifold should be closed.

1. Attach both test hoses to their respective service valve ports. Mid-position manually operated service valves, if present.
2. Install the dispensing valve (closed position) on the refrigerant container. (Single and multiple refrigerant manifolds are available to accommodate one to four 15 oz. cans.)
3. Attach the center charging hose to the refrigerant container valve.
4. Open dispensing valve on the refrigerant valve.
5. Loosen the center charging hose coupler where it connect to the gauge manifold to allow the escaping refrigerant to purge the hose of contaminants.
6. Tighten the center charging hose connector.
7. Purge the low pressure test hose at the gauge manifold.
8. Start the car engine, roll down the car windows and adjust the air conditioner to maximum cooling. The car engine should be at normal operating temperature before proceeding. The heated environment helps the liquid vaporize more efficiently.
9. Crack open the low side hand valve on the manifold. Manipulate the valve so that the refrigerant that enters the system does not cause the low side pressure to exceed 40 psi. Too sudden a surge may permit the entrance of unwanted liquid to the compressor. Since liquids cannot be compressed, the compressor will suf-

Check item / Amount of refrigerant	Almost no refrigerant	Insufficient	Suitable	Too much refrigerant
Temperature of high pressure and low pressure lines	Almost no difference between high pressure and low pressure side temperature	High pressure side is warm and low pressure side is fairly cold	High pressure side is hot and low pressure side is cold	High pressure side is abnormally hot.
State in sight glass	Bubbles flow continuously. **Bubbles will disappear and something like mist will flow when refrigerant is nearly gone.**	The bubbles are seen at intervals of 1 - 2 seconds	Almost transparent. Bubbles may appear when engine speed is raised and lowered. **No clear difference exists betwen these two conditions.**	No bubbles can be seen
Pressure of system	High pressure side is abnormally low	Both pressure on high and low pressure sides are slightly low	Both pressures on high and low pressure sides are normal	Both pressures on high and low pressure sides are abnormally high.
Repair	**Stop compressor immediately** and conduct an overall check.	Check for gas leakage repair as required, replenish and charge system		Discharge refrigerant from service valve of low pressure side

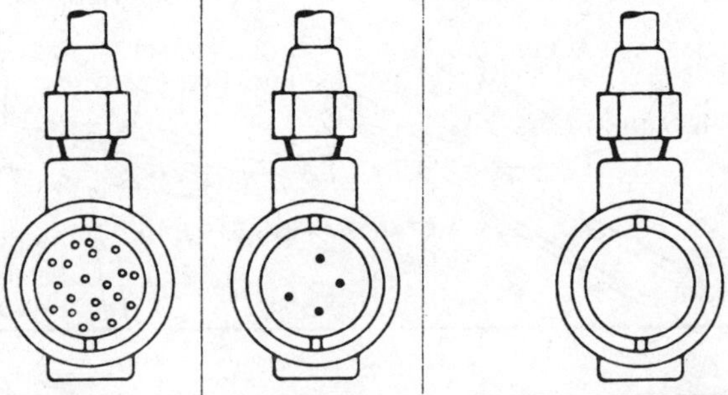

Using a sight glass to determine the relative refrigerant charge

fer damage if compelled to attempt it. If the suction side of the system remains in a vacuum the system is blocked. Locate and correct the condition before proceeding any further.

NOTE: *Placing the refrigerant can in a container of warm water (no hotter than +125°F [+51.6°C]) will speed the charging process. Slight agitation of the can is helpful too, but be careful not to turn the can upside down.*

1978–86

Systems Without Sight Glass

When charging the system, attach only the low pressure line to the low pressure gauge port, located on the accumulator. Do not attach the high pressure line to any service port or allow it to remain attached to the pump after evacuation. Be sure both the high and the low pressure control valves are closed on the gauge set. To complete the charging of the system, follow the outline below:

1. Start the engine and allow it to run at idle, with the cooling system at normal operating temperature.
2. Attach the center gauge hose to a single or multican dispenser.
3. With the multican dispenser inverted, allow one pound of the contents of one or two 14 oz. cans to enter the system through the low pressure side by opening the gauge low pressure valve.
4. Close the low pressure gauge control valve and turn the A/C system on to engage the compressor. Place the blower motor in its high mode.
5. Open the low pressure gauge control valve and draw the remaining charge into the system.
6. Close the low pressure gauge control valve and the refrigerant source valve, on the multican dispenser. Remove the low pressure hose from the accumulator quickly to avoid loss of refrigerant through the Schraeder valve.
7. Install the protective cap on the gauge ports and check for leakage.
8. Test the system for proper operation.

NOTE: *This book contains testing and charging procedures for your Chevrolet Van's air conditioning system. More comprehensive testing, diagnosis and service procedures may be found in CHILTON'S GUIDE TO AIR CONDITIONING AND REPAIR, book part number 7580, available at your local retailer.*

Windshield Wipers

Intense heat from the sun, snow and ice, road oils and the chemicals used in windshield

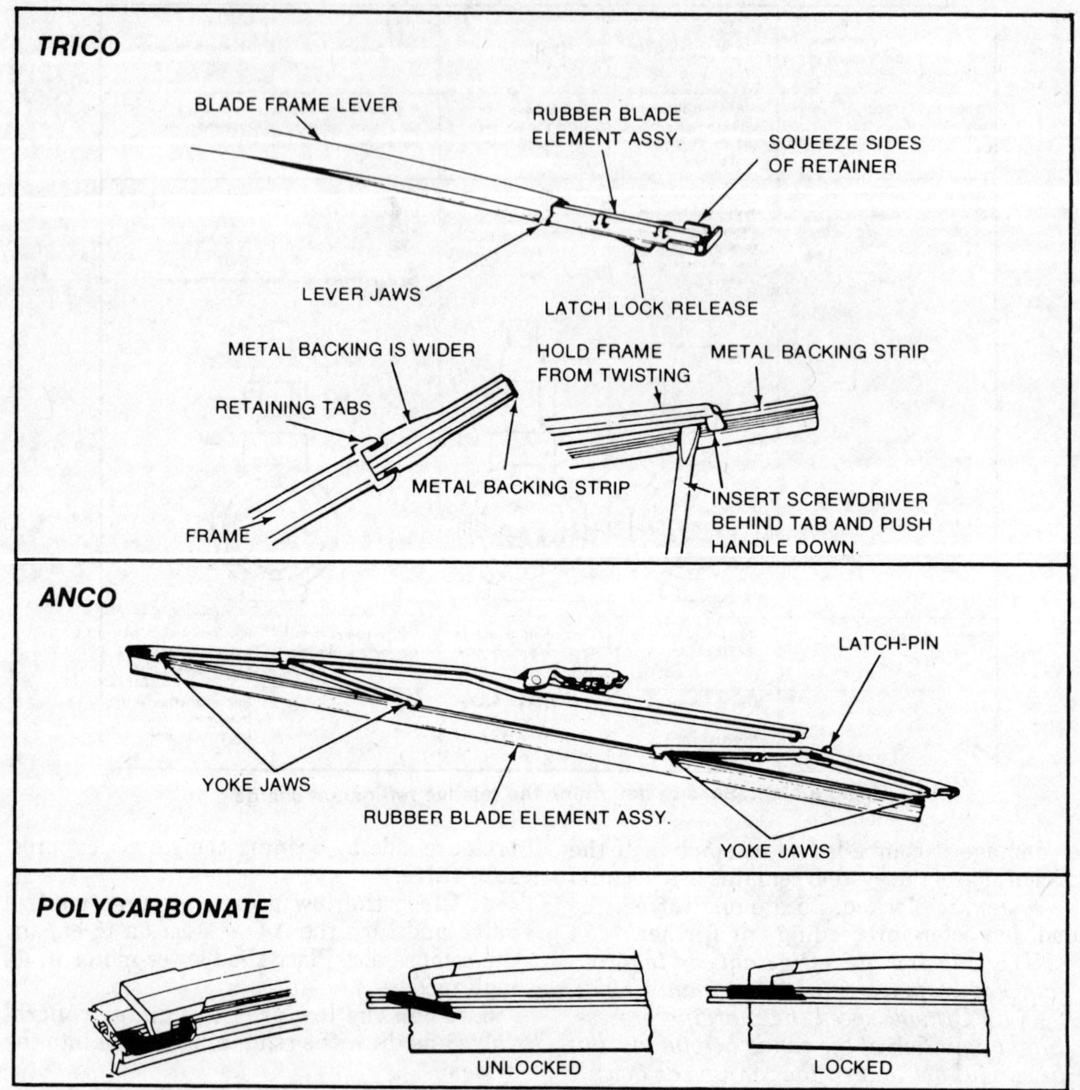

Windshield wiper blade refills

washer solvents combine to deteriorate the rubber wiper refills. The refills should be replaced about twice a year or whenever the blades begin to streak or chatter.

WIPER REFILL REPLACEMENT

Normally, if the wipers are not cleaning the windshield properly, only the refill has to be replaced. The blade and arm usually require replacement only in the event of damage. It is not necessary to remove the arm or the blade to replace the refill (rubber part), though you may have to position the arm higher on the glass. You can do this by turning the key on and operating the wipers. When they are positioned where they are accessible, turn the key off.

There are several types of refills and your vehicle could have any kind, since aftermarket blades and arms may not use exactly the same type refill as the original equipment.

Most Trico styles use a release button that is pushed down to allow the refill to slide out of the yoke jaws. The new refill slides in an locks in place. Some Trico refills are removed by locating where the metal backing strip or the refill is wider and inserting a small screwdriver blade between the frame and metal backing strip. Press down to release the refill from the retaining tab.

The Anco style is unlocked at one end by squeezing the metal tabs, and the refill is slid out of the frame jaws. When the new refill is installed, the tabs will click into place, locking the refill.

The polycarbonate type is held in place by a

locking lever that is pushed downward out of the groove in the arm to free the refill. When the new refill is installed, it will lock in place automatically.

No matter which type of refill you use, be sure that all of the frame claws engage the refill. Before operating the wipers, be sure that no part of the metal frame is contacting the windshield.

Tires and Wheels

The tires should be rotated as specified in the Maintenance Intervals chart. Refer to the accompanying illustrations for the recommended rotation patterns.

The tires on your truck should have built-in tread wear indicators, which appear as ½" (12.7mm) bands when the tread depth gets as low as $^1/_{16}$" (1.6mm). When the indicators appear in 2 or more adjacent grooves, it's time for new tires.

For optimum tire life, you should keep the tires properly inflated, rotate them often and have the wheel alignment checked periodically.

Some late models have the maximum load

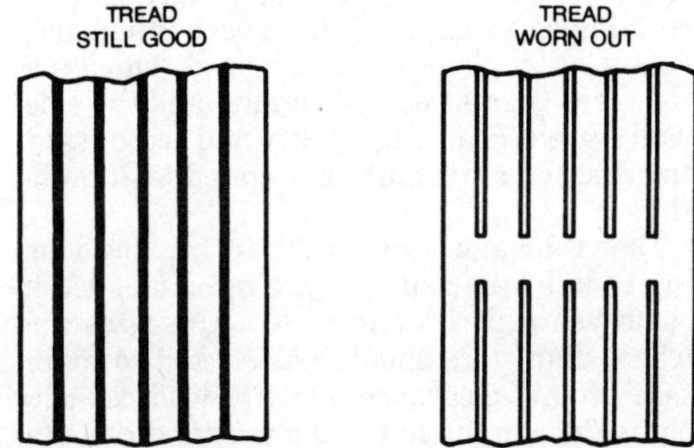

Tire tread wear indicators appear as solid bands when the tire is worn out

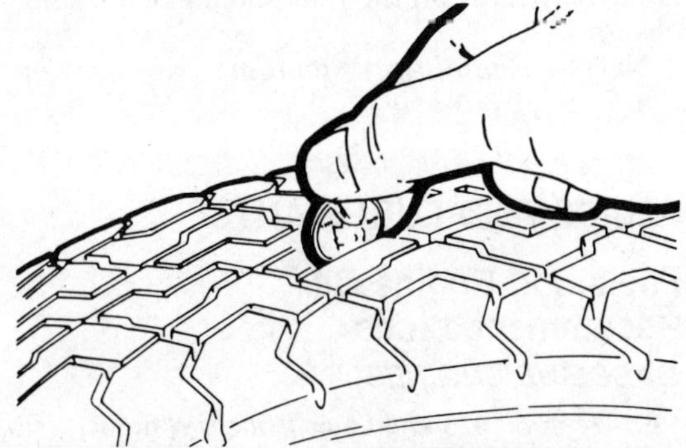

Tread depth can be checked with a penny; when the top of Lincoln's head is visible, it's time for new tires

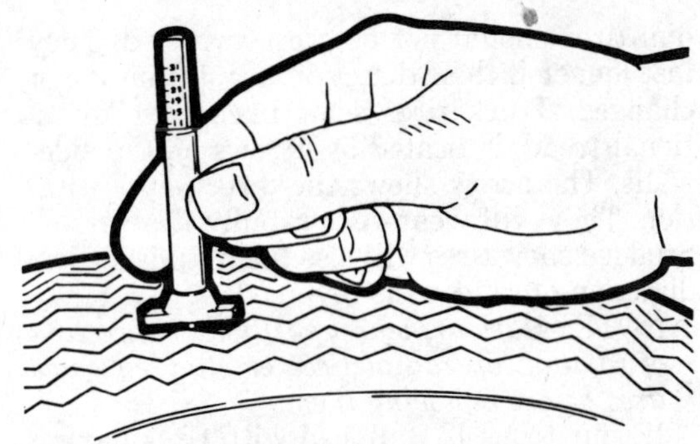

Tread depth can also be checked with an inexpensive gauge made for the purpose

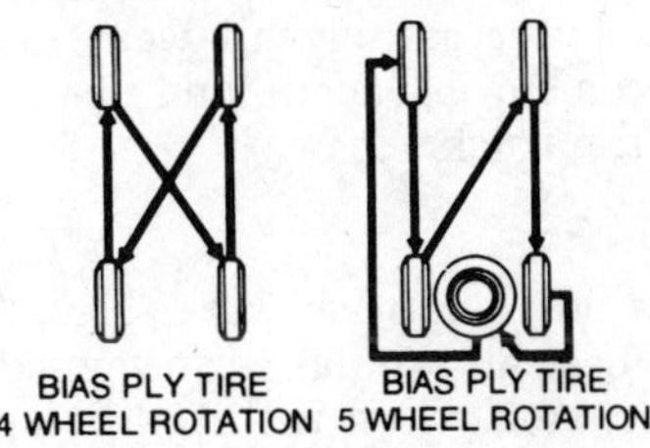

This rotation pattern is for bias or bias-belted tires only

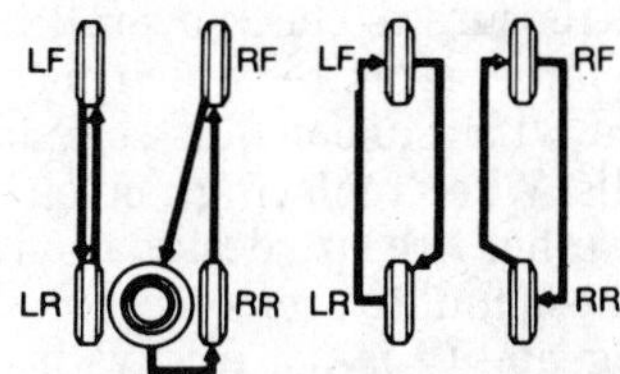

This rotation pattern is for radical tires; it can also be used for bias or bias-belted tires if you wish. The radial spare can be used on the left side, too, but don't change its direction of rotation once used

pressures listed in the V.I.N. plate on the left door frame. In general, pressure of 28–32 psi would be suitable for highway use with moderate loads and passenger car type tires (load range B, non-flotation) of original equipment size. Pressures should be checked before driving, since pressure can increase as much as 6 psi due to heat. It is a good idea to have an accurate gauge and to check pressures weekly. Not all gauges on service station air pumps are to be trusted. In general, truck type tires require higher pressures and flotation type tires, lower pressures.

TIRE ROTATION

It is recommended that you have the tires rotated every 6,000 miles. There is no way to give a tire rotation diagram for every combination of tires and vehicles, but the accompanying diagrams are a general rule to follow. Radial tires should not be cross-switched. They last longer if their direction of rotation is not changed. Truck tires sometimes have directional tread, indicated by arrows on the sidewalls. The arrow shows the direction of rotation. They will wear very rapidly if reversed. Studded snow tires will lose their studs if their direction of rotation is reversed.

NOTE: *Mark the wheel position or direction of rotation on radial tires or studded snow tires before removing them.*

If your truck is equipped with tires having different load ratings on the front and the rear, the tires should not be rotated front to rear. Rotating these tires could affect tire life (the tires with the lower rating will wear faster, and could become overloaded), and upset the handling of the truck.

TIRE USAGE

The tires on your truck were selected to provide the best all around performance for normal operation when inflated as specified. Oversize tires (Load Range D) will not increase the maximum carrying capacity of the vehicle, although they will provide an extra margin of tread life. Be sure to check overall height before using larger size tires which may cause interference with suspension components or wheel wells. When replacing conventional tire sizes with other tire size designations, be sure to check the manufacturer's recommendations. Interchangeability is not always possible because of differences in load ratings, tire dimensions, wheel well clearances, and rim size. Also due to differences in handling characteristics, 70 Series and 60 Series tires should be used only in pairs on the same axle. Radial tires should be used only in sets of four.

The wheels must be the correct width for the tire. Tire dealers have charts of tire and rim compatibility. A mismatch can cause sloppy handling and rapid tread wear. The old rule of thumb is that the tread width should match the rim width (inside bead to inside bead) within 1" (25.4mm). For radial tires, the rim width should be 80% or less of the tire (not tread) width.

The height (mounted diameter) of the new tires can greatly change speedometer accuracy, engine speed at a given road speed, fuel mileage, acceleration, and ground clearance. Tire manufacturers furnish full measurement specifications. Speedometer drive gears are available for correction.

NOTE: *Dimensions of tires marked the same size may vary significantly, even among tires from the same manufacturer.*

The spare tire should be usable, at least for low speed operation, with the new tires.

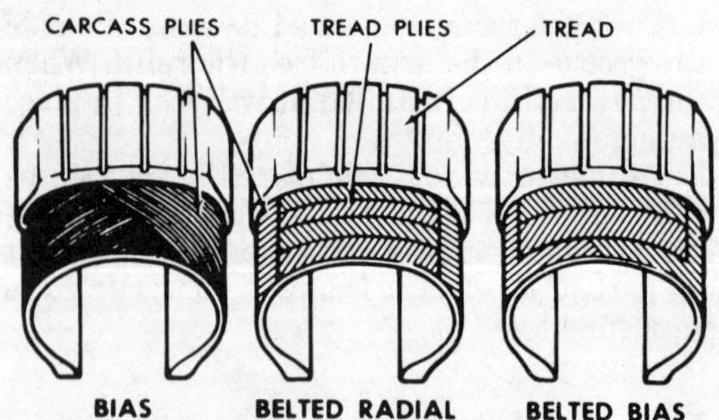

Types of tire construction

TIRE DESIGN

For maximum satisfaction, tires should be used in sets of five. Mixing or different types (radial, bias/belted, fiberglass belted) should be avoided. Conventional bias tires are constructed so that the cords run bead-to-bead at an angle. Alternate plies run at an opposite angle. This type of construction gives rigidity to both tread and sidewall. Bias/belted tires are similar in construction to conventional bias ply tires. Belts run at an angle and also at a 90° angle to the bead, as in the radial tire. Tread life is improved considerably over the conventional bias tire. The radial tire differs in construction, but instead of the carcass plies running at an angle of 90° to each other, they run at an angle of 90° to the bead. This gives the tread a great deal of rigidity and the sidewall a great deal of flexibility and accounts for the characteristic bulge associated with radial tires.

Chevrolet and GMC trucks are capable of using radial tires and they are recommended in some years. If they are used, tire sizes and wheel diameters should be selected to maintain ground clearance and tire load capacity equivalent to the minimum specified tire. Radial tires should always be used in sets of five, but in an emergency radial tires can be used with caution on the rear axle only. If this is done, both tires on the rear should be of radial design.

NOTE: *Radial tires should never be used on only the front axle.*

FLUIDS AND LUBRICANTS

Fuels and Engine Oil Recommendations

GASOLINE ENGINES

1967–74 and 1975 and Later Models Without Catalytic Converter

Chevrolet and GMC trucks are designed to operate on regular grades of fuel (1967–71) commonly sold in the U.S. and Canada. In 1972–74 (and 1975 later models without catalytic converter), unleaded or low-lead fuels of approximately 91 octane (Research Octane) or higher are recommended. General Motors recommends the use of low-leaded or unleaded fuels (0–0.5 grams per gallon) to reduce particulate and hydrocarbon pollutants.

Use of a fuel which is too low in anti-knock quality will result in spark knock. Since many factors affect operating efficiency, such as altitude, terrain and air temperature, knocking many result even though you are using the recommended fuel. If persistent knocking occurs, it may be necessary to switch to a slightly higher grade of gasoline to correct the problem. In the case of late model engines, switching to a premium fuel would be an unnecessary expense. In these engines, a slightly higher grade of gasoline (regular) should be used only when persistent knocking occurs. Continuous or excessive knocking may result in engine damage.

NOTE: *Your engine's fuel requirement can change time, mainly due to carbon buildup, which changes the compression ratio. If you engine pings, knocks, or runs on, switch to a higher grade of fuel and check the ignition timing as soon as possible. If you must use unleaded fuel, sometimes a change of brands will cure the problem. If is is necessary to retard the timing from specifications, don't change it more than about 4°. Retarded timing will reduce power output and fuel mileage, and it will increase engine temperature.*

1975 and Later Models with Catalytic Converter

Chevrolet and GMC trucks with Gross Vehicle Weight Ratings (GVWR) which place them in the heavy duty emissions class do not require a catalytic converter. However, almost all 1975 and later light duty emissions trucks have a catalytic converter. The light duty classification applies to all trucks with a GVWR under 6,000 lbs. through 1978, except for 1978 trucks sold in California. 1978 California models and all 1979 models with GVWR's under 8,500 lbs. fall into the light duty category. In 1980 and later, the light duty classification applies to all trucks with GVWR's under 8,600 lbs.

The catalytic converter is a muffler shaped device installed in the exhaust system. It contains platinum and palladium coated pellets which, through catalytic action, oxidize hydrocarbon and carbon monoxide gases into hydrogen, oxygen, and carbon dioxide.

The design of the converter requires the exclusive use of unleaded fuel. Leaded fuel renders the converter inoperative, raising exhaust emissions to legal levels. In addition, the lead in the gasoline coats the pellets in the converter, blocking the flow of exhaust gases. This raises exhaust back pressure and severely reduces engine performance. In extreme cases, the exhaust system becomes so clocked that the engine will not run.

Converter equipped trucks are delivered with the label "Unleaded Fuel Only" placed next to the fuel gauge on the instrument panel and next to the gas tank filler opening. In general, any unleaded fuel is suitable for use in these trucks as long as the gas has an octane rating or 87 or more. Octane ratings are posted on the gas pumps. However, in some cases, knocking may occur even though the recommended fuel is being used. The only practical solution for this is to switch to a slightly higher grade of unleaded fuel, or to switch brands of unleaded gasoline.

DIESEL ENGINES

Diesel engine pick-ups require the use of diesel fuel. Two grades of diesel fuel are manufactured, #1 and #2, although #2 grade is generally the only grade available. Better fuel economy results from the use of #2 grade fuel. In some northern parts of the U.S., and in most parts of Canada, #1 grade fuel is available in winter, or a winterized blend of #2 grade is supplied in winter months. If #1 grade is available, it should be used whenever temperatures fall below +20°F (–7°C). Winterized #2 grade may also be used at these temperatures. However, unwinterized #2 grade should not be used below +20°F (–7°C). Cold temperatures cause unwinterized #2 grade to thicken (it actually gels), blocking the fuel lines and preventing the engine from running.

Do not use home heating oil or gasoline in the diesel pick-up. Do not attempt to thin unwinterized #2 diesel fuel with gasoline. Gasoline line or home heating oil will damage the engine and void the manufacturer's warranty.

Engine

OIL RECOMMENDATIONS

The SAE grade number indicates the viscosity of the engine oil, or its ability to lubricate under a given temperature. The lower the SAE grade number, the lighter the oil; the lower the viscosity, the easier it is to crank the engine in cold weather.

The API (American Petroleum Institute) designation indicates the classification of engine oil for use under given operating conditions. Only oils designated for "Service SF" should be used. These oils provide maximum

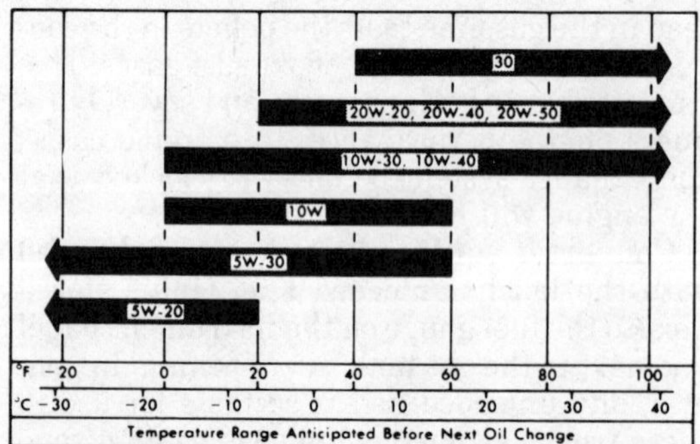

NOTES: 1. SAE 5W and 5W-20 are not recommended for sustained high speed driving.
2. SAE 5W-30 is recommended for all seasons in Canada

Gasoline Engine Oil Viscosity Chart

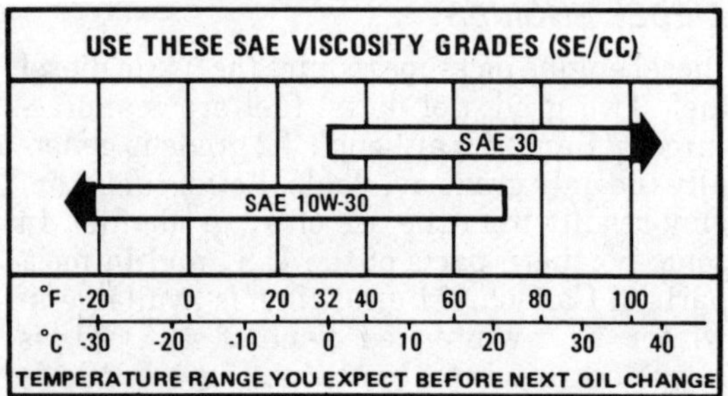

Diesel Engine Oil Viscosity Chart

engine protection. Both the SAE grade number and the API designation can be found on the top of a can of oil.

NOTE: *Non-detergent should not be used.*

Oil viscosities should be chosen from those oils recommended for the lowest anticipated temperatures during the oil change interval.

The multi-viscosity oils offer the important advantage of being adaptable to temperature extremes. They allow easy starting at low temperatures, yet give good protection at high speeds and engine temperatures. This is a decided advantage in changeable climates or in long distance driving.

Diesel engines also require SF engine oil. In addition, the oil must qualify for a CC rating. The API has a number of different diesel engine ratings, including CB, CC, and CD.

NOTE: *1981 and later diesel engines can use wither SF/CC, SF/CD.*

The diesel engine in the Chevrolet and GMC trucks require SF/CC rated oil. DO NOT use an oil if the designation CD appears anywhere on the oil can. Use SF/CC engine oil only. Do not use an oil labeled only SF or only CC. Both designations must appear.

For recommended oil viscosities, refer to the chart. 10W-30 grade oils are not recommended for sustained high speed driving.

Single viscosity oil (SAE 30) is recommended for sustained high speed driving.

SYNTHETIC OIL

There are excellent synthetic and fuel-efficient oils available that, under the right circumstances, can help provide better fuel mileage and better engine protection. However, these advantages come at a price, which can be three or four times the price per quart of conventional motor oils.

Before pouring any synthetic oils into your car's engine, you should consider the condition of the engine and the type of driving you do. Also, check the truck's warranty conditions regarding the use of synthetics.

Generally, it is best to avoid the use of synthetic oil in both brand new and older, high mileage engines. New engines require a proper break-in, and the synthetics are so slippery that they can prevent this. Most manufacturers recommend that you wait at least 5,000 miles before switching to a synthetic oil. Conversely, older engines are looser and tend to use more oil. Synthetics will slip past worn pats more readily than regular oil, and will be used up faster. If your car already leaks and/or uses oil (due to worn parts and bad seals or gaskets), it will leak and use more with a slippery synthetic inside.

Consider your type of driving. If most of your accumulated mileage is on the highway at higher, steadier speeds, a synthetic oil will reduce friction and probably help deliver fuel mileage. Under such ideal highway conditions, the oil change interval can be extended, as long as the oil filter will operate effectively for the extended life of the oil. If the filter can't do its job for this extended period, dirt and sludge will build up in your engine's crankcase, sump, oil pump and lines, no matter what type of oil is used. If using synthetic oil in this manner, you should continue to change the oil filter at the recommended intervals.

Trucks used under harder, stop-and-go, short hop circumstances should always be serviced more frequently, and for these cars synthetic oil may not be a wise investment. Because of the necessary shorter change interval needed for this type of driving, you cannot take advantage of the long recommended change interval of most synthetic oils.

Finally, most synthetic oil are not compatible with conventional oils and cannot be added to them. This means you should always carry a couple of quarts of synthetic oil with you while on a long trip, as not all service stations carry this oil.

Engine

OIL LEVEL CHECK

The engine oil should be checked on a regular basis, ideally at each fuel stop. If the van is used for trailer towing or for heavy duty use, it would be safer to check it more often.

When checking the oil level it is best that the oil be at operating temperature, although checking the level immediately after stopping will give a false reading because all of the oil will not yet have drained back into the crankcase. Be sure that the van is resting on a level surface, allowing time for the oil to drain back into the crankcase.

1. Open the hood or engine compartment and locate the dipstick. Remove it from the tube. The oil dipstick is located on the passenger's side of 6 cylinder engines and on the driver's side of V8s.
2. Wipe the dipstick with a clean rag.
3. Insert the dipstick fully into the tube, and remove it again. Hold the dipstick horizontally

Check engine crankcase oil level with the dipstick

The oil level should show between the "ADD" and "FULL" marks on the dipstick

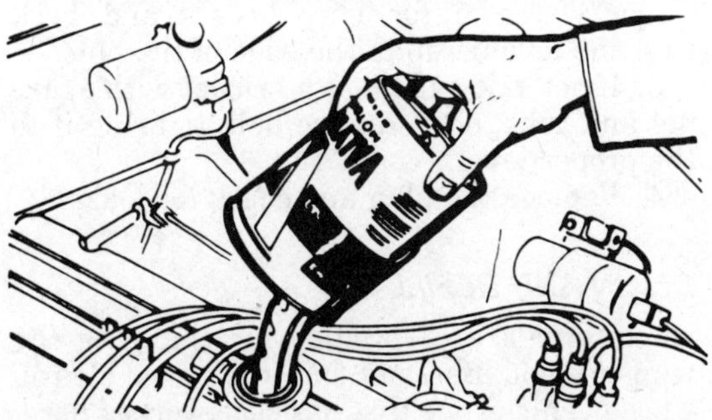

Add oil through the capped opening in the valve cover

and read the oil level. The level should be between the "FULL" and "ADD OIL" marks. If the oil level is at or below the "ADD OIL" mark, oil should be added as necessary. Oil is added through the capped opening on the valve cover(s). See Oil and Fuel Recommendations for proper viscosity and oil to use.

4. Replace the dipstick and check the level after adding oil. Be careful not to overfill the crankcase. There is about 1 quart between the marks.

OIL AND FILTER CHANGE

Engine oil should be changed according to the schedule in the Maintenance Interval Chart. Under conditions such as:

- Driving in dusty conditions
- Continuous trailer pulling or RV use
- Extensive or prolonged idling
- Extensive short trip operation in freezing temperatures (when the engine is not thoroughly warmed up)
- Frequent long runs at high speeds and high ambient temperatures
- Stop-and-go service such as delivery trucks, the oil change interval and filter replacement interval should be cut in half. Operation of the engine in severe conditions such as a dust storm may require an immediate oil and filter change.

Chevrolet and GMC recommended changing both the oil and filter during the first oil change and the filter every other oil change thereafter. Fro the small price of an oil filter, it's cheap insurance to replace the filter at every oil change. One of the larger filter manufacturers points out in its advertisements that not changing the filter leaves one quart of dirty oil in the engine. This claim is true and should be kept in mind when changing your oil.

NOTE: *The oil filter on the diesel engines must be changed every oil change.*

To change the oil, the truck should be on a level surface, and the engine should be at operating temperature. This is to ensure that the foreign matter will be drained away along with the oil, and not left in the engine to form sludge. You should have available a container

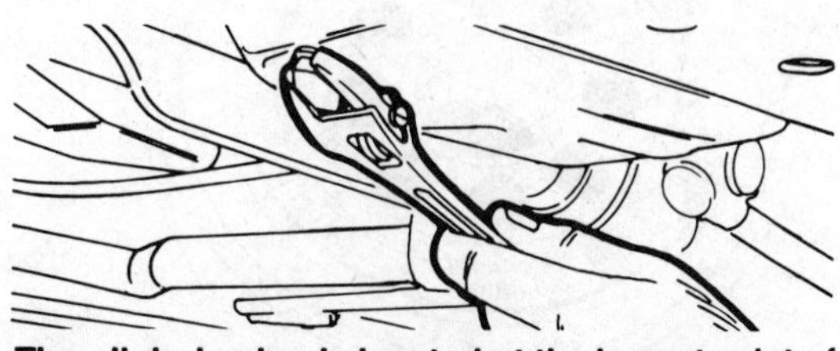

The oil drain plug is located at the lowest point of the engine oil pan

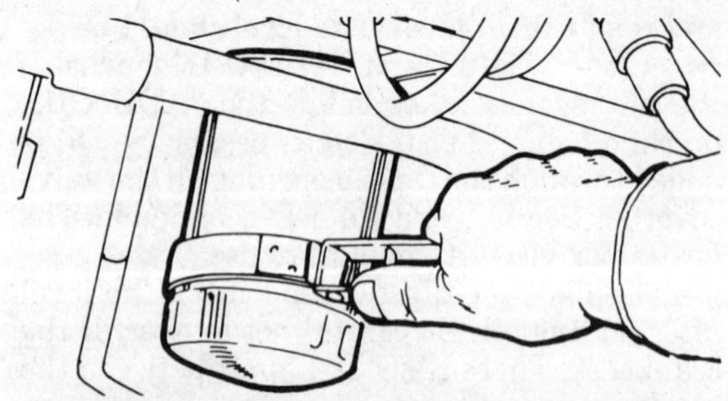

Use a strap wrench to loosen the oil filter; install the new filter by hand

that will hold a minimum of 8 quarts of liquid, a wrench to fit the old drain plug, a spout for pouring in new oil, and a rag or two, which you will always need. If the filter is being replaced, you will also need a band wrench or filter wrench to fit the end of the filter.

NOTE: *If the engine is equipped with an oil cooler, this will also have to be drained, using the drain plug. Be sure to add enough oil to fill the cooler in addition to the engine.*

1. Position the truck on a level surface and set the parking brake or block the wheels. Slide a drain pan under the oil drain plug.
2. From under the truck, loosen, but do not remove the oil drain plug. Cover your hand with a rag or glove and slowly unscrew the drain plug.

CAUTION: *The engine oil will be HOT. Keep your arms, face and hands clear of the oil as it drains out.*

3. Remove the plug and let the oil drain into the pan.

NOTE: *Do not drop the plug into the drain pan.*

4. When all of the oil has drained, clean off the drain plug and put it back into the hole. Remember to tighten the plug 20 ft.lb. (30 ft.lb. for diesel engines).
5. Loosen the filter with a band wrench or special oil filter cap wrench. On most Chevrolet engines, especially the V8s, the oil filter is next to the exhaust pipes. Stay clear of these, since even a passing contact will result in a painful burn.

NOTE: *On trucks equipped with catalytic converters stay clear of the converter. The outside temperature of a hot catalytic converter can approach 1,200°F.*

6. Cover your hand with a rag, and spin the filter off by hand.
7. Coat the rubber gasket on a new filter with a light film of clean engine oil. Screw the filter onto the mounting stud and tighten according to the directions on the filter (usually hand tight one turn past the point where the gasket contacts the mounting base). Don't overtighten the filter.
8. Refill the engine with the specified amount of clean engine oil.
9. Run the engine for several minutes, checking for leaks. Check the level of the oil and add oil if necessary.

When you have finished this job, you will notice that you now possess four or five quarts of dirty oil. The best thing to do with it is to pour it into plastic jugs, such as milk or antifreeze containers. Then, if you are on good terms with you gas station man, he might let you pour it into his used oil container for recycling. Otherwise, the only thing to do with it is to put the containers into the trash.

Coat the gasket on the new oil filter with a film of oil

Manual Transmission

FLUID RECOMMENDATION

Where ambient temperatures are consistently above freezing, use SAE 80W-90 GL-5. For vehicles normally operated in cold climates, use SAE 80W GL-5 gear lubricant.

FLUID LEVEL CHECK

Check the lubricant level at the interval specified in the maintenance chart.

1. With the truck parked on a level surface, remove the filler plug from the side of the transmission case. Be careful not to take out the drain plug at the bottom.
2. If lubricant begins to trickle out of the hole, there is enough. If not, carefully insert a finger (watch out for sharp threads) and check that the level is up to the edge of the hole.
3. If not, add sufficient lubricant with a funnel and tube, or a squeeze bulb to bring it to the proper level.
4. Replace the plug and check for leaks.

DRAIN AND REFILL

No intervals are specified for changing the transmission lubricant, but it is a good idea on a used vehicle, one that has been worked hard, or one driven in deep water. The vehicle should

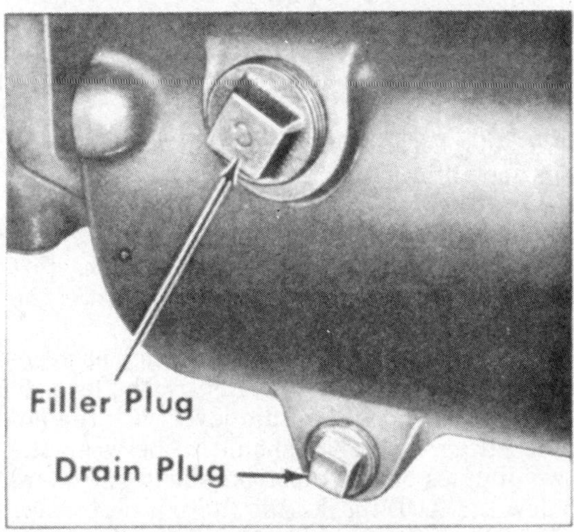

Manual transmission fill and drain plugs

be on a level surface and the lubricant should be at operating temperature.

1. Position the truck on a level surface.
2. Place a pan of sufficient capacity under the transmission drain plug.
3. Remove the upper (fill) plug to provide a vent opening.
4. Remove the lower (drain) plug and let the lubricant drain out. The 1976–82 Tremec top cover 3-speed is drained by removing the lower extension housing bolt.
5. Replace the drain plug.
6. Add lubricant with a suction gun or squeeze bulb.
7. Reinstall the filler plug. Run the engine and check for leaks.

Automatic Transmission

FLUID RECOMMENDATIONS

Use only high quality automatic transmission fluids that are identified by the name DEXRON® or DEXRON®II.

LEVEL CHECK

Check the level of the fluid at the specified interval. The fluid level should be checked with the engine at normal operating temperature and running. If the truck has been running at high speed for a long period, in city traffic on a hot day, or pulling a trailer, let it cool down for about thirty minutes before checking the level.

1. Park on the level with the engine running and the shift lever in Park.
2. Remove the dipstick at the rear of the engine compartment. Cautiously feel the end of the dipstick with your fingers. Wipe it off and replace it, then pull it again and check the level of the fluid on the dipstick.
3. If the fluid felt cool, the level should be

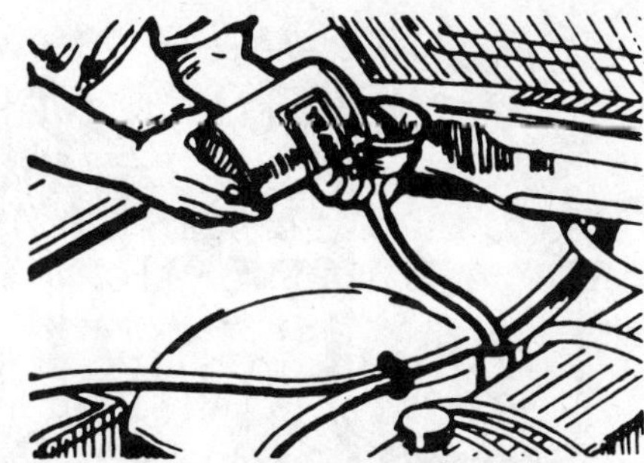
Add automatic transmission fluid through the automatic transmission dipstick tube, using a funnel

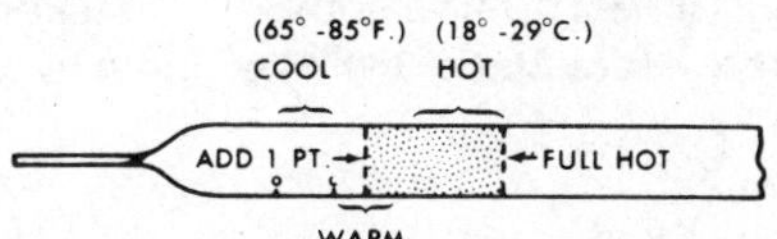

NOTE: DO NOT OVERFILL. It takes only one pint to raise level from ADD to FULL with a hot transmission.

Automatic transmission dipstick markings

between the two dimples below ADD. If it was too hot to hold, the level should be between the ADD and FULL marks.

4. If the fluid is at or below the ADD mark, add fluid through the dipstick tube. One pint raises the level from ADD to FULL when the fluid is hot. The correct fluid to use is DEXRON®II. Be certain that the transmission is not overfilled, this will cause foaming, fluid loss, and slippage.

PAN AND FILTER SERVICE/DRAIN AND REFILL

The fluid should be drained with the transmission warm. It is easier to change the fluid if the truck is raised somewhat from the ground, but this is not always easy without a lift. The transmission must be level for it to drain properly.

1. Place a shallow pan underneath to catch the transmission fluid (about 5 pints). On earlier models, the transmission pan has a drain plug. Remove this and drain the fluid. For later models, loosen all the pan bolts, then pull one corner down to drain most of the fluid. If it sticks, VERY CAREFULLY pry the pan loose. You can buy aftermarket drain plug kits that makes this operation a bit less messy, once installed.

   NOTE: *If the fluid removed smells burnt, serious transmission troubles, probably due to overheating, should be suspected.*

2. Remove the pan bolts and empty out the pan. On some models, there may not be much room to get at the screws at the front of the pan.

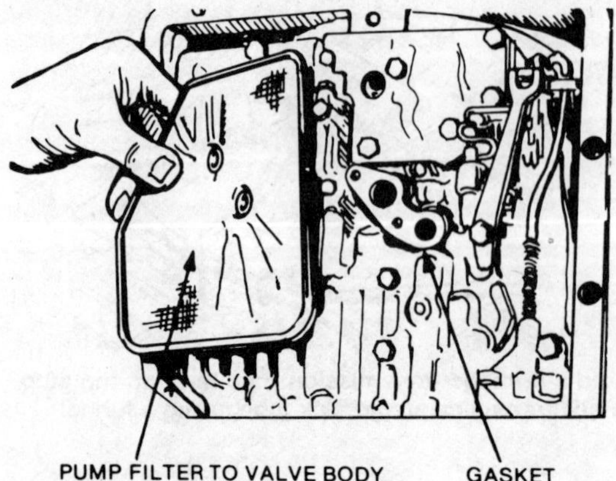

The Turbo Hydra-Matic 350 filter mounts to the valve body

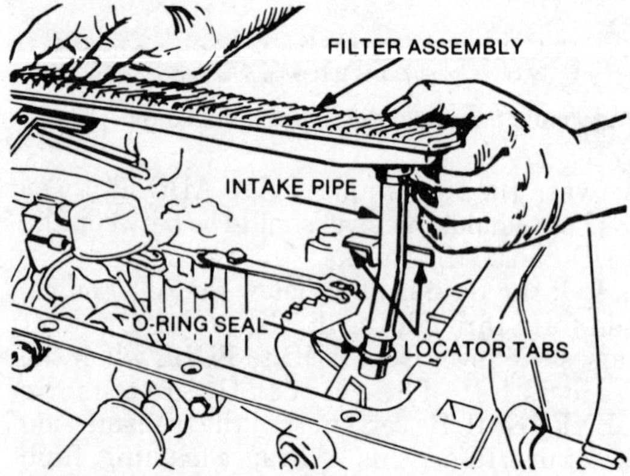

The Turbo Hydra-Matic 400 filter has an O-ring on the intake pipe; check the condition of this O-ring, and replace as necessary

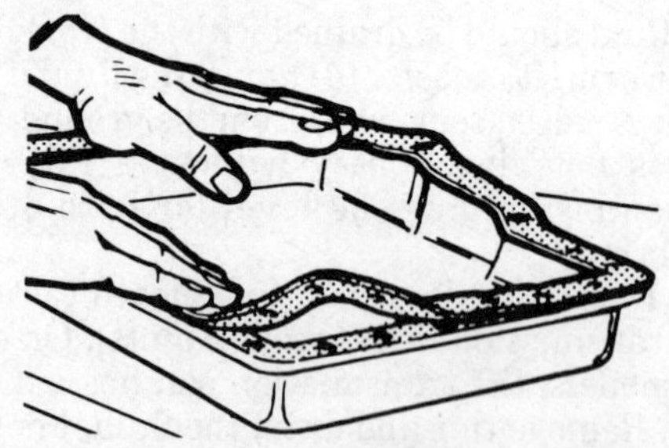
Install the new gasket to the pan

3. Clean the pan with solvent and allow it to air dry. If you use a rag to wipe it out, you risk leaving bits of lint and threads in the transmission.
4. Remove the filter or strainer retaining bolts. On the Turbo Hydra-Matic 400, there are two screws securing the filter or screen to the valve body. A reusable strainer may be found on some models. The strainer may be cleaned in solvent and air dried thoroughly. The filter and gasket must be replaced.
5. Install a new gasket and filter.
6. Install a new gasket on the pan, and tighten the bolts evenly to 12 foot pounds in a criss-cross pattern.
7. Add DEXRON® or DEXRON®II transmission fluid through the dipstick tube. The correct amount is in the Capacities Chart. Do not overfill.
8. With the gearshift lever in PARK, start the engine and let it idle. Do not race the engine.
9. Move the gearshift lever through each position, holding the brakes. Return the lever to PARK, and check the fluid level with the engine idling. The level should be between the two dimples on the dipstick, about 1/4" (6mm) below the ADD mark. Add fluid, if necessary.
10. Check the fluid level after the truck has been driven enough to thoroughly warm up the transmission. Details are given under Fluid Level Checks earlier in the Chapter. If the transmission is overfilled, the excess must be drained off. Overfilling causes aerated fluid, resulting in transmission slippage and probable damage.

Rear Axle Differential

FLUID RECOMMENDATION

Rear axles use SAE 80W-90 GL-5 gear oil. Positraction® axles must use special lubricant available from dealers. If the special fluid is not used, noise, uneven operation, and damage will result. There is also a Positraction® additive used to cure noise and slippage. Positraction axles have an identifying tag, as well as a warning sticker near the jack or on the rear wheel well.

FLUID LEVEL CHECK

Lubricant levels in the rear axle should be checked as specified in the Maintenance chart. To check the lubricant level:

1. Park on level ground.
2. Remove the filler plug from the differential housing cover.
3. If lubricant trickles out, there is enough. If not, carefully insert a finger and check that the level is up to the bottom of the hole. Front axles should be full up to the level of the hole when warm, and 1/2" (12.7mm) below when cool.
4. Lubricant may be added with a funnel or a squeeze bulb. Rear axles use SAE 80W-90 GL-5 gear lubricant.

Positraction® limited slip axles must use a special lubricant available from dealers. If the special fluid is not used, noise, uneven operation, and damage will result. There is also a Positraction® additive to cure noise and slip-

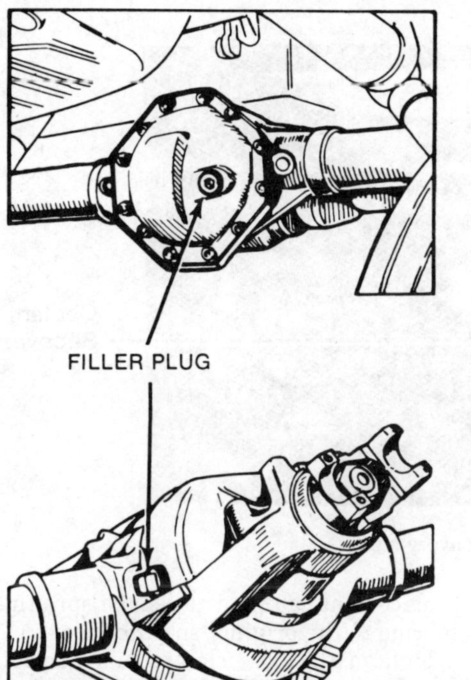

The rear axle filler plug may be in either of the two locations shown here

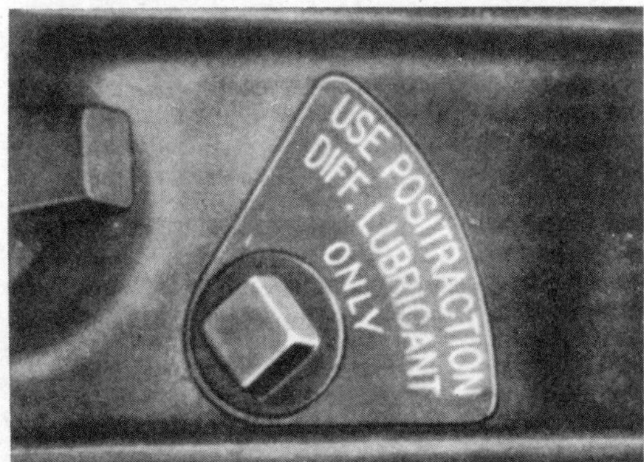

Positraction rear axle identification tag

page. Positraction® axles have an identifying tag, as well as a warning sticker near the jack or on the rear wheel well.

REAR AXLE DRAIN AND REFILL

No intervals are specified for changing axle lubricant, but it is a good idea, especially if you have driven in water over the axle vents.

1. Park the vehicle on the level with the axles at normal operating temperature.
2. Place a pan of at least 6 pints capacity under the differential housing.
3. Remove the filler plug.
4. If you have a drain plug, remove it. If not, unbolt and remove the differential cover.
5. Replace the drain plug, or differential cover. Use a new gasket if the differential cover has been removed.
6. Lubricant may be added with a suction gun or squeeze bulb. Rear axles use SAE 80W-90 gear oil. Positraction® axles must use special lubricant available from dealers. If the special fluid is not used, noise, uneven operation, and damage will result. There is also a Positraction® additive used to cure noise and slippage. Positraction axles have an identifying tag, as well as a warning sticker near the jack or on the rear wheel well. Rear axle lubricant level should be up to the bottom of the filler plug opening.

Cooling System

The coolant level should be checked at each fuel stop, ideally, to prevent the possibility of overheating and serious engine damage. If not, it should at least be checked once each month.

The cooling system was filled at the factory with a high quality coolant solution that is good for year around operation and protects the system from freezing down to -20°F (-29°C) (-32°F [-36°C] in Canada). It is good for two full calendar years or 24,000 miles, whichever occurs first, provided that the proper concentration of coolant is maintained.

The 1973 and later cooling system differs slightly from those used on 1967–72 trucks. The 1973 and later system incorporates a plastic expansion tank connected to the radiator by a hose from the base of the radiator filler neck. The hot coolant level on 1973 and later trucks should be at the FULL HOT mark on the expansion tank and the cold coolant level should be at the FULL COLD mark on the tank. Do not remove the radiator cap to check the coolant level on 1973 and later trucks. On 1967–72 trucks, the cold coolant level should be approximately 3″ (76mm) below the bottom of the filler neck, and the hot level should be 1–1½″ (25.4–38.1mm) below the bottom of the filler neck.

FLUID RECOMMENDATION

Coolant mixture in Chev/GMC Vans is 50/50 ethylene glycol and water for year round use. Use a good quality antifreeze with water pump lubricants, rust inhibitors and other corrosion inhibitors along with acid neutralizers.

LEVEL CHECK

1. On 1973 and later models, check the level on the see-through expansion tank. On earlier models it will be necessary to CAREFULLY remove the radiator cap.

CAUTION: *The radiator coolant is under*

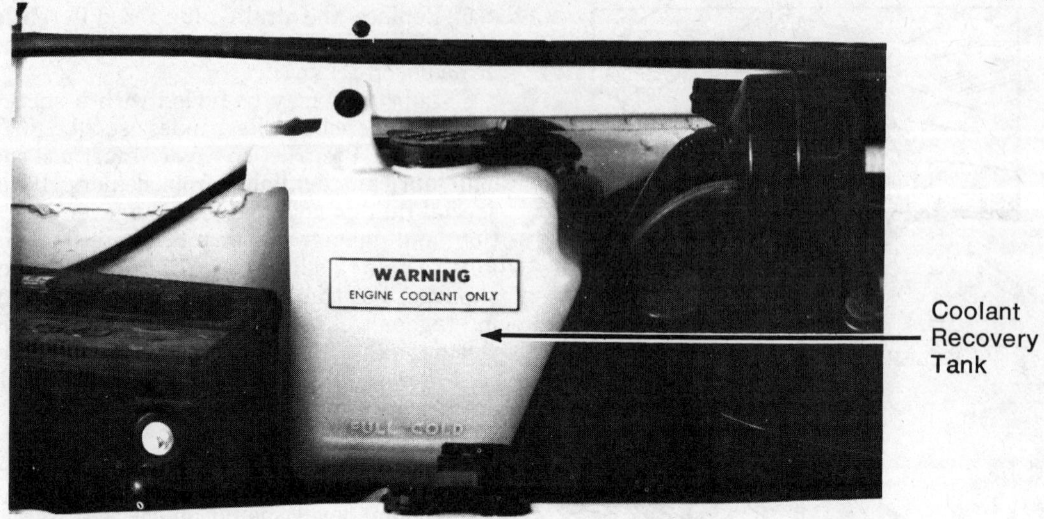

Typical coolant recovery tank

pressure when hot. To avoid the danger of physical harm, coolant level should be checked or replenished only when the engine is cold. To remove the radiator cap when the engine is hot, first cover the cap with a thick rag, or wear a heavy glove for protection. Press down on the cap slightly and slowly turn it counterclockwise until it reaches the first stop. Allow all the pressure to vent (indicated when the hissing sound stops). When the pressure is released, press down on the cap and continue to rotate it counterclockwise. Some radiator caps have a lever for venting the pressure, but you should still exercise extreme caution when removing the cap.

2. Check the level and, if necessary, add coolant to the proper level. Use a 50/50 mix of ethylene glycol antifreeze and water. Alcohol or methanol base coolants are not recommended. Antifreeze solutions should be used, even in summer, to prevent rust and to take advantage of the solution's higher boiling point compared to plain water. This is imperative on air conditioned trucks; the heater core can freeze if it isn't protected. On 1974 and later models, coolant should be added through the coolant recovery tank, not the radiator filler neck.

CAUTION: *Never add large quantities of cold coolant to a hot engine. A cracked engine block may result.*

3. Replace the plug.

Each year the cooling system should be serviced as follows:

• Wash the radiator cap and filler neck with clean water.

• Check the coolant for proper level and freeze protection.

• Have the system pressure tested (15 psi). If a replacement cap is installed, be sure that it conforms to the original specifications.

• Tighten the hose clamps and inspect all hoses. Replace hoses that are swollen, cracked or otherwise deteriorated.

• Clean the frontal area of the radiator core and the air conditioning condenser, if so equipped.

DRAINING, FLUSHING AND TESTING THE COOLING SYSTEM AND COOLANT

The cooling system in you car accumulates some internal rust and corrosion in its normal operation. A simple method of keeping the system clean is known as flushing the system. It is performed by circulating a can of radiator flush through the system, and then draining and refilling the system with the normal coolant. Radiator flush is marketed by several different manufacturers, and is available in cans at auto departments, parts stores, and many hardware stores. This operation should be performed every 30,000 miles or once a year.

To flush the cooling system:

CAUTION: *When draining the coolant, keep in mind that cats and dogs are attracted by the ethylene glycol antifreeze, and are quite likely to drink any that is left in an uncovered container or in puddles on the ground. This will prove fatal in sufficient quantity. Always drain the coolant into a sealable container. Coolant should be reused unless it is contaminated or several years old.*

1. Drain the existing antifreeze and coolant. Open the radiator and engine drain petcocks (located near the bottom of the radiator and engine block, respectively), or disconnect the bottom radiator hose at the radiator outlet.

NOTE: *Before opening the radiator petcock,*

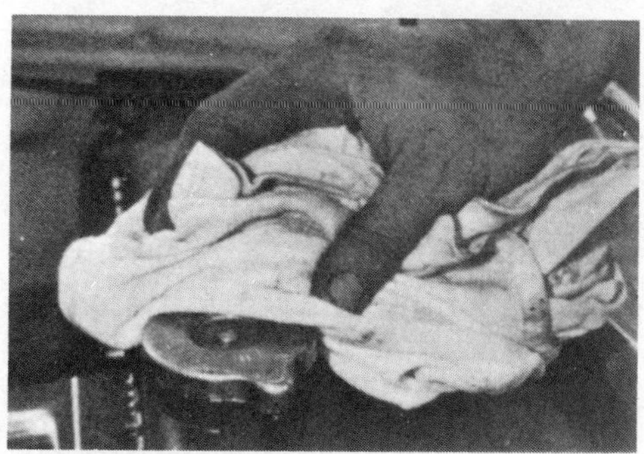
If you must remove the radiator cap when hot, cover the cap with a thick rag

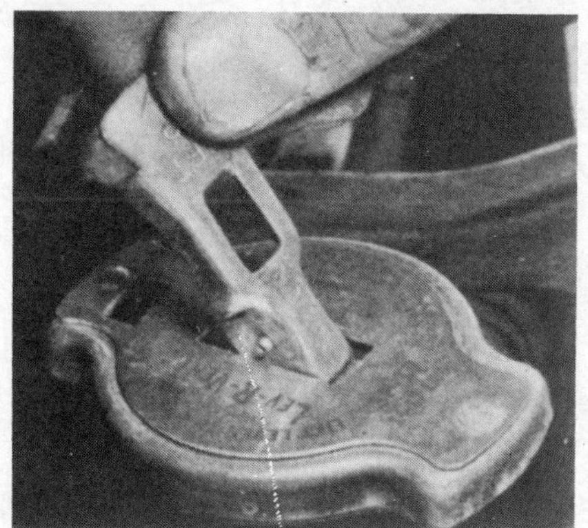
Some radiator caps have levers to vent pressure before the cap is removed

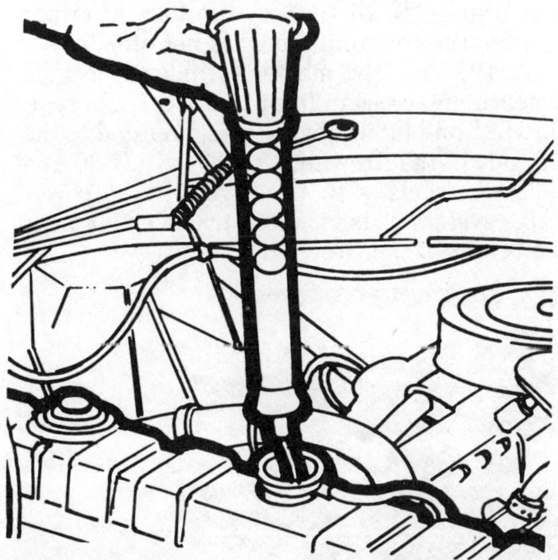
Coolant protection can be checked with a simple float-type tester

spray it with some penetrating oil. Be aware that if the engine has been run up to operating temperature, the coolant emptied will be HOT.

2. Close the petcock or reconnect the lower hose and fill the system with water – hot water if the system has just been run.

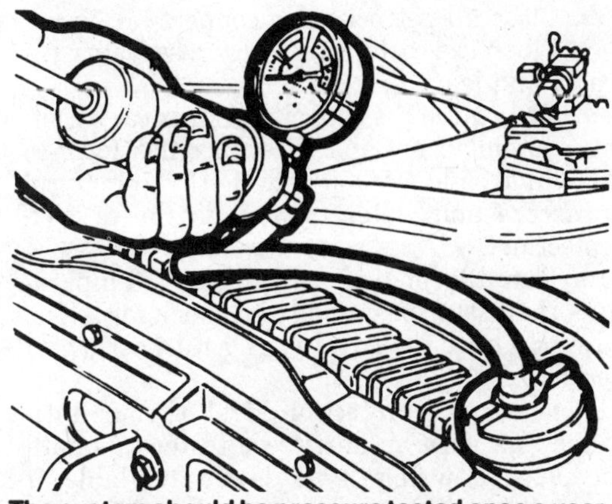
The system should be pressure tested once a year

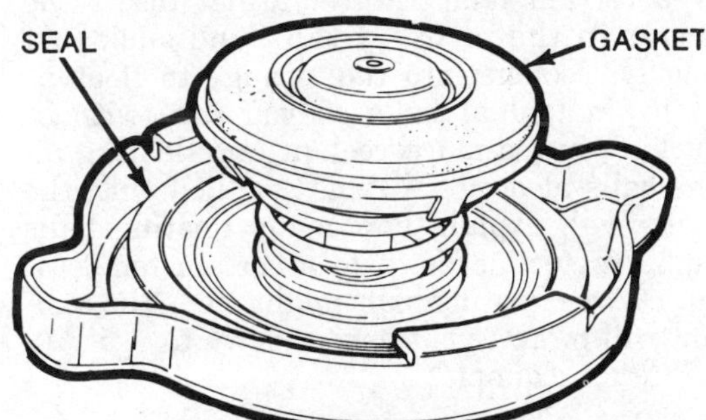

Check the radiator cap's rubber gasket and metal seal for deterioration at least once a year

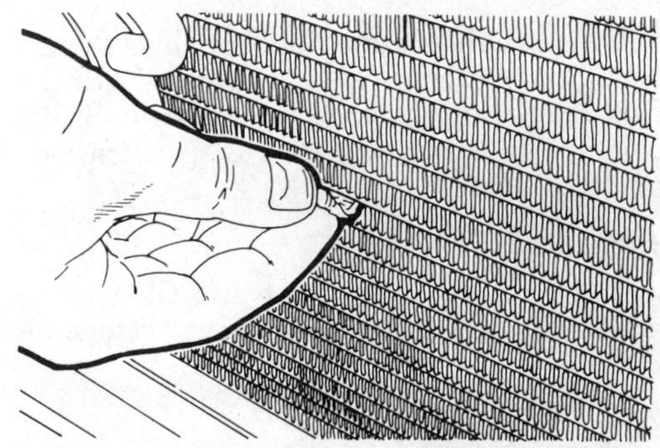
Remove any debris from the radiator's cooling fins

3. Add a can of quality radiator flush to the radiator or recovery tank, following any special instructions on the can.

4. Idle the engine as long as specified on the can of flush, or until the upper radiator hose gets hot.

5. Drain the system again. There should be quite a bit of scale and rust in the drained water.

6. Repeat this process until the drained water is mostly clear.

7. Close all petcocks and connect all hoses.
8. Flush the coolant recovery reservoir with water and leave empty.
9. Determine the capacity of your car's cooling system (see Capacities specifications in this guide. Add a 50/50 mix of ethylene glycol antifreeze and water to provide the desired protection.
10. Run the engine to operating temperature, then stop the engine and check for leaks. Check the coolant level and top up if necessary.
11. Check the protection level of your antifreeze mix with an antifreeze tester (a small, inexpensive syringe type device available at any auto parts store). The tester has five or six small colored balls inside, each of which signify a certain temperature rating. Insert the tester in the recovery tank and suck just enough coolant into the syringe to float as many individual balls as you can (without sucking in too much coolant and floating all the balls at once). A table supplied with the tester will explain how many floating balls equal protection down to a certain temperature (three floating balls might mean the coolant will protect your engine down to +5°F (–15°C), for example.

1967–69 master cylinder access plate

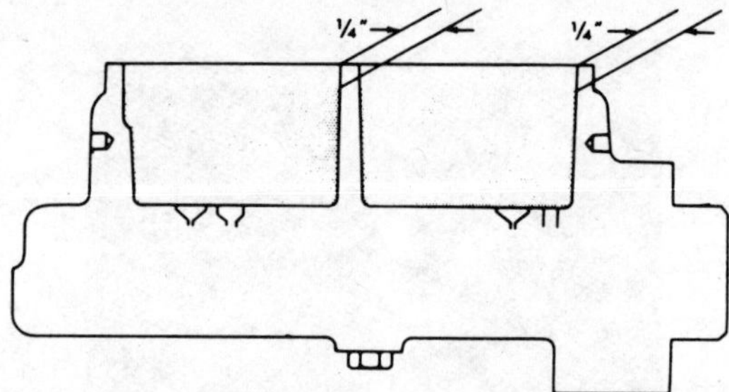

Master cylinder fluid level

Master Cylinder

FLUID RECOMMENDATIONS

Only high quality brake fluids, such as General Motors Supreme No. 11 Hydraulic Brake Fluid, Delco Supreme No. 11 Hydraulic Brake Fluid or fluids meeting DOT-3 specifications should be used.

LEVEL CHECK

Beginning 1967, Chevrolet and GMC vans were equipped with a dual braking system, allowing a vehicle to be brought to a safe stop in the event of failure in either front or rear brakes. The dual master cylinder has 2 entirely separate reservoirs, one connected to the front brakes and the other connected to the rear brakes. In the event of failure in either portion, the remaining part is not affected.

On 1967–69, the master cylinder is located beneath an access in front of the driver's seat. On 1971 and later models, it is mounted to the left side of the firewall. On 1973–75 G-30 and G-3500 models with the Hydro-Boost power brake system, it is mounted transversely near the center of the firewall.

1973–75 Hydro-Boost master cylinder

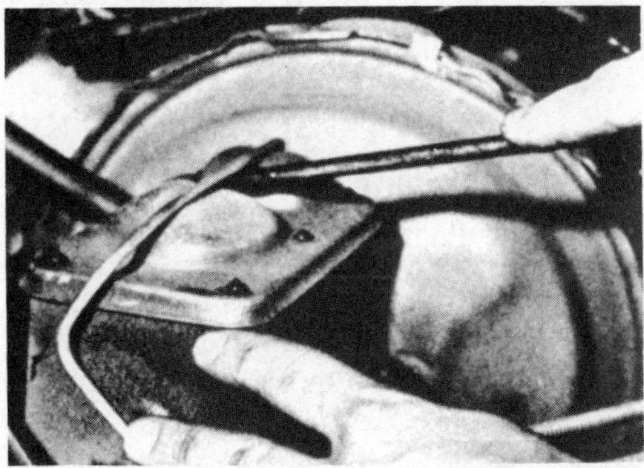

Pry the retaining bail from the top of the master cylinder

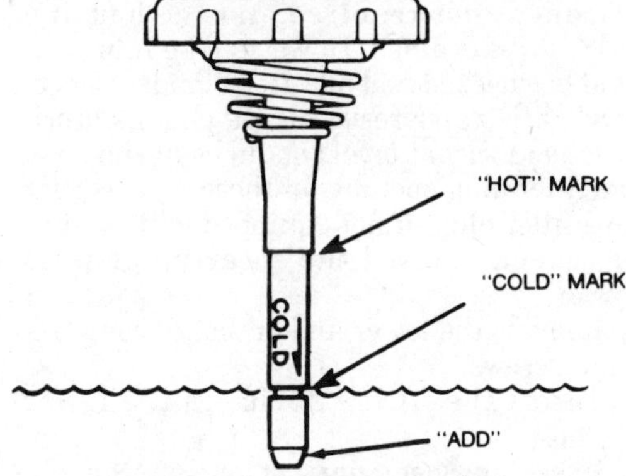

Power steering reservoir dipstick

1. Clean all of the dirt from around the cover of the master cylinder.
2. Be sure that the vehicle is resting on a level surface. If necessary, remove the floor mat and access cover.
3. Carefully pry the clip from the top of the master cylinder to release the cover.
4. The fluid level should be approximately ¼″ (6mm) from the top of the master cylinder. If not, add fluid until the level is correct. Replacement fluid should be Delco Supreme No. 11, DOT 3, or its equivalent.

   NOTE: *It is normal for the fluid level to fall as the disc brake ads wear.*

   CAUTION: *Brake fluid dissolves paint. It also absorbs moisture from the air. Never leave a container or the master cylinder uncovered any longer than necessary.*
5. Install the cover of the master cylinder. On most models there is a rubber gasket under the cover, which fits into 2 slots on the cover. Be sure that this is seated properly.
6. Push the clip back into place and be sure that it seats in the groove on the top of the cover.
7. As necessary, replace the access cover and floor mat.

Power Steering Pump

FLUID RECOMMENDATION

The power steering reservoir should be filled with GM Power Steering fluid, or its equivalent. Automatic Transmission Fluid DEXRON® or DEXRON®II is also satisfactory.

POWER STEERING RESERVOIR LEVEL CHECK

Check the dipstick in the pump reservoir when the fluid is at operating temperature. The fluid should be between the HOT and COLD marks. If the fluid is at room temperature, the fluid should be between the ADD and COLD marks. The fluid does not require periodic changing.

On systems with a remote reservoir, the level should be maintained approximately ½–1″ (12.7–25.4mm) from the top with the wheels in the full left turn position.

Steering Gear

FLUID RECOMMENDATION

On 1967–69 models, the steering gear should be filled with water resistant EP Chassis Lubricant that meets General Motors Specification GM 6031M.

Beginning 1970, no lubrication is needed for the life of the gear, except in the event of seal replacement or overhaul, when the gear should be refilled with a 13 oz. container of Steering Gear Lubricant (Part No. 1051052) which meets GM Specification GM 4673M, or its equivalent.

NOTE: *On these models do not use EP Chassis Lubricant.*

FLUID LEVEL CHECK

1967–69

The steering gear is filled at the factory with a water resistant grease. Seasonal change of the

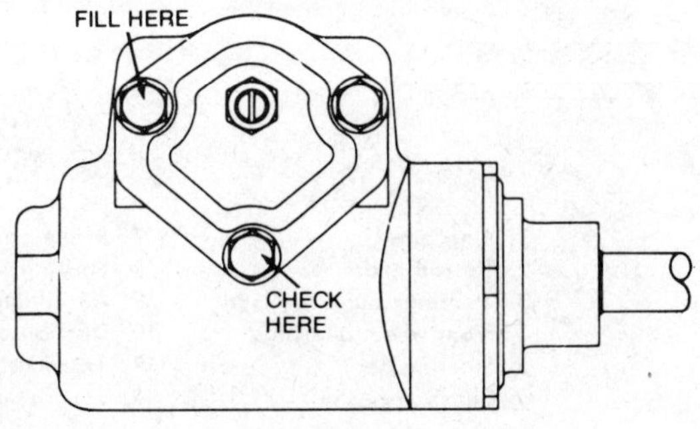

Steering box lubrication point

lubricant is not required and the housing should not be drained. However, the lubricant should be checked and additions made, as necessary, with water resistant EP chassis lubricant. The lubricant level should be at the level of the filler plug opening on those models that have a filler plug. If not equipped with a filler plug, check and fill the steering gear as follows:

1. Remove the lower and outboard cover retaining screws.
2. Insert the filling device in the lower screw hole.
3. Inject lubricant until it appears on the other screw hole. The gear is now filled to the correct level.
4. Replace the lower and outboard cover retaining screws.

1970–86

The steering gear is factory filled with a lubricant which does not require seasonal change. The housing should not be drained. No lubricant is required for the life of the gear.

The gear should be inspected for seal leakage. Look for solid grease, not an oily film. If a seal is replaced or the gear overhauled, the gear should be filled with Part No. 1051052, which is a 13 oz. container of Steering Gear lubricant which meets GM Specifications. Do not use EP Chassis Lube to lubricate the gear and do not overfill.

Chassis Greasing

Refer to the diagrams for chassis points to be lubricated. Not all vehicles have all the fittings illustrated. Water resistant EP chassis lubricant (grease) conforming to GM specification 6031-M should be used for all chassis grease points.

Body Lubrication

HOOD LATCH AND HINGES

Clean the latch surfaces and apply clean engine oil to the latch pilot bolts and the spring anchor. Also lubricate the hood hinges with engine oil. Use a chassis grease to lubricate all the pivot points in the latch release mechanism.

DOOR HINGES

The gas tank filler door and truck doors should be wiped clean and lubricated with clean engine oil once a year. The door lock cylinders and latch mechanisms should be lubricated pe-

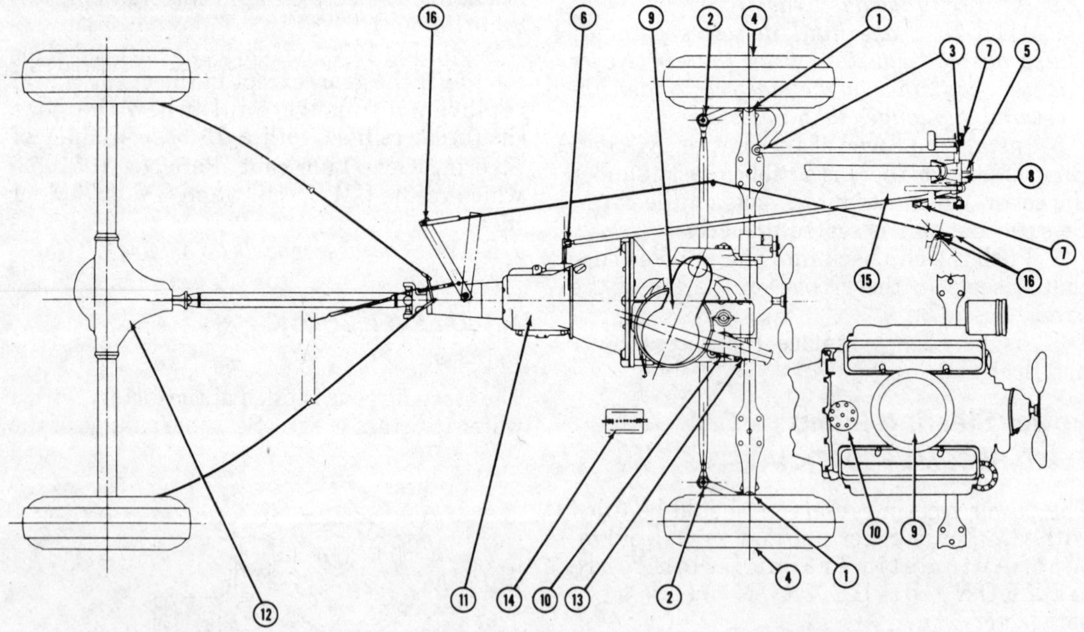

Typical 1967–69 chassis lubrication chart

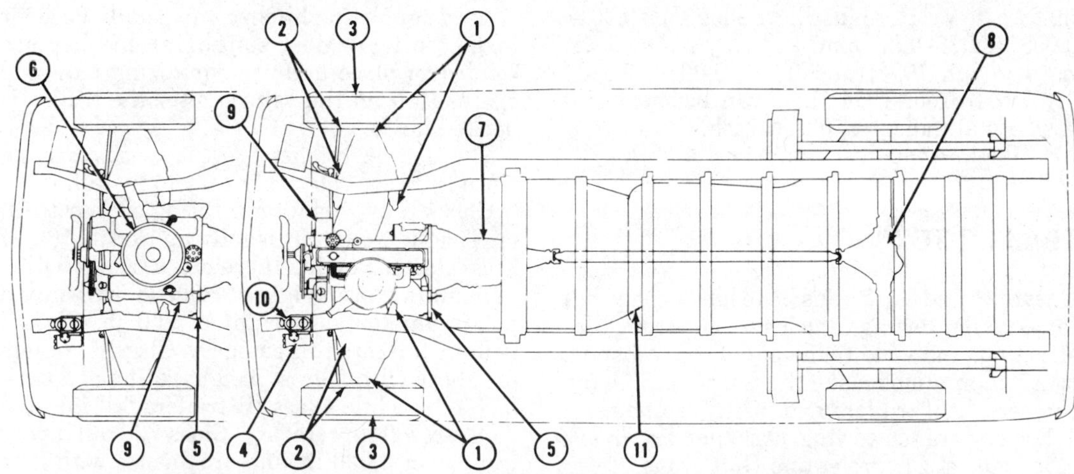

1970 and later chassis lubrication points

riodically with a few drops of graphite lock lubricant or a few shots of silicone spray.

Front Wheel Bearings

Only the front wheel bearings require periodic maintenance. A premium high melting point grease meeting GM specification 6031-M must be used. Long fiber type greases must not be used. This service is recommended at the intervals in the Maintenance Intervals Chart or whenever the van has been driven in water up to the hubs.

1. Remove the wheel and tire assembly, and the brake drum or brake caliper.
2. Remove the hub and disc as an assembly. Remove the caliper mounting bolts and insert a block between the brake pads as the caliper is removed. Remove the caliper and wind it out of the way. Do not allow the caliper to hang from the brake hose
3. Pry out the grease cap, cotter pin, spindle nut, and washer, then remove the hub. Do not drop the wheel bearings.
4. Remove the outer roller bearing assembly from the hub. The inner bearing assembly will remain in the hub and may be removed after prying out the inner seal. Discard the seal.
5. Clean all parts in solvent (air dry) and check for excessive wear and damage.
6. Using a hammer and drift, remove the bearing races from the hub. When installing new races, make sure that they are not cocked and that they are fully seated against the hub shoulder.
7. Pack both wheel bearings using high melting point wheel bearing grease for disc brakes. Ordinary grease will melt and ooze out ruining the pads. Place a healthy glob of grease in the palm of one hand and force the edge of the bearing into it so that the grease fills the bearing. Do this until the whole bearing is packed. Grease packing tools are available to make this job a lot less messy. There are also tools that also make it possible to grease the inner bearing without removing it from the spindle.
8. Place the inner bearing in the hub and install a new inner seal, making sure that the seal flange faces the bearing race.
9. Carefully install the wheel hub over the spindle.
10. Using your hands, firmly press the outer bearing into the hub. Install the spindle washer and nut.
11. To adjust the bearings through 1971 models, tighten the adjusting nut to 15 ft.lb. while rotating the hub. Back the nut off one flat ($^1/_{16}$ turn) and insert a new cotter pin. If the nut and spindle hole do not align, back the nut off slightly. There should be 0.001–0.008" (0.025–0.203mm) end play in the bearing. This can be measured with a dial indicator, if you wish. Install the dust cap, wheel and tire.
12. To adjust the bearings on the 1972 and later models, spin the wheel hub by hand and tighten the nut until it is just snug (12 ft.lb.). Back off the nut until it is loose, then tighten it finger tight. Loosen the nut until either hole in the spindle lines up with a slot in the nut and

insert a new cotter pin. There should be 0.001–0.008" (0.025–0.203mm) end play in the bearing through 1973, and 0.001–0.005" (0.025–0.127mm) from 1974. This can be measured with a dial indicator, if you wish.

13. Replace the dust cap, wheel and tire.

TRAILER TOWING

Chevrolet and GMC vans have long been popular as trailer towing vehicles. Their strong construction, and wide range of engine/transmission combinations make them ideal for towing campers, boat trailers and utility trailers.

Factory trailer towing packages are available on most Chevrolet and GMC vans, if you are installing a trailer hitch and wiring on your van, there are a few thing that you ought to know.

Trailer Weight

Trailer weight is the first, and most important, factor in determining whether or not your vehicle is suitable for towing the trailer you have in mind. The horsepower-to-weight ratio should be calculated. The basic standard is a ratio of 35:1. That is, 35 pounds of GVW for every horsepower.

To calculate this ratio, multiply you engine's rated horsepower by 35, then subtract the weight of the vehicle, including passengers and luggage. The resulting figure is the ideal maximum trailer weight that you can tow. One point to consider: a numerically higher axle ratio can offset what appears to be a low trailer weight. If the weight of the trailer that you have in mind is somewhat higher than the weight you just calculated, you might consider changing your rear axle ratio to compensate.

Hitch Weight

There are three kinds of hitches: bumper mounted, frame mounted, and load equalizing.

Bumper mounted hitches are those which attach solely to the vehicle's bumper. Many states prohibit towing with this type of hitch, when it attaches to the vehicle's stock bumper, since it subjects the bumper to stresses for which it was not designed. Aftermarket rear step bumpers, designed for trailer towing, are acceptable for use with bumper mounted hitches.

Frame mounted hitches can be of the type which bolts to two or more points on the frame, plus the bumper, or just to several points on the frame. Frame mounted hitches can also be of the tongue type, for Class I towing, or, of the receiver type, for classes II and III.

Load equalizing hitches are usually used for large trailers. Most equalizing hitches are welded in place and use equalizing bars and chains to level the vehicle after the trailer is hooked up.

The bolt-on hitches are the most common, since they are relatively easy to install.

Check the gross weight rating of your trailer. Tongue weight is usually figured as 10% of gross trailer weight. Therefore, a trailer with a maximum gross weight of 2,000 lb. will have a maximum tongue weight of 200 lb. Class I trailers fall into this category. Class II trailers are those with a gross weight rating of 2,000–3,500 lb., while Class III trailers fall into the 3,500–6,000 lb. category. Class IV trailers are those over 6,000 lb. and are for use with fifth wheel trucks, only.

When you've determined the hitch that you'll need, follow the manufacturer's installation instructions, exactly, especially when it comes to fastener torques. The hitch will subjected to a lot of stress and good hitches come with hardened bolts. Never substitute an inferior bolt for a hardened bolt.

Wiring

wiring the car for towing is fairly easy. There are a number of good wiring kits available and these should be used, rather than trying to design your own. All trailers will need brake lights and turn signals as well as tail lights and side marker lights. Most states require extra marker lights for overwide trailers. Also, most states have recently required back-up lights for trailers, and most trailer manufacturers have been building trailers with back-up lights for several years.

Additionally, some Class I, most Class II and just about all Class III trailers will have electric brakes.

Add to this number an accessories wire, to operate trailer internal equipment or to charge the trailer's battery, and you can have as many as seven wires in the harness.

Determine the equipment on your trailer and buy the wiring kit necessary. The kit will contain all the wires needed, plus a plug adapter set which included the female plug, mounted on the bumper or hitch, and the male plug, wired into, or plugged into the trailer harness.

When installing the kit, follow the manufacturer's instructions. The color coding of the wires is standard throughout the industry.

One point to note: some domestic vehicles, and most imported vehicles, have separate turn signals. On most domestic vehicles, the brake lights and rear turn signals operate with the same bulb. For those vehicles with separate turn signals, you can purchase an isolation unit so that the brake lights won't blink whenever the turn signals are operated, or, you can go to your local electronics supply house and buy four diodes to wire in series with the brake and turn signal bulbs. Diodes will isolate the brake and turn signals. The choice is yours. The isolation units are simple and quick to install, but far more expensive than the diodes. The diodes, however, require more work to install properly, since they require the cutting of each bulb's wire and soldering in place of the diode.

One, final point, the best kits are those with a spring loaded cover on the vehicle mounted socket. This cover prevent dirt and moisture from corroding the terminals. Never let the vehicle socket hang loosely. Always mount it securely to the bumper or hitch.

Cooling

ENGINE

One of the most common, if not THE most common, problem associated with trailer towing is engine overheating.

With factory installed trailer towing packages, a heavy duty cooling system is usually included. Heavy duty cooling systems are available as optional equipment on most GM vehicles, with or without a trailer package. If you have one of these extra capacity systems, you shouldn't have any overheating problems.

If you have a standard cooling system, without an expansion tank, you'll definitely need to get an aftermarket expansion tank kit, preferably one with at least a 2 quart capacity. These kits are easily installed on the radiator's overflow hose, and come with a pressure cap designed for expansion tanks.

Another helpful accessory is a Flex Fan. These fan are large diameter units are designed to provide more airflow at low speeds, with blades that have deeply cupped surfaces. The blades then flex, or flatten out, at high speed, when less cooling air is needed. These fans are far lighter in weight than stock fans, requiring less horsepower to drive them. Also, they are far quieter than stock fans.

If you do decide to replace your stock fan with a flex fan, note that if your van has a fan clutch, a spacer between the flex fan and water pump hub will be needed.

Aftermarket engine oil coolers are helpful for prolonging engine oil life and reducing overall engine temperatures. Both of these factors increase engine life.

While not absolutely necessary in towing Class I and some Class II trailers, they are recommended for heavier Class II and all Class III towing.

Engine oil cooler systems consist of an adapter, screwed on in place of the oil filter, a remote filter mounting and a multi-tube, finned heat exchanger, which is mounted in front of the radiator or air conditioning condenser.

TRANSMISSION

An automatic transmission is usually recommended for trailer towing. Modern automatics have proven reliable and, of course, easy to operate, in trailer towing.

The increased load of a trailer, however, causes an increase in the temperature of the automatic transmission fluid. Heat is the worst enemy of an automatic transmission. As the temperature of the fluid increases, the life of the fluid decreases.

It is essential, therefore, that you install an automatic transmission cooler. The cooler, which consists of a multi-tube, finned heat exchanger, is usually installed in front of the radiator or air conditioning compressor, and hooked inline with the transmission cooler tank inlet line. Follow the cooler manufacturer's installation instructions.

Select a cooler of at least adequate capacity, based upon the combined gross weights of the van and trailer.

Cooler manufacturers recommend that you use an aftermarket cooler in addition to, and not instead of, the present cooling tank in your vans radiator. If you do want to use it in place of the radiator cooling tank, get a cooler at least two sizes larger than normally necessary.

One note: transmission cooler can, sometimes, cause slow or harsh shifting in the transmission during cold weather, until the fluid has a chance to come up to normal operating temperature. Some coolers can be purchased with or retrofitted with a temperature bypass valve which will allow fluid flow through the cooler only when the fluid has reached operating temperature, or above.

PUSHING AND TOWING

Pushing

Chevrolet and GMC vans with manual transmissions can be push started, but this is not recommended if you value the appearance of your van.

To push start, make sure that both bumpers are in reasonable alignment. Bent sheet metal and inflamed tempers are both common results from misaligned bumpers when push starting.

Turn the ignition key to ON and engage High gear. Depress the clutch pedal. When a speed of about 10 mph is reached, slightly depress the gas pedal and slowly release the clutch. The engine should start.

Never get an assist by having your vehicle towed. Automatic transmission equipped vans cannot be started by pushing.

Towing

Chevrolet and GMC vans can be towed on all four wheels (flat towed) at speeds of less than 35 mph for distances less than 50 miles, providing that the axle, driveline and engine/transmission are normally operable. The transmission should be in Neutral, the engine off, the steering unlocked, and the parking brake released.

The rear wheels must be raised off the ground or the driveshaft disconnected when the transmission if not operating properly, or when speeds of over 35 mph will be used or when towing more than 50 miles.

Do not attach chains to the bumpers or bracketing. All attachments must be made to the structural members. Safety chains should be used. It should also be remembered that power steering and brake assists will not be working with the engine off.

JUMP STARTING

ALL EXCEPT DIESELS

Jump starting is the only way to start an automatic transmission model with a weak battery, and the best method for a manual transmission model.

CAUTION: *Do not attempt this procedure on a frozen battery; it will probably explode. Do not attempt in a sealed Delco Freedom battery showing a light color in the charge indicator.*

1. Turn off all electrical equipment. Place the automatic transmission in Park or the manual in Neutral and set the parking brake.

2. Make sure that the two vehicles are not touching. It is a good idea to keep the engine running in the booster vehicle.

3. Remove the caps from both batteries and cover the openings with cloths. This isn't necessary on batteries with the sponge type flame arrestor filler/vent caps. It isn't possible on the Freedom battery.

4. Attach one end of a jumper cable to the positive (+) terminal of the booster battery. The red cable is usually positive. Attach the other end to the positive terminal of the discharged battery.

CAUTION: *Be very careful about these connections. An alternator and regulator can be destroyed in a remarkably short time if battery polarity is reversed.*

5. Attach one end of the other cable (the black one) to the negative (–) terminal of the booster battery. Attach the other end to a ground point such as the alternator bracket in the engine of the truck being started. Do not connect it to the battery.

CAUTION: *Be careful not to lean over the battery while making this last connection.*

6. If the engine will not start, disconnect the batteries as soon as possible. If this is not done, the two batteries will soon reach a state of equilibrium, with both too weak to start an engine. This is no problem if the engine of the booster vehicle is running fast enough to keep up the charge. Lengthy cranking can also damage the starter.

7. Reverse the procedure exactly to remove the jumper cables. Discard the rags, because they may have acid on them.

NOTE: *It is recognized that some or all of the precautions outlined in this procedure are often ignored with no harmful results. However, the procedure outlined is the only fully safe, foolproof one.*

DIESELS

Jump Starting a Dual Battery Diesel

All GM V8 diesels are equipped with two 12 volt batteries. The batteries are connected in parallel circuit (positive terminal to positive terminal, negative terminal to negative terminal). Hooking the batteries up in parallel circuit increases battery cranking power without increasing total battery voltage output (12 volts). On the other hand, hooking two 12 volt batteries up in a series circuit (positive terminal to negative terminal, positive terminal to negative terminal) increases total battery output to 24 volts (12 volts + 12 volts).

CAUTION: *NEVER hook the batteries up in a series circuit or the entire electrical system will go up in smoke.*

In the event that a dual battery diesel must be jump started, use the following procedure.

1. Open the hood and locate the batteries. On GM diesels, the manufacturer usually suggests using the battery on the driver's side of the car to make the correction.

2. Position the donor car so that the jumper cables will reach from its battery (must be 12 volt, negative ground) to the appropriate battery in the diesel. Do not allow the cars to touch.

3. Shut off all electrical equipment on both vehicles. Turn off the engine of the donor car, set the parking brakes on both vehicles and block the wheels. Also, make sure both vehi-

cles are in Neutral (manual transmission models) or Park (automatic transmission models).

4. Using the jumper cables, connect the positive (+) terminal of the donor car battery to the positive terminal of one (not both) of the diesel batteries.

5. Using the second jumper cable, connect the negative (–) terminal of the donor battery to a solid, stationary, metallic point on the diesel (alternator bracket, engine block, etc.). Be very careful to keep the jumper cables away from moving parts (cooling fan, alternator belt, etc.) on both vehicles.

6. Start the engine of the donor can and run it at moderate speed.

7. Start the engine of the diesel.

8. When the diesel starts, disconnect the battery cables in the reverse order of attachment.

JACKING

The jack supplied with the van was meant for changing tires. It was not meant to support a van while you crawl under it and work. Whenever it is necessary to get under a van to perform service operations, always be sure that it is adequately supported, preferably by jackstands at the proper points.

If your van is equipped with a Positraction or locking rear axle, do not run the engine for any reason with one rear wheel off the ground. Power will be transmitted through the rear

CAUTION:
APPLY PARKING BRAKE. BLOCK DIAGONALLY OPPOSITE WHEEL.

WHEEL REMOVAL
REMOVE HUB CAP WITH WRENCH HANDLE. LOOSEN, BUT DO NOT REMOVE WHEEL NUTS BEFORE USING JACK.

JACK OPERATION
WITH LEVER AT PROPER SETTING, OPERATE WRENCH FROM SIDE TO SIDE TO RAISE OR LOWER VEHICLE.

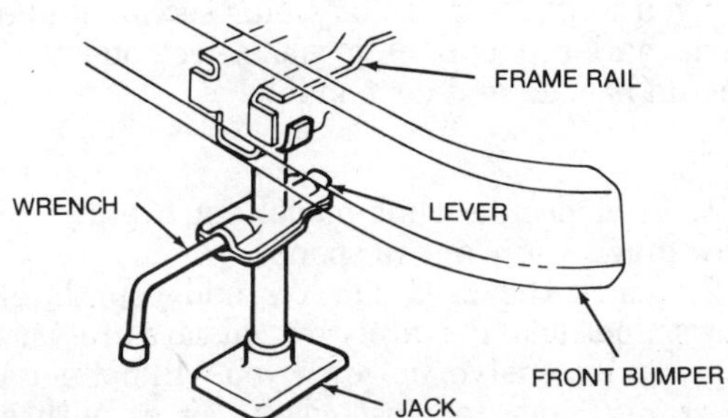

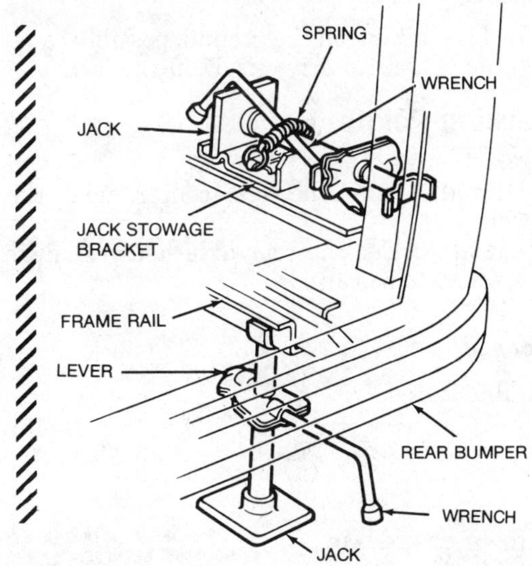

Jacking points—1968–70

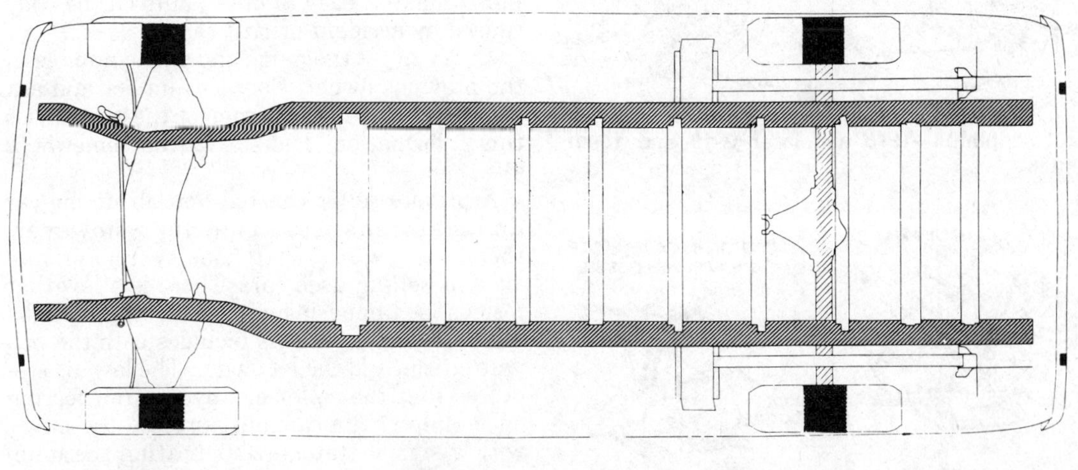

Garage lifting points—1971 and later

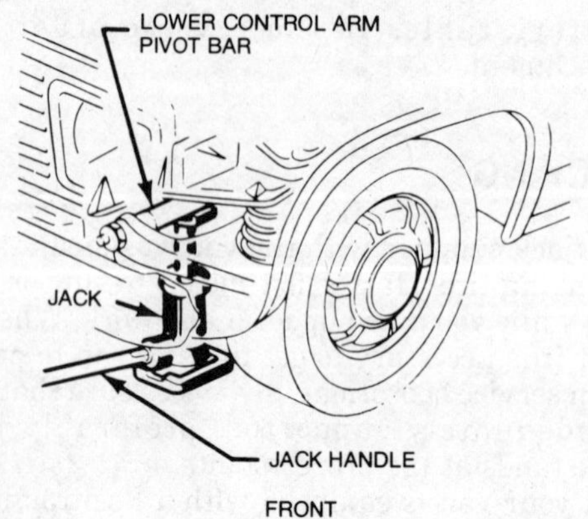

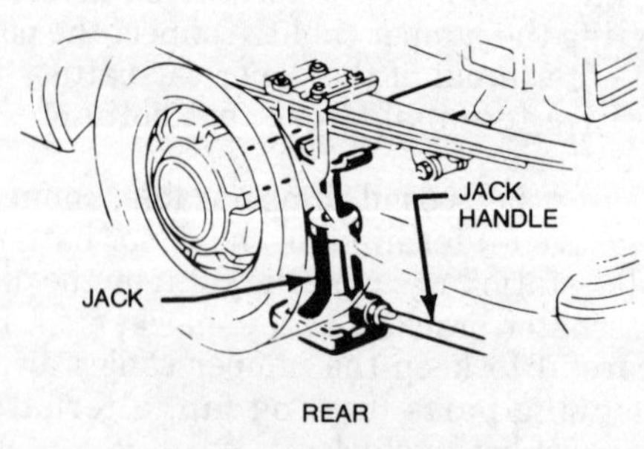

Jacking points—1971–74

wheel remaining on the ground, possibly causing the vehicle to drive itself off the jack.

Jacking Points

1967

• Front: Under the axle center, near the spring seat.

• Rear: Under the rear axle housing, near the wheel to be raised.

1968–86

As illustrated.

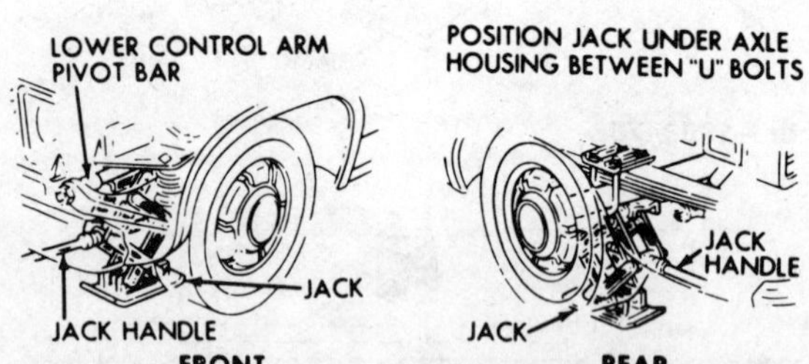

Jacking points—1975 and later G-10 and 1500 series

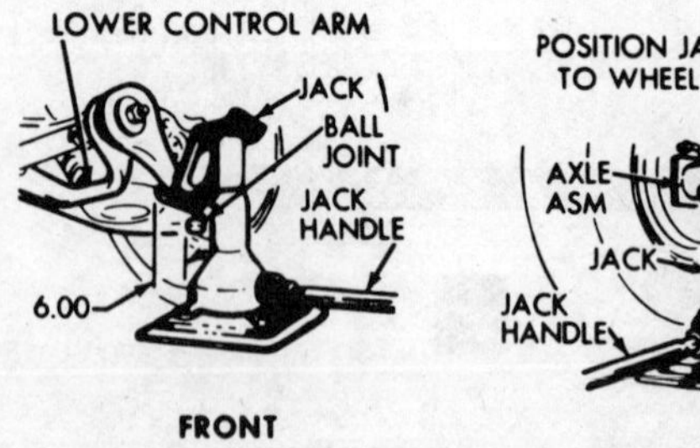

Jacking points—1975 and later G-20, G-30, 2500 and 3500 series

HOW TO BUY A USED CAR

Many people believe that a two or three year old used car is a better buy than a new car. This may be true. The new car suffers the heaviest depreciation in the first two years, but is not old enough to present a lot of costly repair problems. Whatever the age of the used car you might want to buy, this section and a little patience will help you select one that should be safe and dependable.

TIPS

1. First decide what model you want, and how much you want to spend.

2. Check the used car lots and your local newspaper ads. Privately owned cars are usually less expensive, however you will not get a warranty that, in most cases, comes with a used car purchased from a lot.

3. Never shop at night. The glare of the lights make it easy to miss faults on the body caused by accident or rust repair.

4. Try to get the name and phone number of the previous owner. Contact him/her and ask about the car. If the owner of the lot refuses this information, look for a car somewhere else.

A private seller can tell you about the car and maintenance. Remember, however, there's no law requiring honesty from private citizens selling used cars. There is a law that forbids the tampering with or turning back the odometer mileage. This includes both the private citizen and the lot owner. The law also requires that the seller or anyone transferring ownership of the car must provide the buyer with a signed statement indicating the mileage on the odometer at the time of transfer.

5. Write down the year, model and serial number before you buy any used car. Then dial

1-800-424-9393, the toll free number of the National Highway Traffic Administration, and ask if the car has ever been included on any manufacturer's recall list. If so, make sure the needed repairs were made.

6. Use the Used Car Checklist in this section and check all the items on the used car you are considering. Some items are more important than others. You know how much money you can afford for repairs, and, depending on the price of the car, may consider doing any needed work yourself. Beware, however, of

Maintenance Intervals

See text for procedures concerning regular maintenance.

NOTE: *Heavy-duty operation (trailer towing, prolonged idling, severe stop-and-start driving) should be accompanied by a 50% increase in maintenance. Cut the interval in half for these conditions. Figures given are maintenance intervals when service should be performed.*

Maintenance	1967–70	1971–74	1975–86
Air Cleaner (Check and Clean)			
Paper element ①	24,000 mi (replace)	24,000 mi (replace)	30,000 mi (replace) ⑥
PCV Valve (Replace)	12 mo/12,000 mi	12 mo/12,000 mi	12 mo/15,000 mi ⑦ ⑧
Evaporative Canister			
Replace filter	—	12 mo/12,000 mi	24 mo/30,000 mi ⑧
Engine Oil			
Check	Each fuel stop	Each fuel stop	Each fuel stop
Replace	4 mo/6,000 mi	4 mo/6,000 mi	6 mo/7,500 mi ⑨⑬⑭
Engine Oil Filter (Replace)	At 1st oil change; then every 2nd	At 1st oil change; then every 2nd	At 1st oil change; then every 2nd ⑬
Fuel Filter			
Replace ⑮	12,000 mi	12,000 mi	12 mo/15,000 mi ⑥⑫
Powerguide Transmission Fluid			
Check	6,000 mi	6,000 mi	
Replace	24,000 mi ⑥	24,000 mi	—
Turbo Hydra-Matic Fluid & Filter			
Check fluid	6,000 mi	6,000 mi	Each oil change
Change fluid	24,000 mi	24,000 mi	30,000 mi
Replace filter	24,000 mi	24,000 mi	30,000 ⑧ ⑩
Manual transmission (All)			
Check lubricant	6,000 mi	4 mo/6,000 mi	6 mo/7,500 mi ⑨
Add lubricant	As necessary	As necessary	As necessary
Battery			
Lubricate terminal felt washer	6,000 mi ④	—	—
Clean terminal	6,000 mi	As necessary	As necessary
Check electrolyte level	Twice monthly	Twice monthly	Twice monthly
Coolant level	Each fuel stop	Each fuel stop	Each fuel stop
Front Wheel Bearings			
Lubricate	30,000 mi	30,000 mi ③	30,000 mi ⑧⑪
Front and Rear Axle Lube			
Check	6,000 mi	6,000 mi	6 mo/7,500 mi ⑨
Replace	24,000 mi	24,000 mi	1st 15,000 mi w/Positraction
Brake Fluid (Master Cylinder)			
Check fluid level	6,000 mi	6,000 mi	6 mo/7,500 mi ⑨
Add fluid	As necessary	As necessary	As necessary
Manual Steering Gear Lubricant			
Check level	36,000 mi ②	36,000 mi ②	30,000 mi
Add lubricant	As necessary ②	②	②
Power Steering Reservoir			
Check fluid level	At each oil change	At each oil change	6 mo/7,500 mi
Add fluid	As necessary	As necessary	As necessary

Maintenance Intervals (cont.)

Maintenance	1967–70	1971–74	1975–86
Rotate Tires	6,000 mi	6,000 mi	Radial—1st 7,500 mi, then every 15,000 mi Bias Belted—every 7,500 mi
Chassis Lubrication	See Chassis Lubrication charts	See Chassis Lubrication charts	See Chassis Lubrication charts
Drive Belts			
Check and adjust (as necessary)	6,000 mi	6,000 mi	6 mo/7,500 mi

—Not applicable
mi—Miles
mo—Months
① Paper element air cleaners should be rotated 180° each time they are checked
② From 1970 on, no lubrication of the manual steering gear is recommended. The gear should be inspected for leaks at the seal (lubricant leaks, not filmy oil leaks). Seasonal change of the lubricant is not required and the housing should not be drained.
③ 24,000 miles in 1972–72
④ May be equipped with a felt terminal washer
⑤ 20 Series—every 12,000 miles
⑥ 12,000 mi in heavy duty emissions vehicles
⑦ 24 mo/30,000 mi 1976–86
⑧ 24,000 mi in heavy duty emission vehicles
⑨ 4 mo/6,000 mi in heavy duty emission vehicles
⑩ 60,000 mi 1976–78, 100,000 mi 1979–86, light duty emissions vehicles
⑪ 12,000 mi in four wheel drive vehicles
⑫ 24 mo/24,000 mi in California 350 and 400 engines through 1977; 12,000 mi on 1979–86 heavy duty emissions vehicles
⑬ Change at 3,000 mile intervals for 350 Diesel; 6,000 miles for 1981 and later models
⑭ Change at 5,000 mile intervals for 379 (6.2L) Diesel; or every 2,500 miles when operating under extreme temperatures, extended high speed or idle conditions, or frequent trailer towing.
⑮ Figures include diesel fuel filters

Capacities

Year	Model	Engine Displacement Cu in.	Engine Crankcase (qts)		Transmission (pts)			Drive Axle (pts)	Gasoline Tank (gals)	Cooling System (qts)	
					Manual						
			With Filter	Without Filter	3-spd	4-spd	Automatic			With Heater	Without Heater
1967	All	6-230	5	4	2.5	3	4②	3.5①	16	13	12
		6-250	5	4	2.5	3	4②	3.5①	16	13	12
		8-283	5	4	2.5	3	4②	3.5①	16	18	17
1968	All	6-230	5	4	2.5	3	4②	3.5①	16	13	17
		6-250	5	4	2.5	3	4②	3.5①	16	13	17
		8-307	5	4	2.5	3	4②	3.5①	16	18	17
1969	All	6-230	5	4	2.5	3	4②	4.5	24.5	13	12
		6-250	5	4	2.5	3	4②	4.5	24.5	13	12
		8-307	5	4	2.5	3	4②	4.5	24.5	18	17
1970	All	6-250	5	4	2.5	3	4②	4.5	24.5③	13	12
		8-307	5	4	2.5	3	4②	4.5	24.5③	18	17
		8-350	5	4	2.5	3	4②	4.5	24.5③	18	17

Capacities (cont.)

Year	Model	Engine Displacement Cu in.	Engine Crankcase (qts) With Filter	Engine Crankcase (qts) Without Filter	Transmission (pts) Manual 3-spd	Transmission (pts) Manual 4-spd	Transmission (pts) Automatic	Drive Axle (pts)	Gasoline Tank (gals)	Cooling System (qts) With Heater	Cooling System (qts) Without Heater
1971	All	6-250	5	4	2.5	—	4②	4.5	24.5③	13	12
		8-307	5	4	2.5	—	4②	4.5	24.5③	18	17
		8-350	5	4	2.5	—	4②	4.5	24.5③	18	17
1972	All	6-250	5	4	2.5	—	5	⑤	24.5③	13	12
		8-307	5	4	2.5	—	5	⑤	24.5③	16④	15④
		8-350	5	4	2.5	—	5	⑤	24.5③	16④	15④
1973	All	6-250	5	4	2.5	—	5	⑤	21	13	12
		8-307	5	4	2.5	—	5	⑤	21	16④⑥	15④⑥
		8-350	5	4	2.5	—	5	⑤	21	16④⑥	15④⑥
1974	All	6-250	5	4	2.5	—	5	⑤	21	13	12
		8-350	5	4	2.5	—	5	⑤	21	16④⑥	15④⑥
1975	All	6-250	5	4	3.2	—	5	4.3	21/36	15	—
	20, 2500	6-292	6	5	3.2	—	5	3.5	21/36	14.8	—
	30, 3500	6-292	6	5	3.2	—	5	5.4	21/36	14.8	—
	All	8-350 2 bbl	5	4	3.2	—	5	4.3	21/36	17.5	—
	10, 1500	8-350 4 bbl	5	4	3.2	—	5	4.3	21/36	18	—
	20, 2500	8-350 4 bbl	5	4	4.6	—	5	3.5	21/36	18	—
	30, 3500	8-350 4 bbl	5	4	4.6	—	5	5.4	21/36	18	—
	20, 2500	8-400	5	4	—	—	5	3.5	21/36	19.9	—
	30, 2500	8-400	5	4	—	—	5	5.4	21/36	19.9	—
1976	All	6-250	5	4	3.2	—	5	4.3	21/36	15	—
	20, 2500	6-292	6	5	3.2	—	5	3.5	21/36	14.8	—
	30, 3500	6-292	6	5	3.2	—	5	5.4	21/36	14.8	—
	10, 1500	8-350	5	4	4.6	—	5	4.3	21/36	18	—
1976	20, 2500	8-350	5	4	4.6	—	5	3.5	21/36	18	—
	30, 3500	8-350	5	4	4.6	—	5	5.4	21/36	18	—
	20, 2500	8-400	5	4	—	—	5	3.5	21/36	19.9	—
	30, 3500	8-400	5	4	—	—	5	5.4	21/36	19.9	—
1977–78	All	6-250	5	4	3.2	—	5	3.5	22/33	15	—
	20, 2500	6-292	6	5	3.2	—	5	3.5	22/33	14.8	—
	30, 3500	6-292	6	5	3.2	—	5	5.4	22/33	14.8	—
	All	8-305	5	4	3.2	—	5	3.5	22/33	18	—
	10, 20, 1500, 2500	8-350	5	4	4.6⑦	—	5	3.5	22/33	18	—
	30, 3500	8-350	5	4	4.6⑦	—	5⑧	5.4	22/33	18	—
	20, 2500	8-400	5	4	—	—	5	3.5	22/33	19.9	—
	30, 3500	8-400	5	4	—	—	5⑧	5.4	22/33	19.9	—

Capacities (cont.)

Year	Model	Engine Displacement Cu in.	Engine Crankcase (qts) With Filter	Engine Crankcase (qts) Without Filter	Transmission (pts) Manual 3-spd	Transmission (pts) Manual 4-spd	Transmission (pts) Automatic	Drive Axle (pts)	Gasoline Tank (gals)	Cooling System (qts) With Heater	Cooling System (qts) Without Heater
1979–80	All	6-250	5	4	3.2	—	5	3.5	22/33	17	—
	All	8-305	5	4	3.2⑦	—	5	3.5	22/33	19.5	—
	10, 20 1500, 2500	8-350	5	4	3.2⑦	—	5	3.5	22/33	20	—
	30, 3500	8-350	5	4	3.2⑦	—	5	3.5	22/33	20	—
	All	8-400	5	4	3.2⑦	—	5	3.5	22/33	20	—
1981–82	All	6-250	5	4	3.0	—	6	⑨	22/33	20	—
	All	8-305	5	4	3.0	—	6	⑨	22/33	20	—
	All	8-350LD	5	4	3.0	—	6	⑨	22/23	22	—
	All	8-350HD	5	4	3.0	—	7	⑨	22/33	22	—
1983–86	All	6-250	5	4	3	8	⑩	⑨	22/33	14.5	—
	All	6-262	5	4	3	8	6.3	⑨	22/33	17	—
	All	8-305	5	4	3	8	⑩	⑨	22/33	17	—
	All	8-350	5	4	3	8	⑩	⑨	22/33	17	—
	All	8-379 Diesel	7	—	3	8	⑩	⑨	22/33	24	—

LD: Light Duty; HD: Heavy Duty
① 4.5 pts with heavy-duty differential.
② Turbo Hydra-Matic 400—7.5 pts (1967–68). Turbo Hydra-Matic 350—5 pts (1969–74).
③ 22 gallons with Evaporative Emission Canister.
④ Increase by 1 qt for G—10 models with special radiator.
⑤ G—10, G—1500 van—3.5 pts.
G—10, G—1500 Sportvan and G—20, G—2500—5.0 pts.
G—30 and G—3500—6.5 pts.
⑥ 18 qts with air conditioning.
⑦ 4 pts with top-cover Tremec three-speed and Saginaw three-speed
⑧ 7 pts with 10,000 lb or higher GVW.
⑨ 8½ in. ring gear—4.2 pts
8⅞ in. ring gear (Chevrolet)—4.5 pts (3.5 pts 1977–82)
9¾ in. ring gear (Dana) 6.0 pts.
10½ in. ring gear (Chevrolet)—6½ pts
10½ in. ring gear (Dana)—7.2 pts
12½ in. ring gear (Chevrolet)—26.8 pts
⑩ Turbo Hydra-Matic 350—6 pts
Turbo Hydra-Matic 400—7 pts
Turbo Hydra-Matic 700R4—10 pts

trouble in areas that will affect operation, safety or emission. Problems in the Used Car Checklist break down as follows:

1–8: Two or more problems in these areas indicate a lack of maintenance. You should beware.

9–13: Indicates a lack of proper cars, however, these can usually be corrected with a tune-up or relatively simple parts replacement.

14–17: Problems in the engine or transmission can be very expensive. Walk away from any car with problems in both of these areas.

7. If you are satisfied with the apparent condition of the car, take it to an independent diagnostic center or mechanic for a complete check. If you have a state inspection program, have it inspected immediately before purchase, or specify on the bill of sale that the sale is conditional on passing state inspection.

8. Road test the car–refer to the Road Test Checklist in this section. If your original evaluation and the road test agree–the rest is up to you.

USED CAR CHECKLIST

NOTE: *The number on the illustrations refer to the numbers on this checklist.*

1. Mileage: Average mileage is about 12,000 miles per year. More than average mileage may indicate hard usage. 1975 and later catalytic converter equipped models may need converter service at 50,000 miles.

2. Paint: Check around the tailpipe, molding and windows for overspray indicating that the car has been repaired.

3. Rust: Check fenders, doors, rocker panels, window moldings, wheelwells, floorboards, under floormats, and in the truck for signs of rust. Any rust at all will be a problem. There is no way to check the spread of rust, except to replace that part or panel.

4. Body appearance: Check the moldings, bumpers, grille, vinyl roof, glass, doors, trunk lid and body panels for general overall condition. Check for misalignment, loose holdown clips, ripples, scratches in glass, rips or patches in the top. Mismatched paint, welding in the trunk, severe misalignment of body panels or ripples may indicate crash work.

5. Leaks: Get down and look under the car. There are no normal leaks, other than water from the air conditioning condenser.

6. Tires: Check the tire air pressure. A common trick is to pump the tire pressure up to make the car roll easier. Check the tread wear, open the trunk and check the spare too. Uneven wear is a clue that the front end needs alignment. See the troubleshooting chapter for clues to the causes of tire wear.

7. Shock absorbers: Check the shock absorbers by forcing downward sharply on each corner of the car. Good shocks will not allow the car to bounce more than twice after you let go.

8. Interior: Check the entire interior. You're looking for an interior condition that agrees with the overall condition of the car. Reasonable wear is expected, but be suspicious of new seatcovers on sagging seats, new pedal pads, and worn armrests. These indicate an attempt to cover up use. Pull back the carpets and look for evidence of water leaks or flooding. Look for missing hardware, door handles, control knobs, etc. Check lights and signal operations. Make sure all accessories (air conditioner, heater, radio, etc.) work. Check windshield wiper operation.

9. Belts and Hoses: Open the hood and check all belts and hoses for wear, cracks or weak spots.

10. Battery: Low electrolyte level, corroded terminals and/or cracked case indicate a lack of maintenance.

11. Radiator: Look for corrosion or rust in the coolant indicating a lack of maintenance.

12. Air filter: A dirty air filter usually means a lack of maintenance.

13. Ignition Wires: Check the ignition wires for cracks, burned spots, or wear. Worn wires will have to be replaced.

14. Oil level: If the oil level is low, chances are the engine uses oil or leaks. Beware of water in the oil (cracked block), excessively thick oil (used to quiet a noisy engine), or thin, dirty oil with a distinct gasoline smell (internal engine problems).

15. Automatic Transmission: Pull the transmission dipstick out when the engine is running. The level should read Full, and the fluid should be clear or bright red. Dark brown or

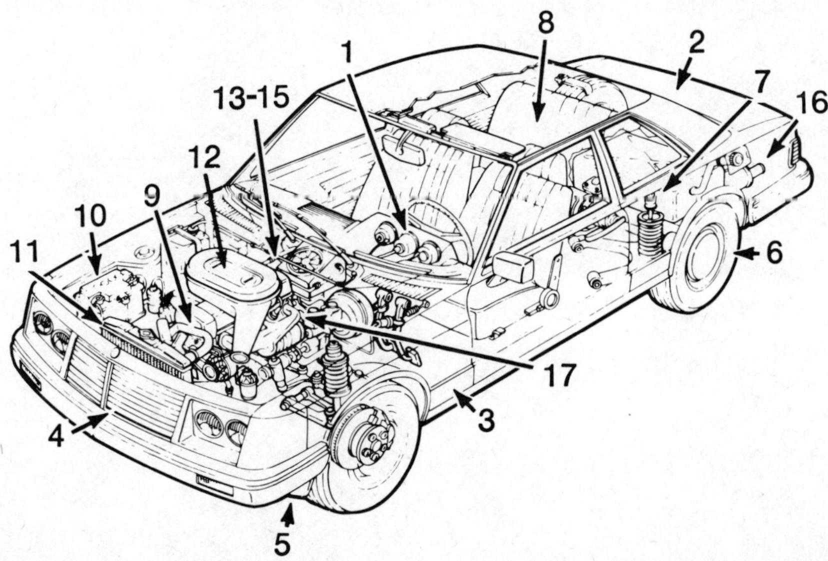

You should check these points when buying a used car. The "Used Car Checklist" gives an explanation of the numbered items

black fluid that has distinct burnt odor signals a transmission in need of repair or overhaul.

16. Exhaust: Check the color of the exhaust smoke. Blue smoke indicates, among other problems, worn rings. Black smoke can indicate burnt valves or carburetor problems. Check the exhaust system for leaks; it can be expensive to replace.

17. Spark Plugs: Remove one of the spark plugs (the most accessible will do). And engine in good condition will show plugs with a light tan or gray deposit on the firing tip. See the color Tune-up tips section for spark plug conditions.

ROAD TEST CHECK LIST

1. Engine Performance: The car should be peppy whether cold or warm, with adequate power and good pickup. It should respond smoothly through the gears.

2. Brakes: They should provide quick, firm stops with no noise, pulling or brake fade.

3. Steering: Sure control with no binding, harshness, or looseness and no shimmy in the wheel should be expected. Noise or vibration from the steering wheel when turning the car means trouble.

4. Clutch (Manual Transmission): Clutch action should give quick, smooth response with easy shifting. The clutch pedal should have about 1–1½" (25.4–38.1mm) of free play before it disengages the clutch. Start the engine, set the parking brake, put the transmission in first gear and slowly release the clutch pedal. The engine should begin to stall when the pedal is ½–¾ of the way up.

5. Automatic Transmission: The transmission should shift rapidly and smoothly, with no noise, hesitation, or slipping.

6. Differential: No noise or thumps should be present. Differentials have no normal leaks.

7. Driveshaft, Universal Joints: Vibration and noise could mean driveshaft problems. Clicking at low speed or coast conditions means worn U-joints.

8. Suspension: Try hitting bumps at different speeds. A car that bounces has weak shock absorbers. Clunks mean worn bushings or ball joints.

9. Frame: Wet the tires and drive in a straight line. Tracks should show two straight lines, not four. Four tire tracks indicate a frame bent by collision damage. If the tires can't be wet for this purpose, have a friend drive along behind you and see if the car appears to be traveling in a straight line.

Tune-Up and Performance Maintenance

2

TUNE-UP PROCEDURES

Neither tune-up nor troubleshooting can be considered independently since each has a direct relationship with the other.

It is advisable to follow a definite and thorough tune-up procedure. Tune-up consists of three separate steps: Analysis, the process of determining whether normal wear is responsible for performance loss, and whether parts require replacement or service; parts replacement or service; and adjustment, where engine adjustments are performed.

The manufacturer's recommended interval for tune-ups is every 12,000 miles or 12 months, whichever comes first for 1970–74, and 22,500 miles or 18 months for 1975–86, except for heavy duty emission models, which use the 12 mo/12,000 miles schedule in all years. These intervals should be shortened if the truck is subjected to severe operating conditions such as trailer pulling, or if starting and running problems are noticed. It is assumed that the routine maintenance described in Chapter 1 has been kept up, as this will have an effect on the results of the tune-up. All the applicable tune-up steps should be followed, as each adjustment complements the effects of the others. If the tune-up (emission control) sticker in the engine compartment disagrees with the information presented in the Tune-up Specifications chart in this chapter, the sticker figures must be followed. The sticker information reflects running changes made by the manufacturer during production. The light duty sticker is usually found on the underhood sheet metal above the grille. The heavy duty sticker is usually on top of the air cleaner.

Diesel engines do not require tune-ups per say, as there is no ignition system.

Troubleshooting is a logical sequence of procedures designed to locate a particular cause of trouble. The Troubleshooting chapter of this book is general in nature (applicable to most vehicles), yet specific enough to locate the problem.

It is advisable to read the entire chapter before beginning a tune-up, although those who are more familiar with tune-up procedures may wish to go directly to the instructions.

Spark Plugs

REPLACEMENT

1. Disconnect each spark plug wire by twisting and pulling on the rubber cap, not on the wire. Carbon core wires can be internally broken rather easily.

Diesel Tune-Up Specifications ⑧

Year	Engine No. Cyl Displacement (cu in.)	Fuel Pump Pressure (psi)	Compression (lbs.)	Intake Valve Opens (deg)	Idle Speed (rpm) ●
1983–86	8-379	5.5–6.5 ①	275 min.	NA	575/550 ②

NOTE: The underhood specifications sticker often reflects tune-up specifications changes made in production. Sticker figures must be used if they disagree with those in this chart.

● Where two idle speed figures appear separately by a slash, the first is for manual trans, the second is for auto trans.

① Transfer pump pressure given—injector opening pressure for used injector—1500 psi

② '83–'84 slow idle: 650 rpm; fast idle: 800 rpm

NA—Not available

Tune-Up Specifications 1967–81

When analyzing compression results, look for uniformity among cylinders rather than specific pressures.

Year	Engine Cu in. Displacement	Spark Plugs Orig Type	Spark Plugs Gap (in.)	Distributor Point Dwell (deg)	Distributor Point Gap (in.)	Ignition Timing* (deg) ▲ MT	Ignition Timing* (deg) ▲ AT	Intake Valve Opens (deg)	Fuel Pump Pressure (psi)	(See Text) Curb Idle Speed (rpm)* MT	(See Text) Curb Idle Speed (rpm)* AT	Solenoid or Base Idle Speed (rpm)* MT	Solenoid or Base Idle Speed (rpm)* AT
1967	6-230	46N	.035	31–34	0.019	4B	4B	48	3–4.5	700	500	See Text	See Text
	6-250	46N	.035	31–34	0.019	4B	4B	62	3–4.5	700	500	See Text	See Text
	8-283	44	.035	28–32	0.019	6A ②	4B	36	5–6.5	700	600 ③	See Text	See Text
1968	6-230	46N	.035	31–34	0.019	TDC ②	4B	48	3–4.5	700	500	See Text	See Text
	6-250	46N	.035	31–34	0.019	TDC ②	4B	16	3–4.5	700	500	See Text	See Text
	8-307	44S	.035	28–32	0.019	2B	2B	28	5–6.5	700	600 ③	See Text	See Text
1969	6-230	R46N	.035	31–34	0.019	TDC	4B	16	3–4.5	700	550	See Text	See Text
	6-250	R46N	.035	31–34	0.019	TDC	4B	16	3–4.5	700	550	See Text	See Text
	8-307	R44	.035	28–32	0.019	2B	2B	28	5–6.5	700	600	See Text	See Text
1970	6-250	R46T	.035	31–34	0.019	TDC	4B	16	3.5–4.5	See Text	See Text	See Text	See Text
	8-307	R45	.035	28–32	0.019	2B	8B	28	5–6.5	See Text	See Text	See Text	See Text
	8-350	R44	.035	28–32	0.019	TDC	4B	28	7–8.5	See Text	See Text	See Text	See Text
1971	6-250	R46TS	.035	31–34	0.019	TDC	4B	16	3.5–4.5	See Text	See Text	See Text	See Text
	8-307	R45TS	.035	28–32	0.019	2B	2B	28	5–6.5	See Text	See Text	See Text	See Text
	8-350	R44TS	.035	28–32	0.019	4B	4B	28	7–8.5	See Text	See Text	See Text	See Text
1972	6-250	R46T	.035	31–34	0.019	4B	4B	16	3.5–4.5	See Text	See Text	See Text	See Text
	8-307	R44T	.035	28–32	0.019	4B	8B	28	5–6.5	See Text	See Text	See Text	See Text
	8-350	R44T	.035	28–32	0.019	4B	8B	28	7–8.5	See Text	See Text	See Text	See Text
1973	6-250LD	R46T	.035	31–34	0.019	6B	6B	16	3.5–4.5	See Text	See Text	See Text	See Text
	8-307 LD	R44T	.035	28–32	0.019	4B	8B	28	5–6.5	See Text	See Text	See Text	See Text
	8-350 LD	R44T	.035	28–32	0.019	8B	12B	28	7–8.5	See Text	See Text	See Text	See Text
	6-250 HD	R46T	.035	31–34	0.019	4B	4B	16	3.5–4.5	See Text	See Text	See Text	See Text
1973	8-307 HD	R44T	.035	28–32	0.019	TDC	TDC	28	5–6.5	See Text	See Text	See Text	See Text
	8-350 HD	R44T	.035	28–32	0.019	4B	4B	28	7–8.5	See Text	See Text	See Text	See Text

1974	6-250	R46T	.035	31–34	0.019	8B	8B	16	3.5–4.5	See Text	See Text	See Text	See Text
	8-350 (2-bbl)	R44T	.035	29–31	0.019	TDC	8B	28	7–8.5	See Text	See Text	See Text	See Text
	8-350 (4-bbl) LD	R44T	.035	29–31	0.019	8B	8B	44	7–8.5	See Text	See Text	See Text	See Text
	8-350 (4-bbl) HD	R44T	.035	29–31	0.019	8B	12B	44	7–8.5	See Text	See Text	See Text	See Text
1975	6-250	R46TX	.060	Electronic		10B	10B	16	3.5–4.5	900	550	See Text	See Text
	6-292	R44TX	.060	Electronic		8B	8B	33	3.5–4.5	600	600	See Text	See Text
	8-350 (2-bbl)	R44TX	.060	Electronic		①	6B	28	7–8.5	①	600	See Text	See Text
	8-350 (4-bbl) LD	R44TX	.060	Electronic		6B	6B	28	7–8.5	800	600	See Text	See Text
	8-350 (4-bbl) HD	R44TX	.060	Electronic		8B(2B)	8B(2B)	28	7–8.5	600(700)	600(700)	See Text	See Text
	8-400	R44TX	.060	Electronic		—	4B(8B)	28	7–8.5	—	700	See Text	See Text
1976	6-250	R46TS	.035	Electronic		6B	10B	16	3.5–4.5	900(1000) ④	550(600) ④	See Text	See Text
	6-292	R44T	.035	Electronic		8B	8B	33	3.5–4.5	600	600 N	See Text	See Text
	8-350 (2-bbl)	R45TS	.045	Electronic		2B	6B	28	7–8.5	800	600	See Text	See Text
	8-350 (4-bbl) LD	R45TS	.045	Electronic		8B(6B)	8B(6B)	28	7–8.5	800	600	See Text	See Text
	8-350 (4-bbl) HD	R44TX	.060	Electronic		8B(2B)	8B(2B)	28	7–8.5	600(700)	600(700) N	See Text	See Text
	8-400	R44TX	.060	Electronic		—	4B	28	7–8.5	—	700 N	See Text	See Text
1977	6-250	R46TS	.035	Electronic		8B(6B)	12B(10B)	16	3.5–4.5	750(850) ④	600 ④	425	425D
	6-292	R44T	.035	Electronic		8B	8B	33	3.5–4.5	600	600 N	450	450 N
	8-305	R45TS	.045	Electronic		8B	8B	28	7–8.5	600	500	700	650 N
	8-350 LD	R45TS	.045	Electronic		8B(6B)	8B(6B)	28	7–8.5	700	500	—	650 D
	8-350 HD	R44T (F44TX)	.045 (.060)	Electronic		8B(2B)	8B(2B)	28	7–8.5	700	700 N	—	—
	8-400	R44T	.045	Electronic		—	4B(2B)	28	7–8.5	—	700 N	—	—
1978	6-250	F46TS	.035	Electronic		8B	8B(10B) ⑥	16	4.5–6	750	600 ⑤	425	425D
	6-292	R44T	.035	Electronic		8B	8B	33	4.5–6	600	600	450	450 N
	8-305	R45TS	.045	Electronic		4B	4B	28	7.5–9	600	500	—	—
	8-350 LD	R45TS	.045	Electronic		8B	8B	28	7.5–9	600(700)	500	—	600 D
	8-350 HD	R44T (R44TX)	.045 (.060)	Electronic		8B(2B)	8B(2B)	28	7.5–9	700	700	—	—

Tune-Up Specifications 1967–81 (cont.)

When analyzing compression results, look for uniformity among cylinders rather than specific pressures.

Year	Engine Cu in. Displacement	Spark Plugs Orig Type	Spark Plugs Gap (in.)	Distributor Point Dwell (deg)	Distributor Point Gap (in.)	Ignition Timing* (deg) ▲ MT	Ignition Timing* (deg) ▲ AT	Intake Valve Opens (deg)	Fuel Pump Pressure (psi)	(See Text) Curb Idle Speed (rpm)* MT	(See Text) Curb Idle Speed (rpm)* AT	Solenoid or Base Idle Speed (rpm)* MT	Solenoid or Base Idle Speed (rpm)* AT
	8-400 LD ⑦	R45TS	.045	Electronic		—	4B	28	7.5–9	—	500	—	600 D
	8-400 HD	R44T	.045	Electronic		—	4B(2B)	28	7.5–9	—	700	—	—
1979	6-250	R46TS	.035	Electronic		10B ⑨	10B ⑨	16	4.5–6	750	600	425	425 D
	8-305	R45TS	.045	Electronic		6B	6B	28	7.5–9	700	600	600	500 D
	8-350 ⑩	R45TS	.045	Electronic		8B	8B	28	7.5–9	700	500	—	600 D
	8-400 ⑩	R45TS	.045	Electronic		—	4B	28	7.5–9	—	500	—	600 D
1980–81	6-250	R46TS	.035	Electronic		10B	8B ⑪	—	4–6	750	650 (D)	—	—
	8-305 (2-bbl)	R45TS	.045	Electronic		8B	8B	—	7–9	700	600 (D)	—	—
	8-305 (4-bbl)	R45TS	.045	Electronic		6B	4B	—	7–9	700	500 (D)	—	—
	8-350	R45TS	.045	Electronic		8B ⑫	8B ⑬	—	7–9	700	500 (D) ⑭	—	—

*Figures in parentheses are for California and high altitude and are given only if they differ from the 49 state specification. Automatic transmission idle speeds are set in Drive, unless specified otherwise.

▲At idle speed with vacuum advance hose disconnected and plugged, unless specified otherwise in the text

① See the underhood specifications sticker
② Without air pump system—4B
③ Without air pump system—500 rpm
④ Air conditioner on
⑤ 49 state without A/C—550
⑥ High alt.—12B
⑦ California only
⑧ G—20, G—30, 2500, 3500 series in Calif.—6B
⑨ G—20, G—30, 2500, 3500 series in Calif.—8B
⑩ Some G—30/3500 series vans differ. Check the underhood emission sticker.
⑪ High Alt.: 10B
⑫ Fed. 1 ton models: 4B
Calif. ¾ & 1 ton models: 6B
⑬ 1 ton models: 6B
⑭ 1 ton models: 700 (N)
Calif. ½ & ¾ ton models: 550 (D)

N—Transmission in Neutral
D—Transmission in Drive
HD (Heavy Duty) 1971 G—30, 3500; 1972–73 G—30, 3500 except passenger models; 1974–78 G—20, 2500, 30, 3500
LD (Light Duty) All 1967–69; 1979–71 G—10, 1500, 20, 2500; 1972–73 G—10, 1500, 20, 2500; 1972–73 G—30, 3500 passenger models; 1974–78 G—10, 1500

NOTE: *The underhood specifications sticker often reflects tune-up specifications changes made in production. Sticker figures must be used if they disagree with those in this chart.*

Part numbers in this chart are not recommendations by Chilton for any product by brand name.

Tune-Up Specifications 1982–86

When analyzing compression results, look for uniformity among cylinders rather than specific pressures.

Year	Engine Cu In. Displacement	Spark Plugs Orig Type	Spark Plugs Gap (in.)	Distributor	Ignition Timing● (deg)▲ MT	Ignition Timing● (deg)▲ AT	Fuel Pump Pressure (psi)	Curb Idle Speed (rpm)● MT	Curb Idle Speed (rpm)● AT
1982	6-250	R45TS	.045	Electronic	①	①	4–6	①	①
	8-305	R45TS	.045	Electronic	①	①	7–9	①	①
	8-350	R45TS	.045	Electronic	①	①	7–9	①	①
1983	6-250	R45TS	.045	Electronic	①	①	4–6	①	①
	8-305	R45TS	.045	Electronic	①	①	7–9	①	①
	8-350	R45TS	.045	Electronic	①	①	7–9	①	①
	8-379	Diesel	—	—	①	①	—	①	①
1984	6-250	R45TS	.045	Electronic	①	①	4–6	①	①
	8-305	R45TS	.045	Electronic	①	①	7–9	①	①
	8-350	R45TS	.045	Electronic	①	①	7–9	①	①
	8-379	Diesel	—	—	①	①	—	①	①
1985–86	6-252	R43CTS	①	Electronic	①	①	4–6.5	③	③
	8-305	R45TS	①	Electronic	①	①	4–6.5	③	③
	8-350	R45TS	②	Electronic	①	①	4–6.5	③	③
	8-379	—	—	Diesel	—	—	6.5–9	650	650④

NOTE: The underhood specifications sticker often reflects tune-up changes made in production. Sticker figures must be used if they disagree with those in this chart.

NOTE: Part numbers in this chart are not recommendations by Chilton for any product by brand name.

NOTE: All engines use hydraulic valve lifters.

● Figures in parentheses are for California, and are given only if they differ from the 49 state specification. Automatic transmission idle speeds are set in Drive, unless specified otherwise.

▲ At idle speed with vacuum advance hose disconnected and plugged, unless specified otherwise in the text.

N—Transmission in Neutral
D—Transmission in Drive
HD—Heavy Duty
LD—Light Duty
① See the underhood specifications sticker
② Vehicles w/HD emissions use R44T
③ If equipped w/ECM, no adjustment required
④ Adjust w/AT in Park
⑤ California only
⑥ G-20, G-30, 2500, 3500 series in Calif.—6B
⑦ G-20, G-30, 2500, 3500 series in Calif.—8B
⑧ Some G-30/3500 series vans differ. Check the underhood emission sticker.
⑨ High Alt.—10B
⑩ Fed 1 ton models—4B
Calif ¾ and 1 ton models—6B
⑪ 1 ton models—6B
⑫ 1 ton models—700(N)
Calif. ½ and ⅓ ton models—550 (D)

2. If the wires are dirty or oily, wipe them clean with a cloth dampened in kerosene and then wipe them dry. If the wires are cracked, they should be replaced. Make sure to get the radio noise suppression type.

3. Blow or brush the dirt away from each of the spark plugs. This can be done by loosening the plugs and cranking the engine with the starter.

4. Remove each spark plug with a spark plug socket; ⅝″ for plug designations with a T, $^{13}/_{16}$″ for the rest. The T, or tapered seat, plugs are used in all but 1967–70 V8s and 1967–69 sixes. Make sure that the socket is all the way down on the plug to prevent it from slipping and cracking the porcelain insulator. On some V8s, the plugs are more accessible from under the truck.

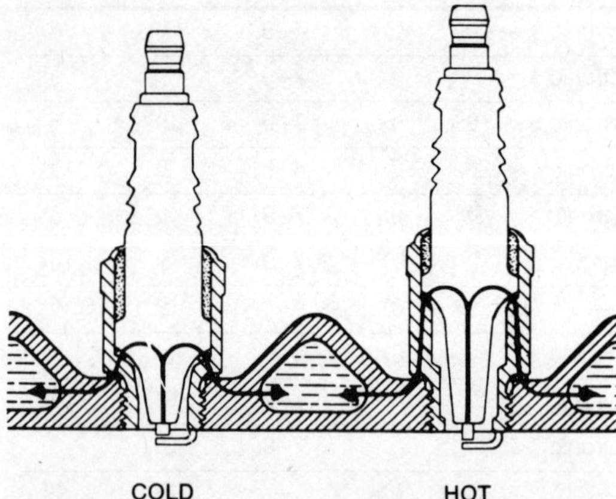

The plug with the higher heat range is on the right; it has a longer heat flow path and thus operates at a higher tip temperature. It should be used for slower driving and light load conditions which promote carbon accumulation

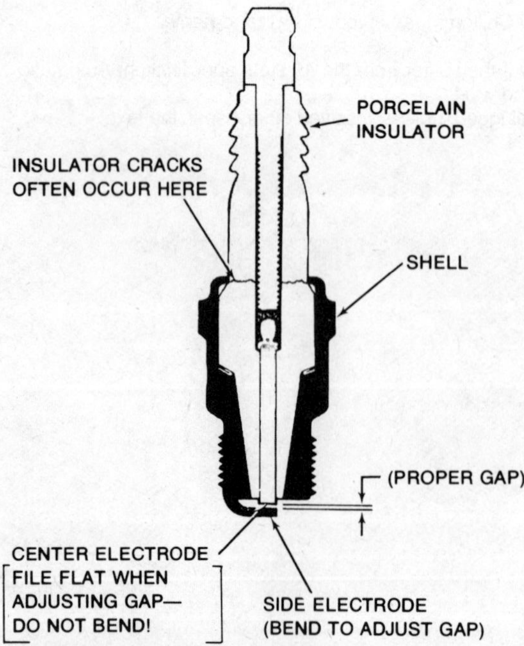

Spark plug cutaway

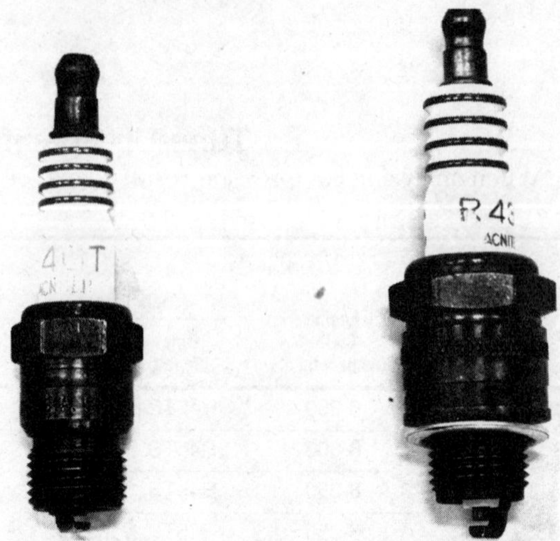

The early type spark plug is on the right. It takes a $^{13}/_{16}$ in. socket and requires a gasket. The later tapered seat plug is on the left. It takes a ⅝ in. socket and needs no gasket. The letter T indicates the taper seat plug

5. Refer to the color section in this book for details on evaluating plug condition. In general, a tan or medium gray color (rust red with some unleaded fuels) on the business end of the plug indicates normal combustion conditions. A spark plug's useful life is about 12,000 miles (more with HEI electronic ignition). Thus it would make sense to throw away the plugs if it has been 12,000 miles or more since the last tune-up. Most professional mechanics won't waster their time cleaning used plugs. There is too much chance of unsatisfactory performance and a customer comeback. Refer to the Tune-Up Specifications chart for the proper spark plug type.

The letter codes on the General Motors original equipment type plus are read this way:

- R – resistor
- S – extended tip
- T – tapered seat
- X – wide gap

The numbers indicate heat range. Hotter running plugs have higher numbers.

6. If the plugs are to be reused, file the center and side electrodes flat with a small, fine file. Heavy or baked on deposits can be carefully scraped off with a small knife blade or the scraper tool on a combination spark plug tool. Check the gap between the two electrodes with

a spark plug gap gauge. The round wire type is the most accurate. If the gap is not as specified, use the adjusting device on the gap gauge to bend the outside electrode to correct.

NOTE: *Always check the gap on new plugs.*

Be careful not to bend the electrode too far or too often, because excessive bending may cause it to break off and fall into the combustion chamber. This would require cylinder head removal to reach the broken piece, and could result in cylinder wall, ring, or valve damage.

7. Clean the plug threads with a wire brush. If you choose to lubricate the threads, use only one drop of engine oil.

8. Screw the plugs in finger tight. Tighten them with the plug socket. If a torque wrench is available, tighten them to 15 ft.lb. for plug designation with a T, and 25 ft.lbs for the rest.

9. Reinstall the wires. If there is any doubt as to their proper locations, refer to the Firing Order illustrations.

The color insert found in the center of the book can help you determine the condition of your spark plugs, and what caused that condition.

Spark Plug Wires

Every 10,000 miles, inspect the spark plug wires for burns, cuts, or breaks in the insulation. Check the boots and the nipples on the distributor cap. Replace any damaged wiring.

Every 30,000 miles or so, the resistance of the wires should be checked with an ohmmeter. Wires with excessive resistance will cause misfiring, and may make the engine difficult to start in damp weather. Generally, the useful life of the cables is 45,000–60,000 miles.

To check resistance, remove the distributor cap, leaving the wires in place. Connect one lead of an ohmmeter to an electrode within the cap. Connect the other lead to the corresponding spark plug terminal (remove it from the spark plug for this test). Replace any wire which shows a resistance over 30,000Ω. Generally speaking, however, resistance should not be over 25,000Ω, and 30,000Ω must be considered the outer limit of acceptability.

It should be remembered that resistance is also a function of length. The longer the wire, the greater the resistance. Thus, if the wires on your car are longer than the factory originals, the resistance will be higher, possibly outside these limits.

When installing new wires, replace them one at a time to avoid mixups. Start by replacing the longest one first. Install the boot firmly over the spark plug. Route the wire over the same path as the original. Insert the nipple firmly onto the tower on the distributor cap, then install the cap cover and latches to secure the wires.

FIRING ORDERS

To avoid possible cross-wiring, replace spark plug wires one at a time.

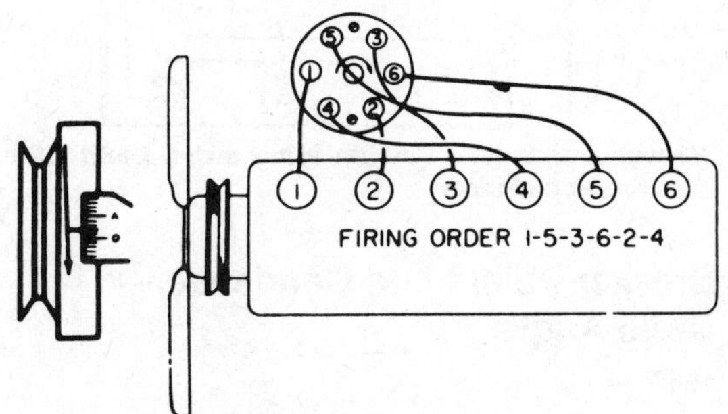

Six-cylinder firing order. Distributor rotation—clockwise

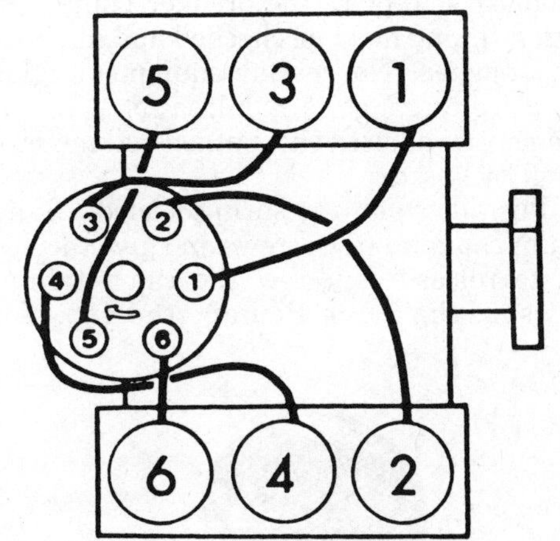

4.3 L V6 firing order

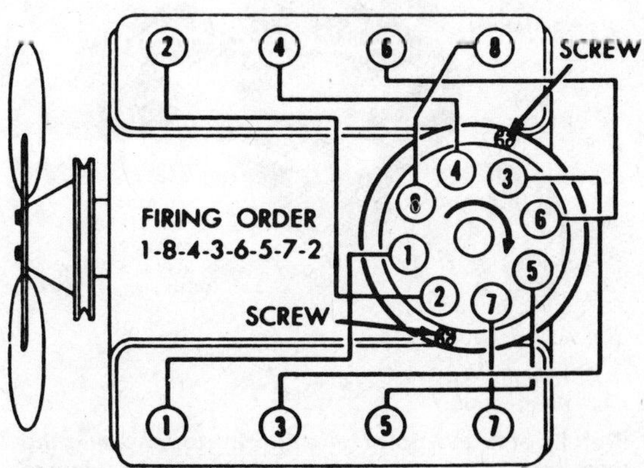

V8 with electronic ignition firing order. Distributor rotation—clockwise

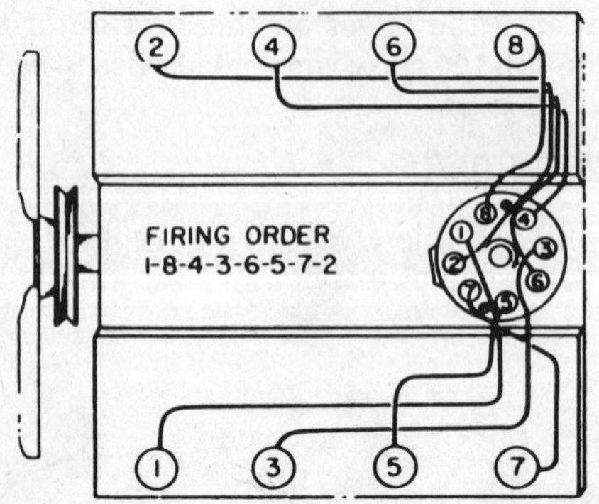

V8 with points-type ignition firing order. Distributor rotation—clockwise

Breaker Points and Condenser—Dwell Angle

1967–74

The usual procedure is to replace the condenser each time the point is replaced. Although this is not always necessary, it is easy to do at this time and the cost is negligible. Every time you adjust or replace the breaker points, the ignition timing must be checked and, if necessary, adjusted. No special equipment other than a feeler gauge is required for point replacement or adjustment, but a dwell meter is strongly advised.

1. Push down on the spring loaded V8 distributor cap retaining screws and give them ½ turn to release. Unscrew the cap retaining screws on the 6-cyl. Remove the cap. You might have to unclip or detach some or all of the plug wires to remove the cap.

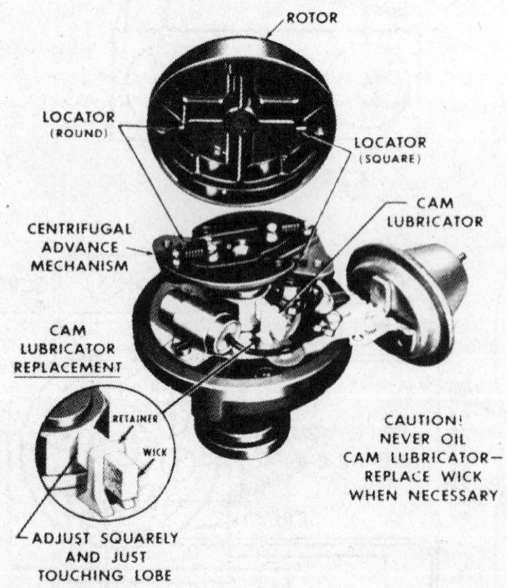

Details of the V8 point type distributor showing the cam lubricator and the square peg in the square hole arrangement that prevents incorrect rotor installation

2. Clean the cap inside and out with a clean rag. Check for cracks and carbon paths. A carbon path shows up as a dark line, usually from the cap sockets or inside terminals to a ground. Check the condition of the carbon button inside the center of the cap and the inside terminals. Replace the cap as necessary.

3. Pull the 6-cylinder rotor up and off the shaft. Remove the two screws and lift the round V8 rotor off. There is less danger of losing the screws if you just back them out all the way and lift them off with the rotor. Clean off the metal outer tip if it is burned or corroded. Don't file it. Replace the rotor as necessary or if one came with your tune-up kit.

4. Remove the radio frequency interference shield if your 1973–74 V8 distributor has one. Watch out for those little screws! The factory says that the points don't need to be replaced if they are only slightly rough or pitted. However, sad experience shows that it is more economical and reliable in the long run to replace the point set while the distributor is open, than to have to do this at a later (and possibly more inconvenient) time.

5. Pull off the two wire terminals from the point assembly. One wire comes from the condenser and the other comes from within the distributor. The terminals are usually held in place by spring tension only. There might be a clamp screw securing the terminals on some older versions. There is also available a one piece point/condenser assembly for V8s. The radio frequency interference shield isn't needed with this set. Loosen the point set holddown screw(s). Be very careful not to drop any of these little screws inside the distributor. If this happens, the distributor will probably have to be removed to get at the screw. If the holddown screw is lost elsewhere, it must be replaced with one that is no longer than the original to avoid interference with the distributor workings. Remove the point set, even if it is to be reused.

6. If the points are to be reused, clean them

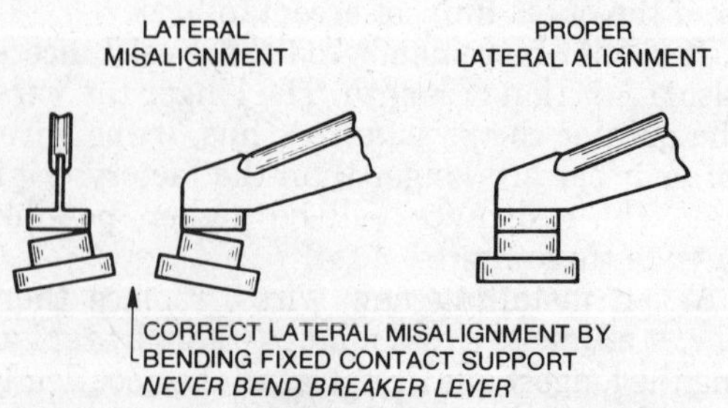

Breaker point alignment

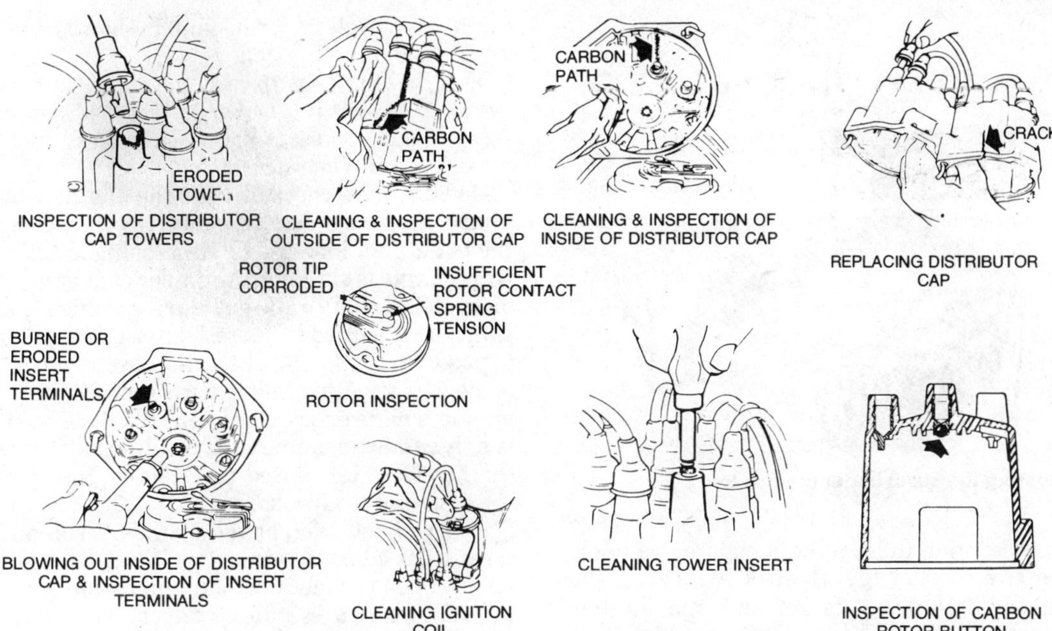

Inspection points for the distributor, rotor, cap and coil

with a few strokes of a special point file. This is done with the points removed to prevent tiny metal filings getting into the distributor. Don't use sandpaper or emery cloth; they will cause rapid point burning.

7. Loosen the condenser holddown screw and slide the condenser out of the clamp. This will save you a struggle with the clamp, condenser, and the tiny screw when you install the new one. If you have the type of clamp that is permanently fastened to the condenser, remove the screw and the condenser. Don't lose the screw.

8. Attend to the distributor cam lubricator. If you have the round kind, turn it around on its shaft at the first tune-up and replace it at the second. If you have the long kind, switch ends at the first tune-up and replace it at the second.

NOTE: *Don't oil or grease the lubricator. The foam is impregnated with a special lubricant.*

If you didn't get any lubricator at all, or if it looks like someone took it off, don't worry. You don't really need it. Just rub a matchhead size dab of high melting point grease on the cam lobes. You can buy special distributor cam lube.

9. Install the new condenser. If you left the clamp in place, just slide the new condenser into the clamp.

10. Replace the point set and tighten the screws on a V8. Leave the screw slightly loose on a six. Replace the two wire terminals, making sure that the wires don't interfere with anything. Some V8 distributors have a ground wire that must go under one of the screws.

11. Check that the contacts meet squarely. If they don't, bend the tab supporting the fixed contact.

NOTE: *If you are installing preset points on a V8, go ahead to Step 16. If they are preset, it will say so on the package. It would be a good idea to make a quick check on point gap, anyway. Sometimes those preset points aren't.*

12. Turn the engine until a high point on the cam that opens the points contacts the rubbing block on the point arm. You can turn the engine by hand if you can get a wrench on the crankshaft pulley nut, or you can grasp the fan belt and turn the engine with the spark plugs removed.

CAUTION: *If you try turning the engine by hand, be very careful not to get your fingers pinched in the pulleys.*

On a stick shift you can push it forward in High gear. Another alternative is to bump the starter switch or use a remote starter switch.

13. On a six, there is a screwdriver slot near the contact. Insert a screwdriver and lever the points open or closed until they appear to be at about the gap specified in the Tune-up Specifications. On a V8, simply insert a ⅛" allen wrench into the adjustment screw and turn. The wrench sometimes comes with a tune-up kit.

14. Insert the correct size feeler gauge and adjust the gap until you can push the gauge in and out between the contacts with a slight drag, but without disturbing the point arm.

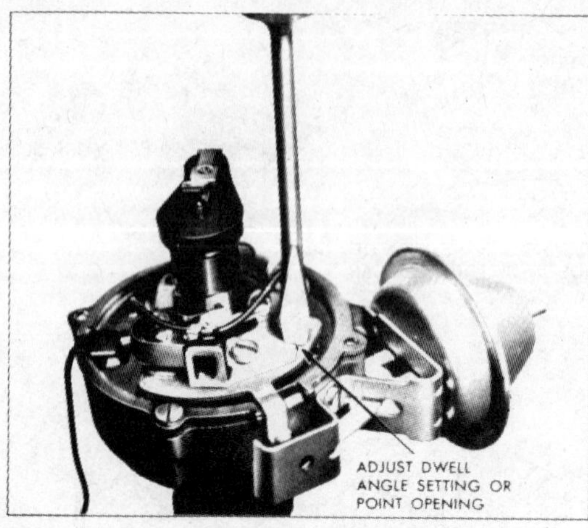

Adjusting the six cylinder distributor

This operation takes a bit of experience to obtain the correct feel. Check by trying the gauges 0.001–0.002" larger and smaller than the setting size. The larger one should disturb the point arm, while the smaller one should not drag at all. Tighten the 6-cylinder point set holddown screw. Recheck the gap, because it often changes when the screw is tightened.

15. After all the point adjustments are complete, pull a white business card through (between) the contacts to remove any traces of oil. Oil will cause rapid contact burning.

NOTE: *You can adjust 6-cylinder dwell at this point, if you wish. Refer to Step 18.*

16. Replace the 1973–74 V8 radio frequency interference shield, if any. You don't need it if you are installing the one piece point/condenser set. Push the rotor firmly down into place. It will only go one way. Tighten the V8 rotor screws. If the rotor is not installed properly, it will probably break when the starter is operated.

17. Replace the distributor cap.

18. If a dwell meter is available, check the dwell. The dwell meter hookup is shown in the Troubleshooting Section.

NOTE: *This hookup may not apply to electronic, capacitive discharge, or other special ignition systems. Some dwell meters won't work at all with such systems.*

Dwell can be checked with the engine running or cranking. Decrease dwell by increasing the point gap; increase by decreasing the gap. Dwell angle is simply the number of degrees of distributor shaft rotation during which the points stay closed. Theoretically, if the point gap is correct, the dwell should also be correct or nearly so. Adjustment with a dwell meter produces more exact, consistent results since it is a dynamic adjustment. If dwell varies more than 3° from idle speed to 1,750 engine rpm, the distributor is worn.

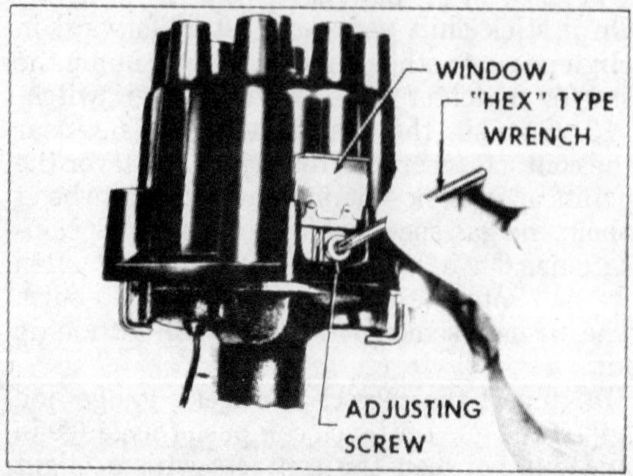

Setting the dwell on the V8 distributor

19. To adjust dwell on a 6-cylinder, trial and error point adjustments are required. On a V8, simply open the metal window on the distributor and insert a ⅛" allen wrench. Turn until the meter shows the correct reading. Be sure to snap the window closed.

20. An approximate dwell adjustment can be made without a meter on a V8. Turn the adjusting screw clockwise until the engine begins to misfire, then turn it out ½ turn.

21. If the engine won't start, check:

a. That all the spark plug wires are in place.

b. That the rotor has been installed.

c. That the two (of three) wires inside the distributor are connected.

d. That the points open and close when the engine turns.

e. That the gap is correct and the holddown screw (on a 6-cylinder) is tight.

22. After the first 200 miles or so on a new set of points, the point gap often closes up due to initial rubbing block wear. For best performance, recheck the dwell (or gap) at this time. This quick initial wear is the reason why the factory recommends 0.003" more gap on new points.

23. Since changing the gap affects the ignition timing, the timing should be checked and adjusted as necessary after each point replacement or adjustment.

1975 and Later

These engines use the breakerless HEI (High Energy Ignition) system. Since there is no mechanical contact, there is no wear or need for periodic service. There is an item in the distributor that resembles a condenser. It is a radio interference suppression capacitor which requires no service.

High Energy Ignition (HEI) System

The General Motors HEI system is a pulse-triggered, transistorized controlled, inductive discharge ignition system. Except on early inline 6-cylinder models, the entire HEI system is contained within the distributor cap. Inline 6-cylinder engines through 1977 have an external coil. Otherwise, the systems are the same.

The distributor, in addition to housing the mechanical and vacuum advance mechanisms, contains the ignition coil (except on 1975–77 inline 6-cylinder engines), the electronic control module, and the magnetic triggering device. The magnetic pick-up assembly contains a permanent magnet, a pole piece with internal teeth, and a pick-up coil (not to be confused with the ignition coil).

In the HEI system, as in other electronic ignition systems, the breaker points have been replaced with an electronic switch – a transistor – which is located within the control module. This switching transistor performs the same function the points did in a conventional ignition system. It simply turns coil primary current on and off at the correct time. Essentially then, electronic and conventional ignition systems operate on the same principle.

The module which houses the switching transistor is controlled (turned on and off) by a magnetically generated impulse induced in the pick-up coil. When the teeth of the rotating timer align with the teeth of the pole piece, the induced voltage in the pick-up coil signals the electronic module to open the coil primary circuit. The primary current then decreases, and a high voltage is induced in the ignition coil secondary windings which is then directed through the rotor and high voltage leads (spark plug wires) to fire the spark plugs.

In essence then, the pick-up coil module system simply replaces the conventional breaker points and condenser. The condenser found within the distributor is for radio suppression purposes only and had nothing to do with the ignition process. The module automatically controls the dwell period, increasing it with increasing engine speed. Since dwell is automatically controlled, it cannot be adjusted. The module itself is non-adjustable and non-repairable and must be replaced if found defective.

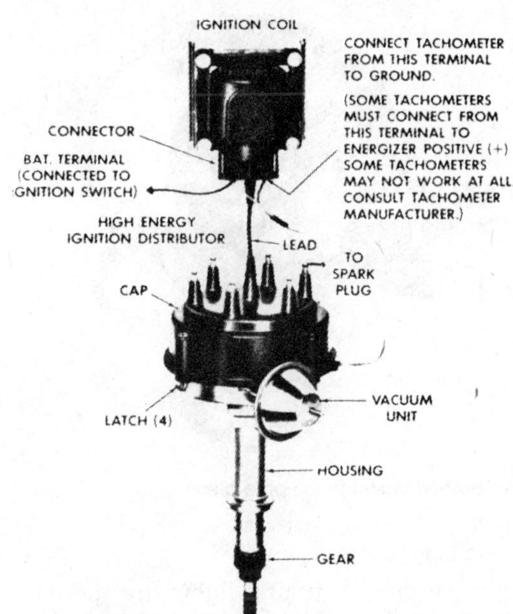

Six-cylinder HEI distributor, 1975–77. 1978 and later models have the coil in the distributor cap

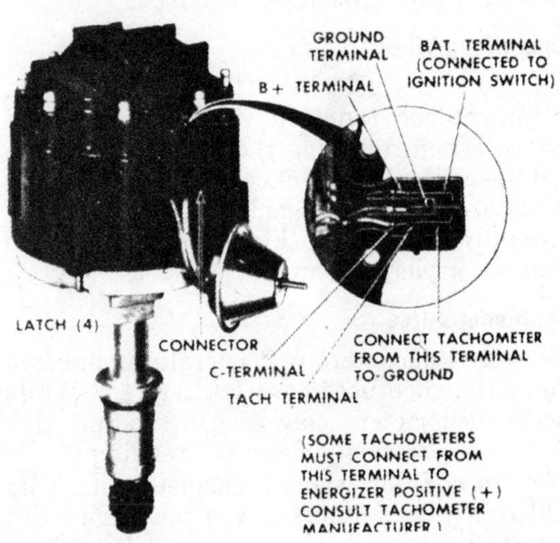

V8 HEI distributor

The module connectors are two different sizes and will only connect one way

HEI SYSTEM PRECAUTIONS

Before going on to troubleshooting, it might be a good idea to take note of the following precautions:

The toothed wheel is the pole piece

Timing Light Use

Inductive pick-up timing lights are the best kind to use if your van is equipped with HEI. Timing lights which connect between the spark plug and the spark plug wire occasionally (not always) give false readings.

Spark Plug Wires

The plug wires used with HEI systems are of a different construction than conventional wires. When replacing them, make sure you get the correct wires, since conventional wires won't carry the voltage. Also, handle them carefully to avoid cracking or splitting them and never pierce them.

Tachometer Use

Not all tachometers will operate or indicate correctly when used on a HEI system. While some tachometers may give a reading, this does not necessarily mean the reading is correct. In addition, some tachometers hook up differently from others. If you can't figure out whether or not your tachometer will work on your car, check with the tachometer manufacturer. Dwell readings, of course, have no significance at all.

HEI Systems Testers

Instruments designed specifically for testing HEI systems are available from several tool manufacturers. Some of these will even test the module itself. However, the tests given in the following section will require only a ohmmeter and a voltmeter.

NOTE: *This book contains simple test procedures for your Chevrolet/GMC Van's electronic ignition. More comprehensive testing on this system and other electronic control systems on your van can be found in CHILTON'S GUIDE TO ELECTRONIC ENGINE CONTROLS, book part number 7535, available at your local retailer.*

ADJUSTMENTS

Ignition Timing

Timing should be checked at each tune-up and any time the points are adjusted or replaced. It isn't likely to change much with HEI. The timing marks consist of a notch on the rim of the crankshaft pulley or vibration damper and a graduated scale attached to the engine front (timing) cover. A stroboscopic flash (dynamic) timing light must be used, as a static light is too inaccurate for emission controlled engines.

There are three basic types of timing light available. The first is a simple neon bulb with two wire connections. One wire connects to the spark plug terminal and the other plugs into the end of the spark plug wire for the No. 1 cylinder, thus connecting the light in series with the spark plug. This type of light is pretty dim and must be held very closely to the timing marks to be seen. Sometimes a dark corner has to be sought out to see the flash at all. This type of light is very inexpensive. The second type operates from the vehicle battery—two alligator clips connect to the battery terminals, while an adapter enables a third clip to be connected between No. 1 spark plug and wire. This type is a bit more expensive, but it provides a nice bright flash that you can see even in bright sunlight. It is the type most often seen in professional shops. The third type replaces the battery power source with 100 volt current.

Some timing lights have other features built into them, such as dwell meters, or tachometers. These are convenient, in that they reduce the tangle of wires under the hood when you're working, but may duplicate the functions of tools you already have. One worthwhile feature, which is becoming more of a necessity with higher voltage ignition systems, is an inductive pickup. The inductive pickup clamps around the No. 1 spark plug wire, sensing the surges of high voltage electricity as they are sent to the plug. The advantage is that no mechanical connection is inserted between the wire and the plug. The advantage is that no mechanical connection is inserted between the wire and the plug, which eliminates false signals to the timing light. A timing light with an inductive pickup should be used on HEI systems.

To check and adjust the timing:

1. Warm up the engine to normal operating temperature. Stop the engine and connect the timing light to the No. 1 (left front on V8, front on 6-cylinder) spark plug wire, wither at the

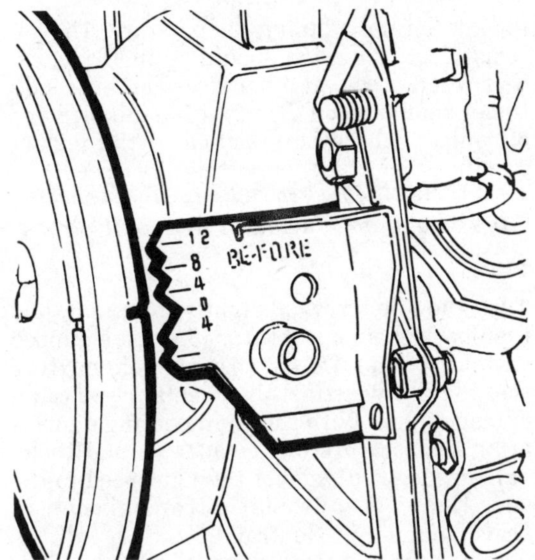

Typical ignition timing marks

plug or at the distributor cap. You can also use the No. 6 wire, if it is more convenient. No. 6 is the rear cylinder on a 6-cylinder, and the third cylinder back on the right bank of a V8. Numbering is illustrated earlier in this Chapter.

NOTE: *Do not pierce the plug wire insulation with HEI; it will cause a miss. The best method is an inductive pickup timing light.*

Clean off the timing marks and mark the pulley or damper notch and timing scale with white chalk.

2. Disconnect and plug the vacuum line at the distributor. This is done to prevent any distributor vacuum advance. Check the underhood emission sticker for any other hoses or wires which may need to be disconnected.

3. Start the engine and adjust the idle speed to that specified in the Tune-up Specifications chart. With automatic transmission, set the specified idle speed in Park. It will be too high, since it is normally (in most cases) adjusted in Drive. You can disconnect the idle solenoid, if any, to get the speed down. Otherwise, adjust the idle speed screw. This is done to prevent any centrifugal (mechanical) advance. The tachometer hookup for 1967–74 models is the same as the dwell meter hookup shown in the Troubleshooting section. On 1975 and later HEI systems, the tachometer connects to the TACH terminal on the distributor or on the coil (6-cylinder through 1977) and to a ground. Some tachometers must connect to the TACH terminal and to the positive battery terminal. Some tachometers won't work with HEI.

CAUTION: *Never ground the HEI TACH terminal; serious system damage will result.*

4. Aim the timing light at the pointer marks. Be careful not to touch the fan, because it may appear to be standing still. If the pulley or damper notch isn't aligned with the proper timing mark (see the Tune-up Specifications chart), the timing will have to be adjusted.

NOTE: *TDC or Top Dead Center corresponds to 0°B, or BTDC, or Before Top Dead Center may be shown as BEFORE. A, or ATDC, or After Top Dead Center may be shown as AFTER.*

5. Loosen the distributor base clamp locknut. You can buy trick wrenches which make this task a lot easier on V8s. Turn the distributor slowly to adjust the timing, holding it by the body and not the cap. Turn the distributor in the direction of rotor rotation (found in the Firing Order illustration) to retard, and against the direction of rotation to advance.

6. Tighten the locknut. Check the timing again, in case the distributor moved slightly as you tightened it.

7. Replace the distributor vacuum line. Correct the idle speed.

8. Stop the engine and disconnect the timing light.

Diesel Injection Timing

8–379 cu. in. Diesels

For the engine to be properly timed, the marks on the top of the engine front cover must be aligned with the marks on the injection pump flange. The engine must be OFF when the timing is reset.

NOTE: *On 49-state 379s, the marks are scribe lines. On California 379s, the marks are half circles.*

1. Loosen the three pump retaining nuts. If the marks are not aligned, adjustment is necessary.

2. Loosen the three pump retaining nuts.

3. Align the mark on the injection pump

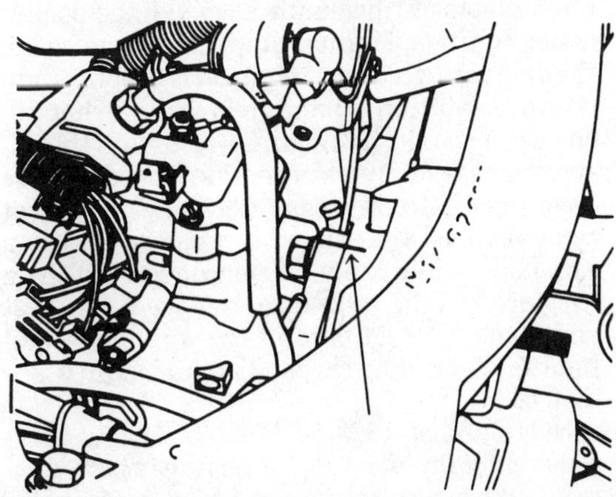
Diesel injection timing marks, 379 shown. Marks shown are in alignment

with the mark on the front cover. Tighten the nuts to 30 ft.lb.

NOTE: *Use a 3/4" open end wrench on the nut at the front of the injection pump to aid in rotating the pump to align the marks.*

4. Adjust the throttle linkage if necessary.

Valve Leash

All engines covered in this guide are equipped with hydraulic valve lifters. Engines so equipped operate with zero clearance in the valve train. Because of this the rocker arms are non-adjustable. The hydraulic lifters themselves do not require any adjustment as part of the normal tune-up, although they occasionally become noisy (especially on high mileage engines) and need to be replaced. In the event of cylinder head removal or any operation that requires disturbing or removing the rocker arms, the rocker arms have to be adjusted. Please refer to Chapter 3. Hydraulic lifter service is also covered in Chapter 3.

Carburetor

In most cases, the mixture screws have limiter caps, but in later years the mixture screws are concealed under staked-in plugs. Idle mixture is adjustable only during carburetor overhaul, and requires the addition of propane as an artificial mixture enrichener. For these reasons, mixture adjustments are not covered here for affected models.

See the emission control label in the engine compartment for procedures and specifications not supplied here.

NOTE: *See Carburetor Identification in Chapter 4 for carburetor I.D. specifics.*

IDLE SPEED AND MIXTURE ADJUSTMENT

These procedures require the use of a tachometer. Tachometer hookup was explained earlier under Ignition Timing, Step 3. In some cases, the degree of accuracy required is greater than that available on a hand-held unit; a shop tachometer would be required to follow the instructions exactly. If the idle speed screws have plastic limiter caps (1971–82), it is not recommended that they be removed unless a satisfactory idle cannot be obtained with them in place. If the caps are removed, exhaust emissions may go beyond the specified legal limits. This can be checked on an exhaust gas analyzer.

NOTE: *Most 1973 and later 4-bbl carburetors have an internal fuel passage restriction. Beyond a certain limited point, turning the idle mixture screws out has no further richening effect.*

Idle speed and mixture are set with the engine at normal running temperature. The automatic transmission should be in Drive, except when specified otherwise. The air conditioner should be off for adjusting mixture and off unless otherwise specified in the text or specifications chart for setting idle speed.

CAUTION: *Block the wheels, set the parking brake, and don't stand in front of the truck.*

1967

Turn the idle screw(s) slightly in to seat, and then back them out 2 turns (3 when equipped with air pump). Do not turn the idle mixture screws tightly against their seats or you could damage them. With the engine idling at operating temperature (air cleaner on and choke valve wide open), adjust the idle speed to the specified rpm (automatic transmission in Drive; manual in Neutral.

Adjust the mixture screw to obtain the highest steady idle speed, then adjust the idle speed screw to the specified rpm. Adjust the mixture screw in to obtain a 20 rpm drop, then back the screw out 1/4 turn. Repeat this operation on the second mixture screw, if so equipped. Readjust the idle speed screw as necessary until the specified rpm is reached.

1968–69

Turn the idle mixture screw(s) in to seat and then back them out 3 turns. Don't turn the screws in tightly or you will damage them. Bring the engine to its operating temperature (air cleaner installed and choke valve open), and adjust the idle speed screw to obtain the specified rpm (automatic transmission in Drive, manual transmission in Neutral).

NOTE: *On air conditioned models, turn the air conditioner off except on 6-cylinder engines with automatic transmission. On these models idle speed is set with the air conditioning on.*

Set the idle mixture screw(s) to give the highest steady idle speed. Adjust the idle speed to the specified rpm. Set the idle speed for engines with idle solenoids as follows: set the idle speed to 500 rpm by turning the idle solenoid hex bolt. Disconnect the solenoid wire and check the idle speed. De-energizing the solenoid will allow the throttle lever to seat against the carburetor idle screw. Turn the carburetor idle screw to obtain 400 rpm.

Turn the mixture screw(s) in to get a 20 rpm drop. Turn the mixture screw out 1/4 turn. Repeat for the second mixture screw, if so equipped. Readjust the idle speed screw, as necessary, to obtain the specified idle rpm.

1970–71

On all vehicles, disconnect the FUEL TANK line from the vapor canister. Remember to reconnect the line after setting the idle speed and mixture. The engine should be at operating temperature with the choke valve and air cleaner damper door fully open, air conditioning OFF and parking brake ON.

6-cylinder Engine, 10 Series: Turn the mixture screw in until it lightly contacts the seat, then back out 4 turns. Adjust the solenoid screw to obtain 800 rpm with manual transmission in Neutral or 630 rpm with automatic transmission in Drive. Adjust the mixture screw to obtain 750 rpm with manual transmission in Neutral or automatic in Drive. Electrically disconnect the solenoid and set the carburetor idle speed screw to obtain 400 rpm and connect the solenoid. Reconnect the vacuum line.

6-cylinder Engine, 20 & 30 Series: Disconnect and plug the distributor vacuum line. Turn the mixture screws in until they lightly contact the seats and back the screw(s) out 4 turns. On manual transmission models, adjust the carburetor idle speed screw to obtain 600 rpm in Neutral. Then adjust the mixture screw to obtain 550 rpm in Neutral. On automatic transmission models, adjust the solenoid screw to obtain 550 rpm with transmission in Drive. Adjust the mixture screw to obtain 500 rpm with transmission in Drive. Disconnect the solenoid and set the carburetor idle speed screw to obtain 400 rpm and connect the solenoid. Reconnect the distributor vacuum line on all models.

Adjusting the idle solenoid, 1970–71

8–307, 10 Series: Disconnect and plug the distributor vacuum line. Turn the mixture screws in until they lightly contact the seats then back them out 4 turns. Adjust the carburetor idle speed screw to obtain 800 rpm with manual transmission in Neutral. Adjust the mixture screw to obtain 630 rpm with automatic transmission in Drive. Adjust the mixture screws in equally to obtain 700 rpm with manual transmission in Neutral or 600 rpm with automatic transmission in Drive. Disconnect the solenoid and set the carburetor idle speed screw to obtain 450 rpm and reconnect the solenoid. Reconnect the vacuum line.

1970 8–307, 20 & 30 Series: Set the mixture screws for maximum idle rpm and adjust the idle speed screw to obtain 700 rpm with manual transmission in Neutral or 600 rpm with automatic transmission in Drive. Adjust the

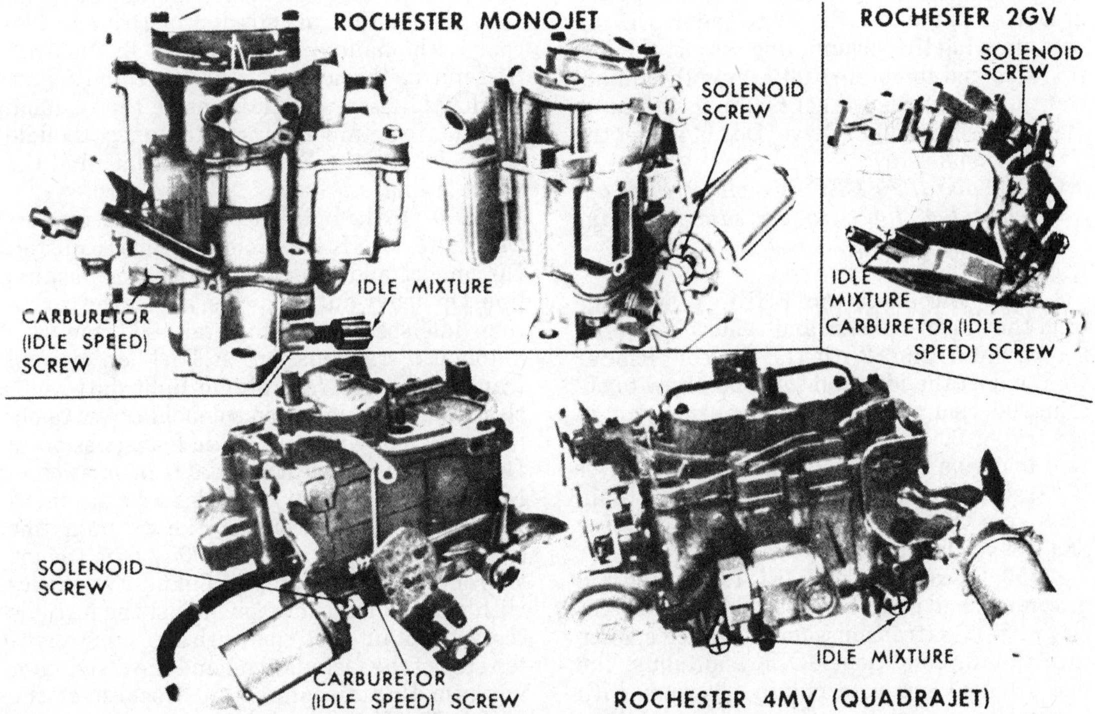

Idle speed and mixture screws, 1970–71

mixture screws equally to obtain a 20 rpm drop, then back the idle screw on manual transmission models to obtain 700 rpm with the transmission in Neutral. On automatic transmission models, adjust the solenoid screw to obtain 600 rpm with the transmission in Drive. Disconnect the solenoid electrically and set the carburetor idle screw to obtain 450 rpm and reconnect the solenoid. Reconnect the vacuum line.

1970–71 8–350, 20 & 30 Series: Disconnect and plug the distributor vacuum line. Turn the mixture screws in until they lightly contact the seats and back them out 4 turns. Adjust the carburetor idle speed screw to obtain 775 rpm (manual transmission in Neutral) or 630 rpm (automatic transmission in Drive). Adjust the mixture screws equally to obtain 700 rpm (manual transmission in Neutral) or 600 rpm (automatic transmission in Drive). Reconnect the vacuum line.

1972

The engine should be at normal operating temperature with the choke valve fully open, parking brake ON and the drive wheels blocked. All carburetors are equipped with idle mixture limiter caps, which provide for only a small adjustment range. Normally, if they are removed, the CO content of the exhaust should be checked to be sure that it meets Federal Emission Control limits.

6–250: Disconnect the FUEL TANK line from the vapor canister. Remember to reconnect it after making the adjustment. Disconnect and plug the vacuum line. Adjust the idle stop solenoid to obtain 700 rpm with manual transmission in Neutral or 600 rpm with automatic transmission in Drive. Do not adjust the CEC solenoid screw.

CAUTION: *If the CEC solenoid screw is adjusted out of limits, a decrease in engine braking may result.*

Reconnect the vacuum line.

8–307: Disconnect the FUEL TANK line from the vapor canister and remove and plug the vacuum line. With the air conditioner OFF, adjust the idle stop solenoid screw to obtain 900 rpm with manual transmission in Neutral or 600 rpm with automatic transmission in Drive. With transmission in Park or Neutral, adjust the fast idle speed to obtain 1850 rpm. Reconnect the FUEL TANK line and the vacuum line.

8–350: Disconnect the FUEL TANK line and disconnect and plug the vacuum line. On vehicles with TCS (transmission controlled spark), turn the air conditioner OFF and adjust the idle solenoid screw to obtain 800 rpm with manual transmission in Neutral or 600 rpm with automatic transmission in Drive. On vehicles without TCS, adjust the carburetor speed screw to obtain 600 rpm with transmission in Neutral. Place the fast idle cam follower on the 2nd step of the fast idle cam, turn the air conditioner OFF and adjust the fast idle to 1350 rpm with manual transmission in Neutral or automatic transmission in Drive. Reconnect the FUEL TANK and vacuum lines.

1973–74

All adjustments should be made with the engine at operating temperature, choke valve fully open, air conditioning OFF, parking brake ON and drive wheels blocked.

6–250: Disconnect the FUEL TANK line and the distributor vacuum line. Plug the vacuum line. Adjust the idle stop solenoid by turning the hex nut to obtain:

- 700 rpm (1973) or 850 rpm (1974) on manual transmission in Neutral
- 600 rpm (1973–74) on automatic transmission in Drive

Do not adjust the CEC solenoid on 1973 vehicles or a decrease in engine braking may result. Place automatic transmission in Neutral and adjust the fast idle to 1800 rpm, on the top step of the fast idle cam. Reconnect the FUEL TANK and vacuum lines.

1973 8–307: On light duty vehicles, disconnect the FUEL TANK line from the vapor canister and plug the distributor vacuum line. Adjust the idle stop solenoid to obtain 600 rpm with automatic transmission in Drive or 900 rpm with manual transmission in Neutral. Disconnect the idle stop solenoid and adjust the low idle screw located inside the solenoid hex nut, to obtain 450 rpm. Reconnect the idle stop solenoid, the FUEL TANK line, and the vacuum line.

8–350: On the light duty vehicles, disconnect the FUEL TANK line from the vapor canister. Disconnect and plug the distributor vacuum line. On heavy duty vehicles, adjust the carburetor idle speed screw to obtain 600 rpm with automatic transmission in Park or manual transmission in Neutral. On light duty vehicles, adjust the idle stop solenoid screw to obtain 600 rpm with automatic transmission in Drive or 900 rpm with manual transmission in Neutral. On light duty vehicles with automatic transmission, reconnect the vacuum line and adjust the fast idle to 1600 rpm on the top step of the fast idle cam. On light duty vehicles with manual transmission, adjust the fast idle screw to obtain 1300 rpm with the screw on the top step of the fast idle cam and the distributor vacuum line disconnected. Reconnect the FUEL TANK line and the vacuum line.

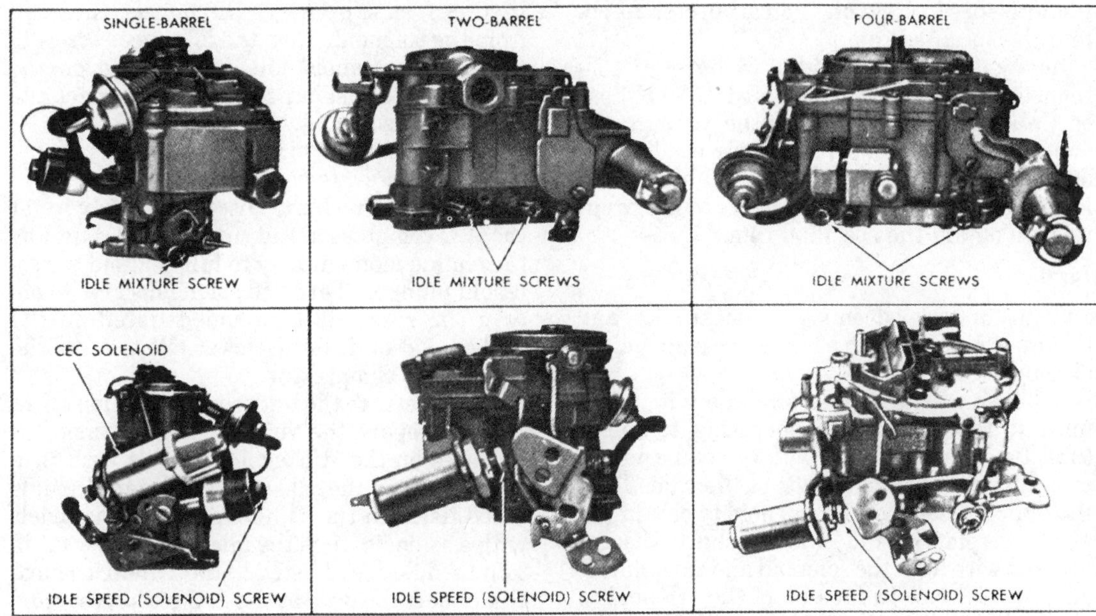

Idle speed and mixture screws, 1972–75

1975

6-cylinder: Do not disconnect the distributor vacuum line. Disconnect the vapor canister FUEL TANK hose. With automatic transmission in Drive and manual in Neutral, adjust the solenoid to get the specified idle speed. Use a 1/8″ allen wrench in the end of the solenoid body to set the low idle speed to 450 rpm with the solenoid wire disconnected. Reset the idle speed with the air conditioning on, except on the 250 engine.

V8 with the 2-bbl carburetor: Disconnect the vapor canister FUEL TANK hose. Leave the distributor vacuum advance hose in place. Adjust the idle speed screw to get the specified idle sped with automatic in Drive and manual in Neutral.

Light duty V8 with 4-bbl carburetor: Disconnect the vapor canister FUEL TANK hose. Leave the distributor vacuum advance hose in place. Disconnect the solenoid wire. Place automatic in Drive and manual in Neutral. Turn the low idle speed screw on the carburetor to get about 450 rpm. Connect the solenoid wire and open the throttle slightly, so that the solenoid plunger can extend. Turn the plunger screw to get the specified idle speed.

Heavy duty V8 with 4-bbl carburetor: This adjustment is the same as for 1974. Reset the idle speed with the air conditioner on.

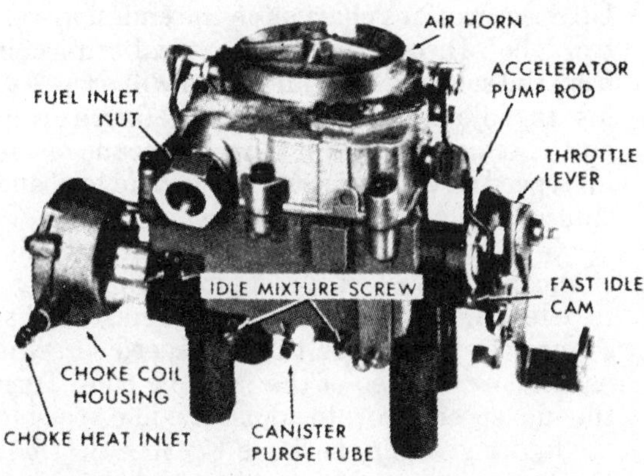

Rochester 2GC, 1975

1976

6-cylinder: Disconnect and plug the CARBURETOR and PCV vapor canister hoses on the 250. Disconnect the canister FUEL TANK hose on the 292. If the engine has a vacuum advance hose running directly from the vacuum source to the distributor vacuum advance unit, disconnect and plug it. Turn the air conditioner on, only on the 292. Set the manual transmission in Neutral. Set the 250 automatic in Drive and the 292 in Neutral. Turn the solenoid to get the specified idle speed. Disconnect the solenoid wire and turn off the air conditioner. Use a 1/8″ allen wrench in the end of the solenoid body to set the low idle speed to 450 rpm.

V8 with two barrel carburetor: This procedure is the same as 1975, except that the canister hose can be left in place.

Light duty V8 with 4-bbl carburetor: Place the automatic in Drive and manual in Neutral. Set the idle speed screw on the carburetor to obtain the specified rpm.

Heavy duty V8 with 4-bbl carburetor: Disconnect the vapor canister FUEL TANK hose on California models. Leave the vacuum advance hose in place. Turn the air conditioner on. Set the automatic in Park and manual in Neutral. Set the idle speed screw on the carburetor to obtain the specified rpm.

1977

See the underhood emission sticker for any hoses or wires that may need to be disconnected.

1 bbl: Start the engine and allow it to run until it reaches normal operating temperature. Be sure the choke is fully open and the cam follower is off the steps of the cam. Turn the nut on the end of the solenoid to obtain the specified rpm. See the Tune-up chart. Disconnect the wire from the solenoid and turn the ⅛" allen head screw in the end of the solenoid to set the base idle to specification. Refer to the Tune-up chart or the underhood emission sticker. Reconnect the wire.

2 and 4 bbl: Be sure the ignition timing is correct. Refer to the underhood emission sticker in order to prepare the vehicle for adjustment.

On carburetors without a solenoid: Be sure the idle speed screw is on the low step of the fast idle cam. Turn the screw to obtain the idle specified in the Tune-Up chart.

On carburetors with a solenoid: Turn the idle screw to obtain the idle speed specified in the Tune-Up chart. Disconnect the electrical lead from between the solenoid and the A/C compressor at the compressor and turn the A/C On. Place the automatic transmission in Drive. Open the throttle momentarily to fully extend the solenoid plunger. Turn the solenoid screw to obtain the base idle speed as specified in the Tune-Up chart or on the emission sticker. Reconnect the electrical lead at the compressor.

1978

1-bbl: The idle speed adjusting procedure is the same as 1977. Refer to the Tune-Up chart for the correct idle speed.

2-bbl: Be sure the ignition timing is correct. Refer to the underhood emission sticker in order to prepare the vehicle for adjustment.

On carburetors without a solenoid: This procedure is the same as 1977. See the Tune-Up chart for the correct idle speed.

On models with a solenoid and without air conditioning: Rev the engine momentarily to fully extend the solenoid plunger. Turn the solenoid screw to obtain the curb idle speed listed in the Tune-Up chart. Disconnect the wire from the solenoid. Turn the idle speed screw to obtain the solenoid idle speed listed on the underhood emission sticker. Reconnect the wire at the solenoid.

On models with air conditioning: Turn the idle speed screw to obtain the idle speed listed in the Tune-Up chart. Disconnect the wire at the A/C compressor and turn the A/C On. Rev the engine momentarily to fully extend the solenoid plunger. Turn the solenoid screw to obtain the solenoid idle speed listed on the underhood emission sticker. Reconnect the wire at the compressor.

4-bbl: Refer to the underhood emission sticker and prepare the vehicle for adjustment as specified on the sticker. On models without a solenoid, turn the idle speed to obtain the idle speed listed in the Tune-Up chart. On models with a solenoid, turn the idle speed screw to obtain the idle speed listed in the Tune-Up chart. Disconnect the wire at the A/C compressor and turn the A/C On. Rev the engine momentarily to fully extend the solenoid plunger. Turn the solenoid screw to obtain the solenoid idle speed listed on the underhood emission sticker. Reconnect the A/C wire at the compressor.

1979 and Later Idle Speed Adjustment

Idle mixture is not adjustable in these years, except for the heavy duty emission V8s equipped with the 4-bbl M4MC.

All adjustments should be made with the engine at normal operating temperature, air cleaner on, choke open, and air conditioning off, unless otherwise noted. Set the parking brake and block the rear wheels. Automatic transmissions should be set in Drive, manuals in Neutral, unless otherwise noted in the procedures or on the emission control label.

• 6–250 Engine: Check the emission control label for any special instructions. Open the throttle slightly to allow the solenoid plunger to extend. Turn the solenoid screw to adjust the curb idle to the figure given in the Tune-Up Specifications chart or on the emission control label. Disconnect the electrical connector from the solenoid. The idle speed will drop. Adjust the idle to the basic idle speed figure given on the emission control label by means of the idle speed screw. Connect the solenoid lead and shut off the engine.

• 6–262 and 8–305 Engines: Check the emission control label in the engine compartment to determine which hoses, if any, must be disconnected. Make sure the idle speed screw is on the low (L) step of the fast idle cam. Turn the idle speed screw to adjust the idle speed to the figure given in the Tune-Up Specifications chart or on the emission control label.

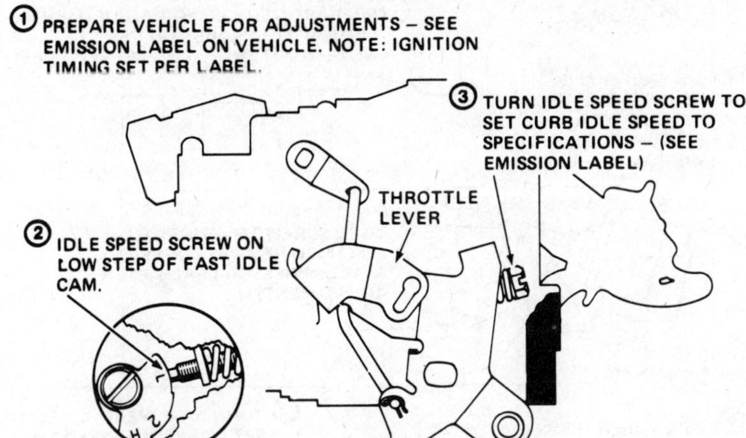

1977–78 2 bbl idle speed adjustment—without solenoid

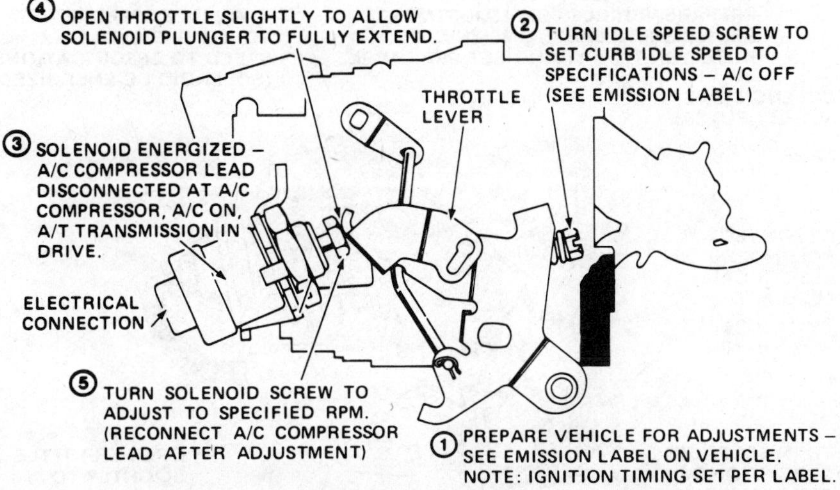

1977–78 2 bbl idle speed adjustment—with solenoid

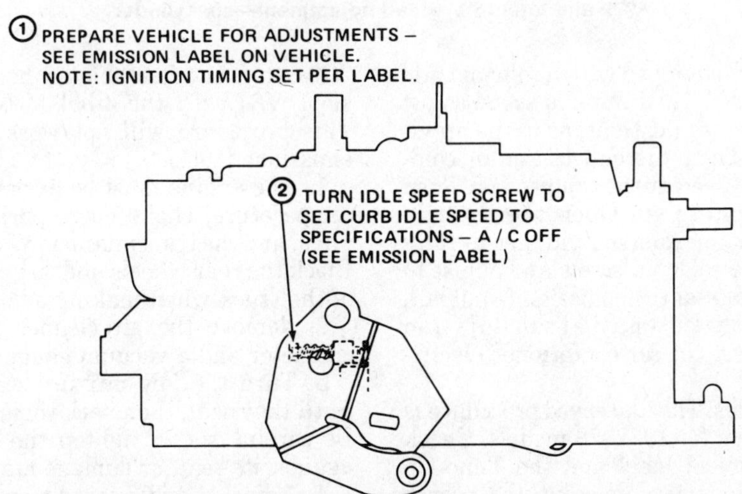

1977 and later 4 bbl idle speed adjustment—without solenoid

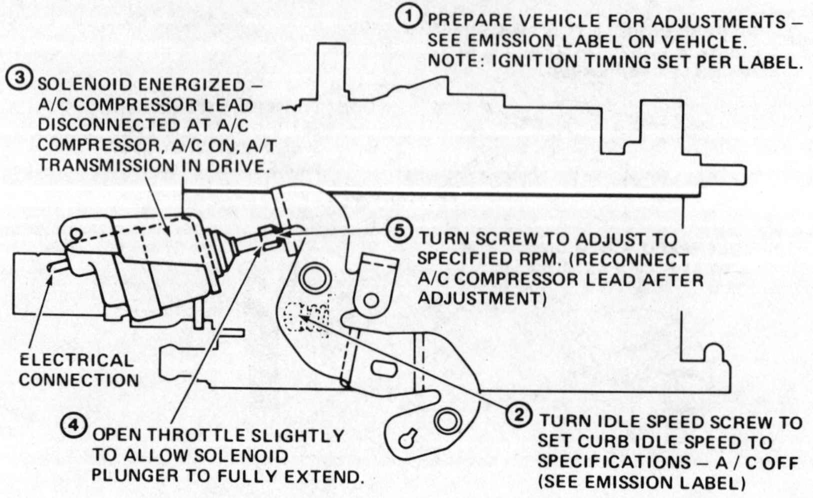

1977 and later 4 bbl and 1979 and later 2 bbl (V8 only) idle speed adjustment—with solenoid

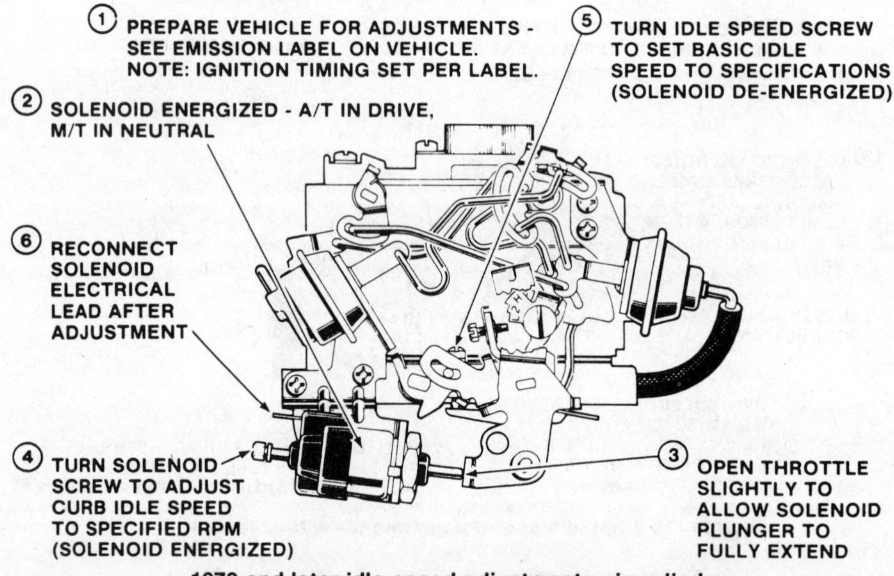

1979 and later idle speed adjustment—six cylinder

On carburetors equipped with a solenoid (air conditioned trucks): turn the idle speed screw to set the idle to specifications, as in the previous paragraph. Then, disconnect the air compressor electrical lead at the compressor. Turn the air conditioning on. Open the throttle slightly to allow the solenoid plunger to fully extend. Turn the solenoid screw and adjust to 700 rpm with manual transmission (Neutral), or 600 rpm with automatic transmission (Drive). Reconnect the air conditioner electrical lead.

• 8–350 Engines: The idle speed procedure is the same as given for 1977–78 models. Check the emission control label and the Tune-Up Specifications chart to determine the proper idle speeds.

Mixture is adjustable on heavy duty emissions V8s with the 4-bbl M4MC carburetor. This procedure will not work on light duty emissions trucks.

1. The engine must be at normal operating temperature, choke open, parking brake applied, and the transmission in Park or Neutral. Block the rear wheels and do not stand in from of the truck when making adjustments.
2. Remove the air cleaner. Connect a tachometer and a vacuum gauge to the engine.
3. Turn the idle mixture screws in lightly until they seat, then back them out two turns. Be careful not to tighten the mixture screw against its seat, or damage may result.
4. Adjust the idle speed screw to obtain the

engine rpm figure specified on the emission control label.

5. Adjust the idle mixture screws equally to obtain the highest engine speed.

6. Repeat Steps 4 and 5 until the best idle is obtained.

7. Shut off the engine, remove the tachometer and vacuum gauge, and install the air cleaner.

Diesel Fuel Injection

IDLE SPEED ADJUSTMENT

379 V8 Diesel

NOTE: *A special tachometer suitable for diesel engines must be used. A gasoline engine type tach will not work with the diesel engine.*

1. Set the parking brake and block the drive wheels.

2. Run the engine up to normal operating temperature. The air cleaner must be mounted and all accessories turned off.

3. Install the diesel tachometer as per the manufacturer's instructions.

4. Adjust the low idle speed screw on the fuel injection pump to 650 rpm in Neutral or Park for both manual and automatic transmissions.

NOTE: *All idle speeds are to be set within 25 rpm of the specified values.*

5. Adjust the fast idle speed as follows:

a. Remove the connector from the fast idle solenoid. Use an insulated jumper wire from the battery positive terminal to the solenoid terminal to energize the solenoid.

b. Open the throttle momentarily to ensure that the fast idle solenoid plunger is energized and fully extended.

c. Adjust the extended plunger by turning the hex-head screw to an engine sped of 800 rpm in Neutral.

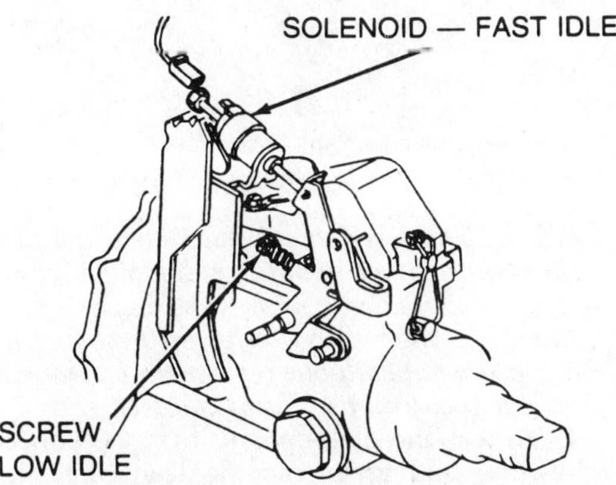

379 (6.2L) diesel injection pump showing idle adjustments

d. Remove the jumper wire and reinstall the connector to the fast idle solenoid.

6. Disconnect and remove the tachometer.

TROUBLESHOOTING THE HEI SYSTEM

The symptoms of a defective component within the HEI system are exactly the same as those you would encounter in a conventional system. Some of these symptoms are:

- Hard or no starting
- Rough idle
- Poor fuel economy
- Engine misses under load or while accelerating.

If you suspect a problem in your ignition system, there are certain preliminary checks which you should carry out before you begin to check the electronic portions of the system. First, it is extremely important to make sure the vehicle battery is in a good state of charge. A defective or poorly charged battery will cause the various components of the ignition system to read incorrectly when they are being tested. Second, make sure all wiring connections are clean and tight, not only at the battery, but also at the distributor cap, ignition coil, and at the electronic control module.

Since the only change between electronic and conventional ignition systems is in the distributor component area, it is imperative to check the secondary ignition circuit first. If the secondary circuit checks out properly, then the engine condition is probably not the fault of the ignition system. To check the secondary ignition system, perform a simple spark test. Remove one of the plug wires and insert some sort of extension in the plug socket. An old spark plug with the ground electrode removed makes a good extension. Hold the wire and extension about ¼" away from the block and crank the engine. If a normal spark occurs, then the problem is most likely not in the ignition system. Check for fuel system problems, or fouled spark plugs.

If, however, there is no spark or a weak spark, then further ignition system testing will have to be done. Troubleshooting techniques fall into two categories, depending on the nature of the problem. The categories are (1) Engine cranks, but won't start or (2) Engine runs, but runs rough or cuts out.

Engine Fails to Start

If the engine won't start, perform a spark test as described earlier. If no spark occurs, check for the presence of normal battery voltage at the battery (BAT) terminal in the distributor cap. The ignition system must be in the ON position for this test. Either a voltmeter or a test light may be used for this test. Connect the test light wire to ground and the probe end to the BAT terminal at the distributor. If the light comes on, you have voltage on the distributor. If the light fails to come on, this indicates an open circuit in the ignition primary wiring leading to the distributor. In this case, you will have to check wiring continuity back to the ignition switch using a test light. If there is battery voltage at the BAT terminal, but no spark at the plugs, then the problem lies within the distributor assembly. Go on to the distributor components test section.

Engine Runs, but Rough or Cuts Out

1. Make sure the plug wires are in good shape first. There should be no obvious cracks or breaks. You can check the plug wires with an ohmmeter, but do not pierce the wires with a probe. Check the chart for the correct plug wire resistance.

2. If the plug wires are OK, remove the cap assembly, and check for moisture, cracks, chips, or carbon tracks, or any other high voltage leaks or failures. Replace the cap if you find any defects. Make sure the timer wheel rotates when the engine is cranked. If everything is all right so far, go on to the distributor components test section.

Distributor Components Testing

If the trouble has been narrowed down to the units within the distributor, the following tests can help pinpoint the defective component. An ohmmeter with both high and low ranges should be used. These tests are made with the cap assembly removed and the battery wire disconnected.

1. Connect an ohmmeter between the TACH and BAT terminals in the distributor cap. The primary coil resistance should be $<1\Omega$ (zero or nearly zero).

2. To check the coil secondary resistance, connect an ohmmeter between the rotor button and the BAT terminal. Then connect the ohmmeter between the ground terminal and the rotor button. The resistance in both cases should be between 6,000 and 30,000Ω.

3. Replace the coil only if the readings in step one and two are infinite.

HEI Plug Wire Resistance Chart

Wire Length	Minimum	Maximum
0–15 inches	3000 ohms	10,000 ohms
15–25 inches	4000 ohms	15,000 ohms
25–35 inches	6000 ohms	20,000 ohms
Over 35 inches		25,000 ohms

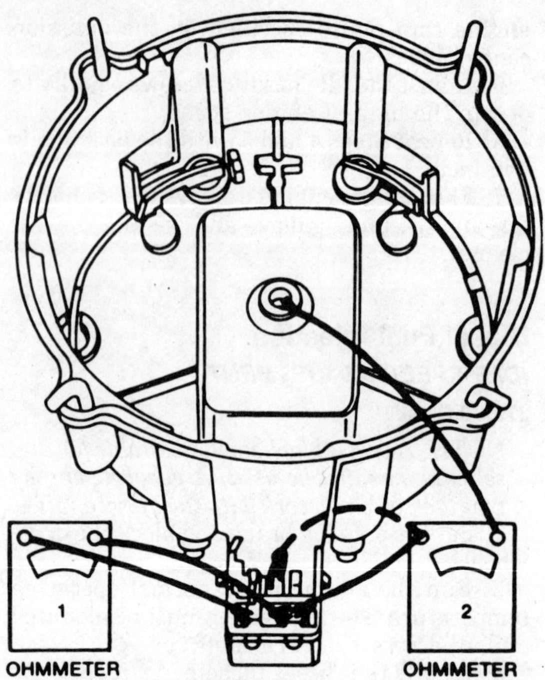

Checking coil resistance on the HEI system. Ohmmeter 1 shows the primary coil resistance connection. Ohmmeter 2 shows the secondary resistance connection. 1980 models shown, others similar

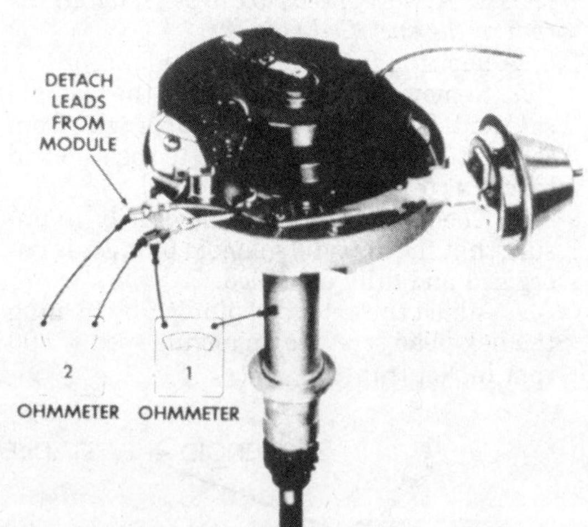

Checking the pick-up coil

NOTE: *These resistance checks will not disclose shorted coil windings. This condition can be detected only with scope analysis or a suitably designed coil tester. If these instruments are unavailable, replace the coil with a known good coil as a final coil test.*

4. To test the pick-up coil, first disconnect the white and green module leads. Set the ohmmeter on the high scale and connect it between a ground and either the white or green

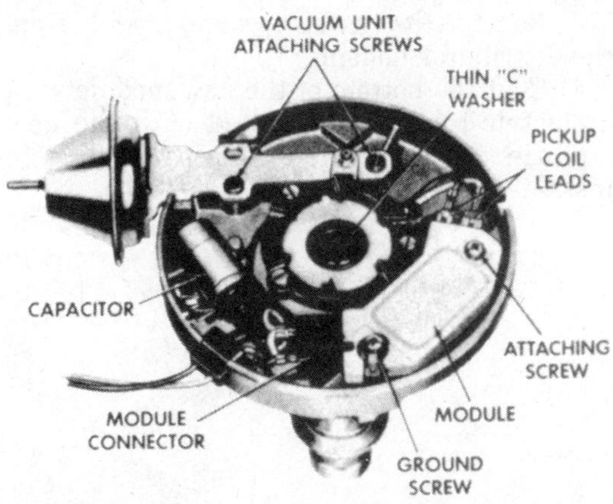

Distributor base and components

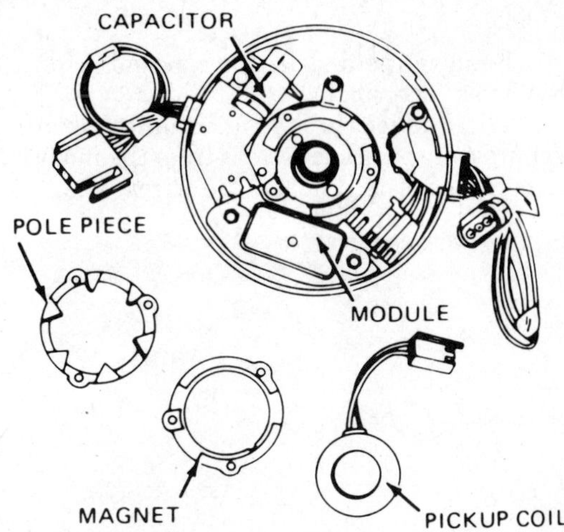

Pickup coil removed and disassembled

lead. Any resistance measurement less than infinity requires replacement of the pick-up coil.

5. Pick-up coil continuity is tested by connecting the ohmmeter (on low range) between the white and green leads. Normal resistance is between 650 and 850Ω, or 500 and 1,500Ω on 1977 and later models. Move the vacuum advance arm while performing this test. This will detect any break in coil continuity. Such a condition can cause intermittent misfiring. Replace the pick-up coil if the reading is outside the specified limits.

6. If no defects have been found at this time, and you still have a problem, then the module will have to be checked. If you do not have access to a module tester, the only possible alternative is a substitution test. If the module fails the substitution test, replace it.

COMPONENT REPLACEMENT

Integral Ignition Coil

1. Disconnect the feed and module wire terminal connectors from the distributor cap.
2. Remove the ignition set retainer.
3. Remove the 4 coil cover-to-distributor cap screws and coil cover.
4. Remove the 4 coil-to-distributor cap screws.
5. Using a blunt drift, press the coil wire spade terminals up out of the distributor cap.
6. Lift the coil up out of the distributor cap.
7. Remove and clean the coil spring, rubber seal washer and coil cavity of the distributor cap.
8. Coat the rubber seal with a dielectric lubricant furnished in the replacement ignition coil package.
9. Reverse the above procedures to install.

Distributor Cap

1. Remove the feed and module wire terminal connectors from the distributor cap.
2. Remove the retainer and spark plug wires from the cap.
3. Depress and release the 4 distributor cap-to-housing retainers and lift off the cap assembly.
4. Remove the 4 coil cover screws and cover.
5. Using a finger or a blunt drift, push the spade terminals up out of the distributor cap.
6. Remove all 4 coil screws and lift the coil, coil spring and rubber seal washer out of the cap coil cavity.
7. Using a new distributor cap, reverse the above procedures to assemble, being sure to clean and lubricate the rubber seal washer with dielectric lubricant.

Rotor

1. Disconnect the feed and module wire connectors from the distributor.
2. Depress and release the 4 distributor cap-to-housing retainers and lift off the cap assembly.
3. Remove the two rotor attaching screws and rotor.
4. Reverse the above procedure to install.

Vacuum Advance

1. Remove the distributor cap and rotor as previously described.
2. Disconnect the vacuum hose from the vacuum advance unit.
3. Remove the two vacuum advance retaining screws, pull the advance unit outward, rotate and disengage the operating rod from its tang.
4. Reverse the above procedure to install.

Module

1. Remove the distributor cap and rotor as previously described.

2. Disconnect the harness connector and pick-up coil spade connectors from the module. Be careful not to damage the wires when removing the connector.

3. Remove the two screws and module from the distributor housing.

4. Coat the bottom of the new module with dielectric lubricant supplied with the new module. Reverse the above procedure to install.

Engine and Engine Overhaul 3

ENGINE ELECTRICAL

Ignition Coil

TESTING/REMOVAL AND INSTALLATION

1. A six cylinder EST distributor with coil-in-cap is illustrated, the 8-cyl EST distributor is similar.
2. Detach the wiring connector from the distributor cap.
3. Turn the four latches and remove the cap and coil assembly from the lower housing.
4. Connect ohmmeter. Test 1.
5. Reading should be zero, or nearly zero. If not replace coil.
6. Connect ohmmeter both ways. Test 2. Use the high scale. Replace coil only if both readings are infinite.
7. If coil is good, go to step 13.
8. Remove coil cover attaching screws and lift off cover.
9. Remove ignition coil attaching screws and lift coil with leads from cap.
10. Remove ignition coil arc seal.
11. Clean with soft cloth and inspect cap for defects. Replace if necessary.
12. Assemble the new coil and cover to cap.
13. On all distributors, including distributors with Hall Effect Switch identified in step 27, remove rotor and pick-up coil leads from module.
14. Connect ohmmeter Test 1 and then test 2.
15. If vacuum unit is used, connect a vacuum source to the vacuum unit. Replace the vacuum unit if inoperative. Observe the ohmmeter throughout vacuum range: flex leads by hand without vacuum to check for intermittent opens.
16. Test 1 should real infinite at all times. Test 2 should read steady at one value within 500–1,500Ω range.

NOTE: *Ohmmeter may deflect if operating vacuum unit causes teeth to align. This is not a defect.*

17. If pickup coil is defective go to step 18. If coil is okay, go to step 23.
18. Mark distributor shaft and gear so they can be reassembled in the same position.
19. Drive out poll pin.
20. Remove gear and pull shaft assembly from distributor.
21. Remove three attaching screws and remove the magnetic shield.

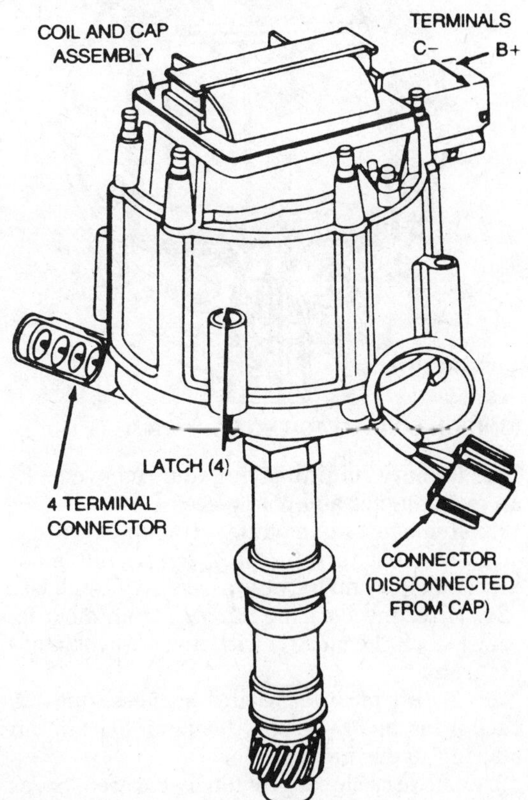

"COIL IN CAP" DISTRIBUTOR

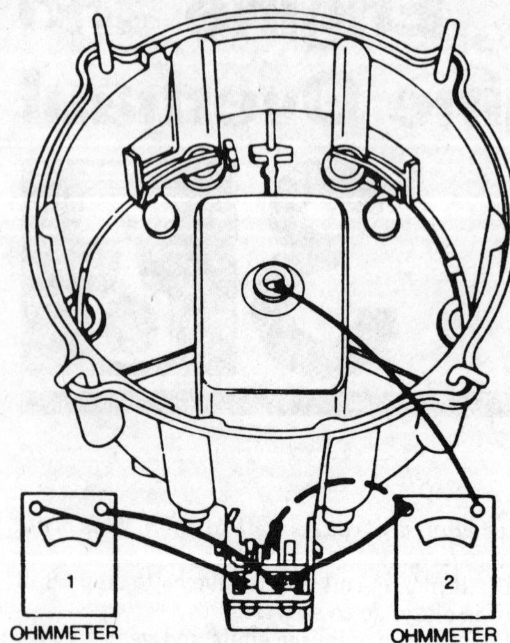

TESTING IGNITION COIL

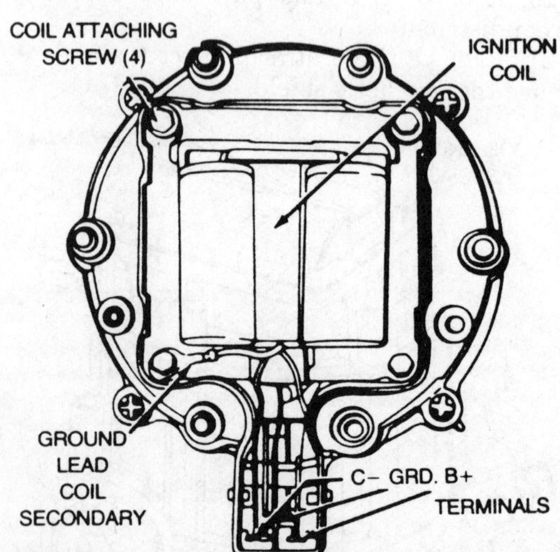

IGNITION COIL ATTACHING SCREWS

22. Remove retaining ring and remove pickup coil, magnet and pole piece.
23. Remove two module attaching screws, and the capacitor attaching screw. Lift module, capacitor and harness assembly from base.
24. Disconnect wiring harness from module.
25. Check the module with an approved module tester.
26. Install module, wiring harness, and capacitor assembly. Use silicone lubricant on housing under module.
27. The procedures previously covered, Steps 1–26, also apply to distributors with Hall Effect Switches.

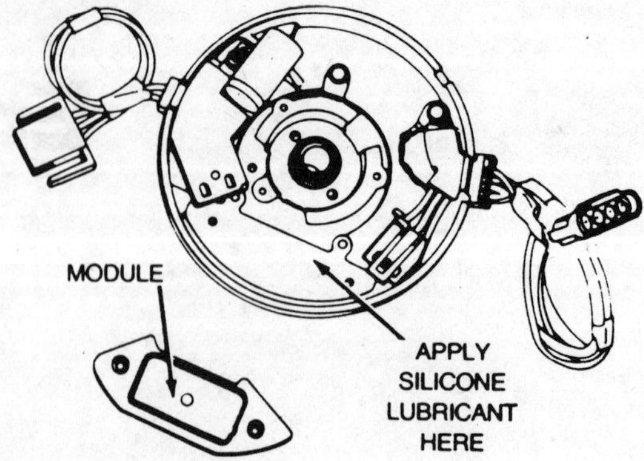

MODULE REMOVED

Ignition Module

REMOVAL AND INSTALLATION

1. Remove distributor cap and rotor.
2. Remove two module attaching screws, and capacitor attaching screw. Lift module, capacitor and harness assembly from base.
3. Disconnect wiring harness from module.
4. Check module with approved module tester.
5. Install module, wiring harness, and capacitor assembly. Use silicone lubricant on housing under module.

Distributor

REMOVAL AND INSTALLATION

1967–74

1. Remove the distributor cap and position it out of the way.
2. Disconnect the primary coil wire (the thin wire) and the vacuum advance hose.
3. Scribe a mark on the distributor body and the engine block showing their relationship. Mark the distributor housing to show the direction in which the rotor is pointing. Note the positioning of the vacuum advance unit.
4. Remove the holddown bolt and clamp and remove the distributor.

To install the distributor with the engine undisturbed:

5. Reinsert the distributor into its opening, aligning the previously made marks on the housing and the engine block.
6. The rotor may have to be turned either way a slight amount before inserting the distributor to align the rotor-to-housing marks.
7. Install the retaining clamp and bolt. Install the distributor cap, primary wire, and the vacuum hose.
8. Start the engine and check the ignition timing.

To install the distributor with the engine disturbed (the engine was turned while the

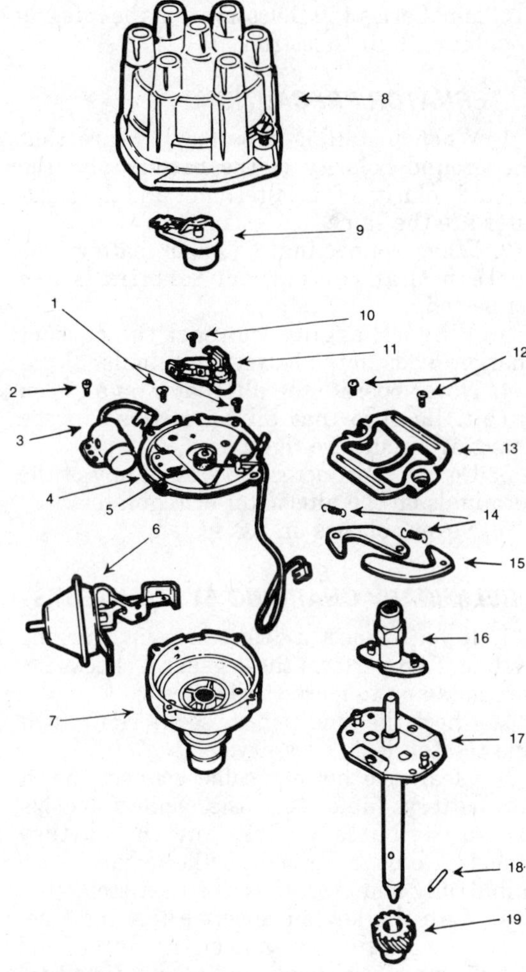

1. Breaker plate attaching screws
2. Condenser screw
3. Condenser
4. Breaker plate assembly
5. Cam lubricator
6. Vacuum control assembly
7. Housing
8. Distributor cap
9. Rotor
10. Contact point attaching screw
11. Contact point assembly
12. Weight cover attaching screws
13. Weight cover
14. Weight springs
15. Advance weights
16. Cam assembly
17. Mainshaft assembly
18. Roll pin
19. Drive gear

Six cylinder point type distributor

distributor was out) or to install a new distributor:

9. Turn the engine to bring the No. 1 piston to the top of its compression stroke. This may be determined by covering the No. 1 spark plug hole with your thumb and slowly turning

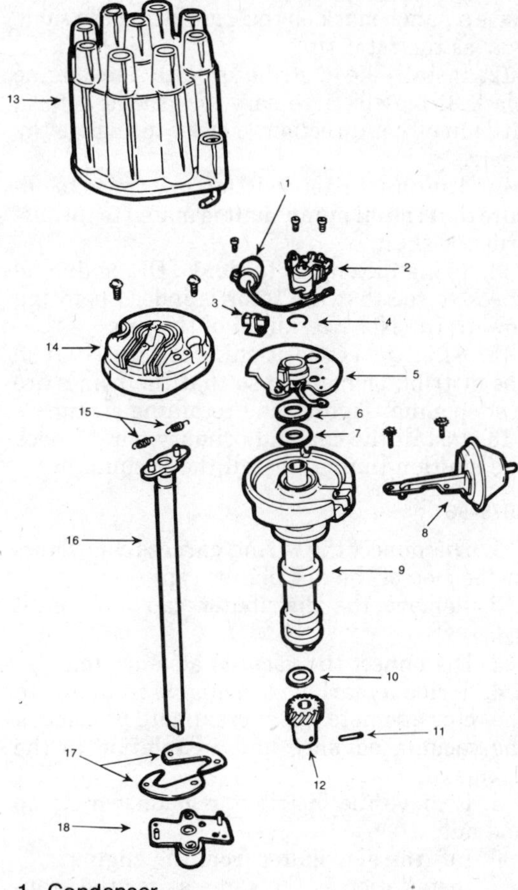

1. Condenser
2. Contact point assembly
3. Cam lubricator (through 1972)
4. Retaining pin
5. Breaker plate
6. Felt washer
7. Plastic seal
8. Vacuum advance unit
9. Housing
10. Shim washer
11. Drive gear pin
12. Drive gear
13. Cap
14. Rotor
15. Weight springs
16. Mainshaft
17. Advance weights
18. Cam weight base assembly

V8 point type distributor

the engine over. When the timing mark on the crankshaft pulley aligns with the 0 on the timing scale and your thumb is pushed out by compression, No. 1 piston is at top dead center (TDC). If you don't feel compression, you've got No. 6 at TDC.

10. Install the distributor to the engine block so that the vacuum advance unit points in the correct direction.

11. Turn the rotor so that it will point to the No. 1 terminal in the cap. Some distributors

have a punch mark on the gear facing the same way as the rotor tip.

12. Install the distributor into the engine block. It may be necessary to turn the rotor a little in either direction in order to engage the gears.

13. Tap the starter switch a few times to ensure that the oil pump shaft is mated to the distributor shaft.

14. Bring the engine to No. 1 TDC again and check to see that the rotor is indeed pointing toward the No. 1 terminal of the cap.

15. After correct positioning is assured, turn the distributor housing so that the points are just opening. Tighten the retaining clamp.

16. Install the cap and primary wire. Check the ignition timing. Install the vacuum hose.

1975–86

1. Disconnect the wiring harness connectors at the side of the distributor cap.
2. Remove the distributor cap and set it aside.
3. Disconnect the vacuum advance line.
4. Scribe a mark on the engine in line with the rotor and note the approximate position of the vacuum advance unit in relation to the engine.
5. Remove the distributor holddown clamp and nut.
6. Lift the distributor from the engine.
7. Installation is the same as for the standard (1967–74) distributor.

Alternator

Three basic alternators are used: the 5.5″ (140mm) Series 1D Delcotron, the 6.2″ (158mm) Series 150 Delcotron and the integral regulator 10 SI Delcotron.

ALTERNATOR PRECAUTIONS

1. When installing a battery, ensure that the ground polarity of the battery and the ground polarity of the alternator and the regulator are the same.
2. When connecting a jumper battery, be certain that the correct terminals are connected.
3. When charging, connect the correct charger leads to the battery terminals.
4. Never operate the alternator on an open circuit. Be sure that all connections in the charging circuit are tight.
5. Do not short across or ground any of the terminals on the alternator or regulator.
6. Never polarize an AC system.

PRELIMINARY CHARGING SYSTEM TESTS

1. If you suspect a defect in your charging system, first perform these general checks before going on to more specific tests.
2. Check the condition of the alternator belt and tighten it if necessary.
3. Clean the battery cable connections at the battery. Make sure the connections between the battery wires and the battery clamps are good. Reconnect the negative terminal only and proceed to the next step.
4. With the key off, insert a test light between the positive terminal on the battery and the disconnected positive battery terminal clamp. If the test light comes on, there is a short in the electrical system of the van. The

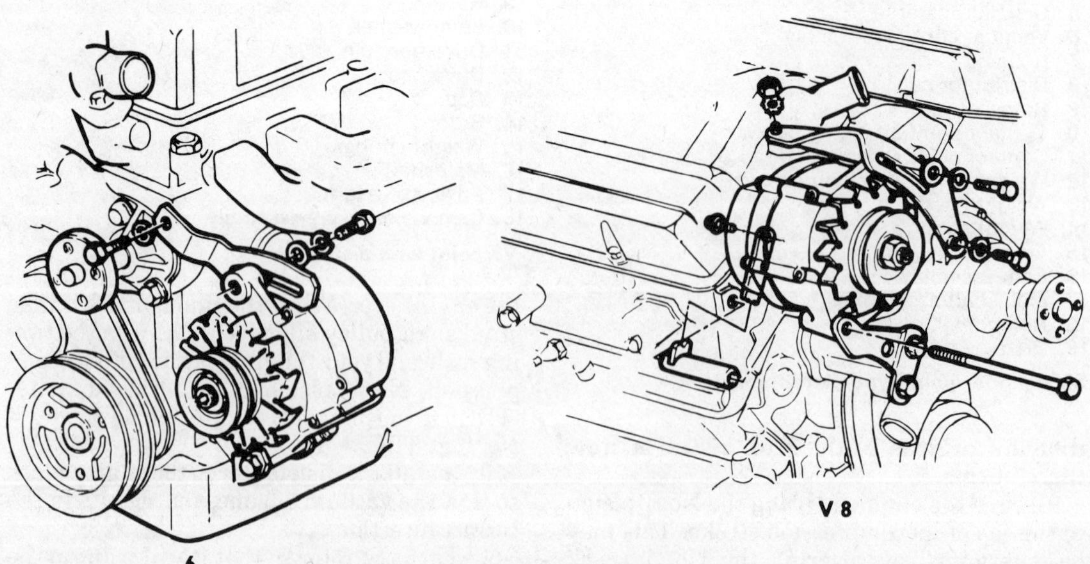

Typical alternator mounting

short must be repaired before proceeding. If the light does not come on, proceed to the next step.

NOTE: *If the van is equipped with an electric shock, the clock must be disconnected.*

5. Check the charging system wiring for any obvious breaks or shorts.

6. Check the battery to make sure it is fully charged and in good condition.

CHARGING SYSTEM OPERATIONAL TEST

NOTE: *You will need a current indicator to perform this test. If the current indicator is to give an accurate reading, the battery cables must be the same gauge and length as the original equipment.*

1. With the engine running and all electrical systems turned off, place a current indicator over the positive battery cable.

2. If a charge of roughly five amps is recorded, the charging system is working. If a draw of about five amps is recorded, the system is not working. The needle moves toward the battery when a charge condition is indicated, and away from the battery when a draw condition is indicated.

3. If a draw is indicated, proceed with further testing. If an excessive charge (10–15 amps) is indicated, the regulator may be at fault.

ALTERNATOR OUTPUT TEST—ALTERNATOR WITH EXTERNAL REGULATOR

1. You will need a tachometer and a voltmeter for this test. You will also need a jumper wire.

2. Connect the tachometer to the engine.

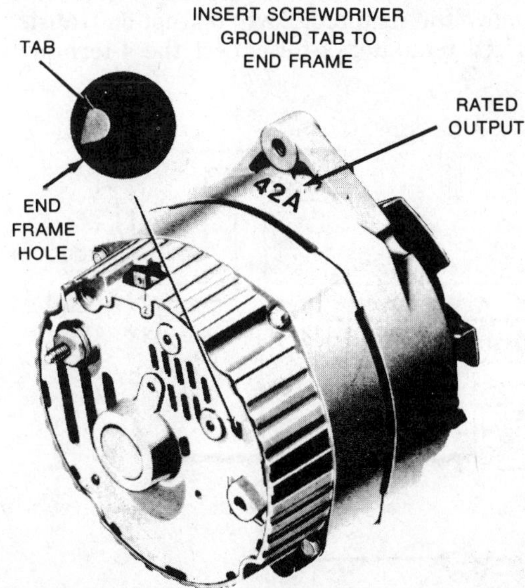

Alternator test hole and power rating location

3. Disconnect the wiring harness at the voltage regulator. With a jumper wire, connect the **F** wire to the number **3** wire in the wire harness plug.

4. Connect a voltmeter across the battery terminals, the positive voltmeter lead to the positive battery terminal and the negative lead to the negative terminal. Note the reading.

5. Start the engine and let it idle.

6. Gradually raise the engine speed to 1,500–2,000 rpm. The reading on the voltmeter should increase 1.0–2.0v over the initial reading. If there is no increase in the reading, the alternator is defective and must be repaired. If the increase is greater than 2v, then the regulator is defective and must be adjusted or replaced. (See voltage adjustment in the regular section.)

OUTPUT TEST—ALTERNATOR WITH INTEGRAL REGULATOR

1. You will need an ammeter for this test.

2. Disconnect the battery ground cable.

3. Disconnect the wire from the battery terminal on the alternator.

4. Connect the ammeter negative lead to the battery terminal wire removed in step three, and connect the ammeter positive lead to the battery terminal on the alternator.

5. Reconnect the battery ground cable and turn on all electrical accessories. If the battery is fully charged, disconnect the coil wire and bump the starter a few times to partially discharge it.

6. Start the engine and run it until you obtain a maximum current reading on the ammeter.

7. If the current is not within ten amps of the rated output of the alternator, the alternator is working properly. If the current is not within ten amps, insert a screwdriver in the test hole in the end frame of the alternator and ground the tab in the test hole against the side of the hole.

8. If the current is now within ten amps of the rated output, remove the alternator and have the voltage regulator replaced. If it is still below ten amps of rated output, have the alternator repaired.

REMOVAL AND INSTALLATION

1. Disconnect the battery ground cable to prevent diode damage.

2. Disconnect and tag all wiring to the alternator.

3. Remove the alternator brace bolt.

4. Remove the drive belt.

5. Support the alternator and remove the mounting bolts. Remove the alternator.

6. Install the unit using the reverse procedure of removal. Adjust the belt to have ½" (12.7mm) depression under thumb pressure on its longest run.

Regulator

REMOVAL AND INSTALLATION

1967–72

1. Disconnect the ground cable from the battery.
2. Disconnect the wiring harness from the regulator.
3. Remove the mounting screws and remove the regulator.
4. Make sure that the regulator base gasket is in place before installation.
5. Clean the attaching area for proper grounding.
6. Install the regulator. Do not overtighten the mounting screws, as this will cancel the cushioning effect of the rubber grommets.

1973 and Later

The regulator on these models is an integral part of the alternator. Alternator disassembly is required to replace it.

VOLTAGE ADJUSTMENT

1967–72

The standard voltage regulator from 1967–72 is a conventional double contact unit, although an optional double contact unit, although an optional transistorized regulator was available. Voltage adjustment procedures are the same for both types except for the point of adjustment. The double contact adjusting screw is located under the cover and the transistor-

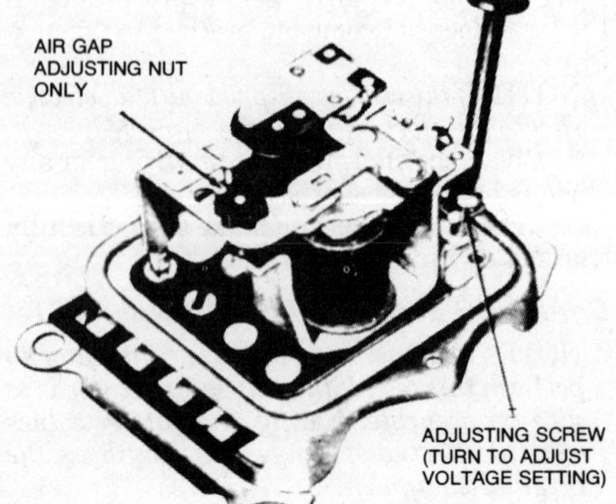

Conventional regulator voltage adjustment

ized regulator is adjusted externally after removing an allen screw from the adjustment hole.

1. Insert a 0.25Ω–25 watt fixed resistor into the charging circuit at the horn relay junction block, between both leads and the terminal. Use a 0.50Ω–25 watt resistor for 1971–72.
2. Install a voltmeter as shown.
3. Warm the engine by running it for several minutes at 1,500 rpm or more.
4. Cycle the voltage regulator by disconnecting and reconnecting the regulator connector.
5. Read the voltage on the voltmeter. If it is between 13.5 and 15.2, the regulator does not need adjustment or replacement. If the voltage is not within these limits, leave the engine running at 1,500 rpm.
6. Disconnect the 4-terminal connector and remove the regulator cover (except on transistorized regulators). Reconnect the 4-terminal

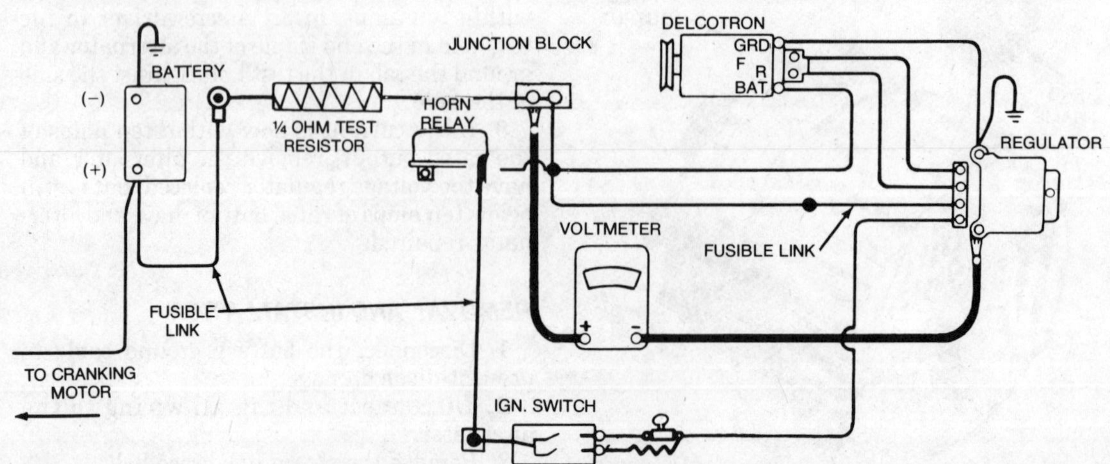

Regulator voltage setting circuit for 1967–72 models

Transistorized voltage regulator adjustment

connector and adjust the voltage to between 14.2 and 14.6 volts by turning the adjusting screw while observing the voltmeter.

7. Disconnect the terminal, install the cover, then reconnect the terminal.
8. Continue running the engine at 1,500 rpm to re-establish the regulator internal temperature.
9. Cycle the regulator by disconnecting/reconnecting the regulator connector. Check the voltage. If the voltage is between 13.5 and 15.2, the regulator is good.

CAUTION: *Always disconnect the regulator before removing or installing the cover in order to prevent damage by short circuiting.*

1973 and Later

On 1973 and later models, the 10 SI Delcotron is used which is equipped with an integral regulator that cannot be adjusted.

Battery

Refer to Chapter 1 for details on the battery.

REMOVAL AND INSTALLATION

1. Disconnect the negative (ground) cable terminal and then the positive cable terminal. Special pullers are available to remove clamp type battery terminals.

NOTE: *To avoid sparks, always disconnect the battery ground cable first, and connect it last.*

2. Remove the holddown clamp.
3. Remove the battery, being careful not to spill the acid.

NOTE: *Spilled acid can be neutralized with a backing soda/water solution. If you somehow get acid in your eyes, flush with lots of water and visit a doctor.*

4. Clean the cable terminals of any corrosion, using a wire brush tool or an old jackknife inside and out.
5. Install the battery. Replace the hold down clamp.
6. Connect the positive and then the negative cable terminal. Do not hammer them in place. The terminals should be coated lightly (externally) with grease or petroleum jelly to prevent corrosion.

CAUTION: *Make absolutely sure that the battery is connected properly before you start the engine. Reversed polarity can destroy your alternator and regulator in a matter of seconds.*

Starter

REMOVAL AND INSTALLATION

The following is a general procedure for all vans, and may vary slightly depending on model and series.

1. Disconnect the battery ground cable at the battery.
2. Raise and support the vehicle.
3. Disconnect and tag all wires at the solenoid terminal.

NOTE: *1975 and later starters do not require the R terminal. The High Energy Ignition System does not need a cable from solenoid to ignition coil.*

4. Reinstall all nuts as soon as they are removed, since the thread sizes are different.
5. Remove the front bracket from the starter and the two mounting bolts. On engines with a solenoid heat shield, remove the front bracket upper bolt and detach the bracket from the starter.
6. Remove the front bracket bolt or nut. Lower the starter front end first, and then remove the unit from the van.
7. Reverse the removal procedures to install the starter. Torque the two mounting bolts to 25–35 ft.lb.

STARTER OVERHAUL

Brush Replacement

1. Disconnect the field coil connectors from the starter motor solenoid terminal.
2. Remove the through bolts.
3. Remove the end frame and the field frame from the drive housing.
4. Disassemble the brush assembly from the field frame by releasing the spring and removing the supporting pin. Pull the brushes and the brush holders out and disconnect the wiring.
5. Install the new brushes into the holders.
6. Assemble the brush holder using the spring and position the unit on the supporting pin.

Alternator and Regulator Specifications

	Alternator			Regulator						
					Field Relay			Regulator		
Year	Part No. or Manufacturer	Field Current @ 12V	Output (amps)	Part No. or Manufacturer	Air Gap (in.)	Point Gap (in.)	Volts to Close	Air Gap (in.)	Point Gap (in.)	Volts at 85° F
1967	1100695	2.2–2.6	32	1119515	0.015	0.030	2.3–3.7	0.067	0.014	13.8–14.8
	1100696	2.2–2.6	42	1119515	0.015	0.030	2.3–3.7	0.067	0.014	13.8–14.8
	1100750	2.2–2.6	61	1119515	0.015	0.030	2.3–3.7	0.067	0.014	13.8–14.8
	1100754	3.7–4.4	62	1116378	0.011–0.018	0.020–0.030	2.5–3.5	NA	NA	13.7–14.8
1968	—	2.2–2.6	37	—	0.015	0.030	2.3–3.7	0.067	0.014	13.8–14.8
	—	2.2–2.6	42	—	0.015	0.030	2.3–3.7	0.067	0.014	13.8–14.8
	—	2.2–2.6	61	—	0.015	0.030	2.3–3.7	0.067	0.014	13.8–14.8
	—	3.7–4.4	62	—	0.011–0.018	0.020–0.030	2.5–3.5	NA	NA	13.8–14.8
1969–70	1100834, 38	2.2–2.6	37	1119515	0.015	0.030	2.3–2.7	0.067	0.014	13.8–14.8
	1100839, 41, 42	2.2–2.6	42	1119515	0.015	0.030	2.3–2.7	0.067	0.014	13.8–14.8
	1100843, 49	2.2–2.6	61	1119515	0.015	0.030	2.3–2.7	0.067	0.014	13.8–14.8
	—	3.7–4.4	62	1116378	0.011–0.018	0.020–0.030	2.5–3.5	NA	NA	13.8–14.8
	1100825	22.–2.6	61	1119515	0.015	0.030	2.3–2.7	0.067	0.014	13.8–14.8
	1100833 ①	2.2–2.6	61			Integral with alternator				
1971–72	1100834	2.2–2.6	37	1119515	0.015	0.030	2.3–2.7	0.067	0.014	13.8–14.8
	1100839	2.2–2.6	42	1119515	0.015	0.030	2.3–2.7	0.067	0.014	13.8–14.8
	1100849	2.2–2.6	61	1119515	0.015	0.030	2.3–2.7	0.067	0.014	13.8–14.8
1973–86	See Casing Stamp				Integral with alternator					

—Not available
NA Not Applicable
① 10 SI Integral Alternator

7. Install the unit in the starter motor and attach the wiring.
8. Position the field frame over the armature.
9. Install the through bolts.
10. Connect the field coil connectors to the solenoid.

Starter Drive Replacement

1. Remove the starter motor as previously outlined.
2. Disconnect the field coil connections from the solenoid terminal.
3. Remove the through bolts.
4. Remove the commutator end frame, the field frame assembly and the armature assembly from the housing.
5. Remove the armature assembly from the housing. On some models it may be necessary to remove the solenoid and the shift lever assembly from the housing first.
7. Slide a small piece of ½″ (12.7mm) pipe

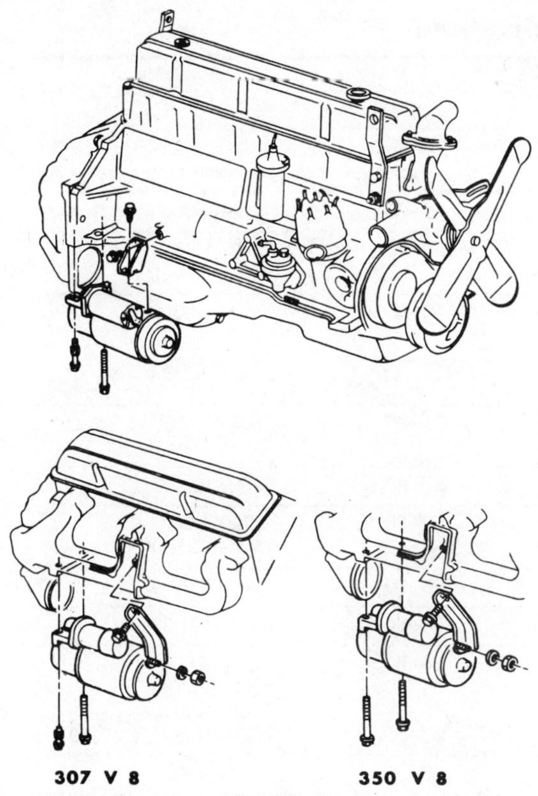

Typical starter motor mounting

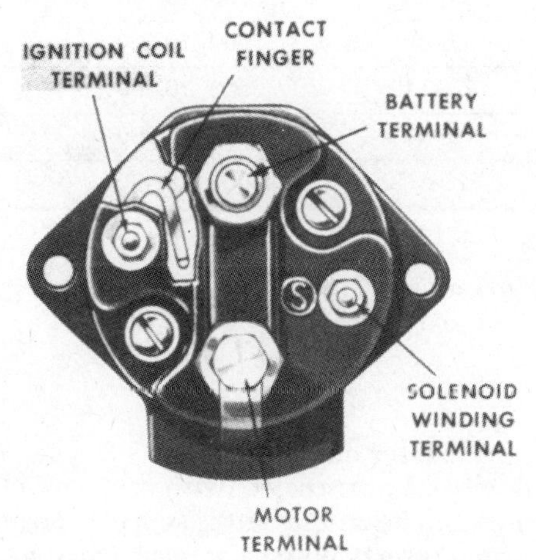

Starter solenoid terminals (typical)

over the end of the shaft so the end of the pipe butts against the edge of the retainer. Carefully tap the end of the pipe with a hammer, driving the retainer towards the armature end of the snapring.

8. Remove the snapring from the groove.

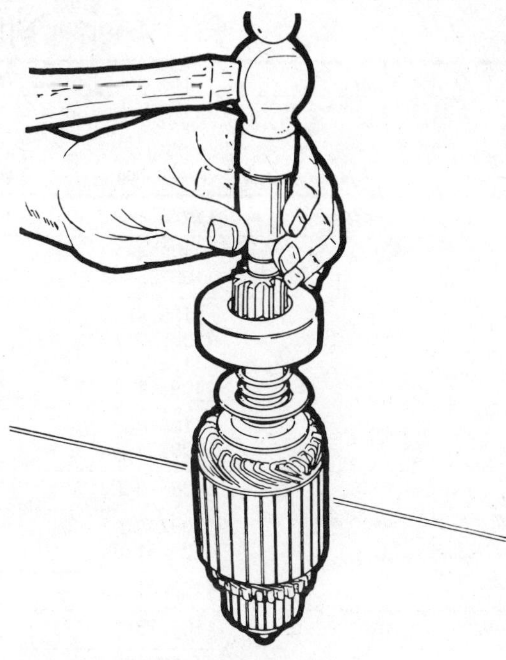

Driving the retainer off the snap ring

9. Slide the retainer and clutch off the shaft.
10. To assemble the drive mechanism, slide the drive assembly onto the armature shaft after lubricating it with silicone.

ENGINE MECHANICAL

Design

All Chevrolet and GMC van engines are water cooled, overhead valve powerplants, using cast iron cylinder blocks and heads.

The 230 and 250 cu in., inline six cylinder engine crankshaft has seven main bearings, with the thrust taken by No. 7. This results in a very rigid crankshaft assembly. The camshaft is low in the block and driven by gears rather than the usual chains and sprockets. Fairly long pushrods actuate the valves through ball mounted rocker arms. This engine has changed very little over the years, giving a great interchangeability of parts. A major change was introduced in 1975. This is an integral cylinder head and intake manifold casting. The integral design results in better emission control and more power and economy. The 292 six, introduced in 1975, is similar to the 250 in design but with a longer stroke. It has special valves with rotators, aluminum bearings, a larger oil capacity, larger crankpins, longer connecting rods, and a number of other heavy duty features derived from its years of use in heavier trucks.

Starter Specifications

		Starter ③		
			No Load Test	
Year	Identification	Volts	Amps ①	rpm
1967–69	1107372 ①	10.6	55–95	3800–6000
1970–75	1108744 1108788 ②	9	50–80	5500–10,500
	1108747 1108780 ②	9	50–80	3500–6000
	1108748 1108781 ②	9	65–90	7500–10,500
	1108748 1108781 ②	9	65–90	7500–10,500
1976	1108778 ②	9	50–80	5500–10,500
	1108780 ②	9	50–80	3500–6000
	1108781 ②	9	65–90	7500–10,500
	1108781 ②	9	65–90	7500–10,500
1977–82	1108778 ②	9	50–80	5500–10,500
	1187780 ②	9	50–80	3500–6000
	1109056 ②	9	50–80	5500–10,500
	1109052 ②	9	65–95	7500–10,500
	1108776 ②	9	65–95	7500–10,500
	1108776 ②	9	65–95	7500–10,500
1983–86	1109561	9	50–75	6000–11,900
	1109535	9	45–70	7000–11,900
	1998241	10	65–95	7500–10,500
	1998244	10	60–85	6800–10,500
	1998211	10	65–95	7500–10,500
	1998396	10	70–110	6500–10,700
	1998397	10	70–110	6500–10,700
	1109563	10	120–210	9000–13,400

① Solenoid included
② "R" terminal removed
③ Brush spring tension is 35 oz. for all starters. Lock test is not recommended.

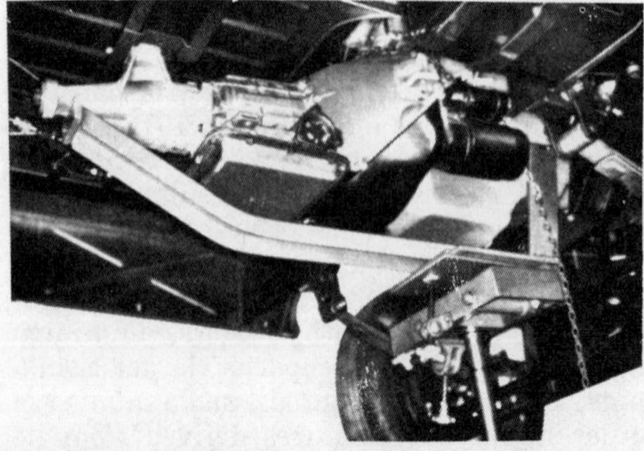

Engine supported for removal—1967–70

The 4.3 Liter engines are 90° V6 type, over head valve, water cooled, with cast iron block and heads. The crankshaft is supported by four precision insert main bearings, with crankshaft thrust taken at the number 4 (rear) bearing. The camshaft is supported by four plain bearings and is chain driven. Motion from the camshaft is transmitted to the valves by hydraulic lifters, pushrods, and ball type rocker arms. The valve guides are integral in the cylinder head. The connecting rods are forged steel, with precision insert type crankpin bearings. The piston pins are a press fit in the connecting rods. The pistons are cast aluminum alloy and the piston pins are a floating fit in the piston.

The small block family of V8 engines, 283 - 305 - 307 - 350 - 400 cu in., are all derived from the innovative design of the original 1955 265 cu in. Chevrolet V8. This engine introduced the ball mounted rocker arm design, replacing the once standard shaft mounted rocker arms. There is extensive interchangeability of components among these engines, extending to the several other small block displacement sizes available in passenger cars. The 400 cu in. version differs in block design; it does not have cooling passages between the cylinders, as on the smaller V8s.

NOTE: *Don't confuse the Chevrolet/GMC van 400 with the big block engine used in passenger cars, identified variously as 396, 400, or 402 cu in. The small block engine can quickly be identified by the placement of the distributor at the rear.*

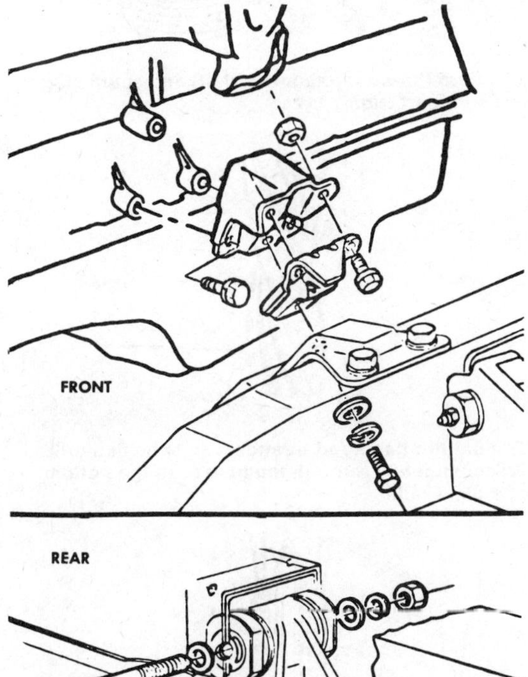

Engine mounts—1967–70

A new V8 diesel of 379 cu in. (6.2L) was introduced for the vans in 1983. This engine is built by Chevrolet; GM's Detroit Diesel Division aided in much of the engine's design. The 379 is even stronger, component by component, than the 350 diesel. Designed "from the block up" as a diesel, it utilizes robust features such as four-bolt main bearing caps.

Engine Overhaul Tips

Most engine overhaul procedures are fairly standard. In addition to specific parts replacement procedures and complete specifications for your individual engine, this chapter also is a guide to accept rebuilding procedures. Examples of standard rebuilding practice are shown and should be used along with specific details concerning your particular engine.

Competent and accurate machine shop services will ensure maximum performance, reliability and engine life.

In most instances it is more profitable for the do-it-yourself mechanic to remove, clean and inspect the component, buy the necessary parts and deliver these to a shop for actual machine work.

On the other hand, much of the rebuilding work (crankshaft, block, bearings, piston rods, and other components) is well within the scope of the do-it-yourself mechanic.

TOOLS

The tools required for an engine overhaul or parts replacement will depend on the depth of your involvement. With a few exceptions, they will be the tools found in a mechanic's tool kit (see Chapter 1). More in-depth work will require any or all of the following:

- a dial indicator (reading in thousandths) mounted on a universal base
- micrometers and telescope gauges
- jaw and screw type pullers
- scraper
- valve spring compressor
- ring groove cleaner
- piston ring expander and compressor
- ridge reamer
- cylinder hone or glaze breaker
- Plastigage®
- engine stand

Use of most of these tools is illustrated in this chapter. Many can be rented for a one time use from a local parts jobber or tool supply house specializing in automotive work.

Occasionally, the use of special tools is called for. See the information on Special Tools and

Safety Notice in the front of this book before substituting another tool.

INSPECTION TECHNIQUES

Procedures and specifications are given in this chapter for inspecting, cleaning and assessing the wear limits of most major components. Other procedures such as Magnaflux® and Zyglo® can be used to locate material flaws and stress cracks. Magnaflux® is a magnetic process applicable only to ferrous materials. The Zyglo® process coats the material with a fluorescent dye penetrant and can be used on any material Check for suspected surface cracks can be more readily made using spot check dye. The dye is sprayed onto the suspected area, wiped off and the area sprayed with a developer. Cracks will show up brightly.

OVERHAUL TIPS

Aluminum has become extremely popular for use in engines, due to its low weight. Observe the following precautions when handling aluminum parts:

• Never hot tank aluminum parts (the caustic hot tank solution will eat the aluminum.

• Remove all aluminum parts (identification tag, etc.) from engine parts prior to the tanking.

• Always coat threads lightly with engine oil or antiseize compounds before installation, to prevent seizure.

• Never over torque bolts or spark plugs especially in aluminum threads.

Stripped threads in any component can be repaired using any of several commercial repair kits (Heli-Coil®, Microdot®, Keenserts®, etc.).

When assembling the engine, any parts that will be frictional contact must be prelubed to provide lubrication at initial start-up. Any product specifically formulated for this purpose can be used, but engine oil is not recommended as a prelube.

When semi-permanent (locked, but removable) installation of bolts or nuts is desired, threads should be cleaned and coated with Loctite® or other similar, commercial nonhardening sealant.

REPAIRING DAMAGED THREADS

Several methods of repairing damaged threads are available. Heli-Coil®, Keenserts® and Microdot® are among the most widely used. All involve basically the same principle – drilling out stripped threads, tapping the hole and installing a prewound insert – making welding, plugging and oversize fasteners unnecessary.

Two types of thread repair inserts are usually supplied – a standard type for most Inch Coarse, Inch Fine, Metric Course and Metric Fine thread sizes and a spark lug type to fit most spark plug port sizes. Consult the individual manufacturer's catalog to determine

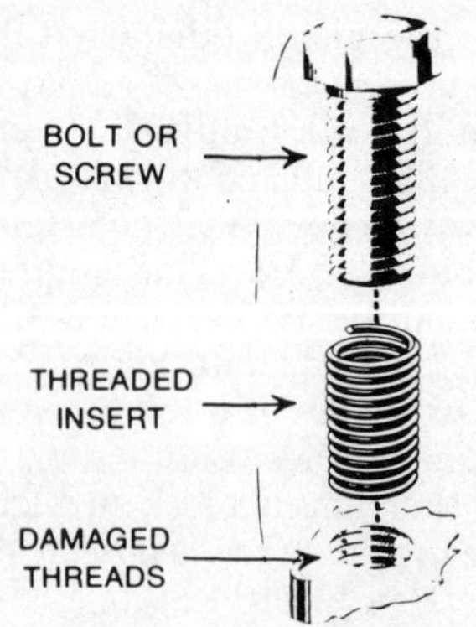

Damaged bolt holes can be repaired with thread repair inserts

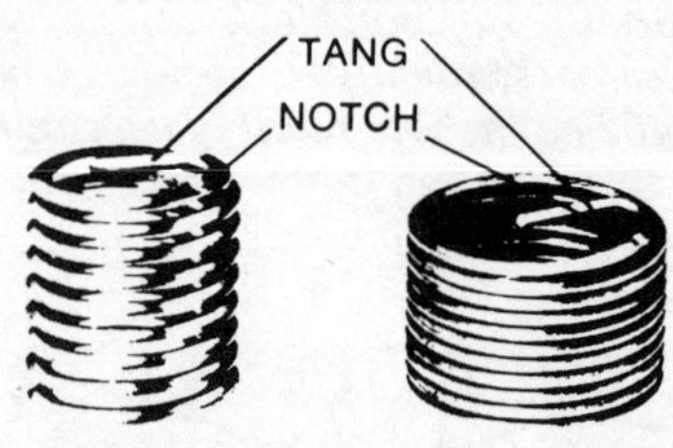

Standard thread repair insert (left) and spark plug thread insert (right)

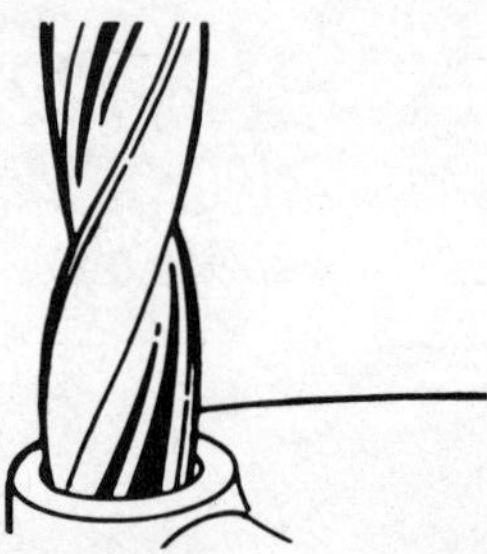

Drill out the damaged threads with specified drill. Drill completely through the hole or to the bottom of a blind hole

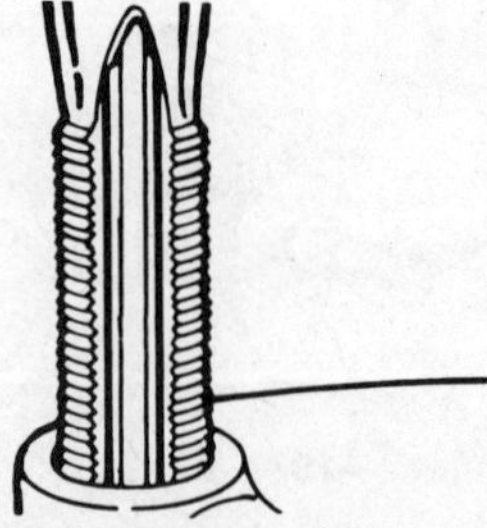

With the tap supplied, tap the hole to receive the thread insert. Keep the tap well oiled and back it out frequently to avoid clogging the threads

Standard Torque Specifications and Fastener Markings

In the absence of specific torques, the following chart can be used as a guide to the maximum safe torque of a particular size/grade of fastener.

- There is no torque difference for fine or coarse threads.
- Torque values are based on clean, dry threads. Reduce the value by 10% if threads are oiled prior to assembly.
- The torque required for aluminum components or fasteners is considerably less.

U.S. Bolts

SAE Grade Number	1 or 2			5			6 or 7		
Number of lines always 2 less than the grade number.									
Bolt Size (Inches)—(Thread)	Maximum Torque			Maximum Torque			Maximum Torque		
	Ft./Lbs.	Kgm	Nm	Ft./Lbs.	Kgm	Nm	Ft./Lbs.	Kgm	Nm
¼—20	5	0.7	6.8	8	1.1	10.8	10	1.4	13.5
—28	6	0.8	8.1	10	1.4	13.6			
5/16—18	11	1.5	14.9	17	2.3	23.0	19	2.6	25.8
—24	13	1.8	17.6	19	2.6	25.7			
⅜—16	18	2.5	24.4	31	4.3	42.0	34	4.7	46.0
—24	20	2.75	27.1	35	4.8	47.5			
7/16—14	28	3.8	37.0	49	6.8	66.4	55	7.6	74.5
—20	30	4.2	40.7	55	7.6	74.5			
½—13	39	5.4	52.8	75	10.4	101.7	85	11.75	115.2
—20	41	5.7	55.6	85	11.7	115.2			
9/16—12	51	7.0	69.2	110	15.2	149.1	120	16.6	162.7
—18	55	7.6	74.5	120	16.6	162.7			
⅝—11	83	11.5	112.5	150	20.7	203.3	167	23.0	226.5
—18	95	13.1	128.8	170	23.5	230.5			
¾—10	105	14.5	142.3	270	37.3	366.0	280	38.7	379.6
—16	115	15.9	155.9	295	40.8	400.0			
⅞— 9	160	22.1	216.9	395	54.6	535.5	440	60.9	596.5
—14	175	24.2	237.2	435	60.1	589.7			
1— 8	236	32.5	318.6	590	81.6	799.9	660	91.3	894.8
—14	250	34.6	338.9	660	91.3	849.8			

Metric Bolts

Relative Strength Marking	4.6, 4.8			8.8		
Bolt Markings						
Bolt Size Thread Size x Pitch (mm)	Maximum Torque			Maximum Torque		
	Ft./Lbs.	Kgm	Nm	Ft./Lbs.	Kgm	Nm
6 x 1.0	2–3	.2–.4	3–4	3–6	.4–.8	5–8
8 x 1.25	6–8	.8–1	8–12	9–14	1.2–1.9	13–19
10 x 1.25	12–17	1.5–2.3	16–23	20–29	2.7–4.0	27–39
12 x 1.25	21–32	2.9–4.4	29–43	35–53	4.8–7.3	47–72
14 x 1.5	35–52	4.8–7.1	48–70	57–85	7.8–11.7	77–110
16 x 1.5	51–77	7.0–10.6	67–100	90–120	12.4–16.5	130–160
18 x 1.5	74–110	10.2–15.1	100–150	130–170	17.9–23.4	180–230
20 x 1.5	110–140	15.1–19.3	150–190	190–240	26.2–46.9	160–320
22 x 1.5	150–190	22.0–26.2	200–260	250–320	34.5–44.1	340–430
24 x 1.5	190–240	26.2–46.9	260–320	310–410	42.7–56.5	420–550

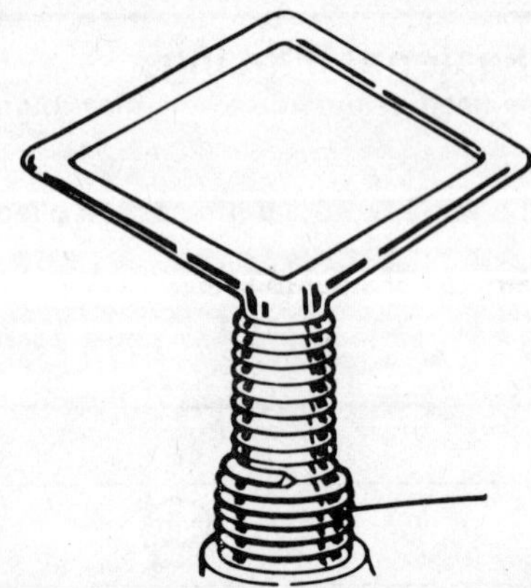

Screw the threaded insert onto the installation tool until the tang engages the slot. Screw the insert into the tapped hole until it is ¼–½ turn below the top surface. After installation break off the tang with a hammer and punch

exact applications. Typical thread repair kits will contain a selection of prewound threaded inserts, a tap (corresponding to the outside diameter threads of the insert) and an installation tool. Spark plug inserts usually differ because they require a tap equipped with pilot threads and a combined reamer/tap section. Most manufacturers also supply blister-packed thread repair inserts separately in addition to a master kit containing a variety of taps and inserts plus installation tools.

Before effecting a repair to a threaded hole, remove any snapped, broken or damaged bolts or studs. Penetrating oil can be used to free frozen threads. The offending item can be removed with locking pliers or with a screw or stud extractor. After the hole is clear, the thread can be repaired, as follows:

Checking Engine Compression

A noticeable lack of engine power, excessive oil consumption and/or poor fuel mileage measured over an extended period are all indicators of internal engine war. Worn piston rings, scored or worn cylinder bores, blown head gaskets, sticking or burnt valves and worn valve seats are all possible culprits here. A check of each cylinder's compression will help you locate the problems.

As mentioned in the Tools and Equipment section of Chapter 1, a screw-in type compression gauge is more accurate that the type you simply hold against the spark plug hole, although it takes slightly longer to use. It's worth it to obtain a more accurate reading. Follow the procedures below for gasoline and diesel engined trucks.

GASOLINE ENGINES

1. Warm up the engine to normal operating temperature.
2. Remove all spark plugs.
3. Disconnect the high tension lead from the ignition coil.
4. On fully open the throttle either by operating the carburetor throttle linkage by hand or by having an assistant floor the accelerator pedal.
5. Screw the compression gauge into the no.1 spark plug hole until the fitting is snug.

   NOTE: *Be careful not to crossthread the plug hole. On aluminum cylinder heads use extra care, as the threads in these heads are easily ruined.*
6. Ask an assistant to depress the accelerator pedal fully on both carbureted and fuel injected trucks. Then, while you read the compression gauge, ask the assistant to crank the engine two or three times in short bursts using the ignition switch.
7. Read the compression gauge at the end of each series of cranks, and record the highest of these readings. Repeat this procedure for each of the engine's cylinders. Compare the highest reading of each cylinder to the compression pressure specification in the Tune-Up Specifications chart in Chapter 2. The specs in this chart are maximum values.

A cylinder's compression pressure is usually acceptable if it is not less than 80% of maximum. The difference between each cylinder should be no more than 12–14 pounds.

8. If a cylinder is unusually low, pour a tablespoon of clean engine oil into the cylinder through the spark plug hole and repeat the compression test. If the compression comes up after adding the oil, it appears that the cylinder's piston rings or bore are damaged or worn. If the pressure remains low, the valves may not be seating properly (a valve job is needed), or the head gasket may be blown near that cylinder. If compression in any two adjacent cyl-

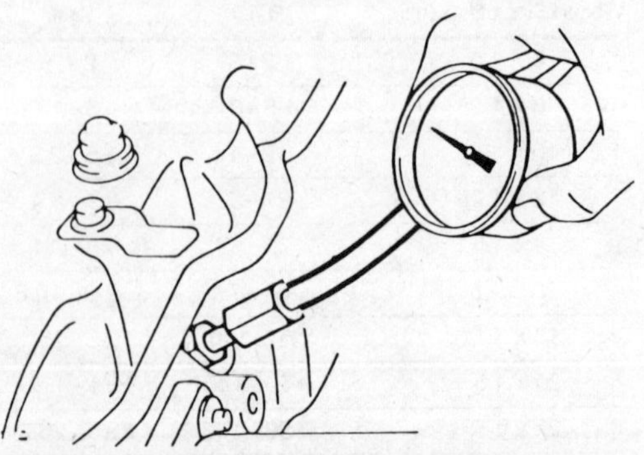

The screw-in type compression gauge is more accurate

inders is low, and if the addition of oil doesn't help the compression, there is leakage past the head gasket. Oil and coolant water in the combustion chamber can result from this problem. There may be evidence of water droplets on the engine dipstick when a head gasket has blown.

Diesel Engines

Checking cylinder compression on diesel engines is basically the same procedure as on gasoline engines except for the following:

1. A special compression gauge adaptor suitable for diesel engines (because these engines have much greater compression pressures) must be used.
2. Remove the injector tubes and remove the injectors from each cylinder.

   NOTE: *Don't forget to remove the washer underneath each injector; otherwise, it may get lost when the engine is cranked.*

3. When fitting the compression gauge adaptor to the cylinder head, make sure the bleeder of the gauge (if equipped) is closed.
4. When reinstalling the injector assemblies, install new washers underneath each injector.

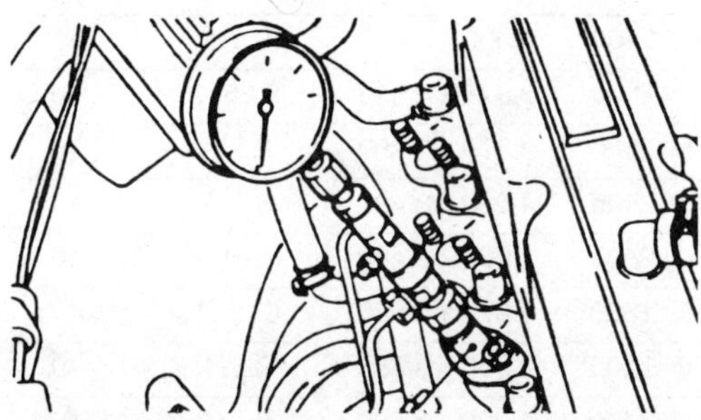

Diesel engines require a special compression gauge adaptor

Engine

REMOVAL AND INSTALLATION

1967–70

The engine and transmission are removed as a unit from below the vehicle.

1. Disconnect the battery cables.
2. Drain the cooling system. Remove the air cleaner.

   CAUTION: *When draining the coolant, keep in mind that cats and dogs are attracted by the ethylene glycol antifreeze, and are quite likely to drink any that is left in an uncovered container or in puddles on the ground. This will prove fatal in sufficient quantity. Always drain the coolant into a sealable container. Coolant should be reused unless it is contaminated or several years old.*

3. Remove the engine splash shield(s).
4. Disconnect the neutral safety switch wire from the automatic transmission.
5. Disconnect the upper and lower radiator hoses from the radiator.
6. Disconnect the wires from the starter solenoid, alternator, temperature switch, oil pressure switch and ignition coil.
7. Disconnect the following components:
   a. Accelerator linkage at the bellcrank on the manifold.
   b. Choke cable at the carburetor.
   c. Fuel line from the fuel pump.
   d. Heater hoses at the engine.
   e. Oil pressure gauge line (if used).
   f. All vacuum lines at the engine.
   g. Power steering lines at the pump.
   h. Engine ground straps; and the exhaust pipes at the manifold. Hang the exhaust pipes out of the way from the frame.
8. Disconnect the A/C compressor mounting bracket and position the compressor out of the way. Also remove the condenser from in front of the radiator. Position it out of the way. DO NOT DISCONNECT ANY OF THE REFRIGERANT LINES.
9. Remove the fan and pulley.
10. Remove the clutch cross-shaft.
11. Remove the driveshaft. If the plug for the driveshaft opening in the transmission is not easily accessible, drain the transmission.
12. Disconnect the speedometer cable at the transmission.
13. Disconnect the shift linkage at the transmission.
14. Disconnect the clutch linkage.
15. Remove the bolt which holds the starter wire harness clip and the engine ground strap from the flywheel housing.
16. Disconnect the automatic transmission cooler lines at both ends and remove the cooler lines. Plug the openings.
17. Place a jack under the engine and transmission and install safety chains. Take the weight off the engine mounts.
18. Remove the engine mount bolts and the engine mount crossmember. Check to be sure that all necessary components are removed or disconnected.
19. Slowly lower the engine/transmission assembly, pulling it to the rear to clear the front axle.
20. Depending on the service required, separate the engine/transmission and mount the engine on a stand.
21. Installation is the reverse of removal. Be sure to check all fluid capacities and check for leaks.

General Engine Specifications

Year	Engine Cu in. Displacement	Carburetor Type	Horsepower @ rpm ■	Torque @ rpm (ft. lbs.) ■	Bore and Stroke (in.)	Compression Ratio	Oil Pressure @ 2000 rpm
1967	6-230	1 bbl	140 @ 4400	220 @ 1600	3.875 x 3.250	8.5:1	38
	6-250	1 bbl	155 @ 4200	235 @ 1600	3.875 x 3.530	8.5:1	38 ①
	8-283	2 bbl	175 @ 4400	275 @ 2400	3.875 x 3.000	9.1:1	38 ①
1968	6-230	1 bbl	140 @ 4400	220 @ 1600	3.875 x 3.250	8.5:1	58
	6-250	1 bbl	155 @ 4200	235 @ 1600	3.875 x 3.530	8.5:1	58
	8-307	2 bbl	200 @ 4600	300 @ 2400	3.875 x 3.250	9.0:1	58
1969	6-230	1 bbl	140 @ 4400	220 @ 1600	3.875 x 3.250	8.5:1	58
	6-250	1 bbl	155 @ 4200	235 @ 1600	3.875 x 3.530	8.5:1	58
	8-307	2 bbl	200 @ 4600	300 @ 2400	3.875 x 3.250	9.0:1	58
1970	6-250	1 bbl	155 @ 4200	235 @ 1600	3.875 x 3.530	8.5:1	40
	8-307	2 bbl	200 @ 4600	300 @ 2400	3.875 x 3.250	9.0:1	40
	8-350	2 bbl	255 @ 4600	355 @ 3000	4.000 x 3.480	9.0:1	40
1971	6-250	1 bbl	145 @ 4200	235 @ 1600	3.875 x 3.530	8.5:1	40
	8-307	2 bbl	200 @ 4600	300 @ 2400	3.875 x 3.250	8.5:1	40
	8-350	2 bbl	255 @ 4600	355 @ 3000	4.000 x 3.480	9.0:1	40
1972	6-250	1 bbl	110 @ 3800	185 @ 1600	3.875 x 3.530	8.5:1	40
	8-307	2 bbl	130 @ 4000	230 @ 2400	3.875 x 3.250	8.5:1	40
	8-350	2 bbl	175 @ 4000	290 @ 2400	4.000 x 3.480	8.5:1	40
1973	6-250	1 bbl	100 @ 3800	175 @ 2000	3.875 x 3.530	8.25:1	40
	8-307	2 bbl	115 @ 3600	225 @ 2000	3.875 x 3.250	8.5:1	40
	8-350	2 bbl	155 @ 4000	255 @ 2400	4.000 x 3.480	8.5:1	40
	8-350	4 bbl	175 @ 4400	270 @ 2400	4.000 x 3.480	8.5:1	40
1974	6-250	1 bbl	100 @ 3600	175 @ 1800	3.875 x 3.530	8.25:1	40
	8-350	2 bbl	145 @ 3600	250 @ 2200	4.000 x 3.480	8.5:1	40
	8-350	4 bbl	160 @ 3800	255 @ 2400	4.000 x 3.480	8.5:1	40
1975	6-250	1 bbl	105 @ 3800	185 @ 1200	3.875 x 3.530	8.25:1	40
	6-292	1 bbl	120 @ 3600	215 @ 2000	3.875 x 4.120	8.0:1	40
	8-350	2 bbl	145 @ 3800	250 @ 2200	4.000 x 3.480	8.5:1	40
	8-350	4 bbl	160 @ 3800	250 @ 2400	4.000 x 3.480	8.5:1	40
	8-400	4 bbl	175 @ 3600	290 @ 2800	4.125 x 3.750	8.5:1	40
1976	6-250	1 bbl	105 @ 3800	185 @ 1200	3.875 x 3.530	8.25:1	40
	6-292	1 bbl	120 @ 3600	215 @ 2000	3.875 x 4.120	8.0:1	40
	8-350	2 bbl	145 @ 3800	250 @ 2200	4.000 x 3.480	8.5:1	40
	8-350 LD	4 bbl	165 @ 3800	260 @ 2400	4.000 x 3.480	8.5:1	40
	8-350 HD	4 bbl	165 @ 3800	255 @ 2800	4.000 x 3.480	8.5:1	40
	8-400	4 bbl	175 @ 3600	290 @ 2800	4.125 x 3.750	8.5:1	40
1977	6-250	1 bbl	110 @ 3800	195 @ 1600	3.875 x 3.530	8.25:1	40
	6-292	1 bbl	120 @ 3600	215 @ 2000	3.875 x 4.120	8.0:1	40
	8-305	2 bbl	145 @ 3800	245 @ 2400	3.736 x 3.480	8.5:1	40

General Engine Specifications (cont.)

Year	Engine Cu in. Displacement	Carburetor Type	Horsepower @ rpm ■	Torque @ rpm (ft. lbs.) ■	Bore and Stroke (in.)	Compression Ratio	Oil Pressure @ 2000 rpm
1977	8-350 LD	4 bbl	165 @ 3800	260 @ 2400	4.000 x 3.480	8.5:1	40
	8-350 HD	4 bbl	165 @ 3800	255 @ 2800	4.000 x 3.480	8.5:1	40
	8-400	4 bbl	175 @ 3600	290 @ 2800	4.125 x 3.750	8.5:1	40
1978	6-250	1 bbl	110 @ 3800	195 @ 1600	3.876 x 3.530	8.3:1	40
	6-292	1 bbl	120 @ 3600	215 @ 2000	3.876 x 4.120	8.0:1	40
	8-305	2 bbl	145 @ 3800	245 @ 2400	3.736 x 3.480	8.5:1	40
	8-350 LD	4 bbl	165 @ 3800	260 @ 2400	4.000 x 3.480	8.5:1	40
	8-350 HD	4 bbl	165 @ 3800	255 @ 2800	4.000 x 3.480	8.5:1	40
	8-400	4 bbl	175 @ 3600	290 @ 2800	4.125 x 3.750	8.5:1	40
1979–80	6-250	2 bbl	130 @ 3500	210 @ 2400	3.876 x 3.530	8.3:1	40
	8-305	2 bbl	140 @ 4000	240 @ 2000	3.736 x 3.480	8.4:1	45
	8-350 Fed.	4 bbl	165 @ 3800	270 @ 2000	4.000 x 3.480	8.2:1	45
	8-350 Cal.	4 bbl	155 @ 3800	260 @ 2000	4.000 x 3.480	8.2:1	45
	8-400 Fed.	4 bbl	175 @ 3600	290 @ 2800	4.125 x 3.750	8.5:1	40
	8-400 Cal.	4 bbl	165 @ 3600	290 @ 2000	4.125 x 3.750	8.5:1	40
1981	6-250	2 bbl	130 @ 4000	210 @ 2000	3.870 x 3.530	8.3:1	40–60
	8-305	2 bbl	135 @ 4200	235 @ 2400	3.740 x 3.480	8.5:1	45
	8-305	4 bbl	155 @ 4400	252 @ 2400	3.740 x 3.480	9.2:1	45
	8-350	4 bbl	165 @ 3800	275 @ 2000	4.000 x 3.480	8.2:1	45
1982	6-250	2 bbl	130 @ 4000	210 @ 2000	3.870 x 3.530	8.3:1	40–60
	8-305	4 bbl	140 @ 4200	240 @ 2400	3.740 x 3.480	8.5:1	45
	8-350	4 bbl	175 @ 4000	275 @ 2000	4.000 x 3.480	8.2:1	45
1983–86	6-250	2 bbl	120 @ 4000	205 @ 2000	3.870 x 3.530	8.3:1	40–60
	6-262	4 bbl	150 @ 4000	225 @ 2400	4.000 x 3.480	9.3:1	40–60
	8-305 ②	4 bbl	160 @ 4400	235 @ 2000	3.740 x 3.480	8.5:1	45
	8-305 ③	4 bbl	155 @ 4000	245 @ 1600	3.740 x 3.480	9.2:1	45
	8-350 ②	4 bbl	165 @ 3800	275 @ 1600	4.000 x 3.480	8.2:1	45
	8-350 ③	4 bbl	155 @ 4000	240 @ 2800	4.000 x 3.480	8.2:1	45
	8-379	Diesel	140 @ 3600	240 @ 2000	3.980 x 3.800	21.5:1	45

■Starting 1972, horsepower and torque are SAE net figures. They are measured at the rear of the transmission with all accessories installed and operating. Since the figures vary when a given engine is installed in different models, some are representative rather than exact.

① Oil pressure at 1500 rpm

② 49-states

③ Calif

HD Heavy Duty Emissions

LD Light Duty Emissions

Fed.—All states except California

Cal.—California

Crankshaft and Connecting Rod Specifications

All measurements are given in in.

		Crankshaft				Connecting Rod		
Year	Engine Displacement (cu. in.)	Main Brg Journal Dia	Main Brg Oil Clearance	Shaft End-Play	Thrust on No.	Journal Diameter	Oil Clearance	Side Clearance
1967	6-230	2.2983–2.2993	.0003–.0029	.002–.006	7	1.999–2.000	.0007–.0027	.009–.014
	6-250	2.2983–2.2993	.0003–.0029	.002–.006	7	1.999–2.000	.0007–.0027	.009–.014
	8-283	①	③	.003–.011	5	1.999–2.000	.0007–.0027	.009–.013
1968	6-230	2.2983–2.2993	.0003–.0029	.002–.006	7	1.9999–2.000	.0007–.0027	.009–.014
	6-250	2.2983–2.2993	.0003–.0029	.002–.006	7	1.999–2.000	.0007–.0027	.009–.014
	8-307	2.4484–2.4493 ②	.0008–.0020 ④	.003–.011	5	2.099–2.100	.0007–.0027	.009–.013
1969	6-230	2.2983–2.2993	.0003–.0029	.002–.006	7	1.999–2.000	.0007–.0027	.009–.014
	6-250	2.2983–2.2993	.0003–.0029	.002–.006	7	1.999–2.000	.0007–.0027	.009–.014
	8-307	2.4484–2.4493 ②	.0008–.0020 ④	.003–.011	5	2.099–2.100	.0007–.0028	.009–.013
1970	6-250	2.2983–2.2993	.0003–.0029	.002–.006	7	1.999–2.000	.0007–.0027	.009–.014
	8-307, 350	2.4484–2.4493 ②	.0003–.0015 ⑤	.002–.006	5	2.099–2.100	.0007–.0028	.008–.014
1971	6-250	2.2983–2.2993	.0003–.0029	.002–.006	7	1.999–2.000	.0007–.0027	.009–.014
	8-307, 350	2.4484–2.4493 ②	.0008–.0015 ⑤	.002–.006	5	2.099–2.100	.0007–.0028	.008–.014
1972	6-250	2.2983–2.2993	.0003–.0029	.002–.006	7	1.999–2.000	.0007–.0027	.009–.014
	8-307, 350	2.4484–2.4493 ②	.0008–.0015 ⑤	.002–.006	5	2.099–2.100	.0007–.0028	.008–.014
1973–74	6-250	2.2983–2.2993	.0003–.0029	.002–.006	7	1.999–2.000	.0007–.0027	.006–.014
	8-307, 350	2.4484–2.4493 ②	.0008–.0015 ⑤	.002–.006	5	2.099–2.100	.0013–.0035	.008–.014
1975–76	6-250	2.2983–2.2993	.0003–.0029	.002–.006	7	1.999–2.000	.0007–.0027	.006–.017
	6-292	2.2983–2.2993	.0008–.0034	.002–.006	7	2.099–2.100	.0007–.0027	.006–.017
	8-350	2.4484–2.4493 ②	.0011–.0023 ⑥	.002–.006	5	2.199–2.200	.0013–.0035	.008–.014
	8-400	2.6484–2.6493 ⑦	.0011–.0023 ⑥	.002–.006	5	2.199–2.200	.0013–.0035	.008–.014
1977	6-250	2.2983–2.2993	.0003–.0029	.002–.006	7	1.999–2.000	.0007–.0027	.006–.017
	6-292	2.2983–2.2993	.0008–.0034	.002–.006	7	2.099–2.100	.0007–.0027	.006–.017

Crankshaft and Connecting Rod Specifications (cont.)

All measurements are given in in.

		Crankshaft				Connecting Rod		
Year	Engine Displacement (cu. in.)	Main Brg Journal Dia	Main Brg Oil Clearance	Shaft End-Play	Thrust on No.	Journal Diameter	Oil Clearance	Side Clearance
1977	8-305	2.4481–2.4490 ⑧	.0011–.0023 ⑥	.002–.006	5	2.199–2.200	.0013–.0035	.008–.014
	8-350	2.4481–2.4490 ⑧	.0011–.0023 ⑥	.002–.006	5	2.199–2.200	.0013–.0035	.008–.014
	8-400	2.6484–2.6493 ⑦	.0011–.0023 ⑥	.002–.006	5	2.199–2.200	.0013–.0035	.008–.014
1978	6-250	2.2983–2.2993	.0003–.0029	.002–.006	7	1.999–2.000	.0007–.0027	.006–.017
	6-292	2.2983–2.2993	.0008–.0034	.002–.006	5	2.099–2.100	.0007–.0027	.006–.017
	8-305, 350	2.4481–2.4490 ⑧	.0011–.0023 ⑥	.002–.006	5	2.0988–2.0998	.0013–.0035	.008–.014
	8-400	2.6484–2.6493 ⑦	.0011–.0023 ⑥	.002–.006	5	2.0988–2.0998	.0013–.0035	.008–.014
1979–82	6-250	2.2979–2.2994	.0010–.0024 ⑨	.002–.006	7	1.999–2.000	.0010–.0030	.006–.017
	8-305, 350	2.4481–2.4490 ⑧	.0011–.0023 ⑥	.002–.006	5	2.0988–2.0998	.0013–.0035	.008–.014
	8-400	2.6484–2.6493 ⑦	.0011–.0023 ⑥	.002–.006	5	2.0988–2.0998	.0013–.0035	.008–.014
1983–86	6-250	2.2979–2.2994	.0010–.0024 ⑨	.002–.006	7	1.999–2.000	.0010–.0026	.006–.017
	6-262	⑫	⑬	.002–.006	Rear	2.2497–2.2487	0.010–0.0032	0.007–0.015
	8-305, 350	2.4481–2.4490 ⑧	.0011–.0023 ⑥	.002–.006	5	2.0988–2.0998	.0013–.0035	.008–.014
	8-379 Diesel	2.9494–2.9504 ⑩	.0018–.0032 ⑪	.002–.007	5	2.398–2.399	—	.007–.024

① No. 1—2.2987–2.2997
Nos. 2–4—2.2978–2.2988
No. 5—2.2978–2.2988
② No. 5—2.4479–2.4488
③ No. 1—.0008–.0020
Nos. 2–4—.0018–.0020
No. 5—.0010–.0032
④ No. 5—.0010–.0026
⑤ Nos. 2–4—.0006–.0018
No. 5—.0008–.0023
⑥ No. 1—.0008–.0020
No. 5—.0017–.0033
⑦ No. 5—2.6479–2.6488
⑧ No. 1—2.4484–2.4493
No. 5—2.4479–2.4488
⑨ No. 7—.0016–.0035
⑩ No. 5—2.9492–2.9502
⑪ No. 5—.0022–.0037
⑫ Front—2.4484–2.4493
Int—2.4481–2.4990
Rear—2.4479–2.4488
⑬ Front—.0008–.0020
Int—.0011–.0023
Rear—.0017–.0032

1971–73

On these vehicles, the engine is removed as a unit with the front suspension.

1. Remove the engine cover.
2. Disconnect the battery ground strap from the engine, and at the battery.
3. Drain the cooling system and disconnect the heater hoses at the engine. Disconnect the radiator hoses at the radiator.

CAUTION: *When draining the coolant, keep in mind that cats and dogs are attracted by the ethylene glycol antifreeze, and are quite likely to drink any that is left in an uncovered container or in puddles on the ground. This will prove fatal in sufficient quantity. Always drain the coolant into a sealable container. Coolant should be reused unless it is contaminated or several years old.*

4. Disconnect the automatic transmission cooler lines at the radiator.
5. Remove the fan guard and radiator.
6. Disconnect the oil pressure gauge.
7. Disconnect the engine wiring harness at the dash panel junction block.
8. Disconnect the alternator wires from the rear of the alternator.

Valve Specifications

Year	Engine No. Cyl Displacement (cu in.)	Seat Angle (deg)	Face Angle (deg)	Spring Test Pressure (lbs @ in.)	Spring Installed Height (in.) ①	Stem to Guide Clearance (in.)		Stem Diameter (in.)	
						Intake	Exhaust	Intake	Exhaust
1967	6-230	46	45	60 @ 1.66	$1\frac{21}{32}$	.0010–.0027	.0015–.0032	.3414	.3414
	6-250	46	45	60 @ 1.66	$1\frac{21}{32}$	.0010–.0027	.0015–.0032	.3414	.3414
	8-283	46	45	82 @ 1.66	$1\frac{21}{32}$	.0010–.0027	.0010–.0027	.3414	.3414
1968	6-230	46	45	60 @ 1.66	$1\frac{21}{32}$	.0010–.0027	.0015–.0032	.3414	.3414
	6-250	46	45	60 @ 1.66	$1\frac{21}{32}$	.0010–.0027	.0015–.0032	.3414	.3414
	8-307	46	45	82 @ 1.66	$1\frac{21}{32}$	.0010–.0027	.0010–.0027	.3414	.3414
1969	6-230	46	45	60 @ 1.66	$1\frac{21}{32}$	.0010–.0027	.0015–.0032	.3414	.3414
	6-250	46	45	60 @ 1.66	$1\frac{21}{32}$	.0010–.0027	.0015–.0032	.3414	.3414
	8-307	46	45	60 @ 1.66	$1\frac{21}{32}$	.0010–.0027	.0010–.0027	.3414	.3414
1970	6-250	46	45	60 @ 1.66	$1\frac{21}{32}$	.0010–.0032	.0015–.0032	.3414	.3414
	8-307	46	45	80 @ 1.70	$1\frac{23}{32}$	.0010–.0027	.0010–.0027	.3414	.3414
	8-350	46	45	80 @ 1.70	$1\frac{23}{32}$	.0010–.0027	.0010–.0027	.3414	.3414
1971	6-250	46	45	60 @ 1.66	$1\frac{21}{32}$	.0010–.0027	.0015–.0032	.3414	.3414
	8-307	46	45	80 @ 1.70	$1\frac{23}{32}$	.0010–.0027	.0010–.0027	.3414	.3414
	8-350	46	45	80 @ 1.70	$1\frac{23}{32}$	.0010–.0027	.0010–.0027	.3414	.3414
1972	6-250	46	45	60 @ 1.66	$1\frac{21}{32}$	.0010–.0027	.0015–.0032	.3414	.3414
	8-307	46	45	80 @ 1.70	$1\frac{23}{32}$	.0010–.0027	.0010–.0027	.3414	.3414
	8-350	46	45	80 @ 1.70	$1\frac{23}{32}$	.0010–.0027	.0010–.0027	.3414	.3414
1973	6-250	46	45	60 @ 1.66	$1\frac{21}{32}$	.0010–.0027	.0015–.0032	.3414	.3414
	8-307	46	45	80 @ 1.70 ②	$1\frac{5}{8}$	.0010–.0027	.0010–.0027	.3414	.3414
	8-350	46	45	80 @ 1.70 ②	$1\frac{23}{32}$	.0010–.0027	.0010–.0027	.3414	.3414
1974	6-250	46	45	60 @ 1.66	$1\frac{21}{32}$	.0010–.0027	.0015–.0032	.3414	.3414
	8-350	46	45	80 @ 1.70 ②	$1\frac{23}{32}$	.0010–.0027	.0010–.0027	.3414	.3414
1975–77	6-250	46	45	60 @ 1.66	$1\frac{21}{32}$	.0010–.0027	.0015–.0032	.3414	.3414

Valve Specifications (cont.)

Year	Engine No. Cyl Displacement (cu in.)	Seat Angle (deg)	Face Angle (deg)	Spring Test Pressure (lbs @ in.)	Spring Installed Height (in.) ①	Stem to Guide Clearance (in.)		Stem Diameter (in.)	
						Intake	Exhaust	Intake	Exhaust
1975–77	6-292	46	45	89 @ 1.69	1 5/8	.0010–.0027	.0010–.0027	.3414	.3414
	8-305	46	45	80 @ 1.70 ②	1 23/32 ③	.0010–.0027	.0010–.0027	.3414	.3414
	8-350	46	45	80 @ 1.70 ②	1 23/32 ③	.0010–.0027	.0010–.0027	.3414	.3414
	8-400	46	45	80 @ 1.70 ②	1 23/32 ③	.0012–.0029	.0012–.0029	.3414	.3414
1978–82	6-250	46	45	60 @ 1.66	1 21/32	.0010–.0027	.0015–.0032	.3414	.3414
	6-292	46	46	82 @ 1.66	1 21/32	.0010–.0027	.0015–.0032	.3414	.3414
	8-305	46	45	80 @ 1.70 ②	1 21/32 ③	.0010–.0027	.0010–.0027	.3414	.3414
	8-350	46	45	80 @ 1.70 ②	1 23/32	.0010–.0027	.0010–.0027	.3414	.3414
	8-400	46	45	80 @ 1.70 ②	1 23/32 ③	.0010–.0027	.0012–.0029	.3414	.3414
1983–86	6-250	46	45	175 @ 1.26	1.66	.0010–.0027	.0015–.0032	.3414	.3414
	6-262	46	45	194–206 @ 1.25	1 23/32	.0010–.0027	.0015–.0032	.3414	.3414
	8-305	46	45	200 @ 1.25 ④	1 21/32 ③	.0010–.0027	.0010–.0027	.3414	.3414
	8-350	46	45	200 @ 1.25 ④	1 23/32 ③	.0010–.0027	.0010–.0027	.3414	.3414
	8-379 Diesel	46	45	740 @ 1.40	1 13/16	.0010–.0027	.0010–.0027	—	—

① ± 1/32 in.
② Exhaust—80 @ 1.61 in.
③ Exhaust—1 19/32 starting 1977, 1 5/8 earlier
④ Exhaust—200 @ 1.16

9. Disconnect the TCS system electrical leads at the CEC valve on the carburetor and at the temperature switch. Remove the harness from the clips and position it out of the way.

10. Disconnect the evaporative emission control system lines at the rocker cover and the carburetor. Position these out of the way.

11. Disconnect the accelerator linkage at the bellcrank on the firewall.

12. Disconnect the power brake vacuum line at the intake manifold.

13. Disconnect the A/C compressor mounting bracket and position the compressor out of the way. Also remove the condenser from in front of the radiator. Position it out of the way.

14. Raise and support the vehicle. Disconnect the following items:

a. Fuel line at the fuel pump.
b. Engine ground straps.
c. Steering idler arm at the frame.
d. Steering pitman arm at the steering gear.
e. Battery cable from the starter.
f. TCS switch at the transmission (position the wiring harness to one side).
g. Exhaust pipe at the manifold (remove the exhaust system).

Ring Side Clearance
(in.)

Year	Engine No. Cyl Displacement (cu in.)	Top Compression	Bottom Compression	Oil Control
'67–'69	6-230	.0012–.0027	.0012–.0027	.005 max
'67–'86	6-250	.0012–.0027	.0012–.0032	.005 max
'85–'86	6-262	.0012–.0032	.0012–.0032	.002–.007
'75–'78	6-292	.0020–.0040	.0020–.0040	.005–.0055
'67	8-283	.0012–.0027	.0012–.0032	.005 max
'68–'73	8-307	.0007–.0027	.0012–.0032	.005 max
'70–'86	8-305, 350, 400	.0012–.0032	.0012–.0032	.002–.007
'83–'86	8-379 Diesel	.0030–.0070	.0015–.0031	.0016–.0038

Ring Gap
(in.)

Year	Engine No. Cyl Displacement (cu in.)	Top Compression	Bottom Compression	Oil Control
'67–'86	6-250, 292	.010–.020	.010–.020	.015–.055
'85–'86	6-262	.010–.020	.010–.025	.015–.055
'67	8-283	.0010–.0020	.0010–.0020	.015–.055
'68–'73	8-307	.010–.020	.010–.020	.015–.055
'69–'76	8-350, 400	.010–.020	.013–.025	.015–.055
'77–'86	8-305, 350, 400	.010–.020	.010–.025	.015–.055
'83–'86	8-379 Diesel	.0012–.022	.030–.040	.0098–.0200

h. Transmission at the crossmember.
i. Stabilizer bar at the frame brackets.

15. Disconnect the shock absorbers from the frame or lower control arm and position them out of the way.
16. Disconnect the clutch and transmission linkage and remove the clutch crossmember.
17. Remove the driveshaft and install a plug in the transmission extension.
18. Disconnect the front brake line at the equalizer 'T' and disconnect the rear brake line at the left frame rail.
19. Disconnect the rear brake line at the right frame rail.
20. Remove the transmission support frame-to-crossmember attaching nuts, but do not remove the bolts.
21. Remove the 6 (3 on each side) frame-to-crossmember attaching bolts.
22. Remove the 4 (2 on each side) frame-to-upper control arm inside attaching bolts.
23. Lower the vehicle on a jack and support it so that the weight is on supports but the wheels and suspension are at curb height.
24. Install wooden blocks between the oil pan and crossmember to stabilize the engine.
25. Position a floor jack under the vehicle so that the jack pad is aligning under the trans-

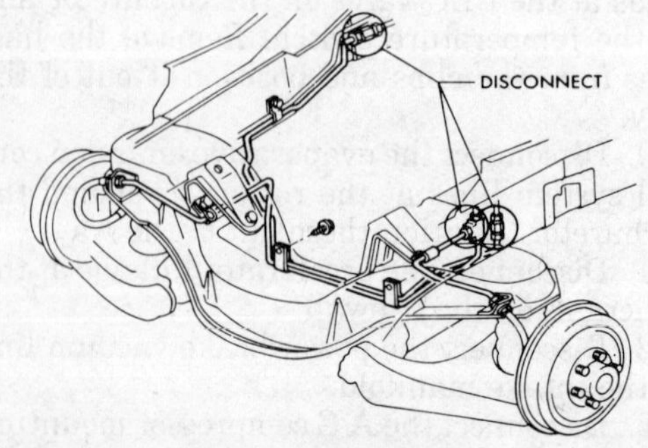

Brake line disconnects—1971–73

Torque Specifications

(ft. lb.)

Year	Engine No. Cyl Displacement (cu in.)	Cylinder Head Bolts	Rod Bearing Bolts	Main Bearing Bolts	Crankshaft Bolt	Flywheel to Crankshaft bolts	Manifold	
							Intake	Exhaust
'67–'71	6-230, 250	95	35	65	—	60	30 ①	25 ②
'72	6-250	95	35	65	—	60	30	25 ②
'73–'74	6-250	95	35	65	—	60	35	30 ②
'75–'86	6-250	95 ⑤	36	65	—	60	—	30 ③
'75–'78	6-292	95	40	65	—	110	35	30 ②
'67	8-283	65	35	80	—	60	30	20
'68	8-307	65	35	80	—	60	30	20 ④
'69–'73	8-307, 350	65	45	70	—	60	30	20 ④
'74–'86	6-262, 8-305, 350, 400	65	45	70	60	60	30	20 ④
'83–'86	8-379 Diesel	100	48	⑥	150	—	31	22

① End bolts—20
② Exhaust to intake
③ 20 on four end bolts with intake manifold integral with head.
④ Inside bolts on 307 and 350—30
⑤ Left-hand front bolt: 85 ft. lbs.
⑥ Inner: 111—Outer: 100

Piston Clearance

Year	Engine No. Cyl Displacement (cu in.)	Piston to Bore Clearance (in.)
'67–'68	6-230	.0005–.0011
'69	6-230	.0005–.0014
'67–'68	6-250	.0005–.0011
'69	6-250	.0005–.0014
'70–'77	6-250	.0005–.0015
'78–'86	6-250	.0010–.0020
'85–'86	6-262	.0007–.0017
'75–'78	6-292	.0026–.0036
'67	8-283	.0005–.0011
'86	8-305	.0007–.0017
'68–'70	8-307	.0005–.0011
'71–'73	8-307	.0012–.0018
'70	8-350	.0012–.0022
'71–'76	8-350	.0007–.0013
'77–'86	8-350	.0007–.0017
'75–'80	8-400	.0014–.0024
'83–'86	8-379 Diesel	.0040–.0050

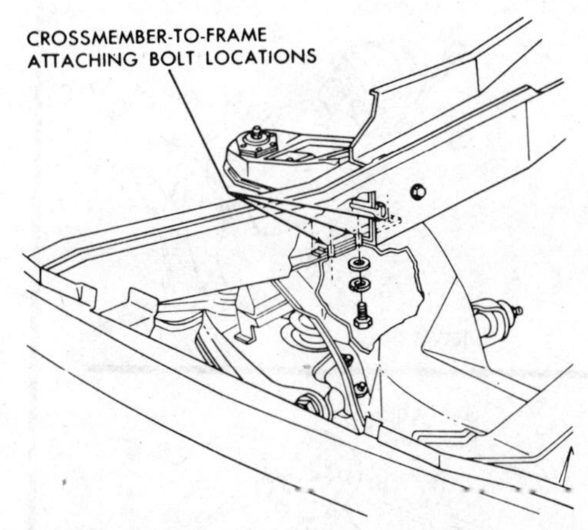

Crossmember-to-frame attaching bolts—1971–73

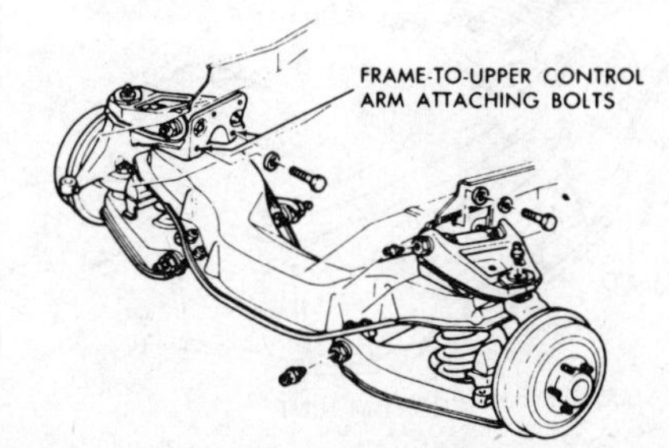

Suspension-to-frame attaching bolts—1971–73

Floor jack under the engine/transmission

mission. Use a block of wood between the jack pad and transmission and support the transmission.

26. Remove the transmission support crossmember.

27. Remove the remaining 4 (2 on each side) suspension-to-frame outside retaining bolts.

28. Slowly raise the vehicle, leaving the suspension and power train on the floor until there is sufficient clearance to remove the engine. Check to be sure that all necessary components are disconnected.

29. Roll the power train/suspension assembly to the work area and support the transmission extension with a jackstand. Remove the floor jack.

30. Place a floor jack under the suspension crossmember and raise the assembly until the weight is on the jack.

31. Attach a hoist to the engine at the lifting brackets.

32. Remove the engine mount throughbolts and remove the engine assembly from the crossmember.

33. Remove the manual transmission and clutch as follows:

a. Remove the clutch housing rear bolts.

b. Remove the bolts attaching the clutch housing to the engine and remove the transmission and clutch as a unit.

NOTE: *Support the transmission as the last bolt is being removed to prevent damaging the clutch.*

c. Remove the starter and clutch housing rear cover.

d. Loosen the clutch mounting bolts a little at a time to prevent distorting the disc until spring pressure is released. Remove all

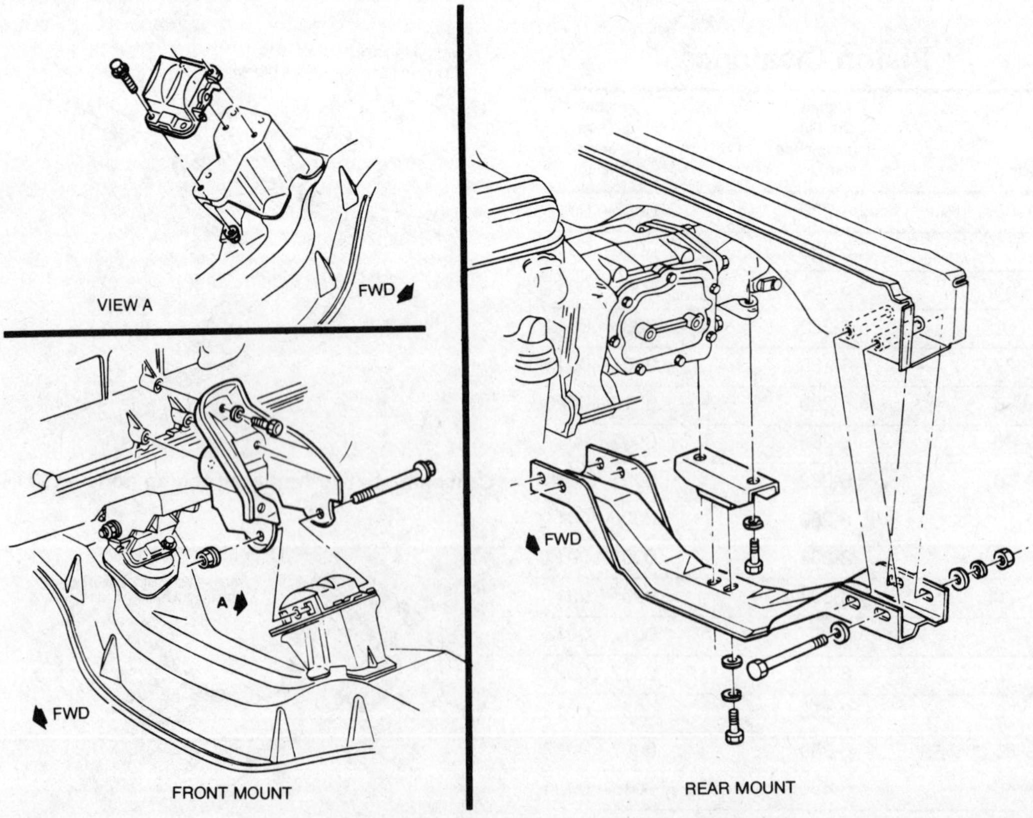

1971 and later six cylinder engine mounts

of the bolts, the clutch disc and the pressure plate.

34. Remove the automatic transmission as follows:

a. Lower the engine and support it on blocks.

b. Remove the starter and converter housing underpan.

c. Remove the flywheel-to-converter attaching bolts.

d. Support the transmission on blocks.

e. Disconnect the throttle linkage and vacuum modulator on the Powerglide. Disconnect the detent cable on the Turbo Hydra-Matic.

f. Remove the transmission-to-engine mounting bolts.

g. Remove the blocks from the engine only and glide the engine away from the transmission.

35. Mount the engine a on a stand.

36. Installation is the reverse of removal. Bleed the front and rear brakes, check all fluid levels, start the engine and check for leaks.

1974–76

The engines on these vehicles are removed through the front of the vehicle. A portable boom type hoist is necessary for this job.

1. Remove the grille. It is attached with screws.

2. Drain the cooling system and disconnect the heater hoses at the engine. Disconnect the radiator hoses at the engine.

CAUTION: *When draining the coolant, keep in mind that cats and dogs are attracted by the ethylene glycol antifreeze, and are quite likely to drink any that is left in an uncovered container or in puddles on the ground. This will prove fatal in sufficient quantity. Always drain the coolant into a sealable container. Coolant should be reused unless it is contaminated or several years old.*

3. Disconnect the A/C compressor mounting bracket and position the compressor out of the way. Also remove the condenser from in front of the radiator. Position it out of the way. DO NOT DISCONNECT ANY OF THE REFRIGERANT LINES.

4. Disconnect the automatic transmission cooler lines at the radiator. Remove the fan guard and radiator.

5. Remove the radiator upper tie bar and radiator support.

6. Disconnect the battery cables at the battery and at the radiator support baffle.

7. Disconnect the engine wiring harness at the junction block on the firewall.

8. Disconnect the oil pressure gauge if equipped.

Engine removal—1974 and later

9. Raise and support the van. Disconnect the following items:

a. Fuel line at the fuel pump.

b. Engine ground straps.

c. Battery cables at the frame mounted clip.

d. Speedometer cable at the transmission.

e. Exhaust pipes from the manifolds (remove the exhaust system).

f. Transmission at the crossmember.

10. Disconnect the clutch linkage or the transmission linkage and remove the clutch cross-shaft.

11. Remove the driveshaft. Plug the opening in the extension housing of the transmission.

12. Remove the engine mount through-bolts.

13. Remove the crossmember-to-engine mount bracket (right side only) attaching bolts, but do not remove the bracket.

14. Lower the vehicle and support it approximately 12" (305mm) from the floor.

15. Remove the engine access cover.

16. Remove the air cleaner.

17. Disconnect the carburetor throttle linkage. Disconnect and plug the fuel line from the carburetor and remove the carburetor.

19. Disconnect the spark plug wires from the spark plugs and position them out of the way.

20. Remove the ignition coil and rear lifting bracket.

21. Securely attach a boom hoist to the engine.

22. With the aid of an assistant, slowly raise the engine to take the weight off the engine mounts. Remove the right mount frame bracket and mount.

23. Continue raising the engine and move it forward out of the van. Check often to be sure that all necessary components are disconnected.

24. Remove the transmission as outlined in Steps 33 or 34 of the 1971–73 procedure.

25. Installation is the reverse of removal. Check all fluids and check for leaks.

1977–78

1. Scribe matchmarks on the hood hinges for reassembly and remove the hood and the grille. Remove the grille cross brace.
2. Disconnect the negative battery cable, then the positive battery cable, at the battery.
3. Remove the air cleaner.
4. Drain the cooling system and disconnect the heater hoses and radiator hoses at the radiator.

CAUTION: *When draining the coolant, keep in mind that cats and dogs are attracted by the ethylene glycol antifreeze, and are quite likely to drink any that is left in an uncovered container or in puddles on the ground. This will prove fatal in sufficient quantity. Always drain the coolant into a sealable container. Coolant should be reused unless it is contaminated or several years old.*

5. Disconnect the A/C compressor mounting bracket and position the compressor out of the way. Also remove the condenser from in front of the radiator. Position it our of the way. DO NOT DISCONNECT ANY OF THE REFRIGERANT LINES.
6. Remove the radiator and the fan shroud.
7. Disconnect and label the wiring at the starter solenoid, alternator, temperature sending switch, oil pressure switch and the coil. Disconnect the engine ground strap.
8. Disconnect:
   a. the accelerator at the intake manifold.
   b. the fuel line from the tank at the fuel pump (plug the line).
   c. the hoses at the fuel vapor storage canister (if so equipped).
   d. the vacuum line to the power brake booster at the manifold (if so equipped).
9. Remove the power steering pump mounting bolts and lay the pump aside. Do not disconnect any of the lines.
10. Raise the van on a hoist and drain the crankcase.
11. Disconnect the exhaust pipe at the manifold. If equipped with a catalytic converter, disconnect the converter bracket at the rear transmission mount.
12. Remove the starter motor.
13. Remove the flywheel splash shield or the converter cover, as applicable.
14. On vans with automatic transmissions, remove the converter-to-flywheel attaching bolts.
15. Remove the engine mount through bolts.
16. Remove the bell housing bolts.
17. Lower the van.
18. Using a floor jack, raise the transmission.
19. Attach a boom hoist to the engine and raise the engine slightly.
20. Remove the engine mount-to-engine brackets.
21. Remove the engine.
22. Reverse the removal procedure to install.

1979–86

1. Disconnect the negative battery cable, then the positive battery cable, at the battery. On the V6 remove the glove box.
2. Drain the cooling system.

CAUTION: *When draining the coolant, keep in mind that cats and dogs are attracted by the ethylene glycol antifreeze, and are quite likely to drink any that is left in an uncovered container or in puddles on the ground. This will prove fatal in sufficient quantity. Always drain the coolant into a sealable container. Coolant should be reused unless it is contaminated or several years old.*

3. Remove the engine cover.
4. Remove the air cleaner. On the V8 remove the air stove pipe. On the V6 remove the outside air duct.
5. On the V6 remove the head light bezels and the grille. On inline six cylinder, remove the grille cross brace and the grille. On the V8, remove the upper radiator support the grille and the lower grille valance.
6. Disconnect the radiator hoses at the radiator.
7. On the V8, remove the radiator coolant reservoir bottle. On the V6, remove the power steering reservoir and the hood release cable.
8. If the van is equipped with an automatic transmission, remove the fluid cooler lines from the radiator.

CAUTION: *Discharging the air conditioning refrigerant should only be attempted by those who have the proper tools and training to do so, as serious personal injury may result. The refrigerant will instantly freeze any surface it comes in contact with, including your eyes.*

9. Discharge the air conditioning system and remove the A/C vacuum reservoir. On the V8, remove the A/C condenser from in front of the radiator. On the six cylinder, remove the A/C compressor.
10. Remove the windshield wiper jar and bracket.
11. Disconnect the accelerator linkage at the carburetor and remove the carburetor.
12. Remove the radiator support bracket and remove the radiator and the shroud.
13. On all six cylinders, remove the A/C compressor mounting bracket and position the compressor out of the way.
14. On the V6 and V8, disconnect the engine wiring harness from the firewall connection. On the inline six cylinder, disconnect the wir-

ing at the alternator, distributor, oil pressure and temperature sending switches and the starter motor.

15. On the V6 and V8:

a. Disconnect the heater hoses at the engine.

b. Remove the thermostat housing.

c. Remove the oil filler pipe and the engine dipstick tube.

d. Remove the cruise control servo, servo bracket and transducer.

e. Remove the distributor cap.

f. Remove the diverter valve.

g. Remove the coolant hose at the intake manifold and the PCV valve.

h. Remove the transmission dipstick tube and the accelerator cable at the tube.

i. Remove the air conditioning idler pulley.

j. Remove the lower fan shroud and filler panel.

k. Remove the hood latch support.

l. Remove the condenser.

16. Raise the vehicle and drain the engine oil.

17. Remove the fuel line from the fuel tank and at the fuel pump.

18. Disconnect the exhaust pipe at the manifold.

On the V6 only:

a. Remove the strut rods at the torque converter or flywheel underpan.

b. Remove the torque converter or flywheel cover.

c. Remove the starter.

d. Remove the flex plate to torque converter bolts (automatic transmissions).

e. Remove the bell housing to engine bolts.

f. Remove the engine mounting through bolts.

Lower the van, support the transmission and remove the engine

19. Remove the driveshaft and plug the end of the transmission.

20. Disconnect the transmission shift linkage and the speedometer cable.

21. Remove the transmission mounting bolts.

22. On the inline six cylinder with manual transmission, disconnect the clutch linkage and remove the clutch cross shaft.

23. On the V8, remove the engine mount bracket-to-frame bolts.

24. Remove the engine mount through bolts.

25. On the inline six cylinder:

a. Lower the van and attach a lifting device to the engine.

b. Raise the engine slightly and remove the right hand mount from the engine.

26. On the V8: Raise the engine slightly and remove the engine mounts. Support the engine with wood between the oil pan and the crossmember.

27. Remove the engine and transmission as one unit (except the V6). Refer to steps 33 or 34 of the 1971–73 procedure to remove the transmission.

28. Reverse the removal procedure to install.

Valve Cover(s)

REMOVAL AND INSTALLATION

All Engines

1. Remove air cleaner.
2. Disconnect and reposition as necessary any vacuum or PCV hoses that obstruct the valve covers.
3. Disconnect electrical wire(s) (spark plug, etc.) from the valve cover slips.
4. Unbolt and remove the valve cover(s).

NOTE: *Do not pry the covers off if they seem stuck. Instead, gently tap around each cover with a rubber mallet until the old gasket or sealer breaks loose.*

5. To install, use a new valve cover gasket or RTV (or any equivalent) sealer. If using sealer, follow directions on the tube. Install valve cover and tighten cover bolts to 3 ft.lb.

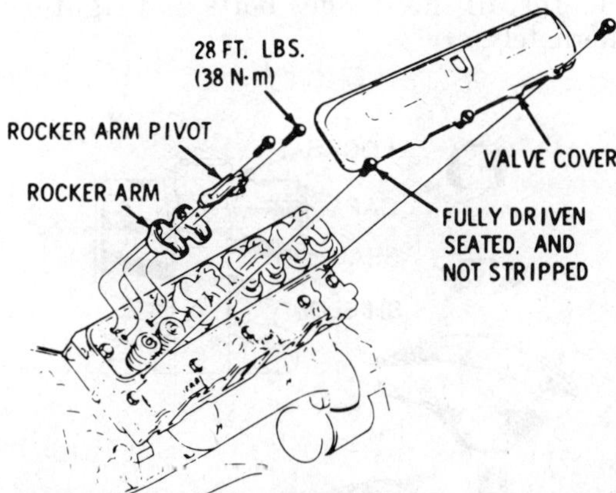

Valve cover and rocker arm removal, gasoline V8 shown. Rocker arms are marked "L" and "R" for left and right

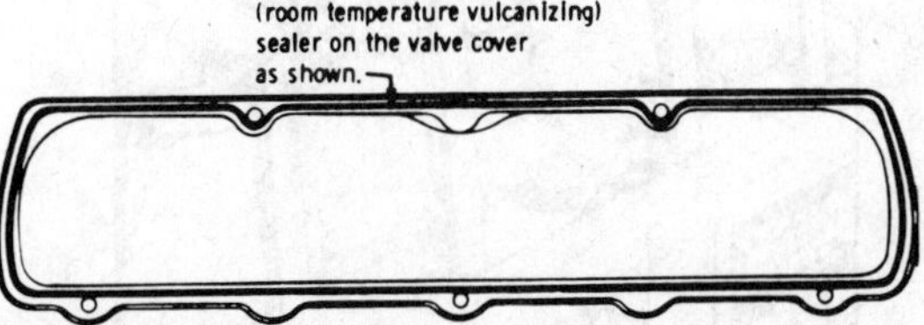

Apply sealer to all valve covers as shown. Always run the sealer bead on the inside edge of the bolt holes on the cover flange

6. Connect and reposition all vacuum and PCV hoses, and reconnect electrical and/or spark plug wires at the cover clips. Install the air cleaner.

Rocker Arms

REMOVAL AND INSTALLATION

All Gasoline Sixes and V8s

1. Remove the valve cover.
2. Remove the rocker arm flanged bolts, and remove the rocker pivots.
3. Remove the rocker arms (and the balls on the V6).

NOTE: *Remove each set of rocker arms/balls (one set per cylinder) as a unit. Only the V6 engines have rocker balls.*

4. To install, position a set of rocker arms, and balls if you have the V6, (for one cylinder) in the proper location.

NOTE: *Install the rocker arms for each cylinder only when the lifters are off the cam lobe and both valves are closed.*

5. Coat the replacement rocker arm/ball with Molycoat® or its equivalent, on the 1986 V6 engine, and the rocker arm and pivot with SAE 90 gear oil on all other engines, and install the pivots.
6. Install the flanges bolts and tighten alternately.

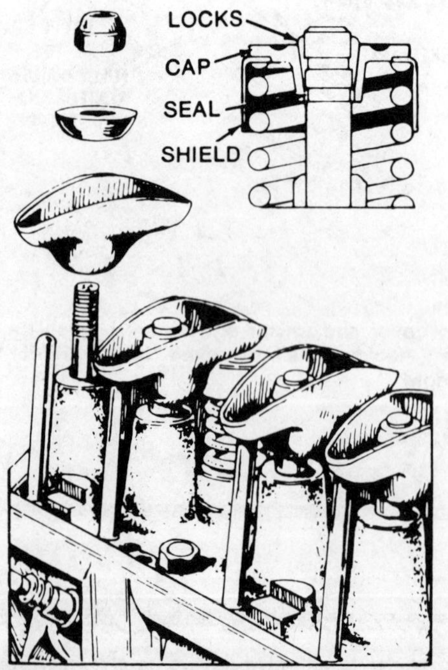

Six-cylinder rocker arm components—all gasoline V8s similar

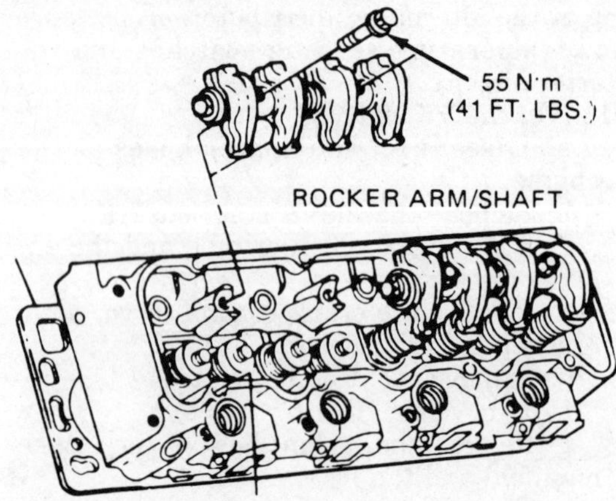

6.2L diesel rocker shaft assemblies

8–379 (6.2L) Diesel

1. Remove the valve cover as previously explained.
2. The rocker assemblies on the 379 are mounted on two short rocker shafts per cylinder head, with each shaft operating four rockers. Remove the two bolts which secure each rocker shaft assembly, and remove the shaft.
3. The rocker arms can be removed from the shaft by removing the cotter pin on the end of each shaft. The rocker arms and springs slide off.
4. To install, make sure first that the rocker arms and springs go back on the shafts in the exact order in which they were removed.

NOTE: *Always install new cotter pins on the rocker shaft ends.*

5. Install the rocker shaft assemblies, torquing the bolts to 41 ft.lb.

Thermostat

REMOVAL AND INSTALLATION

1. Drain the radiator until the level is below the thermostat level (below the level of the intake manifold).

CAUTION: *When draining the coolant, keep in mind that cats and dogs are attracted by the ethylene glycol antifreeze, and are quite likely to drink any that is left in an uncovered container or in puddles on the ground. This will prove fatal in sufficient quantity. Always drain the coolant into a sealable container. Coolant should be reused unless it is contaminated or several years old.*

2. Remove the water outlet elbow assembly from the engine. Remove the thermostat from inside the elbow.
3. Install new thermostat in the reverse order of removal, making sue the spring side is inserted into the elbow. Clean the gasket surfaces on the water outlet elbow and the intake

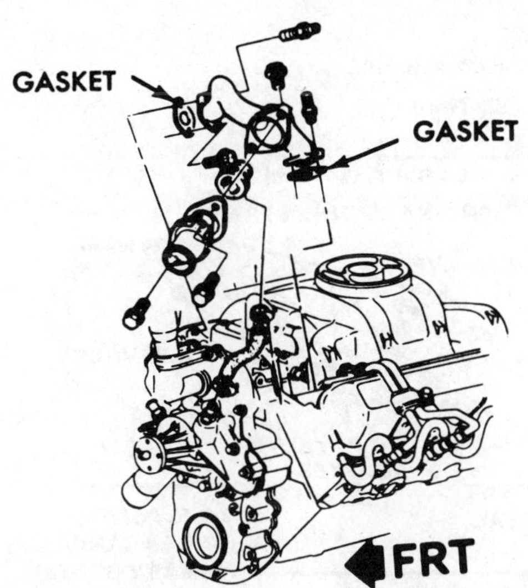

The 379 diesel thermostat is located in the coolant reservoir pipe

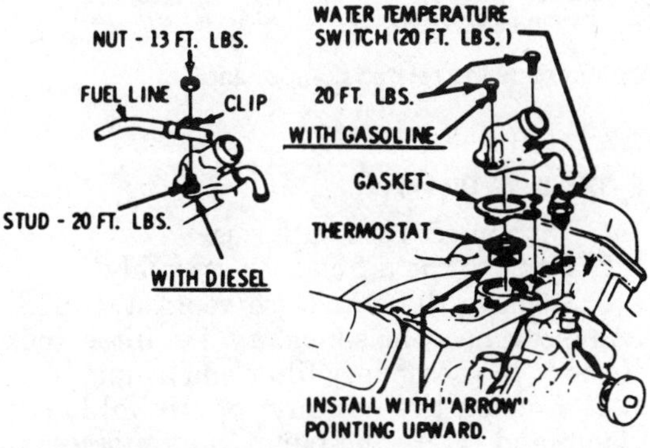

Typical V8 thermostat installation

manifold. Use a new gasket when installing the elbow to the manifold. Refill the radiator to approximately 2½" (64mm) below the filler neck.

Intake Manifold

REMOVAL AND INSTALLATION

Inline 6-Cylinder

1974 and earlier 250 and 292 six cylinder engines use a combined intake and exhaust manifold, both of which are removed together. 1976 and later engines have an intake manifold which is cast integrally with the cylinder head and cannot be removed.

1. Remove the air cleaner assembly and air ducts.
2. Tag and disconnect the throttle linkage at the carburetor. Tag and disconnect the fuel line, vacuum lines, hoses, and electrical connections.
3. Disconnect the transmission downshift linkage (if equipped), and remove the PCV valve from the rocker cover. On models equipped with air injection, disconnect the air supply hose from the check valve on the air injection manifold.
4. Remove the carburetor, with spacer and heat shield (if equipped).
5. Spray the nuts and bolts connecting the exhaust manifold to the exhaust pipe with a rust penetrant, as these are usually quite difficult to remove. Unbolt the exhaust manifold from the pipe.

   NOTE: *It may be necessary to remove the generator rear bracket and/or A/C bracket on some models.*
6. Unbolt the manifold bolts and clamps, and remove the manifold assembly.
7. If you intend to separate the manifolds, remove the single bolt and two nuts at the center of the manifold assembly.
8. Installation is the reverse of removal. When assembling the manifolds, install the connecting bolts loosely first. Place the manifolds on a straight, flat surface and hold them securely during the tightening—this assures the proper mating of surfaces when the manifold assembly is fastened to the head. Stress cracking could occur if the manifolds are not assembled first in this manner. On all manifolds, always use new gaskets between the manifolds and cylinder head.

V6 and V8 Except Diesel

1. Drain the cooling system.

   CAUTION: *When draining the coolant, keep in mind that cats and dogs are attracted by the ethylene glycol antifreeze, and are quite likely to drink any that is left in an uncovered container or in puddles on the ground. This will prove fatal in sufficient quantity. Always drain the coolant into a sealable container. Coolant should be reused unless it is contaminated or several years old.*
2. Remove the air cleaner assembly.
3. Remove the thermostat housing and the bypass hose. It is not necessary to remove the top radiator hose from the thermostat housing.
4. Disconnect the heater hose at the rear of the manifold.
5. Disconnect all electrical connections and vacuum lines from the manifold. Remove the EGR valve if necessary.
6. On vehicles equipped with power brakes remove the vacuum line from the vacuum booster to the manifold.
7. Remove the distributor (if necessary).
8. Remove the fuel line to the carburetor.
9. Remove the carburetor linkage.

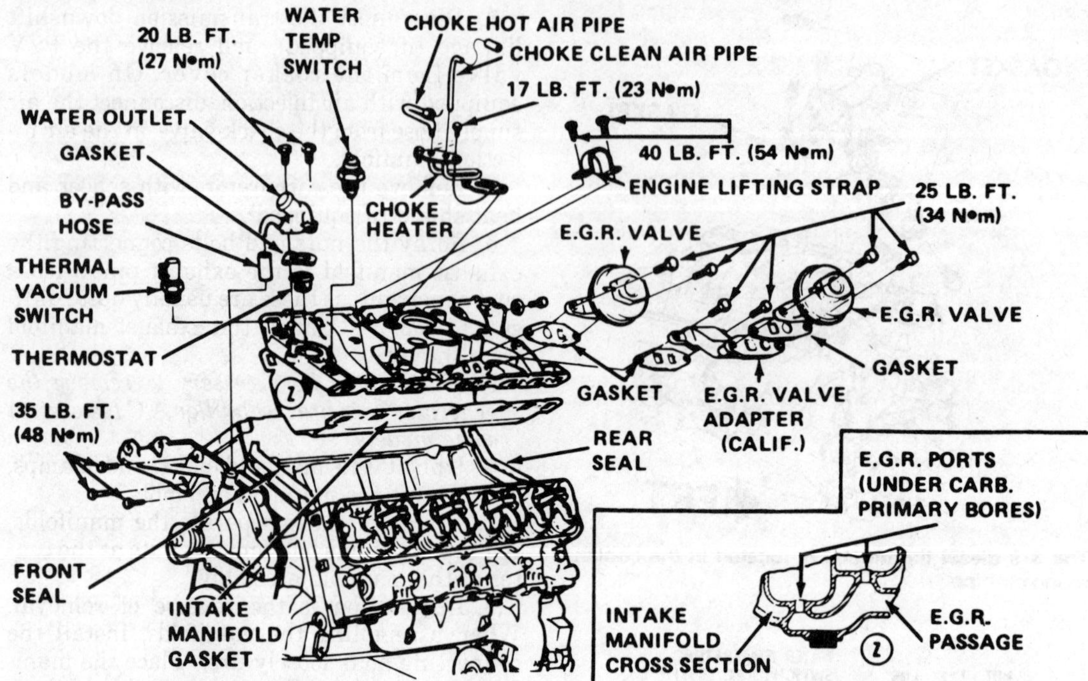

Typical gasoline V8 intake manifold installation showing related components

10. Remove the carburetor.
11. Remove the intake manifold bolts. Remove the manifold and the gaskets. Remember to reinstall the O-ring between the intake manifold and timing chain cover during assembly, if so equipped.
12. Installation is the reverse of removal. Use plastic gasket retainers to prevent the manifold gasket from slipping out of place, if so equipped. On the small block V8s, place a $^{3}/_{16}$" (4.8mm) bead of RTV type silicone sealer on the front and rear ridges of the cylinder block-to-manifold mating surfaces. Extend the bead ½" (12.7mm) up each cylinder head to seal and retain the manifold side gaskets.

NOTE: *Before installing the intake manifold, be sure that the gasket surfaces are thoroughly clean.*

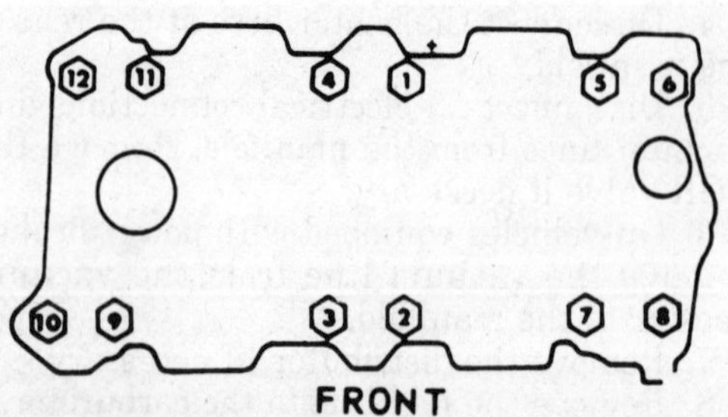

305 and 350 V8 intake manifold bolt torque sequence

8–379 (6.2L) Diesel

1. Disconnect both batteries.
2. Remove the air cleaner assembly.
3. Remove the crankcase ventilator tubes, and disconnect the secondary fuel filter lines. Remove the secondary filter and adaptor.
4. Loosen the vacuum pump holddown clamp and rotate the pump to gain access to the nearest manifold bolt.
5. Remove the EPR/EGR valve bracket, if equipped.
6. Remove the rear air conditioning bracket, if equipped.
7. Remove the intake manifold bolts. The injection line clips are retained by these bolts.
8. Remove the intake manifold.

CAUTION: *If the engine is to be further serviced with the manifold removed, install protective covers over the intake ports.*

9. Clean the manifold gasket surfaces on the cylinder heads and install new gaskets before installing the manifold.

NOTE: *The gaskets have an opening for the EGR valve on light duty installations. An insert covers this opening on heavy duty installations.*

10. Install the manifold. Torque the bolts in the sequence illustrated.
11. The secondary filter must be filled with clean diesel fuel before it is reinstalled.
12. Reverse the remaining removal procedures to complete the installation.

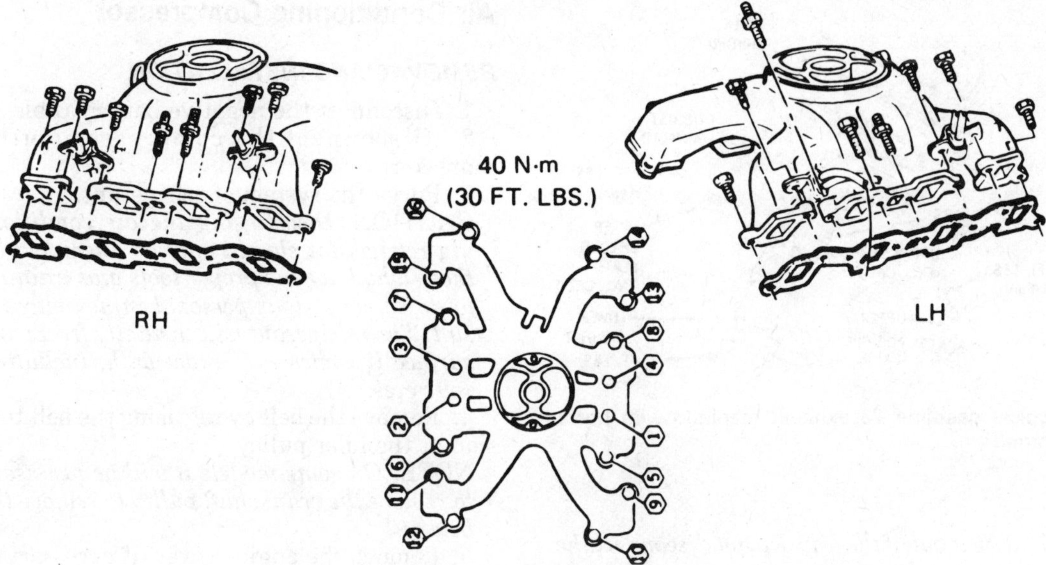

379 diesel intake manifold gasket mounting and bolt torque sequence

Exhaust Manifold

REMOVAL AND INSTALLATION

Inline Six Cylinder

NOTE: *1974 and earlier inline six cylinder exhaust manifold removal and installation procedures are covered under the Intake Manifold procedure (both manifolds are a unit). 1975 and later inline six procedures are covered below.*

1. Disconnect and remove the air cleaner assembly, including the carburetor preheat tube.
2. Disconnect the exhaust pipe at the exhaust manifold. You will probably have to use a liquid rust penetrant to free the bolts.
3. Remove the engine oil dipstick bracket bolt.
4. Liberally coat the manifold nuts with a rust penetrating lubricant. Remove the exhaust manifold bolts and remove the manifold.
5. To install, mount the manifold on the cylinder head and start all bolts.
6. Torque the bolts to specification using the torque sequence illustrated. Complete the installation by reversing the removal procedure.

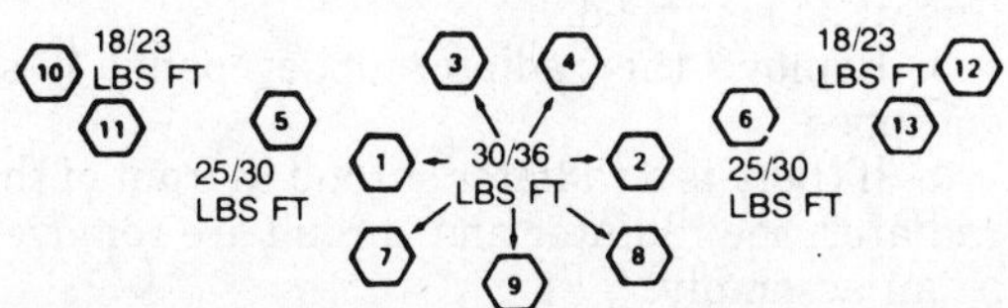

1975 and later inline six exhaust manifold torque sequence—engines with integral intake manifold/cylinder head

Gasoline V6s and V8s

Tab locks are used on the front and rear pairs of bolts on each exhaust manifold. When removing the bolts, straighten the tabs from beneath the car using a suitable tool. When installing the tab locks, bend the tabs against the sides of the bolt, not over the top of the bolt.

1. Remove the air cleaner.
2. Remove the hot air shroud, (if so equipped).
3. Loosen the alternator and remove its lower bracket.
4. Jack up your van and support it with jackstands.
5. Disconnect the crossover pipe from both manifolds.

NOTE: *On models with air conditioning it may be necessary to remove the compressor,*

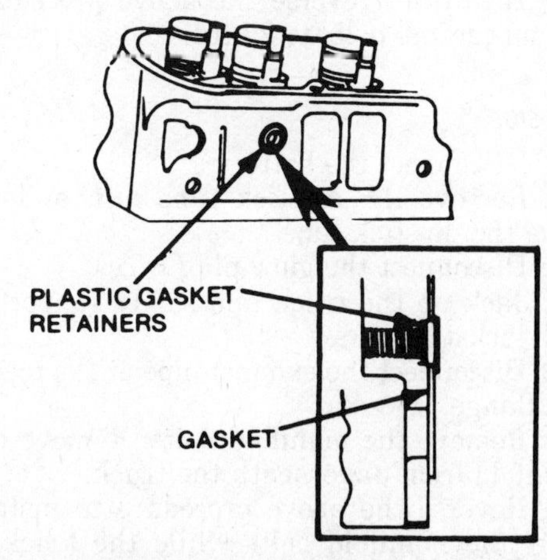

Plastic manifold gasket retainers, gasoline V8s

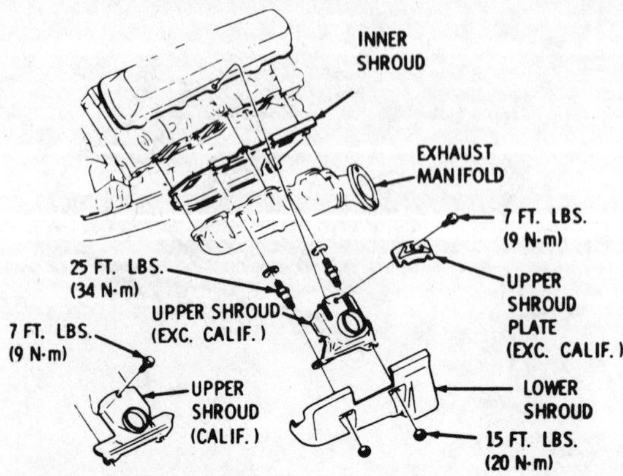

Typical gasoline V8 exhaust manifold with hot air shrouds

and tie it out of the way. Do not disconnect the compressor lines.

6. Remove the manifold bolts and remove the manifold(s). Some models have lock tabs on the front and rear manifold bolts which must be removed before removing the bolts. These tabs can be bent with a drift pin.
7. Installation is the reverse of removal.

8–379 Diesel

RIGHT SIDE

1. Disconnect the batteries.
2. Jack up the truck and safely support it with jackstands.
3. Disconnect the exhaust pipe from the manifold flange and lower the truck.
4. Disconnect the glow plug wires.
5. Remove the air cleaner duct bracket.
6. Remove the glow plug wires.
7. Remove the manifold bolts and remove the manifold.
8. To install, reverse the above procedure and torque the bolts to 25 ft.lb.

LEFT SIDE

1. Disconnect the batteries.
2. Remove the dipstick tube nut, and remove the dipstick tube.
3. Disconnect the glow plug wires.
4. Jack up the truck and safely support it with jackstands.
5. Disconnect the exhaust pipe at the manifold flange.
6. Remove the manifold bolts. Remove the manifold from underneath the truck.
7. Reverse the above procedure to install. Start the manifold bolts while the truck is jacked up first. Torque the bolts to 25 ft.lb.

Air Conditioning Compressor

REMOVAL AND INSTALLATION

1. Disconnect the negative battery cable.
2. Disconnect the compressor clutch connector.
3. Purge the system of refrigerant.

CAUTION: *Discharging the air conditioning refrigerant should only be attempted by those who have the proper tools and training to do so, as serious personal injury may result. The refrigerant will instantly freeze any surface it comes in contact with, including your eyes.*

4. Remove the belt by releasing the belt tension at the idler pulley.

NOTE: *On some models it will be necessary to remove the crankshaft pulley to remove the belt.*

5. Remove the engine cover (if necessary).
6. Remove the air cleaner.
7. Remove the fitting and muffler assembly. Cap and plug all open connections.
8. Remove the compressor bracket.
9. Remove the engine oil tube support bracket bolt and nut.
10. Disconnect the clutch ground lead.
11. Remove the compressor.
12. Drain and measure the oil in the compressor and check for contamination.
13. Replace with fresh oil and reinstall the compressor.
14. Installation is the reverse of the removal procedure.

Radiator

REMOVAL AND INSTALLATION

1. Drain the cooling system.

CAUTION: *When draining the coolant, keep in mind that cats and dogs are attracted by the ethylene glycol antifreeze, and are quite likely to drink any that is left in an uncovered container or in puddles on the ground. This will prove fatal in sufficient quantity. Always drain the coolant into a sealable container. Coolant should be reused unless it is contaminated or several years old.*

2. Disconnect the radiator upper and lower hoses and, if applicable, the transmission coolant lines. Remove the coolant recovery system line, if so equipped.
3. Remove the radiator upper panel if so equipped.
4. If there is a radiator shroud in front of the radiator, the radiator and shroud are removed as an assembly.
5. If there is a fan shroud, remove the shroud attaching screws and let the shroud hang on the fan.

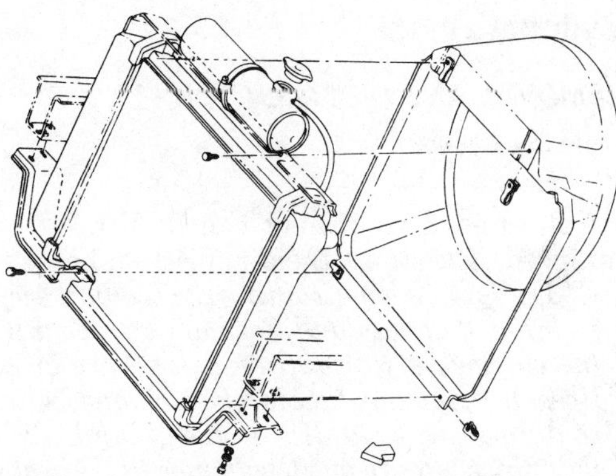

Radiator and shroud mounting (1967–70 six)

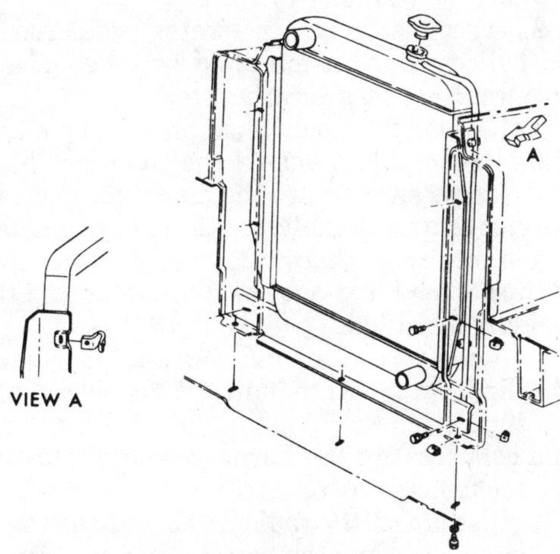

Radiator and shroud mounting (1967–70 V8)

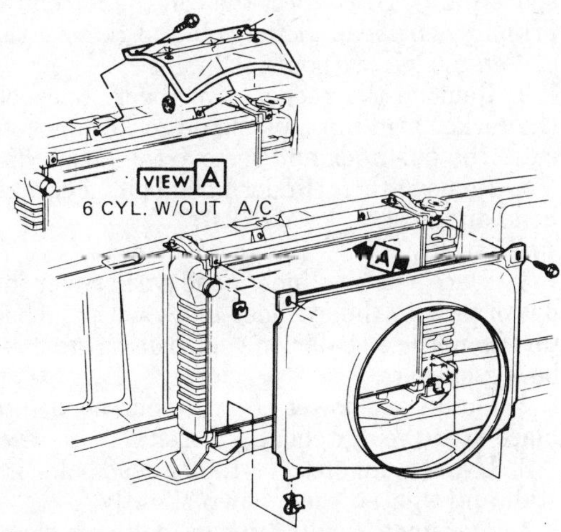

1971 and later radiator shrouds

6. Remove the radiator attaching bolts and remove the radiator.

7. Installation is the reverse of the removal procedure.

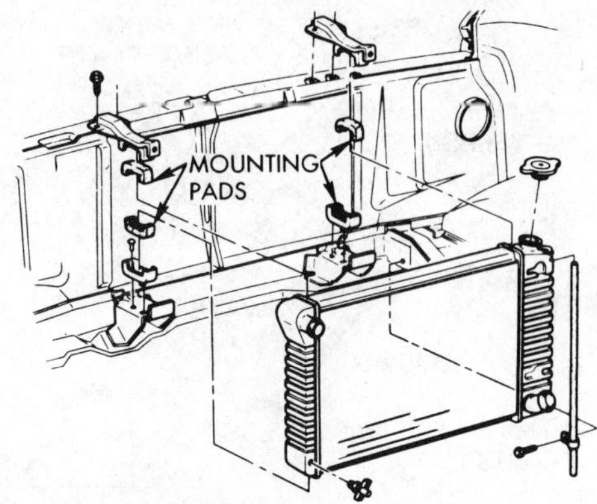

Radiator mounting (1971–74)

Water Pump

REMOVAL AND INSTALLATION

All Engines Except 8–379 (6.2L) Diesel

1. Disconnect the battery.
2. Drain the radiator.

CAUTION: *When draining the coolant, keep in mind that cats and dogs are attracted by the ethylene glycol antifreeze, and are quite likely to drink any that is left in an uncovered container or in puddles on the ground. This will prove fatal in sufficient quantity. Always drain the coolant into a sealable container. Coolant should be reused unless it is contaminated or several years old.*

3. Loosen the alternator and other accessories at their adjusting points, and remove the fan belts from the fan pulley.
4. Remove the fan and pulley.
5. Remove any accessory brackets that might interfere with water pump removal.
6. Disconnect the hose from the water pump inlet and the heater hose from the nipple on the pump. Remove the bolts, pump assembly and old gasket from the timing chain cover.
7. Check the pump shaft bearings for end play or roughness in operation. Water pump bearings usually emit a squealing sound with the engine running when the bearings need to be replaced. Replace the pump if the bearings are not in good shape or have been noisy.
8. To install, make sure the gasket surfaces on the pump and timing chain cover are clean. Install the pump assembly with a new gasket. Tighten the bolts uniformly.
9. The remainder of installation is the reverse of removal. Fill the cooling system and check for leaks at the pump and hose joints. Make sure all of the accessory belts are properly tensioned.

8–379 Diesel

1. Disconnect the batteries.
2. Remove the fan and fan shroud.

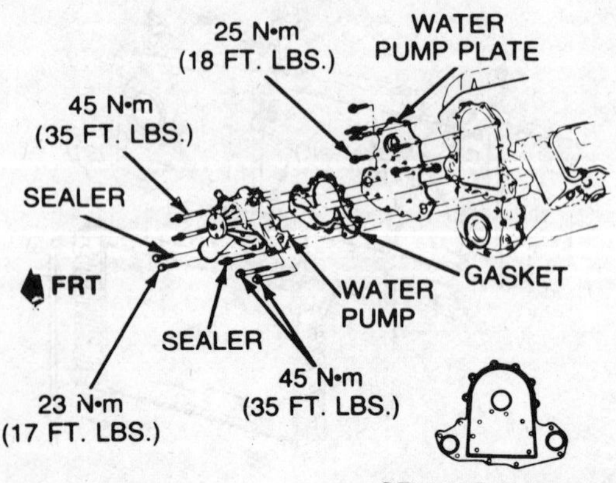

379 diesel water pump assembly. Note sealer application surface

3. Drain the radiator.

CAUTION: *When draining the coolant, keep in mind that cats and dogs are attracted by the ethylene glycol antifreeze, and are quite likely to drink any that is left in an uncovered container or in puddles on the ground. This will prove fatal in sufficient quantity. Always drain the coolant into a sealable container. Coolant should be reused unless it is contaminated or several years old.*

4. If the truck is equipped with air conditioning, remove the A/C hose bracket nuts.
5. Remove the oil filler tube.
6. Remove the generator pivot bolt and remove the generator belt.
7. Remove the generator lower bracket.
8. Remove the power steering belt and secure it out of the way.
9. Remove the air conditioning belt if equipped.
10. Disconnect the by-pass hose and the lower radiator hose.
11. Remove the water pump bolts. Remove the water pump plate and gasket and water pump. If the pump gasket is to be replaced, remove the plate attaching bolts to the water pump and remove (and replace) the gasket.
12. When installing the pump, the flanges must be free of oil. Apply an anaerobic sealer (GM part #1052357 or equvalent) as shown in the accompanying illustration.

NOTE: *The sealer must be wet to the touch when the bolts are torqued.*

13. Attach the water pump and plate assembly. Torque the bolts to specifications.
14. Assemble the remaining components in the reverse order of removal. Fill the cooling system, start the engine and check for leaks.

Cylinder Head

REMOVAL AND INSTALLATION

Inline Six Cylinder

1. Drain the cooling system and remove the air cleaner. Disconnect the PCV hose. If equipped, disconnect the air injection hose.

CAUTION: *When draining the coolant, keep in mind that cats and dogs are attracted by the ethylene glycol antifreeze, and are quite likely to drink any that is left in an uncovered container or in puddles on the ground. This will prove fatal in sufficient quantity. Always drain the coolant into a sealable container. Coolant should be reused unless it is contaminated or several years old.*

2. Disconnect the accelerator pedal rod at the bellcrank on the manifold, and the fuel and vacuum lines at the carburetor.
3. Disconnect the exhaust pipe at the manifold flange, then remove the manifold bolts and clamps and remove the manifolds and carburetor as an assembly. On those 1975 and later engines with the intake manifold integral with the head, remove the carburetor and the exhaust manifold.
4. Remove the fuel and vacuum line retaining clip from the water outlet. Then disconnect the wire harness from the heat sending unit and coil, leaving the harness clear of clips on the rocker arm cover.
5. Disconnect the radiator hose at the water outlet housing and the battery ground strap at the cylinder head.
6. Disconnect the wires and remove the spark plugs. Disconnect the coil-to-distributor primary wire lead at the coil and remove the coil on models without HEI.
7. Remove the rocker arm cover. Back off the rocker arm nuts, pivot the rocker arms to clear the pushrods and remove the pushrods.
8. Remove the cylinder head bolts, cylinder head and gasket.

To install:

1. Place a new cylinder head gasket over the dowel pins in the cylinder block with the bed up. Do not use sealer on composition steel/asbestos gaskets.
2. Guide and lower the cylinder head into place over the dowels and gasket.
3. Use sealant on the cylinder head bolts, install and tighten them down slightly.
4. Tighten the cylinder head bolts a little at a time with a torque wrench in the correct sequence. Final torque should be as specified.
5. Install the valve pushrods down through the cylinder head openings and seat them in their lifter sockets.

6. Install the rocker arms, balls and nuts and tighten the rocker arm nuts until all pushrod play is taken up.

7. Install the thermostat, the thermostat housing and the water outlet using new gaskets. Then connect the radiator hose.

8. Install the temperature sending switch.

9. Install the spark plugs.

10. Use new plug gaskets (if required) and torque to specifications.

11. Install the coil then connect the heat sending unit and the coil primary wires, and the battery ground cable at the cylinder head.

12. Clean the surfaces and install a new gasket over the manifold studs. Install the manifold. Install the bolts and clamps and torque as specified.

13. Connect the throttle linkage.

14. Connect the PCV fuel and vacuum lines and secure the lines in the clip at the water outlet. Connect the air injection line.

15. Fill the cooling system and check for leaks.

16. Adjust the valve lash as explained later.

17. Install the rocker arm cover and position the wiring harness in the clips.

18. Clean and install the air cleaner.

V6s

1. Disconnect the negative battery cable.
2. Remove the engine cover.
3. Remove the intake manifold as described later.
4. Remove the exhaust manifold as describer later.
5. Remove the air pipe at the rear of the head (right cylinder head).
6. Remove the generator mounting bolt at the cylinder head (right cylinder head).
7. Remove the power steering pump and brackets from the cylinder head, and lay them aside (left cylinder head).
8. Remove the air conditioner compressor, and lay it aside (left cylinder head).
9. Remove the rocker arm cover as outlined previously.
10. Remove the spark plugs.
11. Remove the pushrods, as outlined previously.
12. Remove the cylinder head bolts.
13. Remove the cylinder head.
14. Clean all gasket mating surfaces, install a new gasket and reinstall the cylinder head.
15. Install the cylinder heads using new gaskets. Install the gaskets with the head up.

    NOTE: *Coat a steel gasket on both sides with sealer. If a composition gasket is used, do not use sealer.*
16. Clean the bolts, apply sealer to the threads, and install them hand tight.
17. Tighten the head bolts a little at a time in the sequence shown. Head bolt torque is listed in the Torque Specifications chart.
18. Install the intake and exhaust manifolds.
19. Torque the cylinder head bolts to 65 ft.lb. and adjust the rocker arms.
20. Install the remaining components in the reverse of the removal procedure.

Gasoline V8s

1. Remove the intake manifold as described later.
2. Remove the exhaust manifolds as described later and tie out of the way.
3. If the van is equipped with air conditioning, remove the A/C compressor and the forward mounting bracket and lay the compressor aside. Do not disconnect any of the refrigerant lines.
4. Back off the rocker arm nuts and pivot the rocker arms out of the way so that the pushrods can be removed. Identify the pushrods so that they can be installed in their original positions.
5. Remove the cylinder head bolts and remove the heads.
6. Install the cylinder heads using new gaskets. Install the gaskets with the head up.

    NOTE: *Coat a steel gasket on both sides with sealer. If a composition gasket is used, do not use sealer.*
7. Clean the bolts, apply sealer to the threads, and install them hand tight.
8. Tighten the head bolts a little at a time in the sequence shown. Head bolt torque is listed in the Torque Specifications chart.
9. Install the intake and exhaust manifolds.
10. Adjust the rocker arms as explained later.

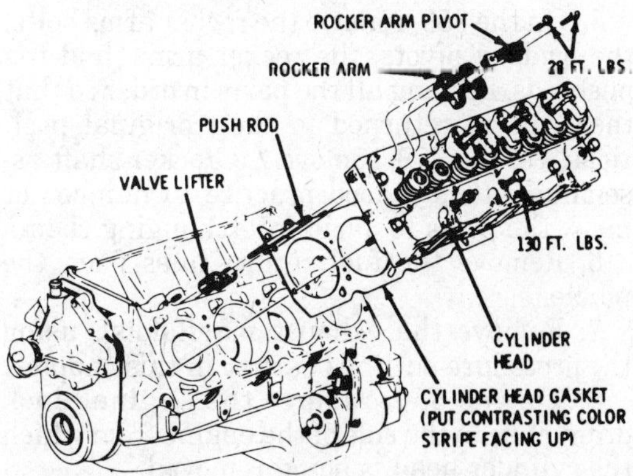

Typical Chevrolet gasoline V8 cylinder head installation, all engines similar

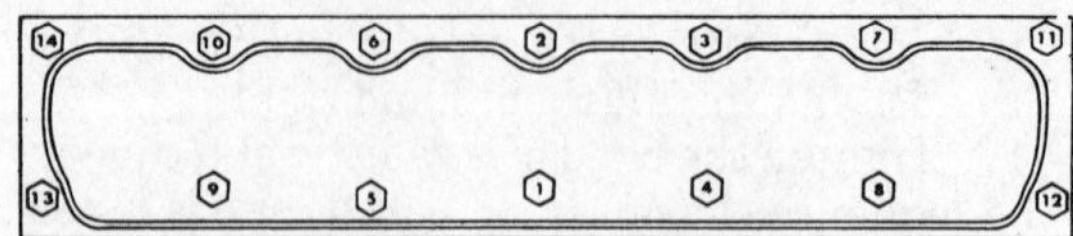

Six cylinder head torque sequence

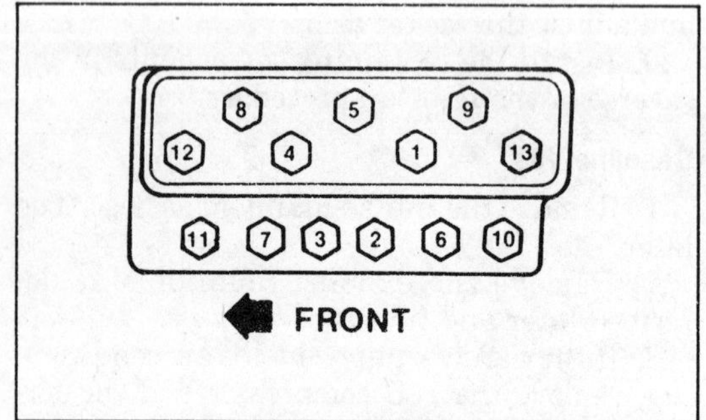

V6 cylinder head bolt tightening sequence.

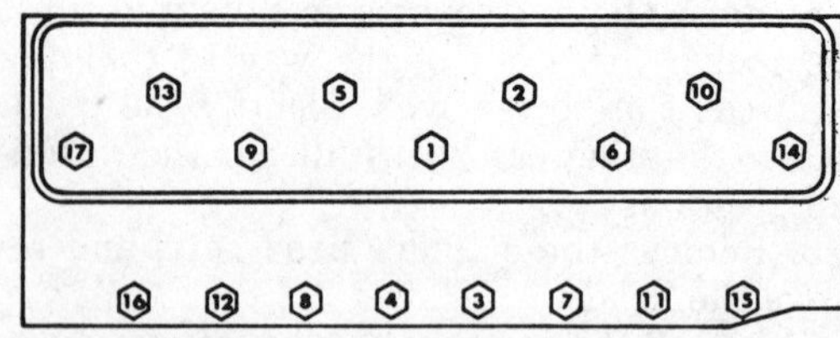

V8 cylinder head torque sequence

Diesel Engines

1. Remove the intake manifold, using the procedure outlined above.
2. Remove the rocker arm cover(s), after removing any accessory brackets which interfere with cover removal.
3. Disconnect and label the glow plug wiring.
4. If the right cylinder head is being removed, remove the ground strap from the head.
5. On the 350, remove the rocker arms bolts, the bridged pivots, the rocker arms, and the pushrods, keeping all the parts in order so that they can be returned to their original positions. On the 379, remove the rocker shaft assemblies. It is a good practice to number or mark the parts to avoid interchanging them.
6. Remove the fuel return lines from the nozzles.
7. Remove the exhaust manifold(s), using the procedure outlined earlier in this chapter.
8. On the 350, remove the engine block drain plug on the side of the engine from which the cylinder head is being removed.
9. Remove the head bolts. Remove the cylinder head.
10. To install, first clean the mating surfaces

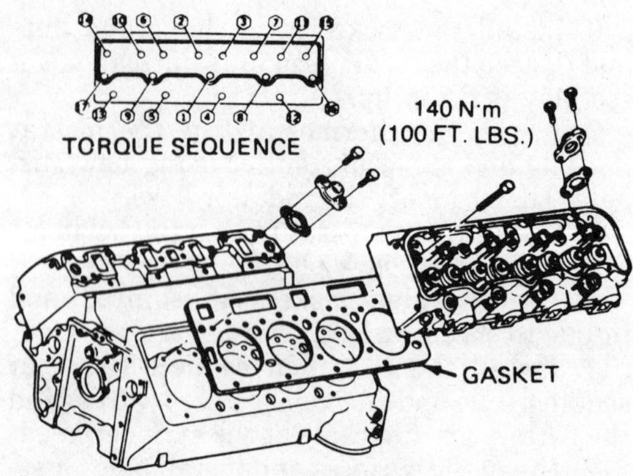

379 diesel cylinder head installation and torque sequence

thoroughly. Install new head gaskets on the engine block. Do NOT coat the gaskets with any sealer on either engine. The gaskets have a special coating that eliminates the need for sealer. The use of sealer will interfere with this coating and cause leaks. Install the cylinder head onto the block.

11. Clean the head bolts thoroughly. On the 350, dip the bolts in clean engine oil and install them into the cylinder block until the heads of the bolts lightly contact the cylinder head. On the 379, the left rear head bolt must be installed into the head prior to head installation. Coat the threads of the 379 cylinder head bolts with sealing compound (GM part #1052080 or equivalent) before installation.
12. On the 350, tighten the bolts in the illustrated sequence to 100 ft.lb. When all the bolts have been tightened to this figure, begin the tightening sequence again, and torque each bolt gradually in the sequence shown until the final torque specified (100 ft.lb.) is met.
13. Install the engine block drain plugs on the 350, the exhaust manifolds, the fuel return lines, the glow plug wiring, and the ground strap for the right cylinder head.
14. Install the valve train assembly. Refer to the Diesel Engine Rocker Arm Replacement in this chapter for the valve lifter bleeding procedures.
15. Install the intake manifold.
16. Install the valve covers. These are sealed with RTV type silicone sealer instead of a gasket. See the Valve Cover procedure for proper sealer application. Install the cover to the head within 10 minutes, while the sealer is still wet.

CLEANING AND INSPECTION

Gasoline Engines

NOTE: *Any diesel cylinder head work should be handled by a reputable machine shop familiar with diesel engines. Disassembly, valve lapping, and assembly can be completed by the following engine procedures.*

One the complete valve train has been removed from the cylinder head(s), the head itself can be inspected, cleaned and machined (if necessary). Set the head(s) on a clean work space, so the combustion chambers are facing up. Begin cleaning the chambers and ports with a hardwood chisel or other non-metallic tool (to avoid nicking or gouging the chamber, ports, and especially the valve seats). Chip away the major carbon deposits, then remove the remainder of carbon with a wire brush fitted to an electric drill.

NOTE: *Be sure that the carbon is actually removed, rather than just burnished.*

After decarbonizing is completed, take the head(s) to a machine shop and have the head hot tanked. In this process, the head is lowered into a hot chemical bath that very effectively cleans all grease, corrosion, and scale from all internal and external head surfaces. Also have the machinist check the valve seats and recut them if necessary. When you bring the clean head(s) home, place them on a clean surface. Completely clean the entire valve train with solvent.

CHECKING FOR HEAD WARPAGE

Lay the head down with the combustion chambers facing up. Place a straight edge across the gasket surface of the head, both diagonally and straight across the center. Using a flat feeler gauge, determine the clearance at the center of the straight edge. If warpage exceeds 0.003" (0.0762mm) in a 6" (152mm) span, or 0.006" (0.152mm) over the total length, the cylinder head must be resurfaced (which is akin to planing a piece of wood). Resurfacing can be performed at most machine shops.

NOTE: *When resurfacing the cylinder head(s) of V8 engines, the intake manifold mounting position is altered, and must be corrected by machining a proportionate amount from the intake manifold flange.*

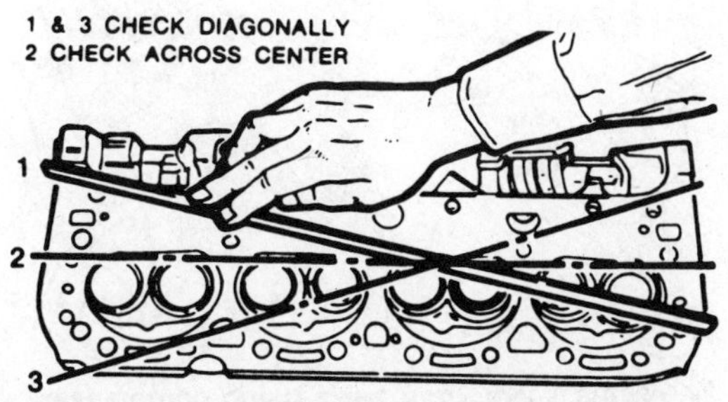

Check the cylinder head mating surface for warpage with a precision straight edge

Have the valve seat concentricity checked at a machine shop

RESURFACING

Cylinder head resurfacing should be done by a qualified machine shop.

Valves and Springs

REMOVAL AND INSTALLATION

Cylinder heads Removed

1. Remove the head(s), and place on a clean surface.
2. Using a suitable spring compressor (for pushrod type overhead valve engines), compress the valve spring and remove the valve spring cap key. Release the spring compressor and remove the valve spring and cap (and valve rotator on some engines).

NOTE: *Use care in removing the keys. They are easily lost.*

3. Remove the valve seals from the intake valve guides. Throw these old seals away, as you'll be installing new seals during reassembly.
4. Slide the valves out of the head from the combustion chamber side.
5. Make a holder for the valves out of a piece of wood or cardboard, as outlined for the pushrods in gasoline engine Cylinder Head Removal. Make sure you number each hole in the cardboard to keep the valves in proper order. Slide the valves out of the head from the combustion chamber side. They MUST be installed as they were removed.

Cylinder Head(s) Installed

It is often not necessary to remove the cylinder head(s) in order to service the valve train. Such is the case when valve seals need to be replaced. Valve seals can be easily replaced with the head(s) on the engine. The only special

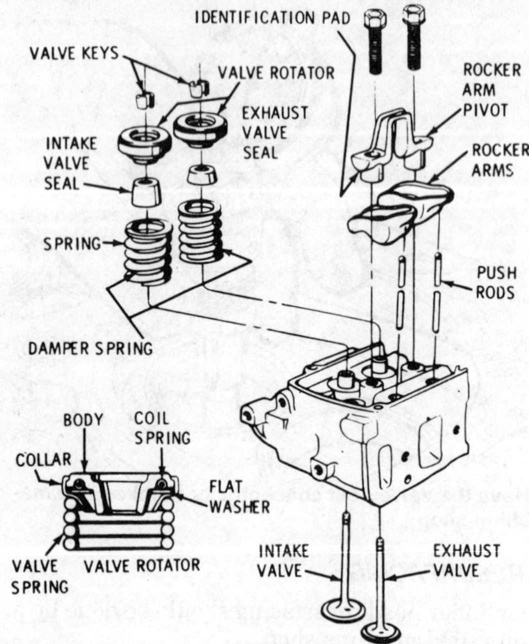

Typical valve train, all gasoline engines similar

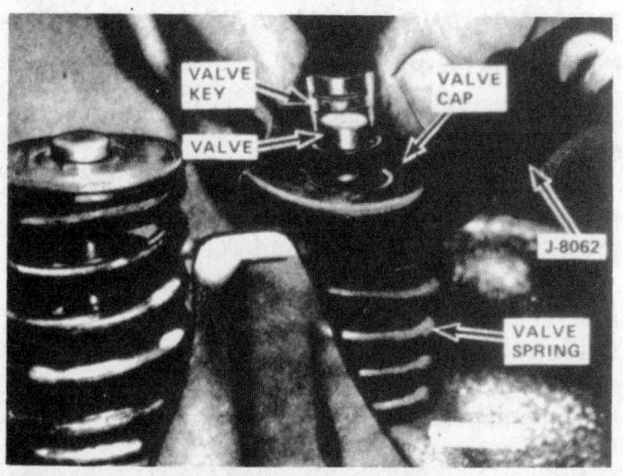

Use care not to lose the valve keys when compressing the valve springs. A dab of grease on the keys holds them in place during installation.

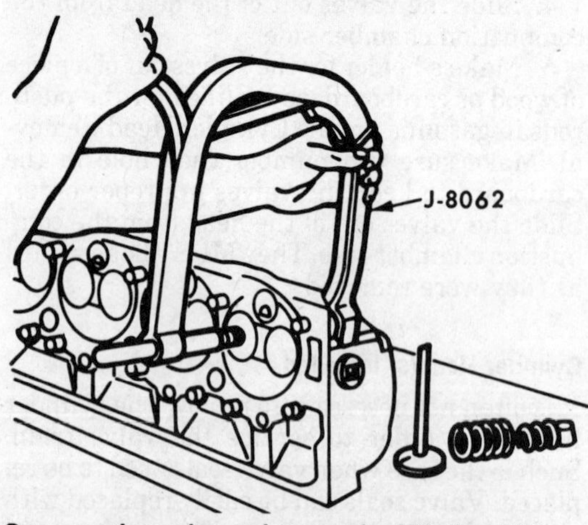

Compressing valve springs on the 379 diesel V8

equipment needed for this job are an air line adapter (sold in most auto parts stores), which screws a compressed air line into the spark plug hole of the cylinder on which you are working, and a valve spring compressor. A source of compressed air is needed, of course.

1. Remove the valve cover as previously detailed.

2. Remove the spark plug, rocker arm and pushrod on the cylinder(s) to be serviced.

3. Install the air line adapter (GM tool #J-23590 or equivalent) into the spark plug hole. Turn on the air compressor to apply compressed air into the cylinder. This keeps the valves up in place.

NOTE: *Set the regulator of the air compressor at least 50 pounds to ensure adequate pressure.*

4. Using the valve spring compressor, compress the valve spring and remove the valve

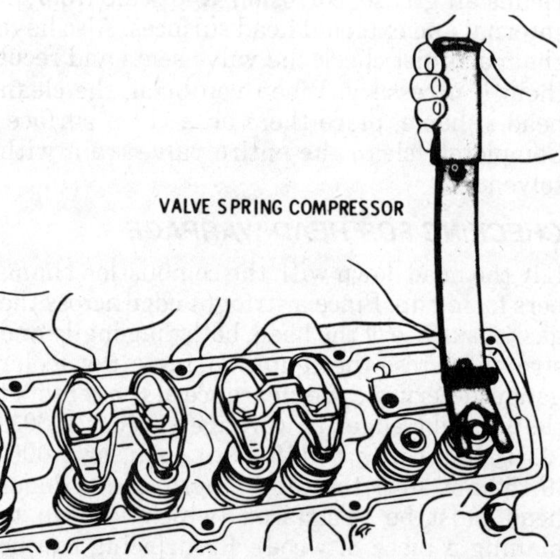

Removing the valve springs

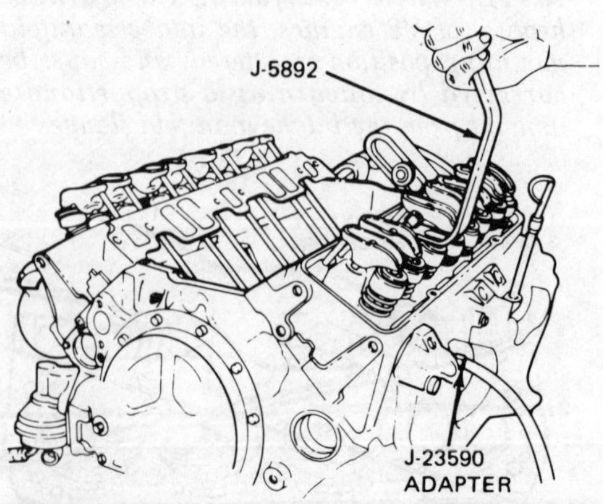

Replacing valve stem seals using compressed air an adapter for the spark plug holes, and a valve spring compressor

keys and keepers, the valve spring and damper.

5. Remove the valve stem seal.

6. To reassemble, oil the valve stem and new seal. Install a new seal over the valve stem. Set the spring, damper and keeper in place. Compress the spring. Coat the keys with grease to hold them onto the valve stem and install the keys, making sure they are seated fully in the keeper. Reinstall the valve cover after adjusting the valves, as outlined in this chapter.

INSPECTION

Inspect the valve faces and seats (in the head) for pits, burned spots and other evidence of poor seating. If a valve face is in such bad shape that the head of the valve must be ground in order to true up the face, discard the valve because the sharp edge will run too hot. The correct angle for valve faces is 45°. We recommend the refacing be done at a reputable machine shop.

Check the valve stem for scoring and burned spots. If not noticeably scored or damaged, clean the valve stem with solvent to remove all gum and varnish. Clean the valve guides using solvent an an expanding wire type valve guide cleaner. If you have access to a dial indicator for measuring valve stem-to-guide clearance, mount it so that the stem of the indicator is at 90° to the valve stem, and as close to the valve guide as possible. Move the valve off its seat, and measure the valve guide-to-stem clearance by rocking the stem back and forth to actuate the dial indicator. Measure the valve stems using a micrometer, and compare to specifications to determine whether stem or guide wear is responsible for the excess clearance. If a dial indicator and micrometer are not available to you, take your cylinder head and valves to a reputable machine shop for inspection.

Some of the engines covered in this guide are equipped with valve rotators, which double as valve spring caps. In normal operation the rotators put a certain degree of wear on the tip of the valve stem. This wear appears as concentric rings on the stem tip. However, if the rotator is not working properly, the wear may appear as straight notches or X patterns across the valve stem tip. Whenever the valves are removed from the cylinder head, the tips should be inspected for improper pattern, which could indicate valve rotator problems. Valve stem tips will have to be ground flat if rotator patterns are severe.

FOR DIMENSIONS, REFER TO SPECIFICATIONS

CHECK FOR BENT STEM

DIAMETER

VALVE FACE ANGLE

1/32" MINIMUM

THIS LINE PARALLEL WITH VALVE HEAD

Critical valve dimensions

Valve Seats

REMOVAL AND INSTALLATION

The valve seats in Chevrolet engines are not removable. Refer all servicing of the valve seats to a qualified machine shop.

Valve Guides

The engines covered in this guide use integral valve guides. That is, they are a part of the cylinder head and cannot be replaced. The guides can, however, be reamed oversize if they are found to be worn past an acceptable limit. Occasionally, a valve guide bore will be oversize as manufactured. These are marked on the inboard side of the cylinder heads on the machined surface just above the intake manifold.

If the guides must be reamed (this service is

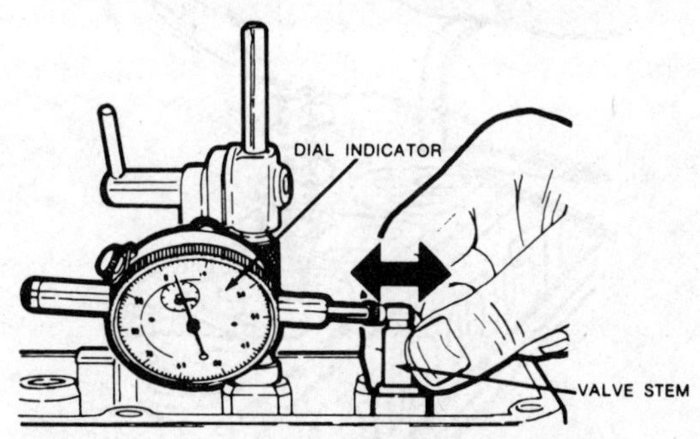

Check the valve stem-to-guide clearance

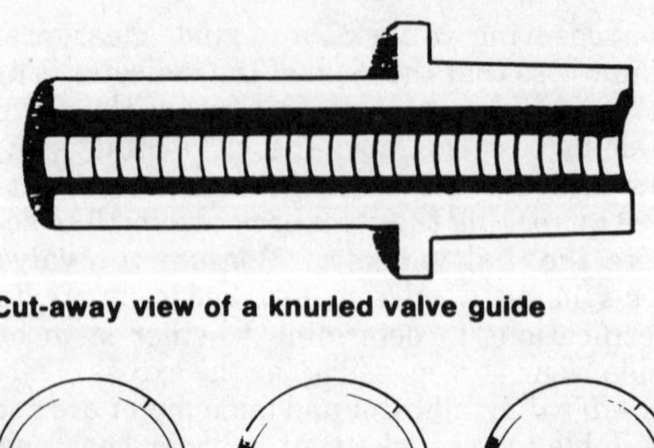

Cut-away view of a knurled valve guide

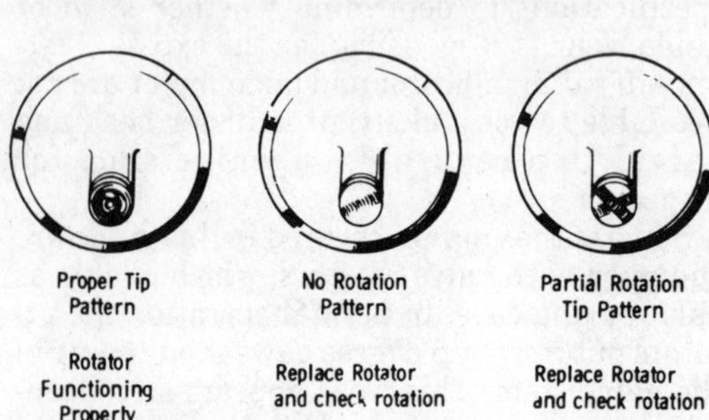

Valve stem wear

available at most machine shops), then valves with oversize stems must be fitted. Valves are usually available in 0.001" (0.0254mm), 0.003" (0.0762mm) and 0.005" (0.127mm) stem oversizes. Valve guides which are not excessively worn or distorted may, in some cases, be knurled rather than reamed. Knurling is a process in which the metal on the valve guide bore is displaced and raised, thereby reducing clearance. Knurling also provides excellent oil control. The option of knurling rather than reaming valve guides should be discussed with a reputable machinist or engine specialist.

LAPPING THE VALVES

When valve faces and seats have been refaced and recut, or if they are determined to be in good condition, the valves must be lapped in to ensure efficient sealing when the valve closes against the seat.

Lapping the valves by hand

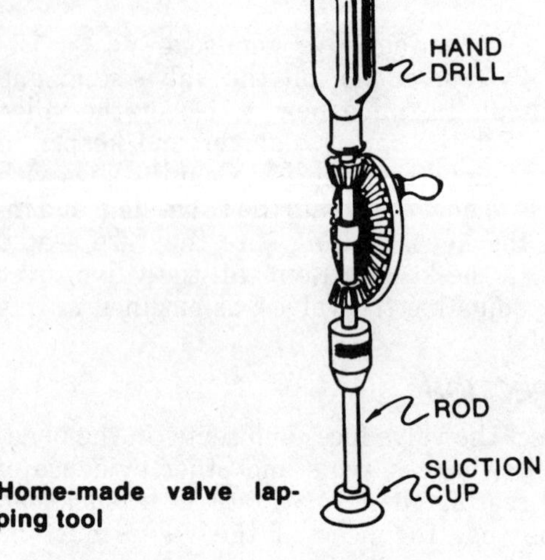

Home-made valve lapping tool

1. Invert the cylinder head so that the combustion chambers are facing up.
2. Lightly lubricate the valve stems with clean oil, and coat the valve seats with valve grinding compound. Install the valves in the head as numbered.
3. Attach the suction cup of a valve lapping tool to a valve head. You'll probably have to moisten the cup to securely attach the tool to the valve.
4. Rotate the tool between the palms. changing position and lifting the tool often to prevent grooving. Lap the valve until a smooth, polished seat is evident (you may have to add a bit more compound after some lapping is done).
5. Remove the valve and tool, and remove ALL traces of grinding compound with solvent soaked rag, or rinse the head with solvent.

NOTE: *Valve lapping can also be done by fastening a suction cup to a piece of drill rod in a hand eggbeater type drill. Proceed as above, using the drill as a lapping tool. Due to the higher speeds involved when using the hand drill, care must be exercised to avoid grooving the seat. Lift the tool and change direction of rotation often.*

Valve Springs

HEIGHT AND PRESSURE CHECK

1. Place the valve spring on a flat, clean surface next to a square.
2. Measure the height of the spring, and rotate it against the edge of the square to measure distortion (out-of-roundness). If spring height varies between springs by more than $^1/_{16}$" (1.5875mm) replace the spring.

A valve spring tester is needed to test spring test pressure, so the valve springs must usually be taken to a professional machine shop for this test. Spring pressure at the installed and compressed heights is checked, and a tolerance

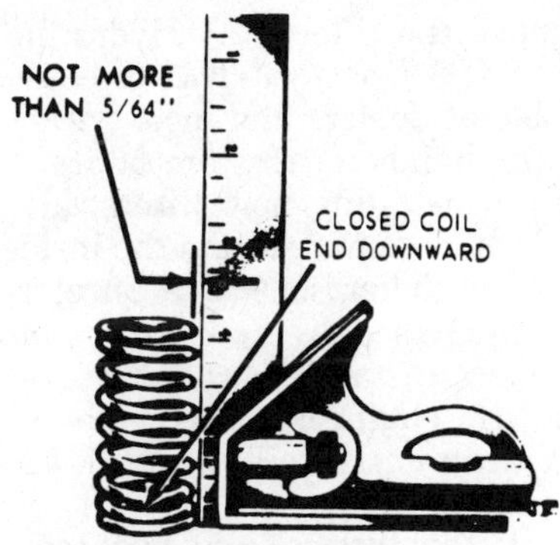

Check the valve spring free length and squareness

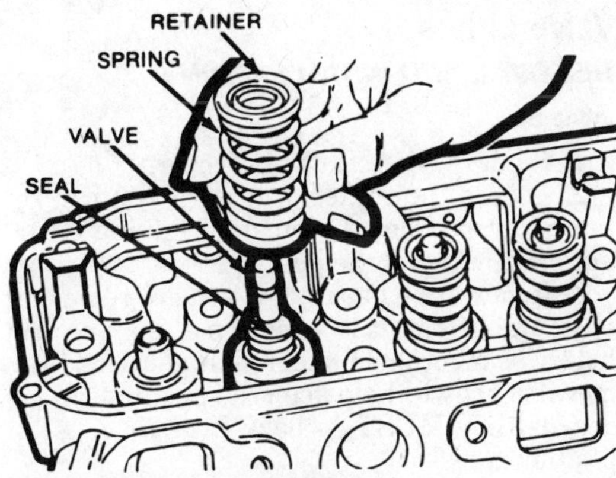

Installing valve stem seals

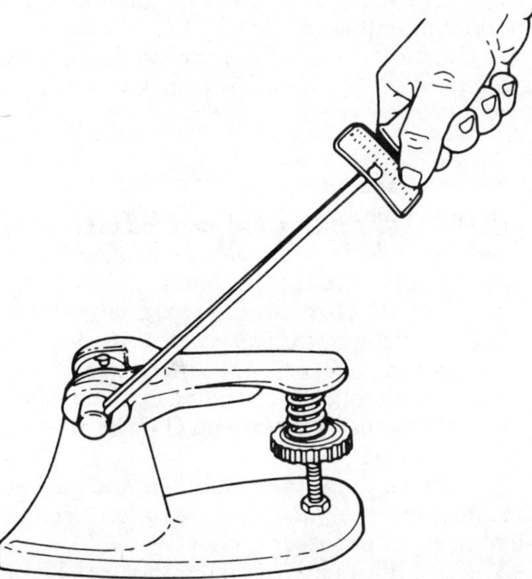
Have the valve spring test pressure checked professionally

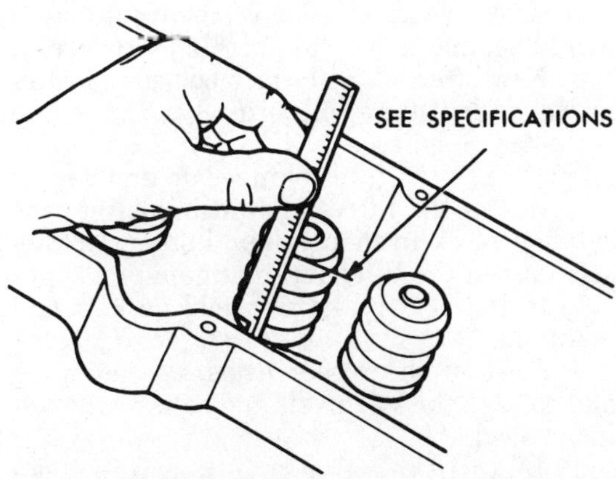

Check valve spring installed height

of plus or minus 5 lbs. is permissible on the springs covered in this guide.

VALVE INSTALLATION

NOTE: *For installing new valve stem seals without removing the cylinder head(s), see the procedure under Valves and Springs–Cylinder Head(s) Installed earlier in this chapter.*

New valve seals must be installed when the valve train is put back together. Certain seals slip over the valve stem and guide boss, while others require that the boss be machined. Teflon guide seals are available. Check with a machinist and/or automotive parts store for a suggestion on the proper seals to use.

NOTE: *Remember that when installing valve seals, a small amount of oil must be able to pass the seal to lubricate the valve guides; otherwise, excessive wear will result.*

To install the valves and rocker assembly:

1. Lubricate the valve stems with clean engine oil.
2. Install the valves in the cylinder head, one at a time, as numbered.
3. Lubricate and position the seals and valve springs, again a valve at a time.
4. Install the spring retainers, and compress the springs.
5. With the valve key groove exposed above the compressed valve spring, wipe some wheel bearing grease around the groove. This will retain the keys as you release the spring compressor.
6. Using needlenose pliers (or your fingers), place the keys in the key grooves. The grease should hold the keys in place. Slowly release the spring compressor. The valve cap or rotator will raise up as the compressor is released, retaining the keys.
7. Install the rocker assembly, and install the cylinder head(s).

Valve Lifters

REMOVAL AND INSTALLATION

Inline Six

1. Remove the rocker arm cover.
2. Loosen the rocker arm until you can rotate it away from the pushrod, giving clearance to the top of the pushrod.
3. Remove the pushrod. If you are replacing all of the lifters, it is wise to make a pushrod holder as mentioned under Cylinder Head Removal. This will help keep the pushrods in order, as they MUST go back in their original positions.
4. Remove the pushrod covers on the side of the block.

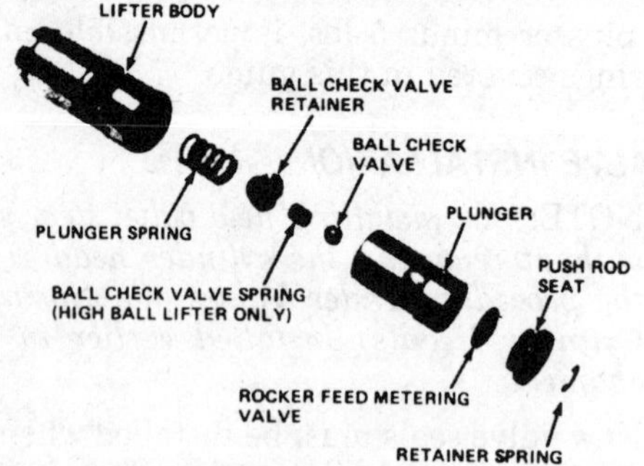

Valve lifter, exploded view

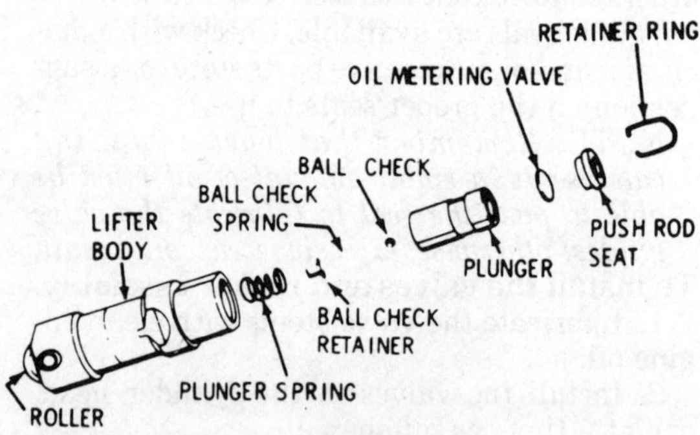

Roller lifter, 379 diesel engine

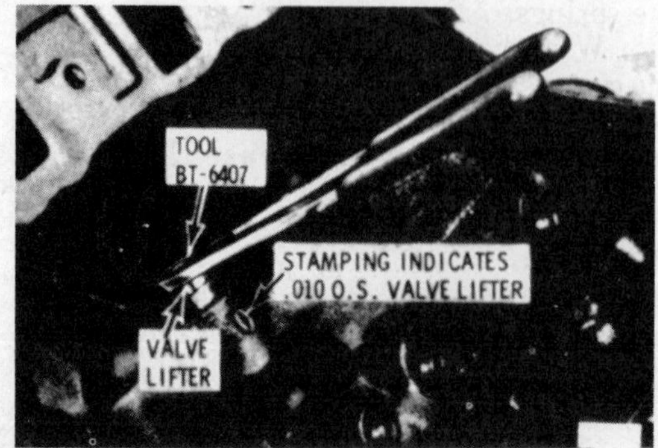

Removing hydraulic valve lifter

5. Remove the lifter(s). A Hydraulic lifter removal tool (GM part #J-3049 or equivalent) is available at dealers and most parts stores, and is quite handy for this procedure.
6. Before installing new lifters, all sealer coating must be removed from the inside. This can be done with kerosene or carburetor cleaning solvent. Also, the new lifters must be primed before installation, as dry lifters will seize when the engine is started. Submerge the lifters in clean engine oil and work the lifter plunger up and down.
7. Install the lifter(s) and pushrod(s) into the cylinder block in their original positions.
8. Pivot the rocker arm back into its original position. With the lifter on the base circle of the camshaft (valve closed), tighten the rocker arm nut to 20 ft.lb. Do not over torque. You will have to rotate the crankshaft to do the individual valves.
9. Replace the pushrod covers using new gaskets. Replace the rocker arm cover, using a new gasket or sealer.

Gasoline V6 and V8

NOTE: *Valve lifters and pushrods should be kept in order so they can be reinstalled in their original position. Some engines will have both standard size and 0.010" (0.254mm) oversize valve lifters as original equipment. The oversize lifters are etched with an* **O** on their sides. The cylinder block will also be marked with an **O** if the oversize lifter is used.

1. Remove the intake manifold and gasket.
2. Remove the valve covers, rocker arm assemblies and pushrods.
3. If the lifters are coated with varnish, apply carburetor cleaning solvent to the lifter body. The solvent should dissolve the varnish in about 10 minutes.
4. Remove the lifters. On diesels, remove the lifter retainer guide bolts, and remove the guides. A special tool for removing lifters is available, and is helpful for this procedure.
5. New lifter MUST be primed before installation, as dry lifters will seize when the engine is started. Submerge the lifters in clean engine oil and work the lifter plunger up and down.
6. Install the lifters and pushrods into the cylinder block in their original order. On diesels, install the lifter retainer guide.
7. Install the intake manifold gaskets and manifold.
8. Position the rocker arms, (rocker arms and balls on the V6) pivots and bolts on the cylinder head.
9. Install the valve covers, connect the spark plug wires and install the air cleaner.

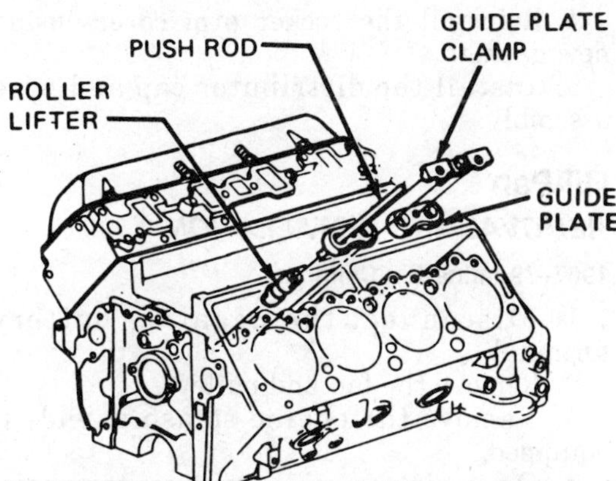

379 diesel lifer and guide plate access through hole

8–379 Diesel

1. Remove the valve covers as previously detailed.
2. Remove the rocker shaft assemblies.
3. Remove the cylinder head(s).
4. Remove the guide clamps and guide plates. It may be necessary to use mechanical fingers to remove the guide plates.
5. Using GM tool #J-29834 or another suitable lifter removal tool and a magnet, remove the lifter(s) through the access in the block.
6. Coat the lifters with clean engine oil before installation. If installing new lifters, they bust be primed first by working the lifter plunger while the lifter is submerged in clean kerosene or diesel fuel. Lifters that have not been primed will seize when the engine is started.
7. Install the lifters in their original positions in the block. A lifter installation tool can be fabricated out of welding rod or similar gauge wire and may help.
8. Install the lifter guide plate and guide plate clamp. The crankshaft must be turned 2 full rotations (720°) after assembly of the lifter guide plate clamp to insure free movement of the lifters in the guide plates.
9. Install the remainder of components in the reverse order of removal.

NOTE: *The pushrods must be installed with their painted ends facing UP.*

VALVE LASH ADJUSTMENT

All engines described in this book use hydraulic lifters, which require no periodic adjustment. In the event of cylinder head removal or any operation that requires disturbing the rocker arms, the rocker arms will have to be adjusted.

1967–71

Normalize the engine temperature by running it for several minutes. Shut the engine off and

Six cylinder valve arrangement

remove the valve cover(s). After valve cover removal, torque the cylinder heads to specification. The use if oil stopper clips, readily available on the market is recommended to prevent oil splatter when adjusting valve lash. Restart the engine. Valve lash is set with the engine warm and idling.

Turn the rocker arm nut counterclockwise until the rocker arm begins to clatter. Reverse the direction and turn the rocker arm down slowly until the clatter just stops. This is the zero lash position. Turn the nut down an additional ¼ turn and wait ten seconds until the engine runs smoothly. Continue with additional ¼ turns, waiting ten seconds each time, until the nut has been turned down 1 full turn from the zero lash position. This one turn, preload adjustment must be performed to allow the lifter to adjust itself and prevents possible interference between the valves and pistons. Noisy lifters should be cleaned or replaced.

1972–86

1. Remove the rocker covers and gaskets.
2. Adjust the valves on the inline six cylinder engines as follows:
   a. Mark the distributor housing with a piece of chalk at No. 1 and 6 plug wire positions. Remove the distributor cap with the plug wires attached.
   b. Crank the engine until the distributor rotor points to No. 1 cylinder and the points are open. At this point, adjust the following valves:
   - No. 1 – Exhaust and Intake
   - No. 2 – Intake
   - No. 3 – Exhaust
   - No. 4 – Intake
   - No. 5 – Exhaust

   c. Back out the adjusting nut until lash is felt at the pushrod, then turn the adjusting nut in until all lash is removed. This can be determined by checking pushrod end play while turning the adjusting nut. When all play has been removed, turn the adjusting nut in 1 full turn.
   d. Crank the engine until the distributor rotor points to No. 6 cylinder and the points are open. The following valves can be adjusted:
   - No. 2 – Exhaust
   - No.3 – Intake
   - No. 4 – Exhaust
   - No. 5 – Intake
   - No. 6 – Intake and Exhaust

3. Adjust the valves on V6 and V8 engines as follows:

a. Crank the engine until the mark on the damper aligns with the TDC or 0° mark on the timing tab and the engine is in No. 1 firing position. This can be determined by placing the fingers on the No. 1 cylinder valves as the marks align. If the valves do not move, it is in No. 1 firing position. If the valves move, it is in No. 6 firing position (No. 4 on the V6) and the crankshaft should be rotated 1 more revolution to the No. 1 firing position.

b. The adjustment is made in the same manner as 6 cylinder engines.

c. With the engine in No. 1 firing position, the following valves can be adjusted:

V6 Engines
- Exhaust – 1, 5, 6,
- Intake – 1, 2, 3,

V8 Engines
- Exhaust – 1,3,4,8
- Intake – 1,2,5,7

d. Crank the engine 1 full revolution until the marks are again in alignment. This is No. 6 firing position (No. 4 on the V6). The following valves can now be adjusted:

V6 Engines
- Exhaust – 2, 3, 4
- Intake – 4, 5, 6

V8 Engines
- Exhaust – 2,5,6,7
- Intake – 3,4,6,8

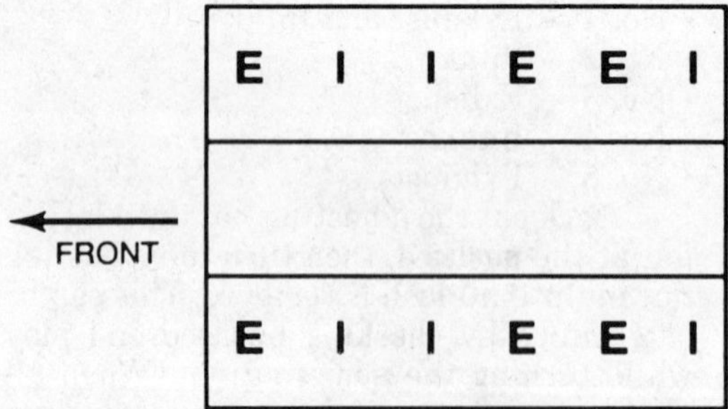

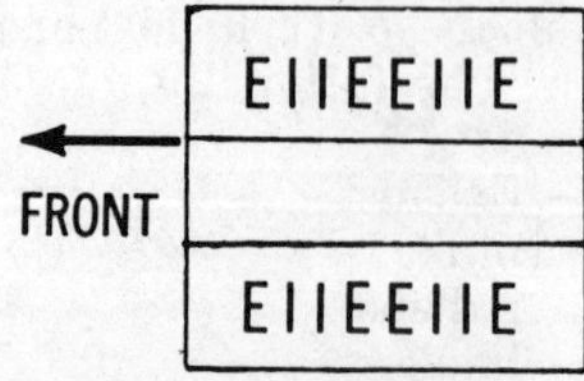

V8 valve arrangement

4. Reinstall the rocker arm covers using new gaskets.

5. Install the distributor cap and wire assembly.

Oil Pan

REMOVAL AND INSTALLATION

1967–79 Inline Six Cylinder

1. Disconnect the negative battery terminal.
2. Remove the fan and pulley.
3. Remove the engine splash shields if equipped.
4. On vehicles with automatic transmissions, disconnect and plug the cooler lines.
5. Drain the radiator and disconnect the lower radiator hose at the radiator.

CAUTION: *When draining the coolant, keep in mind that cats and dogs are attracted by the ethylene glycol antifreeze, and are quite likely to drink any that is left in an uncovered container or in puddles on the ground. This will prove fatal in sufficient quantity. Always drain the coolant into a sealable container. Coolant should be reused unless it is contaminated or several years old.*

6. If equipped, remove the accessory drive pulley and shroud.
7. Install a support under the damper.
8. Place a jack under the support on the damper and jack the engine to clear the front mounts.
9. Remove the crossmember to frame bolts and lower the crossmember to rest on the front springs.
10. Drain the oil and remove the oil pan. Discard the gaskets and seals.
11. Installation is the reverse of removal. Use new gaskets and a new seal in the rear main bearing cap and crankcase front cover. Do not use sealer. Fill the engine with coolant and oil. Start the engine and check for leaks.

1970–75 Inline 6-Cylinder

1. Disconnect the negative battery terminal.
2. Raise and support the vehicle. Disconnect the starter leaving the wires attached and swing it out of the way.
3. If there is not enough clearance, remove the bolts securing the engine mounts to the crossmember and raise the engine high enough to insert a 2″ x 4″ (51mm x 102mm) piece of wood between the engine mounts and the crossmember brackets.
4. Drain the engine oil.
5. Remove the flywheel and converter cover.
6. Remove the oil pan.
7. Clean all gasket surfaces and install a

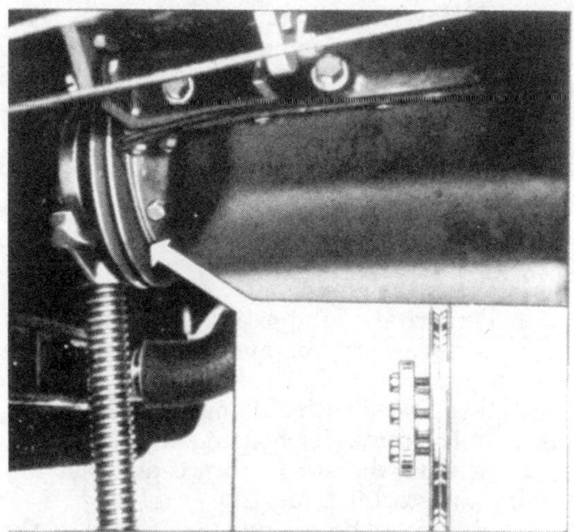

Supporting the engine (1967–69 six cylinder) for oil pan removal

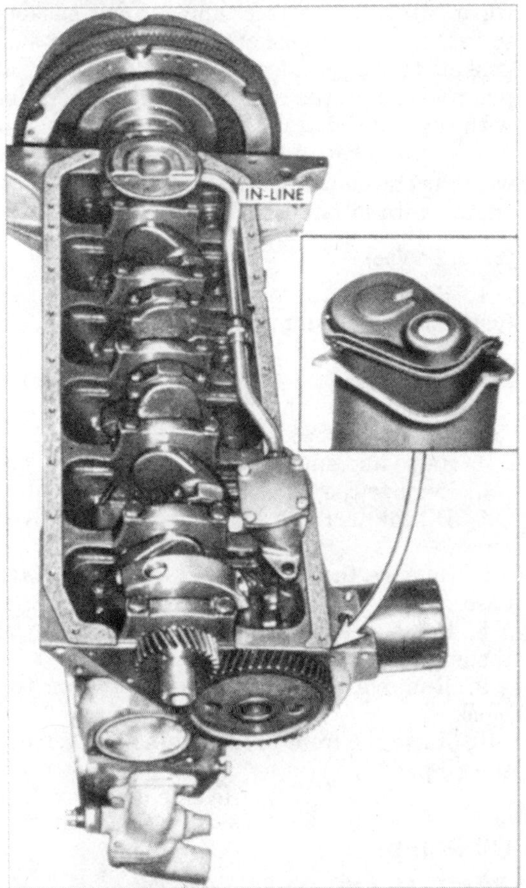

Six cylinder oil pan and gasket seals

new seal in the rear main bearing groove and a new seal in the crankcase front cover. Installation is the reverse of removal. Install new side gaskets on the block, but do not use sealer. Fill the engine with oil and run the engine, checking for leaks.

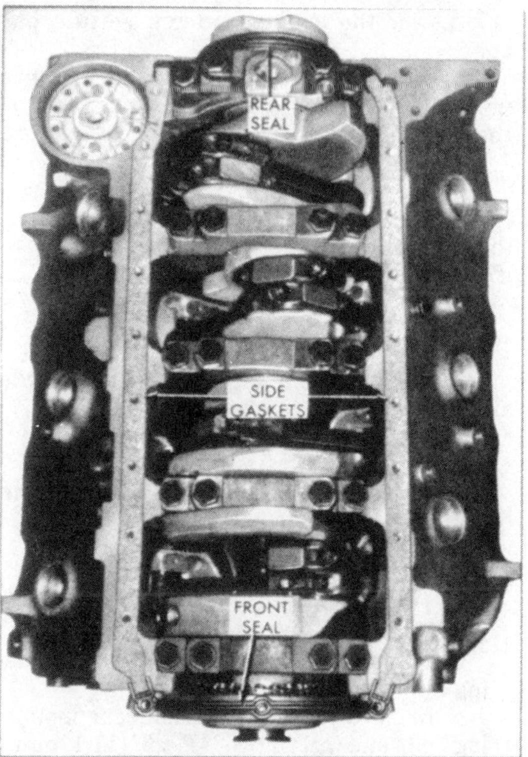

V8 oil pan and gasket seals

Engine blocked for oil pan removal (1970–74 six)

1976–77 Inline 6-Cylinder

1. Disconnect the battery ground cable.
2. Drain the oil.
3. Remove the starter.
4. Remove the manual transmission flywheel splash shield or the automatic transmission converter housing underpan.
5. Support the front of the engine. Remove the engine mount through-bolts.
6. Raise the front of the engine enough to replace the through bolts in the engine half of the mounts.

7. Lower the engine and remove the pan bolts.
8. Clean all gasket surfaces and install a new seal in the rear main bearing cap and on the crankcase front cover. Install new side gaskets to the block, using sealer.
9. Replace the pan.
10. Raise the engine and replace the mount through bolts. Fill the engine with oil and run it, watching for leaks.

1978 and Later Inline 6-Cylinders

1. Disconnect the negative battery cable and remove the engine cover.
2. Remove the air cleaner and studs.
3. Remove the fan finger guard.
4. Remove the radiator upper supporting brackets.
5. Raise the van on a hoist.
6. On vans with manual transmissions:
   a. Disconnect the clutch cross shaft from the left front mounting bracket.
   b. Remove the transmission-to-bell housing upper bolt.
   c. Remove the transmission rear mounting bolts and install two $^{7}/_{16}$" x 3" (11.11mm x 76.2mm) bolts.
   d. Raise the transmission and place small pieces of 2" x 4" wooden blocks in between the mount and the crossmember.
7. Remove the starter motor.
8. Drain the engine oil.
9. Remove the engine mount through bolts.
10. Raise the engine slightly and place small 2" x 4" wooden blocks in between the mount and the block.
11. Remove the flywheel splash shield or the converter cover, as applicable.
12. Remove the oil pan attaching bolts and remove the oil pan.
13. Clean the gasket surface throughly and use a new gasket on installation.
14. Reverse the procedure to install.

4.3 Liter V6

A one piece type oil pan gasket is used.

1. Disconnect the negative battery cable. Raise the vehicle, support it safely, and drain the engine oil.
2. Remove the exhaust crossover pipe.
3. Remove the torque converter cover (on models with automatic transmission).
4. Remove the strut rods at the flywheel cover.
5. Remove the strut rod brackets at the front engine mountings.
6. Remove the starter.
7. Remove the oil pan bolts, nuts and reinforcements.
8. Remove the oil pan and gaskets.
9. Thoroughly clean all gasket surfaces and install a new gasket, using only a small amount of sealer at the front and rear corners of the oil pan.
10. Installation is the reverse of the removal procedure.

Gasoline V8

1. Drain the engine oil.
2. Remove the oil dipstick and tube.
3. If necessary remove the exhaust pipe crossover.
4. If equipped with automatic transmission, remove the converter housing pan.
5. Remove the starter brace and bolt and swing the starter aside.
6. Remove the oil pan and discard the gaskets.
7. Installation is the reverse of removal. Clean all gasket surfaces and use new gaskets to assemble. Use gasket sealer to retain side gaskets to the cylinder block. Install a new oil pan rear seal in the rear main bearing cap slot with the ends butting the side gaskets. Install a new front seal in the crankcase front cover with the ends butting the side gaskets. Fill the engine with oil and check for leaks.

Diesel Engines

1. Remove the vacuum pump and drive (with A/C or the oil pump drive (without A/C).
2. Disconnect the batteries and remove the dipstick.
3. Remove the upper radiator support and fan shroud.
4. Raise and support the car. Drain the oil.
5. Remove the flywheel cover.
6. Disconnect the exhaust and crossover pipes.
7. Remove the oil cooler lines at the filter base.
8. Remove the starter assembly. Support the engine with a jack.
9. Remove the engine mounts from the block.
10. Raise the front of the engine and remove the oil pan.
11. Installation is the reverse of removal.

Oil Pump

REMOVAL AND INSTALLATION

Inline 6-Cylinder

1. Drain the oil and remove the oil pan.
2. Remove the 2 flanged mounting bolts and remove the pickup pipe bolt.
3. Remove the pump and screen as an assembly.
4. To install, align the oil pump driveshafts

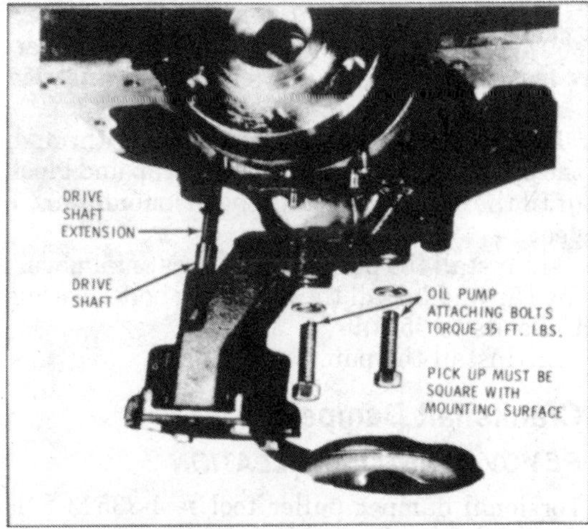

Oil pump installation, typical

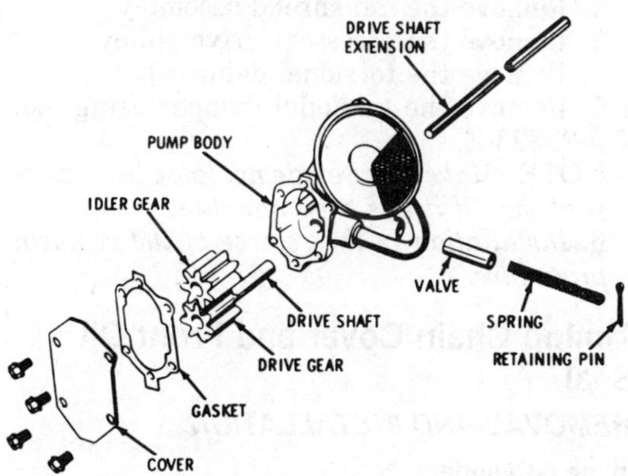

Oil pump exploded view

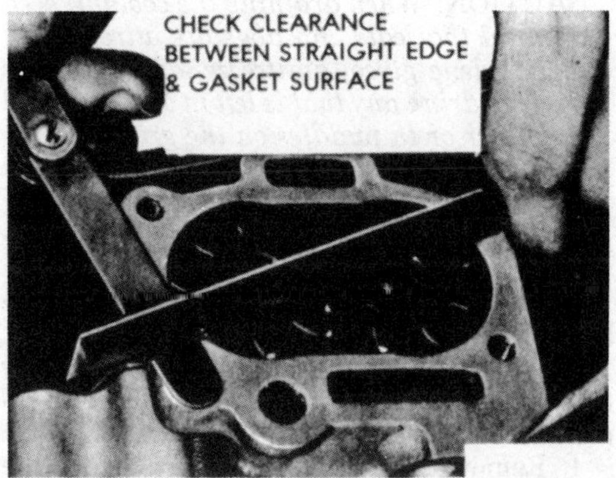

Checking oil pump end clearance

with the distributor tang and install the oil pump. Position the flange over the distributor lower bushing, using no gasket. The oil pump should slide easily into place. If not, remove it and reposition the slot to align with the distributor tang.

5. Reinstall the oil pan and fill the engine with oil.

4.3L V6

1. Remove the oil pan.
2. Remove the bolt attaching the pump to the rear main bearing cap. Remove the pump and the extension shaft, which will come out behind it.
3. If the pump has been disassembled, is being replaced, or for any reason oil has been removed from it, it must be primed. It can either be filled with oil before installing the cover plate (and oil kept within the pump during handling), or the entire pump cavity can be filled with petroleum jelly. IF THE PUMP IS NOT PRIMED, THE ENGINE COULD BE DAMAGED BEFORE IT RECEIVES ADEQUATE LUBRICATION WHEN YOU START IT.
4. Engage the extension shaft with the oil pump shaft. Align the slot on the top of the extension shaft with the drive tang on the lower end of the distributor driveshaft, and then position the pump at the rear main bearing cap so the mounting bolt can be installed. Install the bolt, torquing to 65 ft.lb.
5. Install the oil pan.

V8 and Diesel

1. Drain the oil and remove the oil pan.
2. Remove the bolt (two bolts on diesels) holding the pump to the rear main bearing cap. Remove the pump and extension shaft.
3. To install, assemble the pump and extension shaft to the rear main bearing cap aligning the slot on the top of the extension shaft with the drive tang on the distributor driveshaft. The installed position of the oil pump screen is with the bottom edge parallel to the oil pan rails. Further installation is the reverse of removal.

OVERHAUL

Inline Sixes

1. With the pump removed from the block, remove the four cover attaching screws, the cover, idler gear and drive gear and shaft.
2. Remove the pressure regulator valve and other related valve parts.

CAUTION: *Do not disturb the oil pickup pipe on the screen or body.*

3. Inspect the pump body for excessive wear or cracks, and inspect the pump gears for excessive wear, cracks or damage. Check the shaft for looseness in the housing. It should not be a sloppy fit. Check the inside of the cover for wear that would permit oil to leak past the ends of the gears. Remove any debris from the

surface of the screen, and check the screen for damage. Check the pressure regulator valve plunger for fit in the body.

4. Assembly is the reverse of the disassembly procedure. Tighten the cover screws to 8 ft.lb.

V6/V8 and Diesel

1. Remove the oil pump driveshaft extension.
2. Remove the cotter pin, spring and the pressure regulator valve.

NOTE: *Place your thumb over the pressure regulator bore before removing the cotter pin, as the spring is under pressure.*

3. Remove the oil pump cover attaching screws and remove the oil pump cover and gasket. Clean the pump in solvent or kerosene, and wash out the pickup screen.
4. Remove the drive gear and the idler gear from the pump body.
5. Check the gears for scoring and other damage. Install the gears if in good condition or replace them if damaged. Check gear end clearance by placing a straight edge over the gears and measuring the clearance between the straight edge and the gasket surface with a feeler gauge. End clearance for the gasoline V6 and V8 is 0.002" (0.051mm) to 0.0065" (0.165mm). If end clearance is excessive, check for scores in the cover that would bring the total clearance over the specs.
6. Check the gear side clearance by inserting the feeler gauge between the gear teeth and the side of the pump body. Clearance should be between 0.002" (0.051mm) and 0.005" (0.127mm).
7. Pack the inside of the pump completely with petroleum jelly. DO NOT USE ENGINE OIL. The pump MUST be primed this way or it will not produce any oil pressure when the engine is started.
8. Install the cover screws and tighten alternately and evenly to eight ft.lb.
9. Position the pressure valve into the pump cover, closed end first, then install the spring and retaining pin.

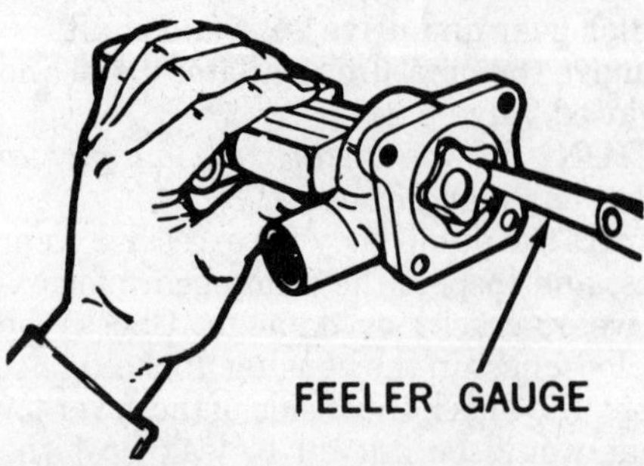

Measuring oil pump side clearance, typical

NOTE: *When assembling the driveshaft extension into the driveshaft, the end of the extension nearest the washers must be inserted into the driveshaft.*

10. Insert the driveshaft extension through the opening in the main bearing cap and block until the shaft mates into the distributor drive gear.
11. Install the pump onto the rear main bearing cap and install the attaching bolts. Torque the bolts to 35 ft.lb.
12. Install the pan.

Crankshaft Damper

REMOVAL AND INSTALLATION

Torsional damper puller tool # J-23523-E is required to perform this procedure.

1. Remove the fan belts, fan and pulley.
2. Remove the fan shroud assembly.
3. Remove the accessory drive pulley.
4. Remove the torsional damper bolt.
5. Remove the torsional damper using tool # J-23523-E.

NOTE: *Make sure you do not loose the crankshaft key, if it has been removed.*

6. *Installation is the reverse of the removal procedure.*

Timing Chain Cover and Front Oil Seal

REMOVAL AND INSTALLATION

Inline 6-Cylinder

1. Drain the engine coolant, remove the radiator hoses, and remove the radiator.

CAUTION: *When draining the coolant, keep in mind that cats and dogs are attracted by the ethylene glycol antifreeze, and are quite likely to drink any that is left in an uncovered container or in puddles on the ground. This will prove fatal in sufficient quantity. Always drain the coolant into a sealable container. Coolant should be reused unless it is contaminated or several years old.*

2. Remove the fan belt and any accessory belts. Remove the fan pulley.
3. A harmonic balancer puller is necessary to pull the balancer. Install the puller and remove the balancer.
4. Remove the two screws which attach the oil pan to the front cover. Remove the screws which attach the front cover to the block. Do not remove the cover yet.
5. Before the front cover is removed, it is necessary to cut the oil fan front seal. Pull the cover forward slightly.
6. Using a sharp knife or razor knife, cut the oil pan front seal flush with the cylinder block on both sides of the cover.

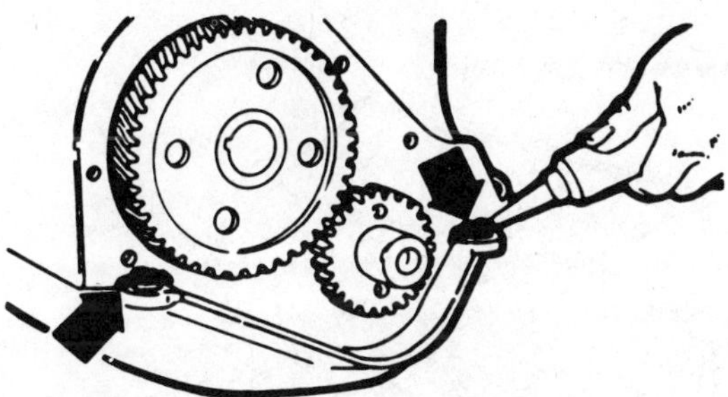

Applying sealer front cover mounting on the 250 inline six

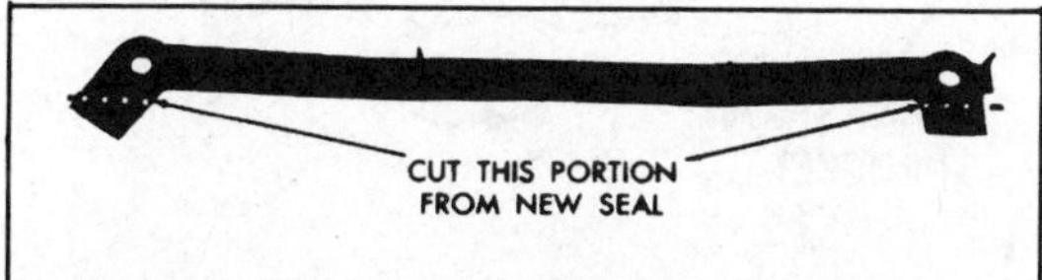

Oil pan front seal modification

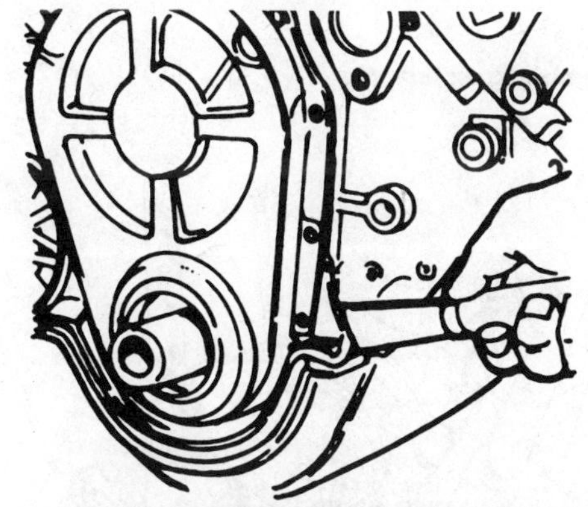

Cut the oil pan seal flush with the front of the block

Installing timing cover, inline six cylinder.

7. Remove the front cover and the attached portion of oil pan seal. Remove the front cover gasket from the block.

8. Install the front cover, first obtain an oil pan front seal. Cut the tabs from the new seal.

9. Install the seal in the front cover, pressing the tips into the holes provided in the cover. Coat the mating area of the front cover with a room temperature vulcanizing (RTV) sealer first.

10. Coat the new front cover gasket with sealer and install it on the cover.

11. Apply a ⅛" (3mm) bead of RTV sealer to the joint formed at the oil pan and cylinder block.

12. Install the front cover.

13. Install the harmonic balancer. Make sure the front cover seal is positioned evenly around the balancer. If you so not have access to a balancer installation tool (and you probably don't), you can either fabricate one using the illustration as a guide, or you can tap the balancer on using a brass or plastic mallet. If you use the last method, make sure the balancer goes on evenly.

14. The rest of the installation is in the reverse order of removal.

Gasoline V6s and V8s

1. Drain the cooling system.

CAUTION: *When draining the coolant, keep in mind that cats and dogs are attracted by the ethylene glycol antifreeze, and are quite likely to drink any that is left in an uncovered container or in puddles on the ground. This will prove fatal in sufficient quantity. Always drain the coolant into a sealable container. Coolant should be reused unless it is contaminated or several years old.*

2. Remove the crankshaft pulley and damper. Remove the water pump. Remove the screws holding the timing case cover to the block and remove the cover and gaskets.

3. Use a suitable tool to pry the old seal out of the front face of the cover.

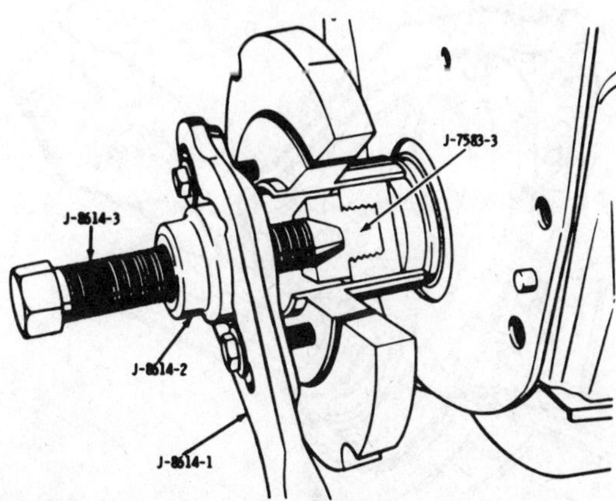

Removing harmonic balancer from end of crankshaft, all gasoline engines similar

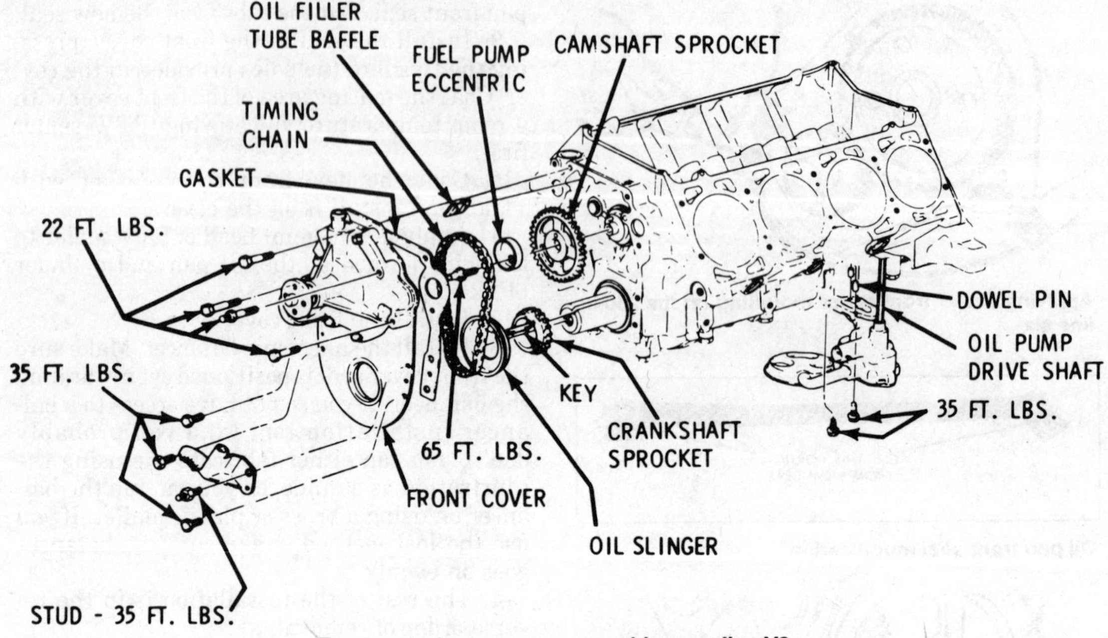

Front cover/water pump assembly, gasoline V8s

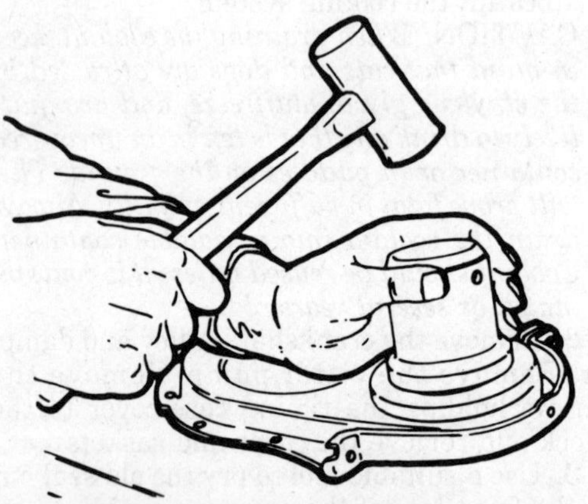

Seal installation with the cover removed

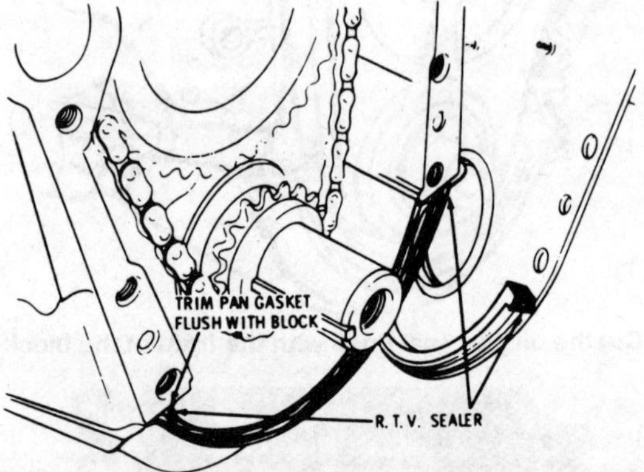

Sealer application

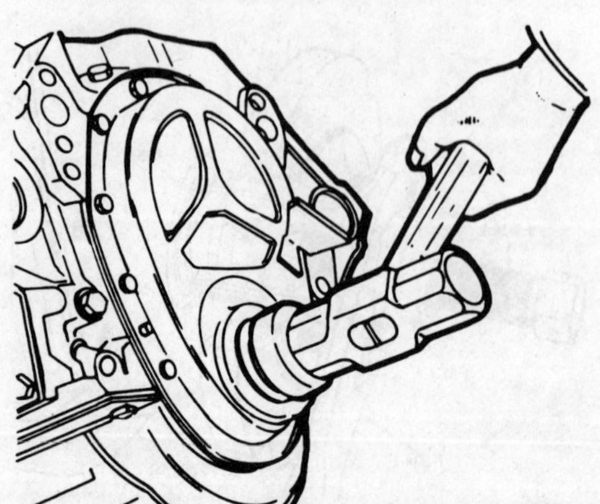

Seal installation with cover installed, V8s

4. Install the new seal so that the open end is toward the inside of the cover.

NOTE: *Coat the lip of the new seal with oil prior to installation.*

5. Check that the timing chain oil slinger is in place against the crankshaft sprocket.
6. Apply sealer to the front cover as shown in the accompanying illustration. Install the cover carefully onto the locating dowels.
7. Tighten the attaching screws to 6–8 ft.lb.

379 Diesel

1. Drain the cooling system.

CAUTION: *When draining the coolant, keep in mind that cats and dogs are attracted by the ethylene glycol antifreeze, and are quite likely to drink any that is left in an uncovered container or in puddles on the ground. This will prove fatal in sufficient quantity. Always drain the coolant into a sealable container. Coolant should be reused unless it is contaminated or several years old.*

2. Remove the water pump as outlined elsewhere in this chapter.
3. Rotate the crankshaft to align the marks on the injection pump driven gear and the camshaft gear as shown in the illustration.
4. Scribe a mark aligning the injection pump flange and the front cover.

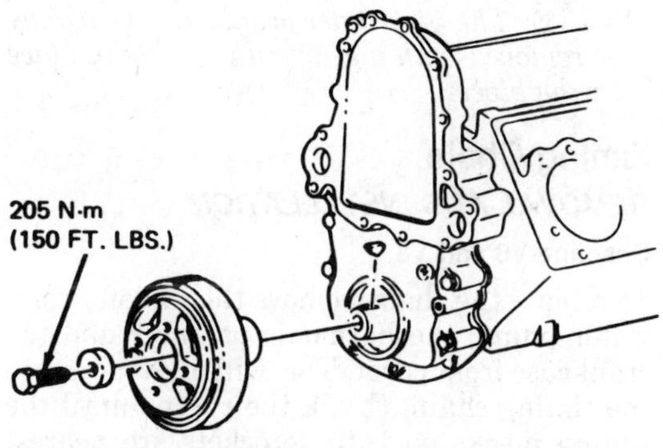

379 diesel crankshaft (torsional) damper. Note key

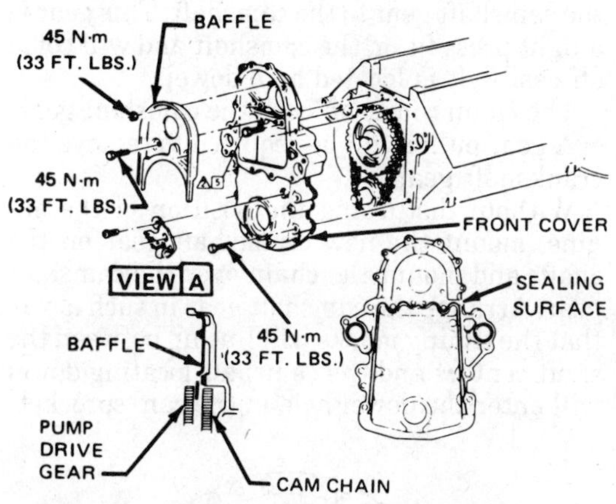

Front cover assembly showing sealer application, 379 diesel

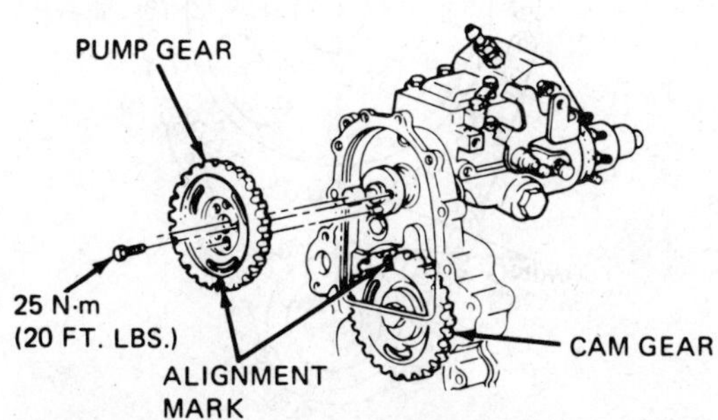

Injection pump and cam gear alignment, 379 diesel

5. Remove the crankshaft pulley and torsional damper.
6. Remove the front cover-to-oil pan bolts (4).
7. Remove the two fuel return line clips.
8. Remove the injection pump retaining nuts from the front cover.
9. Remove the baffle. Remove the remaining cover bolts, and remove the front cover.
10. If the front cover oil seal is to be replaced, it can now be pried out of the cover with a suitable prying tool. Press the new seal into the cover evenly.

NOTE: *The oil seal can also be replaced with the front cover installed. Remove the torsional damper first, then pry the old seal out of the cover using a suitable prying tool. Use care not to damage the surface of the crankshaft. Install the new seal evenly into the cover and install the damper.*

11. To install the front cover, first clean both sealing surfaces until all traces of old sealer are gone. Apply a 2mm bead of sealant (GM sealant #1052357 or equivalent) to the sealing surface as shown in the illustration. Apply a bead of RTV type sealer to the bottom portion of the front cover which attached to the oil pan. Install the front cover.
12. Install the baffle.
13. Install the injection pump, making sure the scribe marks on the pump and front cover are aligned.
14. Install the injection pump driven gear, making sure the marks on the cam gear and pump are aligned. Be sure the dowel pin and the three holes on the pump flange are also aligned.
15. Install the fuel line clips, the front cover-to-oil bolts, and the torsional damper and crankshaft pulley. Torque the pan bolts to 4–7 ft.lb., and the damper bolt to 140–162 ft.lb.

Timing Gears

REMOVAL AND INSTALLATION

Inline Sixes

The camshaft in these engines is gear driven, unlike the chain driven cams in V8s. The removal of the timing gear requires removal of the camshaft.

1. After the cam is removed, place the camshaft and gear in an arbor press and remove the gear from the cam. Many well equipped machine shops have this type of equipment if you need the gear pressed off.
2. Installation is in the reverse order of removal. The clearance between the camshaft and the thrust plate should be 0.001–0.005″ (0.0254–0.127mm) on both engines. If less

than 0.005" (0.127mm) clearance exists, the spacer ring should be replaced. If more than 0.005" (0.127mm) clearance, the thrust plate should be replaced.

CAUTION: *The thrust plate must be positioned so that the Woodruff key in the shaft does not damage it when the shaft is pressed out of the gear. Support the hub of the gear or the gear will be seriously damaged.*

NOTE: *The 6-cylinder crankshaft gear may be removed with a gear puller while in place on the block.*

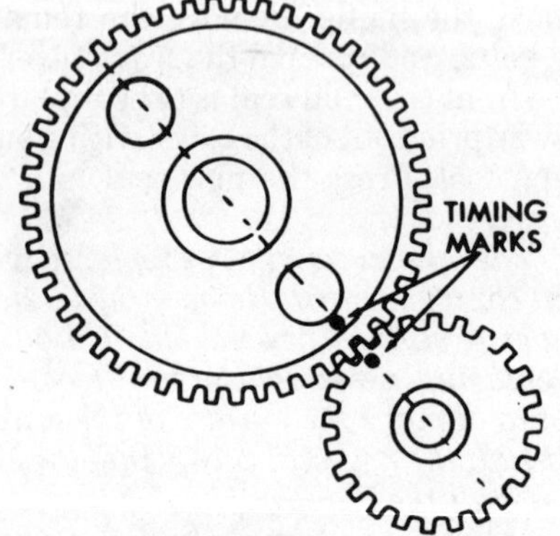

Inline six-cylinder timing gear alignment

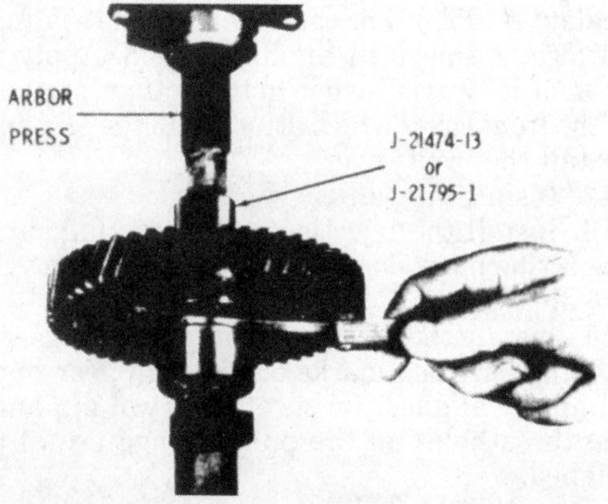

Installing camshaft timing gear and checking thrust plate end clearances. Inline sixes

Access holes in the inline six cylinder camshaft gear for the camshaft thrust plate screws

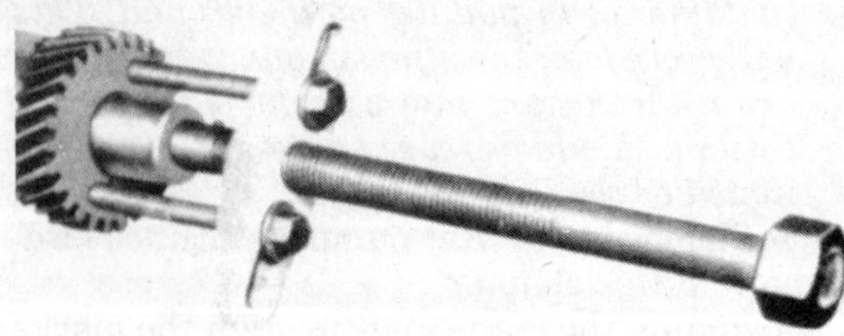

Crankshaft gear puller. Inline sixes

Timing Chain

REMOVAL AND INSTALLATION

Gasoline V6 and V8

To replace the chain, remove the radiator core, water pump, the harmonic balancer and the crankcase front cover. This will allow access to the timing chain. Crank the engine until the timing marks on both sprockets are nearest each other and in line between the shaft centers. Then take out the three bolts that hold the camshaft gear to the camshaft. This gear is a light press fit on the camshaft and will come off easily. It is located by a dowel.

The chain comes off with the camshaft gear.

A gear puller will be required to remove the crankshaft gear.

Without disturbing the position of the engine, mount the new crankshaft gear on the shaft, and mount the chain over the camshaft gear. Arrange the camshaft gear in such a way that the timing marks will line up between the shaft centers and the camshaft locating dowel will enter the dowel hole in the cam sprocket.

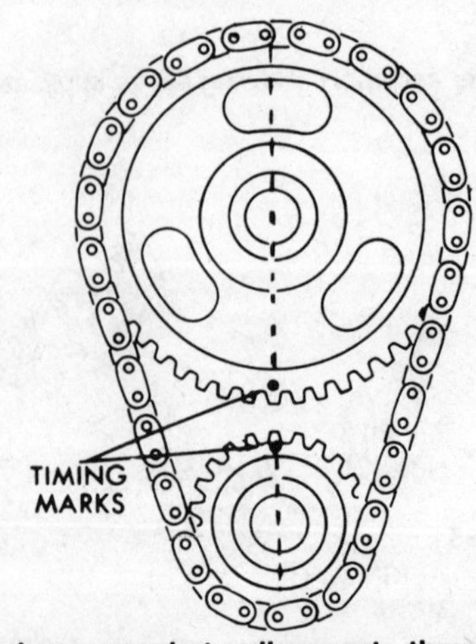

V8 timing sprocket alignment through 1978

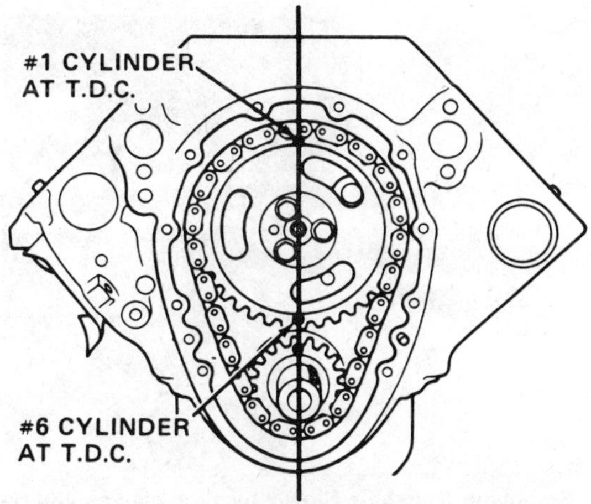

V8 timing sprocket alignment, 1979 and later

Gasoline V8 crankshaft sprocket removal

Place the cam sprocket, with its chain mounted over it, in position on the front of the car and pull up with the three bolts that hold it to the camshaft.

After the gears are in place, turn the engine two full revolutions to make certain that the timing marks are in correct alignment between the shaft centers.

End play of the camshaft is zero.

8–379 Diesel

1. Remove the front cover as previously detailed.
2. Remove the bolt and washer attaching the camshaft gear. Remove the injection pump gear.
3. Remove the camshaft sprocket, timing chain and crankshaft sprocket as a unit.
4. To install, the cam sprocket, timing chain and crankshaft sprocket as a unit, aligning the timing marks on the sprockets as shown in the illustration.
5. Rotate the crankshaft 360° so that the camshaft gear and the injection pump gear are

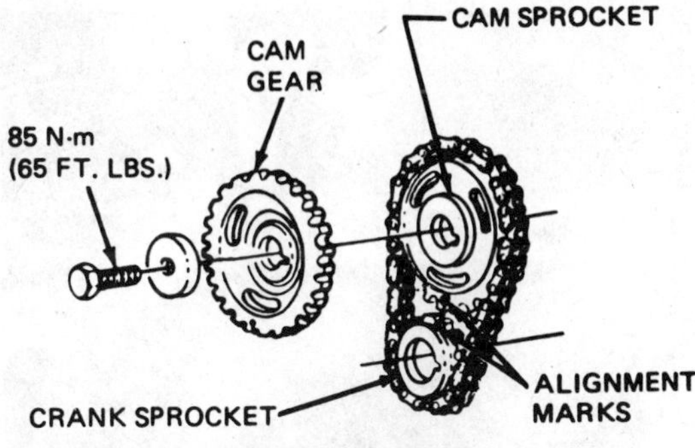

379 diesel timing chain assembly

aligned as shown in the illustration (accompanying the 379 Diesel Front Cover Removal Procedure).

6. Install the front cover as previously detailed. The injection pump must be retimed since the timing chain assembly was removed. See Chapter 2 for this procedure.

Camshaft

REMOVAL AND INSTALLATION

Inline 6-Cylinder

1. Remove the grille. Remove the radiator hoses and remove the radiator.
2. Remove the timing gear cover.
3. Remove the valve cover and gasket, loosen all the rocket arm nuts, and pivot the rocker arms clear of the pushrods.
4. Remove the distributor and the fuel pump.
5. Remove the pushrods. Remove the coil and then remove the side cover. Remove the valve lifters.
6. Remove the two camshaft thrust plate retaining screws by working through the holes in the camshaft gear.
7. Remove the camshaft and gear assembly by pulling it out through the front of the block.
8. If either the camshaft or the camshaft gear is being renewed, the gear must be pressed off the camshaft. The replacement parts must be assembled in the same way. When placing the gear on the camshaft, press the gear onto the shaft until it bottoms against the gear spacer ring. The end clearance of the thrust plate should be 0.001– 0.005″ (0.0254–0.127mm).
9. Prelube the camshaft lobes with clean engine oil and then install the camshaft assembly in the engine. Be careful not to damage the bearings.
10. Turn the crankshaft and the camshaft gears so that the timing marks align. Push the camshaft into position and install and torque the thrust plate bolts to 7 ft.lb.

Checking camshaft gear runout, inline six engines

11. Check camshaft and crankshaft gear runout with a dial indicator. Camshaft gear runout should not exceed 0.004" (0.1016mm) and crankshaft gear runout should not be above 0.003" (0.0762mm).

12. Using a dial indicator, check the backlash at several points between the camshaft and crankshaft gear teeth. Backlash should be 0.004–0.006" (0.1016–0.152mm).

13. Install the timing gear cover. Install the harmonic balancer.

14. Install the valve lifters and the pushrods. Install the side cover. Install the coil and the fuel pump.

15. Install the distributor and set the timing. Pivot the rocker arms over the pushrods and adjust the valves.

16. Install the radiator, hoses and grille.

Gasoline V6 and V8

1. Disconnect the battery.

2. Drain and remove the radiator.

CAUTION: *When draining the coolant, keep in mind that cats and dogs are attracted by the ethylene glycol antifreeze, and are quite likely to drink any that is left in an uncovered container or in puddles on the ground. This will prove fatal in sufficient quantity. Always drain the coolant into a sealable container. Coolant should be reused unless it is contaminated or several years old.*

3. Disconnect the fuel line at the fuel pump. Remove the pump on 1978 and later models.

4. Disconnect the throttle cable and the air cleaner.

5. Remove the alternator belt, loosen the alternator bolts and move the alternator to one side.

6. Remove the power steering pump from its brackets and move it out of the way.

7. Remove the air conditioning compressor from its brackets and move the compressor out of the way without disconnecting the lines.

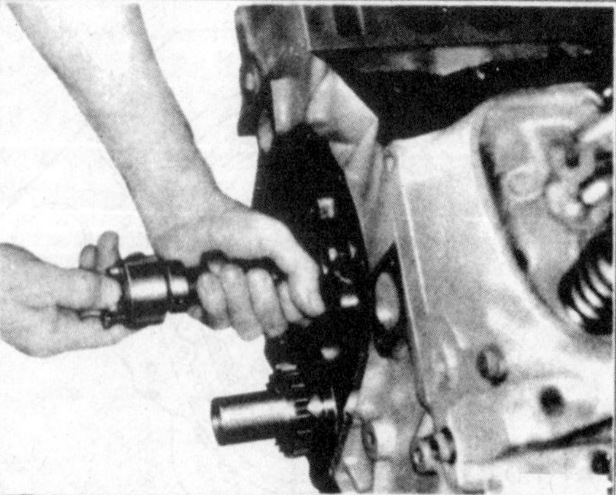

Removing camshaft. Slowly turn the cam as you remove it

8. Disconnect the hoses from the water pump.

9. Disconnect the electrical and vacuum connections.

10. Mark the distributor as to location in the block. Remove the distributor.

11. Raise the car and drain the oil pan.

12. Remove the exhaust crossover pipe and starter motor.

13. Disconnect the exhaust pipe at the manifold.

14. Remove the harmonic balancer and pulley.

15. Support the engine and remove the front motor mounts.

16. Remove the flywheel inspection cover.

17. Remove the engine oil pan.

18. Support the engine by placing wooden blocks between the exhaust manifolds and the front crossmember.

19. Remove the engine front cover.

20. Remove the valve covers.

21. Remove the intake manifold, oil filler pipe, and temperature sending switch.

22. Mark the lifters, pushrods, and rocker arms as to location so that they may be installed in the same position. Remove these parts.

23. If the car is equipped with air conditioning, discharge the A/C system and remove the condenser.

24. Remove the fuel pump eccentric, camshaft gear, oil slinger, and timing chain. Remove the camshaft thrust plate (on front of camshaft) if equipped.

25. Carefully remove the camshaft from the engine.

26. Inspect the shaft for signs of excessive wear or damage.

27. Liberally coat camshaft and bearing with heavy engine oil or engine assembly lubricant and insert the cam into the engine.
28. Align the timing marks on the camshaft and crankshaft gears. See Timing Chain Replacement for details.
29. Install the distributor using the locating marks made during removal. If any problems are encountered, see Distributor Installation.
30. To install, reverse the removal procedure but pay attention to the following points:
   a. Install the timing indicator before installing the power steering pump bracket.
   b. Install the flywheel inspection cover after installing the starter.
   c. Replace the engine oil and radiator coolant.

8–379 Diesel

1. Disconnect the battery.
2. Jack up the truck and safely support it with jackstands.
3. Drain the cooling system, including the block.

CAUTION: *When draining the coolant, keep in mind that cats and dogs are attracted by the ethylene glycol antifreeze, and are quite likely to drink any that is left in an uncovered container or in puddles on the ground. This will prove fatal in sufficient quantity. Always drain the coolant into a sealable container. Coolant should be reused unless it is contaminated or several years old.*

4. Disconnect the exhaust pipes at the manifolds. Remove the fan shroud.
5. Lower the truck.
6. Remove the radiator and fan.
7. Remove the vacuum pump, and remove the intake manifolds as previously detailed.
8. Remove the injection pump and lines as outlined in Chapter 4.Make sure you cap all injection lines to prevent dirt from entering the system, and tag the lines for later installation.
9.Remove the water pump.
10. Remove the injection pump drive gear.
11. Scribe a mark aligning the line on the injection pump flange to the front cover.
12. Remove the injection pump from the cover.
13. Remove the power steering pump and the generator and lay them aside.
14. If the truck is equipped with air conditioning, remove the compressor (with the lines attached) and position it out of the way.

CAUTION: *DO NOT disconnect the air conditioning lines unless you are familiar with this procedure.*

15. Remove the valve covers.
16. Remove the rocker shaft assemblies and pushrods. Place the pushrods in order in a rack (easily by punching holes in a piece of heavy cardboard and numbering the holes) so that they can be installed in correct order.
17. Remove the thermostat housing and the crossover from the cylinder heads.
18. Remove the cylinder heads as previously detailed, with the exhaust manifolds attached.
19. Remove the valve lifter clamps, guide plates and valve lifters. Place these parts in a rack so they can be installed in the correct order.
20. Remove the front cover.
21. Remove the timing chain assembly.
22. Remove the fuel pump.
23. Remove the camshaft retainer plate.
24. If the truck is equipped with air conditioning, remove the A/C condenser mounting bolts. Have an assistant help in lifting the condenser out of the way.
15. Remove the camshaft by carefully sliding it out of the block.

Whenever a new camshaft installed, GM recommends replacing all the valve lifters, as well as the oil filter. The engine oil must be changed. These measures will help ensure proper wear characteristics of the new camshaft.

1. Coat the camshaft lobes with Molykote® or an equivalent lube. Liberally tube the camshaft journals with clean engine oil and install the camshaft carefully.
2. Install the camshaft retainer plate and torque the bolts to 20 ft.lb.
3. Install the fuel pump.
4. Install the timing chain assembly as previously detailed.
5. Install the front cover as previously detailed.
6. Install the valve lifters, guide plates and clamps, and rotate the crankshaft as previously outlined so that the lifters are free to travel.
7. Install the cylinder heads.
8. Install the pushrods in their original order. Install the rocker shaft assemblies, then install the valve covers.
9. Install the injection pump to the front cover, making sure the lines on the pump and the scribe line on the front cover are aligned.
10. Install the injection pump driven gear, making sure the gears are aligned. Retime the injection pump.
11. Install the remaining engine components in the reverse order of removal. Make the necessary adjustments (drive belts, etc.) and refill the cooling system.

CAMSHAFT INSPECTION

Completely clean the camshaft with solvent, paying special attention to cleaning the oil holes. Visually inspect the cam lobes and bearing journals for excessive wear. If a lobe is questionable, have the cam checked at a reputable machine shop. If a journal or lobe is worn, the camshaft must be reground or replaced. Also have the camshaft checked for straightness on a dial indicator.

NOTE: *If a cam journal is worn, there is a good chance that the bushings are worn.*

Camshaft Bearings

REMOVAL AND INSTALLATION

If excessive camshaft wear is found, or if the engine is completely rebuilt, the camshaft bearings should be replaced.

NOTE: *The front and rear bearings should be removed last, and installed first. Those bearings act as guides for the other bearings and pilot.*

1. Drive the camshaft rear plug from the block.
2. Assemble the removal puller with its shoulder on the bearing to be removed. Gradually tighten the puller nut until the bearing is removed.
3. Remove the remaining bearings, leaving the front and rear for last. To remove these, reverse the position of the puller, so as to pull the bearings towards the center of the block. Leave the tool in this position, pilot the new front and rear bearings on the installer, and pull them into position.
4. Return the puller to its original position and pull the remaining bearings into position.

NOTE: *You must make sure that the oil holes of the bearings and block align when installing the bearings. If they don't align, the camshaft will not get proper lubrication and may seize or at least be seriously damaged. To check for correct oil hole alignment, use a piece of brass rod with a 90° bend in the end as shown in the illustration. Check all oil hole openings. The wire must enter each hole, or the hole is not properly aligned.*

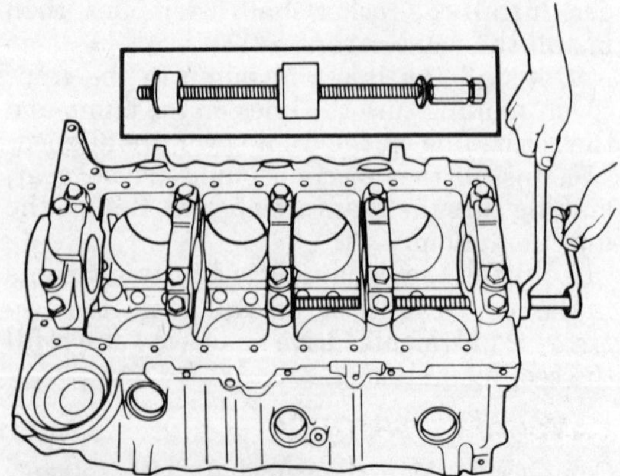

Camshaft bearing removal and installation tool

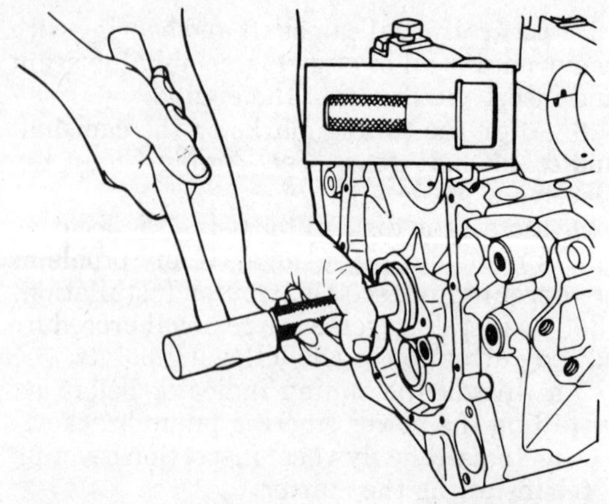

Installing front cam bearing on 379 diesel. Bearing tool is illustrated inset. Method is similar on other engines

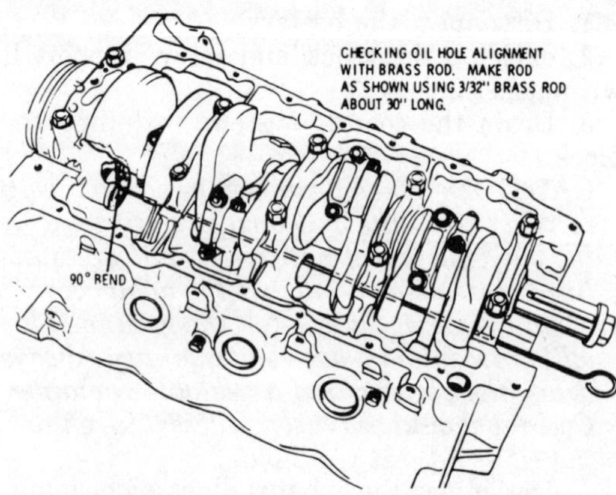

Make this simple tool to check camshaft bearing oil hole alignment

5. Replace the camshaft rear plug, and stake it into position. On the 8–379 diesel, coat the outer diameter of the new plug with GM sealant #1052080 or equivalent, and install it flush to $^1/_{32}$" (0.794mm) deep.

Pistons and Connecting Rods

REMOVAL AND INSTALLATION

Before removing the pistons, the top of the cylinder bore must be examined for a ridge. A ridge at the top of the bore is the result of normal cylinder wear, caused by the piston rings only traveling so far up the bore in the course of the piston stroke. The ridge can be felt by hand. It must be removed before the pistons are removed.

A ridge reamer is necessary for this operation. Place the piston at the bottom of its stroke, and cover it with a rag. Cut the ridge away with the ridge reamer, using extreme care to avoid cutting too deeply. Remove the rag, and remove the cuttings that remain on the piston with a magnet and a rag soaked in clean oil. Make sure the piston top and cylinder bore are absolutely clean before moving the piston.

1. Remove intake manifold and cylinder head or heads.
2. Remove oil pan.
3. Remove oil pump assembly if necessary.
4. Matchmark the connecting rod cap to the connecting rod with a scribe. Each cap must be reinstalled on its proper rod in the proper direction. Remove the connecting rod bearing cap and the rod bearing. Number the top of each piston with silver paint or a felt tip pen for later assembly.
5. Cut lengths of ⅜" (9.53mm) diameter hose to use as rod bolt guides. Install the hose over the threads of the rod bolts, to prevent the bolt threads from damaging the crankshaft journals and cylinder walls when the piston is removed.
6. Squirt some clean engine oil onto the cylinder wall from above, until the wall is coated. Carefully push the piston and rod assembly up and out of the cylinder by tapping on the bottom of the connecting rod with a wooden hammer handle.
7. Place the rod bearing and cap back on the connecting rod, and install the nuts temporarily. Using a number stamp or punch, stamp the cylinder number on the side of the connecting rod and cap. This will help keep the proper piston and rod assembly on the proper cylinder.

NOTE: *On all V8s, starting at the front the right bank cylinders are 2-4-6-8 and the left bank 1-3-5-7. On the V6 engine even number cylinders 2-4-6 are in the right bank, odd number cylinders 1-3-5 are in the left bank, when viewed from the rear of the engine.*

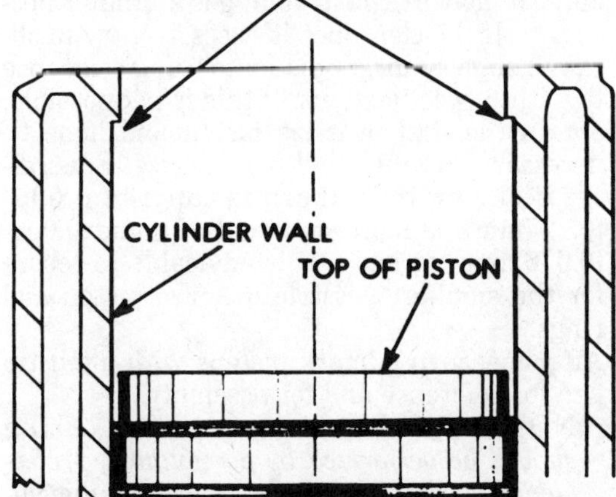

Ridge formed by piston rings at the top of their travel

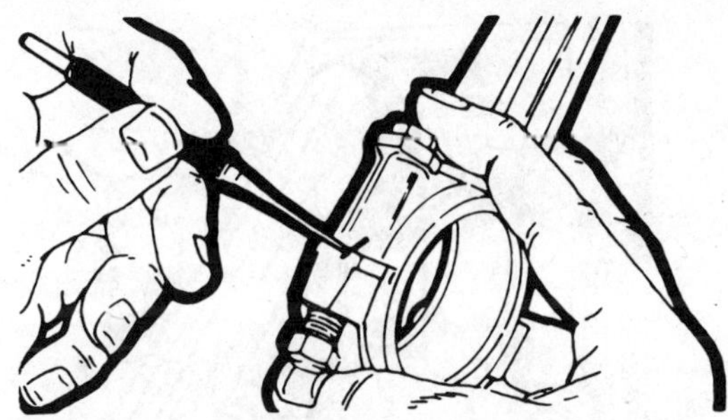

Match the connecting rods to their caps with a scribe mark

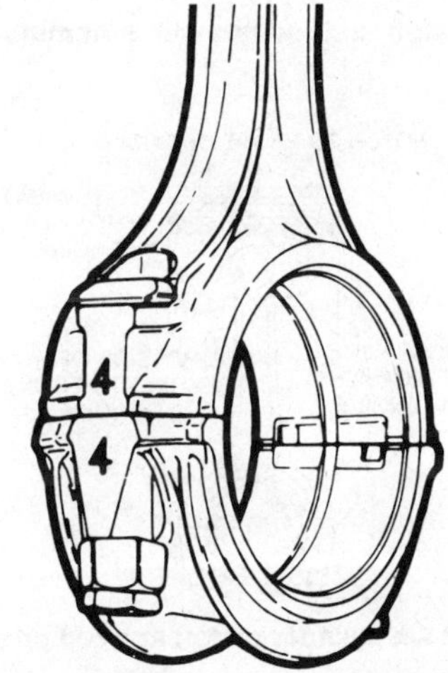

Match the connecting rods to their cylinders with a number stamp

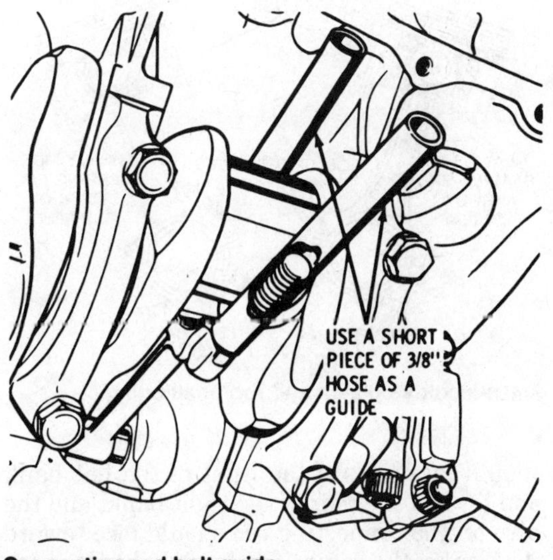

Connecting rod bolt guide

8. Remove remaining pistons in similar manner.

On all gasoline engines, the notch on the piston will face the front of the engine for assembly. The chamfered corners of the bearing caps

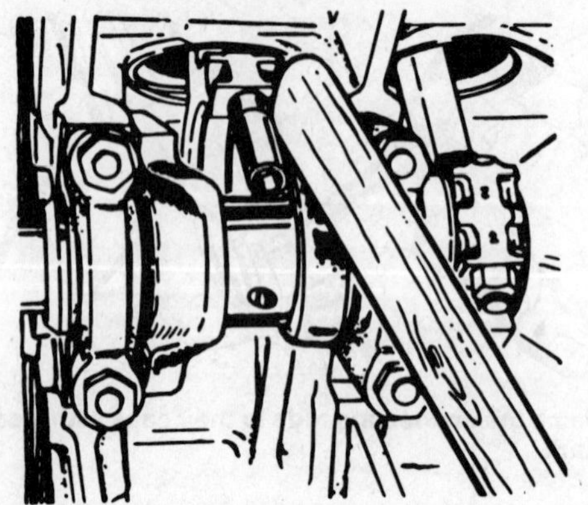
Push the piston and rod out with a hammer handle

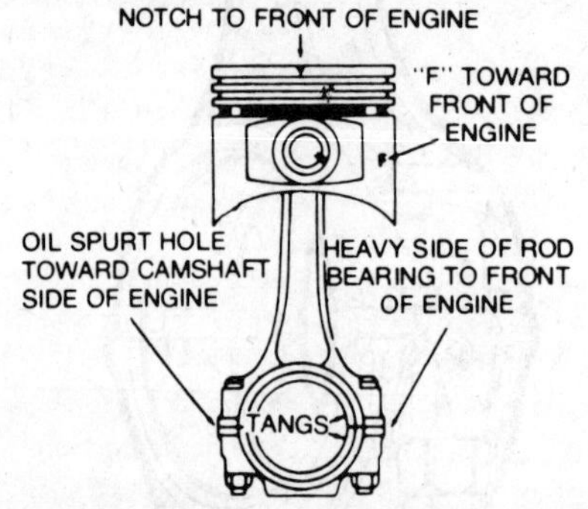

250 and 292 six cylinder piston and rod positioning

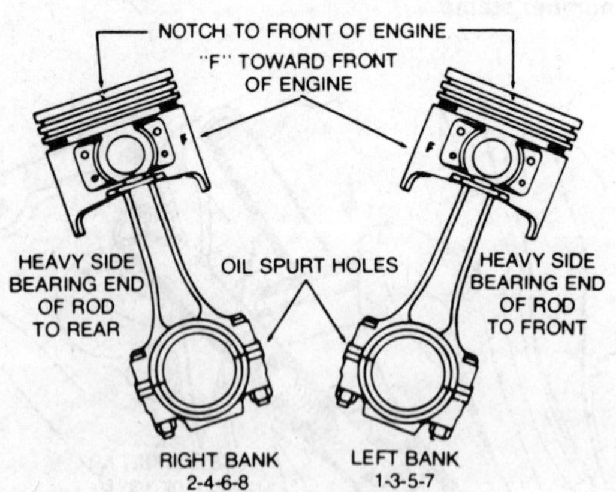

Small-block V8 piston and rod positioning

should face toward the front of the left bank and toward the rear of the right bank, and the boss on the connecting rod should face toward the front of the engine for the right bank and to the rear of the engine on the left bank.

On the 379 diesel, install the piston and rod assemblies with the rod bearing tang slots on the side opposite the camshaft.

On various engines, the piston compression rings are marked with a dimple, a letter **T**, a letter **O**, **GM** or the word **TOP** to identify the side of the ring which must face toward the top of the piston.

Piston Ring and Wrist Pin

REMOVAL

Some of the engines covered in this guide utilize pistons with pressed in wrist pins. These must be removed by a special press designed for this purpose. Other pistons have their wrist pins secured by snaprings, which are easily removed with snapring pliers. Separate the piston from the connecting rod.

A piston ring expander is necessary for removing piston rings without damaging them. Any other method (screwdriver blades, pliers. etc.) usually results in the rings being bent, scratched or distorted, or the piston itself being damaged. When the rings are removed, clean the ring grooves using an appropriate ring groove cleaning tool, using care not to cut too deeply. Thoroughly clean all carbon and varnish from the piston with solvent.

CAUTION: *Do not use a wire brush or caustic solvent (acids, etc.) on pistons.*

Inspect the pistons for scuffing, scoring, cracks, pitting, or excessive ring groove wear. If these are evident, the piston must be replaced.

The piston should also be checked in relation to the cylinder diameter. Using a telescoping gauge and micrometer, or a dial gauge, measure the cylinder bore diameter perpendicular (90°) to the piston pin, 2½" (63.5mm) below the cylinder block deck (surface where the block mates with the heads). Then, with the micrometer, measure the piston perpendicular to its wrist pin on the shirt. The difference between the two measurements is the piston clearance. If the clearance is within specifications or slightly below (after the cylinders have been bored or honed), finish honing is all that is necessary. If the clearance is excessive, try to obtain a slightly larger piston to bring clearance to within specifications. If this is not possible, obtain the first oversize piston and hone (if necessary, bore) the cylinder to size. Generally, if the cylinder bore is tapered 0.005" (0.127mm) or more or is out-of-round 0.003" (0.0762mm) or more, it is advisable to rebore for the smallest possible oversize piston and rings.

After measuring, mark pistons with a felt tip pen for reference and for assembly.

NOTE: *Cylinder honing and/or boring should be performed by a reputable, professional mechanic with the proper equipment. In some cases, cleanup honing can be done*

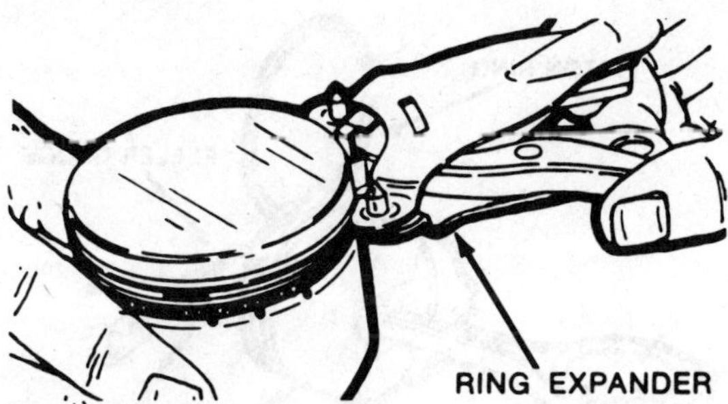

Remove the piston rings

Install the piston lock-rings, if used

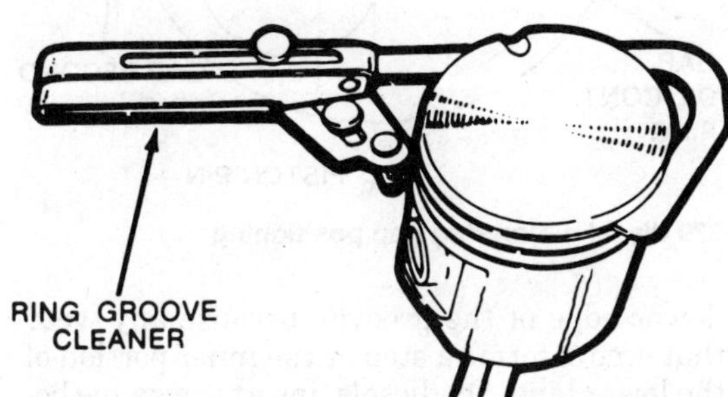

Clean the piston ring grooves using a ring groove cleaner

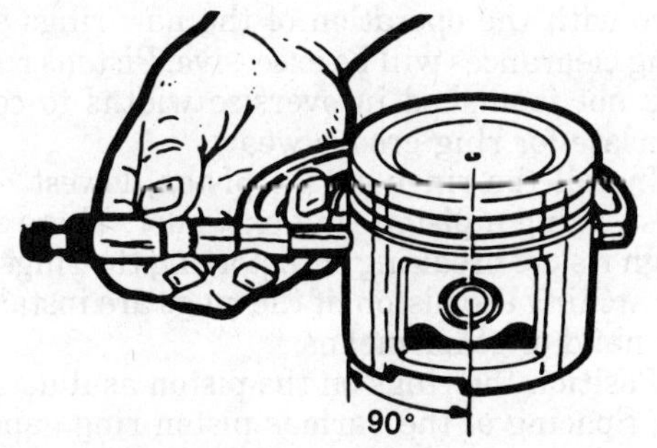

Measuring the piston prior to fitting

with the cylinder block in the car, but most excessive honing and all cylinder boring must be done with the block stripped and removed from the car.

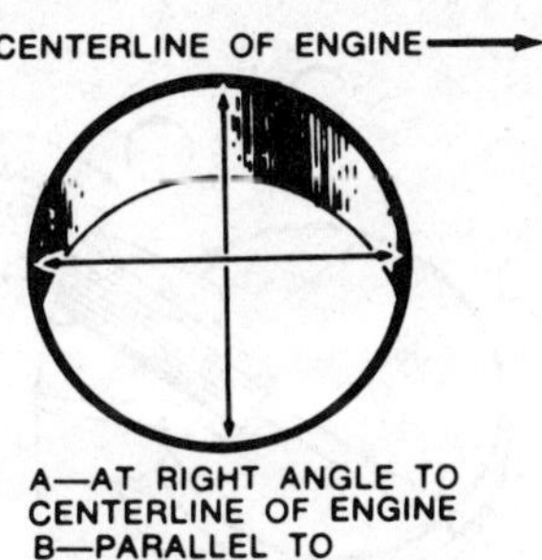

Cylinder bore measuring points

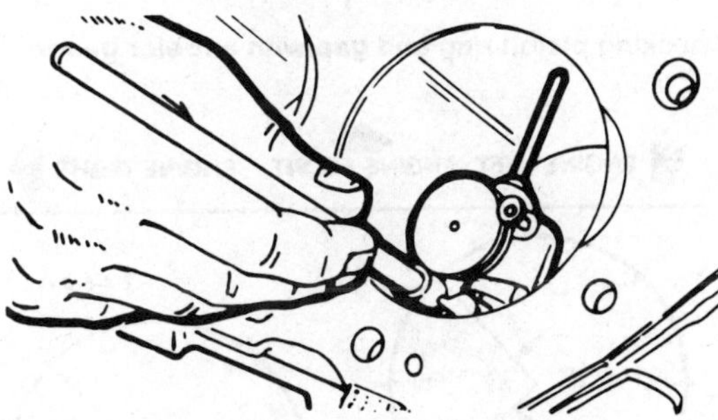
Measuring cylinder bore with a dial gauge

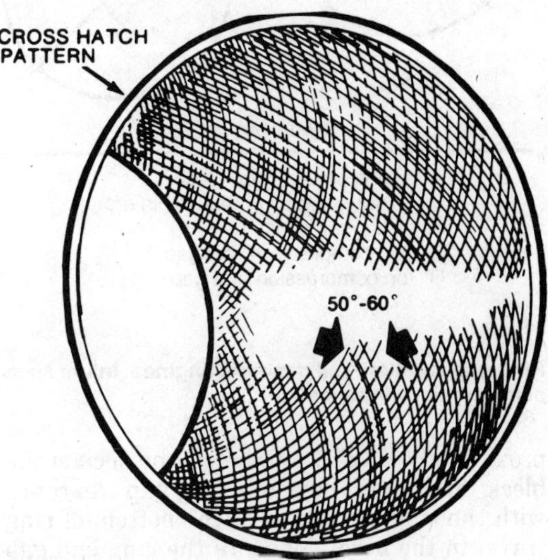

Cylinder bore cross-hatching after honing

PISTON RING END GAP

Piston ring end gap should be checked while the rings are removed from the pistons. Incorrect end gap indicates that the wrong size rings are being used; ring breakage could occur.

Compress the piston rings to be used in a cylinder, one at a time, into that cylinder. Squirt clean oil into the cylinder, so that the rings and the top 2″ (51mm) of cylinder wall are coated. Using an inverted piston, press the rings ap-

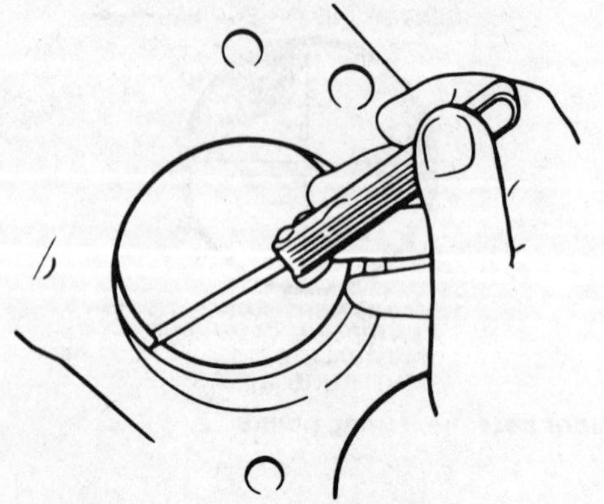

Checking piston ring end gap with a feeler gauge

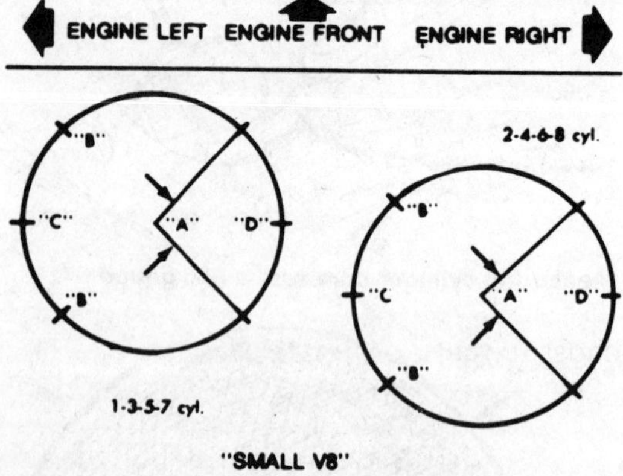

"A" oil ring spacer gap
(tang in hole or slot within arc)
"B" oil ring rail gaps
"C" 2nd compression ring gap
"D" top compression ring gap

Ring gap location—all gasoline engines. Inline sixes same on all cylinders also

proximately 1″ (25.4mm) below the deck of the block (on diesels, measure ring gap clearance with the ring positioned at the bottom of ring travel in the bore). Measure the ring end gap with a feeler gauge, and compare to the Ring Gap chart in this chapter. Carefully pull the ring out of the cylinder and file the ends squarely with a fine file to obtain the proper clearance.

PISTON RING SIDE CLEARANCE CHECK AND INSTALLATION

Check the piston to see that the ring grooves and oil return holes have been properly cleaned. Slide a piston ring into its groove, and check the side clearance with a feeler gauge. On gasoline engines, make sure you insert the gauge between the ring and its lower land

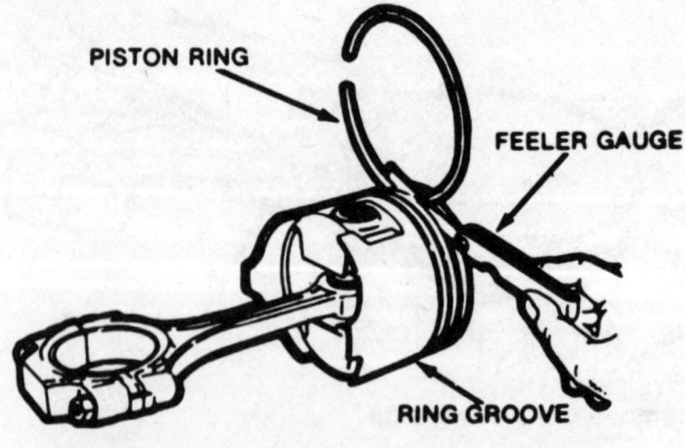

Checking piston ring side clearance

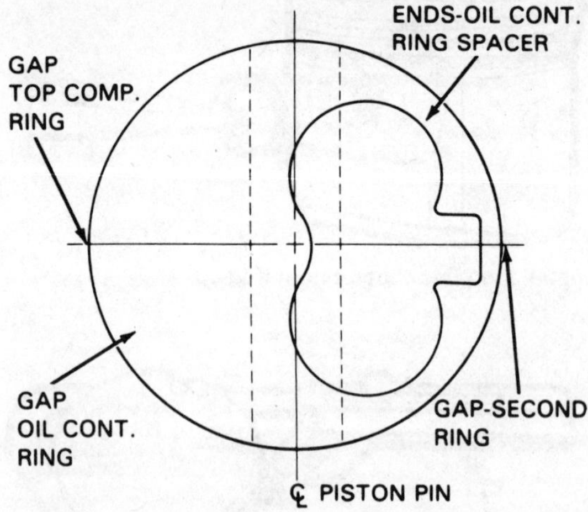

379 diesel piston ring gap positioning

(lower edge of the groove), because any wear that occurs forms a step at the inner portion of the lower land. On diesels, insert the gauge between the ring and the upper land. If the piston grooves have worn to the extent that relatively high steps exist on the lower land, the piston should be replaced, because these will interfere with the operation of the new rings and ring clearances will be excessive. Pistons rings are not furnished in oversize widths to compensate for ring groove wear.

Install the rings on the piston, lowest ring first, using a piston ring expander. There is a high risk of breaking or distorting the rings, or scratching the piston, if the rings are installed by hand or other means.

Position the rings on the piston as illustrated. Spacing of the various piston ring gaps is crucial to proper oil retention and even cylinder wear. When installing new rings, refer to the illustration diagram furnished with the new parts.

Connecting Rod Bearings

Connecting rod bearings for the engine covered in this guide consist of two halves or shells which are interchangable in the rod and cap. When the shells are placed in position, the ends extend slightly beyond the rod and cap surfaces so that when the rod bolts are torqued the shells will be capped tightly in place to insure positive seating and to prevent turning. A tang holds the shells in place.

NOTE: *The ends of the bearing shell must never be filed flush with the mating surface of the rod and cap.*

If a rod bearing becomes noisy or is worn so that its clearance on the crank journal is sloppy, a new bearing of the correct undersize must be selected and installed since there is a provision for adjustment.

CAUTION: *Under no circumstances should the rod end or cap be filed to adjust the bearing clearance, nor should shims of any kind be used.*

Inspect the rod bearings while the rod assemblies are out of the engine. If the shells are scored or show flaking, they should be replaced. If they are in good shape check for proper clearance on the crank journal (see below). Any scoring or ridges on the crank journal means the crankshaft must be replaced, or reground and fitted with undersized bearings.

CHECKING BEARING CLEARANCE AND REPLACING BEARINGS

NOTE: *Make sure connecting rods and their caps are kept together, and that the caps are installed in the proper direction.*

Replacement bearings are available in standard size, and in undersizes for reground crankshafts. Connecting rod-to-crankshaft bearing clearance is checked using Plastigage® at either the top or bottom of each crank journal. The Plastigage® has a range of 0.001"–0.003" (0.0254–0.0762mm).

1. Remove the rod cap with the bearing shell. Completely clean the bearing shell and the crank journal, and blow any oil from the oil hole in the crankshaft; Plastigage® is soluble in oil.
2. Place a piece of Plastigage® lengthwise along the bottom center of the lower bearing shell, then install the cap with shell and torque the bolt or nuts to specification. DO NOT turn the crankshaft with Plastigage® in the bearing.
3. Remove the bearing cap with the shell. The flattened Plastigage® will be found sticking to either the bearing shell or crank journal. Do not remove it yet.
4. Use the scale printed on the Plastigage® envelope to measure the flattened material at its widest point. The number within the scale which most closely corresponds to the width of the Plastigage® indicates bearing clearance in thousandths of an inch.
5. Check the specifications chart in this chapter for the desired clearance. It is advisable to install a new bearing if clearance exceeds 0.003" (0.0762mm). However, if the bearing is in good condition and is not being checked because of bearing noise, bearing replacement is not necessary.
6. If you are installing new bearings, try a standard size, then each undersize in order until one is found that is within the specified limits when checked for clearance with Plastigage®. Each undersize shell has its size stamped on it.
7. When the proper size shell is found, clean off the Plastigage®, oil the bearing thoroughly, reinstall the cap with its shell and torque the rod bolt nuts to specification.

NOTE: *With the proper bearing selected and the nuts torqued, it should be possible to move the connecting rod back and forth freely*

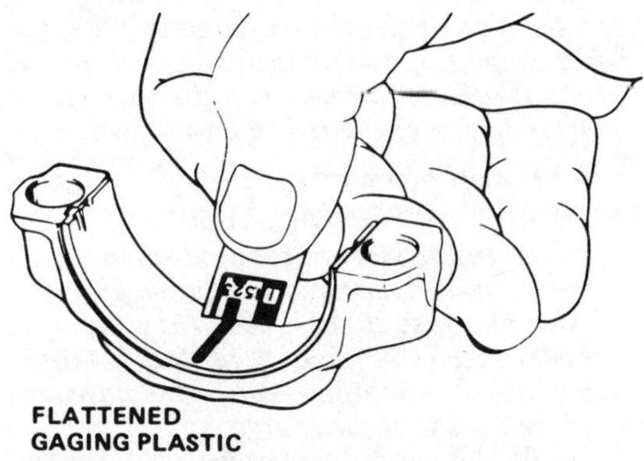

Checking rod bearing clearance with Plastigage® or equivalent

Undersize marks are stamped on the bearing shells. Tangs fit in the notches in the rod and cap

on the crank journal as allowed by the specified connecting rod and clearance. If the rod cannot be moved, either the rod bearing is too far undersize or the rod is misaligned.

PISTON AND CONNECTING ROD ASSEMBLY AND INSTALLATION

NOTE: *In 1985 GM introduced engines with silicone coated pistons. If your engine has these pistons, if replaced, they must be replaced with silicone coated pistons. Substituting another type of piston could reduce the life of the engine.*

Install the connecting rod to the piston, making sure piston installation notches and any marks on the rod are in proper relation to one another. Lubricate the wrist pin with clean engine oil, and install the pin into the rod and piston assembly, either by hand or by using a wrist pin press as required. Install snaprings if equipped, and rotate them in their grooves to make sure they are seated. To install the piston and connecting rod assembly:

1. Make sure connecting rod big end bearings (including end cap) are of the correct size and properly installed.
2. Fit rubber hoses over the connecting rod bolts to protect the crankshaft journals, as in the Piston Removal procedure. Coat the rod bearings with clean oil.
3. Using the proper ring compressor, insert the piston assembly into the cylinder so that the notch in the top of the piston faces the front of the engine (this assumes that the dimple(s) or other markings on the connecting rods are in correct relation to the piston notch(s).
4. From beneath the engine, coat each crank journal with clean oil. Pull the connecting rod, with the bearing shell in place, into position against the crank journal.
5. Remove the rubber hoses. Install the bearing cap and cap nuts and torque to specification.

NOTE: *When more than one rod and piston assembly is being installed, the connecting rod cap attaching nuts should only be tightened enough to keep each rod in position until all have been installed. This will ease the installation of the remaining piston assemblies.*

6. Check the clearance between the sides of the connecting rods and the crankshaft using a feeler gauge. Spread the rods slightly with a screwdriver to insert the gauge. If clearance is below the minimum tolerance, the rod may be machined to provide adequate clearance. If clearance is excessive, substitute an unworn rod, and recheck. If clearance is still outside specifications, the crankshaft must be welded and reground or replaced.
7. Replace the oil pump if removed and the oil pan.
8. Install the cylinder head(s) and intake manifold.

Using a wooden hammer handle, tap the piston down through the ring compressor and into the cylinder

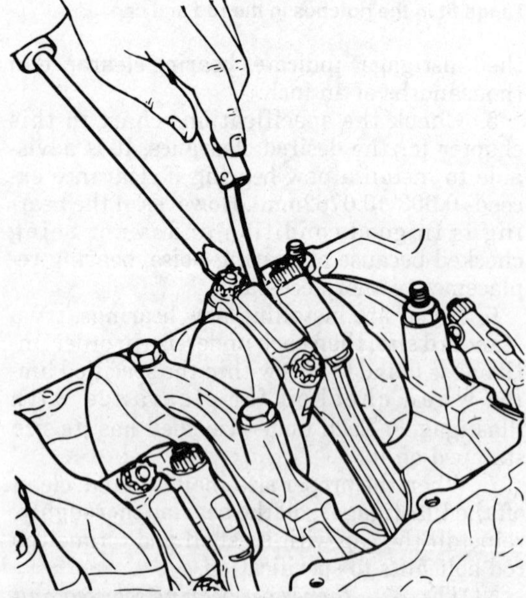

Checking connecting rod side clearance with a feeler gauge. Use a small pry bar to carefully spread the connecting rods

Rear Main Oil Seal

REMOVAL AND INSTALLATION

Both halves of the rear main oil seal can be replaced without removing the crankshaft. Always replace the upper and lower seal together. The lip should face the front of the engine. Be very careful that you do not break the sealing bead in the channel on the outside portion of the seal while installing it. An installation tool can be fabricated to protect the seal bead.

1. Remove the oil pan, oil pump and rear main bearing cap.
2. Remove the oil seal from the bearing cap by prying it out with a suitable tool.
3. Remove the upper half of the seal with a

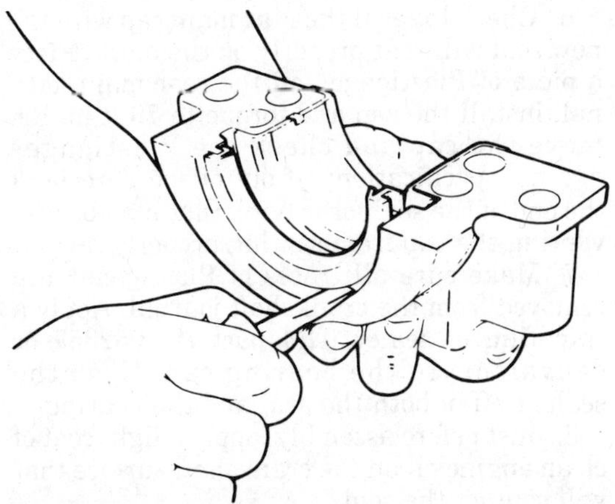

Remove the seal half from the bearing cap without scratching the cap

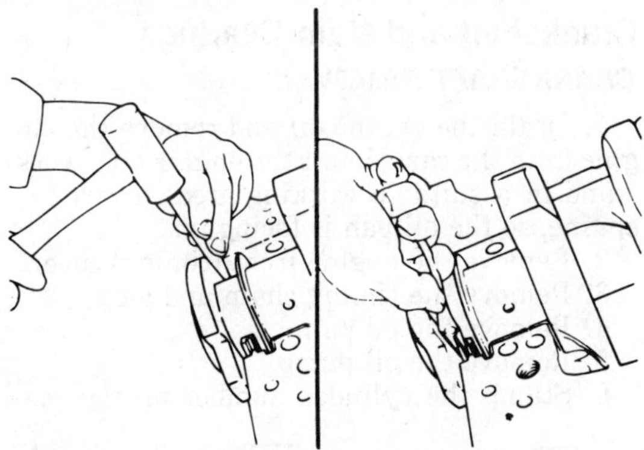

Removing the upper seal half from the block

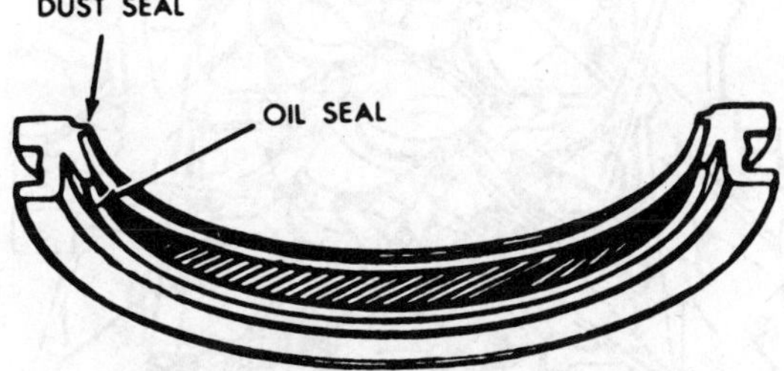

Typical rear main seal half, bearing cap side

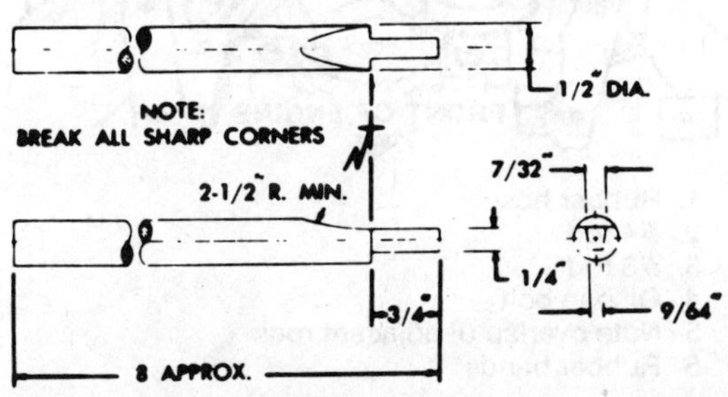

Make a rear main bearing seal packing tool from a wooden dowel.

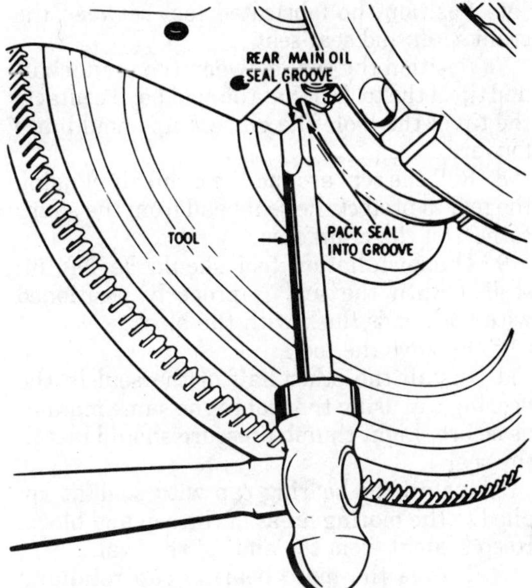

Packing the oil seal

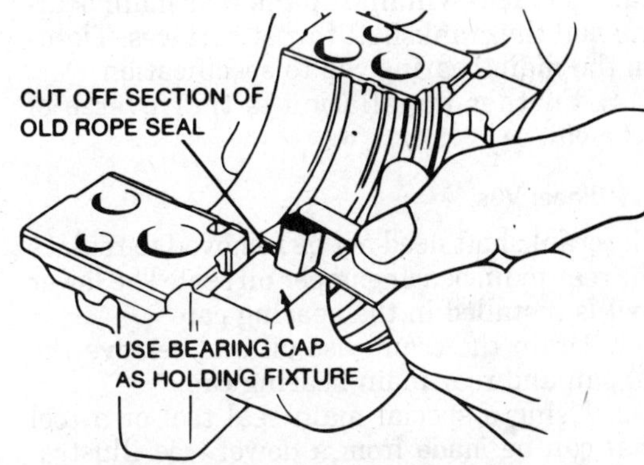

Cutting the lower (bearing cap) seal ends

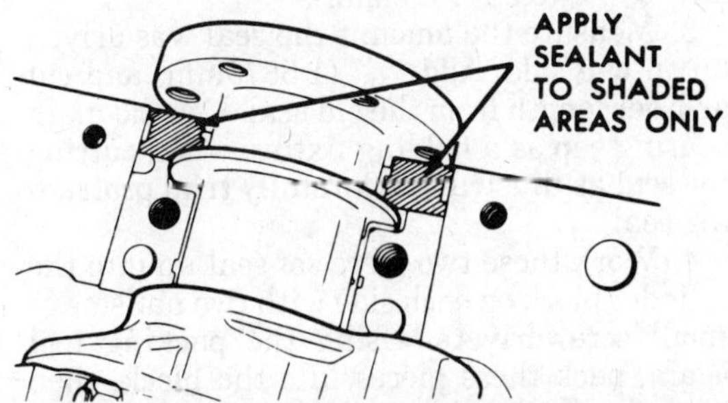

Sealing the bearing cap before final torquing. Apply a bit of oil to the crank journal just before installing the cap

small punch. Drive it around far enough to be gripped with pliers.

4. Clean the crankshaft and bearing cap.

5. Coat the lips and bead of the seal with light engine oil, keeping oil from the ends of the seal.

6. Position the fabricated tool between the crankshaft and seal seat.
7. Position the seal between the crankshaft and tip of the tool so that the seal bead contacts the tip of the tool. The oil seal lip should face forward.
8. Roll the seal around the crankshaft using the tool to protect the seal bead from the sharp corners of the crankcase.
9. The installation tool should be left installed until the seal is properly positioned with both ends flush with the block.
10. Remove the tool.
11. Install the other half of the seal in the bearing cap using the tool in the same manner as before. Light thumb pressure should install the seal.
12. Install the bearing cap with sealant applied to the mating areas of the cap and block. Keep sealant from the ends of the seal.
13. Torque the main bearing cap retaining bolts to 10–12 ft.lb. Tap the end of the crankshaft first rearward, then forward with a lead hammer. This will line up the rear main bearing and the crankshaft thrust surfaces. Tighten the main bearing cap to specification.
14. Further installation is the reverse of removal.

379 Diesel V8s

The crankshaft need not be removed to replace the rear main bearing upper oil seal. The lower seal is installed in the bearing cap.

1. Drain the crankcase oil and remove the oil pan and rear main bearing cap.
2. Using a special main seal tool or a tool that can be made from a dowel (see illustration), drive the upper seal into its groove on each side until it is tightly packed. This is usually ¼–¾" (6.35–19.05mm).
3. Measure the amount the seal was driven up on one side. Add $^1/_{16}$" (1.5875mm) and cut another length from the old seal. Use the main bearing cap as a holding fixture when cutting the seal as illustrated. Carefully trim protruding seal.
4. Work these two pieces of seal up into the cylinder block on each side with two nailsets or small screwdrivers. Using the packing tool again, pack these pieces into the block, then trim the flush with a razor blade or hobby knife as shown. Do not scratch the bearing surface with the razor.

NOTE: *It may help to use a bit of oil on the short pieces of the rope seal when packing it into the block.*

5. Apply Loctite® # 496 sealer or equivalent to the rear main bearing cap and install the rope seal. Cut the ends of the seal flush with the cap.
6. Check to see if the rear main cap with the new seal will seat properly on the block. Place a piece of Plastigage® on the rear main journal, install the cap and torque to 70 ft.lb. Remove the cap and check the Plastigage® against specifications. If out of specs, recheck the end of the seal for fraying that may be preventing the cap from seating properly.
7. Make sure all traces of Plastigage® are removed from the crankshaft journal. Apply a thin film of sealer (GM part # 1052357 or equvalent) to the bearing cap. Keep the sealent off of both the seal and the bearing.
8. Just before assembly, apply a light coat of clean engine oil on the crankshaft surface that will contact the seal.
9. Install the bearing cap and torque to specification.
10. Install the oil pump and oil pan.

Crankshaft and Main Bearings

CRANKSHAFT REMOVAL

1. Drain the engine oil and remove the engine from the car. Mount the engine on a work stand in a suitable working area. Invert the engine, so the oil pan is facing up.
2. Remove the engine front (timing) cover.
3. Remove the timing chain and gars.
4. Remove the oil pan.
5. Remove the oil pump.
6. Stamp the cylinder number on the ma-

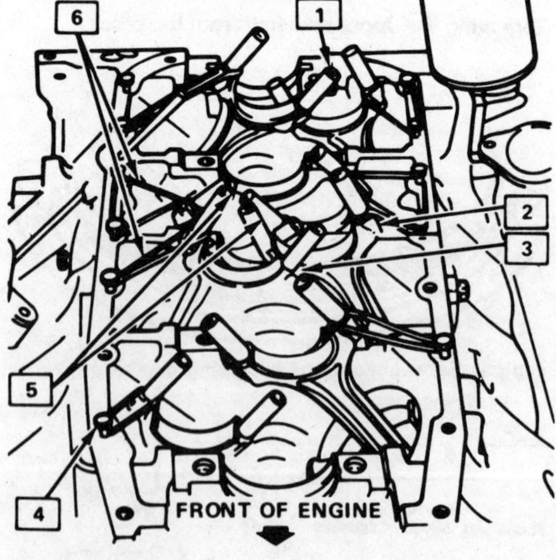

1. Rubber hose
2. #4 rod
3. #3 rod
4. Oil pan bolt
5. Note overlap of adjacent rods
6. Rubber bands

Crankshaft removal showing hose lengths on rod bolts

chined surfaces of the bolt bosses of the connecting rods and caps for identification when reinstalling. If the pistons are to be removed eventually from the connecting rod, mark the cylinder number on the pistons with silver paint or felt tip pen for proper cylinder identification and cap-to-rod location.

7. Remove the connecting rod caps. Install lengths of rubber hose on each of the connecting rod bolts, to protect the crank journals when the crank is removed.

8. Mark the main bearing caps with a number punch or punch so that they can be reinstalled in their original positions.

9. Remove all main bearing caps.

10. Note the position of the keyway in the crankshaft so it can be installed in the same position.

11. Install rubber bands between a bolt on each connecting rod and oil pan bolts that have been reinstalled in the block (see illustration). This will keep the rods from banging on the block when the crank is removed.

12. Carefully lift the crankshaft out of the block. The rods will pivot to the center of the engine when the crank is removed.

MAIN BEARING INSPECTION

Like connecting rod big end bearings, the crankshaft main bearings are shell type inserts that do not utilize shims and cannot be adjusted. The bearings are available in various standard and undersizes. If main bearing clearance is found to be too sloppy, a new bearing (both upper and lower halves) is required.

NOTE: *Factory undersized crankshafts are marked, sometimes with a* **9** and/or a large spot of light green paint. The bearing caps also will have the paint on each side of the undersized journal.

Generally, the lower half of the bearing shell (except No. 1 bearing) shows greater wear and fatigue. If the lower half only shows the effects of normal wear (no heavy scoring or discoloration), it can usually be assumed that the upper half is also in good shape. Conversely, if the lower half is heavily worn or damaged, both halves should be replaced. Never replace one bearing half without replacing the other.

CHECKING CLEARANCE

Main bearing clearance can be checked both with the crankshaft in the car and with the engine out of the car. If the engine block is still in the car, the crankshaft should be supported both front and rear (by the damper and to remove clearance from the upper bearing. Total clearance can then be measured between the lower bearing and journal. If the block has been removed from the car, and is inverted, the crank will rest on the upper bearings and the total clearance can be measured between the lower bearing and journal. Clearance is checked in the same manner as the connecting rod bearings, with Plastigage®.

NOTE: *Crankshaft bearing caps and bearing shells should NEVER be filed flush with the cap-to-block mating surface to adjust for wear in the old bearings. Always install new bearings.*

1. If the crankshaft has been removed, install it (block removed from car). If the block is still in the car, remove the oil pan and oil pump. Starting with the rear bearing cap, remove the cap and wipe all oil from the crank journal and bearing cap.

2. Place a strip of Plastigage® the full width of the bearing, (parallel to the crankshaft), on the journal.

CAUTION: *Do not rotate the crankshaft while the gaging material is between the bearing and the journal.*

3. Install the bearing cap and evenly torque the cap bolts to specification.

4. Remove the bearing cap. The flattened Plastigage® will be sticking to either the bearing shell or the crank journal.

5. Use the graduated scale on the Plastigage® envelope to measure the material at its widest point.

NOTE: *If the flattened Plastigage® tapers toward the middle or ends, there is a difference in clearance indicating the bearing or journal has a taper, low spot or other irregularity. If this is indicated, measure the crank journal with a micrometer.*

6. If bearing clearance is within specifications, the bearing insert is in good shape. Replace the insert if the clearance is not within specifications. Always replace both upper and lower inserts as a unit.

7. Standard, 0.001″ (0.0254mm) or 0.002″ (0.051mm) undersize bearings should produce the proper clearance. If these sizes still produce too sloppy a fit, the crankshaft must be reground for use with the next undersize bearing. Recheck all clearances after installing new bearings.

8. Replace the rest of the bearings in the same manner. After all bearings have been checked, rotate the crankshaft to make sure there is no excessive drag. When checking the No. 1 main bearing, loosen the accessory drive belts (engine in car) to prevent a tapered reading with the Plastigage®.

MAIN BEARING REPLACEMENT

Engine Out of Car

1. Remove and inspect the crankshaft.
2. Remove the main bearings from the bear-

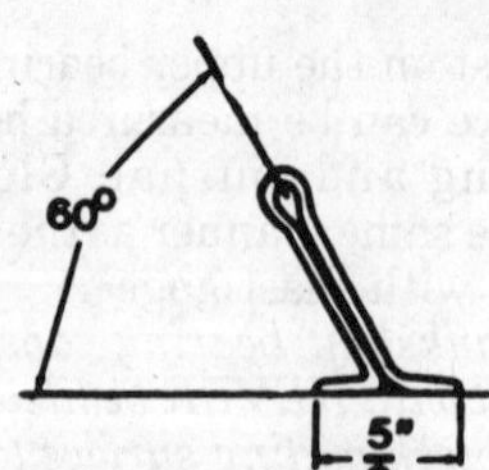

Home-made bearing roll-out pin

Roll-out pin installed for removing upper half of main bearing

ing saddles in the cylinder block and main bearing caps.

3. Coat the bearing surfaces of the new, correct size main bearings with clean engine oil and install them in the bearing saddles in the block and in the main bearing caps.

4. Install the crankshaft. See Crankshaft Installation.

Engine in Car

1. With the oil pan, oil pump and spark plugs removed, remove the cap from the main bearing needing replacement and remove the bearing from the cap.

2. Make a bearing roll out pin, using a bent cotter pin as shown in the illustration. Install the end of the pin in the oil hole in the crankshaft journal.

3. Rotate the crankshaft clockwise as viewed from the front of the engine. This will roll the upper bearing out of the block.

4. Lube the new upper bearing with clean engine oil and insert the plain (unnotched) end between the crankshaft and the indented or notched side of the block. Roll the bearing into place, making sure that the oil holes are aligned. Remove the roll pin from the oil hole.

5. Lube the new lower bearing and install the main bearing cap. Install the main bearing cap, making sure it is positioned in proper direction with the matchmarks in alignment.

6. Torque the main bearing cap bolts to specification.

NOTE: *See Crankshaft Installation for thrust bearing alignment.*

CRANKSHAFT END PLAY AND INSTALLATION

When main bearing clearance has been checked, bearings examined and/or replaced, the crankshaft can be installed. Thoroughly clean the upper and lower bearing surfaces, and lube them with clean engine oil. Install the crankshaft and main bearing caps.

Dip all main bearing cap bolts in clean oil, and torque all main bearing caps, excluding the thrust bearing cap, to specifications (see the Crankshaft and Connecting Rod chart in this chapter to determine which bearing is the thrust bearing). Tighten the thrust bearing bolts finger tight. To align the thrust bearing, pry the crankshaft the extent of its axial travel several times, holding the last movement toward the front of the engine. Add thrust washers if required for proper alignment. Torque the thrust bearing cap to specifications.

To check crankshaft end play, pry the crankshaft to the extreme rear of its axial travel, then to the extreme front of its travel. Using a feeler gauge, measure the end plat at the front of the rear main bearing. End play may also be measured at the thrust bearing. Install a new rear main bearing oil seal in the cylinder block and main bearing cap. Continue to reassemble the engine.

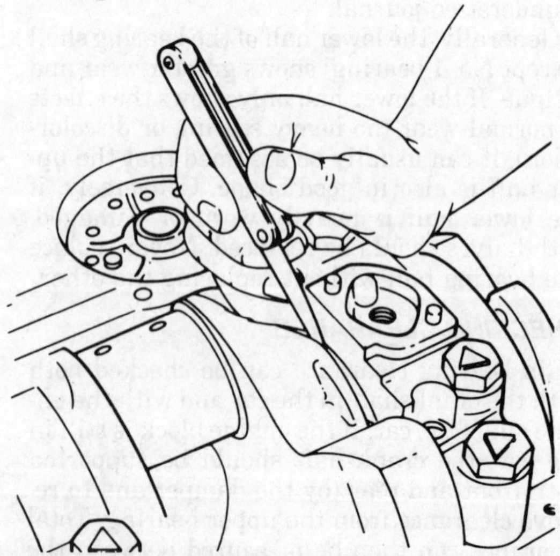

Measuring crankshaft end play at the front of the rear main bearing

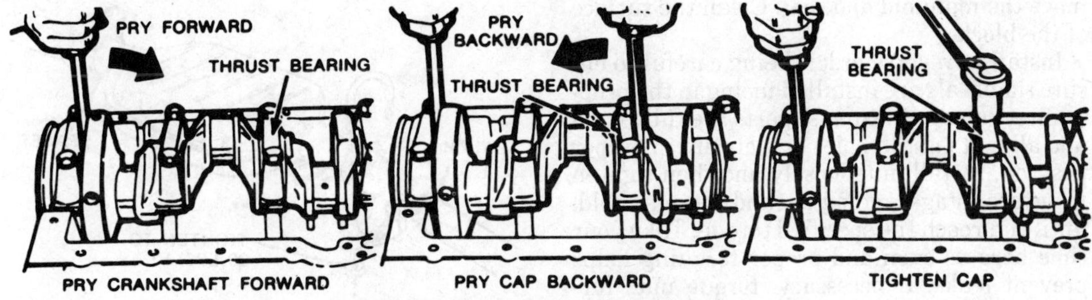

Aligning the crankshaft thrust bearing

Flywheel and Ring Gear

REMOVAL AND INSTALLATION

The ring gear is an integral part of the flywheel and is not replaceable.

1. Remove the transmission.
2. Remove the six bolts attaching the flywheel to the crankshaft flange. Remove the flywheel.
3. Inspect the flywheel for cracks, and inspect the ring gear for burrs or worn teeth. Replace the flywheel if any damage is apparent. Remove burrs with a mill file.
4. Install the flywheel. The flywheel will only attach to the crankshaft in one position, as the bolt holes are unevenly spaced. Install the bolts and torque to specification.

Exhaust System

SAFETY PRECAUTIONS

For a number of reasons, exhaust system work can be the most dangerous type of work you can do on your van. Always observe the following precautions:

1. Support the van extra securely. Not only will you often be working directly under it, but you'll frequently be using a lot of force, say, heavy hammer blows, to dislodge rusted parts. This can cause a van that's improperly supported to shift and possibly fall.
2. Wear goggles. Exhaust system parts are always rusty. Metal chips can be dislodged, even when you're only turning rusted bolts. Attempting to pry pipes apart with a chisel makes the chips fly even more frequently.
3. If you're using a cutting torch, keep it a great distance from either the fuel tank or lines. Stop what you're doing and feel the temperature of the fuel bearing pipes on the tank frequently. Even slight heat can expand and/or vaporize fuel, resulting in accumulated vapor, or even a liquid leak, near your torch.
4. Watch where your hammer blows fall. You could easily tap a brake or fuel line when you hit an exhaust system part with a glancing blow. Inspect all lines and hoses in the area where you've been working.

Special Tools

A number of special exhaust system tools can be rented from auto supply houses or local stores that rent special equipment. A common one is a tail pipe expander, designed to enable you to join pipes of identical diameter.

It may also be quite helpful to use solvents designed to loosen rusted bolts or flanges. Soaking rusted parts the night before you do the job can speed the work of freeing rusted parts considerably. Remember that these solvents are are often flammable. Apply only to parts after they are cool!

Exhaust Manifold

REMOVAL AND INSTALLATION

Exhaust manifolds rarely rust, but they may crack due to road damage or thermal shock. The first step is to disconnect the exhaust pipe or crossover pipe by removing the nuts from the manifold studs. Then slide the collar or pull the flanged portion of the exhaust pipe or crossover away. In some cases, you may have to loosen the crossover pipe on the other side in order to gain clearance for easy manifold removal. Make sure you remove and replace seals. If the Early Fuel Evaporation valve is involved remove it and install it later with all new seals.

CAUTION: *Be extremely careful not to contact the hot exhaust pipe, while working underneath the car.*

Remove parts that are in the way. These may include the hot air shroud, or various accessory brackets on the engine. You may have to disconnect the steering shaft on certain vehicles. Disconnect the oxygen sensor, if it's on the manifold.

You'll have to bend back locking tabs that ensure that mounting nuts remain tight. Then, after the mounting nuts are soaked with solvent, loosen and remove them. Finally, remove the manifold and seal. Clean the surface of the block.

Install in reverse order, being careful to ensure that seals are installed facing in the proper direction so all exhaust ports are fully open and all bolt or stud holes or slots are in proper position. Install nuts loosely and then tighten in several stages, going around the manifold, until you reach the specified torque. Take your time here as even and proper torquing helps prevent leaks. If necessary, torque nuts further to align a flat with the locking tab. Then, make sure to bend all tabs over to prevent loosened nuts and leaks.

If the manifold has an oxygen sensor installed in it, you'll have to remove it and install it into the new manifold, using a high temperature sealer on the threads. Make sure you don't forget to reconnect the sensor when the manifold is in place.

Crossover Pipe

REMOVAL AND REPLACEMENT

The crossover pipe (used on V-type engines only) is typically connected to the manifolds by flanged connections or collars. In some cases, bolts that are unthreaded for part of their length are used in conjunction with springs. Make sure you install the springs and that they are in good mechanical condition (no broken coils) when installing the new pipe. Replace ring type seals, also.

Headpipe

REMOVAL AND REPLACEMENT

The headpipe is typically attached to the rear of one exhaust manifold with a flange or collar type connector and flagged to the front of the catalytic converter. Remove nuts and bolts and, if springs are used to maintain the seal, the springs. The pipe may then be separated from the rest of the system at both flanges.

Replace ring seals; inspect springs and replace them if any coils are broken.

Catalytic Converter

REMOVAL AND REPLACEMENT

CAUTION: *Be very careful when working on or near the converter. External temperatures can reach +1,500°F (+816°C) and more, causing severe burns. Removal or installation should only be performed on a cold exhaust system.*

Remove bolts at the flange at the rear end. Then, loosen nuts and remove U-clamp to remove the catalyst. Slide the catalyst out of the outlet pipe. Replace all ring seals. In some cases, you'll have to disconnect an air line com-

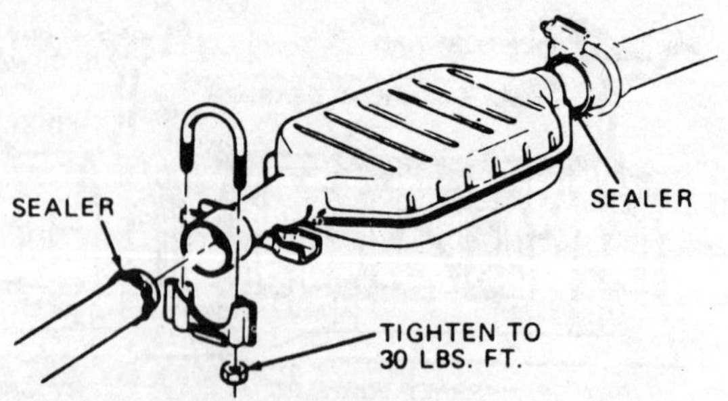

Catalytic Converter G Series

ing from the engine compartment before catalyst removal. In some cases, a hanger supports the converter via one of the flange bolts. Make sure the hanger gets properly reconnected. Also, be careful to retain all parts used to heat shield the converter and reinstall them. Make sure the converter is replaced for proper direction of flow and air supply connections.

Muffler and Tailpipes

REMOVAL AND INSTALLATION

These units are typically connected by flanges at the rear of the converter and at either end of mufflers either by an original weld or by U-clamps working over a pipe connection in which one side of the connection is slightly larger than the other. You may have to cut the original connection and use the pipe expander to allow the original equipment exhaust pipe to be fitted over the new muffler. In this case, you'll have to purchase new U-clamps to fasten the joints. GM recommends that whenever you replace a muffler, all parts to the rear of the muffler in the exhaust system must be replaced. Also, all slip joints rearward of the converter should be coated with sealer before they are assembled.

Be careful to connect all U-clamps or other hanger arrangements so the exhaust system will not flex. Assemble all parts loosely and rotate parts inside one another or clamps on the pipes to ensure proper routing of all exhaust system parts to avoid excessive heating of the floorpan, fuel lines and tank, etc. Also, make sure there is clearance to prevent the system from rattling against spring shackles, the differential, etc. You may be able to bend long pipes slightly by hand to help get enough clearance, if necessary.

While disassembling the system, keep your eye open for any leaks or for excessively close clearance to any brake system parts. Inspect the brake system for any sort of heat damage and repair as necessary.

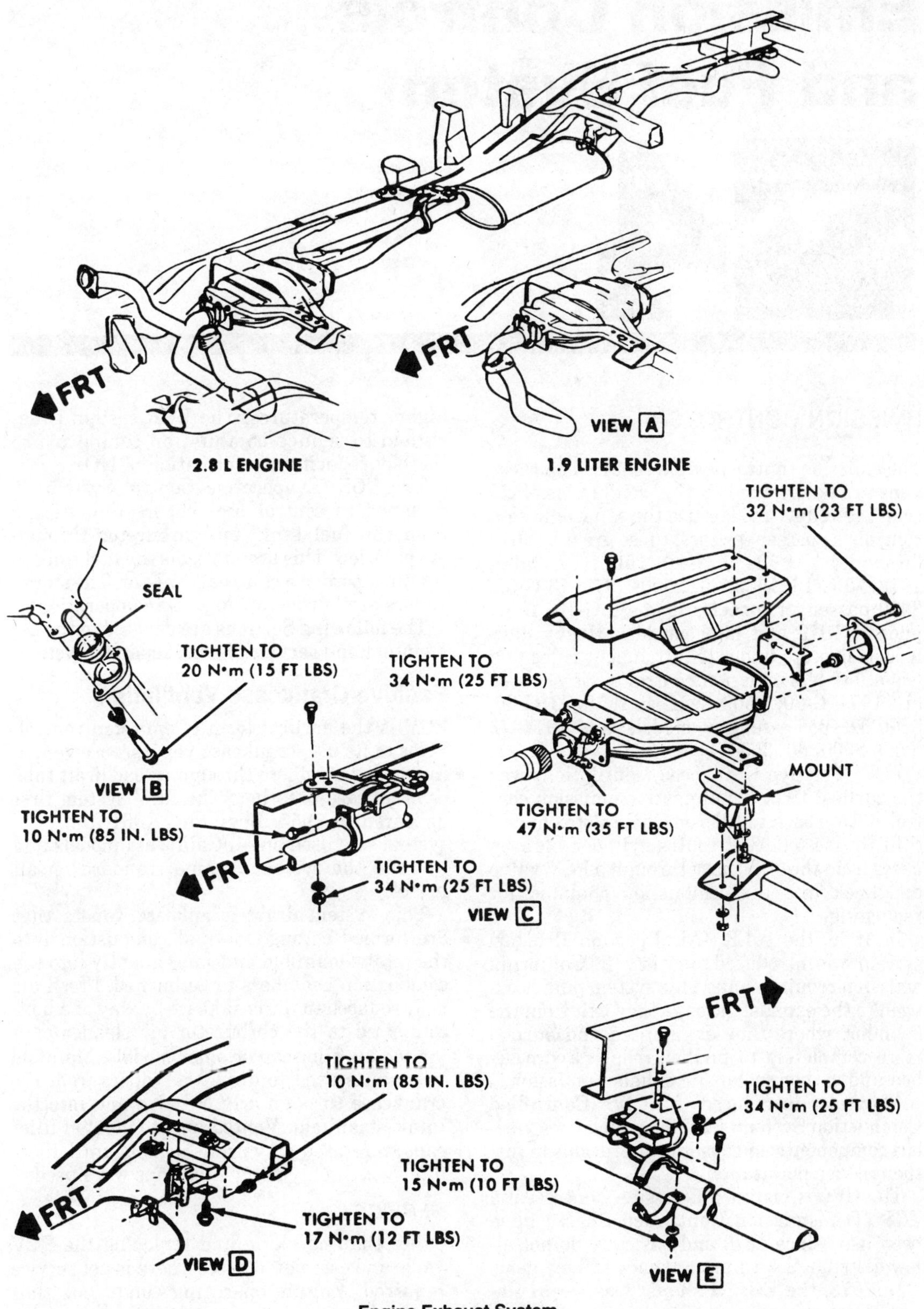

Engine Exhaust System

Emission Controls and Fuel System

EMISSION CONTROLS

The emission control devices required on these vans are determined by the weight classification. Light duty models use the same emission controls as passenger cars; these are all 1967–69 models; 1970–71 G-10, 1500, 20, 2500; 1972–73 G-10, 1500, 20, 2500; 1972–73 G-30, 3500 passenger models; 1974–78 G-10, 1500, and all 1979 and later models. Heavy duty models operate under less stringent rules and use a few less emission control devices; these are 1971 G-30, 3500 models; 1972–73 G-30, 3500 except passengers models; and 1974–78 G-20, 2500, 30, 3500.

PCV (Positive Crankcase Ventilation) was the earliest form of automotive emission control, dating back to 1955 on Chevrolet vehicles. Still in use today, it routes cylinder blow-by gases from the crankcase through a PCV valve and back into the combustion chamber for reburning.

In 1966, the A.I.R. (Air Injection Reactor) system was introduced to satisfy the California emission requirements. This system pumps oxygen to the exhaust gases as they exit from the cylinder, where they are ignited and burned more completely to further reduce hydrocarbon and carbon monoxide exhaust emission.

Chevrolet introduced the CCS (Controlled Combustion System) in 1968, which uses various components and design calibrations to further reduce pollutants.

The CEC (Combined Emission Control) and TCS (Transmission Controlled Spark) have been used since 1970 and basically do not allow distributor vacuum advance in Low gear.

In 1973, the EGR (Exhaust Gas Recirculation) system was developed in response to more stringent Federal exhaust emission standards regarding NOx (oxides of nitrogen). Oxides of nitrogen are formed at higher combustion chamber temperatures and increase with higher temperatures. The EGR system is designed to reduce combustion temperature thereby reducing the formation of NOx.

The ECS (Evaporative Control System) is designed to control fuel vapors that escape from the fuel tank and carburetor through evaporation. This system seals the fuel tank to retain vapors in a charcoal canister. The stored vapors are burned during engine operation.

The following Sections are devoted to the description and service of each separate system.

Positive Crankcase Ventilation

PCV is the earliest form of emission control. Prior to its use, crankcase vapors were vented into the atmosphere through a road draft tube or crankcase breather. The PCV system first appeared in 1955. Beginning 1961, the PCV system was used on all California models and in 1963 the system became standard on all models.

This system draws crankcase vapors that are formed through normal combustion into the intake manifold and subsequently into the combustion chambers to be burned. Fresh air is introduced to the crankcase by way of a hose connected to the carburetor air cleaner or a vented oil filler cap or older models. Manifold vacuum is used to draw the vapors from the crankcase through a PCV valve and into the intake manifold. Vented and nonvented filler caps were used on various models until 1968, after which only nonvented caps were used.

SERVICE

Other than checking and replacing the PCV valve and associated hoses, there is not service required. Engine operating conditions that would direct suspicion to the PCV system are rough idle, oil present in the air cleaner, oil leaks and excessive oil sludging or dilution. If any of the above conditions exist, remove the PCV valve and shake it. A clicking sound indi-

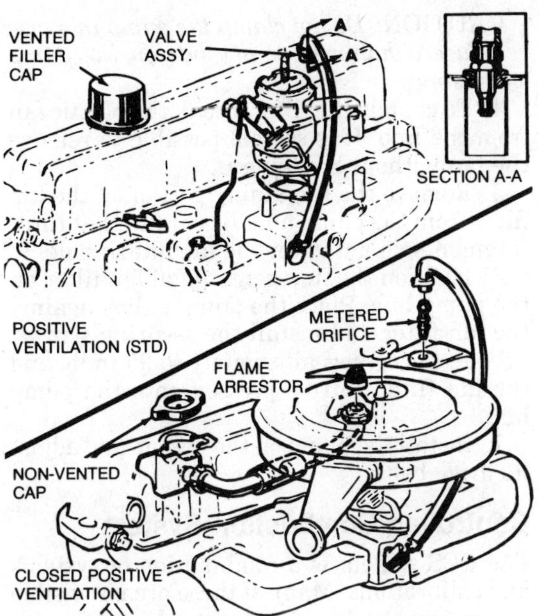

Closed and positive crankcase ventilation systems

cates that the valve is free. If no clicking sound is heard, replace the valve. Inspect the PCV breather in the air cleaner. Replace the breather if it is so dirty that it will not allow gases to pass through. Check all the PCV hoses for condition and tight connections. Replace any hoses that have deteriorated.

Air Injector Reactor (Air Pump)

This system was first introduced on California vans in 1966. The AIR system injects compressed air into the exhaust system, near enough to the exhaust valves to continue the burning of the normally unburned segment of the exhaust gases. To do this it employs an air injection pump and a system of hoses, valves, tubes, etc., necessary to carry the compressed air from the pump to the exhaust manifolds.

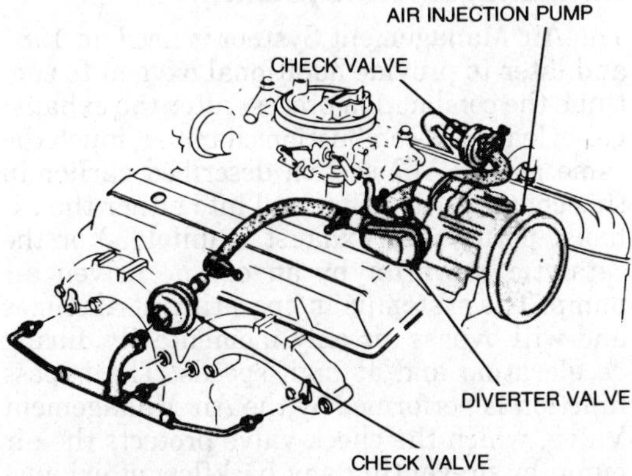

Components of the A.I.R. system

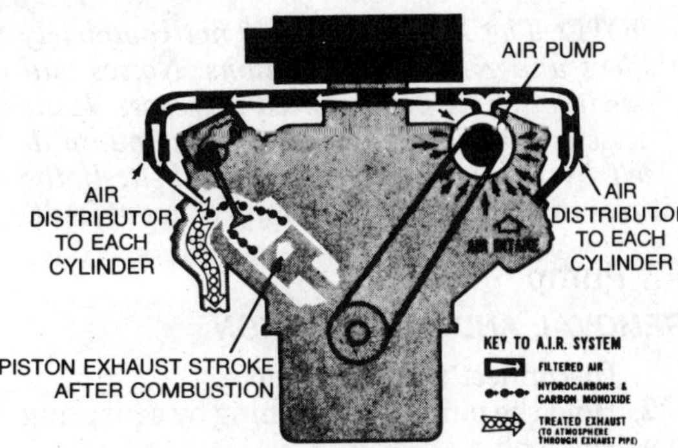

Schematic of the A.I.R. system

A diverter valve is used to prevent backfiring. The valve senses sudden increases in manifold vacuum and ceases the injection of air during dual rich periods. During coasting, this valve diverts the entire air flow through a muffler and during high engine speeds, expels it through a relief valve. Check valves in the system prevent exhaust gases from entering the pump.

TESTING

Check Valve

To test the check valve, disconnect the hose at the diverter valve. Blow into the hose and suck on it. Air should flow only into the engine.

Diverter Valve

Pull off the vacuum line to the top of the valve with the engine running. There should be vacuum in the line. Replace the line. No air should be escaping with the engine running at a steady idle. Open and quickly close the throttle. A blast of air should come out of the valve muffler for at least one second.

Air Pump

Disconnect the hose from the diverter valve. Start the engine and accelerate it to about 1,500 rpm. The air flow should increase as the engine is accelerated. If no air flow is noted or it remains constant, check the following:

1. Drive belt tension.
2. Listen for a leaking pressure relief valve. If it is defective, replace the whole relief/diverter valve.
3. Foreign matter in pump filter openings. If the pump is defective or excessively noisy, it must be replaced.

SERVICE

All hoses and fittings should be inspected for condition and tightness of connections. Check the drive belt for wear and tension periodically.

NOTE: *The A.I.R. system is not completely silent under normal conditions. Noises will rise in pitch as engine speed increases. If the noise is excessive, eliminate the air pump itself by disconnecting the drive belt. If the noise disappears, the air pump is not at fault.*

Air Pump

REMOVAL AND INSTALLATION

1. Disconnect the output hose.
2. Hold the pump from turning by squeezing the drive belt.
3. Loosen the pulley bolts.
4. Loosen the alternator so the belt can be removed.
5. Remove the pulley.
6. Remove the pump mounting bolts and the pump.
7. Install the pump with the mounting bolts loose.
8. Install the pulley and tighten the bolts finger tight.
9. Install and adjust the drive belt.
10. Squeeze the drive belt to prevent the pump from turning.
11. Torque the pulley bolts to 25 ft.lb. Tighten the pump mountings.
12. Check and adjust the belt tension again, if necessary.
13. Connect the hose.
14. If any hose leaks are suspected, pour soapy water over the suspected area with the engine running. Bubbles will form wherever air is escaping.

FILTER REPLACEMENT

1. Disconnect the air and vacuum hoses from the diverter valve.
2. Loosen the pump pivot and adjusting bolts and remove the drive belt.
3. Remove the pivot and adjusting bolts from the pump. Remove the pump and the diverter valve as an assembly.

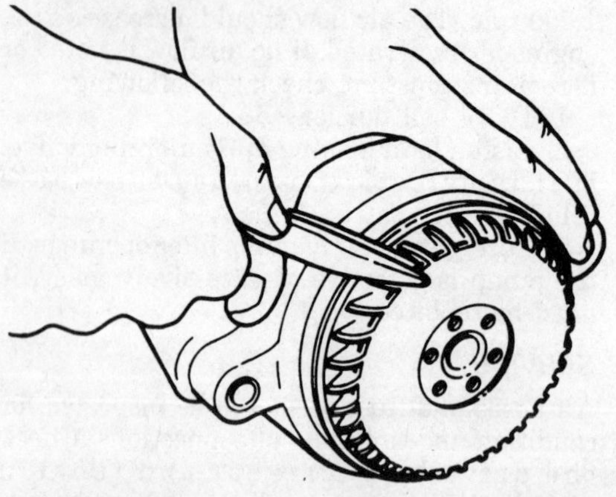

AIR filter removal

CAUTION: *Do not clamp the pump in a vise or use a hammer or pry bar on the pump housing.*

4. To change the filter, break the plastic fan from the hub. It is seldom possible to remove the fan without breaking it.
5. Remove the remaining portion of the fan filter from the pump hub. Be careful that filter fragments do not enter the air intake hole.
6. Position the new centrifugal fan filter on the pump hub. Place the pump pulley against the fan filter and install the securing screws. Torque the screws alternately to 95 in.lb. and the fan filter will be pressed onto the pump hub.
7. Install the pump on the engine and adjust its drive belt.

Controlled Combustion System

The CCS system is a combination of systems and calibrations. Many of these are not visible or serviceable, but are designed into the engine. Originally, in 1968–69, the system was comprised of special carburetion and distributor settings, higher engine operating temperatures and a thermostatically controlled air cleaner. In later years, the thermostatically controlled air cleaner (CHA) was used independently of the other settings on some engines. Likewise, some engines used the special settings without CHA. In 1970, the TCS system was incorporated and the entire system was renamed CEC in 1971. The name reverted to TCS in 1972. In 1973, EGR was also added to the system.

The various systems, CHA, TCS, CEC and EGR are all part of the Controlled Combustion System.

SERVICE

Refer to the CHA, TCS, CEC or EGR Sections for maintenance and service (if applicable).

Air Management System

The Air Management System is used on 1981 and later to provide additional oxygen to continue the combustion process after the exhaust gases leave the combustion chamber; much the same as the AIR system described earlier in this chapter. Air is injected into either the exhaust port(s), the exhaust manifold(s) or the catalytic converter by an engine driven air pump. The system is in operating at all times and will bypass air only momentarily during deceleration and at high speeds. The bypass function is performed by the Air Management Valve, which the check valve protects the air pump by preventing any backflow of exhaust gases.

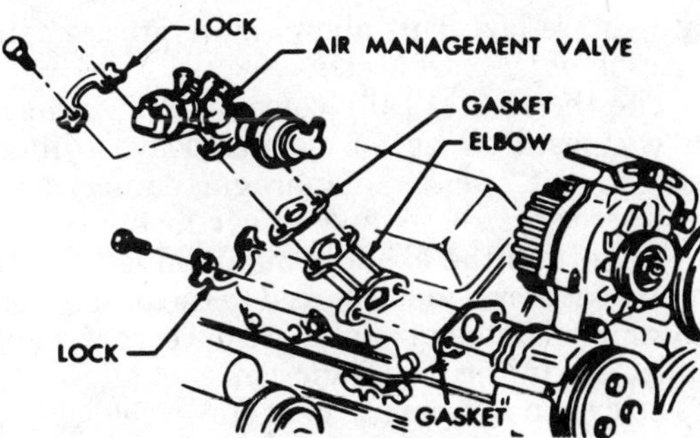

Air management system—typical

The AIR system helps to reduce HC and CO content in the exhaust gases by injecting air into the exhaust ports during cold engine operation. This air injection also helps the catalytic converter to reach the proper temperature quicker during warm-up. When the engine warm (closed loop), the AIR system injects air into the beds of a 3-way converter to lower the HC and CO content in the exhaust.

The Air Management System utilizes the following components:

1. An engine driven air pump.
2. Air management valves (Air Control and Air Switching)
3. Air flow and control hoses
4. Check valves
5. A dual bed, 3-way catalytic converter

The belt driven, vane type air pump is located at the front of the engine and supplies clean air to the system for purposes already stated.

When the engine is cold, the Electronic Control Module (ECM) energizes an air control solenoid. This allows air to flow to the air switching valve. The air switching valve is then energized to direct air into the exhaust ports.

When the engine is warm, the ECM de-energizes the air switching valve, thus directing the air between the beds of the catalytic converter. This then provides additional oxygen for the oxidizing catalyst in the second bed to decrease HC and CO levels, while at the same time keeping oxygen levels low in the first bed, enabling the reducing catalyst to effectively decrease the levels of NOx.

If the air control valve detects a rapid increase in manifold vacuum (deceleration), certain operating modes (wide open throttle, etc.) or if the ECM self diagnostic system detects any problems in the system, air is diverted to the air cleaner or directly into the atmosphere.

The primary purpose of the ECM's divert mode is to prevent backfiring. Throttle closure at the beginning of deceleration will temporarily create air/fuel mixtures which are too rich to burn completely. These mixtures will be come burnable when they reach the exhaust if they are combined with injection air. The next firing of the engine will ignite the mixture causing an exhaust backfire. Momentary diverting of the injection air from the exhaust prevents this.

The Air Management System check valves and hoses should be checked periodically for any leaks, cracks or deterioration.

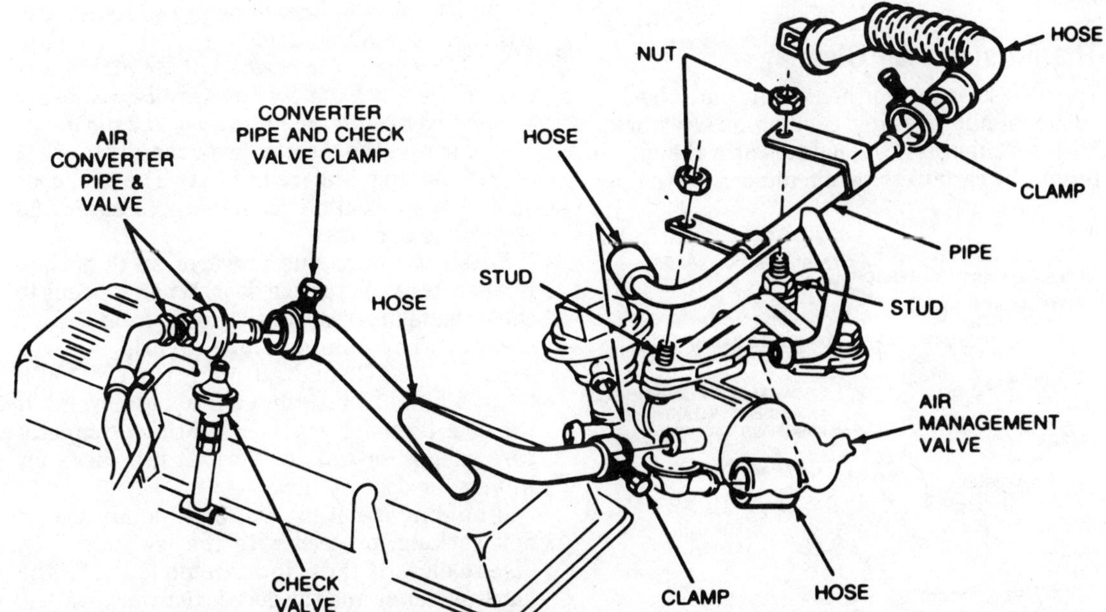

Check valve and hoses—1981 and later air management system

REMOVAL AND INSTALLATION

Air Pump

1. Remove the valves and/or adapter at the air pump.
2. Loosen the air pump adjustment bolt and remove the drive belt.
3. Unscrew the three mounting bolts and then remove the pump pulley.
4. Unscrew the pump mounting bolts and then remove the pump.
5. Installation is in the reverse order of removal. Be sure to adjust the drive bolt tension after installing it.

Check Valve

1. Release the clamp and disconnect the air hoses from the valve.
2. Unscrew the check valve from the air injection pipe.
3. Installation is in the reverse order of removal.

Air Management Valve

1. Disconnect the negative battery cable.
2. Remove the air cleaner.
3. Tag and disconnect the vacuum hose from the valve.
4. Tag and disconnect the air outlet hoses from the valve.
5. Bend back the lock tabs and then remove the bolts holding the elbow to the valve.
6. Tag and disconnect any electrical connections at the valve and then remove the valve from the elbow.
7. Installation is in the reverse order of removal.

Thermostatic Air Cleaner

The use of carburetor heated air dates back to 1960 when it was first used on heavy trucks.

This system is designed to warm the air entering the carburetor when underhood temperatures are low. This allows more precise calibration of the carburetor.

The thermostatically controlled air cleaner is composed of the air cleaner body, a filter, sensor unit, vacuum diaphragm, damper door and associated hoses and connections. Heat radiating from the exhaust manifold is trapped by a heat stove and is ducted to the air cleaner to supply heated air to the carburetor. A movable door in the air cleaner snorkel allows air to be drawn in from the heat stove (cold operation) or from the underhood air (warm operation). Periods of extended idling, climbing a grade or high speed operation are followed by a considerable increase in engine compartment temperature. Excessive fuel vapors enter the intake manifold causing an over-rich mixture, resulting in a rough idle. To overcome this, some engines may be equipped with a hot idle compensator.

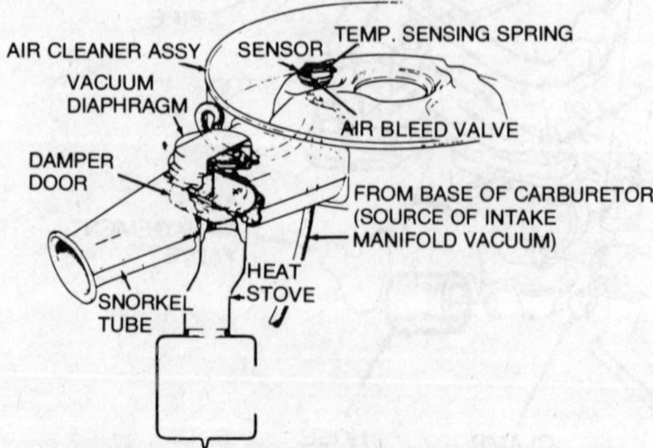

Components of the thermostatically controlled air cleaner

SERVICE

1. Either start with a cold engine or remove the air cleaner from the engine for at least half an hour. While cooling the air cleaner, leave the engine compartment hood open.
2. Tape a thermometer, of known accuracy, to the inside of the air cleaner so that it is near the temperature sensor unit. Install the air cleaner on the engine but do not fasten its securing nut.
3. Start the engine. With the engine cold and the outside temperature less than +90°F (+32°C), the door should be in the HEAT ON position (closed to outside air).

NOTE: *Due to the position of the air cleaner on some trucks, a mirror may be necessary when observing the position of the air door.*

4. Operate the throttle lever rapidly to ½–¾ of its opening and release it. The air door should open to allow outside air to enter and then close again.
5. Allow the engine to warm up to normal temperature. Watch the door. When it opens to the outside air, remove the cover from the air cleaner. The temperature should be over +90°F (+32°C) and no more than +130°F (+54°C); +115°F (+46°C) is about normal. If the door does not work within these temperature ranges, or fails to work at all, check for linkage or door binding.

If binding is not present and the air door is not working, proceed with the vacuum tests, given below. If these indicate no faults in the vacuum motor and the door is not working, the temperature sensor is defective and must be replaced.

Vacuum Motor Test

NOTE: *Be sure that the vacuum hose which runs between the temperature switch and the vacuum motor is not pinched by the retaining clip under the air cleaner. This could prevent the air door from closing.*

1. Check all of the vacuum lines and fittings for leaks. Correct any leaks. If none are found, proceed with the test.

2. Remove the hose which runs from the sensor to the vacuum motor. Run a hose directly from the manifold vacuum source to the vacuum motor.

3. If the motor closes the air door, it is functioning properly and the temperature sensor is defective.

4. If the motor does not close the door and no binding is present in its operation, the vacuum motor is defective and must be replaced.

NOTE: *If an alternate vacuum source is applied to the motor, insert a vacuum gauge in the line by using a T-fitting. Apply at least 9 in.Hg. of vacuum in order to operate the motor.*

Transmission Controlled Spark

Introduced in 1970, this system controls exhaust emissions by eliminating vacuum advance in the lower forward gears.

The 1970 system consists of a transmission switch, solenoid vacuum switch, time delay relay, and a thermostatic water temperature switch. The solenoid vacuum switch is de-energized in the lower gears via the transmission switch and closes off distributor vacuum. The 2-way transmission switch is activated by the shifter shaft on manual transmissions, and by fluid pressure on automatic transmissions. The switch energizes the solenoid in High gear, the plunger extends and uncovers the vacuum port, and the distributor receives full vacuum. The temperature switch overrides the system until the engine temperature reaches +82°F (+28°C). This allows vacuum advance in all gears, thereby preventing stalling after

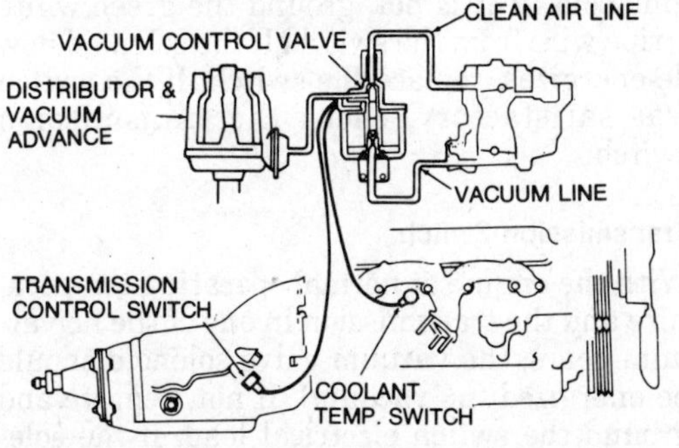

1970 TCS system

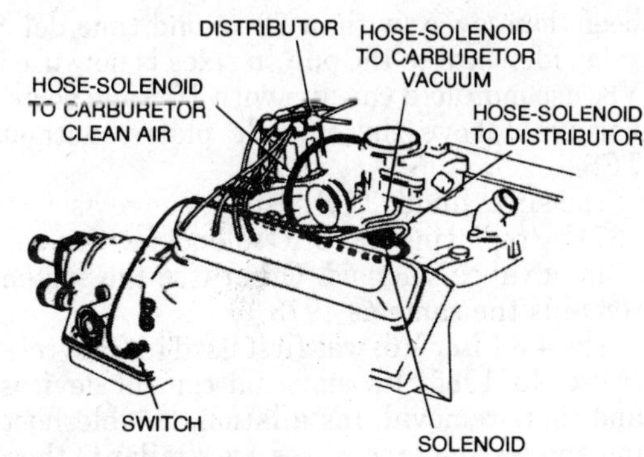

TCS system components

starting. A time delay relay opens fifteen seconds after the ignition is switched on. Full vacuum advance during this delay eliminates the possibility of stalling.

The 1971 system is similar, except that the vacuum solenoid (now called a Combination Emissions Control solenoid) serves two functions. One function is to control distributor vacuum; the added function is to act as a deceleration throttle stop in High gear. This cuts down on emissions when the vehicle is coming to stop in High gear. Two throttle settings are necessary; one for curb idle and one for emission control on coast.

The 1972 six cylinder system is similar to that used in 1971, except that an idle stop solenoid has been added to the system and the name was changed back to TCS. In the energized position, the solenoid maintains engine speed at the predetermined fast idle. When de-energized the solenoid allows the throttle plates to close beyond the normal idle position, thus cutting off the air supply and preventing engine run-on. The six is the only 1972 engine with a CEC valve, which serves the same deceleration function as in 1971. The time delay relay delays full vacuum twenty seconds after the transmission is shifted into High gear. 1972 V8 engines use a vacuum advance solenoid similar to that used in 1970. The solenoid controls distributor vacuum advance and performs no throttle positioning function. The idle stop solenoid used on V8s operates in the same manner as the one on sixes. All air conditioned models have an additional anti-diesel (run-on) solenoid which engages the compressor clutch for 3 seconds after the ignition is switched off. The 1973 TCS system on the six is identical to that on 1972 six, except for recalibration of the temperature switch. The system used on 1973 engines changed slightly from 1972. In place of the CEC solenoid on the six, the V8 continues to use a vacuum advance solenoid. The other differences are: The upshift delay relay, previously located under the instrument panel has been done away with; a 20 second time delay relay identical to the one on sixes is now used; V8s use manifold vacuum with TCS and ported vacuum (above the throttle plates) without TCS.

The six cylinder TCS system was revised for 1974 by replacing the CEC solenoid with a vacuum advance solenoid. Otherwise the system remains the same as 1973.

The 4.3 Liter V6, was first used in Chevrolet trucks in 1985. Its emission control devices, and their removal, installation, troubleshooting and testing procedures are similar to those on the V8s.

The 4.3, 5.0 (RPO LF3), and 5.7L (RPO LS9) engines in California have a Computer Command Control system which controls:

- Fuel control system.
- Air injection reaction (AIR).
- Exhaust gas recirculation (EGR).
- Evaporative Emission Control System (EECS).
- Electronic Spark Timing (EST).
- Electronic Spark Control (ESC) (4.3L CAL.).
- Transmission Converter Clutch (TCC).

An Electronic Control Module (ECM) is the heart of the Computer Command Control System. The ECM uses sensors to get information about engine operation which it uses to vary systems it controls.

The ECM has the ability to do some diagnosis of itself. When it recognizes a problem, it lights a "Service Engine Soon" lamp on the instrument panel. When this occurs, the cause of the light coming on should be checked as soon as reasonably possible, and the malfunction corrected.

All diagnosis and repair of the Computer Command Control system, the Electronic Control Module, and the components they control, should be referred to a qualified technician possessing the proper diagnostic equipment.

TESTING

If there is a TCS system malfunction, first connect a vacuum gauge in the hose between the solenoid valve and the distributor vacuum unit. Drive the vehicle or raise it on a frame lift and observe the vacuum gauge. If full vacuum is available in all gears, check for the following:

1. Blown fuse.
2. Disconnected wire at solenoid operated vacuum valve.
3. Disconnected wire at transmission switch.
4. Temperature override switch energized due to low engine temperature.
5. Solenoid failure.

If no vacuum is available in any gear, check the following:

1. Solenoid valve vacuum lines switched.
2. Clogged solenoid vacuum valve.
3. Distributor or manifold vacuum lines leaking or disconnected.
4. Transmission switch or wire grounded.

Tests for individual components are as follows:

Idle Stop Solenoid

This unit may be checked simply by observing it while an assistant switches the ignition on and off. It should extend further with the current switched on. The unit is not repairable.

Solenoid Vacuum Valve

Check that proper manifold vacuum is available. Connect the vacuum gauge in the line between the solenoid valve and the distributor. Apply 12 volts to the solenoid. If vacuum is still not available, the valve is defective, either mechanically or electrically. The unit is not repairable. If the valve is satisfactory, check the relay next.

Relay

1. With the engine at normal operating temperature and the ignition on, ground the solenoid vacuum valve terminal with the black lead. The solenoid should energize (no vacuum) if the relay is satisfactory.
2. With the solenoid energized as in Step 1, connect a jumper from the relay terminal with the green/white stripe lead to ground. The solenoid should de-energize (vacuum available) if the relay is satisfactory.
3. If the relay worked properly in Steps 1 and 2, check the temperature switch. The relay unit is not repairable.

Temperature Switch

The vacuum valve solenoid should be de-energized (vacuum available) with the engine cold. If it is not, ground the green/white stripe wire from the switch. If the solenoid now de-energizes, replace the switch. If the switch was satisfactory, check the transmission switch.

Transmission Switch

With the engine at normal operating temperature and the transmission in one of the no vacuum gears, the vacuum valve solenoid should be energized (no vacuum). If not, remove and ground the switch electrical lead. If the solenoid energizes, replace the switch.

Exhaust Gas Recirculation

The EGR system and valve were introduced in 1973. Its purpose is to control oxides of nitrogen which are formed during the peak combustion temperatures. The end products of combustion are relatively inert gases derived from the exhaust gases which are directed into the EGR valve to help lower peak combustion temperatures.

The EGR valve contains a vacuum diaphragm operated by manifold vacuum. The vacuum signal port is located in the carburetor body and is exposed to engine vacuum in the off/idle and part throttle operation. In 1974, a thermal delay switch was added to delay operation of the valve during engine warmup, when NOx levels are already at a minimum.

On inline sixes, the EGR valve is located on the intake manifold adjacent to the carburetor. On V6 and V8 engines, the valve is located on the right rear side of the intake manifold adjacent to the rocker arm cover.

SERVICE

The EGR valve is not serivcable, except for replacement. To check the valve, proceed as follows:

1. Connect a tachometer to the engine.
2. With the engine running at normal operating temperature, with the choke valve fully open, set the engine rpm at 2000. The transmission should be in Park (automatic) or Neutral (manual) with the parking brake On and the wheels blocked.
3. Disconnect the vacuum hose at the valve. Make sure that vacuum is available at the valve and look at the tachometer to see if the engine speed increases. If it does, a malfunction of the valve is indicated.
4. If necessary, replace the valve.

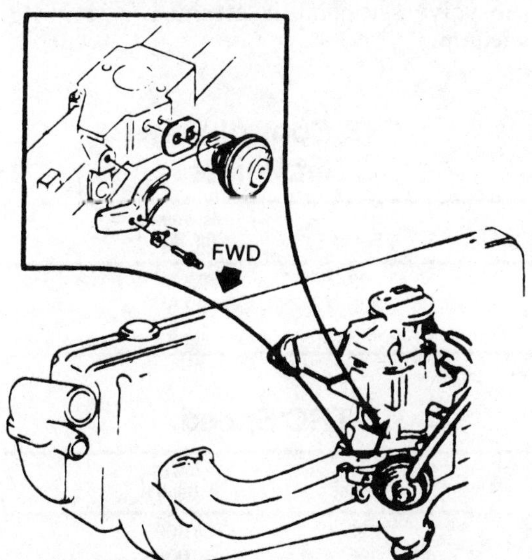

Six cylinder EGR valve

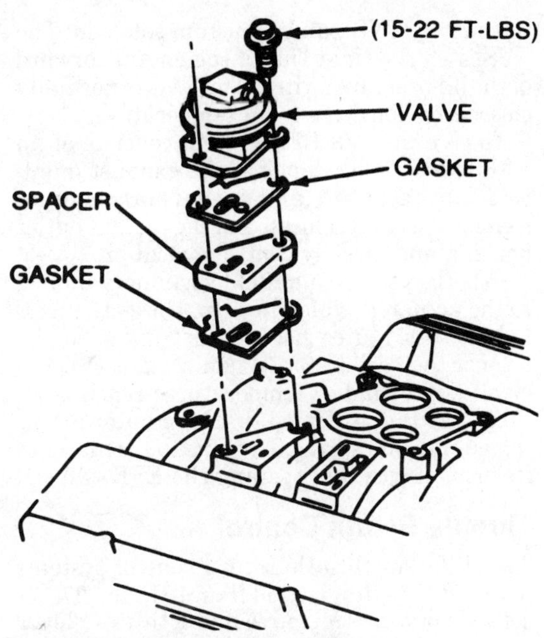

Typical EGR valve mounting, V8s

Evaporation Control System

Introduced on California vehicles in 1970, an nationwide in 1971, this system reduces the amount of escaping gasoline vapors. Float bowl emissions are controlled by internal carburetor modifications. Redesigned bowl vents, reduced bowl capacity, heat shields, and improved intake manifold-to-carburetor insulation serve to reduce vapor loss into the atmosphere. The venting of fuel tank vapors into the air has been stopped. Fuel vapors are now directed through lines to a canister containing an activated charcoal filter. Unburned vapors are trapped here until the engine is started. When the engine is running, the canister is purged by air drawn in by manifold vacuum. The air and fuel vapors are directed into the engine to be burned.

SERVICE

Replace the filter in the engine compartment canister at the intervals shown in the Maintenance Intervals Chart in Chapter 1. If the fuel tank cap requires replacement, ensure that the new cap is the correct part for your truck.

Early Fuel Evaporation System

This system is used on 1975 and later light duty models. The six cylinder system consists of an EFE valve mount at the flange of the exhaust manifold, an actuator, a thermal vacuum switch (TVS), and a vacuum solenoid. The TVS is on the right side of the engine forward of the oil pressure switch. The TVS is normally closed and sensitive to oil temperature.

The V6 and V8 EFE system consists of an EFE valve at the flange of the exhaust manifold, an actuator, and a thermal vacuum switch. The TVS is located in the coolant outlet housing and directly controls vacuum.

In both systems, manifold vacuum is applied to the actuator, which in turn, closes the EFE valve. This routes hot exhaust gases to the base of the carburetor. When coolant (V6/V8) or oil (six cylinder) temperatures reach a set limit, vacuum is denied to the actuator allowing an internal spring to return the actuator to its normal position, opening the EFE valve.

Throttle Return Control

Two different throttle return control systems are used. The first is used from 1975 to 1978. It consists of a control valve and a throttle lever actuator. When the truck is coasting against the engine, the control valve is open to allow vacuum to operate the throttle lever actuator. The throttle lever actuator then pushes the throttle lever slightly open reducing the HC (hydrocarbon) emission level during coasting. When manifold vacuum drops below a predetermined level, the control valve closes, the throttle lever retracts, and the throttle lever closes to the idler position.

The second TRC system is used in 1979 and later. It consists of a throttle lever actuator, a solenoid vacuum control valve, and an electronic speed sensor. The throttle lever actuator, mounted on the carburetor, opens the primary throttle plates a present amount, above normal engine idle speed, in response to a signal from the solenoid vacuum control valve. The valve, mounted at the left rear of the engine above the intake manifold on the six cylinder, or on the thermostat housing mounting stud on the V6 or V8, is held open in response to a signal from the electronic speed sensor. When open, the valve allows a vacuum signal to be sent to the throttle lever actuator. The speed sensor monitors engine speed at the distributor. It supplies an electrical signal to the solenoid valve, as long as a preset engine speed is exceeded. The object of this system is the same as that of the earlier system.

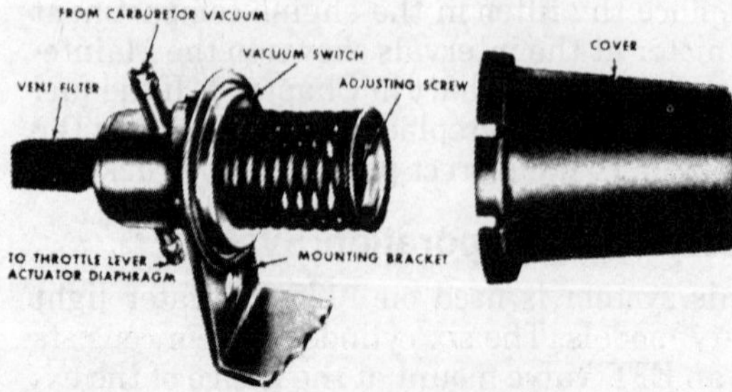

Throttle return control valve through 1978

SERVICE

Control Valve

1975–76

1. Disconnect the valve-to-carburetor hose and connect it to an external vacuum source with a vacuum gauge.
2. Disconnect the valve-to-actuator hose at the connector and connect it to a vacuum gauge.
3. Place a finger firmly over the end of the bleed fitting.
4. Apply a minimum of 23 in.Hg. vacuum to the control valve and seal off the vacuum source. The gauge on the actuator side should read the same as the gauge on the source side. If not, the valve needs adjustment. If vacuum drops off on either side (with the finger still on the bleed fitting), the valve is defective and should be replaced.
5. With a minimum of 23 in.Hg. vacuum in the valve, remove the finger from the bleed fitting. The vacuum level in the actuator side will drop to zero and the reading on the source side will drop to a value that will be the value set point. If the value is not within ½ in.Hg. vacuum of the specified valve set point, adjust the valve.
6. Gently pry off the plastic cover.
7. Turn the adjusting screw in (clockwise) to raise the set point or out (counterclockwise) to lower the set point.
8. Recheck the valve set point.
9. If necessary, repeat the adjustment until the valve set point is attained ± ½ in.Hg. vacuum.

TRS Control Valve Set Points

Engine	Set Point (in. Hg)
292	22.5
305	22.5
350	21.5

TRC Speed

Engine	Setting (rpm)
292	1600
305	1600
350	1500

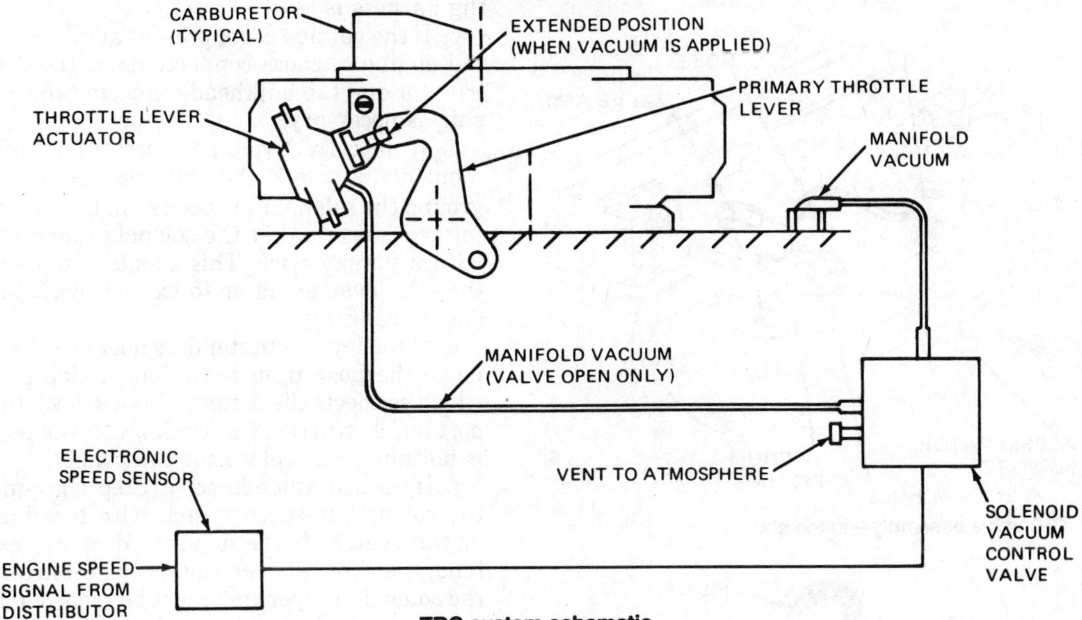

TRC system schematic

1977–78

1. Disconnect the vavle-to-carburetor hose at the carburetor. Connect the hose to an external vacuum source, with an accurate vacuum gauge connected into the line near the valve.
2. Apply a minimum of 25 in.Hg. of vacuum to the control valve vacuum supply fitting while sealing off the vacuum supply between the gauge and the vacuum source. The vacuum gauge will indicate the set point value of the valve.
3. If the gauge reading is not within 0.5 in.Hg. of the specified value (see the chart), the valve must be adjusted. If the trapped vacuum drops off faster than 0.1 in.Hg. per second, the valve is leaking and must be replaced.
4. To adjust the valve set point, follow Steps 6–9 of the 1975–76 adjustment procedure.

Throttle Valve

1975–78

1. Disconnect the valve-to-actuator hose at the valve and connect it to an external vacuum source.
2. Apply 20 in.Hg. vacuum to the actuator and seal the vacuum source. If the vacuum gauge reading drops, the valve is leaking and should be replaced.
3. Check the throttle lever, shaft, and linkage for freedom of operation.
4. Start the engine and warm it to operating temperature.
5. Note the idle rpm.
6. Apply 20 in.Hg. vacuum to the actuator and manually operate the throttle. Allow it to close against the extended actuator plunger. Note the engine rpm.
7. Release and reapply 20 in.Hg. vacuum to the actuator and note the rpm at which the engine speed increases (do not assist the actuator).
8. If the engine speed obtained in Step 7 is not within 150 rpm of that obtained in Step 6, then the actuator may be binding. If the binding cannot be corrected, replace the actuator.
9. Release the vacuum from the actuator and the engine speed should return to within 50 rpm of the speed noted in Steps 4 and 5.

To adjust the actuator:

10. Turn the screw on the actuator plunger until the specified TRC speed range is obtained.

THROTTLE LEVER ACTUATOR

1979 and Later

The checking procedure is the same as for earlier years. Follow Steps 1–9 of the Throttle Valve procedure. Adjustment procedures are covered in the carburetor adjustments section, later in this chapter.

TRC SYSTEM CHECK

1979 and Later

1. Connect a tachometer to the distributor TACH terminal. Start the engine and raise the

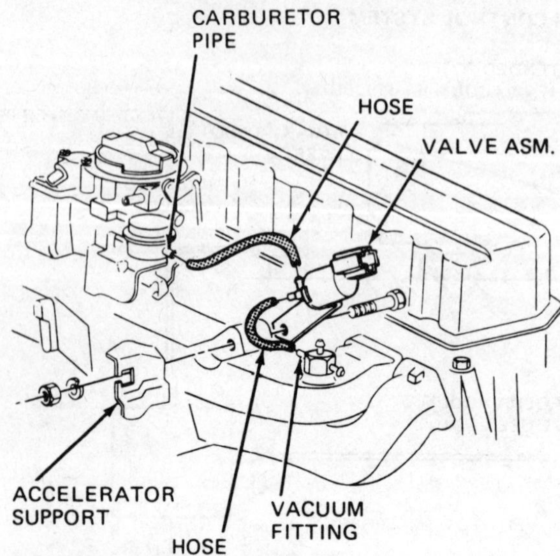

TRC valve assembly—inline six

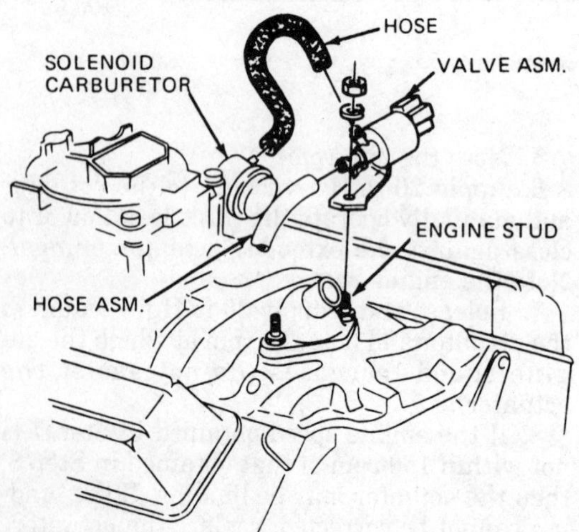

TRC valve assembly—V8s

engine speed to 1890 rpm. The throttle lever actuator on the carburetor should extend.

2. Reduce the engine speed to 1700 rpm. The lever actuator should retract.

3. If the actuator operates outside of the speed limits, the speed switch is faulty and must be replaced. It cannot be adjusted.

4. If the actuator does not operate at all:

a. Check the voltage at the vacuum solenoid and the speed switch with a voltmeter. Connect the negative probe of the voltmeter to the engine ground and the positive probe to the voltage source wire on the component. The positive probe can be inserted on the connector body at the wire side; it is not necessary to unplug the connector. Voltage should be 12 to 14 volts in both cases.

b. If the correct voltage is present at one component but not the other, the engine wiring harness is faulty.

c. If the voltage is not present at all, check the engine harness connections at the distributor and the bulkhead connector and repair as necessary.

d. If the correct voltage is present at both components, check the solenoid operation: ground the solenoid-to-speed switch connecting wire terminal at the solenoid connector with a jumper wire. This should cause the throttle lever actuator to extend, with the engine running.

e. If the lever actuator does not extend, remove the hose from the solenoid side port which connects the actuator hose. Check the port for obstructions or blockage. If the port is not plugged, replace the solenoid.

f. If the actuator extends in Step d, ground the solenoid-to-speed switch wire terminal at the switch. If the actuator does not extend, the wire between the speed switch and the solenoid is open and must be repaired. If the actuator does extend, check the speed switch ground wire for a ground; it should read zero volts with the engine running. Check the speed switch-to-distributor wire for a proper connection. If the ground and distributor wires are properly connected and the actuator still does not extend when the engine speed is above 1890 rpm, replace the speed switch.

5. If the actuator is extended at all speeds:

a. Remove the connector from the vacuum solenoid.

b. If the actuator remains extended, check the solenoid side port orifice for blockage. If plugged, clear and reconnect the system and recheck. If the actuator is still extended, remove the solenoid connector; if the actuator does not retreat, replace the vacuum solenoid.

c. If the actuator retracts with the solenoid connector off, reconnect it and remove the speed switch connector. If the actuator retracts, the problem is in the speed switch, which should be replaced. If the actuator does not retract, the solenoid-to-speed switch wire is shorted to ground in the wiring harness. Repair the short.

Oxygen Sensor

1983 and Later

The oxygen sensor is a spark plug shaped device that is screwed into the exhaust manifold on V8s and into the exhaust pipe on inline sixes. It monitors the oxygen content of the exhaust gases and sends a voltage signal to the Electronic Control Module (ECM). The ECM

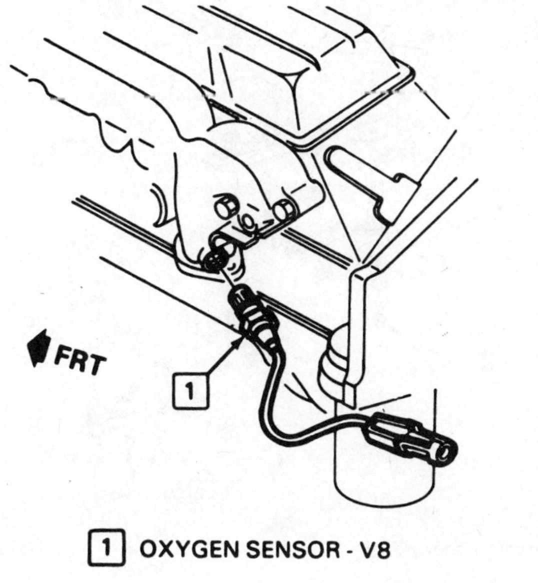

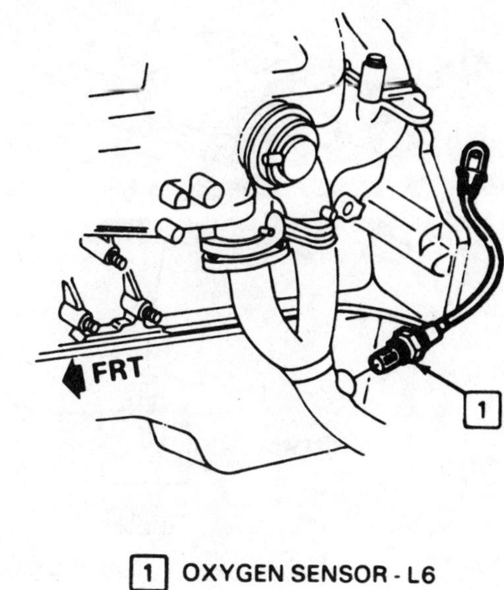

Oxygen sensor locations

monitors this voltage and, depending on the value of the received signal, issues a command to the mixture control solenoid on the carburetor to adjust for rich or lean conditions.

The proper operation of the oxygen sensor depends upon four basic conditions:

1. Good electrical connections. Since the sensor generates low currents, good clean electrical connections at the sensor are a must.
2. Outside air supply. Air must circulate to the internal portion of the sensor. When servicing the sensor, do not restrict the air passages.
3. Proper operating temperatures. The ECM will not recognize the sensor's signals until the sensor reaches approximately +600°F (+316°C).
4. Non-leaded fuel. The use of leaded gasoline will damage the sensor very quickly.

NOTE: *No attempt should be made to measure the output voltage of the sensor. The current drain of any conventional voltmeter would be enough to permanently damage the sensor. No jumpers, test leads, or other electrical connections should ever be made to the sensor. Use these tool ONLY on the ECM side of the harness connector AFTER the oxygen sensor has been disconnected.*

REMOVAL AND INSTALLATION

CAUTION: *The sensor uses a permanently attached pigtail and connector. This pigtail should not be removed from the sensor. Damage or removal of the pigtail or connector could affect the proper operation of the sensor. Keep the electrical connector and louvered end of the sensor clean and free of grease. NEVER use cleaning solvents of any type on the sensor.*

NOTE: *The oxygen sensor may be difficult to remove when the temperature of the engine is below +120°F (+49°C). Excessive force may damage the threads in the exhaust manifold or exhaust pipe.*

1. Disconnect the electrical connector and any attaching hardware.
2. Remove the sensor.
3. Coat the threads of the sensor with a GM antiseize compound (*5613695) before installation. New sensors are precoated with this compound.

NOTE: *The GM antiseize compound is NOT a conventional antiseize paste. The sue of a regular paste may electrically insulate the sensor, rendering it useless. The threads MUST be coated with the proper electrically conductive antiseize compound.*

4. Install the sensor and torque to 30 ft.lb. Use care in making sure the silicone boot is in the correct position to avoid melting it during operation.
5. Connect the electrical connector and attaching hardware if used.

Oxidizing Catalytic Converter

An underfloor oxidizing catalytic converter is used to control hydrocarbon and carbon monoxide emissions on many 1975 and later mod-

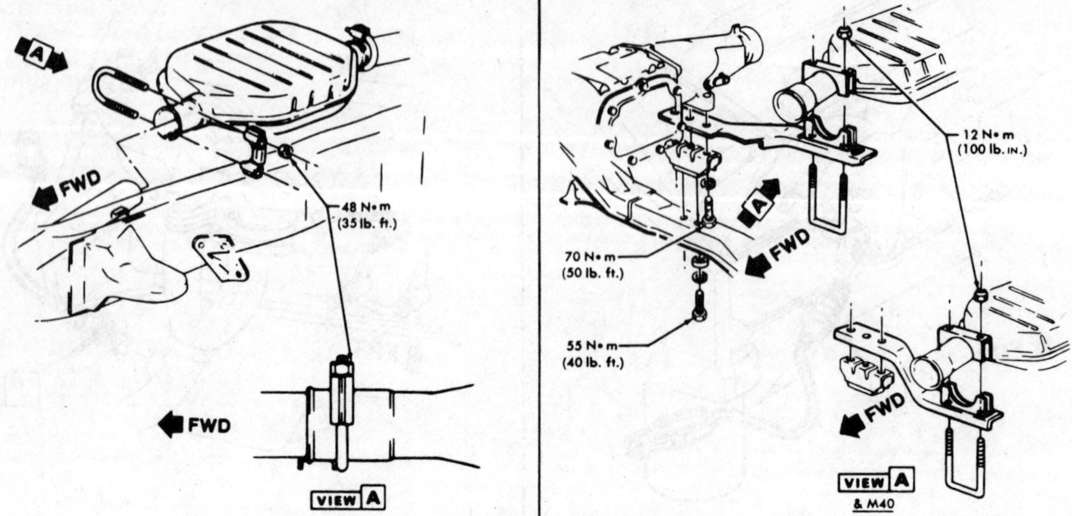

Typical catalytic converter mounting

els. Control is accomplished by placing a catalyst in the exhaust system to enable all exhaust gas flow to pass through it and undergo a chemical reaction before passing into the atmosphere. The chemical reaction involved is the oxidizing of hydrocarbons and carbon monoxide into water vapor and carbon dioxide.

REMOVAL AND INSTALLATION

CAUTION: *Catalytic converter operating temperatures are extremely high. Outside converter temperatures can go well over +1,000°F (+538°C). Use extreme care when working on or around the catalytic converter.*

1. Raise and support the truck.
2. Remove the clamps at the front and rear of the converter.
3. Cut the converter pipes at the front and rear of the converter and remove it.
4. Remove the support from the transmission.
5. Remove the converter pipe-to-exhaust pipe and the converter pipe-to-tailpipe.

To install the converter:

6. Install the exhaust pipe and tailpipe into the converter with sealer.
7. Loosely install the support on the transmission.
8. Install new U-bolts and clamps, check all clearances and tighten the clamps.
9. Lower the truck.

NOTE: *Dealers have equipment to remove and replace the converter contents (pellets) without removing the converter from the exhaust system.*

Pulse Air Injection Reactor System

This system consists of four air valves which inject fresh air into the exhaust system in order to further the combustion process of the exhaust gases. The firing of the engine creates a pulsating flow of exhaust gases, which are of either positive or negative pressure. Negative pressure at the pulse air valve will result in air being injected into the exhaust system. Positive pressure will force the check valve closed and no exhaust gases will flow into the fresh air supply.

Regularly inspect the pulse air valves, pipes, grommets and hose for cracks and leaks. Replace the necessary part if any are found. If a check valve fails, exhaust gases will get into the carburetor through the air cleaner and cause the engine to surge and perform poorly.

If exhaust gases pass through a pulse air valve, the paint will be burned off the rocker arm cover plenum as a result of the excessive heat. The rubber grommets and hose will also deteriorate. Failure of the pulse air valve can also be indicated by a hissing sound.

REMOVAL AND INSTALLATION

1. Remove the air cleaner. Disconnect the rubber hose from the plenum connecting pipe. (See illustration).
2. Disconnect the four check valve fittings at the cylinder head and remove the check valve pipes from the plenum grommets.
3. Disconnect the check valve from the check valve pipe.
4. Assemble the replacement check valve to the check valve pipe.
5. Attach the check valve assembly to the cylinder head as illustrated. Hand tighten the fittings.
6. Using a 1″ (25.4mm) open end wrench as a lever, align the check valve on pipe **A** with the plenum grommet. Using the palm of your

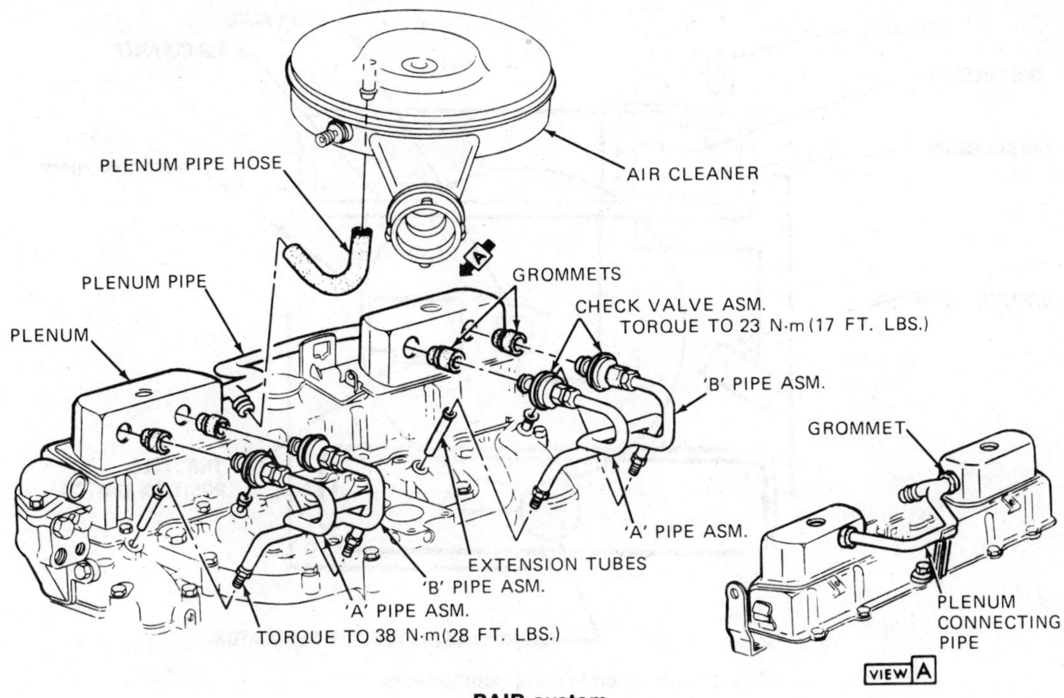

PAIR system

left hand, press the check valve into the grommet. Using a silicone lubricant on the grommet will make thing a little easier. Repeat this procedure for pipe **B** using your left hand for the tool and your right hand for installing the valve in the grommet.

DIESEL ENGINE EMISSIONS CONTROLS

Crankcase Ventilation

A Crankcase Depression Regulator Valve (CDRV) is used to regulate (meter) the flow of crankcase gases back into the engine to be burned. The CDRV is designed to limit vacuum in the crankcase as the gases are drawn from the valve covers through the CDRV and into the intake manifold (air crossover).

Fresh air enters the engine through the combination filter, check valve and oil fill cap. The fresh air mixes with blow-by gases and enters both valve covers. The gases pass through a filter installed on the valve covers and are drawn into connecting tubing.

Intake manifold vacuum acts against a spring loaded diaphragm to control the flow of crankcase gases. Higher intake vacuum levels pull the diaphragm closer to the top of the outlet tube. This reduces the amount of gases being drawn from the crankcase and decreases the vacuum level in the crankcase. As the intake vacuum decreases, the spring pushes the diaphragm away from the top of the outlet tube allowing more gases to flow to the intake manifold.

NOTE: *Do not allow any solvent to come in contact with the diaphragm of the Crankcase Depression Regulator Valve because the diaphragm will fail.*

Exhaust Gas Recirculation (EGR)

To lower the formation of nitrogen oxides (NOx) in the exhaust, it is necessary to reduce combustion temperatures. This is done in the diesel, as in the gasoline engine, by introducing exhaust gases into the cylinders through the EGR valve.

On the 379 diesel, and Exhaust Pressure Regulator (EPR) valve and solenoid operate in conjunction with the EGR valve. The EPR valve's job is to increase exhaust backpressure in order to increase EGR flow (to reduce nitrous oxide emissions). The EPR valve is usually open, and the solenoid is normally closed. When energized by the B+ wire from the Throttle Position Switch (TPS), the solenoid opens, allowing vacuum to the EPR valve, closing it. This occurs at idle. As the throttle is opened, at a calibrated throttle angle, the TPS de-energizes the EPR solenoid, cutting off vacuum to the EPR valve, closing the valve.

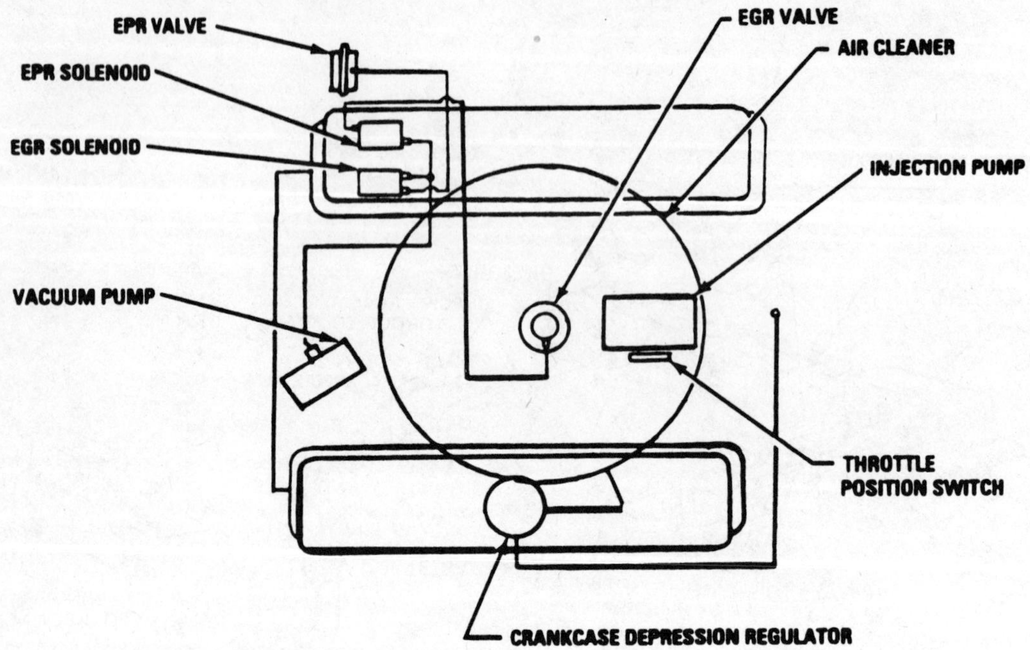

379 diesel emissions components

FUNCTIONAL TESTS OF COMPONENTS

Vacuum Regulator Valve (VRV)

The Vacuum Regulator Valve is attached to the side of the injection pump and regulates vacuum in proportion to throttle angle. Vacuum from the vacuum pump is supplied to port A and vacuum at port B is reduced as the throttle is opened. At closed throttle, the vacuum is 15″; at half throttle, 6″; at wide open throttle there is zero vacuum.

Exhaust Gas Recirculation (EGR) Valve

Apply vacuum to vacuum port. The valve should be fully open at 10.5" and closed below 6″.

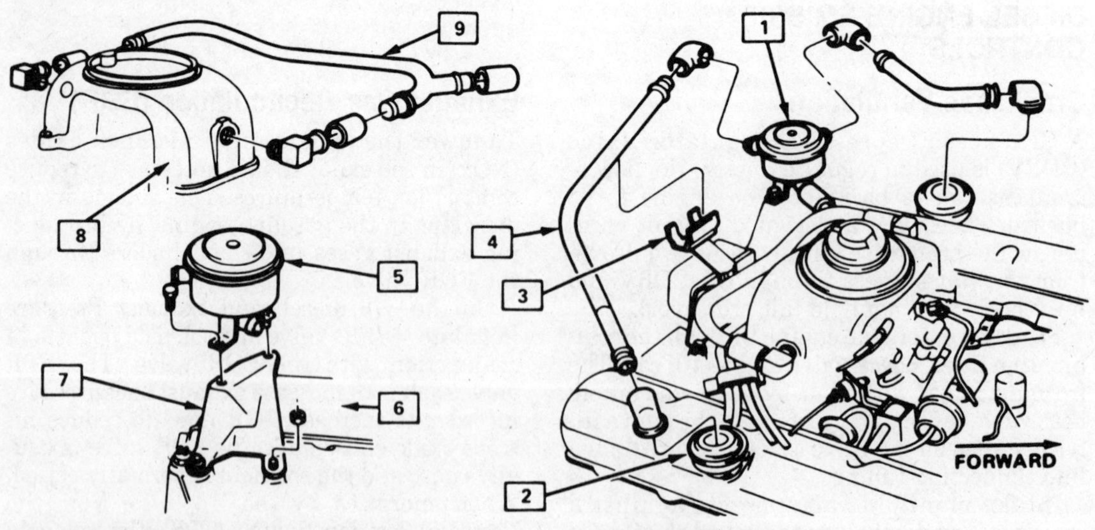

1. Crankcase depression regulator (CDR)
2. Ventilation filter
3. Brace clip
4. Ventilation pipes
5. Crankcase depression regulator (CDR)
6. L.H. valve cover
7. Bracket
8. Air crossover
9. Air crossover to regulator valve pipe

Crankcase ventilation system components, diesels

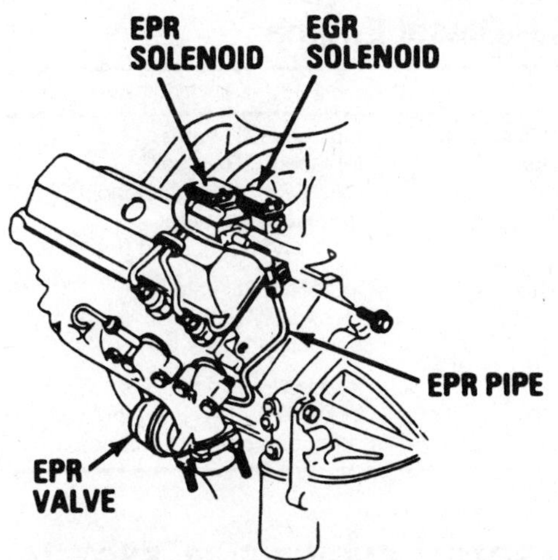

Exhaust Pressure Regulator valve and solenoid, 379 diesels

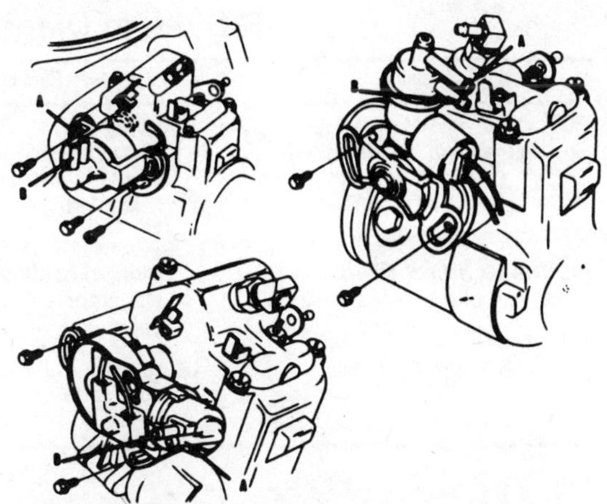

Diesel vacuum regulator valve (VRV), mounted to injection pump

Response Vacuum Reducer (RVR)

Connect a vacuum gauge to the port marked **To EGR valve to T.C.C. solenoid**. Connect a hand operated vacuum pump to the VRV port. Draw a 50.66 kPa (15 in.Hg.) vacuum on the pump and the reading on the vacuum gauge should be lower than the vacuum pump reading as follows:

- 0.75″ Except High Altitude
- 2.5″ High Altitude

Torque Converter Clutch Operated Solenoid

When the torque converter clutch is engaged, an electrical signal energizes the solenoid allowing ports 1 and 2 to be interconnected. When the solenoid is not energized, port 1 is closed and ports 2 and 3 are interconnected.

Solenoid Energized

- Ports 1 and 3 are connected.

Solenoid De-Energized

- Ports 2 and 3 are connected.

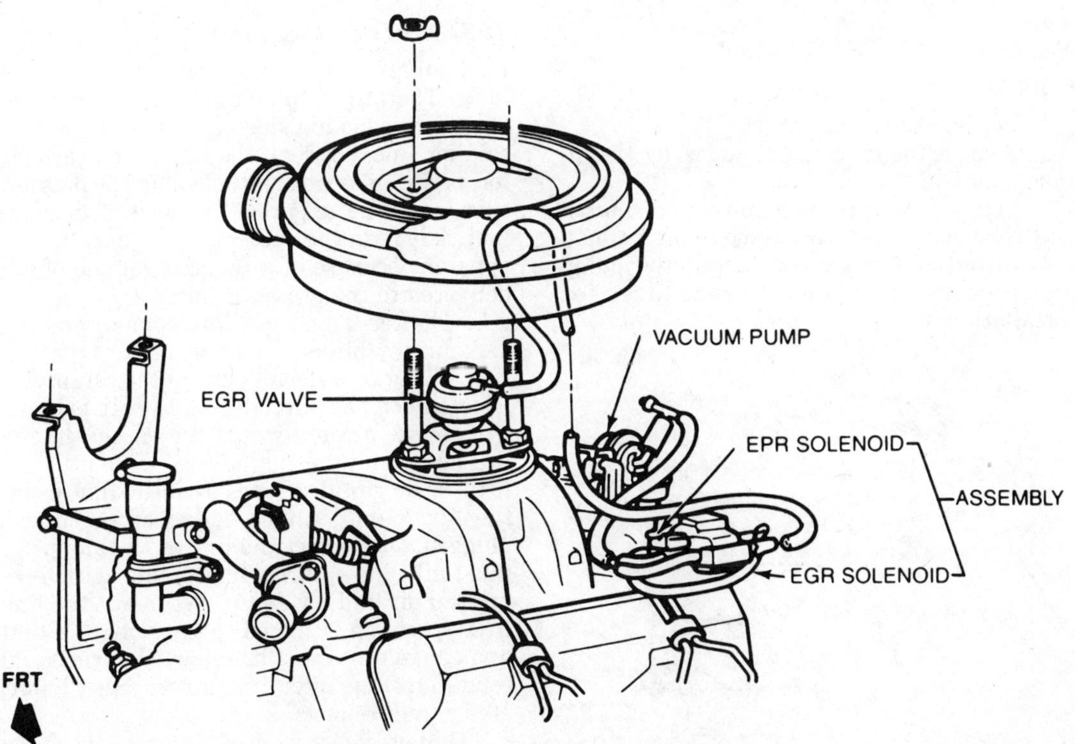

Diesel EGR valve location, 379 (6.2L) engine

EGR System Diagnosis—Diesel Engine

Condition	Possible Causes	Correction
EGR valve will not open. Engine stalls on deceleration. Engine runs rough on light throttle.	Binding or stuck EGR valve. No vacuum to EGR valve. Control valve blocked or air flow restricted.	Replace EGR valve. Replace EGR valve. Check VRV, RVR, solenoid, T.C.C. Operation, Vacuum Pump and connecting hoses.
EGR valve will not close. (Heavy smoke on acceleration).	Binding or stuck EGR valve. Constant high vacuum to EGR valve.	Replace EGR valve. Check VRV, RVR, solenoid, and connecting hoses.
EGR valve opens partially.	Binding EGR valve. Low vacuum at EGR valve.	Replace EGR valve. Check VRV, RVR, solenoid, vacuum pump, and connecting hoses.

Vacuum Pump Diesel Engines

Since the air crossover and intake manifold in a diesel engine is unrestricted (unlike a gasoline engine which has throttle plates creating a venturi effect) there is no vacuum source. To provide vacuum, a vacuum pump is mounted in the location occupied by the distributor in a gasoline engine. This pump supplies the air conditioning servos, the cruise control servos, and the transmission vacuum modulator where required.

The pump is a diaphragm type which needs no maintenance. It is driven by a drive gear on its lower end which meshes with gear teeth on the end of the engine's camshaft.

REMOVAL AND INSTALLATION

8–379

1. Disconnect the batteries.
2. Remove the air cleaner, and cover the intake manifold.
3. Remove the vacuum pump clamp, disconnect the vacuum line and remove the pump.
4. Install a new gasket. Install the pump and reverse the removal procedures for installation.

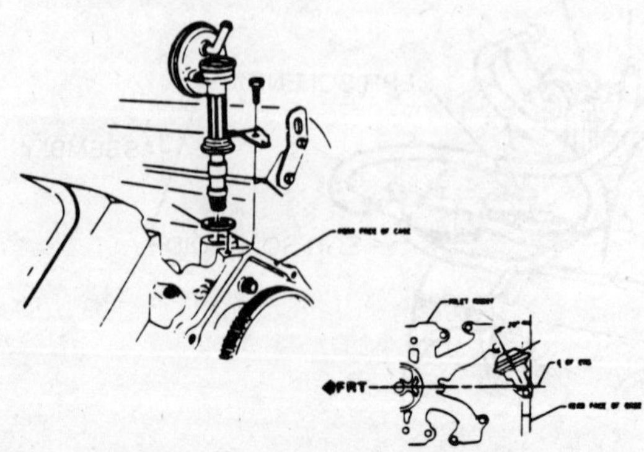

Vacuum pump mounting, 379 (6.2L) engine

GASOLINE ENGINE FUEL SYSTEM

Mechanical Fuel Pump

The fuel pump is a single action AC diaphragm type. All fuel pumps used on inline and V8 engines in vans are diaphragm type and because of design are serviced by replacement only. No adjustments or repairs are possible.

The pump is operated by an eccentric on the camshaft. On six cylinder engines, the eccentric acts directly on the pump rocker arm. On V8 engines, a pushrod between the camshaft eccentric and the fuel pump operates the pump rocker arm.

TESTING THE FUEL PUMP

Fuel pumps should always be tested on the vehicle. The larger line between the pump and tank is the suction side of the system and the smaller line, between the pump and carburetor, is the pressure side. A leak in the pressure side would be apparent because of dripping fuel. A leak in the suction side is usually only apparent because of a reduced volume of fuel delivered to the pressure side.

1. Tighten any loose line connections and look for any kinks or restrictions.
2. Disconnect the fuel line at the carburetor. Disconnect the distributor-to-coil primary wire. Place a container at the end of the fuel line and crank the engine a few revolutions. If little or no gasoline flows from the line, either the fuel pump is inoperative or the line is plugged. Disconnect the line at the pump and the tank; blow through the line with compressed air and try again. Reconnect the line. If the problem is traced to the tank, the tank and gauge unit must be removed to check the condition of the inlet filter screen. See Chapter 10 for tank removal.
3. If fuel flows in good volume, check the fuel pump pressure to be sure.

4. Attach a pressure gauge to the pressure side of the fuel line.

5. Run the engine and note the reading on the gauge. Stop the engine and compare the reading with the specifications listed in the Tune-Up Specifications chart. If the pump is operating properly, the pressure will be as specified and will be constant at idle speed. If pressure varies or is too high or low, the pump should be replaced.

6. Remove the pressure gauge.

REMOVAL AND INSTALLATION

CAUTION: *Never smoke when working around gasoline! Avoid all sources of sparks or ignition. Gasoline vapors are EXTREMELY volatile!*

NOTE: *When you connect the fuel pump outlet fitting, always use 2 wrenches to avoid damaging the pump.*

1. Disconnect the fuel intake and outlet lines at the pump and plug the pump intake line.

2. On V6 and V8 engines, you can remove the upper bolt from the right front engine mounting boss (on the front of the block) and insert a long bolt (⅜-16 x 2") to hold the fuel pump pushrod.

3. Remove the two pump mounting bolts and lockwashers; remove the pump and its gasket.

4. If the rocker arm pushrod is to be removed from the V6s and V8s, remove the two adapter bolts and lockwashers and remove the adapter and its gasket.

5. Install the fuel pump with a new gasket reversing the removal procedure. Heavy grease can be used to hold the fuel pump pushrod up when installing the pump, if you didn't install the long bolt in Step 2. Coat the mating surfaces with sealer.

6. Connect the fuel lines an check for leaks.

Carburetor

REMOVAL AND INSTALLATION

CAUTION: *Never smoke when working around gasoline! Avoid all sources of sparks or ignition. Gasoline vapors are EXTREMELY volatile!*

1. Remove the air cleaner and its gasket.

2. Disconnect the fuel and vacuum lines from the carburetor.

3. Disconnect the choke coil rod or heated air line tube.

4. Disconnect the throttle linkage.

5. On automatic transmission cars, disconnect the throttle valve linkage.

6. Remove the CEC valve vacuum hose and electrical connector.

7. Remove the idle stop electrical wiring from the idle stop solenoid, if so equipped.

8. Remove the carburetor attaching nuts and/or bolts, gasket or insulator, and remove the carburetor.

9. Install the carburetor using a reverse of the removal procedure. Use a new gasket and fill the float bowl with gasoline to ease starting the engine.

IDENTIFICATION

Carburetor identification numbers will generally be found in the following locations:

1 MV, ME: Stamped on the vertical portion of the float bowl, adjacent to the fuel inlet nut.

2 GV, GC: Stamped on the flat section of the float bowl next to the fuel inlet nut.

E2SE, 2SE: Stamped on the vertical surface of the float bowl adjacent to the vacuum tube.

M2MC: Stamped on the vertical surface of the left rear corner of the float bowl.

E4ME, 4 MV, M4MC, M4ME: Stamped on the vertical section of the float bowl, near the secondary throttle lever.

OVERHAUL

Efficient carburetion depends greatly on careful cleaning and inspection during overhaul, since dirt, gum, water, or varnish in or on the carburetor parts are often responsible for poor performance.

Overhaul you carburetor in a clean, dustfree area. Carefully disassembly the carburetor, referring often to the exploded views and directions packaged with the rebuilding kit. Keep all similar and look alike parts segregated during disassembly and cleaning to avoid accidental interchange during assembly. Make a note of all jet sizes.

When the carburetor is disassembled, wash all parts (except diaphragms, electric choke units, pump plunger, and any other plastic, leather, fiber, or rubber parts) in clean carburetor solvent. Do not leave parts in the solvent any longer than is necessary to sufficiently loosen the deposits. Excessive cleaning may remove the special finish from the float bowl and choke valve bodies, leaving these parts unfit for service. Soak all parts in clean solvent and blow them dry with compressed air or allow them to air dry. Wipe clean all cork, plastic, leather, and fiber parts with a clean, lint free cloth.

Blow out all passages and jets with compressed air and be sure that there are no restrictions or blockages. Never use wire or similar tools to clean jets, fuel passages, or air bleeds. Clean all jets and valves separately to avoid accidental interchange.

Check all parts for wear or damage. If wear or damage is found, replace the defective parts.

Especially check the following:

1. Check the float needle and seat for wear. If wear is found, replace the complete assembly.
2. Check the float hinge pin for wear and the float(s) for dents or distortion. Replace the float if fuel has leaked into it.
3. Check the throttle and choke shaft bores for wear or an out-of-round condition. Damage or wear to the throttle arm, shaft, or shaft bore will often require replacement of the throttle body. These parts require a close tolerance of fit; wear may allow air leakage, which could affect starting and idling.

NOTE: *Throttle shafts and bushings are not included in overhaul kits. They can be purchased separately.*

4. Inspect the idle mixture adjusting needles for burrs or grooves. Any such condition requires replacement of the needle, since you will not be able to obtain a satisfactory idle.
5. Test the accelerator pump check valves. They should pass air one way but not the other. Test for proper seating by blowing and sucking on the valve. Replace the valve as necessary. If the valve is satisfactory, wash the valve again to remove breath moisture.
6. Check the bowl cover for warped surfaces with a straightedge.
7. Closely inspect the valves and seats for wear and damage, replacing as necessary.
8. After the carburetor is assembled, check the choke valve for freedom of operation.

Carburetor overhaul kits are recommended for each overhaul. These kits contain all gaskets and new parts to replace those which deteriorate most rapidly. Failure to replace all parts supplied with the kit (especially gaskets) can result in poor performance later.

Some carburetor manufacturers supply overhaul kits of three basic types: minor repair; major repair; and gasket kits.

After cleaning and checking all components, reassemble the carburetor, using new parts and referring to the exploded view. When reassembling, make sure that all screws and jets are tight in their seats, buy do not overtighten as the tips will be distorted. Tighten all screws gradually, in rotation. Do not tighten needle valves into their seats; uneven jetting will result. Always use new gaskets. Be sure to adjust the float level when reassembling.

Carburetor Adjustments

These adjustment are arranged by carburetor model. Most of these vans use General Motors Rochester carburetors. The first number of the carburetor model number indicates the number of barrels, while the last letter indicates the type of choke used. These are V for the manifold mounted choke coil, C for the choke coil mounted on the carburetor, and E for electric choke.

NOTE: *Most of these adjustments require that measurements be made to thousandths of an inch, using some sort of gauge. Drill bits are ideal for this purpose.*

PRELIMINARY CHECKS (ALL CARBURETORS)

The following should be observed before attempting any adjustments.

1. Thoroughly warm the engine. If the engine is cold, be sure that it reaches operating temperature.
2. Check the torque of all carburetor mounting nuts. Also check the intake manifold-to-cylinder head bolts. If air is leaking at any of these points, any attempts at adjustment will inevitably lead to frustration.
3. Check the manifold heat control valve (if used) to be sure that it is free.
4. Check and adjust the choke as necessary.
5. Adjust the idle speed and mixture. If any adjustments are performed that might possibly change the idle speed or mixture, adjust the idle and mixture again when you are finished.

Rochester B (1967)

FLOAT LEVEL AND FLOAT DROP

The air horn must be removed to make this adjustment. The carburetor need not be removed from the manifold.

1. Remove the air cleaner and the air horn.
2. Hold the air horn (with the gasket in place) so that the floats hang free.
3. Measure the distance from the gasket surface to the bottom of the float with a T-scale. The distance should be as specified. If not, bend the tang until the floats are parallel and the specified distance from the gasket. The floats should also be aligned to avoid interference with the bowl.
4. Turn the air horn over so that the float arm closes the needle valve. Bend the tang until the distance is as specified.
5. Reinstall the air horn and adjust the idle speed and mixture.

IDLE VENT

1. Open the throttle and insert the specified gauge between the throttle valve and the bore opposite the idle needle.
2. Adjust by turning the valve on top of the air horn until the vent is just opening.

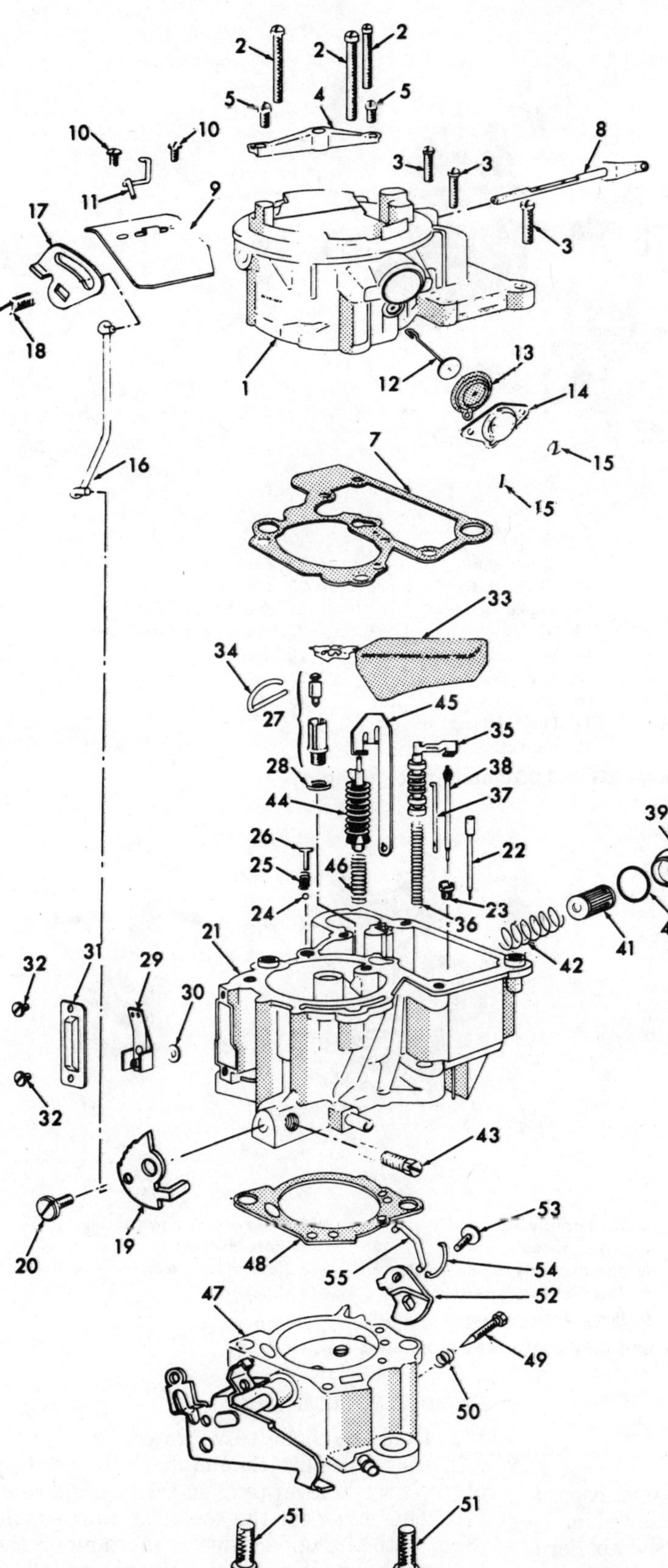

1. Air horn assembly
2. Screw (long)
3. Screw (short)
4. Bracket
5. Screw
7. Air horn gasket
8. Choke shaft and lever assembly
9. Choke valve
10. Screw
11. Lever
12. Vacuum break link assy.
13. Vacuum break diaphragm
14. Cover
15. Screw
16. Choke rod
17. Choke lever
18. Screw
19. Fast idle cam
20. Cam attaching screw
21. Float bowl assembly
22. Idle tube assembly
23. Main metering jet
24. Pump discharge ball
25. Pump discharge spring
26. Pump discharge guide
27. Needle and seat assy.
28. Needle seat gasket
29. Idle compensator assembly
30. Gasket
31. Cover
32. Screw
33. Float assembly
34. Float hinge pin
35. Power piston assembly
36. Power piston spring
37. Power piston rod
38. Metering rod and spring assembly
39. Fuel inlet filter nut
40. Gasket
41. Fuel inlet filter
42. Fuel filter spring
43. Slow idle screw
44. Pump assembly
45. Pump actuating lever
46. Pump return spring
47. Throttle body assembly
48. Gasket
49. Idle needle
50. Idle needle spring
51. Throttle body screw
52. Pump and power lever
53. Screw
54. Link
55. Link

Carter YF Carburetor

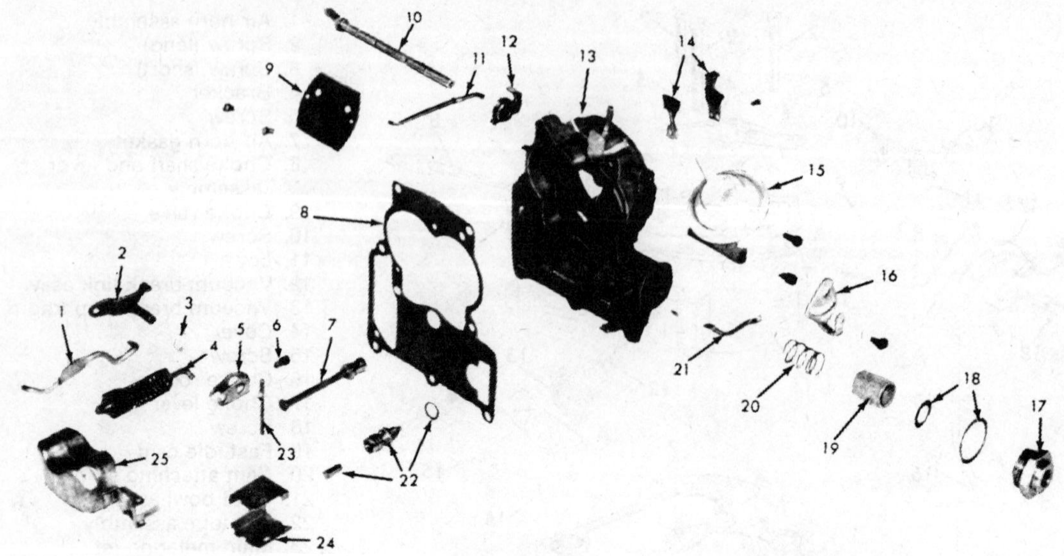

Rochester 2G and 2GV carburetor air horn

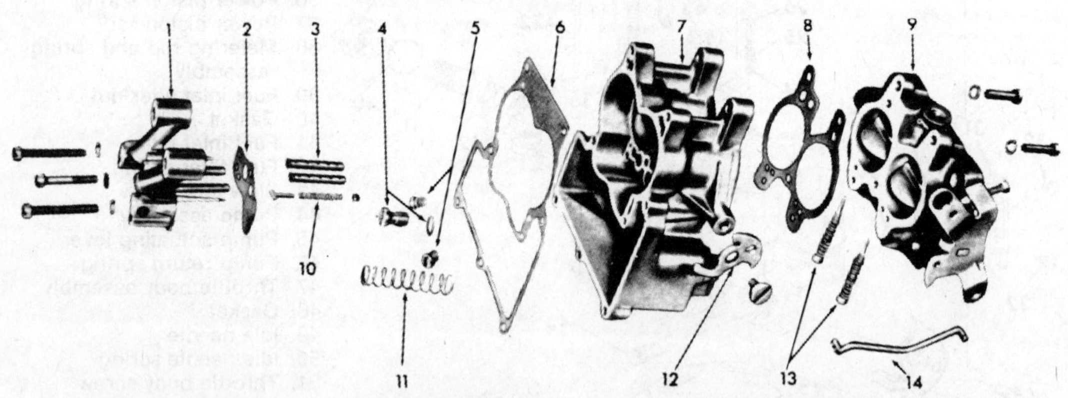

Rochester 2G and 2GV carburetor bowl and throttle body

Carter YF (1967)

IDLE VENT

1. With choke open, back out the idle speed screw until free to close the throttle valve.
2. Insert feeler gauge between the air horn and vent valve. Adjust to get 0.065" (1.651mm) clearance.

FAST IDLE AND CHOKE VALVE

1. Hold the choke valve closed.
2. Close the throttle and mark the position of the throttle lever tang on the fast idle cam.
3. The mark on the fast idle cam should align with the upper edge of the tang on the throttle lever. If not, bend the choke rod as necessary.

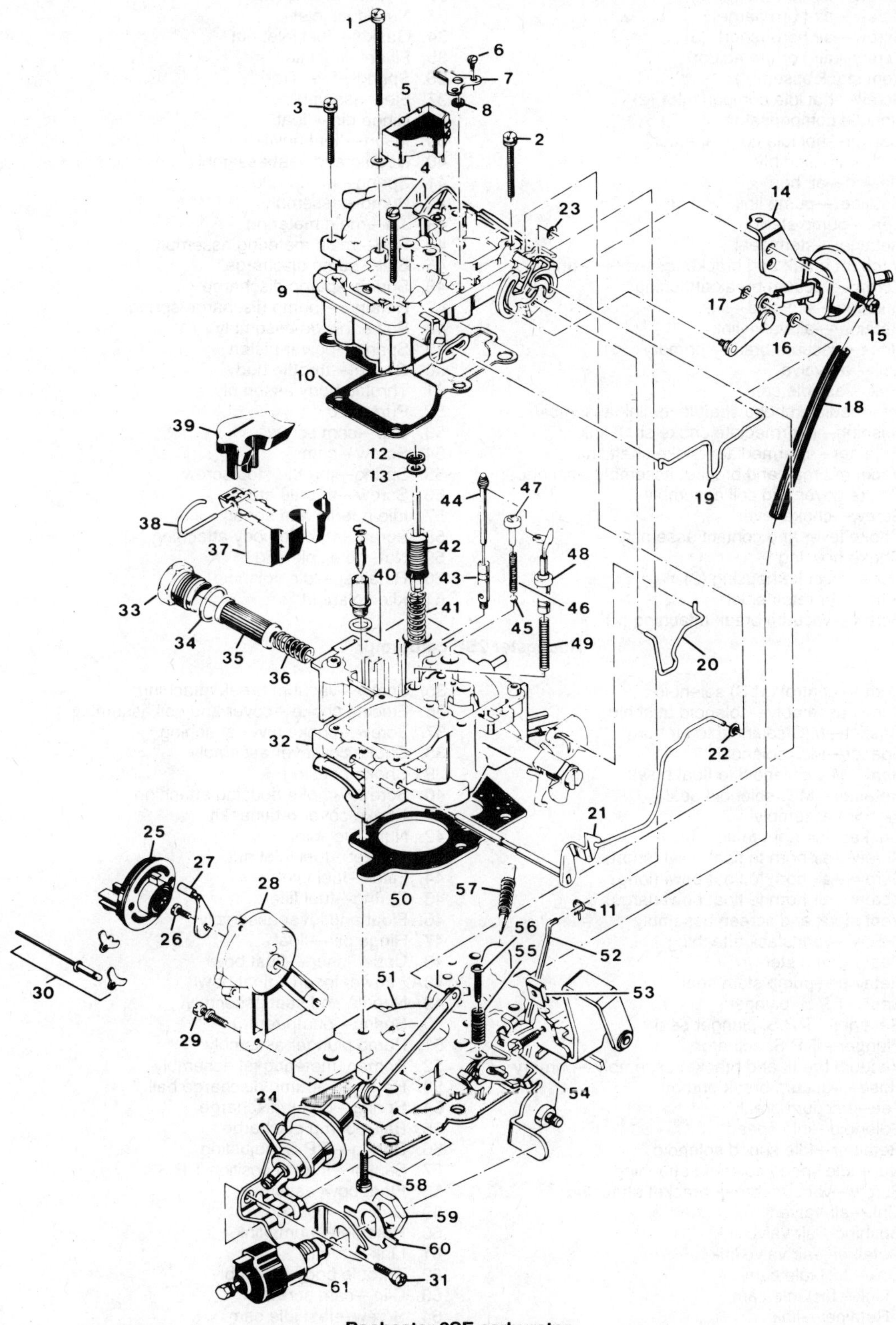

Rochester 2SE carburetor

1. Screw—air horn (long) (2)
2. Screw—air horn (large)
3. Screw—air horn (short) (3)
4. Screw—air horn (medium)
5. Vent stack assembly
6. Screw—hot idle compensator (2)
7. Hot idle compensator
8. Gasket—hot idle compensator
9. Air horn assembly
10. Gasket—air horn
11. Retainer—pump link
12. Seal—pump stem
13. Retainer—stem seal
14. Vacuum break and bracket assembly—primary
15. Screw—vacuum break attaching
16. Bushing—air valve—link
17. Retainer—air valve link
18. Hose—vacuum break—primary
19. Link—air valve
20. Link—fast idle cam
21. Intermediate choke shaft/lever/link assembly
22. Bushing—intermediate choke shaft link
23. Retainer—intermediate choke shaft link
24. Vacuum break and bracket assembly—secondary
25. Choke cover and coil assembly
26. Screw—choke lever
27. Choke lever and contact assembly
28. Choke housing
29. Screw—choke housing (2)
30. Stat cover retainer kit
31. Screw—vacuum break attaching (2)
32. Float bowl assembly
33. Nut—fuel inlet
34. Gasket—fuel inlet nut
35. Filter—fuel inlet
36. Spring—fuel filter
37. Float assembly
38. Hinge pin—float
39. Insert—float bowl
40. Needle and seat assembly
41. Spring—pump return
42. Pump—assembly
43. Jet—main metering
44. Rod—main metering assembly
45. Ball—pump discharge
46. Spring—pump discharge
47. Retainer—pump discharge spring
48. Power piston assembly
49. Spring—power piston
50. Gasket—throttle body
51. Throttle body assembly
52. Pump rod
53. Clip—cam screw
54. Screw—cam
55. Spring—throttle stop screw
56. Screw—throttle stop
57. Idle needle and spring
58. Screw—throttle body attaching (4)
59. Nut—idle solenoid
60. Retainer—idle solenoid
61. Idle solenoid

Rochester 2SE carburetor

1. Mixture control (M/C) solenoid
2. Screw assembly—solenoid attaching
3. Gasket—M/C solenoid to air horn
4. Spacer—M/C solenoid
5. Seal—M/C solenoid to float bowl
6. Retainer—M/C solenoid seal
7. Air horn assembly
8. Gasket—air horn to float bowl
9. Screw—air horn to float bowl (short)
10. Screw—air horn to float bowl (long)
11. Screw—air horn to float bowl (large)
12. Vent stack and screen assembly
13. Screw—vent stack attaching
14. Seal—pump stem
15. Retainer—pump stem seal
16. Seal—T.P.S. plunger
17. Retainer—T.P.S. plunger seal
18. Plunger—T.P.S. actuator
19. Vacuum break and bracket assembly—primary
20. Hose—vacuum break primary
21. Tee—vacuum break
22. Solenoid—idle speed
23. Retainer—idle speed solenoid
24. Nut—idle speed solenoid attaching
25. Screw—vacuum break bracket attaching
26. Link—air valve
27. Bushing—air valve link
28. Retainer—air valve link
29. Link—fast idle cam
29A. Link—fast idle cam
29B. Retainer—link
29C. Bushing—link
30. Hose—vacuum break
31. Intermediate choke shaft/lever/link assembly
32. Bushing—intermediate choke link
33. Retainer—intermediate choke link
34. Vacuum break and link assembly—secondary
35. Screw—vacuum break attaching
36. Electric choke—cover and coil assembly
37. Screw—choke lever attaching
38. Choke coil lever assembly
39. Choke housing
40. Screw—choke housing attaching
41. Choke cover retainer kit
42. Nut—fuel inlet
43. Gasket—fuel inlet nut
44. Filter—fuel inlet
45. Spring—fuel filter
46. Float and lever assembly
47. Hinge pin—float
48. Upper insert—float bowl
48A. Lower insert—float bowl
49. Needle and seat assembly
50. Spring—pump return
51. Pump plunger assembly
52. Primary metering jet assembly
53. Retainer—pump discharge ball
54. Spring—pump discharge
55. Ball—pump discharge
56. Spring—T.P.S. adjusting
57. Sensor—throttle position T.P.S.
58. Float bowl assembly
59. Gasket—float bowl
60. Retainer—pump link
61. Link—pump
62. Throttle body assembly
63. Clip—cam screw
64. Screw—fast idle cam
65. Idle needle and spring assembly
66. Screw—throttle body to float bowl
67. Screw—vacuum break bracket attaching
68. Screw—idle stop
69. Spring—idle stop screw
70. Gasket—insulator flange

Rochester E2SE carburetor

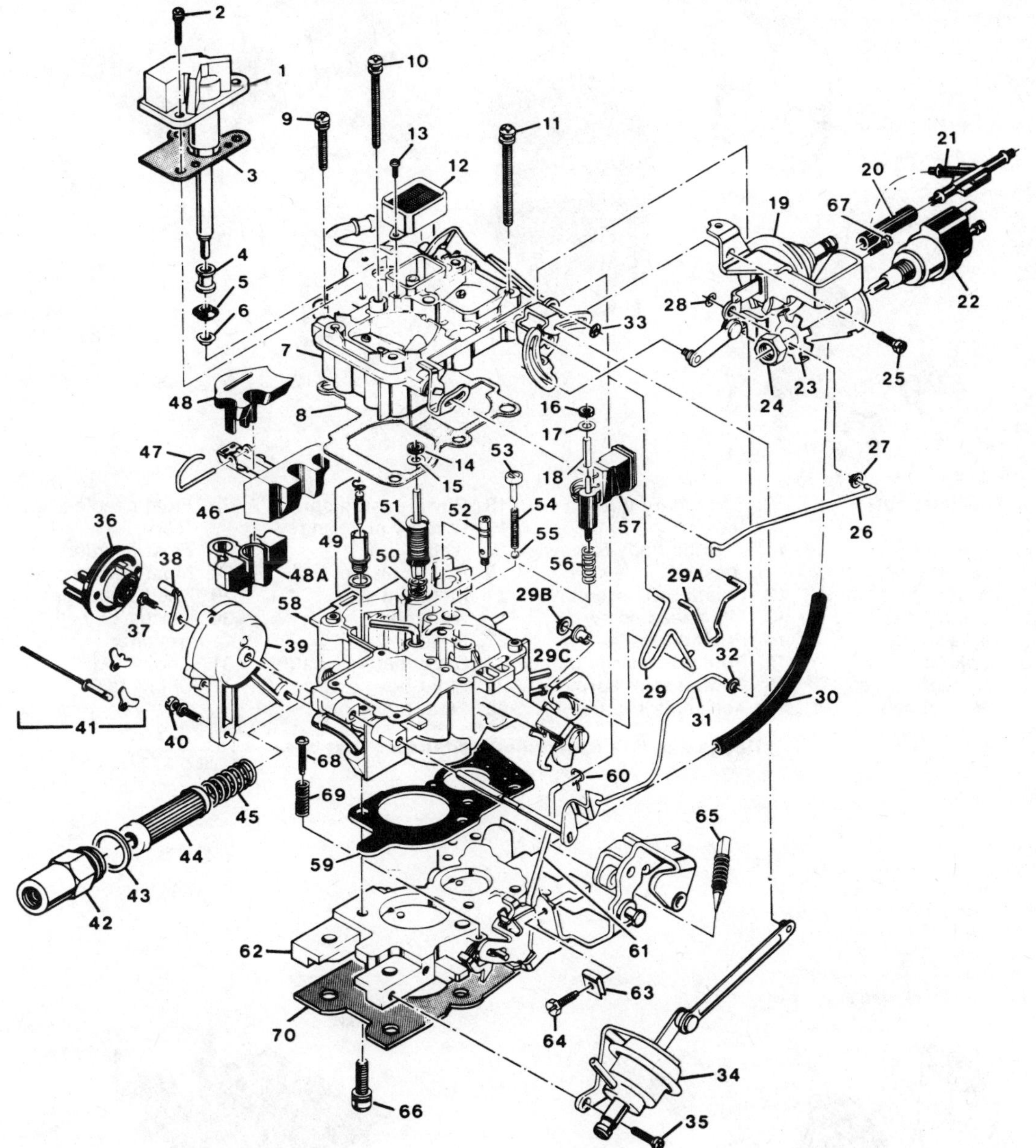

Rochester E2SE carburetor

CHOKE UNLOADER

1. Open the throttle to the wide open position.
2. Using a rubber band, hold the choke valve closed.
3. Bend the unloader tang on the throttle lever to get the proper clearance between the lower edge of the choke valve and the air horn wall.

VACUUM BREAK

1. Hold the vacuum break arm against its stop and hold the choke closed with a rubber band.
2. Bend the vacuum bread link to get the specified distance between the lower edge of the choke valve and the air horn wall.

FLOAT LEVEL

1. Turn the bowl cover upside down and measure the float level by measuring the distance between the float (free end) and the cover. The distance should be $^7/_{32}$" (5.5mm); if not bend the lip of the float, not the float arm.
2. Hold the cover in proper position (not upside down) and measure the amount of float drop from the cover to the float bottom at the end opposite the hinge. This distance should be specified.

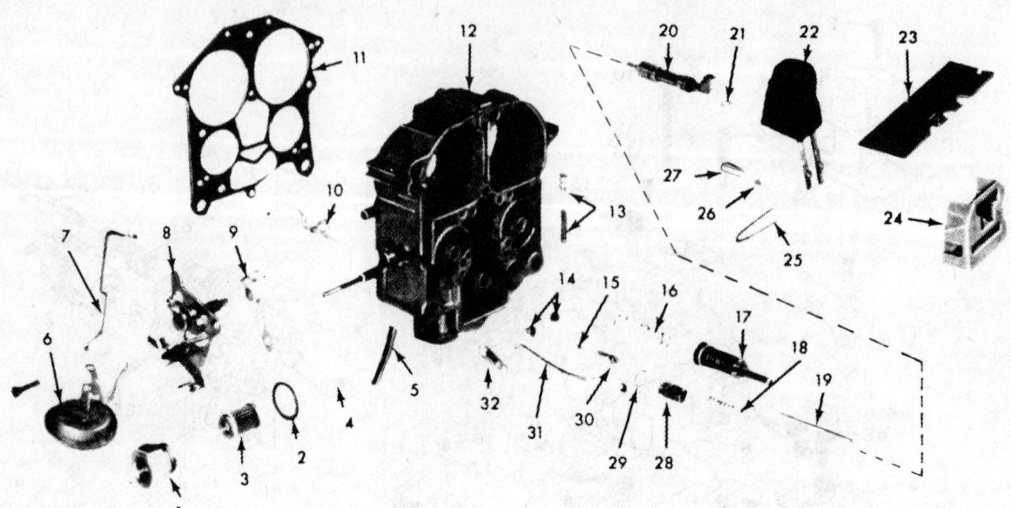

1. Fuel inlet nut
2. Gasket
3. Fuel-filter
4. Fuel filter spring
5. Vacuum break hose
6. Vacuum diaphragm
7. Air valve dashpot
8. Choke control bracket
9. Fast idle cam
10. Secondary throttle lockout
11. Throttle body-to-bowl gasket
12. Float bowl assembly
13. Idle speed screw
14. Primary jets
15. Pump discharge ball
16. Pump return spring
17. Accelerator pump
18. Power piston spring
19. Primary metering rods
20. Power piston
21. Metering rod retainer
22. Float
23. Secondary air baffle
24. Float bowl insert
25. Float hinge pin
26. Float needle pull clip
27. Float needle
28. Float needle seat
29. Needle seat gasket
30. Discharge ball retainer
31. Choke rod
32. Choke lever

Rochester 4MV (Quadrajet) carburetor float bowl

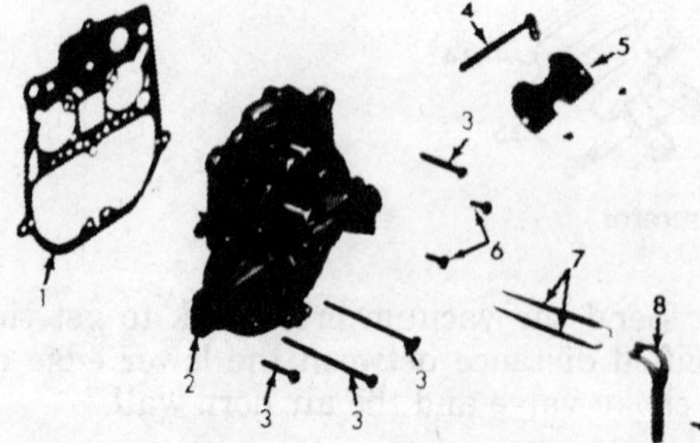

1. Air horn-to-bowl gasket
2. Air horn assembly
3. Air horn-to-bowl retaining screws long, 5 short, counter-sunk—item no. 6)
4. Choke shaft and lever
5. Choke valve
6. Counter-sunk air horn retaining screws
7. Secondary metering rods
8. Metering rod hanger

Rochester 4MV (Quadrajet) carburetor air horn

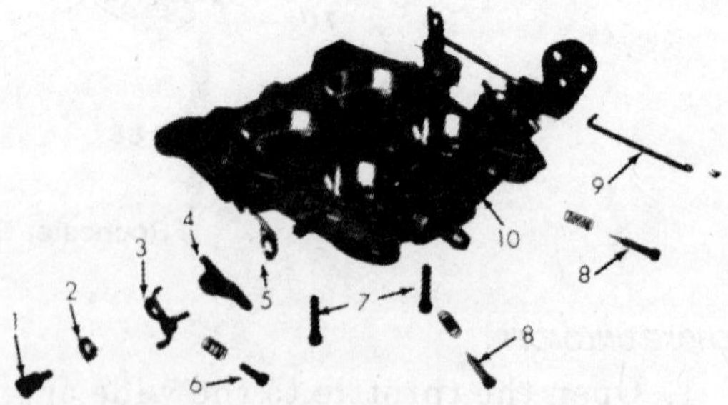

1. Shouldered retaining screw
2. Torsion spring (3-to-4)
3. Fast idle adjusting lever
4. Fast idle cam lever
5. Choke unloader lever
6. Fast idle screw
7. Throttle body-to-bowl screws
8. Idle mixture needle
9. Accelerator pump rod
10. Throttle body assembly

Rochester 4MV (Quadrajet) carburetor throttle body

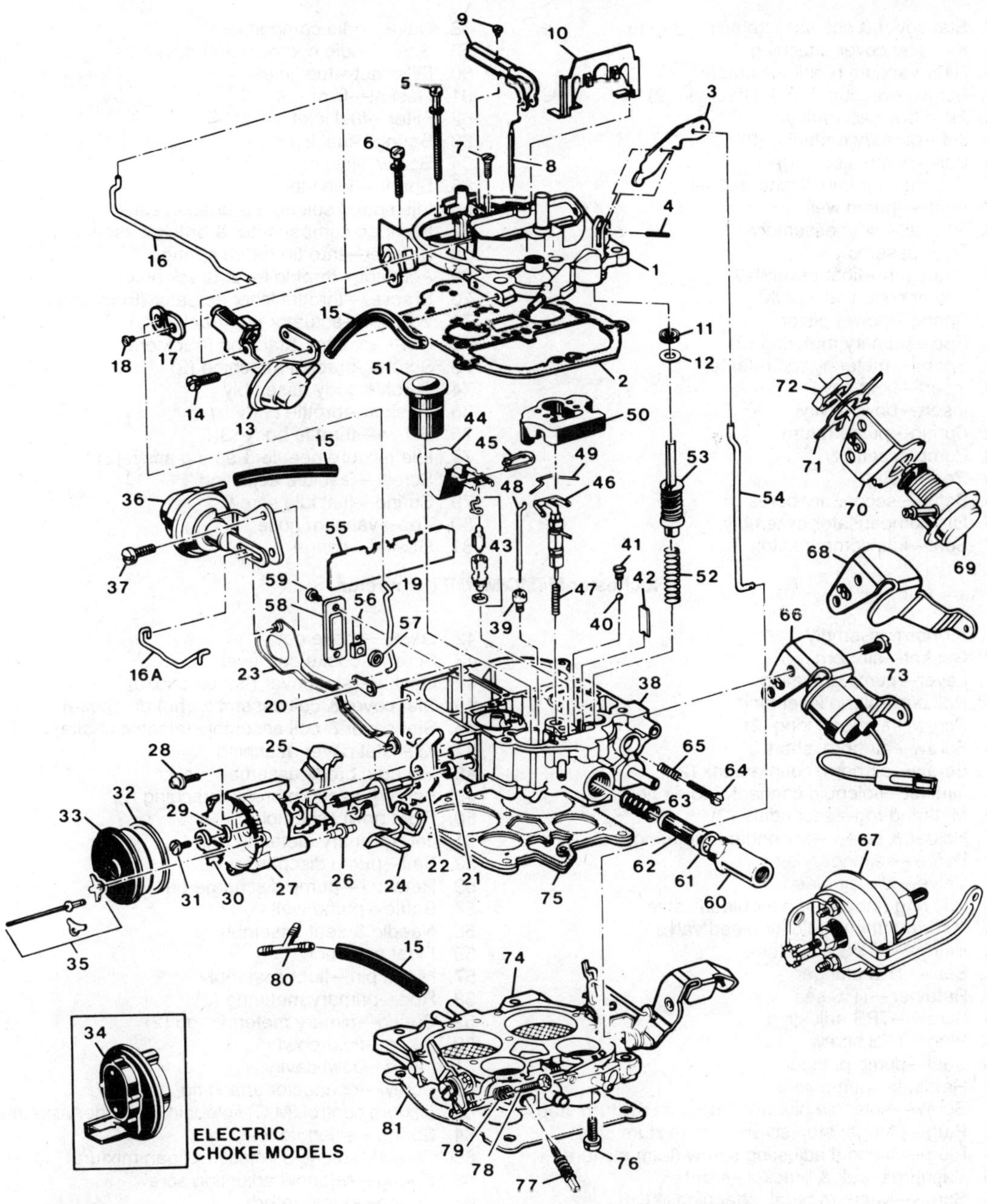

1. Air horn assy.
2. Gasket—air horn
3. Lever—pump actuating
4. Roll pin—pump lever hinge
5. Screw—air horn long
6. Screw—air horn short
7. Screw—air horn countersunk
8. Metering rod—secondary
9. Holder and screw—secondary metering rod
10. Baffle—secondary air
11. Seal—pump plunger
12. Retainer—pump seal
13. Vac. break control & bracket—front
14. Screw—control attaching
15. Hose—vacuum
16. Rod—air valve
16A. Rod—air valve (truck)
17. Lever—choke rod (upper)
18. Screw—choke lever
19. Rod—choke
20. Lever—choke rod (lower)
21. Seal—intermediate choke shaft
22. Lever—secondary lockout
23. Link—rear vacuum break
24. Int. choke shaft & lever
25. Cam—fast idle
26. Seal—choke housing to bowl (hot air choke)
27. Kit—choke housing
28. Screw—choke housing to bowl
29. Seal—intermediate choke shaft (hot air choke)
30. Lever—choke coil
31. Screw—choke coil lever
32. Gasket—stat cover (hot air choke)
33. Stat cover & coil assy. (hot air choke)

Rochester M4MC/M4ME carburetor

34. Stat cover & coil assy. (electric choke)
35. Kit—stat cover attaching
36. Rear vacuum break assembly
37. Screw—vacuum break attaching (2)
38. Float bowl assembly
39. Jet—primary metering (2)
40. Ball—pump discharge
41. Retainer—pump discharge ball
42. Baffle—pump well
43. Needle & seat assembly
44. Float assembly
45. Hinge pin—float assembly
46. Power piston assembly
47. Spring—power piston
48. Rod—primary metering (2)
49. Spring—metering rod retainer
50. Insert—float bowl
51. Insert—bowl cavity
52. Spring—pump return
53. Pump assembly
54. Rod—pump
55. Baffle—secondary bores
56. Idle compensator assembly
57. Seal—idle compensator
58. Cover—idle compensator
59. Screw—idle compensator cover (2)
60. Filter nut—fuel inlet
61. Gasket—filter nut
62. Filter—fuel inlet
63. Spring—fuel filter
64. Screw—idle stop
65. Spring—idle stop screw
66. Idle speed solenoid & bracket assembly
67. Idle load compensator & bracket assembly
68. Bracket—throttle return spring
69. Actuator—throttle lever (truck only)
70. Bracket—throttle lever actuator (truck only)
71. Washer—actuator nut (truck only)
72. Nut—actuator attaching (truck only)
73. Screw—bracket attaching (2)
74. Throttle body assembly
75. Gasket—throttle body
76. Screw—throttle body (3)
77. Idle mixture needle & spring assy. (2)
78. Screw—fast idle adjusting
79. Spring—fast idle screw
80. Tee—vacuum hose
81. Gasket—flange

Rochester M4MC/M4ME carburetor

1. Air horn assembly
2. Gasket—air horn
3. Lever—pump actuating
4. Roll pin—pump lever hinge
5. Screw—air horn, long (2)
6. Screw—air horn, short
7. Screw—air horn, countersunk (2)
8. Gasket—solenoid connector to air horn
9. Metering rod—secondary (2)
10. Holder & screw—secondary metering rod
11. Baffle—secondary air
12. Valve—idle air bleed
13. "O" ring (thick)—idle air bleed valve
14. "O" ring (thin)—idle air bleed valve
15. Plunger—TPS actuator
16. Seal—TPS plunger
17. Retainer—TPS seal
18. Screw—TPS adjusting
19. Plug—TPS screw
20. Seal—pump plunger
21. Retainer—pump seal
22. Screw—solenoid plunger stop (rich mixture stop)
23. Plug—plunger stop screw (rich mixture stop)
24. Plug—solenoid adjusting screw (lean mixture)
25. Vacuum break & bracket—front
26. Screw—vacuum break attaching (2)
27. Hose—vacuum
28. Rod—air valve
29. Lever—choke rod (upper)
30. Screw—choke lever
31. Rod—choke
32. Lever—choke rod (lower)
33. Seal—intermediate choke shaft
34. Lever—secondary lockout
35. Link—rear vacuum break
36. Intermediate choke shaft & lever
37. Cam—fast idle
38. Seal—choke housing to bowl (hot air choke)
39. Choke housing
40. Screw—choke housing to bowl
41. Seal—intermediate choke shaft (hot air choke)
42. Lever—choke coil
43. Screw—choke coil lever
44. Gasket—stat cover (hot air choke)
45. Stat cover & coil assembly (hot air choke)
46. Stat cover & coil assembly (electric choke)
47. Kit—stat cover attaching
48. Vacuum break assembly—rear
49. Screw—vacuum break attaching (2)
50. Float bowl assembly
51. Jet—primary metering (2)
52. Ball—pump discharge
53. Retainer—pump discharge ball
54. Baffle—pump well
55. Needle & seat assembly
56. Float assembly
57. Hinge pin—float assembly
58. Rod—primary metering (2)
59. Spring—pimary metering rod (2)
60. Insert—float bowl
61. Insert—bowl cavity
62. Screw—connector attaching
63. Mixture control (M/C) solenoid & plunger assembly
64. Spring—solenoid tension
65. Screw—solenoid adjusting (lean mixture)
66. Spring—solenoid adjusting screw
67. Spring—pump return
68. Pump assembly
69. Link—pump
70. Baffle—secondary bores
71. Throttle position sensor (TPS)
72. Spring—TPS tension
73. Filter nut—fuel inlet
74. Gasket—filter nut
75. Filter—fuel inlet
76. Spring—fuel filter
77. Screw—idle stop
78. Spring—idle stop screw
79. Idle speed solenoid & bracket assembly
80. Bracket—throttle return spring
81. Idle load compensator & bracket assembly
82. Idle speed control & bracket assembly

Rochester E4ME carburetor

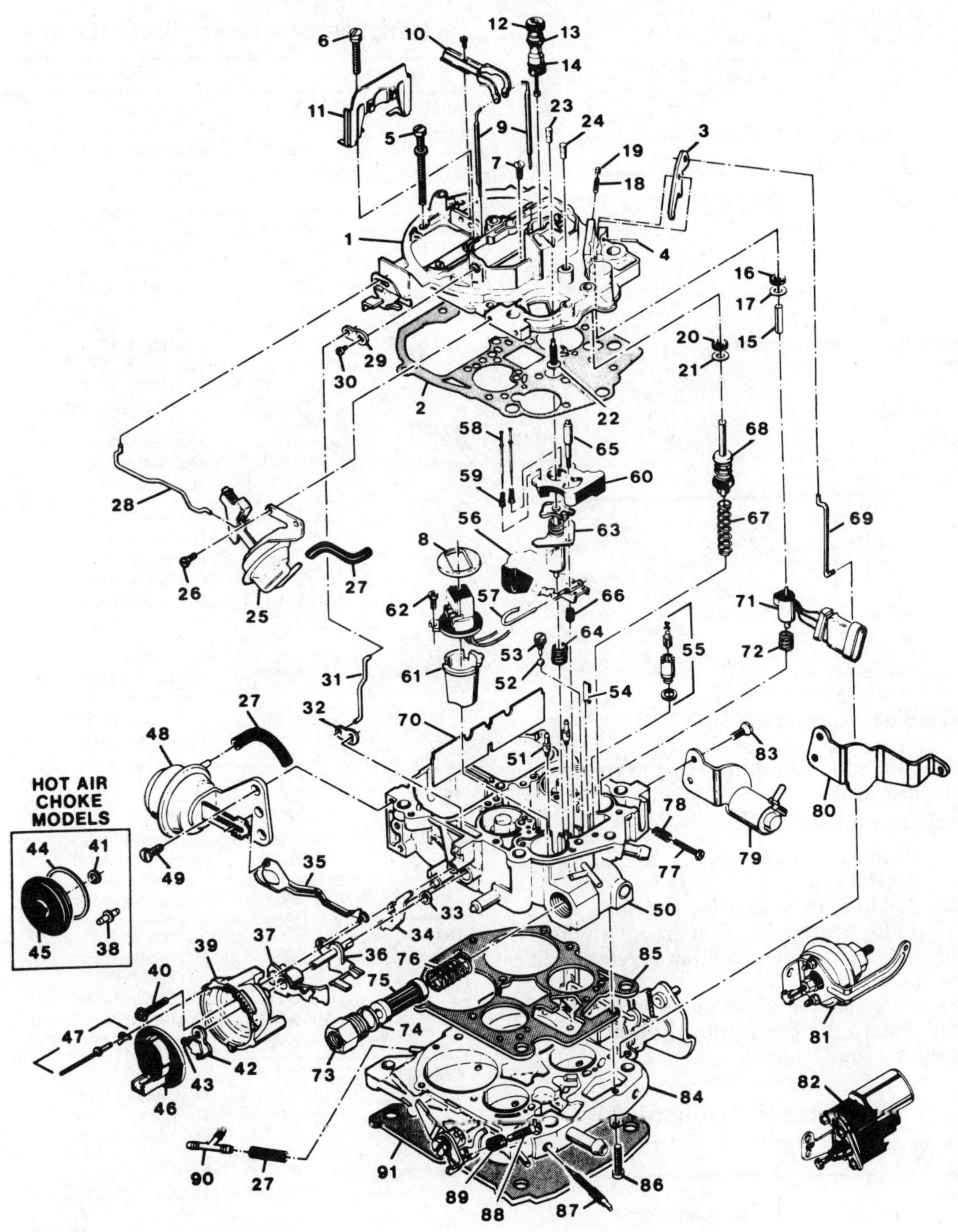

83. Screw—bracket attaching
84. Throttle body assembly
85. Gasket—throttle body
86. Screw—throttle body
87. Idle needle & spring assembly (2)
88. Screw—fast idle adjusting
89. Spring—fast idle screw
90. Tee—vacuum hose
91. Gasket—flange

Rochester E4ME carburetor

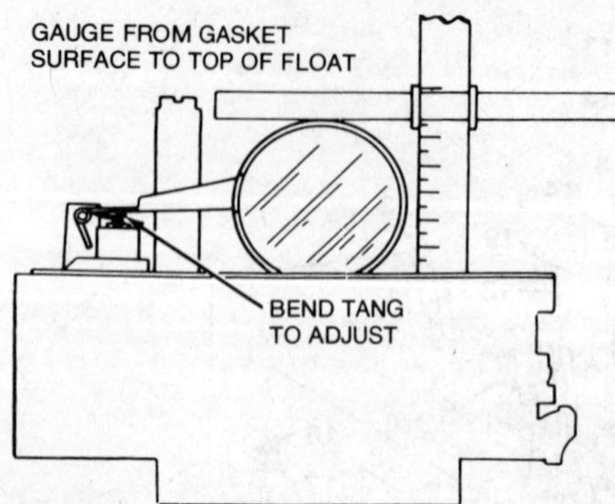

Float level—Rochester B

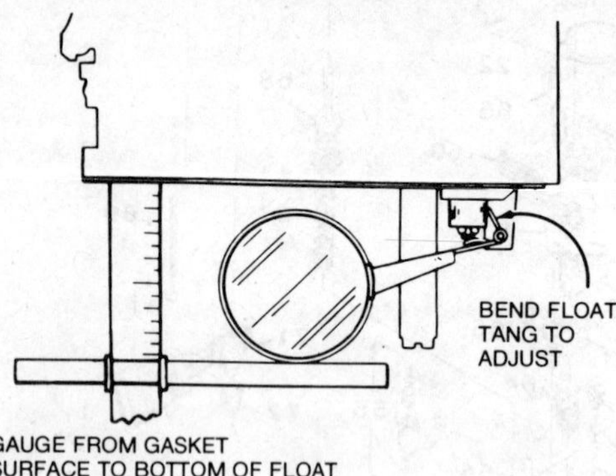

Float drop—Rochester B

3. Make the adjustment by the stop tab on the float arm.

ACCELERATOR PUMP

1. Seat the throttle valve by backing off the idle speed screw.
2. Hold the throttle valve closed.
3. Fully depress the diaphragm shaft and check the contact between lower retainer and the lifter link.
4. This retainer (upper pump spring) should just contact the pump lifter link buy do not compress the spring.

Carburetor Applications

Year	Engine	Carburetor
1967	6-230	Rochester B
		Carter YF
	6-250	Rochester B
		Carter YF
	V8-283	Rochester 2G
1968	6-230	Rochester M
	6-250	Rochester M
	V8-307	Rochester 2G
1969	6-230	Rochester M
	6-250	Rochester M
		Rochester MV
	V8-307	Rochester 2G (1¼ in.)
		Rochester 2GV (1¼ in.)

Carburetor Applications (cont.)

Year	Engine	Carburetor
1970	6-250	Rochester M
		Rochester MV
	V8-307	Rochester 2GV (1¼ in.)
	V8-350	Rochester 2G (1¼ in.)
		Rochester 4MV (Quadrajet)
1971	6-250	Rochester MV
	V8-307	Rochester 2GV
	V8-350	Rochester 4MV (Quadrajet)
1972–73	6-250	Rochester MV
	V8-307, 350	Rochester 2GV
	V8-350	Rochester 4MV (Quadrajet)
1974	6-250	Rochester MV
	8-350	Rochester 2GV
	8-350	Rochester 4MV
1975	6-250	Rochester 1MV
	6-292	Rochester 1MV
	8-350	Rochester 2GC
	8-350 LD	Rochester M4MC
	8-350 HD	Rochester 4MV
	8-400	Rochester 4MV
1976	6-250	Rochester 1MV
	6-292	Rochester 1MV
	8-350	Rochester 2GC
	8-350 LD	Rochester M4MC
	8-350 HD	Rochester 4MV
	8-400	Rochester 4MV
1977	6-250	Rochester 1ME
	6-292	Rochester 1ME
	8-305	Rochester 2GC
	8-350 LD	Rochester M4MC
	8-350 HD	Rochester 4MV
	8-400	Rochester 4MV
1978	6-250	Rochester 1ME
	6-292	Rochester 1ME
	8-305	Rochester 2GC
	8-350 LD	Rochester M4MC
	8-350 HD	Rochester 4MV/M4MC
	8-400	Rochester 4MV/M4MC
1979–80	6-250	Rochester 2SE
	8-305	Rochester M2MC
	8-350	Rochester M4MC
	8-400	Rochester M4MC
1981	6-250	Rochester 2SE
	8-305	Rochester M2ME
	8-305	Rochester M4MC/M4ME
	8-350	Rochester M4MC/M4ME
1982	6-250	Rochester 2SE
	8-305	Rochester M4MC/M4ME
	8-350	Rochester M4MC/M4ME
1983–86	6-250	Rochester 2SE
		Rochester E2SE
	6-262, 8-305	Rochester M4MC/M4ME
		Rochester E4ME
	8-350	Rochester M4MC/M4ME
		Rochester E4ME

LD, HD See the beginning of the Chapter for explanation.

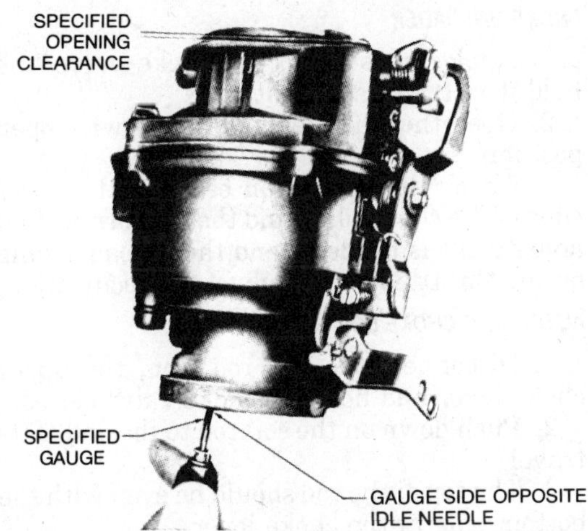

Idle vent adjustment—Rochester B

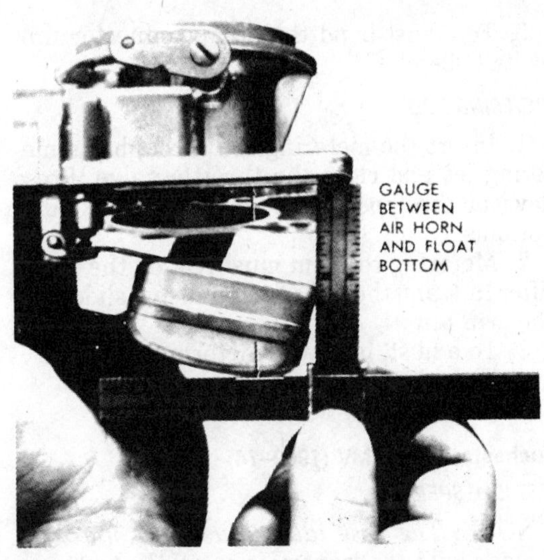

Float drop adjustment—Carter YF

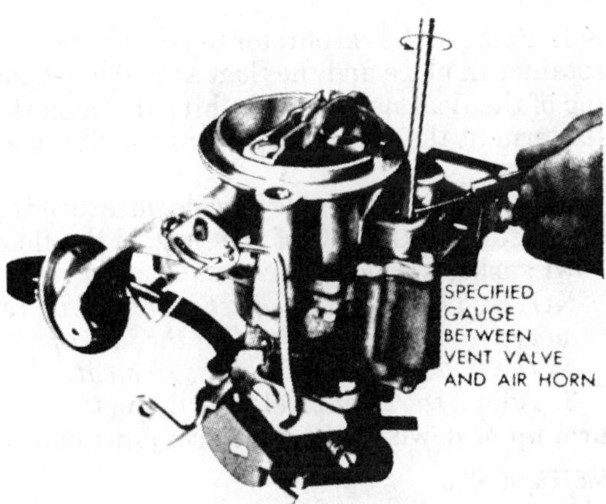

Idle vent adjustment—Carter YF

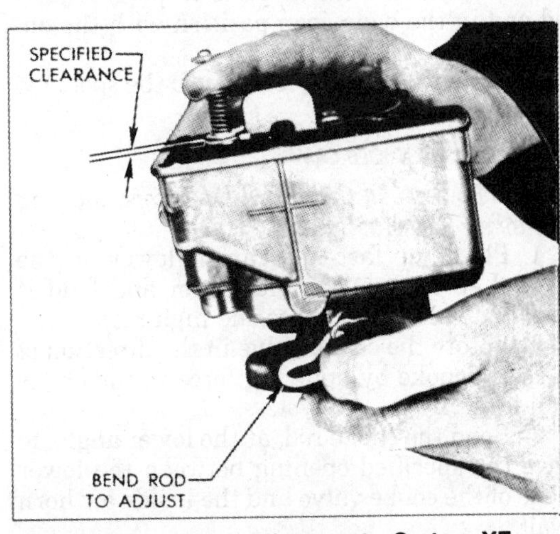

Accelerator pump adjustment—Carter YF

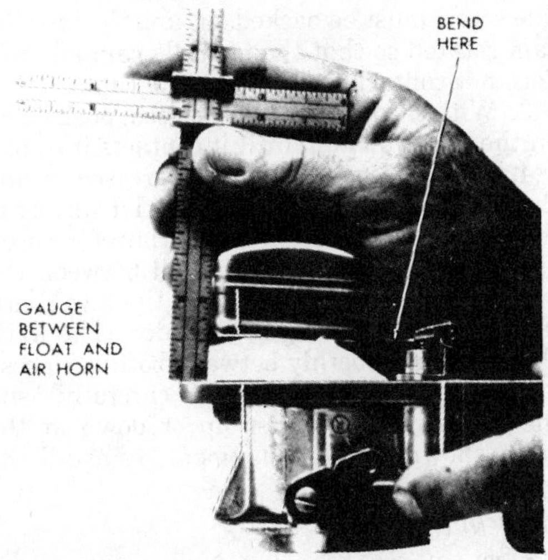

Float level adjustment—Carter YF

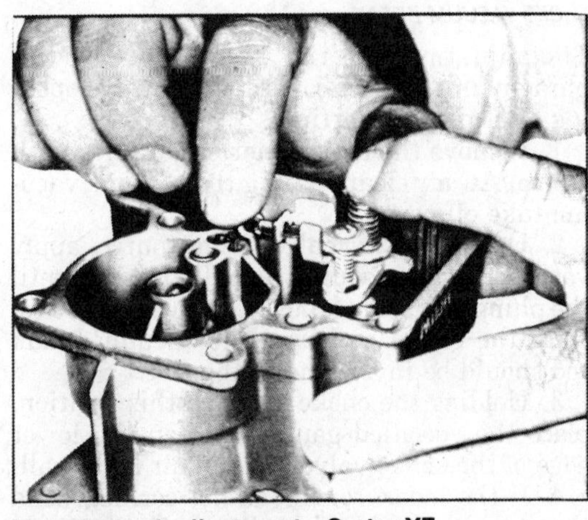
Metering rod adjustment—Carter YF

5. To adjust bend the pump connector link at its U-bend.

METERING ROD

1. Insert the metering rod through the metering jet and close the throttle valve. Press down on the upper pump spring until the pump bottoms.
2. Metering rod arm must rest on the pump lifter link and the rod eye should just slide over the arm pin.
3. To adjust, bend the metering rod arm.

Rochester M and MV (1969–74)

FAST IDLE SPEED

NOTE: *The fast idle adjustment must be made with the transmission in Neutral.*

1. Position the fast idle lever on the high step of the fast idle cam.
2. Be sure that the choke is properly adjusted and in the wide open position with the engine warm.
3. Bend the fast idle lever until the specified speed is obtained.

CHOKE ROD (FAST IDLE CAM)

NOTE: *Adjust the fast idle before making choke rod adjustments.*

1. Place the fast idle cam follower on the second step of the fast idle cam and hold it firmly against the rise to the high step.
2. Rotate the choke valve in the direction of a closed choke by applying force to the choke coil lever.
3. Bend the choke rod, at the lower angle, to give the specified opening between the lower edge of the choke valve and the inside air horn wall.

NOTE: *Measurement must be made at the center of the choke valve.*

CHOKE VACUUM BREAK

The adjustment of the vacuum break diaphragm unit insures correct choke valve opening after engine starting.

1. Remove the air cleaner on vehicles with Therm/AC air cleaner; plug the sensor's vacuum take off port.
2. Using an external vacuum source, apply vacuum to the vacuum break diaphragm until the plunger is seated, push the choke valve toward the closed position. The vacuum break rod should be in the end of the slot.
3. Holding the choke valve in this position, place the specified gauge between the lower edge of the choke valve and the air horn wall.
4. If the measurement is not correct, bend the vacuum break rod at the angle.

CHOKE UNLOADER

1. Apply pressure to the choke valve and hold it in the closed position.
2. Open the throttle valve to the wide open position.
3. Check the dimension between the lower edge of the choke plate and the air horn wall; if adjustment is needed, bend the unloader tang on the throttle lever to adjust to specification.

AUTOMATIC CHOKE COIL ROD

1. Disconnect the coil rod from the upper choke lever and hold the choke valve closed.
2. Push down on the coil rod to the end of its travel.
3. The top of the rod should be even with the bottom hole in the choke lever.
4. To make adjustments, bend the rod at the center.

FLOAT LEVEL

1. Remove the carburetor top. Hold the float retainer in place and the float arm against the top of the float needle by pushing down on the flat arm at the outer end toward the flat bowl casting.
2. Using an adjustable T scale, measure the distance from the tow of the float to the float bowl gasket surface.

NOTE: *The float bowl gasket should be removed and the gauge held on the index point on the float for accurate measurement.*

3. Adjust the float level by bending the float arm up or down at the float arm junction.

METERING ROD

1. Hold the throttle valve wide-open and push down on the metering rod against spring tension, then remove the rod from the main metering jet.
2. In order to check adjustment, the slow idle screw must be backed out and the fast idle cam rotated so that the fast idle cam follower does not contact the steps on the cam.
3. With the throttle valve closed, push down on the power piston until it contacts its stop.
4. With the power piston depressed, swing the metering rod holder over the flat surface of the bowl casting next to the carburetor bore.
5. Insert a specified size drill between the bowl casting sealing beak and the lower surface of the metering rod holder. The drill should slide smoothly between both surfaces.
6. If adjustment is needed, carefully bend the metering rod holder up or down at the point shown. After adjustment, reinstall the metering rod.

IDLE VENT (1967–69)

1. The engine idle must be set at the specified rpm and the choke valve held wide-open so

that the fast idle cam follower is not contacting the cam.

NOTE: *If the carburetor is off the car, a preliminary idle setting can be made by turning the idle speed screw in 1½ turns from the closed throttle valve position.*

2. With the throttle stop screw held against the idle stop screw, the idle vent valve should be open 0.050" (1.27mm). To check, a drill of specified size may be inserted between the top of the air horn casting and the bottom surface of the valve.

3. If adjustment is necessary, turn the slotted vent valve head with a screwdriver. Turning the head clockwise increases the clearance.

NOTE: *On models equipped with an idle stop solenoid, the solenoid must be activated when checking and adjusting the valve.*

C.E.C. SOLENOID (1971–73)

NOTE: *Do not use the C.E.C. valve to set idle rpm.*

1. With the engine running, and transmission in Neutral (manual) or Drive (Automatic), air conditioner OFF, distributor vacuum hose removed and plugged, and fuel tank vapor hose disconnected, manually extend the C.E.C. valve plunger to contact the throttle lever.
2. Adjust the plunger length to obtain the C.E.C. valve rpm.
3. Reconnect the vapor hose and vacuum hose.

Model 1MV, 1ME (1975–78)

FAST IDLE SPEED

1. Check and adjust the idle speed.
2. With the engine at normal operating temperature, air cleaner ON, EGR valve signal line disconnected and plugged and the air conditioning OFF, connect a tachometer.
3. Disconnect the vacuum advance hose at the distributor and plug the line.
4. With the transmission in Neutral (park on automatic), start the engine and set the fast idle cam follower on the high step of the cam.
5. Bend the tang in or out to obtain the fast idle speed.

FAST IDLE CAM (CHOKE ROD)

1. Check and adjust the fast idle speed.
2. Set the fast idle cam follower on the second step of the cam.
3. Apply force to the choke coil rod to hold the choke valve toward the closed position.
4. Measure the clearance between the upper edge (lower 1975) of the choke valve and the inside of the air horn wall.
5. Bend the rod at the lower angle to adjust.

CHOKE UNLOADER

1. Hold the choke valve down by applying light force to the choke coil lever.
2. Open the throttle valve to wide open.
3. Measure the clearance between the upper edge of the choke valve and the air horn wall.
4. If adjustment is necessary, bend the tang on the throttle lever.

FLOAT LEVEL

The adjustment is the same as for the Model MV.

AUTOMATIC CHOKE COIL ROD (1975)

1. Detach the top of the rod. Pull the rod up to the end of its travel. Completely close the choke valve.

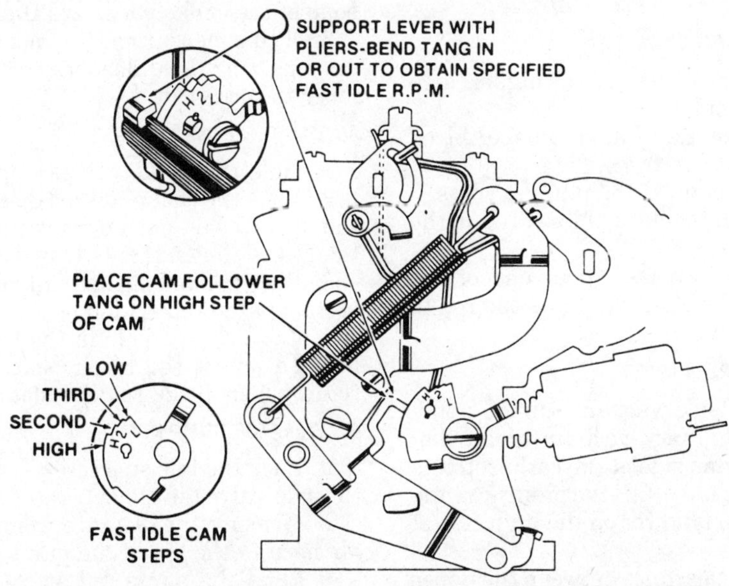

Location of the cam follower and the tang for fast idle adjustment

2. The bottom of the rod should be even with the top of the lever.
3. If adjustment is necessary, bend the rod.

AUTOMATIC CHOKE COIL ROD (1976)

1. Detach the top of the rod. Completely close the choke valve. Push the rod down to the end of its travel.
2. The top of the rod should be even with the bottom of the hole in the choke lever.
3. Bend the rod to adjust.

ELECTRIC CHOKE ADJUSTMENT (1977–78 1ME)

1. Place the cam follower on the highest step of the fast idle cam.
2. Hold the choke valve completely closed.
3. Insert a 0.120" (3.05mm) drill bit through the hole in the end of the choke coil housing lever. It should go into the hole in the casting at about the 11 o'clock position.
4. Bend the choke coil rod to adjust.
5. Loosen the three retaining screws and set the choke coil pointer to the center index mark.

NOTE: *Failure of the electric choke heater circuit will cause the oil pressure light to go on.*

PRIMARY VACUUM BREAK (1975)

1. With an outside vacuum source, apply vacuum to the primary vacuum break diaphragm until the plunger is fully seated. The primary diaphragm is the one on the opposite side from the idle speed solenoid.
2. Measure the clearance between the lower edge of the choke valve and the air horn wall.
3. Bend the vacuum break rod to adjust the clearance. Be sure there is no binding or interference.

PRIMARY VACUUM BREAK (1976–77)

1. Place the cam follower on the highest step of the fast idle cam.
2. Tape over the diaphragm housing bleed hole.
3. Apply vacuum until the plunger seats.
4. Push up on the choke coil lever rod in the end of the slot.
5. Measure between the upper end of the choke valve and the air horn. Bend the rod to adjust.

AUXILIARY VACUUM BREAK (1975)

1. With the outside vacuum source, apply vacuum to the auxiliary vacuum break diaphragm (on the same side of the carburetor as the idle speed solenoid) until the plunger seats.
2. Place the cam follower on the high step of the fast idle cam.
3. Measure the clearance between the upper edge of the choke valve and the air horn wall. Bend the link between the vacuum break and the choke valve to adjust.

Rochester 2G and 2GV (1967–74)

These procedures are for both the 1¼" (31.75mm) and 1½" (38.1mm) models. Where there are differences these are noted. The 1½" model has larger throttle bores and an additional fuel feed circuit to make it suitable for use on the 350 V8.

FAST IDLE CAM (CHOKE ROD)

1. Turn the idle screw onto the second step of the fast idle cam, abutting against the top step.
2. Hold the choke valve toward the closed position and check the clearance between the upper edge of the choke valve and the air horn wall.
3. If this measurement varies from specifications, bend the tang on the choke lever.

CHOKE VACUUM BREAK

1. Apply vacuum to the diaphragm to fully seat the plunger.
2. Push the choke valve in toward the closed position and hold it there.
3. Check the distance between the lower edge of the choke valve and the air horn wall.
4. If this dimension is not within specifications, bend the vacuum break rod to adjust.

CHOKE UNLOADER

1. Hold the throttle valves wide-open and use a rubber band to hold the choke valve toward the closed position.
2. Measure the distance between the upper edge of the choke valve and the air horn wall.
3. If this measurement is not within specifications, bend the unloader tang on the throttle lever to correct it.

AUTOMATIC CHOKE COIL ROD

1. Hold the choke valve completely open.
2. With the choke coil rod disconnected from the upper level, push downward on the end of the rod to the end of its travel.
3. With the rod pushed fully downward, the bottom of the rod should be even with the bottom of the slotted hole in the lever.
4. To adjust the lever, bend it by using a screwdriver in the smaller slot.

ACCELERATOR PUMP ROD

1. Back the idle stop screw out and close the throttle valves in their bores.
2. Measure the distance from the top of the air horn to the top of the pump rod.
3. Bend the pump rod at a lower angle to correct this dimension.

FLOAT LEVEL

Invert the air horn, and with the gasket in place and the needle seated, measure the level as follows:

On nitrophyl floats, measure from the air horn gasket to the lip on the toe of the float.

On brass floats, measure from the air horn gasket to the lower edge of the float seam.

Bend the float tang to adjust the level.

FLOAT DROP

Holding the air horn right side up, measure float drop as follows:

On nitrophyl floats, measure from the air horn gasket to the lip at the toe of the float.

On brass floats, measure from the air horn gasket to the bottom of the float.

Bend the float tang to adjust either type floats.

Model 2GC (1975–78)

ACCELERATOR PUMP ROD

1. Back out the idle speed adjusting screw.
2. Hold the throttle valve completely closed.
3. Measure the distance from the top of the air horn ring to the top of the pump rod.
4. If necessary, bend the pump rod to adjust.

FAST IDLE CAM

1. Place the idle speed screw on the second step of the fast idle cam against the highest step.
2. Measure the clearance between the upper edge of the choke valve and the air horn wall.
3. Bend the choke lever tang to adjust.

CHOKE UNLOADER

1. With the throttle valves wide open, place the choke valve in the closed position.
2. Measure the clearance between the upper edge of the choke valve and the air horn casting.
3. Bend the throttle lever tang to adjust.

INTERMEDIATE CHOKE ROD

1. Remove the thermostatic cover coil, gasket, and inside baffle plate.
2. Place the idle screw on the high step of the fast idle cam.
3. Close the choke valve by pushing up on the intermediate choke lever.
4. Insert a 0.120" (3.05mm) drill bit into the hole inside the choke housing (at about the 11 o'clock position). The edge of the choke lever must align with the edge of the bit.
5. Bend the intermediate choke rod between the two upper bends to adjust.

AUTOMATIC CHOKE COIL

1. Place the idle screw on the high step of the fast idle cam.
2. Loosen the thermostatic choke coil cover retaining screws.
3. Rotate the choke cover against coil tension until the choke valve begins to close. Continue rotating it until the index mark aligns with the specified point on the choke housing. These are: centered (index) except for 1975–76 automatic, which is one notch rich.
4. Tighten the choke cover retaining screws.

CHOKE VACUUM BREAK

1. Disconnect the vacuum hose. Using an outside vacuum source, seat the vacuum diaphragm.
2. Cover the vacuum break bleed hole with a small piece of tape so that the diaphragm will be hold inward.
3. Place the idle speed screw on the high step of the fast idle cam.
4. Hold the choke coil lever inside the choke housing toward the closed choke position.
5. Measure the clearance between the upper edge of the choke valve and the air horn wall.
6. Bend the vacuum break rod to adjust.
7. After adjustment, remove the piece of tape and reconnect the vacuum hose.

FLOAT LEVEL, FLOAT DROP

These procedures are the same as for the model 2GV, covered earlier.

Rochester 2SE (1979–84)

FLOAT ADJUSTMENT

1. Hold the float retainer in place with you hand and push the float down against the needle.
2. Place a ⅛" (3.mm) gauge at the toe of the float, as illustrated.
3. Remove the float and bend the arm as necessary to adjust the level.

FAST IDLE ADJUSTMENT

1. Refer to the underhood emissions sticker. Disconnect and plug any hoses indicted on the sticker.
2. Adjust the curb idle speed as outlined in Chapter Two.
3. Place the fast idle screw on the high step of the fast idle cam.
4. Turn the screw in or out to adjust the fast idle speed.

CHOKE COIL LEVER ADJUSTMENT

Refer to the illustration for this adjustment.

ELECTRIC CHOKE SETTING

1. Loosen the three choke coil retaining screws.
2. Place the fast idle screw on the high step of the fast idle adjusting cam.

3. Set the line on the choke 1 notch counterclockwise from the center mark.

AIR VALVE ROD ADJUSTMENT

1. Fully seat the diaphragm using an outside vacuum source.
2. Be sure the air valve is completely closed.
3. Place a 0.040" (1.016mm) gauge between the rod and the end of the slot in the lever, as illustrated.
4. Bend the rod to obtain 0.040" (1.016mm) clearance.

FAST IDLE CAM CHOKE ROD ADJUSTMENT

1. The choke coil lever and the fast idle adjustments must be correct before performing this adjustment.
2. Install a special choke valve measuring gauge (no. J-26701) on the carburetor.
3. Rotate the degree scale until the zero mark is opposite the pointer.
4. With the choke valve completely open, place the magnet directly on top of the choke valve.
5. Rotate the bubble until it is centered.
6. Rotate the scale to place the 17° mark opposite the pointer.
7. Place the fast idle screw on the second highest step of the fast idle cam.
8. Close the choke by pushing on the intermediate choke lever.
9. Push on the vacuum break lever toward the open choke lever until the lever is against the rear tang on the choke lever.
10. Bend the fast idle cam rod until the bubble on the gauge is centered. Remove the gauge.

PRIMARY SIDE VACUUM BREAK ADJUSTMENT

1. Refer to steps 1–5 of the Fast Idle Cam Choke Rod Adjustment.
2. Rotate the scale to place the specified degree opposite the pointer. Refer to the carburetor specification chart.
3. Fully seat the choke vacuum diaphragm using an outside vacuum source.
4. Hold the choke valve toward the closed position by pushing on the intermediate choke lever.
5. Bend the vacuum break rod until the bubble is centered and remove the gauge.

Rochester M2MC, M2ME (1979–81)

All adjustments for this carburetor are the same as the Rochester M4MC M4ME with the exception of the following:

FAST IDLE ADJUSTMENT

1. Hold the cam follower on the high step of the fast idle cam.
2. Turn the fast idle screw out until the primary throttle valves are closed.
3. Turn the fast idle screw out to contact the lever, then turn the screw in two turns.
4. Check the fast idle speed and adjust by turning the screw.

AUTOMATIC CHOKE COIL – M2MC

1. Install the thermostatic coil and cover with a gasket between the choke cover and the choke housing. The thermostatic coil must be installed in the slot in the inside of the choke coil lever pick-up arm.
2. Place the fast idle cam follower on the high step of the fast idle cam.
3. Rotate the cover and coil assembly counterclockwise until the choke valve just opens.
4. Align the index point on the cover with the specified mark on the choke housing. The setting is 1 notch lean.
5. Tighten the retaining screws.

CHOKE COIL LEVER ADJUSTMENT – M2ME

1. Drill out and remove the cover rivets.
2. Remove the cover and coil.
3. Place the fast idle cam follower on the high step of the cam.
4. Push clockwise upward on the thermostatic coil tang until the choke valve is closed.
5. Insert a 0.120" (3.05mm) gauge rod into the hole in the choke housing.
6. The lower edge of the lever should just touch the gauge rod.
7. Bend the choke rod at its mid-point to adjust.

Rochester 4MV (Quadrajet) (1970–78)

FAST IDLE SPEED

1. Position the fast idle lever on the high step of the fast idle cam.
2. Be sure that the choke is wide open and the engine warm. On 1973–74 manual transmission models, disconnect the distributor vacuum advance hose.
3. Turn the fast idle screw to gain the proper fast idle rpm.

CHOKE ROD (FAST IDLE CAM)

1. Place the cam follower on the second step of the fast idle cam.
2. Close the choke valve by exerting counterclockwise pressure on the external choke lever.
3. Insert a gauge of the proper size between the lower (upper starting 1975) edge of the choke valve and the inside air horn wall.
4. To adjust, bend the choke rod.

VACUUM BREAK

1. Fully seat the vacuum break diaphragm using an outside vacuum source.
2. Open the throttle valve enough to allow the fast idle cam follower to clear the fast idle

cam. Starting 1975, place the cam follower on the high step.

3. The end of the vacuum break rod should be at the outer end of the slot in the vacuum break diaphragm plunger.

4. The specified clearance should register from the lower end of the choke valve to the inside air horn wall.

5. If the clearance is not correct, bend the vacuum break link.

CHOKE UNLOADER

1. Push up on the vacuum break lever and fully open the throttle valves.

2. Measure the distance from the lower (upper starting 1975) edge of the choke valve to the air horn wall.

3. To adjust, bend the tang on the fast idle lever.

AUTOMATIC CHOKE COIL ROD

1. Close the choke valve by rotating the choke coil lever counterclockwise.

2. Disconnect the thermostatic coil rod from the upper lever.

3. Push down on the rod until it contacts the bracket of the coil.

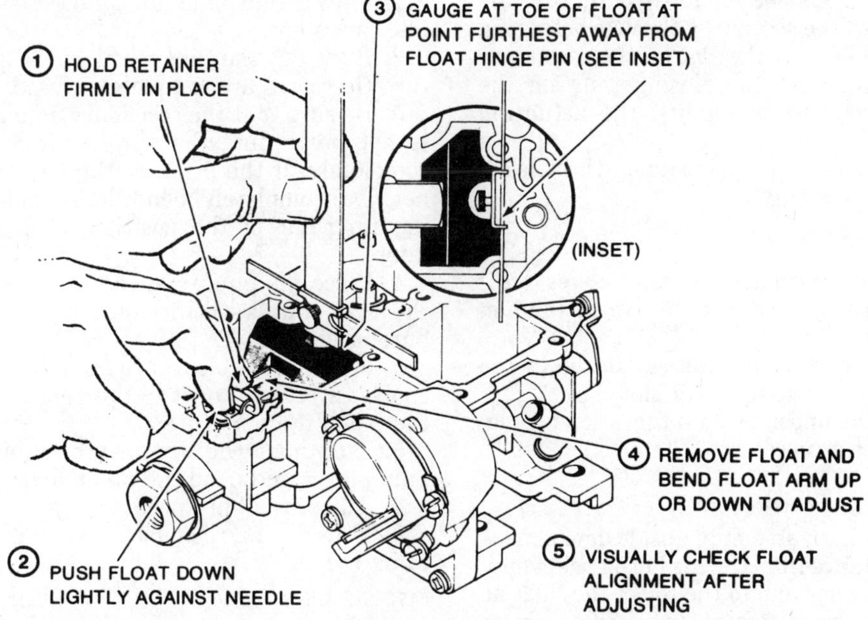

FLOAT ADJUSTMENT

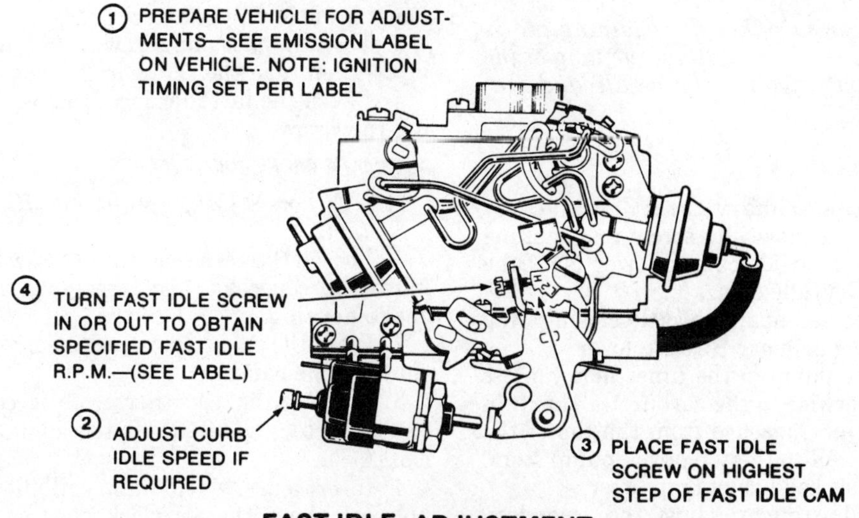

FAST IDLE ADJUSTMENT
(ON VEHICLE)

4. The rod must fit in the notch of the upper lever.

5. If it does not, it must be bent on the curved portion just below the upper lever.

NOTE: *1976 models that hesitate or stall on acceleration during warmup may be cured by installation of a new choke coil no. 460110.*

SECONDARY CLOSING

This adjustment assures proper closing of the secondary throttle plates.

1. Set the slow idle as per instructions in Chapter 2. Make sure that the fast idle cam follower is not resting on the fast idle cam.

2. There should be 0.020" (0.51mm) clearance between the secondary throttle actuating rod and the front of the slot on the secondary throttle lever with the closing tang on the throttle lever resting against the actuating lever.

3. Bend the tang on the primary throttle actuating rod to adjust.

SECONDARY OPENING

1. Open the primary throttle valves until the actuating link contacts the upper tang on the secondary lever.

2. The bottom of the link should be in the center of the secondary lever slot.

3. Bend the upper tang on the secondary lever to adjust as necessary.

FLOAT LEVEL

With the air horn assembly upside down, measure the distance from the air horn gasket surface (gasket removed) to the top of the float at the toe. Measure at a point $^3/_{16}$" (4.76mm) back from the toe for all models except for 1973–76, which should be measured at a point $^1/_{16}$" (1.58mm) back.

NOTE: *Make sure that the retaining pin is firmly hold in place and that the tang of the float is firmly against the needle and seat assembly.*

ACCELERATOR PUMP

1. Close the primary throttle valves by backing out the slow idle screw and making sure that the fast idle cam follower is off the steps of the fast idle cam.

2. Bend the secondary throttle closing tang away from the primary throttle lever.

3. With the pump in the inner hole (unless specified otherwise in the carburetor chart) in the pump lever, measure from the top of the choke valve wall to the top of the pump stem.

4. To adjust, bend the pump lever.

5. After adjusting, readjust the secondary throttle tang and the slow idle screw.

AIR VALVE SPRING

To adjust the air valve spring windup, loosen the allen head lockscrew and turn the adjusting screw counterclockwise to remove all spring tension. With the air valve closed, turn the adjusting screw clockwise the specified number of turns after the torsion spring contacts the pin on the shaft. Hold the adjusting screw in this position and tighten the lockscrew.

Model M4MC, M4ME (1975–86)

ACCELERATOR PUMP ROD

1. Take the fast idle cam follower off the fast idle cam steps.

2. Back out the idle speed screw until the throttle valves are completely closed.

3. Be sure that the secondary actuating rod is not preventing the throttle from closing completely. If the primary throttle valves do not close completely, bend the secondary closing tang out of the position, then readjust later.

4. Place the pump rod in the inner hole in the lever, unless specified otherwise in the carburetor chart.

5. Measure the clearance from the top of the choke valve wall, next to the vent stack, and the top of the pump stem.

6. To adjust the dimension, support the pump lever and bend the pump lever.

7. Adjust the idle speed.

8. If necessary, readjust the secondary actuating rod.

FAST IDLE SPEED

1. Hold the cam follower on the high step of the fast idle cam.

2. Turn the fast idle screw out until the primary throttle valves are closed.

3. Turn the fast idle screw in to contact the lever, then turn the screw in 3 turns.

4. Check the fast idle speed, adjust by turning the screw.

AUTOMATIC CHOKE COIL LEVER

NOTE: *For M4ME, see the M2MC, M2ME Section.*

1. Loosen the three retaining screws and remove the cover and coil assembly from the choke housing.

2. Place the cam follower on the high step of the fast idle cam.

3. Push up on the thermostatic coil tang (counterclockwise) until the choke valve closes.

4. Insert a 0.120" (3.05mm) drill bit into the hole (at about the 4 o'clock position) in the choke housing.

5. The lower edge of the choke coil lever should just contact the side of the bit.

6. Bend the choke rod to adjust.

CHOKE ROD (FAST IDLE CAM)

1. Adjust the fast idle.

2. Place the cam follower on the second step of the fast idle cam firmly against the ride of the high step.

3. Close the choke valve by pushing up on the choke coil lever inside the choke housing.

4. Measure the clearance between the upper edge of the choke valve and the inside of the air horn wall.

5. Bend the tang on the fast idle cam to adjust the clearance. Be sure that the tang lies against the cam after bending it.

6. Recheck the fast idle speed.

AIR VALVE DASHPOT

1. Seat the front vacuum diaphragm using an outside vacuum source.

2. The air valves must be completely closed.

3. Measure the clearance between the air valve dashpot and the end of the slot in the air valve lever. It should be 0.015" (0.381mm).

4. Bend the air valve dashpot to adjust the clearance.

FRONT VACUUM BREAK

1. Remove the thermostatic cover and coil assembly from the choke housing.

2. Place the cam follower on the high step of the fast idle cam.

3. Seat the front vacuum diaphragm using an outside vacuum source.

4. Push up on the inside choke coil lever until the tang on the vacuum break lever contacts the tang on the vacuum break plunger.

5. Measure the clearance between the upper edge of the choke valve and the air horn wall.

6. Turn the adjusting screw on the vacuum break plunger lever to adjust.

7. Reconnect the vacuum hose after adjustment.

REAR VACUUM BREAK

1. Remove the thermostatic cover and coil assembly from the choke housing.

2. Place the cam follower on the high step of the fast idle cam.

3. Plug the bleed hose in the vacuum break unit cover with tape.

4. Seat the rear vacuum diaphragm using an outside vacuum source.

5. Push up the choke coil lever inside the choke housing toward the closed position.

6. With the choke rod in the bottom slot of the choke lever, measure the clearance between the upper edge of the choke valve and air horn wall.

7. Bend the vacuum break rod if necessary to adjust.

8. After adjustment, remove the tape and install the vacuum hose.

CHOKE UNLOADER

1. Install the thermostatic coil and cover with a gasket between the choke cover and the choke housing. The thermostatic coil must be installed in the slot in the inside of the choke coil lever pick-up arm.

2. Hold the throttle valves wide open with the choke valve completely closed. On a warm engine, close the choke valve by pushing up on the tang of the intermediate choke lever which contact the fast idle cam. A rubber band will hold it in position.

3. Measure the distance between the upper edge of the choke valve and the air horn wall.

4. Bend the tang on the fast idle lever to adjust the clearance. Check to be sure that the tang on the fast idle cam lever is contacting the center of the fast idle cam after adjustment.

AIR VALVE SPRING

1. Remove the front vacuum break diaphragm and the air valve dashpot rod.

2. Loosen the lockscrew.

3. Turn the tension adjusting screw counterclockwise until the air valve opens part way.

4. Turn the tension adjusting screw clockwise while tapping lightly on the casting with the handle of a screwdriver.

5. When the air valve just closes, turn the tension adjusting screw clockwise the specified number of turns after the spring contacts the pin.

6. Tighten the lockscrew and reinstall the diaphragm and dashpot rod.

FLOAT LEVEL

Use the procedure given earlier for the model 4MV, measuring at a point $^{3}/_{16}$" (4.76mm) from the toe of the float.

Rochester E2SE 2-bbl.

The model E2SE, introduced on Chevrolet trucks in 1983, is designed as a part of the GM Computer Command Control system (C3). An electrically operated mixture control solenoid differentiates the E2SE from the conventional 2SE series.

A plunger in the end of the above mentioned solenoid is submerged in fuel in the fuel chamber of the float bowl. The plunger is controlled, or pulsed, by electrical signals received from the Electronic Control Module (ECM). The solenoid system is used to control the air/fuel mixture in the primary bore of the carburetor.

① Hold retainer in place
② Push float down lightly against needle
③ Gage at large toe of float, at point farthest from float hinge
④ Remove float and bend float arm up or down to adjust
(Some models have float stabilizer spring. Use care in removing)
⑤ Visually check float alignment

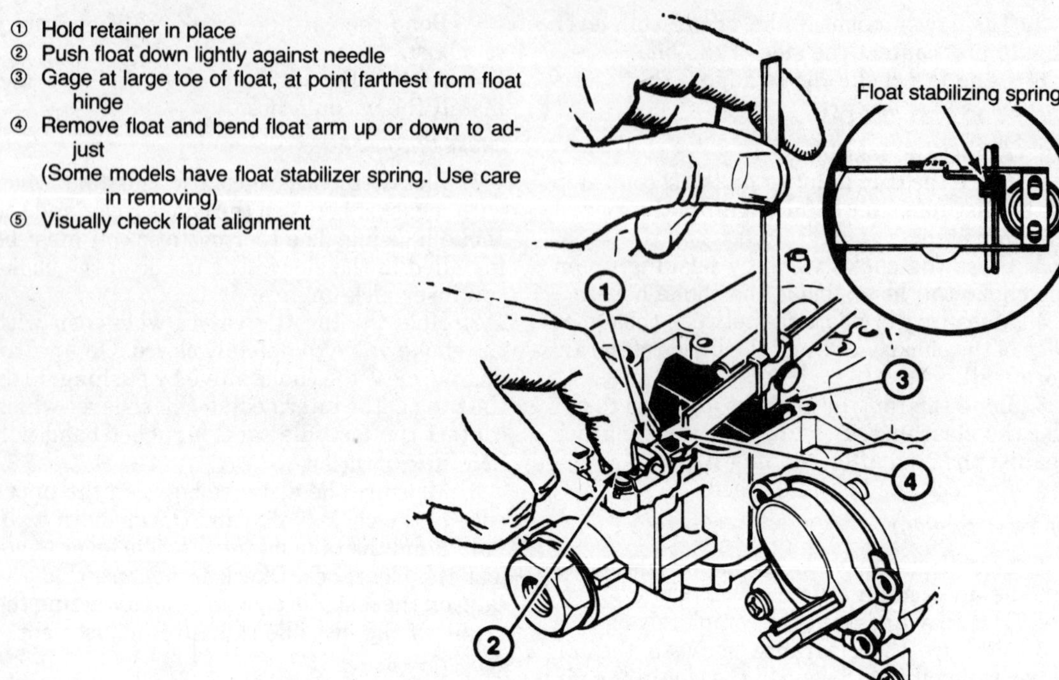

E2SE 2-bbl. float adjustment

NOTE: ON MODELS USING A CLIP TO RETAIN PUMP ROD IN PUMP LEVER, NO PUMP ADJUSTMENT IS REQUIRED. ON MODELS USING THE "CLIPLESS" PUMP ROD, THE PUMP ADJUSTMENT SHOULD NOT BE CHANGED FROM ORIGINAL FACTORY SETTING UNLESS GAUGING SHOWS OUT OF SPECIFICATION. THE PUMP LEVER IS MADE FROM HEAVY DUTY, HARDENED STEEL MAKING BENDING DIFFICULT. DO NOT REMOVE PUMP LEVER FOR BENDING UNLESS ABSOLUTELY NECESSARY.

② GAUGE FROM AIR HORN CASTING SURFACE TO TOP OF PUMP STEM. DIMENSION SHOULD BE AS SPECIFIED.

① THROTTLE VALVES COMPLETELY CLOSED. MAKE SURE FAST IDLE SCREW IS OFF STEPS OF FAST IDLE CAM.

③ IF NECESSARY TO ADJUST. REMOVE PUMP LEVER RETAINING SCREW AND WASHER AND REMOVE PUMP LEVER BY ROTATING LEVER TO REMOVE FROM PUMP ROD. PLACE LEVER IN A VISE, PROTECTING LEVER FROM DAMAGE, AND BEND END OF LEVER (NEAREST NECKED DOWN SECTION).

NOTE: DO NOT BEND LEVER IN A SIDEWAYS OR TWISTING MOTION.

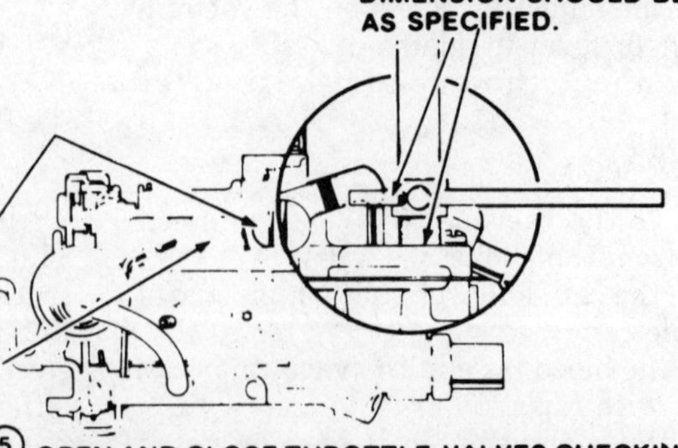

⑤ OPEN AND CLOSE THROTTLE VALVES CHECKING LINKAGE FOR FREEDOM OF MOVEMENT AND OBSERVING PUMP LEVER ALIGNMENT.

④ REINSTALL PUMP LEVER, WASHER AND RETAINING SCREW. RECHECK PUMP ADJUSTMENT ① AND ②. TIGHTEN RETAINING SCREW SECURELY AFTER THE PUMP ADJUSTMENT IS CORRECT.

E2SE 2-bbl. pump adjustment

The model E2SE also has a Throttle Position Sensor (TPS) mounted in the float bowl and is used to signal the ECM as throttle position changes occur. As throttle position changes, a tang on the pump lever moves the TPS plunger, modifying an electrical signal to the ECM. This signal is used in conjunction with signals from various other engine sensors by the ECM to control various engine operating modes.

FLOAT ADJUSTMENT

1. Remove the air horn from the throttle body.
2. Use your fingers to hold the retainer in place, and to push the float down into light contact with the needle.
3. Measure the distance from the tow of the float (furthest from the hinge) to the top of the carburetor (gasket removed).
4. To adjust, remove the float and gently bend the arm to specification. After adjustment, check the float alignment in the chamber.

PUMP ADJUSTMENT

1. With the throttle closed and the fast idle screw off the steps of the fast idle cam, measure the distance from the air horn casting to the top of the pump stem.
2. To adjust, remove the retaining screw and washer and remove the pump lever. Bend the end of the lever to correct the stem height. Do not twist the the lever or bend it sideways.
3. Install the lever, washer and screw and check the adjustment. When correct, open and close the throttle a few times to check the linkage movement and alignment.

NOTE: *No pump adjustment is required on 1981 and later models.*

FAST IDLE ADJUSTMENT

1. Set the ignition timing and curb idle speed, and disconnect the plug hoses as directed on the emission control decal.
2. Place the fast idle screw on the highest step of the cam.

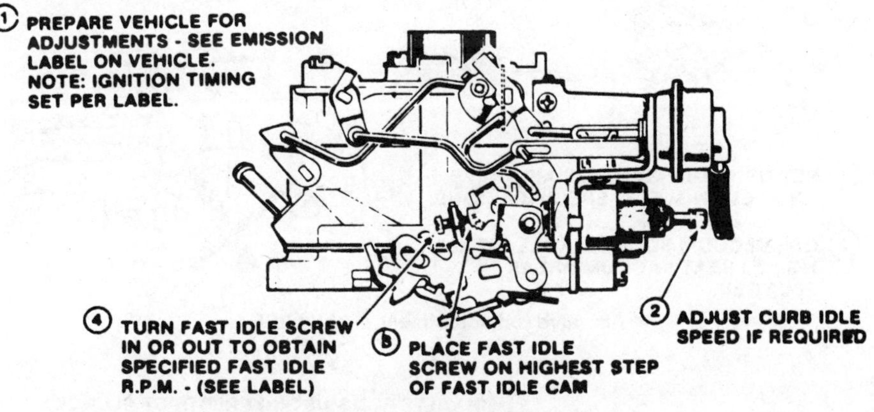

Fast idle adjustment, E2SE 2-bbl.

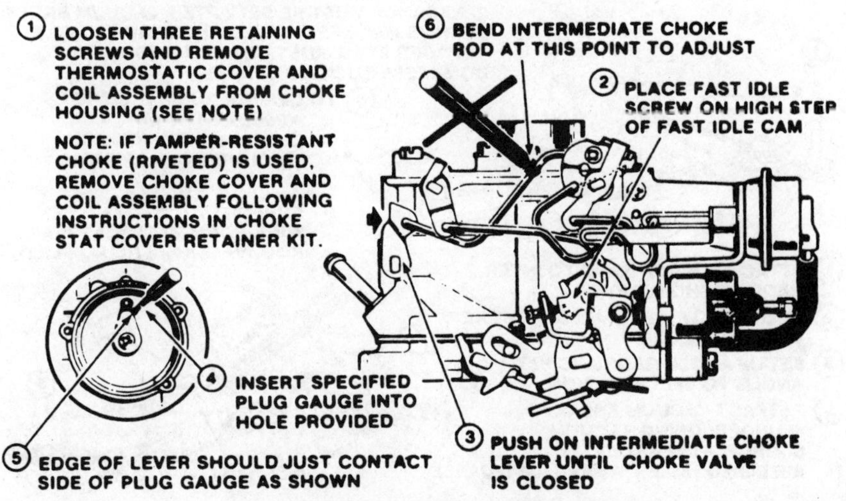

E2SE 2-bbl. choke coil lever adjustment

3. Start the engine and adjust the engine speed to specification with the fast idle screw.

CHOKE COIL LEVER ADJUSTMENT

1. Remove the three retaining screws and remove the choke cover and coil. On models with a riveted choke cover, drill out the three rivets and remove the cover and choke coil.

NOTE: *A choke stat cover retainer kit is required for reassembly.*

2. Place the fast idle screw on the high step of the cam.

3. Close the choke by pushing in on the intermediate choke lever. On front wheel drive models, the intermediate choke lever is behind the choke vacuum diaphragm.

4. Insert a drill or gauge of the specified size into the hole in the choke housing. The choke lever in the housing should be up against the side of the gauge.

5. If the lever does not just touch the gauge, bend the intermediate choke rod to adjust.

AIR VALVE ROD ADJUSTMENT

Refer to the accompanying illustration for this procedure.

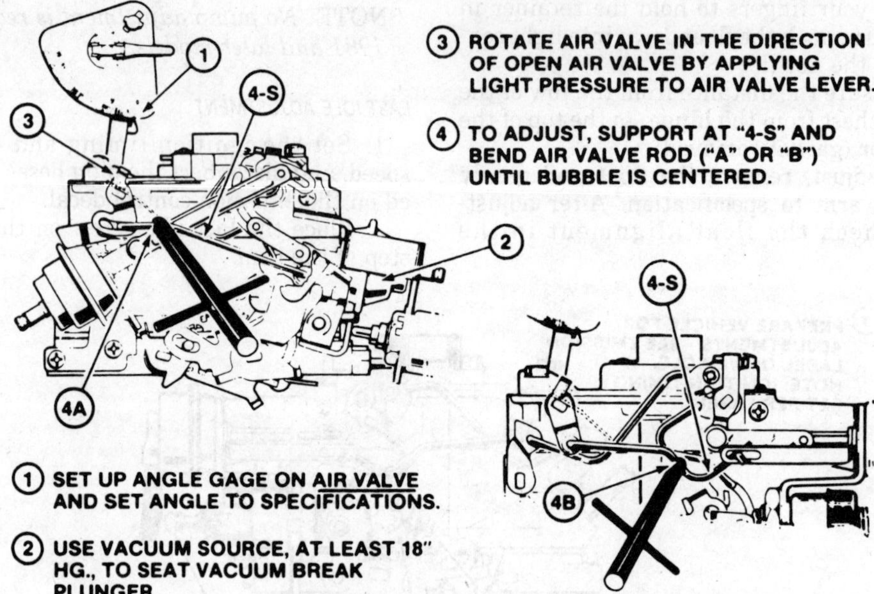

Air valve rod adjustment, 2-bbl. E2SE

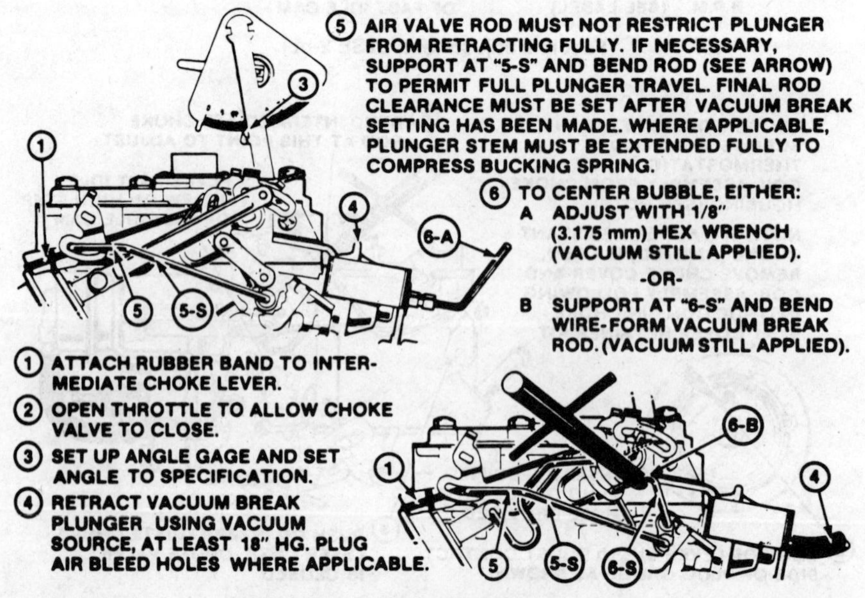

E2SE primary vacuum break adjustment

① Attach rubber band to intermediate choke lever
② Open Throttle to allow choke valve to close
③ Set up angle gage and set angle to specifications
④ Hold throttle lever in wide open position
⑤ Push on choke shaft lever to open choke valve and to make contact with black closing tang
⑥ Adjust by bending tang until bubble is centered

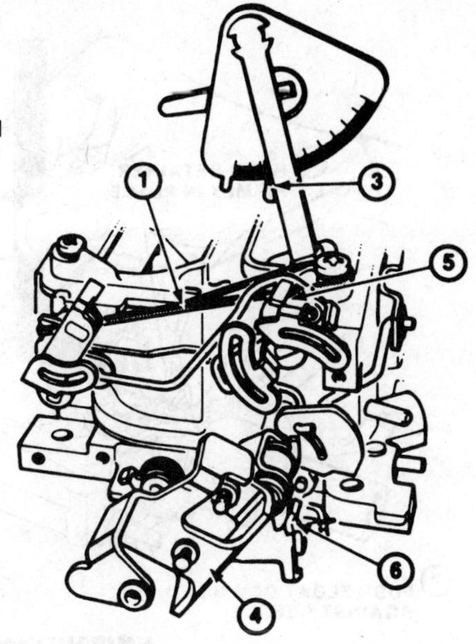

E2SE choke unloader adjustment

PRIMARY SIDE VACUUM BREAK ADJUSTMENT

Refer to the illustration for this procedure.

ELECTRIC CHOKE SETTING

This procedure is only for those carburetors with choke covers retained by screws. Riveted choke covers are preset and nonadjustable.

1. Loosen the three retaining screws.
2. Place the fast idle screw on the high step of the cam.
3. Rotate the choke cover to align the cover mark with the specified housing mark.

CHOKE UNLOADER ADJUSTMENT

Refer to the accompanying illustrations for this procedure.

Rochester E4ME and E4MC Quadrajet 4-bbl

These 4-bbl carburetors feature an electrically operated mixture control solenoid, and are designed as part of the GM Computer Command Control (C3) system. As with the E2SE 2-bbl the electric mixture control solenoid is mounted in the float bowl, and is used to control the air/fuel mixture in the primary bores of the carburetor. The plunger in the solenoid is controlled, or pulsed, by electrical signals received from the Electronic Control Module.

An Idle Speed Control (ISC) assembly, monitored by the ECM, controls engine idle speed. The curb (base) idle is programmed into the ECM and is not adjustable. When the throttle lever is resting against the ISC plunger, the ISC acts as a dashpot on throttle closing. An Idle Speed Solenoid or Idle Load Compensator is used on some models to position the primary throttle valve, providing engine idle speed requirements.

On E4MC models, the Idle Load Compensator (ILC) mounted on the float bowl is used to control curb idle speeds. The ILC uses manifold vacuum to sense changes in engine load (the A/C compressor clutch engaged, for example) and compensates by adjusting throttle angle for the curb idle speed. The ILC uses an spring loaded vacuum sensitive diaphragm whose plunger either extends (vacuum decrease) or retracts (vacuum increase) to adjust throttle angle for curb idle speeds. Both the ISC and ILC are factory adjusted.

FLOAT LEVEL

With the air horn assembly removed, measure the distance from the air horn gasket surface (gasket removed) to the top of the float at the toe ($^1/_{16}$″ (1.58mm) back from the toe).

NOTE: *Make sure the retaining pin is firmly held in place and that the tang of the float is lightly held against the needle and seat assembly.*

Remove the float and bend the float arm to adjust except on carburetors used with the computer controlled systems (E4MC and E4ME). For those carburetors, if the float level is too high, hold the retainer firmly in place and push down on the center of the float to adjust. If the float level is too low on models with the computer controlled system, lift out the metering rods. Remove the solenoid connector screw. Turn the lean mixture solenoid screw in clockwise, counting and recording the exact number of turns until the screw is lightly bot-

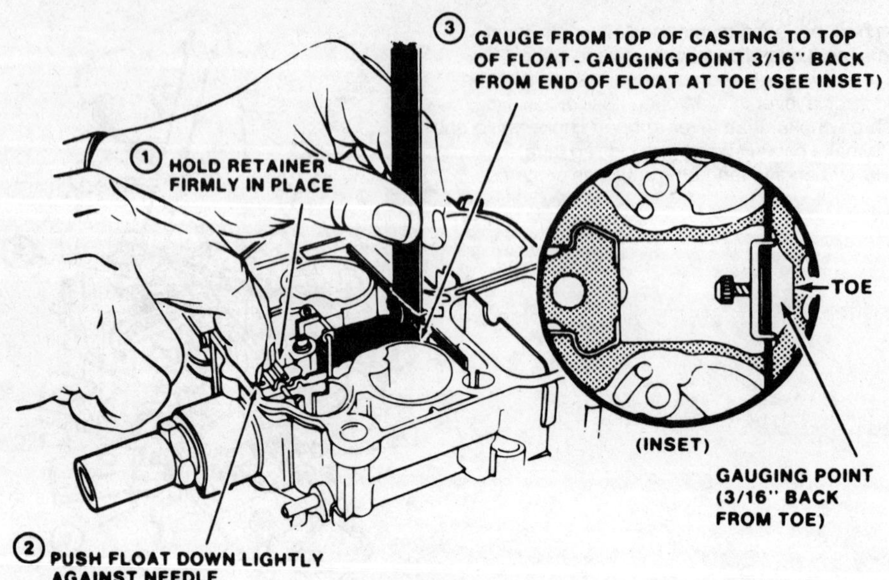

E4ME/MC float level adjustment

tomed in the bowl. Then turn the screw out clockwise and remove. Lift out the solenoid and connector. Remove the float and bend the arm up to adjust. Install the parts, turning the mixture solenoid screw in until it is lightly bottomed, then unscrewing it the exact number of turns counted earlier.

ACCELERATOR PUMP

The accelerator pump is not adjustable on computer controlled carburetors (E4MC and E4ME).

1. Close the primary throttle valves by backing out the slow idle screw and making

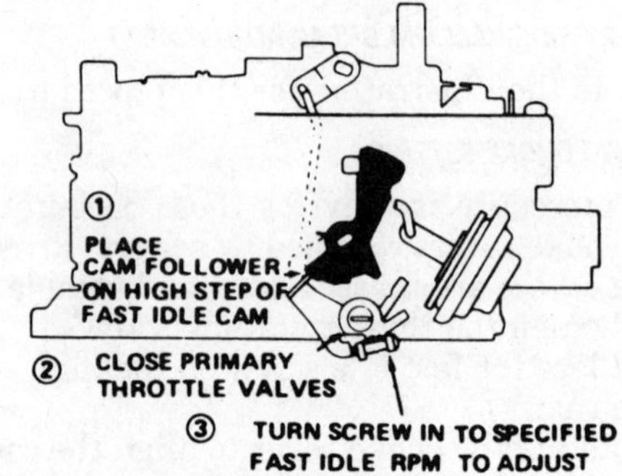

Fast idle adjustment, E4ME/MC

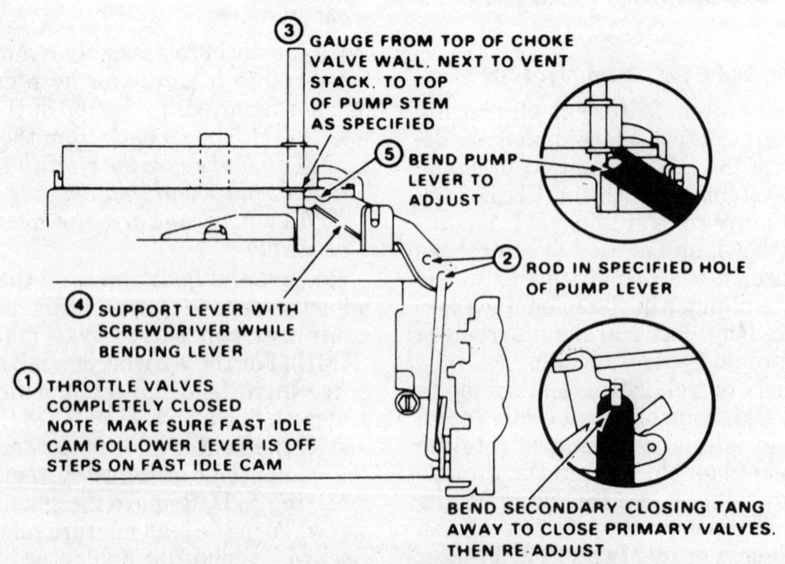

Accelerator pump adjustment, E4ME/MC 4-bbl.

55 WAYS TO IMPROVE FUEL ECONOMY

CHILTON'S
FUEL ECONOMY & TUNE-UP TIPS

Tune-up • Spark Plug Diagnosis • Emission Controls

Fuel System • Cooling System • Tires and Wheels

General Maintenance

CHILTON'S FUEL ECONOMY & TUNE-UP TIPS

Fuel economy is important to everyone, no matter what kind of vehicle you drive. The maintenance-minded motorist can save both money and fuel using these tips and the periodic maintenance and tune-up procedures in this Repair and Tune-Up Guide.

There are more than 130,000,000 cars and trucks registered for private use in the United States. Each travels an average of 10-12,000 miles per year, and, and in total they consume close to 70 billion gallons of fuel each year. This represents nearly ⅔ of the oil imported by the United States each year. The Federal government's goal is to reduce consumption 10% by 1985. A variety of methods are either already in use or under serious consideration, and they all affect you driving and the cars you will drive. In addition to "down-sizing", the auto industry is using or investigating the use of electronic fuel delivery, electronic engine controls and alternative engines for use in smaller and lighter vehicles, among other alternatives to meet the federally mandated Corporate Average Fuel Economy (CAFE) of 27.5 mpg by 1985. The government, for its part, is considering rationing, mandatory driving curtailments and tax increases on motor vehicle fuel in an effort to reduce consumption. The government's goal of a 10% reduction could be realized — and further government regulation avoided — if every private vehicle could use just 1 less gallon of fuel per week.

How Much Can You Save?

Tests have proven that almost anyone can make at least a 10% reduction in fuel consumption through regular maintenance and tune-ups. When a major manufacturer of spark plugs sur-

TUNE-UP

1. Check the cylinder compression to be sure the engine will really benefit from a tune-up and that it is capable of producing good fuel economy. A tune-up will be wasted on an engine in poor mechanical condition.

2. Replace spark plugs regularly. New spark plugs alone can increase fuel economy 3%.

3. Be sure the spark plugs are the correct type (heat range) for your vehicle. See the Tune-Up Specifications.

Heat range refers to the spark plug's ability to conduct heat away from the firing end. It must conduct the heat away in an even pattern to avoid becoming a source of pre-ignition, yet it must also operate hot enough to burn off conductive deposits that could cause misfiring.

The heat range is usually indicated by a number on the spark plug, part of the manufacturer's designation for each individual spark plug. The numbers in bold-face indicate the heat range in each manufacturer's identification system.

Manufacturer	Typical Designation
AC	R **45** TS
Bosch (old)	WA **145** T30
Bosch (new)	HR **8** Y
Champion	RBL **15** Y
Fram/Autolite	41**5**
Mopar	P-**62** PR
Motorcraft	BRF-**4**2
NGK	BP **5** ES-15
Nippondenso	W **16** EP
Prestolite	14GR **5** 2A

Periodically, check the spark plugs to be sure they are firing efficiently. They are excellent indicators of the internal condition of your engine.

On AC, Bosch (new), Champion, Fram/Autolite, Mopar, Motorcraft and Prestolite, a higher number indicates a hotter plug. On Bosch (old), NGK and Nippondenso, a higher number indicates a colder plug.

4. Make sure the spark plugs are properly gapped. See the Tune-Up Specifications in this book.

5. Be sure the spark plugs are firing efficiently. The illustrations on the next 2 pages show you how to "read" the firing end of the spark plug.

6. Check the ignition timing and set it to specifications. Tests show that almost all cars have incorrect ignition timing by more than 2°.

veyed over 6,000 cars nationwide, they found that a tune-up, on cars that needed one, increased fuel economy over 11%. Replacing worn plugs alone, accounted for a 3% increase. The same test also revealed that 8 out of every 10 vehicles will have some maintenance deficiency that will directly affect fuel economy, emissions or performance. Most of this mileage-robbing neglect could be prevented with regular maintenance.

Modern engines require that all of the functioning systems operate properly for maximum efficiency. A malfunction anywhere wastes fuel. You can keep your vehicle running as efficiently and economically as possible, by being aware of your vehicle's operating and performance characteristics. If your vehicle suddenly develops performance or fuel economy problems it could be due to one or more of the following:

PROBLEM	POSSIBLE CAUSE
Engine Idles Rough	Ignition timing, idle mixture, vacuum leak or something amiss in the emission control system.
Hesitates on Acceleration	Dirty carburetor or fuel filter, improper accelerator pump setting, ignition timing or fouled spark plugs.
Starts Hard or Fails to Start	Worn spark plugs, improperly set automatic choke, ice (or water) in fuel system.
Stalls Frequently	Automatic choke improperly adjusted and possible dirty air filter or fuel filter.
Performs Sluggishly	Worn spark plugs, dirty fuel or air filter, ignition timing or automatic choke out of adjustment.

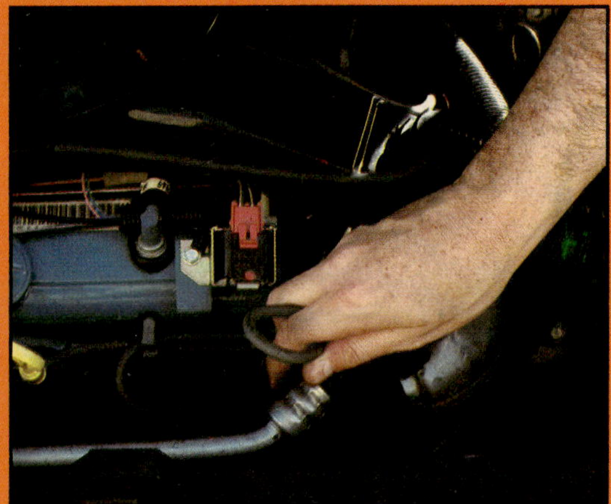

Check spark plug wires on conventional point type ignition for cracks by bending them in a loop around your finger.

Be sure that spark plug wires leading to adjacent cylinders do not run too close together. (Photo courtesy Champion Spark Plug Co.)

7. If your vehicle does not have electronic ignition, check the points, rotor and cap as specified.

8. Check the spark plug wires (used with conventional point-type ignitions) for cracks and burned or broken insulation by bending them in a loop around your finger. Cracked wires decrease fuel efficiency by failing to deliver full voltage to the spark plugs. One misfiring spark plug can cost you as much as 2 mpg.

9. Check the routing of the plug wires. Misfiring can be the result of spark plug leads to adjacent cylinders running parallel to each other and too close together. One wire tends to pick up voltage from the other causing it to fire "out of time".

10. Check all electrical and ignition circuits for voltage drop and resistance.

11. Check the distributor mechanical and/or vacuum advance mechanisms for proper functioning. The vacuum advance can be checked by twisting the distributor plate in the opposite direction of rotation. It should spring back when released.

12. Check and adjust the valve clearance on engines with mechanical lifters. The clearance should be slightly loose rather than too tight.

SPARK PLUG DIAGNOSIS

Normal

APPEARANCE: This plug is typical of one operating normally. The insulator nose varies from a light tan to grayish color with slight electrode wear. The presence of slight deposits is normal on used plugs and will have no adverse effect on engine performance. The spark plug heat range is correct for the engine and the engine is running normally.
CAUSE: Properly running engine.
RECOMMENDATION: Before reinstalling this plug, the electrodes should be cleaned and filed square. Set the gap to specifications. If the plug has been in service for more than 10-12,000 miles, the entire set should probably be replaced with a fresh set of the same heat range.

Oil Deposits

APPEARANCE: The firing end of the plug is covered with a wet, oily coating.
CAUSE: The problem is poor oil control. On high mileage engines, oil is leaking past the rings or valve guides into the combustion chamber. A common cause is also a plugged PCV valve, and a ruptured fuel pump diaphragm can also cause this condition. Oil fouled plugs such as these are often found in new or recently overhauled engines, before normal oil control is achieved, and can be cleaned and reinstalled.
RECOMMENDATION: A hotter spark plug may temporarily relieve the problem, but the engine is probably in need of work.

Incorrect Heat Range

APPEARANCE: The effects of high temperature on a spark plug are indicated by clean white, often blistered insulator. This can also be accompanied by excessive wear of the electrode, and the absence of deposits.
CAUSE: Check for the correct spark plug heat range. A plug which is too hot for the engine can result in overheating. A car operated mostly at high speeds can require a colder plug. Also check ignition timing, cooling system level, fuel mixture and leaking intake manifold.
RECOMMENDATION: If all ignition and engine adjustments are known to be correct, and no other malfunction exists, install spark plugs one heat range colder.

Carbon Deposits

APPEARANCE: Carbon fouling is easily identified by the presence of dry, soft, black, sooty deposits.
CAUSE: Changing the heat range can often lead to carbon fouling, as can prolonged slow, stop-and-start driving. If the heat range is correct, carbon fouling can be attributed to a rich fuel mixture, sticking choke, clogged air cleaner, worn breaker points, retarded timing or low compression. If only one or two plugs are carbon fouled, check for corroded or cracked wires on the affected plugs. Also look for cracks in the distributor cap between the towers of affected cylinders.
RECOMMENDATION: After the problem is corrected, these plugs can be cleaned and reinstalled if not worn severely.

Photos Courtesy Fram Corporation

MMT Fouled

APPEARANCE: Spark plugs fouled by MMT (Methycyclopentadienyl Maganese Tricarbonyl) have reddish, rusty appearance on the insulator and side electrode.
CAUSE: MMT is an anti-knock additive in gasoline used to replace lead. During the combustion process, the MMT leaves a reddish deposit on the insulator and side electrode.
RECOMMENDATION: No engine malfunction is indicated and the deposits will not affect plug performance any more than lead deposits (see Ash Deposits). MMT fouled plugs can be cleaned, regapped and reinstalled.

High Speed Glazing

APPEARANCE: Glazing appears as shiny coating on the plug, either yellow or tan in color.
CAUSE: During hard, fast acceleration, plug temperatures rise suddenly. Deposits from normal combustion have no chance to fluff-off; instead, they melt on the insulator forming an electrically conductive coating which causes misfiring.
RECOMMENDATION: Glazed plugs are not easily cleaned. They should be replaced with a fresh set of plugs of the correct heat range. If the condition recurs, using plugs with a heat range one step colder may cure the problem.

Ash (Lead) Deposits

APPEARANCE: Ash deposits are characterized by light brown or white colored deposits crusted on the side or center electrodes. In some cases it may give the plug a rusty appearance.
CAUSE: Ash deposits are normally derived from oil or fuel additives burned during normal combustion. Normally they are harmless, though excessive amounts can cause misfiring. If deposits are excessive in short mileage, the valve guides may be worn.
RECOMMENDATION: Ash-fouled plugs can be cleaned, gapped and reinstalled.

Detonation

APPEARANCE: Detonation is usually characterized by a broken plug insulator.
CAUSE: A portion of the fuel charge will begin to burn spontaneously, from the increased heat following ignition. The explosion that results applies extreme pressure to engine components, frequently damaging spark plugs and pistons.

Detonation can result by over-advanced ignition timing, inferior gasoline (low octane) lean air/fuel mixture, poor carburetion, engine lugging or an increase in compression ratio due to combustion chamber deposits or engine modification.
RECOMMENDATION: Replace the plugs after correcting the problem.

Photos Courtesy Champion Spark Plug Co.

EMISSION CONTROLS

13. Be aware of the general condition of the emission control system. It contributes to reduced pollution and should be serviced regularly to maintain efficient engine operation.

14. Check all vacuum lines for dried, cracked or brittle conditions. Something as simple as a leaking vacuum hose can cause poor performance and loss of economy.

15. Avoid tampering with the emission control system. Attempting to improve fuel econ-

FUEL SYSTEM

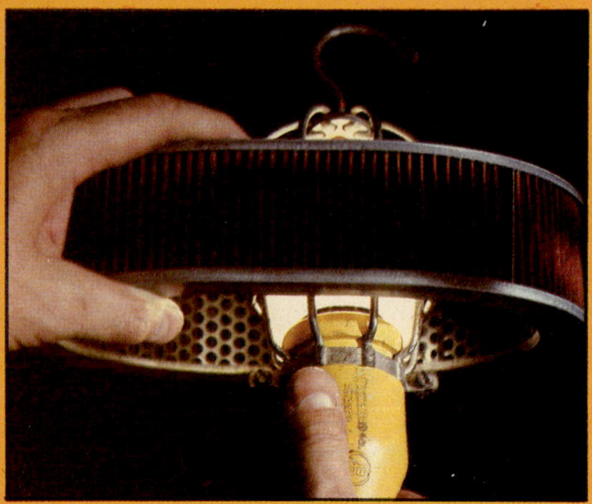

Check the air filter with a light behind it. If you can see light through the filter it can be reused.

Extremely clogged filters should be discarded and replaced with a new one.

18. Replace the air filter regularly. A dirty air filter richens the air/fuel mixture and can increase fuel consumption as much as 10%. Tests show that ⅓ of all vehicles have air filters in need of replacement.

19. Replace the fuel filter at least as often as recommended.

20. Set the idle speed and carburetor mixture to specifications.

21. Check the automatic choke. A sticking or malfunctioning choke wastes gas.

22. During the summer months, adjust the automatic choke for a leaner mixture which will produce faster engine warm-ups.

COOLING SYSTEM

29. Be sure all accessory drive belts are in good condition. Check for cracks or wear.

30. Adjust all accessory drive belts to proper tension.

31. Check all hoses for swollen areas, worn spots, or loose clamps.

32. Check coolant level in the radiator or expansion tank.

33. Be sure the thermostat is operating properly. A stuck thermostat delays engine warm-up and a cold engine uses nearly twice as much fuel as a warm engine.

34. Drain and replace the engine coolant at least as often as recommended. Rust and scale

TIRES & WHEELS

38. Check the tire pressure often with a pencil type gauge. Tests by a major tire manufacturer show that 90% of all vehicles have at least 1 tire improperly inflated. Better mileage can be achieved by over-inflating tires, but never exceed the maximum inflation pressure on the side of the tire.

39. If possible, install radial tires. Radial tires deliver as much as ½ mpg more than bias belted tires.

40. Avoid installing super-wide tires. They only create extra rolling resistance and decrease fuel mileage. Stick to the manufacturer's recommendations.

41. Have the wheels properly balanced.

omy by tampering with emission controls is more likely to worsen fuel economy than improve it. Emission control changes on modern engines are not readily reversible.

16. Clean (or replace) the EGR valve and lines as recommended.

17. Be sure that all vacuum lines and hoses are reconnected properly after working under the hood. An unconnected or misrouted vacuum line can wreak havoc with engine performance.

23. Check for fuel leaks at the carburetor, fuel pump, fuel lines and fuel tank. Be sure all lines and connections are tight.

24. Periodically check the tightness of the carburetor and intake manifold attaching nuts and bolts. These are a common place for vacuum leaks to occur.

25. Clean the carburetor periodically and lubricate the linkage.

26. The condition of the tailpipe can be an excellent indicator of proper engine combustion. After a long drive at highway speeds, the inside of the tailpipe should be a light grey in color. Black or soot on the insides indicates an overly rich mixture.

27. Check the fuel pump pressure. The fuel pump may be supplying more fuel than the engine needs.

28. Use the proper grade of gasoline for your engine. Don't try to compensate for knocking or "pinging" by advancing the ignition timing. This practice will only increase plug temperature and the chances of detonation or pre-ignition with relatively little performance gain.

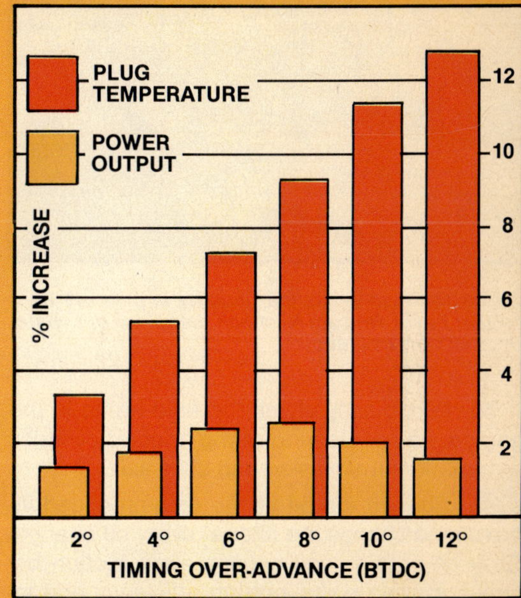

Increasing ignition timing past the specified setting results in a drastic increase in spark plug temperature with increased chance of detonation or preignition. Performance increase is considerably less. (Photo courtesy Champion Spark Plug Co.)

that form in the engine should be flushed out to allow the engine to operate at peak efficiency.

35. Clean the radiator of debris that can decrease cooling efficiency.

36. Install a flex-type or electric cooling fan, if you don't have a clutch type fan. Flex fans use curved plastic blades to push more air at low speeds when more cooling is needed; at high speeds the blades flatten out for less resistance. Electric fans only run when the engine temperature reaches a predetermined level.

37. Check the radiator cap for a worn or cracked gasket. If the cap does not seal properly, the cooling system will not function properly.

42. Be sure the front end is correctly aligned. A misaligned front end actually has wheels going in differed directions. The increased drag can reduce fuel economy by .3 mpg.

43. Correctly adjust the wheel bearings. Wheel bearings that are adjusted too tight increase rolling resistance.

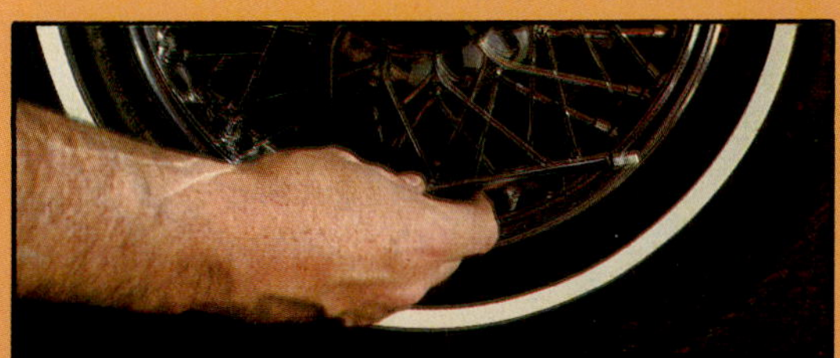

Check tire pressures regularly with a reliable pocket type gauge. Be sure to check the pressure on a cold tire.

GENERAL MAINTENANCE

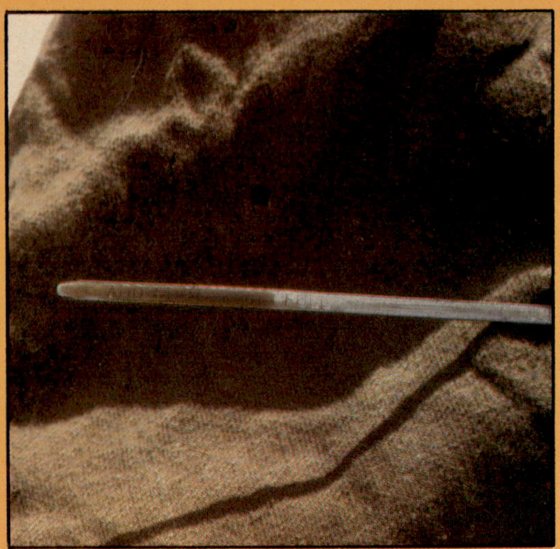

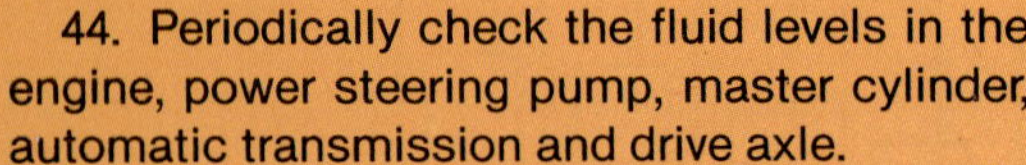

Check the fluid levels (particularly engine oil) on a regular basis. Be sure to check the oil for grit, water or other contamination.

A vacuum gauge is another excellent indicator of internal engine condition and can also be installed in the dash as a mileage indicator.

44. Periodically check the fluid levels in the engine, power steering pump, master cylinder, automatic transmission and drive axle.

45. Change the oil at the recommended interval and change the filter at every oil change. Dirty oil is thick and causes extra friction between moving parts, cutting efficiency and increasing wear. A worn engine requires more frequent tune-ups and gets progressively worse fuel economy. In general, use the lightest viscosity oil for the driving conditions you will encounter.

46. Use the recommended viscosity fluids in the transmission and axle.

47. Be sure the battery is fully charged for fast starts. A slow starting engine wastes fuel.

48. Be sure battery terminals are clean and tight.

49. Check the battery electrolyte level and add distilled water if necessary.

50. Check the exhaust system for crushed pipes, blockages and leaks.

51. Adjust the brakes. Dragging brakes or brakes that are not releasing create increased drag on the engine.

52. Install a vacuum gauge or miles-per-gallon gauge. These gauges visually indicate engine vacuum in the intake manifold. High vacuum = good mileage and low vacuum = poorer mileage. The gauge can also be an excellent indicator of internal engine conditions.

53. Be sure the clutch is properly adjusted. A slipping clutch wastes fuel.

54. Check and periodically lubricate the heat control valve in the exhaust manifold. A sticking or inoperative valve prevents engine warm-up and wastes gas.

55. Keep accurate records to check fuel economy over a period of time. A sudden drop in fuel economy may signal a need for tune-up or other maintenance.

© 1980 Chilton Book Company, Radnor, PA 19089

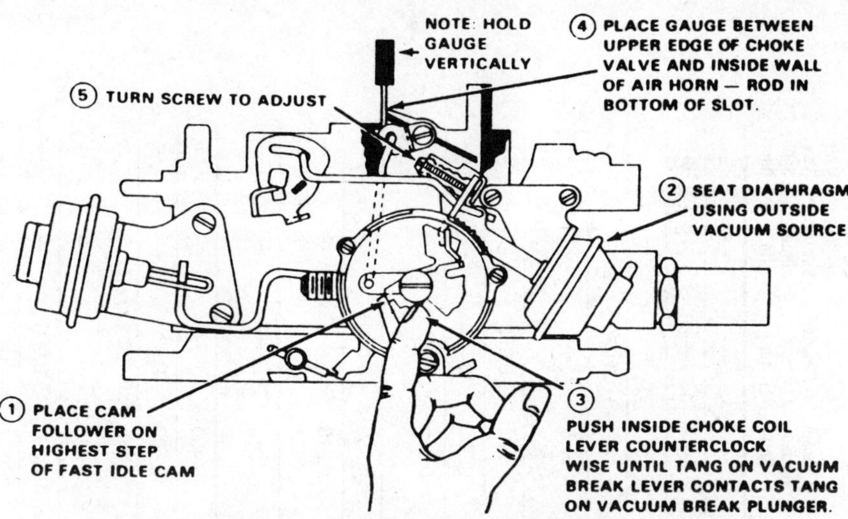

E4ME/MC front vacuum break adjustment

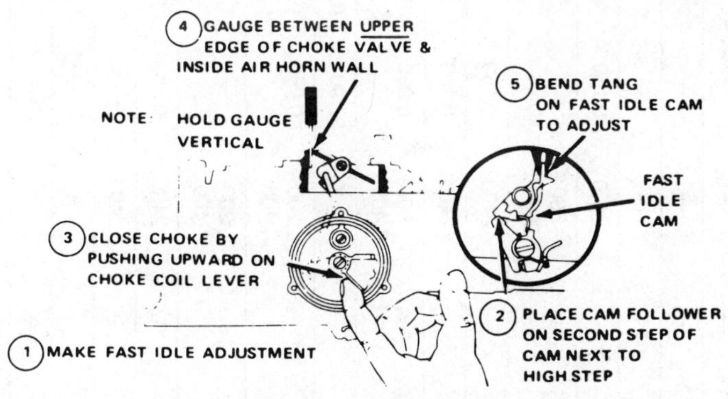

Choke rod (fast idle cam) adjustment—E4ME/MC

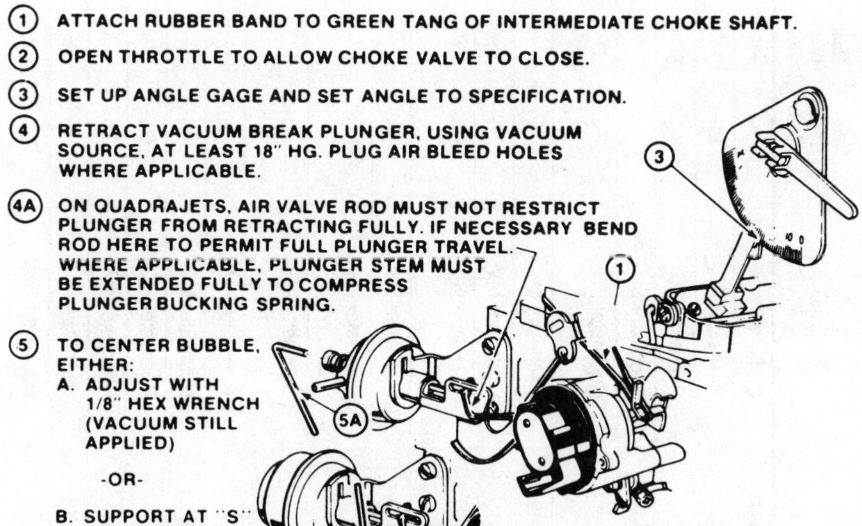

E4ME/MC rear vacuum break adjustment

Carburetor Specifications

Year	Carburetor Model	Float Level (in.)	Float Drop (in.)	Idle Vent (in.)	Accelerator Pump (in.)	Fast Idle Speed (rpm)	Fast Idle Cam Choke Rod (in.)	Primary or Front Choke Vacuum Break (in.)	Choke Unloader (in.)	Metering Rod (in.)	Rear or Auxiliary Vacuum Break (in.)	Air Valve Spring (turns)
1967	Carter YF	7/32	1 3/16	0.065	—	—	—	—	—	—	—	—
	Rochester B	1 9/32	1 3/4	0.066	—	—	—	—	—	—	—	—
	Rochester 2G	3/4 ①	1 29/32	—	1 1/8	—	—	—	—	—	—	—
1968	Rochester M	11/32	—	0.050	—	2400	0.150	—	—	0.070	—	—
	Rochester 2G	3/4	1 3/4	1.000	1 1/8	1800–2000	—	—	—	—	—	—
1969	Rochester M	1/4	—	0.050	—	2400	0.150	—	—	0.070	—	—
	Rochester MV	1/4	—	0.050	—	2400	0.180	2.260	0.350	0.070	—	—
	Rochester 2G	27/32	1 3/4	0.020	1 1/8	1800–2400	0.095	0.130	0.215	—	—	—
1970–71	Rochester MV	1/4	—	—	—	2400	0.190 ②	0.230 ③	0.350	0.070	—	—
	Rochester 2GV	23/32 ④	1 3/4	0.027	1 3/8	2200–2400	0.060	0.140 ⑤	0.215	—	—	—
	Rochester 2G	23/32	1 3/4	0.020	1 17/32	2200–2400	—	—	—	—	—	—
	Rochester 4MV	1/4	—	3/8	5/16	2400	0.100	0.245 ⑦	0.450	—	—	7/16
1972	Rochester MV	1/4	—	—	—	2400	—	⑧	0.500	0.080	—	—
	Rochester 2 GV	21/32	1 9/32	—	—	⑨	—	0.110 ⑩	0.210	—	—	—
	Rochester 4MV	3/16	—	—	—	⑪	—	0.215	0.450	—	—	1/2
1973	Rochester MV	1/4	—	—	—	2400	⑫	0.430 ⑬	0.600 ⑪	0.080	—	—
	Rochester 2GV	21/32 ⑮	1 9/32	—	—	1600	0.150 ⑯	0.080 ⑰	0.215 ⑱	—	—	—
	Rochester 4MV	7/32 ⑳	—	—	—	1600 ⑲	0.430	0.215	0.450	—	—	1/2
1974	Rochester MV 7044021	0.295	—	—	—	1800	0.275	0.350	0.500	0.080	—	—

	7044022	0.295	—	—	—	1800	0.245	0.300	0.500	0.080	—	—
	7044025	0.250	—	—	—	1800	0.245	0.300	0.521	0.070	—	—
	7044321	0.295	—	—	—	2400	0.300	0.375	0.500	0.080	—	—
	Rochester 2GV 7044123	19/32	1 9/32	—	1 9/32	1600	0.200	0.140	0.250	—	—	—
	7044124	19/32	1 9/32	—	1 3/16	1600	0.245	0.130	0.325	—	—	—
	Rochester 4MV 7044214, 7044514	11/32	—	—	13/32	1600	0.430	0.215	0.450	—	—	7/8
	7044218, 7044518	1/4	—	—	13/32	1600	0.430	0.215	0.450	—	—	7/8
	7044219, 7044519	1/4	—	—	13/32	1600	0.430	0.215	0.450	—	—	7/8
	7044224	11/32	—	—	13/32	1600	0.430	0.215	0.450	—	—	7/8
1975	Rochester 1MV 7045004	11/32	—	—	—	1800	0.245	0.300	0.325	0.080	0.150	—
	7045005	11/32	—	—	—	1800	0.275	0.350	0.325	0.080	0.290	—
	7045304	11/32	—	—	—	1800	0.245	0.300	0.325	0.080	0.290	—
	7045305	11/32	—	—	—	1800	0.275	0.350	0.325	0.080	0.290	—
	Rochester 2GC 7045123, 7045124	21/32	31/32	—	1 5/8	—	0.400	0.130	0.350	—	—	—
	Rochester M4MC 7045218, 7045219	15/32	—	—	0.275	1600	0.325	0.180	0.325	—	0.170	3/4
	Rochester 4MV 7045214, 7045584	11/32	—	—	0.275	1600	0.430	0.215	0.450	—	—	7/8
	7045588	11/32	—	—	0.275	1600	0.430	0.230	0.450	—	—	3/4
1976	Rochester 1MV 17056002	11/32	—	—	—	2100	0.130	0.165	0.335	0.080	0.265	—
	17056003	11/32	—	—	—	2100	0.145	0.180	0.335	0.080	WO	—
	17056008, 17056009	1/4	—	—	—	2400	0.150	0.190	0.275	0.070	—	—
	17056302	11/32	—	—	—	2100	0.155	0.190	0.325	0.080	WO	—
	17056303	11/32	—	—	—	2100	0.180	0.225	0.325	0.080	WO	—
	17056308, 17056309	1/4	—	—	—	2400	0.150	0.190	0.275	0.070	—	—

Carburetor Specifications (cont.)

Year	Carburetor Model	Float Level (in.)	Float Drop (in.)	Idle Vent (in.)	Accelerator Pump (in.)	Fast Idle Speed (rpm)	Fast Idle Cam Choke Rod (in.)	Primary or Front Choke Vacuum Break (in.)	Choke Unloader (in.)	Metering Rod (in.)	Rear or Auxiliary Vacuum Break (in.)	Air Valve Spring (turns)
1976	Rochester 2GC 17056123, 17056124	21/32	19/32	—	1 11/16	—	0.260	0.130	0.325	—	—	—
	Rochester M4MC 17056218, 17056219, 17056518, 17056519	5/16	—	—	9/32	1600	0.325	0.185	0.325	—	—	7/8
	Rochester 4MV 7045214	11/32	—	—	9/32	1600	0.290	0.145	0.295	—	—	7/8
	7045225	11/32	—	—	9/32	1600	0.290	0.138	0.295	—	—	3/4
	7045584	11/32	—	—	9/32	1600	0.290	0.155	0.295	—	—	7/8
	7045589	11/32	—	—	9/32	1600	0.290	0.155	0.295	—	—	3/4
1977	Rochester 1ME 17057001	3/8	—	—	—	2100	0.125	0.150	0.325	0.080	—	—
	17057002	3/8	—	—	—	2100	0.110	0.135	0.325	0.080	—	—
	17057004	3/8	—	—	—	2100	0.110	0.135	0.325	0.080	—	—
	17057005	3/8	—	—	—	2100	0.125	0.180	0.325	0.080	—	—
	17057010	3/8	—	—	—	2100	0.110	0.135	0.325	0.080	—	—
	17057302	3/8	—	—	—	2100	0.110	0.135	0.325	0.080	—	—
	17057303	3/8	—	—	—	2100	0.125	0.150	0.325	0.090	—	—
	17057008, 17057009, 17057308, 17057309	5/16	—	—	—	2400	0.150	0.180	0.275	0.065	—	—
	Rochester 2GC 17057108, 17057110, 17057113, 17057123	19/32	1 9/32	—	1 21/32	—	0.260	0.160	0.325	—	—	—
	Rochester M4MC 17057218	7/16	—	—	9/32	1600	0.325	0.160	0.280	—	—	7/8
	17057219	7/16	—	—	9/32	1300	0.325	0.165	0.280	—	—	7/8

	17057222	7/16	—	—	9/32	1600	0.325	0.160	0.280	—	—	7/8
	17057518	7/16	—	—	9/32	1600	0.325	0.165	0.280	—	—	7/8
	17057519	7/16	—	—	9/32	1300	0.325	0.165	0.280	—	—	7/8
	17057522	7/16	—	—	9/32	1600	0.325	0.165	0.280	—	—	7/8
	17057586	7/16	—	—	3/8 ㉒	1600	0.325	0.180	0.280	—	—	7/8
	17057588	7/16	—	—	3/8 ㉒	1600	0.325	0.180	0.280	—	—	7/8
	Rochester 4MV 17057213	11/32	—	—	9/32	1600	0.220	0.115	0.205	—	—	7/8
	17057229	11/32	—	—	9/32	1600	0.220	0.110	0.205	—	—	7/8
	17057514	11/32	—	—	9/32	1600	0.220	0.120	0.225	—	—	7/8
	17057525	11/32	—	—	9/32	1600	0.220	0.120	0.225	—	—	3/4
1978	Rochester 1ME 17058008, 17C58009	5/16	—	—	—	2400	0.275	0.275	0.520	0.065	—	—
	17058017, 17C58312	5/16	—	—	—	2100	0.190	0.250	0.600	0.080	—	—
	17058313	5/16	—	—	—	2100	0.190	0.250	0.600	0.100	—	—
	17058081, 17058082, 17058084	5/16	—	—	—	2000	0.200	0.250	0.450	0.080	—	—
	Rochester 2GC All	19/32	1 9/32	—	1 21/32	㉑	0.260	0.190	0.355	—	—	—
	Rochester M4MC/4MV 17058213, 17058229	15/32	—	—	9/32	1700	0.277	0.123	0.260	—	—	7/8
	17058218, 17058222	7/16	—	—	9/32	1600	0.314	0.157	0.277	—	—	7/8
	17058219	7/16	—	—	9/32	1300	0.314	0.168	0.277	—	—	7/8
	17058514	15/32	—	—	9/32	1600	0.277	0.153	0.287	—	—	7/8
	17058518, 17058522, 17058523, 17058524, 17058586, 17058588	15/32	—	—	9/32	1600	0.314	0.179	0.277	—	—	7/8
	17058519	15/32	—	—	9/32	1300	0.314	0.179	0.277	—	—	7/8
	17058525	7/16	—	—	9/32	1600	0.277	0.153	0.277	—	—	3/4

Carburetor Specifications (cont.)

Year	Carburetor Model	Float Level (in.)	Float Drop (in.)	Idle Vent (in.)	Accelerator Pump (in.)	Fast Idle Speed (rpm)	Fast Idle Cam Choke Rod (in.)	Primary or Front Choke Vacuum Break (in.)	Choke Unloader (in.)	Metering Rod (in.)	Rear or Auxiliary Vacuum Break (in.)	Air Valve Spring (turns)
1979	Rochester 2SE 17059640, 17059642, 17059740	1/8	—	—	9/16	2000	17°	20°	49°	—	37°	—
	17059641	1/8	—	—	9/16	1800	17°	23.5°	49°	—	;37°	—
	17059741, 17059764	1/8	—	—	9/16	2100	17°	20°	49°	—	37°	—
	17059765, 17059767	1/8	—	—	9/16	2100	17°	23.5°	49°	—	37°	—
	Rochester M2MC 17059142, 17059144	15/32	—	—	13/32	1600	0.243	0.171	0.243	—	—	—
	17059143, 17059145	15/32	—	—	13/32	1300	0.243	0.171	0.243	—	—	—
	Rochester M4MC 17059061, 17059201	15/32	—	—	13/32	1300	0.314	—	0.277	—	0.129	7/8
	17059213, 17059215	15/32	—	—	9/32	1900	0.234	0.129	0.260	—	—	1
	17059229, 17059513, 17059515, 17059529, 17059527, 17059528	15/32	—	—	9/32 (22)	1600	0.314	—	0.277	—	0.149	7/8
	All Others	15/32	—	—	13/32	1600	0.314	—	0.277	—	0.129	7/8
1980–81	Rochester 2SE	3/16	—	—	5/8	2000	0.077	0.149 (23)	0.243 (24)	—	0.149	1
	Rochester M2ME	13/32	—	—	5/16	1600	0.243	0.142	—	0.243	—	—
	Rochester M4ME,C	(25)	—	—	9/32 (26)	1800	0.314	0.136	0.277 (28)	—	—	—
1982	Rochester 2SE	3/16	—	—	9/16	(21)	0.077	0.149 (29)	0.277	—	0.243 (30)	1
	Rochester M4ME,C	3/8 (31)	—	—	9/32 (32)	(21)	0.314 (33)	0.129 (34)	0.277 (35)	—	0.179 (36)	7/8 (37)
1983	Rochester 2SE	3/16	—	—	Fixed	(21)	0.077	0.149 (38)	0.277	—	0.243	—
	Rochester E2SE	11/32	—	—	Fixed	(21)	0.077	0.149	0.277	—	0.243	1
	Rochester M4ME,C	13/32 (39)	—	—	9/16	(21)	0.314 (40)	(41)	0.251 (42)	—	0.136 (43)	7/8 (44)
	Rochester E4ME,C	11/32 (45)	—	—	—	(21)	0.110 (46)	(47)	0.243 (48)	—	0.157 (48)	7/8

1984	Rochester 2SE	11/32 (49)	—	—	—	(21)	0.123 (50)	0.179 (51)	0.260 (52)	—	0.195 (53)	1 (54)
	Rochester E2SE	9/32 (55)	—	—	—	(21)	0.164 (56)	0.142 (57)	0.304 (58)	—	0.220 (59)	1/2 (60)
	Rochester M4ME,C	13/32 (61)	—	—	9/32	(21)	0.314 (62)	(63)	0.251 (64)	—	0.149 (65)	7/8 (66)
	Rochester E4ME,C	11/32 (67)	—	—	—	(21)	0.110 (68)	0.157 (69)	0.243 (70)	—	(70)	7/8 (71)

(1) #7026113—5/8 in.
(2) 20 & 30 Series—0.180 in.
(3) 20 & 30 Series—0.260 in.
(4) 1970 20 & 30 Series—27/32 in.
(5) 20 & 30 Series—0.130 in.
(6) Bottom of rod should be even with top of hole
(7) 1970 10 Series w/man. trans.—0.275 in.
(8) Man. Trans.—0.225 in.
Auto Trans.—0.190 in.
All Trans. (H/D)—0.260 in.
(9) 1850 rpm (1 1/4)
2200 rpm (1 1/2)
(10) Auto trans.—0.080 in.
(11) Auto—1500 rpm
Man.—1350 rpm
(12) Auto Trans. (Carb #7043022)—0.245 in.
Man. Trans. (Carb #7043021)—0.275 in.
Carb #7043025—0.350 in.
Carb #7043026 & all California cars—0.375 in.
(13) Man. Trans.—0.300 in.
Auto Trans.—0.350 in.
(14) Auto only and Man. only—0.500 in.
(15) Carb #7043108—25/32 in.
(16) Carb #7043108—0.200 in.
(17) Carb #7043108—0.140 in.
(18) Carb #7043108—0.250 in.
(19) L.D. Man. Trans.—1300 rpm w/o vacuum advance
H.D. Man. Trans.—1600 rpm w/vacuum advance
(20) Carb #'s 7043028, 215—5/16 in.
Carb #'s 7043200, 216—1/4 in.
(21) See the underhood emission sticker
(22) Outer hole
(23) #17081629:0.136
17081720, 1708121,
17081725, 17081726,
17081727:0.179
(24) 17081629, 17081720,
17081725, 17081726,
17081727:0.269
(25) M4MC:3/8"
M4ME:15/32"
(26) #17081524, 17081526:5/16"
(27) 17080213, 17080215,
17080298, 17080507,
17080513:0.234
(28) 17080212, 17080213,
17080215, 17080298,
17080507, 17080512,
17080513:0.251
17081506, 17081508:0.227
17081524, 17081526:0.243
(29) 17082341, 17082342,
17082344, 17082345: 0.179 in.
17082431, 17082433: 0.136 in.
17082482: 0.129 in.
17082486, 17082487,
17082488, 17082489: 0.164 in.
(30) 17082341, 17082342,
17082344, 17082345: 0.234 in.
(31) 17081200, 17081205,
17081206, 17081220,
17081226, 17081227: 15/32 in.
17081290, 17081291,
17081292, 17081506,
17081508, 17081524,
17081526: 13/32 in.
(32) 17081524, 1708526: 5/16 in.
(33) 17080213, 1708215,
17080298, 1708507,
17080513, 0.234 in.
(34) 17080212, 17080512,
17081200, 17081226,
17081227: 0.136 in.
17081524, 17081526: 0.142 in.
(35) 17080212, 17080213,
17080215, 17080298,
17080507, 17080512,
17080513: 0.260 in.
17081506, 17081508: 0.227 in.
17081524, 17081526: 0.243 in.
(36) 17081200, 17081201,
17081205, 17081206,
17081220, 17081226,
17081227: 0.129 in.
17081290, 17081291,
17081292: 0.136 in.
17081506, 17081508,
17081524, 17081526: 0.227 in.
(37) 17080212, 17080512,
17080513: 3/4 turn
17080213, 17080215,
17080298, 17080507: 1 turn
(38) 17083410, 17083412,
17083414, 17083416: 0.129 in.
17083423, 17083429,
17083560, 17083562,
17083565, 17083569: 0.164 in.
(39) 17080213, 17080298,
17080507, 17080513,
17083298, 17083507: 3/8 in.
17082213: 9/32 in.
17080201, 17080205,
17080206, 17080290,
17080291, 17080292: 15/32 in.
(40) 17080213, 17080298,
17080507, 17080513,
17082213, 17083298,
17083507: 0.234 in
(41) 17080213, 17080298,
17080507, 17080513,
17082213, 17083298,
17083507: 0.129 in.
(42) 17080201, 17080205,
17080206, 17080290,
17080291, 17080292: 0.277 in.
17080213, 17080298,
17080507, 17080513,

Carburetor Specifications (cont.)

17082213, 17083298,
17083507: 0.260 in.
(43) 17080201, 17080205,
17080206: 0.129 in.
17080213, 17080298,
17080507, 17080513,
17082213, 17083298,
17083507, 0.179 in.
(44) 17080213, 17080298,
17080507, 17080513,
17082213, 17083298,
17083507: 1 turn
(45) 17083506, 17083508,
17083524, 17083526: 7/16 in.
(46) 17083203, 17083207: 0.243 in.
(47) 17083506, 17083508: 0.157 in.
17083524, 17083526: 0.142 in.
(48) 17083506, 17083508,
17083524, 17083526: 0.227 in.
(49) 17084360, 17084362,
17084364, 17084366: 5/32 in.
17084390, 17084391,
17084392, 17084393: 7/16 in.
(50) 17084390, 17084391,
17084392, 17084393: 0.164 in.
17084410, 17084412,
17084425, 17084427,
17084560, 17084562,
17084569: 0.077 in.
(51) 17084410, 17084412: 0.129 in.
17084425, 17084427: 0.149 in.
17084560, 17084562,
17084569: 0.136 in.
(52) 17084410, 17084412: 0.277 in.
17084390, 17084391,
17084392, 17084393,
17084560, 17084562,
17084569: 0.243 in.
(53) 17084352, 17084353,
17084354, 17084355,
17084364, 17084366: 0.220 in.
17084390, 17084391,
17084392, 17084393,
17084410, 17084412: 0.243 in.
17084425, 17084427: 0.227 in.
17084560, 17084562,
17084569: 0.211 in.
(54) 17084390, 17084391,
17084392, 17084393: 1 1/2 turns
17084410, 17084412,
17084425, 17084427,
17084560, 17084562,
17084569, Not Adjustable
(55) 17084368, 17084370,
17084542: 4/32 in.
17084430, 17084431,
17084434, 17084435: 11/32 in.
17084534, 17084535,
17084537, 17084538,
17084540: 5/32 in.
(56) 17084356, 17084357,
17084358, 17084359,
17084369, 17084370: 0.123 in.
17084430, 17084431,
17084434, 17084435: 0.077 in.
(57) 17084430, 17084431,
17084434, 17084435: 0.149 in.
(58) 17084356, 17084357,
17084358, 17084359,
17084369, 17084370: 0.179 in.
17084430, 17084431,
17084434, 17084435: 0.277 in.
(59) 17084356, 17084357,
17084358, 17084359,
17084369, 17084370: 0.179 in.
17084430, 17084431,
17084434, 17084435: 0.243 in.
(60) 17084356, 17084357,
17084358, 17084359,
17084369, 17084370: 3/4 turn
17084430, 17084431,
17084434, 17084435: 1 turn
Idle mixture screw: 4 turns
Lean mixture screw: 2 1/2 turns
(61) 17080212, 17080213,
17080298, 17082213,
17083298, 17084500,
17084501, 17084502: 3/8 in.
(62) 17080213, 17080298,
17082213, 17083298,
17084500, 17084501: 0.234 in.
(63) 17080212, 17084502: 0.136 in.
17080213, 17080298,
17082213, 17083298,
17084500, 17084501: 0.129 in.
(64) 17080212, 17084502,
17080213, 17080298,
17082213, 17083298,
17084500, 17084501: 0.260 in.
(65) 17080212, 17084502,
17080213, 17080298,
17082213, 17083298,
17084500, 17084501: 0.179 in.
17084226, 17084227,
17084290, 17084292: 0.136 in.
(66) 17080213, 17080298,
17082213, 17083298,
17084500, 17084501: 1 turn
17080212, 17084502: 7/8 turn
(67) 17084507, 17084509,
17084525, 17084527: 14/32 in.
(68) 17084205, 17084209: 0.243 in.
(69) 17084525, 17084527: 0.142 in.
(70) 17084507, 17084509,
17084525, 17084527: 0.227 in.
(71) 17084507, 17084509,
17084525, 17084527: 1 turn

Model 1ME/1M/1MEF

(All measurements in inches)

Year	Carburetor Number	Float Level	Choke Unloader Setting	Choke Setting	Fast Idle Speed (rpm)	Metering Rod Setting	Fast Idle Cam 2nd Step	Choke Vacuum Break
1984–86	17081009	11/32	.520	①	②	.090	.275	.400
	17084329	11/32	.520	①	②	.090	.275	.400
	17085009	11/32	.520	①	②	.090	.275	.400
	17085036	11/32	.520	①	②	.090	.275	.400
	17085044	11/32	.520	①	②	.090	.275	.400
	17085045	11/32	.520	①	②	.090	.275	.400
	17086096	11/32	.520	①	②	.090	.275	.400
	17086101	11/32	.520	①	②	.090	.275	.400
	17086102	11/32	.520	①	②	.090	.275	.400

① Not adjustable
② See emission label under hood

Model E2SE

(All measurements in inches or degrees)

Year	Carburetor Number	Float Level	Choke Coil Lever	Choke Rod ①	Primary Vacuum Break	Secondary Vacuum Break	Air Valve Rod	Choke Unloader
1985–86	17084636	9/32	.085	28°	25°	35°	1°	45°
	17085356	4/32	.085	22°	25°	30°	1°	30°
	17085357	9/32	.085	22°	25°	30°	1°	30°
	17085358	4/32	.085	22°	25°	30°	1°	30°
	17085359	9/32	.085	22°	25°	30°	1°	30°
	17085368	4/32	.085	22°	25°	30°	1°	30°
	17085369	9/32	.085	22°	25°	30°	1°	30°
	17085370	4/32	.085	22°	25°	30°	1°	30°
	17085371	9/32	.085	22°	25°	30°	1°	30°
	17085452	5/32	.085	28°	25°	35°	1°	45°
	17085453	5/32	.085	28°	25°	35°	1°	45°
	17085458	5/32	.085	28°	25°	35°	1°	45°

Note: Specified angle for use with angle degree tool
① All models: Lean mixture screw–2½ turns
Idle mixture screw–4 turns

Model M4MC/M4ME Quadrajet

(All measurements in inches or degrees)

Year	Carburetor Number	Float Level	Pump Rod Hole	Pump Rod Setting	Choke Rod ① Setting	Air Valve Rod	Vacuum Break Front	Vacuum Break Rear	Air Valve Turns	Choke Unloader	Propane Enrichment (rpm)
1985–86	17084500	12/32	inner	9/32	37°	.025	23°	30°	1	40°	②
	17084501	12/32	inner	9/32	37°	.025	23°	30°	1	40°	②

Model M4MC/M4ME Quadrajet (cont.)

(All measurements in inches or degrees)

Year	Carburetor Number	Float Level	Pump Rod Hole	Pump Rod Setting	Choke Rod ① Setting	Air Valve Rod	Vacuum Break Front	Vacuum Break Rear	Air Valve Turns	Choke Unloader	Propane Enrichment (rpm)
1985–86	17084502	12/32	inner	9/32	46°	.025	24°	30°	7/8	40°	②
	17085000	12/32	inner	9/32	46°	.025	24°	30°	7/8	40°	②
	17085001	12/32	inner	9/32	46°	.025	23°	30°	1	40°	②
	17085003	12/32	inner	9/32	46°	.025	23°	—	7/8	35°	②
	17085004	13/32	inner	9/32	46°	.025	23°	—	7/8	35°	②
	17085205	13/32	inner	9/32	20°	.025	26°	38°	7/8	39°	②
	17085206	13/32	inner	9/32	46°	.025	—	26°	7/8	39°	20
	17085208	13/32	inner	9/32	20°	.025	26°	38°	7/8	39°	10
	17085209	13/32	outer	3/8	20°	.025	26°	36°	7/8	39°	50
	17085210	13/32	inner	9/32	20°	.025	26°	38°	7/8	39°	10
	17085211	13/32	outer	3/8	20°	.025	26°	36°	7/8	39°	50
	17085212	13/32	inner	9/32	46°	.025	23°	—	7/8	35°	②
	17085213	13/32	inner	9/32	46°	.025	23°	—	7/8	35°	②
	17085215	13/32	inner	9/32	46°	.025	—	26°	7/8	32°	②
	17085216	13/32	inner	9/32	20°	.025	26°	38°	7/8	39°	②
	17085217	13/32	inner	9/32	20°	.025	26°	36°	1/2	39°	②
	17085219	13/32	inner	9/32	20°	.025	26°	36°	1/2	39°	②
	17085220	13/32	outer	3/8	20°	.025	—	26°	7/8	32°	75
	17085221	13/32	outer	3/8	20°	.025	—	26°	7/8	32°	75
	17085222	13/32	inner	9/32	20°	.025	26°	36°	1/2	39°	20
	17085223	13/32	outer	3/8	20°	.025	26°	36°	1/2	39°	50
	17085224	13/32	inner	9/32	20°	.025	26°	36°	1/2	39°	20
	17085225	13/32	outer	3/8	20°	.025	26°	36°	1/2	39°	50
	17085226	13/32	inner	9/32	20°	.025	—	24°	7/8	32°	20
	17085227	13/32	inner	9/32	20°	.025	—	24°	7/8	32°	20
	17085228	13/32	inner	9/32	46°	.025	—	24°	7/8	39°	30
	17085229	13/32	inner	9/32	46°	.025	—	24°	7/8	39°	30
	17085230	13/32	inner	9/32	20°	.025	—	26°	7/8	32°	20
	17085231	13/32	inner	9/32	20°	.025	—	26°	7/8	32°	40
	17085235	13/32	inner	9/32	46°	.025	—	26°	7/8	39°	80
	17085238	13/32	outer	3/8	20°	.025	—	26°	7/8	32°	75
	17085239	13/32	outer	3/8	20°	.025	—	26°	7/8	32°	75
	17085290	13/32	inner	9/32	46°	.025	—	24°	7/8	39°	30
	17085291	13/32	outer	3/8	46°	.025	—	26°	7/8	39°	100
	17085292	13/32	inner	9/32	46°	.025	—	24°	7/8	39°	30
	17085293	13/32	outer	3/8	46°	.025	—	26°	7/8	39°	100
	17085294	13/32	inner	9/32	46°	.025	—	26°	7/8	39°	②
	17085298	13/32	inner	9/32	46°	.025	—	26°	7/8	39°	②

Note: Specified angle for use with angle degree tool. Choke coil lever setting is .120 in. for all carburetors.

① Second step of fast idle cam

② See Underhood Specifications sticker

Angle Degree to Decimal Conversion
Model M2MC, M2ME and M4MC Carburetor

Angle Degrees	Decimal Equiv. Top of Valve	Angle Degrees	Decimal Equiv. Top of Valve
5	.023	33	.203
6	.028	34	.211
7	.033	35	.220
8	.038	36	.227
9	.043	37	.234
10	.049	38	.243
11	.054	39	.251
12	.060	40	.260
13	.066	41	.269
14	.071	42	.277
15	.077	43	.287
16	.083	44	.295
17	.090	45	.304
18	.096	46	.314
19	.103	47	.322

sure that the fast idle cam follower is off the steps of the fast idle cam.

2. Bend the secondary throttle closing tang away from the primary throttle lever, if necessary, to insure that the primary throttle valves are fully closed.

3. With the pump in the appropriate hole in the pump lever, measure from the top of the choke valve wall to the top of the pump stem.

4. To adjust, bend the pump lever.

5. After adjusting, readjust the secondary throttle tang and the slow idle screw.

DIESEL ENGINE FUEL SYSTEM

Fuel Supply Pump

REMOVAL AND INSTALLATION

The diesel fuel supply pump is serviced in the same manner as the fuel pump on the gasoline engines.

Fuel Filter

See Diesel Fuel Filter in Chapter 1 for service procedures.

WATER IN FUEL (DIESEL)

Water is the worst enemy of the diesel fuel injection system. The injection pump, which is designed and constructed to extremely close tolerances, and the injectors can be easily damaged if enough water if forced through them in the fuel. Engine performance will also be drastically affected, and engine damage can occur.

Diesel fuel is much more susceptible than gasoline to water contamination. Diesel engined trucks are equipped with an indicator lamp system that turns on an instrument panel lamp if water (1 to 2½ gallons) is detected in the fuel tank. The lamp will come on for 2 to 5 seconds each time the ignition is turned on, assuring the driver the lamp is working. If there is water in the fuel, the light will come back on after a 15 to 20 second off delay, and then remain on.

PURGING THE FUEL TANK

8–379

The 379 (6.2L) diesel equipped trucks also have a water-in-fuel warning system. The fuel tank is equipped with a filter which screens out the water and lets it lay in the bottom of the tank below the fuel pickup. When the water level reaches a point where it could be drawn into the system, a warning light flashes in the cab. A built-in siphoning system starting at the fuel tank and going to the rear spring hanger on some models, and at the midway point of the right frame rail on other models permits you to attach a hose at the shut-off and siphon out the water.

If it becomes necessary to drain water from the fuel tank, also check the primary fuel filter for water. This procedure is covered under Diesel Fuel Filter in Chapter 1.

Fuel Injection Pump

REMOVAL AND INSTALLATION

8–379

REMOVAL

1. Disconnect both batteries.
2. Remove the fan and fan shroud.
3. Remove the intake manifold as described in Chapter 3.

4. Remove the fuel lines as described in this chapter.
5. Disconnect the alternator cable at the injection pump, and the detent cable (see illustration) where applicable.

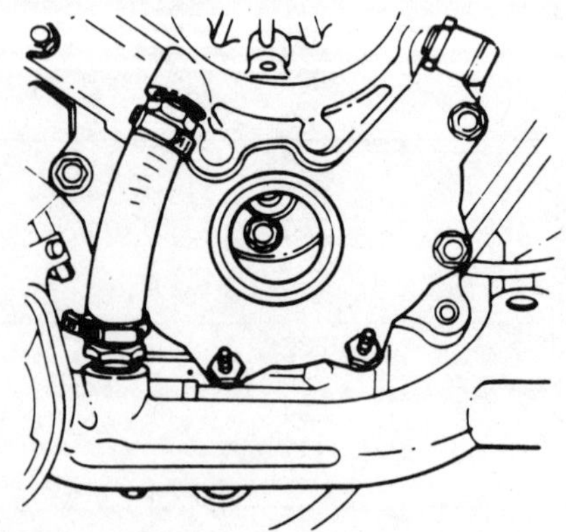

Rotate the crankshaft so the injection pump drive gear bolts become accessable through the hole

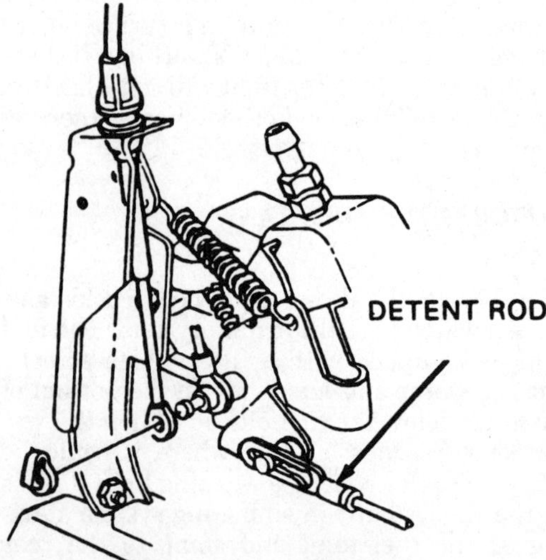

379 diesel accelerator cable linkage

6. Tag and disconnect the necessary wires and hoses at the injection pump.
7. Disconnect the fuel return line at the top of the injection pump.
8. Disconnect the fuel feed line at the injection pump.
9. Remove the air conditioning hose retainer bracket if equipped with A/C.
10. Remove the oil fill tube, including the crankcase depression valve vent hose assembly.
11. Remove the grommet.
12. Scribe or paint a match mark on the front cover and on the injection pump flange.
13. The crankshaft must be rotated in order to gain access to the injection pump drive gear bolts through the oil filler neck hole.
14. Remove the injection pump-to-front cover attaching nuts. Remove the pump and cap all open lines and nozzles.

INSTALLATION

1. Replace the gasket. This is important.
2. Align the locating pin on the pump hub with the slot in the injection pump driven gear. At the same time, align the timing marks.
3. Attach the injection pump to the front cover, aligning the timing marks before torquing the nuts to 30 ft.lb.

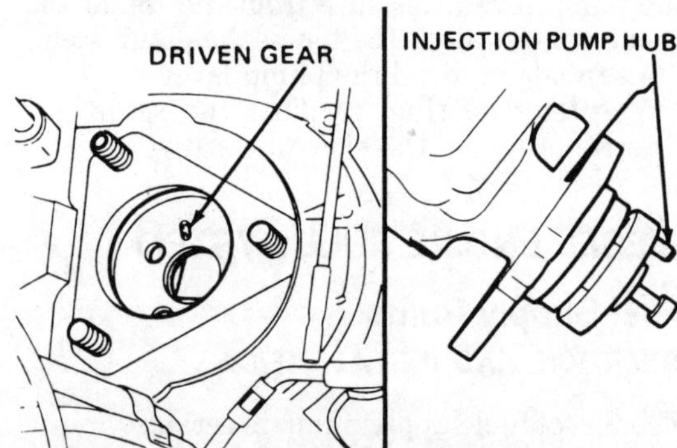

Injection pump locating pin, 379 diesel

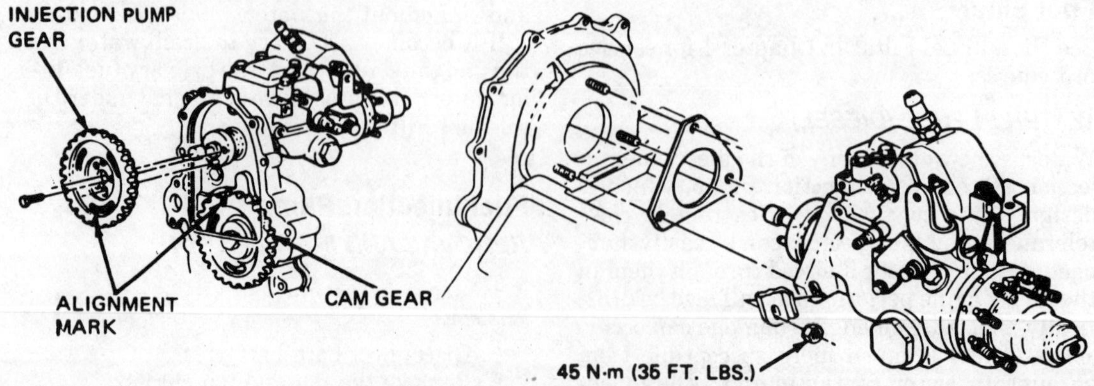

379 diesel injection pump mounting

4. Install the drive gear to injection pump bolts, torquing the bolts to 20 ft.lb.

5. Install the remaining components in the reverse order of removal. Torque the fuel feed line at the injection pump to 20 ft.lb. Start the engine and check for leaks.

Injection Pump Fuel Lines

REMOVAL AND INSTALLATION

8–379

NOTE: *When the fuel lines are to be removed, clean all fuel line fittings thoroughly before loosening. Immediately cap the lines, nozzles and pump fittings to maintain cleanliness.*

1. Disconnect both batteries.
2. Disconnect the air cleaner bracket at the valve cover.
3. Remove the crankcase ventilator bracket and move it aside.
4. Disconnect the secondary filter lines.
5. Remove the secondary filter adapter.
6. Loosen the vacuum pump holddown clamp and rotate the pump in order to gain access to the intake manifold bolt. Remove the intake manifold bolts. The injection line clips are retained by the same bolts.
7. Remove the intake manifold. Install a protective cover (GM part *J-29664-1 or equivalent) so no foreign material falls into the engine.
8. Remove the injection line clips at the loom brackets.
9. Remove the injection lines at the nozzles and cover the nozzles with protective caps.
10. Remove the injection lines at the pump and tag the lines for later installation.
11. Remove the fuel line from the injection pump.
12. Install all components in the reverse order of removal. Follow the illustrations for injection line connection.

Fuel Injectors

REMOVAL AND INSTALLATION

8–379

1. Disconnect the truck's batteries.
2. Disconnect the fuel line clip, and remove the fuel return hose.
3. Remove the fuel injection line as previously detailed.
4. Using GM special tool J-29873, remove the injector. Always remove the injector by

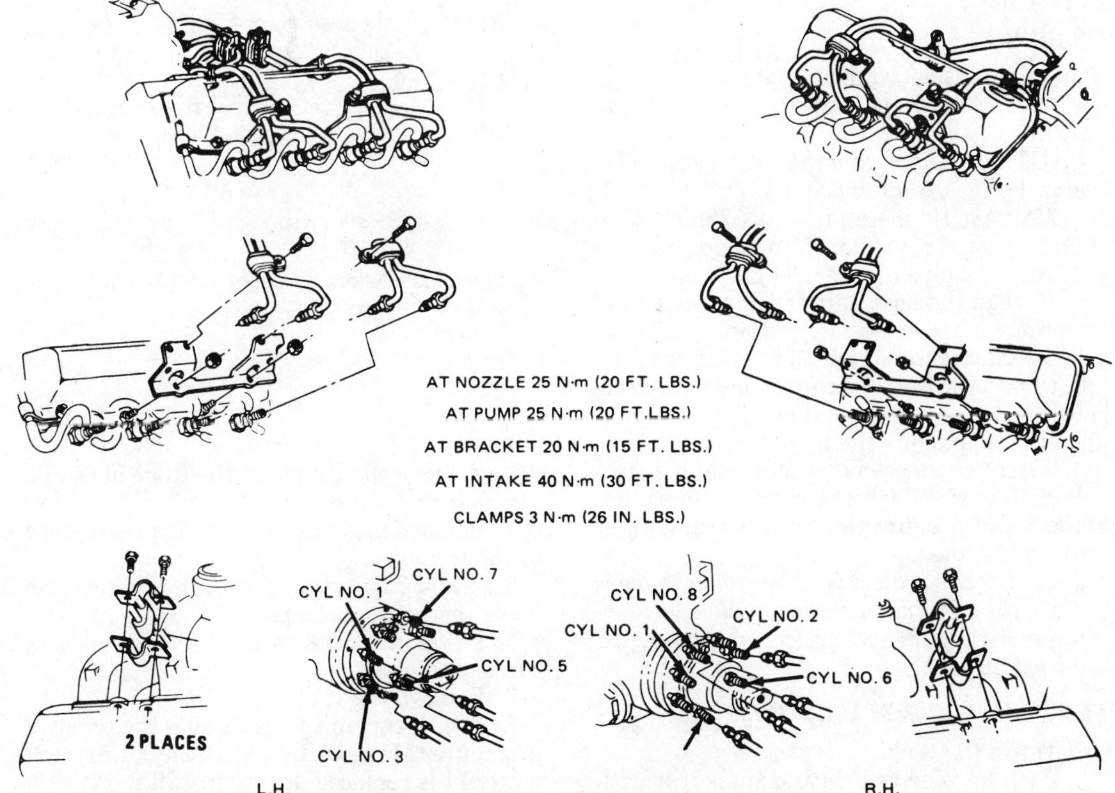

Torque specifications and fuel line routing, 379 diesel

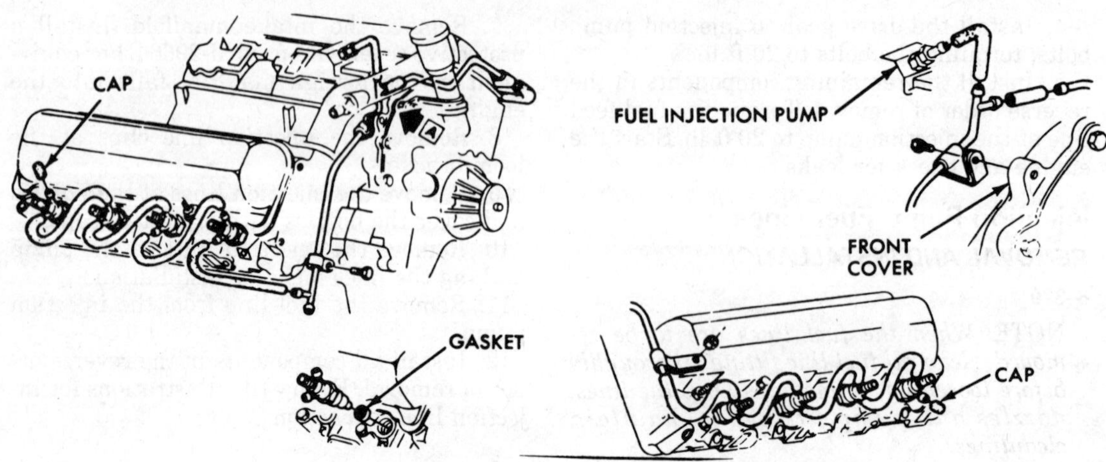

Injector installation, 379 diesel

turning the 30mm hex protion of the injector; turning the round portion will damage the injector. Always cap the injector and fuel lines when disconnected, to prevent contamination.

5. Install the injector with new gasket and torque to 50 ft.lb. Connect the injection line and torque the nut to 20 ft.lb. Install the fuel return hose, fuel line clips, and connnect the batteries.

Fuel Tank

DRAINING

If the vehicle is not equipped with a drain plug, use the following procedure to remove the gasoline.

CAUTION: *Disconnect the battery before beginning the draining operation.*

1. Using a 10' piece of 3/8" (9.525mm) hose cut a flap slit 18" (457mm) from one end.
2. Install a pipe nipple, of slightly larger diameter than the hose, into the opposite end of the hose.
3. Install the nipple end of the hose into the fuel tank with the natural curve of the hose pointing downward. Keep feeding the hose in until the nipple hits the bottom of the tank.
4. Place the other end of the hose in a suitable container and insert a air hose pointing it in the downward direction of the slit and inject air into the line.

NOTE: *If the vehicle is to be stored, always drain the gasoline from the complete fuel system including the carburetor, fuel pump, fuel lines, and tank.*

REMOVAL AND INSTALLATION

1. Drain the tank.
2. Jack up your vehicle and support it with jackstands.

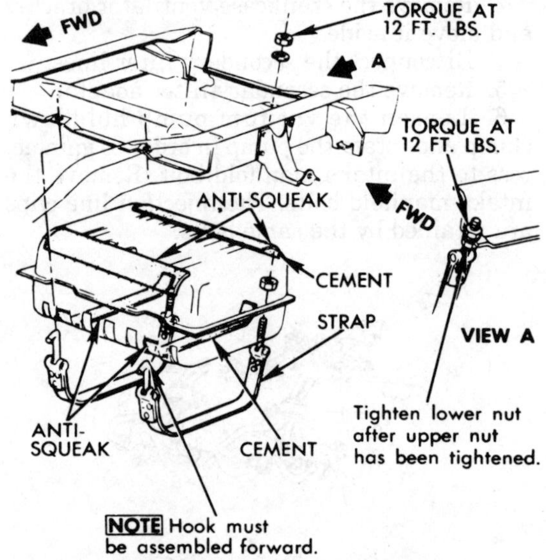

Fuel tank installation, typical of most models

3. Remove the clamp on the filler neck and the vent tube hose.
4. Remove the gauge hose which is attached to the frame.
5. While supporting the tank securely, remove the support straps.
6. Lower the tank until the gauge wiring can be removed.
7. Remove the tank.
8. Install the unit by reversing the removal procedure. Make certain that the antisqueak material is replaced during installation.
9. Lower the vehicle.

Chassis Electrical 5

UNDERSTANDING AND TROUBLESHOOTING ELECTRICAL SYSTEMS

For any electrical system to operate, it must make a complete circuit. This simply means that the power flow from the battery must make a complete circle. When an electrical component is operating, power flows from the battery to the component, passes through the component causing it to perform its function (lighting a light bulb, for example) and then returns to the battery through the ground of the circuit. This ground is usually (but not always) the metal part of the vehicle on which the electrical component is mounted.

Perhaps the easiest way to visualize this is to think of connecting a light bulb with two wires attached to it to your vehicle battery. The battery in your vehicle has two posts (negative and positive). If one of the two wires attached to the light bulb was attached to the negative post of the battery and the other wire was attached to the positive post of the battery, you would have a complete circuit. Current from the battery would flow out one post, through the wire attached to it and then to the light bulb, causing it to light. It would then leave the light bulb, travel through the other wire, and return to the other post of the battery.

The normal automotive circuit differs from this simple example in two ways. First, instead of having a return wire from the bulb to the battery, the light bulb returns the current to the battery through the chassis of the vehicle. Since the negative battery cable is attached to the chassis and the chassis is made of electrically conductive metal, the chassis of the vehicle can se000715 a ground wire to complete the circuit. Secondly, most automotive circuits contain switches to turn components on and off as required.

There are many types of switches, but the most common simply serves to prevent the passage of current when it is turned off. Since the switch is a part of the circle necessary for a complete circuit, it operates to leave an opening in the circuit, and thus an incomplete or open circuit, when it is turned off.

Some electrical components which require a large amount of current to operate also have a relay in their circuit. Since these circuits carry a large amount of current, the thickness of the wire (gauge size) in the circuit is also greater. If this large wire were connected from the component to the control switch on the instrument panel, and then back to the component, a voltage drop would occur in the circuit. To prevent this potential drop in voltage, an electromagnetic switch (relay) is used. The large wires in the circuit are connected from the vehicle battery to one side of the relay, and from the opposite side of the relay to the component. The relay is normally open, preventing current from passing through the circuit. An additional, smaller, wire is connected from the relay to the control switch to the circuit. When the control switch is turned on, it completes the circuit. This closes the relay and allows current to flow from the battery to the component. The horn, headlight, and starter circuits are three which use relays.

You have probably noticed how the vehicle's instrument panel lights get brighter the faster you rev the engine. This happens because you alternator (which supplies the battery) puts out more current at speeds above idle. This is normal. However, it is possible for larger surges of current to pass through the electrical system of your car. If this surge of current were to reach an electrical component, it could burn the component out. To prevent this from happening, fuses are connected into the current supply wires of most of the major electrical systems of your vehicle. The fuse serves to head off the surge at the pass. When an electrical current of excessive power passes through the component's fuse, the fuse blows out and breaks the circuit, saving it from destruction.

The fuse also protects the component from damage if the power supply wire to the component is grounded before the current reaches the component.

There is another important rule to the complete circle circuit. Every complete circuit from a power source must include a component which is using the power from the power source. If you were to disconnect the light bulb (from the previous example of a light bulb being connected to the battery by two wires together (take our word for it-don't try it) the result would literally be shocking. A similar thing happens (on a smaller scale) when the power supply wire to a component or the electrical component itself becomes grounded before the normal ground connection for the circuit. To prevent damage to the system, the fuse for the circuit blows to interrupt the circuit, protecting the components from damage. Because grounding a wire from a power source makes a complete circuit, less the required component to use the power, this phenomenon is called a short circuit. The most common causes of short circuits are: the rubber insulation on a wire breaking or rubbing through to expose the current carrying core of the wire to a metal part of the vehicle, or a short switch.

Some electrical systems on the vehicle are protected by a circuit breaker which is, basically, a self-repairing fuse. When either of the above described events takes place in a system which is protected by a circuit breaker, the circuit breaker opens the circuit the same way a fuse does. However, when either the short is removed from the circuit or the surge subsides, the circuit breaker resets itself and does not have to be replaced as a fuse does.

The final protective device in the chassis electrical system is a fuse link. A fuse link is a wire that acts as a fuse. It is connected between the starter relay and the main wiring harness for the car. This connection is under the hood, very near a similar fuse link which protects all the chassis electrical components. It is the probable cause of trouble when none of the electrical components function, unless the battery is disconnected or dead.

Electrical problems generally fall into one of three areas:

1. The component that is not functioning is not receiving current.
2. The component itself is not functioning.
3. The component is not properly grounded.

Problems that fall into the first category are by far the most complicated. It is the current supply system to the component which contains all the switches, relays, fuses, etc.

The electrical system can be checked with a test light and a jumper wire. A test light is a device that looks like a pointed screwdriver with a wire attached to it. It has a light bulb in its handle. A jumper wire is a piece of insulated wire with an alligator clip attached to each end.

If a light bulb is not working, you must follow a systematic plan to determine which of the three causes is the villain.

1. Turn on the switch that controls the inoperable bulb.
2. Disconnect the power supply wire from the bulb.
3. Attach the ground wire on the test light to a good metal ground.
4. Touch the probe end of the test light to the end of the power supply wire that was disconnected from the bulb. If the bulb is receiving current, the test light will go on.

NOTE: *If the bulb is one which works only when the ignition key is turned on (turn signal), make sure the key is turned on.*

If the test light does not go on, then the problem is in the circuit between the battery and the bulb. As mentioned before, this includes all the switches, fuses, and relays in the system. The problem is an open circuit between the battery and the bulb. If the fuse is blown and, when replaced, immediately blows again, there is a short circuit in the system which must be located and repaired. If there is a switch in the system, bypass it with a jumper wire. This is done by connecting one end of the jumper wire to the power supply wire into the switch, and the other end of the jumper wire to the wire coming out of the switch. If the test light lights with the jumper wire installed, the switch or whatever was bypassed is defective.

NOTE: *Never substitute the jumper wire for the bulb, as the bulb is the component required to use the power from the power source.*

5. If the bulb in the test light goes on, then the current is getting to the bulb that is not working in the vehicle. This eliminates the first of the three possible causes. Connect the power supply wire and connect a jumper wire from the bulb to a good metal ground. Do this with the switch which controls the bulb turned on, and also the ignition switch turned on if it is required for the light to work. If the bulb works with the jumper wire installed, then it has a bad ground. This is usually caused by the metal area on which the bulb mounts to the car being coated with some type of foreign matter or rust.
6. If neither test located the source of the

trouble, then the light bulb itself is defective.

The above test procedure can be applied to any of the components of the chassis electrical system by substituting the component that is not working for the light bulb. Remember that for any electrical system to work, all connections must be clean and tight.

HEATING AND AIR CONDITIONING

Heater, A/C Blower Motor

REMOVAL AND INSTALLATION

1. Disconnect the battery cables. On 1971 and later models, remove the battery.
2. Unclip the blower motor lead wire.
3. On 1967–69 models, scribe the location of the motor flange in relation to the blower case.
4. Remove the blower attaching screws.
5. Remove the blower assembly. It may be necessary to pry gently on the blower flange. Sometimes the sealer acts as an adhesive.
6. If the motor is being replaced, remove the nut attaching the blower wheel to the blower motor shaft and separate the two.
7. Assembly the blower wheel to the motor with the open end away from the motor.
8. If the sealer has hardened or it otherwise useless, apply a new bead of sealer to the mounting flange.
9. Installation of the blower motor and wheel is the reverse of remvoal. Connect the lead wires and the battery cables and check the operation of the motor.

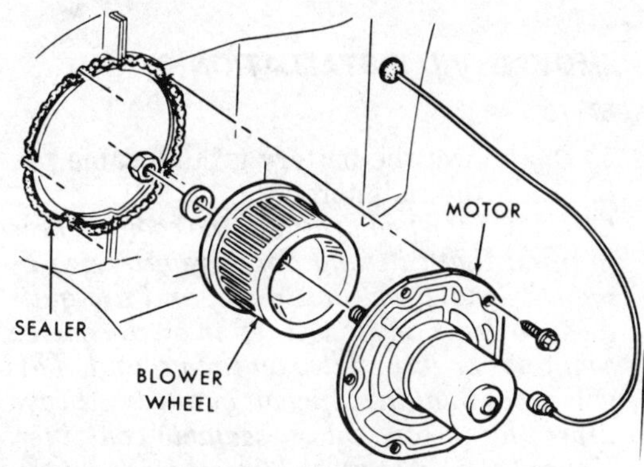

1970–73 blower motor assembly

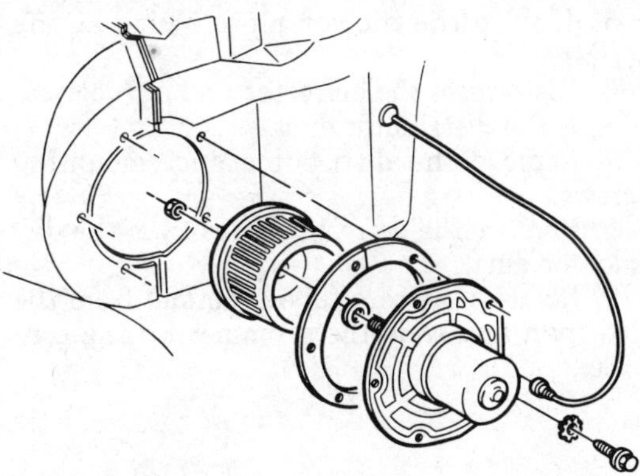

1974–82 blower motor assembly

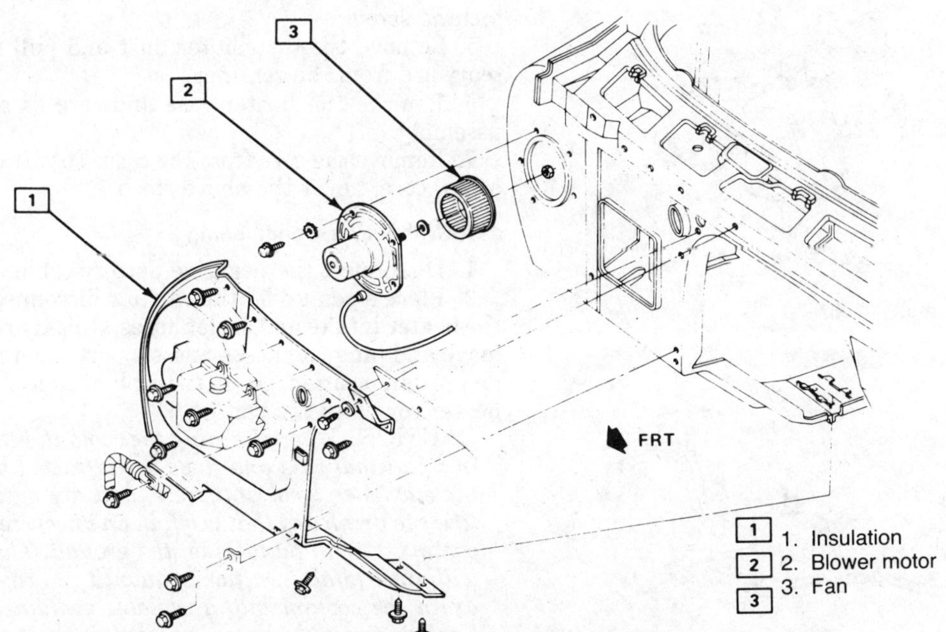

1983 and later blower motor assembly

Core

REMOVAL AND INSTALLATION

1967–70

1. Disconnect the battery ground cable.
2. Drain the radiator.

CAUTION: *When draining the coolant, keep in mind that cats and dogs are attracted by the ethylene glycol antifreeze, and are quite likely to drink any that is left in an uncovered container or in puddles on the ground. This will prove fatal in sufficient quantity. Always drain the coolant into a sealable container. Coolant should be reused unless it is contaminated or several years old.*

3. Disconnect the heater hoses below the toe pan.
4. Remove the glove compartment.
5. Unclip the blower motor wire at the terminal.
6. Disconnect the defroster and air door cables at the distributor duct.
7. Remove the distributor duct mounting screws.
8. Remove the defroster hoses from the distributor duct.
9. Remove the core tube grommet from the floor pan and slide the grommet up the core tube.

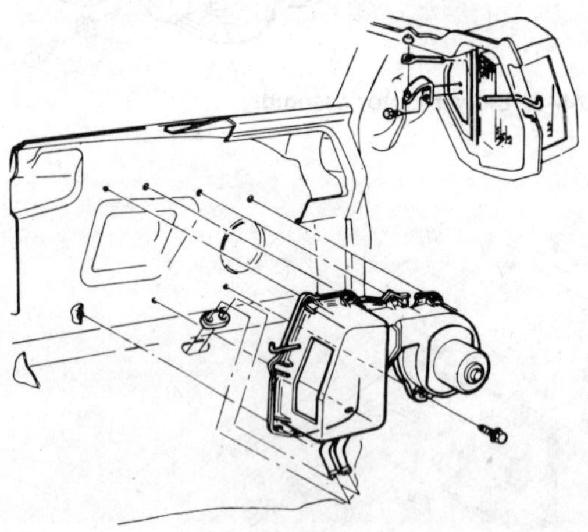

Heater assembly—1967–70

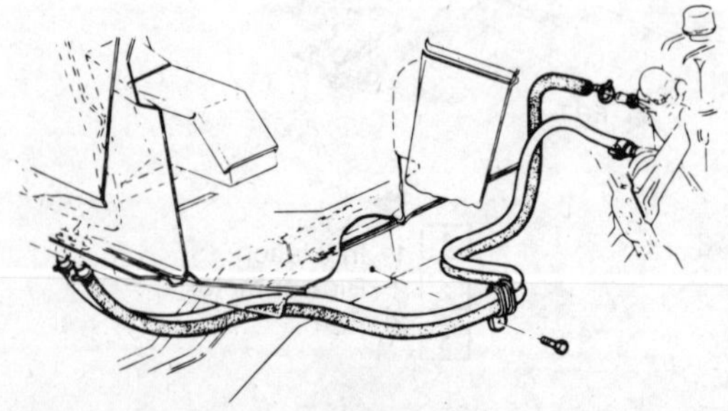

Heater hose routing—1967–70

10. Remove the screw holding the heater case to the toe pan.
11. Pull the case away from the toe pan and slide the core tubes down through the floor pan. When it is clear, pull the assembly out and withdraw the core tubes from the floor pan.
12. Remove the temperature door cable.
13. Remove the core from the case.
14. Installation is the reverse of removal. Fill the cooling system.

All 1971–73 Models, 1974–77 Without Air Conditioning

This procedure applies to models without air conditioning and to those with the floor mounted air conditioner.

1. Disconnect the battery ground cable.
2. Place a pan under the van and disconnect the heater intake and outlet hoses. Quickly, remove and plug the heater hoses and support them in an upright position. Drain the coolant from the heater core into the pan.

CAUTION: *When draining the coolant, keep in mind that cats and dogs are attracted by the ethylene glycol antifreeze, and are quite likely to drink any that is left in an uncovered container or in puddles on the ground. This will prove fatal in sufficient quantity. Always drain the coolant into a sealable container. Coolant should be reused unless it is contaminated or several years old.*

3. Disconnect the right hand air distributor hose from the heater case and put it aide.
4. Pry the eyelet clip from the temperature door cable and remove the Bowden cable attaching screw.
5. Remove the distributor duct and pull it rearward from the retainer.
6. Remove the heater case and core as an assembly.
7. Remove the core from the case. To install a new core, never the above steps.

1978 Without Air Conditioning

1. Disconnect the negative battery cable.
2. Place a pan under the van and disconnect the heater intake and outlet hoses. Quickly remove and plug the hoses and support them in an upright position. Drain the coolant from the heater core into the pan.

CAUTION: *When draining the coolant, keep in mind that cats and dogs are attracted by the ethylene glycol antifreeze, and are quite likely to drink any that is left in an uncovered container or in puddles on the ground. This will prove fatal in sufficient quantity. Always drain the coolant into a sealable container. Coolant should be reused unless it is contaminated or several years old.*

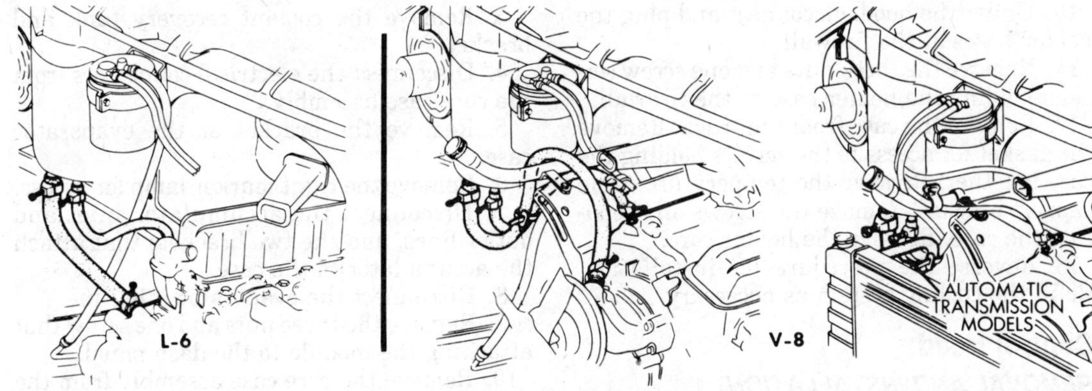

1971 and later heater hose routing

3. Remove the heater distributor duct-to-case attaching screws and the duct-to-engine cover screw. Remove the duct.

4. Remove the screw attaching the defroster duct to the distributor case.

5. Disconnect the temperature door cable. Carefully fold the cable back and out of the way.

6. Remove the three nuts from the engine compartment side of the distributor case and the screw from the passenger compartment side.

7. Remove the heater case and core assembly.

8. Remove the core retaining straps and remove the core.

9. Reverse to install.

1979–86 Without Air Conditioning

1. Refer to steps 1–3 of the 1978 procedure.
2. Remove the engine cover.
3. Remove all the instrument panel attaching screws.
4. Carefully lower the steering column. Raise and support the right side of the instrument panel.
5. Remove the defroster duct-to-case attaching screws and the two screws attaching the distributor to the heater case.
6. Refer to steps 5–9 of the 1978 procedure.

1974–77 With Air Conditioning

These models have the air conditioning equipment mounted under the right side of the instrument panel.

1. Remove the battery.
2. Remove the engine cover.
3. Remove the evaporator/blower shield and bracket.
4. Remove the left floor outlet deflector and bracket.
5. Loosen the steering column to instrument panel reinforcement screws. Remove one screw.
6. Disconnect the speedometer cable at the instrument.
7. Remove the instrument panel to lower reinforcement screws. Move the instrument panel back and detach the radio antenna and wires. Disconnect the brake switch electrical connector.
8. Detach the blower/evaporator support bracket from the door pillar and the engine housing. Move it back for access.
9. Detach the heater hoses at the core (from under the hood). Plug the hoses to prevent spillage.
10. Remove the air inlet valve assembly from the kick panel. Remove the temperature door control cable at the heater case.
11. Remove the heater assembly. Remove the core from the assembly.
12. Reverse the procedure for installation. Tighten the column screw to 22 ft.lb. Refill the cooling system as necessary.

1978–86 With Air Conditioning

1. Disconnect the battery ground cable.
2. Remove the engine cover.
3. Remove the steering column to instrument panel bolts. Lower the column carefully.
4. Remove the upper and lower instrument panel attaching screws. Remove the radio support bracket screw.
5. Raise and support the right side of the instrument panel.
6. Remove the lower right instrument panel bracket.
7. Remove the vacuum actuator from the kick panel.
8. Disconnect the temperature cable and vacuum hoses at the case. Remove the heater distributor duct from over the engine hump.
9. Remove the two defroster duct to firewall attaching screws below the windshield.

10. Under the hood, disconnect and plug the heater hoses at the firewall.
11. Remove the three nuts and one screw (inside) holding the heater case to the firewall.
12. Remove the case from the truck. Remove the gasket for access to the screws holding the case together. Remove the temperature cable support bracket. Remove the screws and separate the case. Remove the heater core.
13. Reverse the procedure for installation. Refill the cooling system as necessary.

Control Head

REMOVAL AND INSTALLATION

1. Disconnect the negative battery cable.
2. Remove the headlamp switch control knob.
3. Remove the instrument panel bezel.
4. Remove the control screws.
5. Disconnect the temperature cable eyelet clip and retainer.
6. Remove the control lower right mounting tab through the dash opening.
7. Remove the upper tab and the lower right tab.
8. Disconnect the electrical harness.
9. Disconnect the vacuum harness.
8. Remove the control assembly.
9. Installation is the reverse of the removal procedure.

Evaporative Core

REMOVAL AND INSTALLATION

1. Disconnect the negative battery cable.
2. Purge the system of refrigerant.
3. Remove the coolant recovery tank and bracket.
4. Disconnect the electrical connectors from the core case assembly.
5. Remove the bracket at the evaporator case.
6. Remove the right marker lamp for access.
7. Disconnect the accumulator inlet and outlet lines, and the two brackets that attach the accumulator to the case.
8. Disconnect the evaporator inlet line.
9. Remove the three nuts and one screw that attaching the module to the dash panel.
10. Remove the core case assembly from the vehicle.
11. Remove the screws, separate the case sections and remove the evaporator core.
12. Installation is the reverse of the removal procedure.

NOTE: *Add 3 ounces of 525 viscosity refrigerant oil to the condenser if a new one is installed.*

RADIO

REMOVAL AND INSTALLATION

1967–70

1. Disconnect the battery ground cable.
2. Remove the knobs, washers, and nuts from the radio shafts.
3. Detach any support brackets.
4. Lower the radio and detach the wiring for power, speaker, and antenna.
5. Remove the radio. Reverse the procedure for installation.

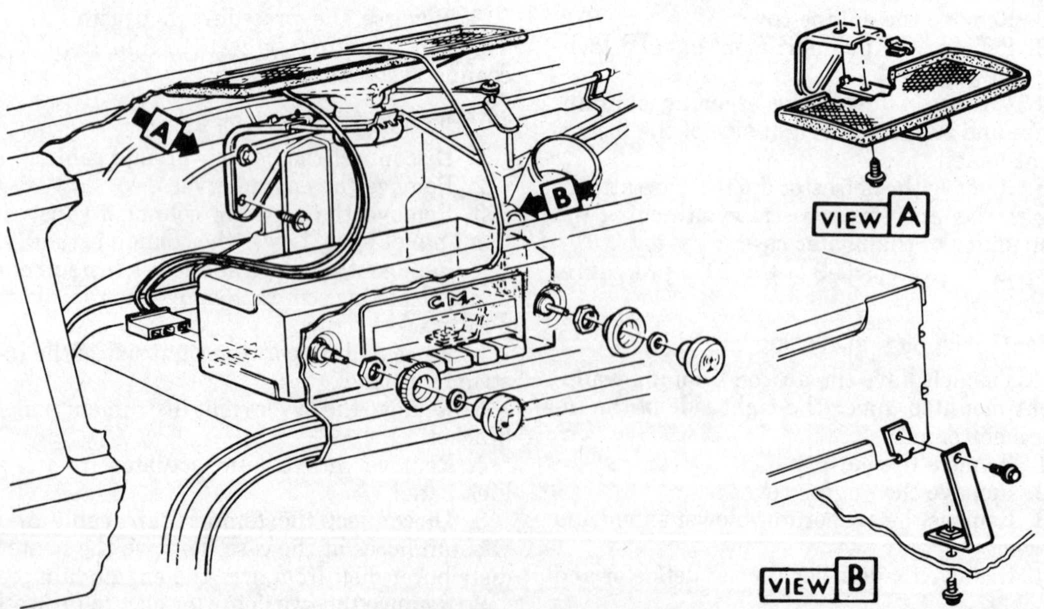

Radio installation—1971–73

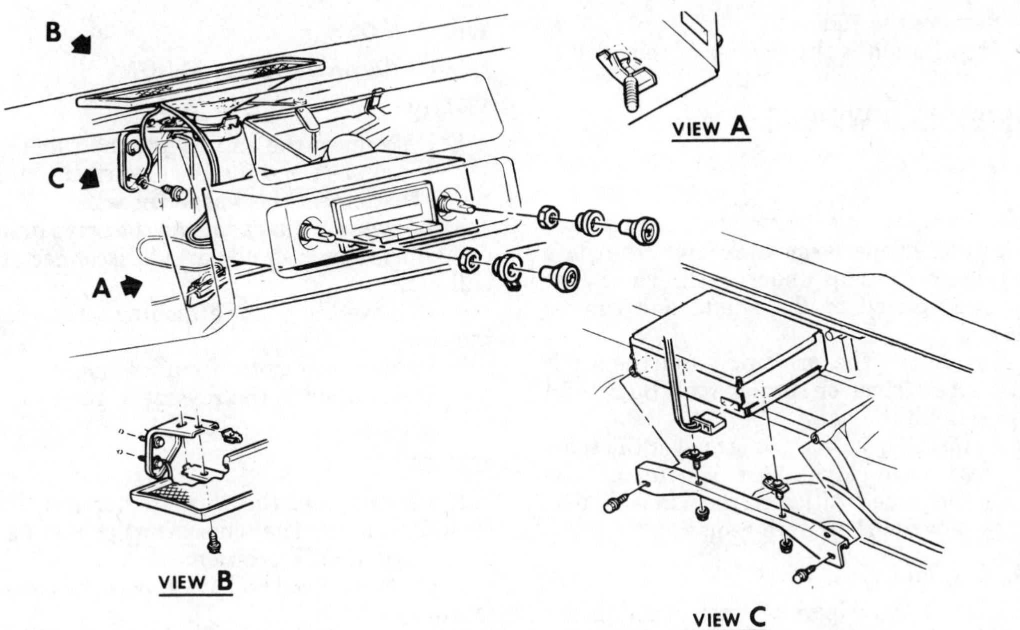

1974–77 radio installation

1971–86

1. Disconnect the ground cable from the battery.
2. Remove the engine cover.
3. Remove the air cleaner from the carburetor.
4. On models through 1977, remove the stud in the carburetor which holds the air cleaner.
5. Cover the carburetor with a clean rag.
6. Remove the knobs, washers and nuts from the front of the radio.
7. Remove the rear bracket screw and bracket from the radio.
8. Remove the radio through the engine access area. Lower the radio far enough to detach the wiring.

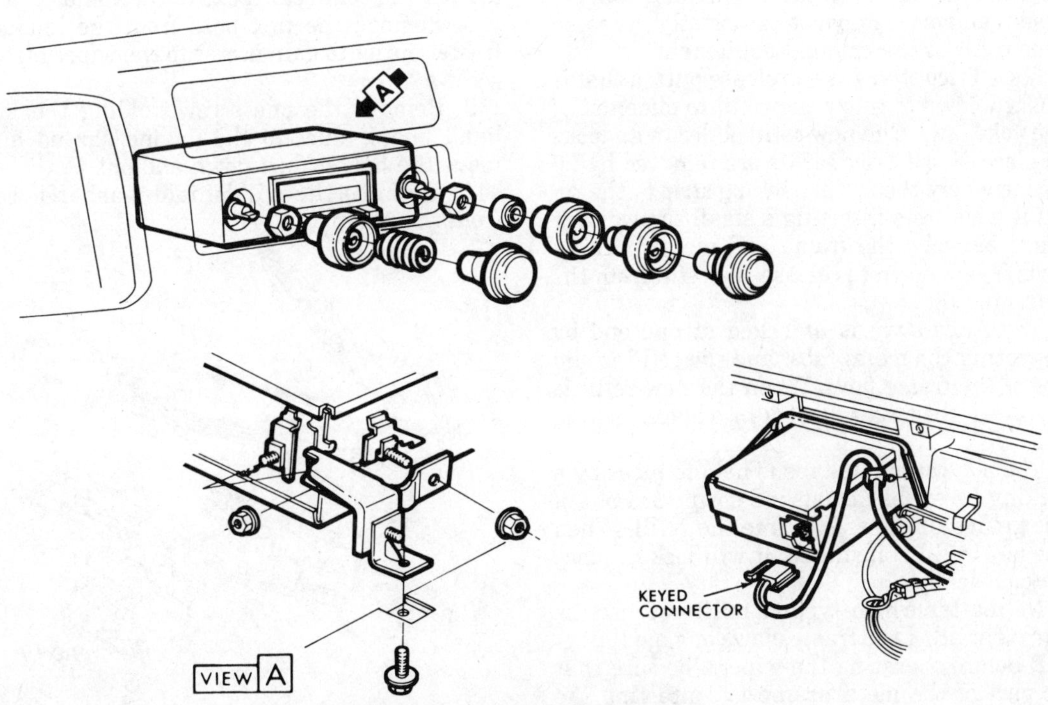

1978 and later radio installation

9. Remove the radio.
10. Installation is the reverse of removal.

WINDSHIELD WIPERS

Blade and Arm

REMOVAL AND INSTALLATION

1. Pull the wiper arms away from the glass and release the clip underneath. The wiper arms are splined to the shafts and can be pulled off.
2. To remove the arm, pry underneath it with a screwdriver or similar tool. Be careful not to scratch the paint.
3. To install, position the arm over the shaft and press down. Make sure you install the arms in the same position on the windshield as they were when they were removed.

BLADE REFILL

Normally, if the wipers are not cleaning the windshield properly, only the refill has to be replaced. The blade and arm usually require replacement only in the event of damage. It is not necessary to remove the arm or the blade to replace the refill (rubber part), though you may have to position the arm higher on the glass. You can do this by turning the key on and operating the wipers. When they are positioned where they are accessible, turn the key off.

There are several types of refills and your vehicle could have any kind, since aftermarket blades and arms may not use exactly the same type refill as the original equipment.

Most Trico styles use a release button that is pushed down to allow the refill to slide out of the yoke jaws. The new refill slides in an locks in place. Some Trico refills are removed by locating where the metal backing strip or the refill is wider and inserting a small screwdriver blade between the frame and metal backing strip. Press down to release the refill from the retaining tab.

The Anco style is unlocked at one end by squeezing the metal tabs, and the refill is slid out of the frame jaws. When the new refill is installed, the tabs will click into place, locking the refill.

The polycarbonate type is held in place by a locking lever that is pushed downward out of the groove in the arm to free the refill. When the new refill is installed, it will lock in place automatically.

No matter which type of refill you use, be sure that all of the frame claws engage the refill. Before operating the wipers, be sure that no part of the metal frame is contacting the windshield.

Wiper Motor

REMOVAL AND INSTALLATION

1967–70

1. Disconnect the battery ground cable.
2. Disconnect and tag the electrical connections. Disconnect the washer hoses.
3. Loosen the nuts securing the drive link to the wiper motor crank arm. Disconnect the ball joint.
4. Remove the motor attaching screws from the cowl.
5. Remove the motor from its mount.
6. Installation is the reverse of removal.

1971–86

1. Be sure that the wiper motor arm is in PARK position. The wiper arms should be in their normal OFF position.
2. Open the hood and disconnect the battery ground cable.
3. Remove the exposed cowl cover screws with the hood up.
4. Remove the wiper arms. This can be done by pulling the wiper arms away from the glass to release the clip underneath. The wiper arms are splined to the shafts and can be pulled off.
5. Remove the remaining screws securing the cowl panel and remove it.
6. Loosen the nuts holding the transmission linkage to the wiper motor crank arm.
7. Disconnect the power feed to the wiper arm at the connector next to the radio.
8. Remove the flex hose from the left defroster outlet to gain access to the wiper motor screws.
9. Remove the one screw holding the left hand heater duct to the engine shroud and move the heater duct down and out.
10. Remove the windshield washer hoses from the pump.

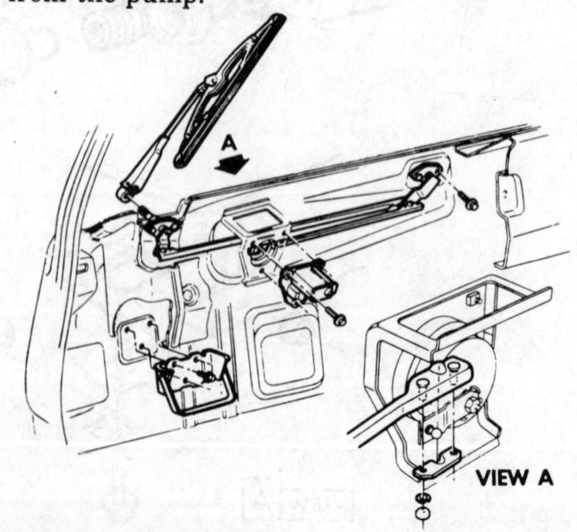

Wiper motor—1967–70

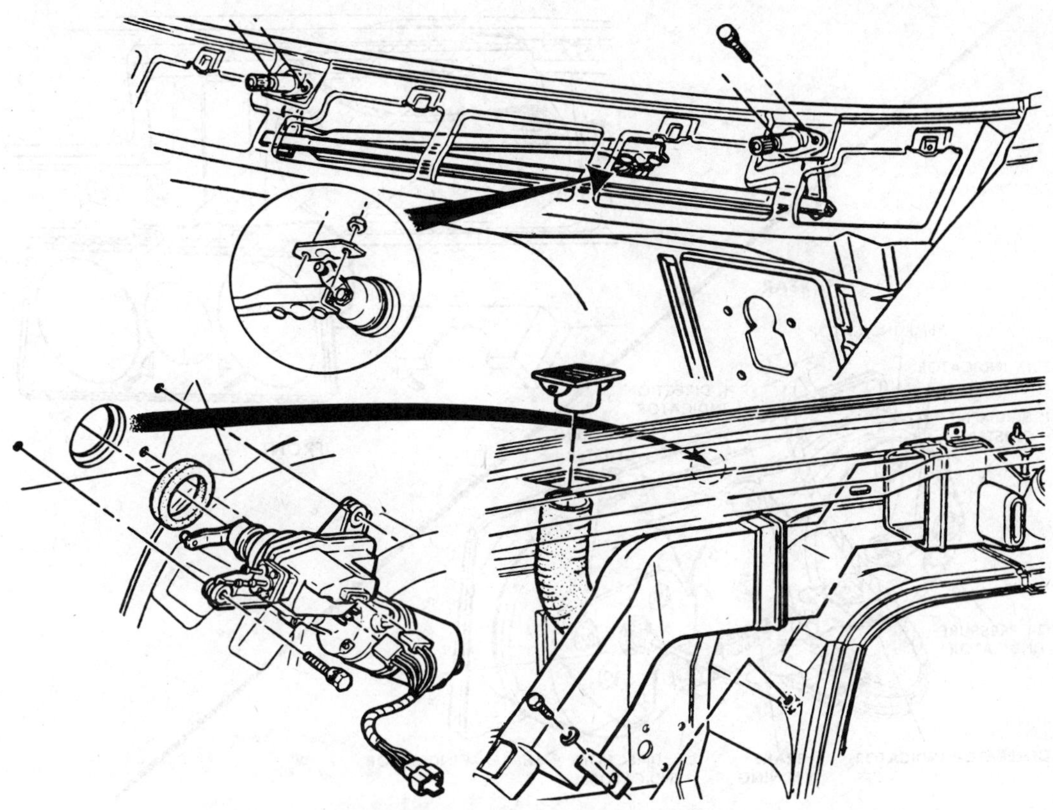

1971 and later windshield wiper motor

11. Remove the 3 screws holding the wiper motor to the cowl and lift the wiper motor out from under the dash.

12. Installation is the reverse of removal. Install the wiper motor in the PARK position.

Wiper Linkage

REMOVAL AND INSTALLATION

1. Be sure that the wiper motor is in PARK position. The wiper arms should be in their normal OFF position.
2. Open the hood and disconnect the battery ground cable.
3. Remove the exposed cowl cover screws with the hood up.
4. Remove the wiper arms. This can be done by pulling the wiper arms away from the glass to release the clip underneath. The wiper arms are splined to the shafts and can be pulled off.
5. Remove the remaining screws securing the cowl panel and remove it.
6. Remove the screws and nuts securing the transmission linkage to the wiper motor crank arm. Disconnect the ball joint and remove the linkage.
7. Installation is the reverse of removal.

INSTRUMENTS AND SWITCHES

INSTRUMENT CLUSTER

The entire cluster may be removed from the vehicle for servicing the instruments and gauges. The illuminating and indicator lamps can be removed and replaced without removing the entire cluster. On earlier models, the lamps and bulbs are clip retained and can be easily snapped in or out. Later models use plastic bulb holders that are twist-locked through a laminated plastic printed circuit in the luster housing.

REMOVAL AND INSTALLATION

1967–70

1. Disconnect the battery ground cable.
2. Disconnect the speedometer cable at the head.
3. Remove the two nuts attaching the cluster to the dash panel. The cluster can now be pulled clear of the dash.
4. Disconnect all wires and bulbs, noting their respective locations.
5. Remove the cluster.
6. Installation is the reverse of removal.

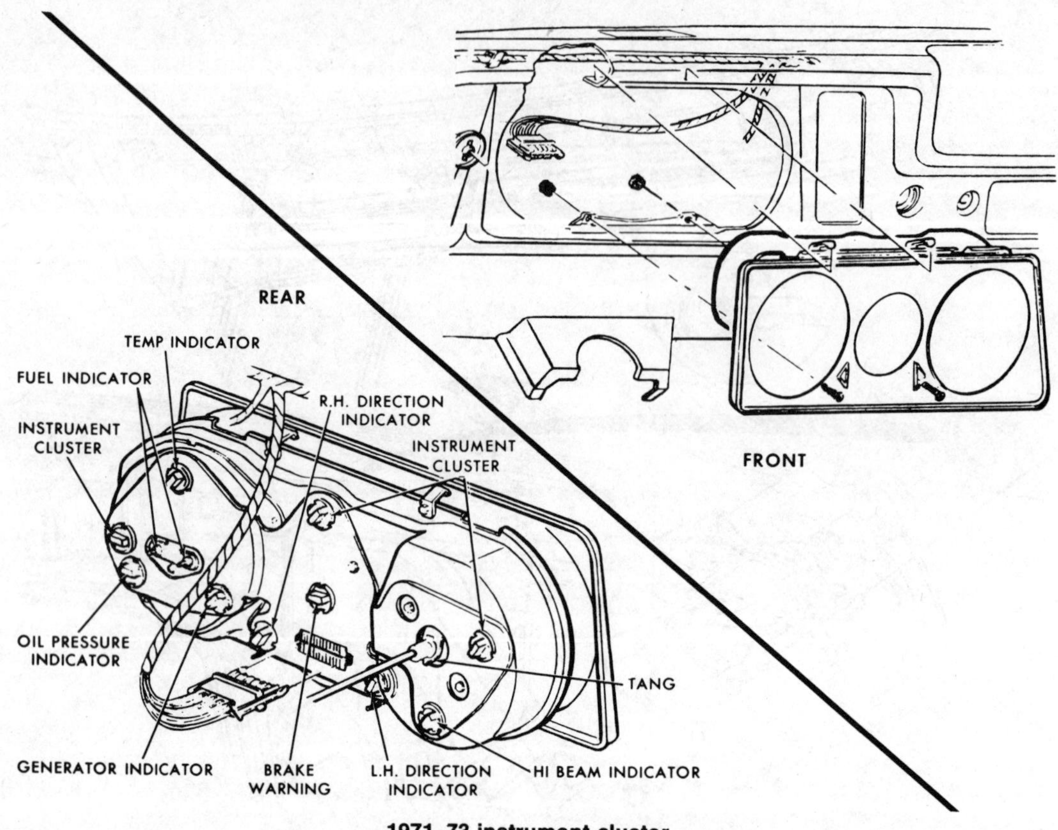

1971–73 instrument cluster

1971–86

1. Open the hood and disconnect the battery ground cable.
2. Reach up under the dash and disconnect the speedometer cable by first depressing the tang on the rear of the speedometer head and detaching the cable as the tang is depressed.
3. Unplug the instrument panel harness connector.
4. Disconnect and plug the oil pressure gauge line (if equipped).
5. Remove the nuts from the instrument cluster bezel and remove bezel.
6. Pull the top of the cluster away from instrument panel and lift out the bottom of the cluster.
7. Remove the cluster.
8. Installation is the reverse of removal. The clips at the top of the cluster slip into the openings in the instrument panel after the bottom of the cluster is installed.

Wiper and Washer Switch

REMOVAL AND INSTALLATION

1967–72

The windshield wiper switch is mounted on the left side of the instrument panel, and are reached by removing the left side trim panel. Electrical connections must be disconnected at the rear of the switch before removing the switch unit from the dash. Be sure to note how the wires are connected before removing. The switch units are fixed to the instrument panel by two or four screws.

Head Light Switch

The headlight switch is mounted on the left hand side of the instrument panel. To remove the switch, disconnect the negative battery cable and remove the left instrument panel trim plate. Remove the retaining nut securing the switch, and disconnect the electrical connector from the back of the switch. The switch can now be removed. Reverse the procedure for installation.

Back-up Light Switch

REMOVAL AND INSTALLATION

Manual Transmission

The back-up light switch is located on the left side of the transmission case. To remove:

1. Disconnect the negative battery cable.
2. Disconnect the back-up switch harness.
3. Remove the back-up switch and the seal.

4. Installation is the reverse of the removal procedure.

Automatic Transmission

The back-up light switch is located on the left side of the transmission case. To remove:

1. Disconnect the negative battery cable.
2. Disconnect the back-up switch assembly harness.
3. Place the gear selector in neutral.
4. Squeeze the switch tangs together and lift out the switch assembly.
5. Installation is the reverse of the removal procedure.

Turn Signal Switch

REMOVAL AND INSTALLATION

1967–72

1. Disconnect the battery ground cable.
2. Remove the steering wheel, preload spring, and cancelling cam.
3. Remove the shift lever roll pin and shift lever (if applicable).
4. Remove the turn signal lever screw and the lever.
5. Push the hazard warning knob in. This must be done to avoid damaging the switch.
6. Disconnect the switch wires from the chassis harness located under the dash.
7. Remove the mast jacket upper bracket.
8. Remove the switch wiring cover from the column.
9. Unscrew the mounting screws and remove the switch, bearing housing, switch cover, and shift housing from the column.
10. Installation is the reverse or removal.

Combination Turn Signal/Wiper Washer Switch

REMOVAL AND INSTALLATION

1973 and Later

1. Disconnect the battery ground cable. Remove the steering wheel.
2. Remove the switch cancelling spring and cam.
3. Remove the column to instrument panel trim plate, if any.
4. Disconnect the switch wiring harness at the half-moon connector.
5. Pry the wiring harness protector out of the column retaining slots.
6. Mark their locations, then remove each wire from the half-moon connector.
7. Remove the turn signal lever screw and the lever.
8. On tilt columns, remove the automatic transmission dial and needle. Remove the cap and bulb from the housing cover. Unscrew and remove the tilt release lever. The directional signal housing cover has to be pulled off the column; there is a special tool used for this.
9. Remove the three switch screws and remove the switch, guiding the wiring harness through the opening.
10. On installation, tape the switch wires and guide them through the housing opening. On tilt columns, the directional signal housing cover must be tapped back into place.

Ignition Switch

REMOVAL AND INSTALLATION

1967–72

1. Raise the hood and disconnect the battery ground cable.
2. Remove the lock cylinder by inserting the key in the switch and turning it to the ACC position. Insert a piece of stiff wire in the small hole in the cylinder face and push in to depress the plunger. Continue to turn the key counterclockwise until the lock cylinder can be removed.
3. Remove the metallic ignition switch nut.
4. Pull the ignition switch out from behind the dash, and remove the "theft resistant" connector. A screwdriver can be used to unsnap the locking tangs from the connector.
5. Snap the connectors into place on a new switch.
6. Put the switch into position from behind the dash, first installing the ground ring and then the ignition switch nut.
7. Install the lock cylinder.
8. Reconnect the battery cable.
9. Installation is the reverse or removal.

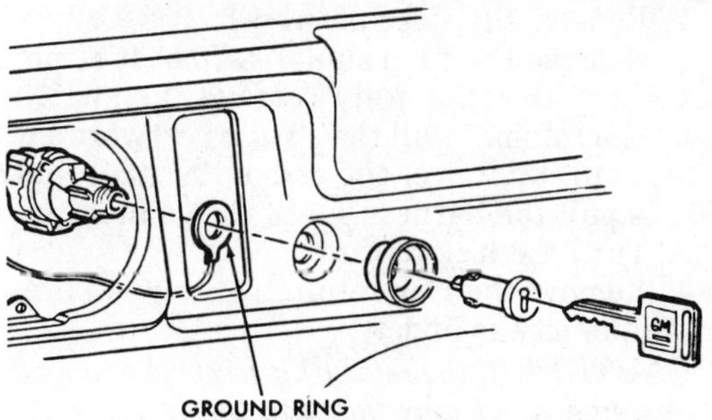

Typical ignition switch—1967–72

Lock Cylinder

REMOVAL AND INSTALLATION

1973–78

1. Remove the steering wheel and turn signal switch.

NOTE: *It is not necessary to completely re-*

move the turn signal switch. Pull the switch over the end of the shaft – no further.

2. Place lock cylinder in Run position.

CAUTION: *Do not remove the ignition key buzzer.*

3. Insert a small drift pin into the turn signal housing slot. Keeping the drift pin to the right side of the slot, break the housing flash loose and depress the spring latch at the lower end of the lock cylinder. Remove the lock cylinder.

NOTE: *Considerable force may be necessary to break this casting flash, buy be careful not to damage any other parts. When ordering a new lock cylinder, specify a cylinder assembly. This will same assembling the cylinder, washer, sleeve and adapter.*

4. To install, hold the lock cylinder sleeve and rotate the knob clockwise against the stop. Insert the cylinder into the housing, aligning the key and keyway. Hold a 0.070" (1.778mm) drill between the lock bezel and housing. Rotate the cylinder counterclockwise, maintaining a light pressure until the drive section of the cylinder mates with the sector. Push in until the snapring pops into the grooves. Remove drill. Check cylinder operation.

CAUTION: *The drill prevents forcing the lock cylinder inward beyond its normal position. The buzzer switch and spring latch can hold the lock cylinder in too far. Complete disassembly of the upper bearing housing is necessary to release an improperly installed lock cylinder.*

1979 and Later

1. Remove the steering wheel.
2. Remove the turn signal switch. It is not necessary to completely remove the switch from the column. Pull the switch rearward far enough to slip it over the end of the shaft, but do not pull the harness out of the column.
3. Turn the lock to Run.
4. Remove the lock retaining screw and remove the lock cylinder.

CAUTION: *If the retaining screw is dropped on removal, it may fall into the column, requiring complete disassembly of the column to retrieve the screw.*

5. To install, rotate the key to the stop while holding onto the cylinder.
6. Push the lock all the way in.
7. Install the screw. Tighten the screw to 3 ft.lb. for regular columns, 2 ft.lb. for adjustable columns.
8. Install the turn signal switch and the steering wheel.

1973 AND LATER IGNITION SWITCH REMOVAL AND INSTALLATION

The switch is on the steering column, behind the instrument panel.

1. Lower the steering column, making sure that it is supported.

CAUTION: *Extreme care is necessary to prevent damage to the collapsible column.*

2. Make sure the switch is in the Lock position. If the lock cylinder is out, pull the switch rod up to the stop, then go down 1 detent.
3. Remove the two screws and the switch.
4. Before installation, make sure the switch is in the Lock position.
5. Install the switch using the original screws.

CAUTION: *Use of screws that are too long could prevent the column from collapsing on impact.*

6. Replace the column.

Speedometer Cable

REMOVAL AND INSTALLATION

1. Disconnect the speedometer cable from the rear of the speedometer head. Unscrew through 1972, unclip from 1973.
2. Remove the old cable by pulling it out from the speedometer end of the cable housing. If the old cable is broken, the speedometer cable will have to be disconnected from the transmission and the cable removed from the other end.
3. Lubricate the lower ¾ of the new cable with speedometer cable lubricant and feed the cable into the cable housing.
4. Connect the speedometer cable to the speedometer head and to the transmission if disconnected there.

LIGHTING

Headlight

REMOVAL AND INSTALLATION

NOTE: *Some 1978 and later models have rectangular headlights. Otherwise the following removal and installation procedures apply.*

1. Remove the headlight bezel by releasing the attaching screws.
2. Remove the spring (if any) from the retaining ring and turn the unit to disengage it from the headlamp adjusting screws.
3. Disconnect the wiring harness connector.

NOTE: *Do not disturb the adjusting screws.*

4. Remove the retaining ring and the headlamp.

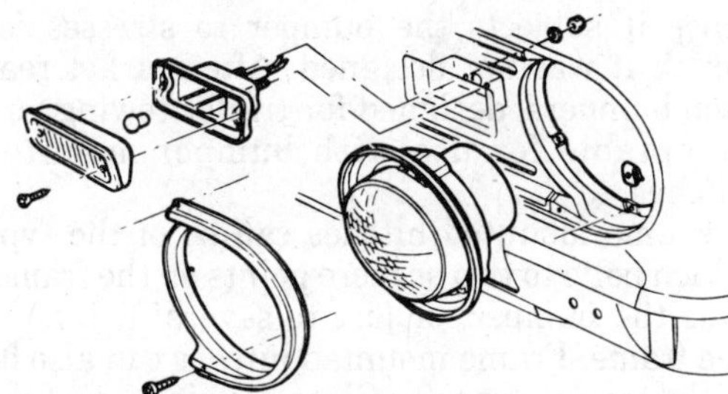

Headlight assembly—1967–70

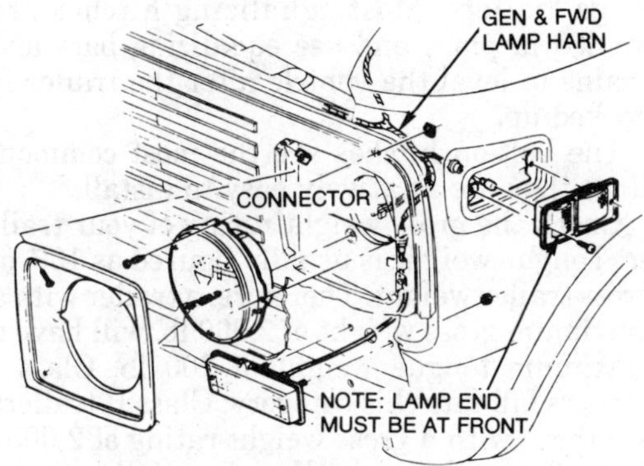

1971 and later headlight assembly (rectangular headlights are similar)

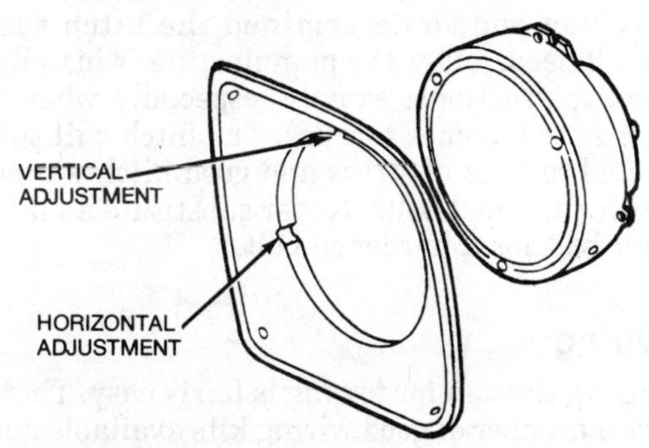

Headlight adjusting screws—typical

5. Position the new sealed beam unit in the retaining ring.

NOTE: *The number which is molded into the lens must be at the top.*

6. Attach the wiring connector.

7. Install the headlamp assembly, twisting the ring slightly to engage the adjusting screws.

8. Install the retaining ring spring and check the operation of the unit. Install the bezel.

HEADLIGHT AIMING

The headlights must be properly aimed to provide the best, safest road illumination. The

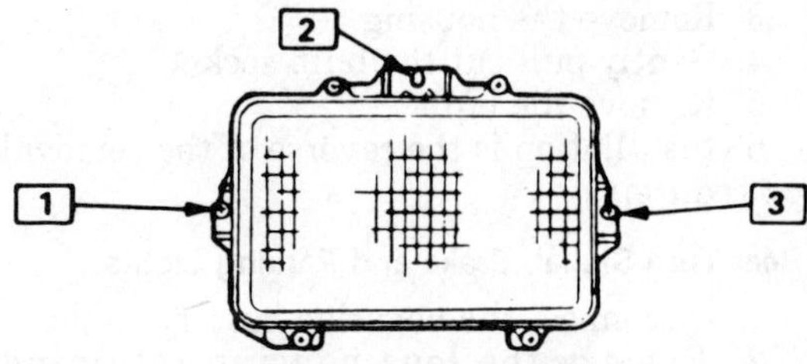

1. Horizontal adj. screw-RH
2. Vertical adj. screw
3. Horizontal adj. screw-LH

Headlight aiming. Round headlight models similar

lights should be checked for proper aim, and adjusted if necessary, after installing a new sealed beam unit or if the front end sheet metal has been replaced. Certain state and local authorities have requirements for headlight aiming and you should check these before adjusting.

NOTE: *The truck's fuel tank should be about half full when adjusting the headlights. Tires should be properly inflated, and if a heavy load is carried, it should remain there.*

Horizontal and vertical aiming of each sealed beam unit is provided by two adjusting screws, which move the mounting ring in the body against the tension of the coil spring. There is no adjustment for focus; this is done during headlight manufacturing.

Signal and Marker Lights

REMOVAL AND INSTALLATION

Front Turn Signal and Parking Lights

1. Disconnect the negative battery cable.
2. Remove the four bezel retaining screws.
3. Remove the bezel.
4. Remove the three park lamp retaining screws.
5. Remove the parking lamp.
6. Disconnect the electrical connector from the parking lamp and install a new bulb.
7. Installation is the reverse of the removal procedure.

Front Side Marker Lights

1. Disconnect the negative battery cable.
2. Remove the two retaining screws.
3. Remove the side marker lamp.
4. Remove the bulb from the lamp and install a new bulb.
5. Installation is the reverse of the removal procedure.

Rear Side Marker Lights

1. Disconnect the negative battery cable.
2. Remove the housing retaining screws.

3. Remove the housing.
4. Gently pull out the bulb socket.
5. Remove the bulb.
6. Installation is the reverse of the removal procedure.

Rear Turn Signal, Brake and Parking Lights

1. Disconnect the negative battery cable.
2. Remove the lens housing retaining screws.
3. Remove the lamp housing.
4. Remove the bulb socket by squeezing the retention lock and rotating the socket counterclockwise.
5. Remove the bulb.
6. Installation is the reverse of the removal procedure.

TRAILER TOWING

Vans have long been popular as trailer towing vehicles. Their strong construction, and wide range of engine/transmission combinations make them ideal for towing campers, boat trailers and utility trailers.

Factory trailer towing packages are available on most GM vehicles. However, if you are installing a trailer hitch and wiring on your Van, there are a few thing that you ought to know.

Trailer Weight

Trailer weight is the first, and most important, factor in determining whether or not your vehicle is suitable for towing the trailer you have in mind. The horsepower-to-weight ratio should be calculated. The basic standard is a ratio of 35:1. That is, 35 pounds of GVW for every horsepower.

To calculate this ratio, multiply you engine's rated horsepower by 35, then subtract the weight of the vehicle, including passengers and luggage. The resulting figure is the ideal maximum trailer weight that you can tow. One point to consider: a numerically higher axle ratio can offset what appears to be a low trailer weight. If the weight of the trailer that you have in mind is somewhat higher than the weight you just calculated, you might consider changing your rear axle ratio to compensate.

Hitch Weight

There are three kinds of hitches: bumper mounted, frame mounted, and load equalizing.

Bumper mounted hitches are those which attach solely to the vehicle's bumper. Many states prohibit towing with this type of hitch, when it attaches to the vehicle's stock bumper, since it subjects the bumper to stresses for which it was not designed. Aftermarket rear step bumpers, designed for trailer towing, are acceptable for use with bumper mounted hitches.

Frame mounted hitches can be of the type which bolts to two or more points on the frame, plus the bumper, or just to several points on the frame. Frame mounted hitches can also be of the tongue type, for Class I towing, or, of the receiver type, for classes II and III.

Load equalizing hitches are usually used for large trailers. Most equalizing hitches are welded in place and use equalizing bars and chains to level the vehicle after the trailer is hooked up.

The bolt-on hitches are the most common, since they are relatively easy to install.

Check the gross weight rating of your trailer. Tongue weight is usually figured as 10% of gross trailer weight. Therefore, a trailer with a maximum gross weight of 2,000 lb. will have a maximum tongue weight of 200 lb. Class I trailers fall into this category. Class II trailers are those with a gross weight rating of 2,000–3,500 lb., while Class III trailers fall into the 3,500–6,000 lb. category. Class IV trailers are those over 6,000 lb. and are for use with fifth wheel trucks, only.

When you've determined the hitch that you'll need, follow the manufacturer's installation instructions, exactly, especially when it comes to fastener torques. The hitch will subjected to a lot of stress and good hitches come with hardened bolts. Never substitute an inferior bolt for a hardened bolt.

Wiring

Wiring the van for towing is fairly easy. There are a number of good wiring kits available and these should be used, rather than trying to design your own. All trailers will need brake lights and turn signals as well as tail lights and side marker lights. Most states require extra marker lights for overwide trailers. Also, most states have recently required back-up lights for trailers, and most trailer manufacturers have been building trailers with back-up lights for several years.

Additionally, some Class I, most Class II and just about all Class III trailers will have electric brakes.

Add to this number an accessories wire, to operate trailer internal equipment or to charge the trailer's battery, and you can have as many as seven wires in the harness.

Determine the equipment on your trailer and buy the wiring kit necessary. The kit will contain all the wires needed, plus a plug adapter set which included the female plug, mounted on the bumper or hitch, and the male plug, wired into, or plugged into the trailer harness.

When installing the kit, follow the manufacturer's instructions. The color coding of the wires is standard throughout the industry.

One point to note: some domestic vehicles, and most imported vehicles, have separate turn signals. On most domestic vehicles, the brake lights and rear turn signals operate with the same bulb. For those vehicles with separate turn signals, you can purchase an isolation unit so that the brake lights won't blink whenever the turn signals are operated, or, you can go to your local electronics supply house and buy four diodes to wire in series with the brake and turn signal bulbs. Diodes will isolate the brake and turn signals. The choice is yours. The isolation units are simple and quick to install, but far more expensive than the diodes. The diodes, however, require more work to install properly, since they require the cutting of each bulb's wire and soldering in place of the diode.

One, final point, the best kits are those with a spring loaded cover on the vehicle mounted socket. This cover prevents dirt and moisture from corroding the terminals. Never let the vehicle socket hang loosely; always mount it securely to the bumper or hitch.

Cooling

ENGINE

One of the most common, if not THE most common, problems associated with trailer towing is engine overheating.

With factory installed trailer towing packages, a heavy duty cooling system is usually included. Heavy duty cooling systems are available as optional equipment on most GM vehicles, with or without a trailer package. If you have one of these extra-capacity systems, you shouldn't have any overheating problems.

If you have a standard cooling system, without an expansion tank, you'll definitely need to get an aftermarket expansion tank kit, preferably one with at least a 2 quart capacity. These kits are easily installed on the radiator's overflow hose, and come with a pressure cap designed for expansion tanks.

Another helpful accessory is a Flex Fan. These fan are large diameter units are designed to provide more airflow at low speeds, with blades that have deeply cupped surfaces. The blades then flex, or flatten out, at high speed, when less cooling air is needed. These fans are far lighter in weight than stock fans, requiring less horsepower to drive them. Also, they are far quieter than stock fans.

If you do decide to replace your stock fan with a flex fan, note that if your van has a fan clutch, a spacer between the flex fan and water pump hub will be needed.

Aftermarket engine oil coolers are helpful for prolonging engine oil life and reducing overall engine temperatures. Both of these factors increase engine life.

While not absolutely necessary in towing Class I and some Class II trailers, they are recommended for heavier Class II and all Class III towing.

Engine oil cooler systems consist of an adapter, screwed on in place of the oil filter, a remote filter mounting and a multi-tube, finned heat exchanger, which is mounted in front of the radiator or air conditioning condenser.

TRANSMISSION

An automatic transmission is usually recommended for trailer towing. Modern automatics have proven reliable and, of course, easy to operate, in trailer towing.

The increased load of a trailer, however, causes an increase in the temperature of the automatic transmission fluid. Heat is the worst enemy of an automatic transmission. As the temperature of the fluid increases, the life of the fluid decreases.

It is essential, therefore, that you install an automatic transmission cooler.

The cooler, which consists of a multi-tube, finned heat exchanger, is usually installed in front of the radiator or air conditioning compressor, and hooked inline with the transmission cooler tank inlet line. Follow the cooler manufacturer's installation instructions.

Select a cooler of at least adequate capacity, based upon the combined gross weights of the Van and trailer.

Cooler manufacturers recommend that you use an aftermarket cooler in addition to, and not instead of, the present cooling tank in your vans radiator. If you do want to use it in place of the radiator cooling tank, get a cooler at least two sizes larger than normally necessary.

One note, transmission cooler can, sometimes, cause slow or harsh shifting in the transmission during cold weather, until the fluid has a chance to come up to normal operating temperature. Some coolers can be purchased with or retrofitted with a temperature bypass valve which will allow fluid flow through the cooler only when the fluid has reached operating temperature, or above.

CIRCUIT PROTECTION

FUSIBLE LINKS

Fusible links are sections of wire, with special insulation, designed to melt under electrical overload. Replacements are simply spliced into the wire in most cases. Circuits protected by fusible links, 1967–74, are: engine wiring, battery charging, alternator, and headlights. For 1975–86, the circuits are: high beam indicator, air conditioning hi-blower, horn, and ignition.

Fusible Link Repair

1. Determine the circuit that is damaged.
2. Disconnect the negative battery terminal.
3. Cut the damaged fuse link from the harness and discard it.
4. Identify and procure the proper fuse link and butt connectors.
5. Strip the wire about ½″ (12.7mm) on each end.
6. Connect the fusible link and crimp the butt connectors making sure that the wires are secure.
7. Solder each connection with resin core solder, and wrap the connections with plastic electrical tape.
8. Reinstall the wire in the harness.
9. Connect the negative battery terminal and test the system for proper operation.

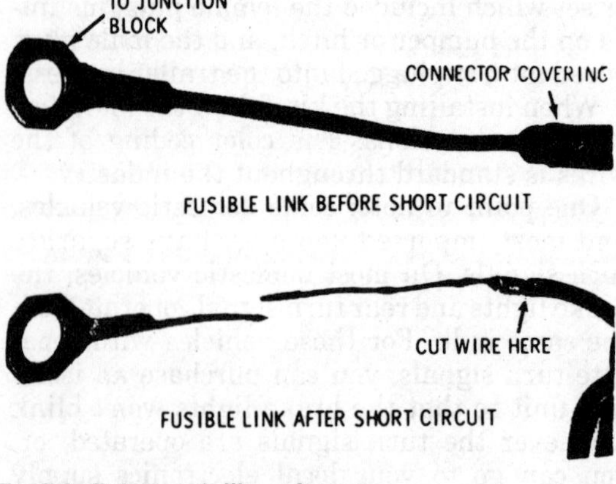

Fusible links work like a fuse

CIRCUIT BREAKERS

A circuit breaker is a electrical switch which breaks the circuit in case of an overload. All models have a circuit breaker in the headlight switch to protect the headlight and parking light systems. An overload may cause the lights to flash on and off. 1974–75 wiper motors have a circuit breaker at the motor. 1975–86 rear mounted air conditioners have a circuit breaker at the firewall.

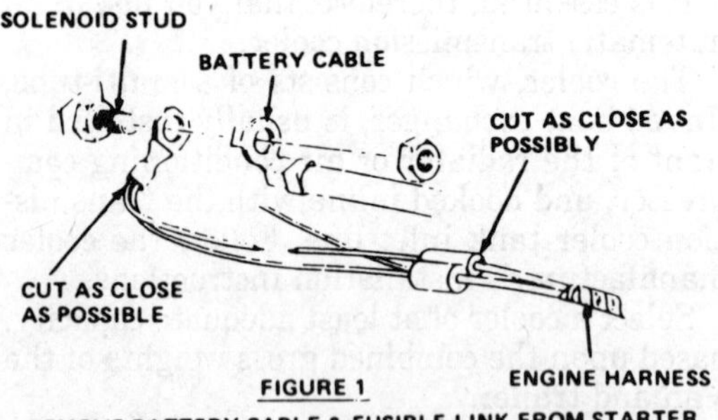

FIGURE 1
REMOVE BATTERY CABLE & FUSIBLE LINK FROM STARTER SOLENOID AND CUT OFF DEFECTIVE WIRE AS SHOWN TWO PLACES.

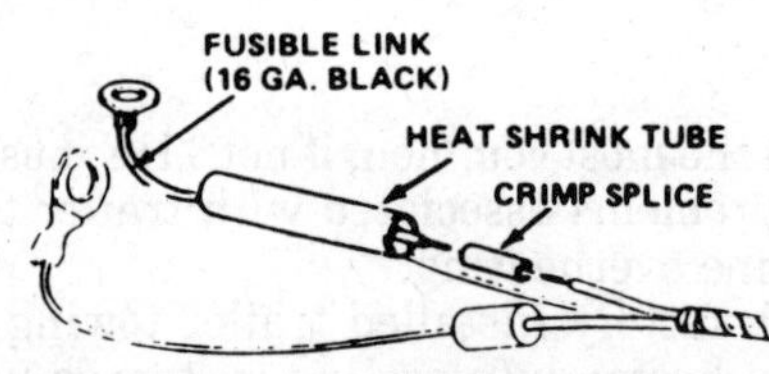

FIGURE 2
STRIP INSULATION FROM WIRE ENDS. PLACE HEAT SHRINK TUBE OVER REPLACEMENT LINK. INSERT WIRE ENDS INTO CRIMP SPLICE AS SHOWN. NOTE: PUSH WIRES IN FAR ENOUGH TO ENGAGE WIRE ENDS.

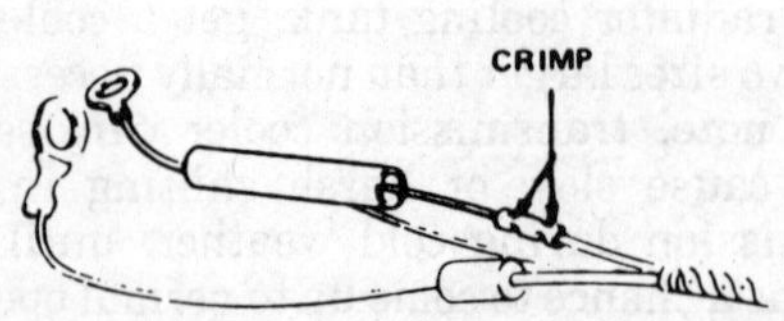

FIGURE 3
CRIMP SPLICE WITH CRIMPING TOOL TWO PLACES TO BIND BOTH WIRES.

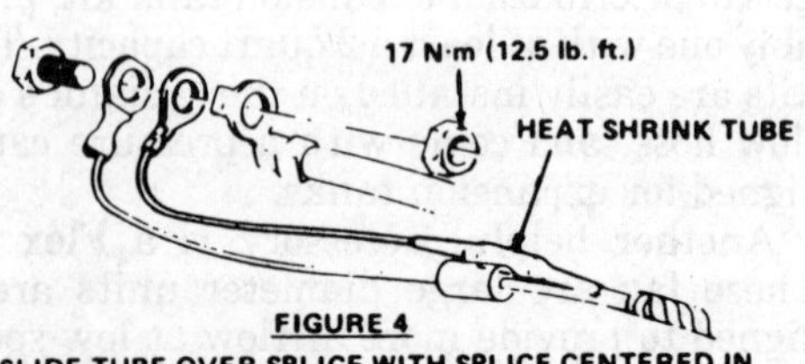

FIGURE 4
SLIDE TUBE OVER SPLICE WITH SPLICE CENTERED IN TUBE. APPLY LOW TEMPERATURE HEAT TO SHRINK TUBE AROUND WIRES & SPLICE. REASSEMBLE LINKS & BATTERY CABLE.

Fusible link repair

FUSES AND FLASHERS

The fuse block is mounted to the firewall, inside the truck, to the left of the steering column. The turn signal flasher and hazard warning flasher plug into the fuse block. Each fuse receptacle is marked as to the circuits it protects and the correct amperage. In-line fuses are also used to protect some circuits. These are: 1972–86 ammeter, 1973–74 rear air conditioner, and 1975–86 auxiliary heater.

NOTE: *A special heavy duty turn signal flasher is required to properly operate the turn signals when a trailer's lights are connected to the system.*

WIRING DIAGRAMS

Wiring diagrams are not included in this book. As vans have become more complex, and available with longer and longer option lists, wiring diagrams have grown in size and complexity. It has become virtually impossible to provide a readable reproduction in a reasonable number of pages. Information on ordering wiring diagrams from the manufacturer can be found in the owners manual.

Drive Train 6

MANUAL TRANSMISSION

Most 3-speed transmissions are the very simialr Saginaw and Muncie side cover units. These may be told apart by the shape of the side cover. The Saginaw has a single bolt centered at the top edge of the side cover, while the Muncie has two bolts along the top edge. The Muncie was discontinued in 1978. Some 1976–80 models use the top cover Tremec 3-speed. All 3-speeds use side mounted external linkage and a column shift. A column shifted 4-speed Warner T-10 transmission was optional in 1968–69 only.

REMOVAL AND INSTALLATION

1967

1. Drain the lubricant from the transmission.
2. Remove the driveshaft.
3. Remove the screws holding the steering jacket grommet to the floor and slide the grommet up the jacket out of the way.
4. Remove the accelerator pedal and floor mat.
5. Remove the transmission cover and the floor pans (if equipped).
6. Disconnect the speedometer cable at the transmission rear bearing retainer.
7. Remove the top 2 screws attaching the transmission the bellhousing. Insert 2 guide pins in these holes. They will support the weight of the transmission and keep it level while it is being removed.
8. Remove the flywheel underpan and remove the lower screws attaching the transmission to the bellhousing.
9. Slide the transmission straight back on the guide pins until the mainshaft is free of the splines in the clutch disc.
10. Remove the transmission from the vehicle.
11. Installation is the reverse of removal. Fill the transmission with the specified amount and type of fluid. Road test the vehicle to be sure that the transmission and clutch operate properly.

1968–70

1. Drain the lubricant from the transmission.
2. Disconnect the speedometer cable.
3. Remove the shift controls from the transmission.
4. On vehicles with the 4-speed transmission, remove the floor mat, transmission floor pan cover and place the transmission gearshift in Neutral. Remove the transmission gearshift lever and cover.
5. Place a clean cloth over the opening in the side of the 4-speed transmission.
6. Disconnect the backup light switch.
7. Disconnect the driveshaft and remove it.
8. Support the transmission with a suitable jack.
9. Place a protective shield between the radiator and fan.
10. Support the engine with a floor jack.
11. Remove the engine rear mount-to-transmission attaching bolts.
12. Carefully lower both the engine and transmission to clear the support bracket.
13. Visually, make sure that all necessary parts have been disconnected or removed.
14. Remove the flywheel housing underpan and the mounting bolts from the transmission.
15. Support the clutch release bearing to prevent its falling from the flywheel housing when the transmission is removed.
16. Move the transmission assembly straight out of the bellhousing. Be sure that it is supported firmly to be sure that the clutch is not damaged.
17. Installation is the reverse of removal. Apply a very light coating of high temperature

grease to the mainshaft to be sure that the clutch and transmission mainshaft slide freely.

18. Torque the flywheel housing-to-transmission mounting nuts to 40–50 ft.lb. Torque the rear engine mount-to-bracket nuts to 55–75 ft.lb. Fill the transmission with lubricant. Road test the vehicle.

1971–86

1. Raise and support the van.
2. Drain the transmission. The 1976–80 Tremec top cover transmission is drained by removing the lower case to extension housing bolt.
3. Disconnect the speedometer cable, back-up light and TCS switch.
4. Remove the shift controls from the transmission.
5. Disconnect the driveshaft and remove it from the vehicle.
6. Support the transmission with a floor jack.
7. Inspect the transmission to be sure that all necessary components have been removed or disconnected.
8. Mark the front of the crossmember to be sure that it is installed correctly.
9. Support the clutch release bearing to prevent it from falling out of the flywheel housing when the transmission is removed.
10. Remove the flywheel housing under pan and transmission mounting bolts.
11. Move the transmission slowly away from the engine, keeping the mainshaft in alignment with the clutch disc hub. Be sure that the transmission is supported.
12. Remove the transmission from under the vehicle.
13. Installation is the reverse of removal. Lightly coat the mainshaft with high temperature grease. Do not use much grease, since, under normal operation, the grease will be thrown onto the clutch, causing it to fail.
14. Tighten the transmission to flywheel housing bolts to 55 ft.lb. through 1972, and to 75 ft.lb. for 1973 and later. Fill the transmission with lubricant. Road test the vehicle.

Linkage Adjustment

3-Speed Column Shift

The gearshift linkage should be adjusted each time it is disturbed or removed.

1. Install the control rods to both of the levers and set both shifter levers in the Neutral position.
2. Align both shifter tube levers on the mast jacket in Neutral. Install a $^{3}/_{16}''$–$^{7}/_{32}''$ (4.76–5.56mm) gauge to hold them in place. The gauge is inserted in the holes of the levers.
3. Connect the control rods to the tube levers, making sure that the clamps and tube levers are properly positioned in Neutral.
4. Remove the gauge and move the gearshift lever through all positions to be sure that the adjustment is correct in all positions.

4-Speed Column Shift (1968–69)

1. Raise and support the van.
2. Place the shifter lever in Neutral.
3. Disconnect the 1st/2nd shift rod from the cross-shaft lever. Disconnect the 3rd/4th shift rod from the transmission lever. Disconnect the reverse cable from the reverse lever, by removing the C-clip. If necessary, manually operate the transmission and put it in Neutral.
4. Remove the engine splash shield. Install a fabricated pin through the upper control shaft bracket into the cutouts in the shaft levers and into the hole in the base of the control shaft.
5. Adjust the swivel on the end of the 1st/2nd rod to freely enter the cross-shaft lever hole. Reconnect the rod to the lever.
6. Adjust the swivel on the end of the 3rd/4th rod to freely enter the transmission lever. Reconnect the rod to the lever.
7. Adjust the swivel on the end of the reverse cable to freely enter the hole in the reverse lever. If there is not enough room for adjustment, move the cable assembly to the front or rear using the cable-to-bracket attaching nuts. Install the washer and C-clip. Tighten the swivel locknut.
8. Remove the fabricated pin, reinstall the splash shields and lower the vehicle.

CLUTCH

Adjustments

LINKAGE AND FREE PLAY

This adjustment is for the amount of clutch pedal free travel before the throwout bearing contacts the clutch release fingers. It is required periodically to compensate for clutch lining wear. Incorrect adjustment will cause gear grinding and clutch slippage or wear.

NOTE: *If you have a problem with grinding when shifting into gear, shorten the pedal stop bumper to 3/8″ (9.5mm) and readjust the linkage.*

1. Disconnect the clutch fork return spring at the fork on the clutch housing.
2. Loosen the outer adjusting nut (A) and back it off approximately ½″ (12.7mm) from the swivel.

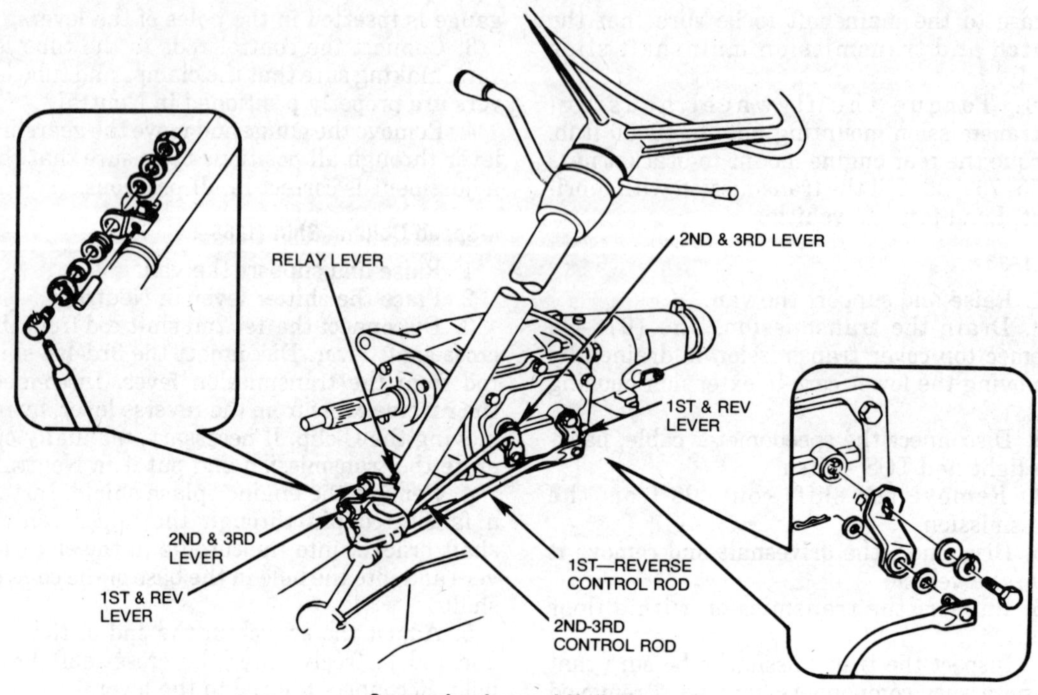

3-speed column shift linkage

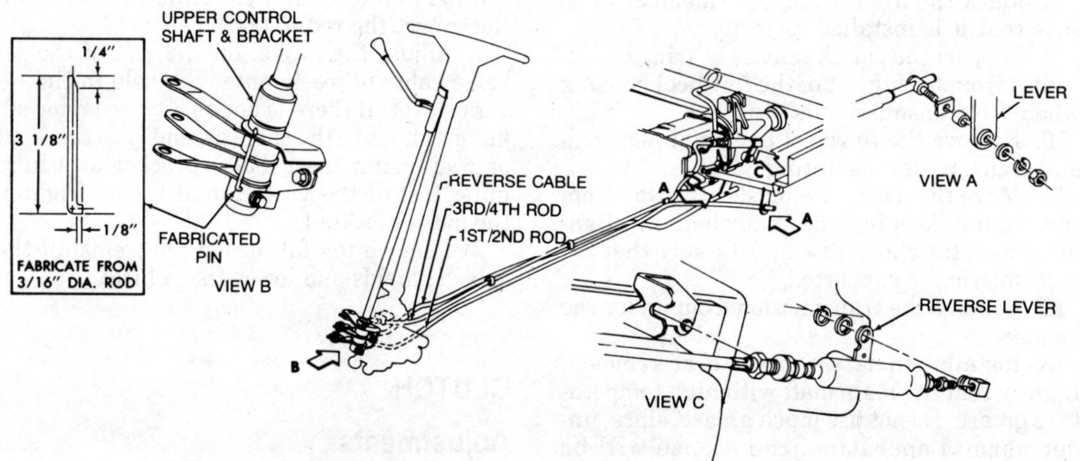

4-speed column shift linkage

3. Hold the clutch fork pushrod against the fork to move the throwout bearing against the clutch fingers. The pushrod will slide through the swivel at the cross-shaft.

4. Adjust the inner adjusting nut (B) to obtain $^{3}/_{16}$″–¼″ (4.76–6.35mm) clearance between nut (B) and the swivel. The clearance should be ¼″ (6.35mm) for 1973 and later models.

5. Release the pushrod, connect the return spring and tighten the outer nut (a) to lock the swivel against the inner nut (B).

6. Check the free travel at the pedal and readjust as necessary. It should be ¾–1″ (19–15mm) through 1973 and 1¼–1½″ (32–38mm) starting 1974.

Driven Disc and Pressure Plate

REMOVAL AND INSTALLATION

CAUTION: *The clutch driven disc contains asbestos, which has been determined to be a cancer causing agent. Never clean clutch surfaces with compressed air! Avoid inhaling any dust from any clutch surface! When*

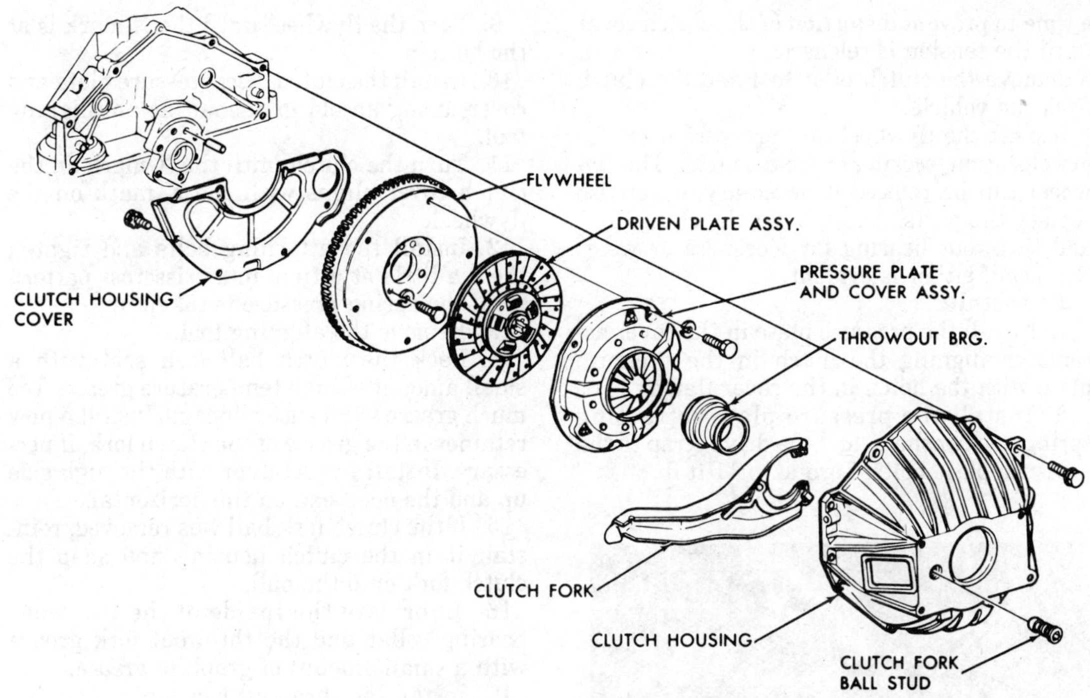

Exploded view of a typical diaphragm clutch

cleaning clutch surfaces, use a commercially available brake cleaning fluid.

There are two types of clutch pressure plates used, diaphragm and coil spring. In general, the larger heavy duty clutches are usually of the coil spring pressure plate type. Most removal and installation details are similar for both types.

Diaphragm Spring Pressure Plate

1. Remove the transmission as previously outlined.

2. Disconnect the fork pushrod and remove the flywheel housing. Remove the clutch throwout bearing from the fork.

3. Remove the clutch fork by pressing it away from the ball mounting with a screwdriver until the fork snaps loose from the ball or remove the ball stud from the clutch housing.

4. Install a pilot tool (an old mainshaft makes a good pilot tool) to hold the clutch while you are removing it.

NOTE: *Before removing the clutch from the flywheel, matchmark the flywheel, the clutch cover and one of the pressure plate lugs. These parts must be reassembled in their original positions as they are a balanced assembly.*

5. Loosen the clutch attaching bolts one turn at

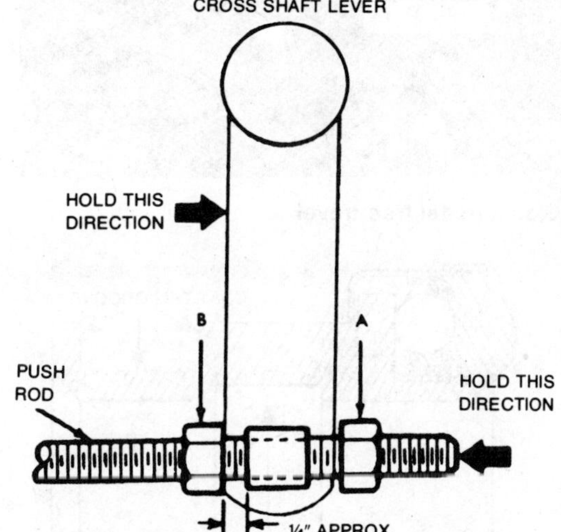

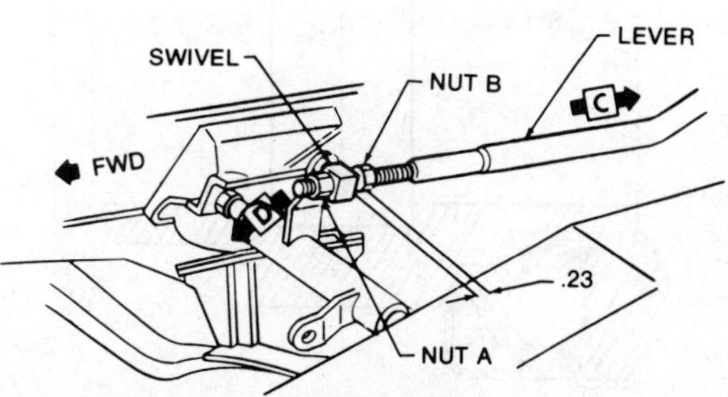

Clutch pedal free travel adjustment

a time to prevent distortion of the clutch cover until the tension is released.

6.Remove the clutch pilot tool and the clutch from the vehicle.

Inspect the flywheel and pressure plate for discoloration, scoring or wear marks. The flywheel can be refaced if necessary, otherwise replace the parts. Also inspect the clutch fork and throwout bearing for looseness or wear. Replace if either is evident.

To install:

7. Install the pressure plate in the cover assembly, aligning the notch in the pressure plate with the notch in the cover flange.

8. Install the pressure plate retracting spring, lockwashers, and the drive strap to the pressure plate bolts. Torque to 11 ft.lb.

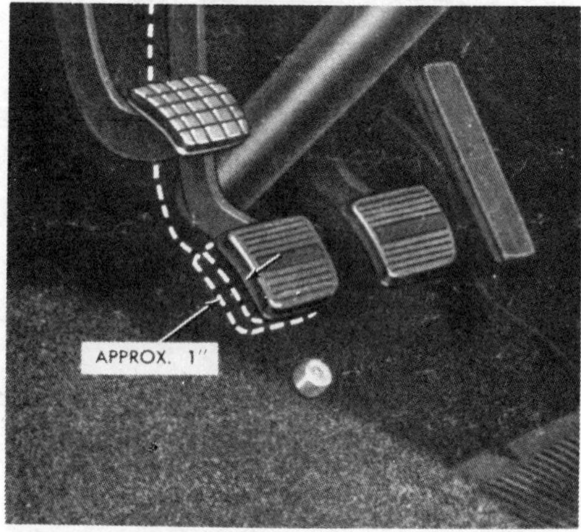

Clutch pedal free travel

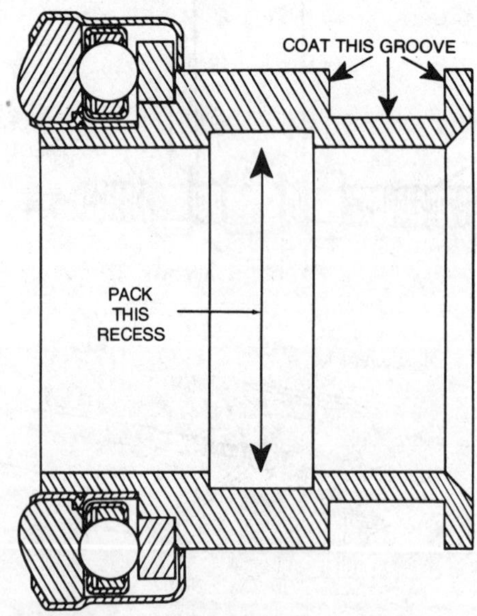

Lubrication points on the clutch throwout bearing

9. Turn the flywheel until the X mark is at the bottom.

10. Install the clutch disc, pressure plate and cover, using an old mainshaft as an aligning tool.

11. Turn the clutch until the X mark on the clutch cover aligns with the X mark on the flywheel.

12. Install the attaching bolts and tighten them a little at a time in a crisscross pattern until the spring pressure is taken up.

13. Remove the aligning tool.

14. Pack the clutch ball fork seat with a small amount of high temperature grease. Too much grease will cause slippage. Install a new retainer in the groove of the clutch fork, if necessary. Install the retainer with the high side up and the open end on the horizontal.

15. If the clutch fork ball was removed, reinstall it in the clutch housing and snap the clutch fork onto the ball.

16. Lubricate the inside of the throwout bearing collar and the throwout fork groove with a small amount of graphite grease.

17. Install the throwout bearing.

18. Install the flywheel housing and transmission.

19. Further installation is the reverse of removal. Adjust the clutch linkage.

Coil Spring Pressure Plate

Basically, the same procedures apply to diaphragm clutch removal as to the coil spring clutch removal.

When loosening the clutch holding bolts, loosen them only a turn or two at a time in order to avoid bending the rim of the cover. It will be helpful to place wood or metal spacers, about 3/8" (9.5mm) thick, between the clutch levers and the cover to hold the levers down as the holding bolts are being removed or when the clutch is being removed from the engine.

Master Cylinder

REMOVAL AND INSTALLATION

1. Disconnect the negative battery cable.
2. Remove the lower steering column covers.
3. Remove the lower left side air conditioning duct (if necessary).
4. Remove the retainer clip and washer from the pushrod.
5. Disconnect the pushrod and remove the wave washer.
6. Disconnect the reservoir hose.
7. Disconnect the secondary cylinder hydraulic line from the master cylinder.
8. Remove the nuts that secure the master cylinder and remove the master cylinder.

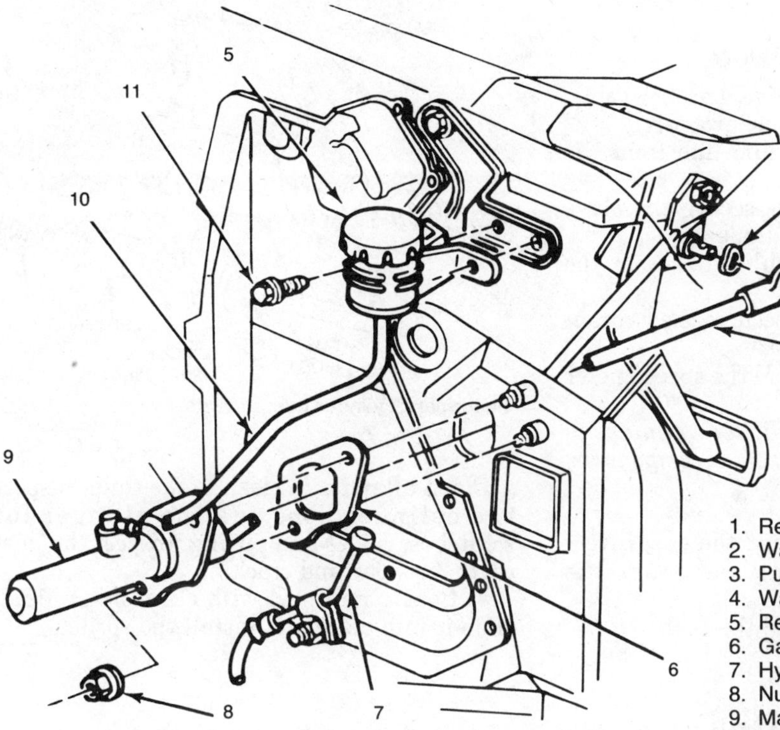

1. Retainer
2. Washer
3. Pushrod
4. Wave Washer
5. Reservoir
6. Gasket
7. Hydraulic line, secondary cylinder
8. Nut
9. Master cylinder
10. Reservoir Hose
11. Screw

Master cylinder and reservoir

9. Scrape all gasket material from the master cylinder and the cowl.

10. Remove the screws that secure the reservoir and remove the reservoir.

OVERHAUL

1. Remove the adapter and the seal from the master cylinder.

2. Pull the dust cover back and remove the snapring.

3. Shake the pushrod and the plunger out of the master cylinder and remove the following:

- The front seal.
- The spring.
- The support.
- The rear seal and the shim.

Clean all parts in clean brake fluid. Inspect the cylinder bore and the plunger for scratches, ridges and pitting. Inspect the dust cover for wear and cracking.

4. Lubricate all seals with clean brake fluid.

5. Install the shim and a new seal with the flat against the shim.

6. Install the support and the spring.

7. Install a new seal.

8. Coat the cylinder boar with clean brake fluid and slide the plunger and the pushrod in.

9. Push the pushrod in and install the snapring.

10. Coat the inside of the dust cover with grease and slide it into place.

11. Install a new seal and the adapter, and install the master cylinder.

12. Installation is the reverse of the removal procedure.

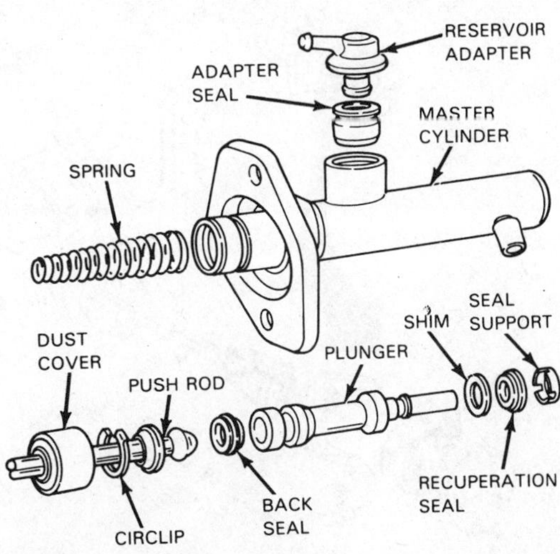

Master Cylinder - Exploded View

Slave Cylinder

REMOVAL AND INSTALLATION

1. Disconnect the negative battery cable. Raise and support the vehicle properly.
2. Disconnect the hydraulic line from the slave cylinder.
3. Remove the nuts that secure the slave cylinder and remove the cylinder.
4. Disconnect the hydraulic line from the master cylinder.
5. Remove the nut that secures the hydraulic line and remove the line.
6. Reinstall the nut to hold the speedometer cable in place.

NOTE: *Cover all hydraulic line openings to keep dirt and moisture out of the components.*

OVERHAUL

1. Remove the pushrod and the dust cover.
2. Remove the snapring and shake the plunger out.
3. Remove the spring and the seal.

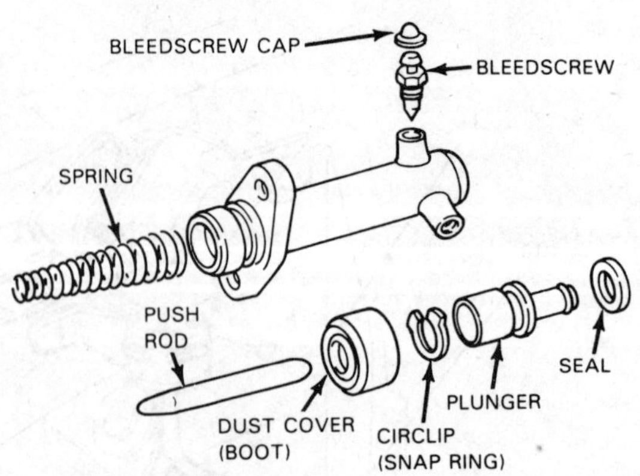

Secondary cylinder components

Clean all parts in clean brake fluid. Inspect the cylinder bore and the plunger for scratches, ridges and pitting. Inspect the dust cover for wear and cracking.

4. Coat a new seal with clean brake fluid, slide it into place and install the spring.

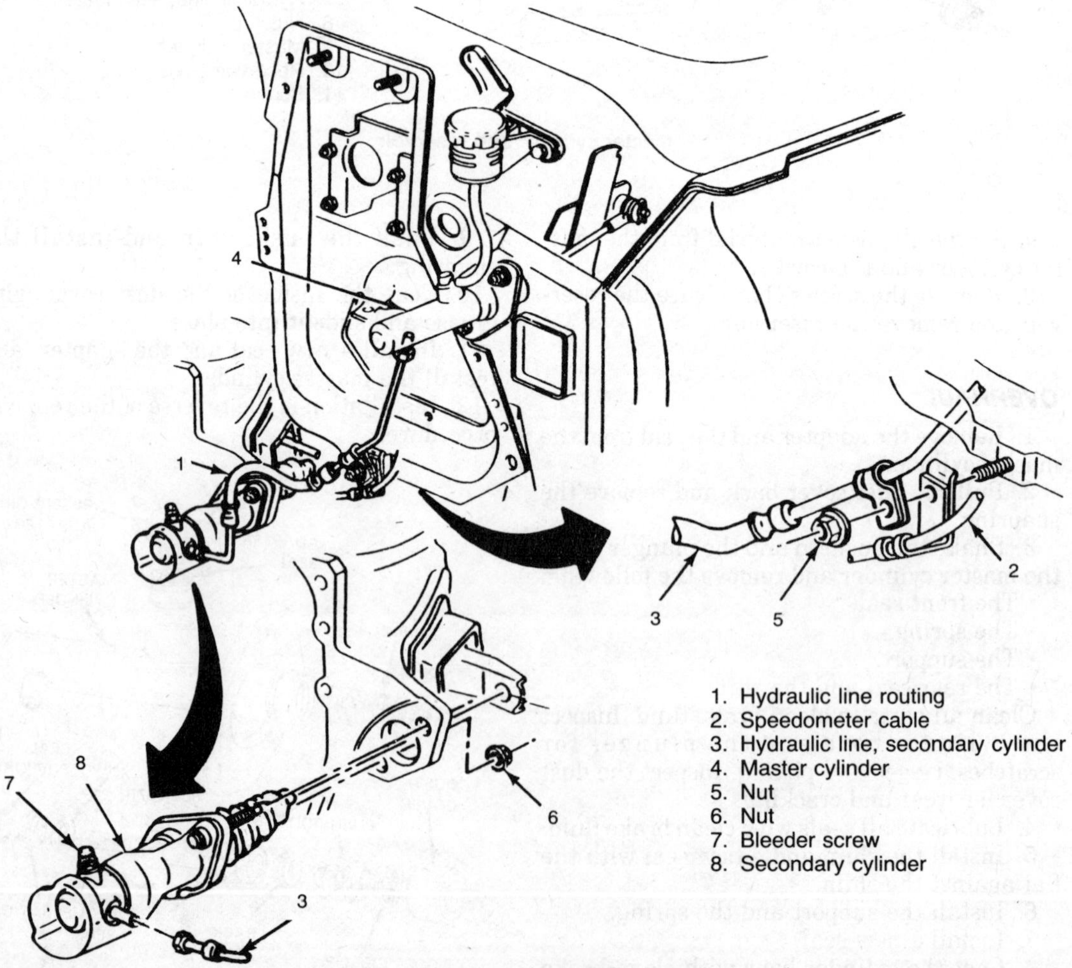

1. Hydraulic line routing
2. Speedometer cable
3. Hydraulic line, secondary cylinder
4. Master cylinder
5. Nut
6. Nut
7. Bleeder screw
8. Secondary cylinder

Secondary cylinder and hydraulic line

5. Coat the hydraulic bore with clean brake fluid and slide the plunger in.

6. Push the plunger in and install the snapring.

7. Coat the inside of the dust cover with grease and slide it into place.

8. Install the pushrod and install the slave cylinder.

9. Installation is the reverse of the removal procedure.

AUTOMATIC TRANSMISSION

Three automatic transmissions are used. The 2-speed Powerglide was last used in 1971. The 3-speed Turbo Hydra-Matic 350 was introduced in 1969. A heavier duty Turbo Hydra-Matic 400 is used on 1977–86 G-20, G-30 and 3500 350 and 400 V8s. Some 1980 and later transmissions use the Torque Converter Clutch system. 1982 and later models are available with a Turbo Hydra-Matic 700-R4 4 speed automatic which incorporates the torque converter clutch. No band adjustments are necessary or possible on Turbo Hydra-Matic transmissions; they use clutches instead of bands.

Identification

The transmissions can be quickly identified visually: the word Powerglide is embossed on the right side of the Powerglide case; the Turbo Hydra-Matic 350 has an almost square shaped pan with the right rear corner cut off diagonally; the 400 has an irregularly shaped pan. The Turbo Hydra-Matic 350 has a cable operated downshift linkage connected the the carburetor throttle linkage, while the 400 has an electrical downshift switch on the accelerator linkage.

Fluid Pan and Filter

REMOVAL AND INSTALLATION

The fluid should be drained with the transmission warm. It is easier to change the fluid if the truck is raised somewhat from the ground, but this is not always easy without a lift. The transmission must be level for it to drain properly.

1. Place a shallow pan underneath to catch the transmission fluid (about 5 pints). On earlier models, the transmission pan has a drain plug. Remove this and drain the fluid. For later models, loosen all the pan bolts, then pull one corner down to drain most of the fluid. If it sticks, VERY CAREFULLY pry the pan loose. You can buy aftermarket drain plug kits that makes this operation a bit less messy, once installed.

NOTE: *If the fluid removed smells burnt, serious transmission troubles, probably due to overheating, should be suspected.*

2. Remove the pan bolts and empty out the pan. On some models, there may not be much room to get at the screws at the front of the pan.

3. Clean the pan with solvent and allow it to air dry. If you use a rag to wipe it out, you risk leaving bits of lint and threads in the transmission.

4. Remove the filter or strainer retaining bolts. On the Turbo Hydra-Matic 400, there are two screws securing the filter or screen to the valve body. A reusable strainer may be found on some models. The strainer may be cleaned in solvent and air dried thoroughly. The filter and gasket must be replaced.

5. Install a new gasket and filter.

6. Install a new gasket on the pan, and tighten the bolts evenly to 12 foot pounds in a criss-cross pattern.

7. Add DEXRON® or DEXRON®II transmission fluid through the dipstick tube. The correct amount is in the Capacities Chart. Do not overfill.

8. With the gearshift lever in PARK, start the engine and let it idle. Do not race the engine.

9. Move the gearshift lever through each position, holding the brakes. Return the lever to PARK, and check the fluid level with the engine idling. The level should be between the two dimples on the dipstick, about ¼" (6mm) below the ADD mark. Add fluid, if necessary.

10. Check the fluid level after the truck has been driven enough to thoroughly warm up the transmission. Details are given under Fluid Level Checks earlier in the Chapter. If the

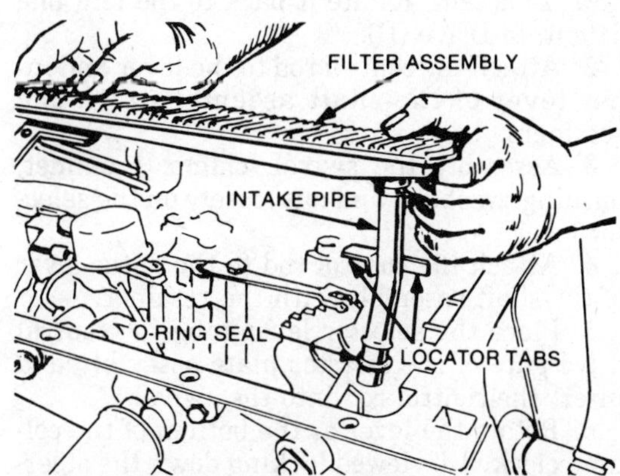

The Turbo Hydra-Matic 400 filter has an O-ring on the intake pipe; check the condition of this O-ring, and replace as necessary

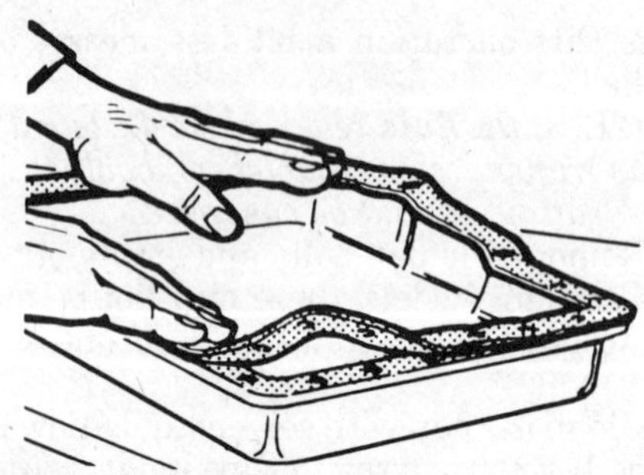

Install the new gasket to the pan

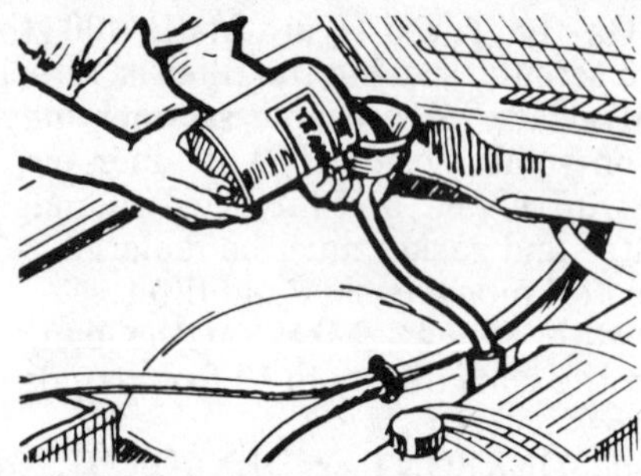

Transmission fluid is added through the dipstick tube

transmission is overfilled, the excess must be drained off. Overfilling causes aerated fluid, resulting in transmission slippage and probable damage.

Adjustments

SHIFT LINKAGE

Powerglide

1. Loosen the shift rod adjusting nut at the bottom of the steering column. Set the transmission lever in Drive (D). Determine Drive by shifting the lever all the way to the right to the Low (L) detent. Rotate it back to the left, one detent, to Drive (D).
2. Attach the control rod to the lever and inner lever of the shaft assembly with the retainers.
3. Assembly the swivel, clamp, grommet, bushing, washers, and nut loosely on the selector lever.
4. Attach the control rod to the outer lever of the shaft assembly with the retainer.
5. Place the selector lever tang in Neutral drive gate of the selector plate assembly and insert the control rod into the swivel.
6. Rotate the lever at the bottom of the column clockwise viewed looking down the steering column, until the tang contacts the Drive side of the Neutral/Drive gate.
7. Tighten the nut.

Turbo Hydra-Matic 350, 400, and 700-R4

THROUGH 1976

1. Lift the selector lever toward the steering wheel and allow the selector lever to be positioned in Drive by the detent. Do not use the selector lever pointer as a reference.
2. Release the selector lever. The lever should not be able to go into Low unless the lever is lifted.
3. Lift the selector lever toward the steering wheel and allow the lever to be positioned in Neutral by the transmission detent.
4. Release the selector lever. The lever should not be able to engage reverse unless the lever is lifted. A properly adjusted linkage will prevent the lever from moving beyond both the Neutral and Drive detents unless the lever is lifted.
5. If adjustment is required, remove the screw and spring washer from the swivel clamp.
6. Set the transmission lever in Neutral by moving it counterclockwise to 1 and then 3 detents clockwise.
7. Put the transmission selector lever in Neutral as determined by the mechanical stop in the steering column.
8. Assembly the swivel spring and washer to the lever and tighten.

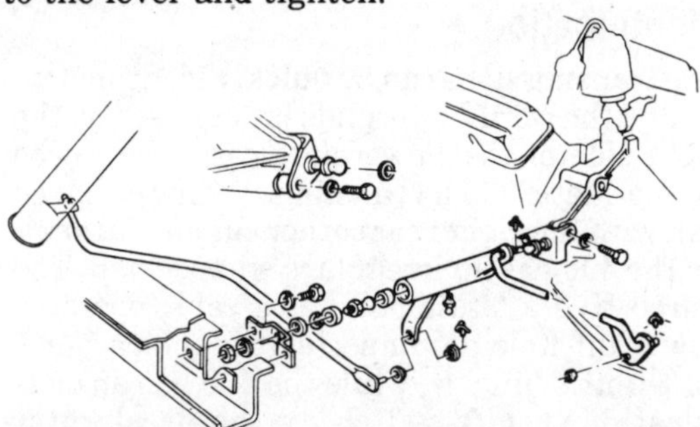

Turbo Hydra-Matic shift linkage adjustment —through 1976

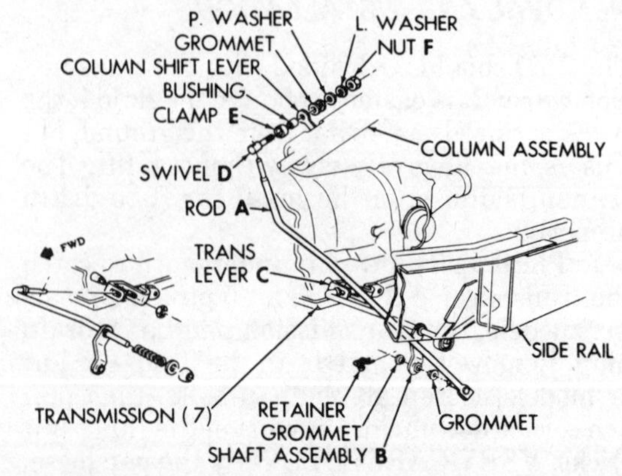

1977 and later shift linkage adjustment

9. Readjust the Neutral safety switch if necessary.

10. If the indicator pointer fails to line up properly with the gear symbol, adjust the position of the pointer and scale.

1977–81

CAUTION: *Perform the procedure exactly and in the order presented. Failure to do so may lead to premature transmission failure due to operation without the controls in the full detent positon. Such operation will result in reduced oil pressure, and therefore only partial engagement of the drive clutches. Partial engagement of the clutches with sufficient pressure to cause apparent normal operation will result in transmission failure after only a few miles of operation.*

1. Remove the nut (F) and slide off the washers, grommet, bushing and clamp (E). Remove swivel (D).
2. Remove the retainer, grommets and the transmission lever (C) from the shaft assembly.
3. Set the transmission lever (C) in the Neutral position either by moving the lever (C) counterclockwise to the L1 position, then clockwise 3 steps to the Neutral position, or by moving the lever (C) clockwise to the Park position, then counterclockwise 2 steps to the Neutral position.
4. Set the column shift lever in the Neutral position by rotating the shift lever until it locks into the stop in the column. Do not use the gear select pointer as a reference to position the column shift lever.
5. Attach rod (A) to the shaft assembly (B) as shown.
6. Slide the swivel (D) and the clamp (E) onto rod (A). Align the column shift lever and loosely attach the assembly.
7. Hold the column shift lever against the Neutral stop, on the Park postion side.
8. Tighten the nut (F) to 18 ft.lb.
9. Adjust the indicator needle if necessary. It may also be necessary to adjust the neutral start switch.

1982 AND LATER

1. Set the trans lever **A** in the neutral position by moving it clockwise to the **Park** detent, then counterclockwise 2 dents to **Neutral**.
2. Set the column shift lever to the **Neutral** gate notch, by rotating it until the shift lever drops into the **Neutral** gate. Do not use the indicator pointer as a reference to position the shift lever, as this will not be accurate.
3. Attach rod **C** to the transmission shaft assembly as shown.
4. Slide the swivel and clamp onto rod **C** and align it with the column shift lever. Complete the attachment.
5. Hold the column lever against the **Neutral** stop on the **Park** position side. Tighten the nut.

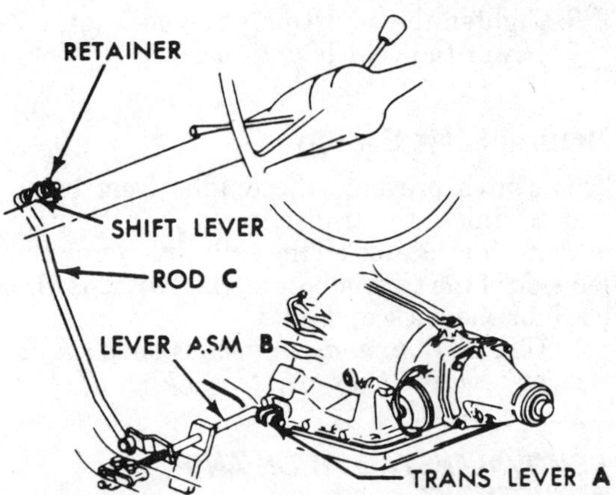

1982 and later Turbo Hydra-Matic automatic transmission linkage adjustment, column shift shown

POWERGLIDE LOW BAND ADJUSTMENT

Only the Powerglide transmission has bands requiring adjustment; the Turbo Hydra-Matic uses non-adjustable clutches.

1. Raise and support the vehicle.
2. Place the selector lever in Neutral.
3. Remove the protective cap from the low band adjusting screw on the left side of the transmission.
4. Loosen the adjusting screw locknut ¼ turn and hold it in this position with a wrench.
5. Using an in.lb. torque wrench, adjust the band adjusting screw to 70 in.lb., and back the screw off 4 complete turns for a band that has been in operation 6,000 miles or more; or, 3 complete turns for a band that has been in operation less than 6,000 miles.

NOTE: *The back-off figure is not approximate; it must be exact.*

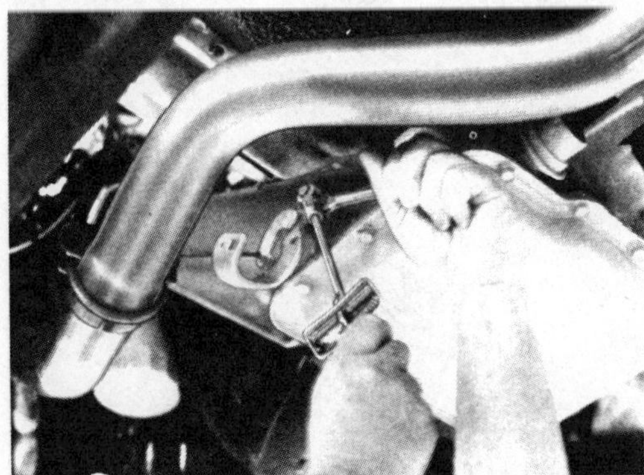

Adjusting the Powerglide low band

6. Tighten the adjusting screw locknut.
7. Lower the vehicle and road test.

Neutral Start Switch

This switch prevents the engine from being started unless the transmission is in Neutral or Park. It is located on the shift linkage on the left side of the transmission. The switch is also used for the back-up lights.

NOTE: *The manual transmission back-up light switch is on the rear of the transmission.*

REMOVAL/INSTALLATION AND ADJUSTMENT

1. Loosen the clamp on the switch actuating rod on models through 1973 or loosen the switch mounting screws on 1974 and later models.
2. Make sure the transmission is in Neutral.
3. Insert a pin through the hole in the switch actuating arm into the switch body to hold the switch in the Neutral position. Adjust as necessary to make the pin fit.
4. Tighten the adjustment. Remove the pin.
5. Check that the engine can be started only in Park and Neutral and that the backup lights go on only in Reverse. Adjust as necessary.

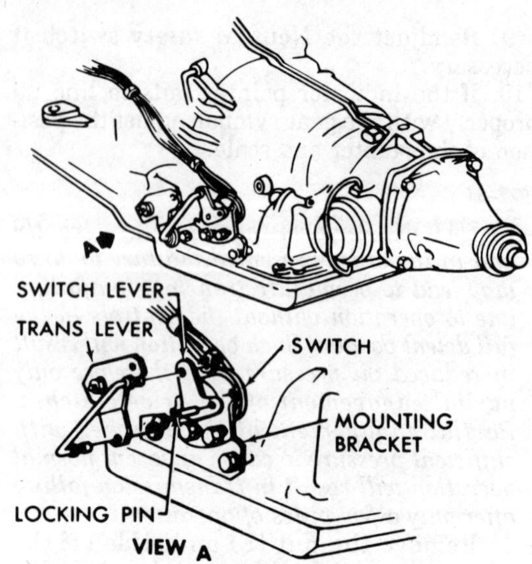

1974 and later neutral start safety switch

DOWNSHIFT ADJUSTMENT

Powerglide

1967–70 INLINE 6-CYLINDER

1. With the accelerator depressed, the bell crank on the engine must be in the wide open throttle position.
2. The firewall lever must be $\frac{1}{64}$–$\frac{1}{16}$" (0.39–

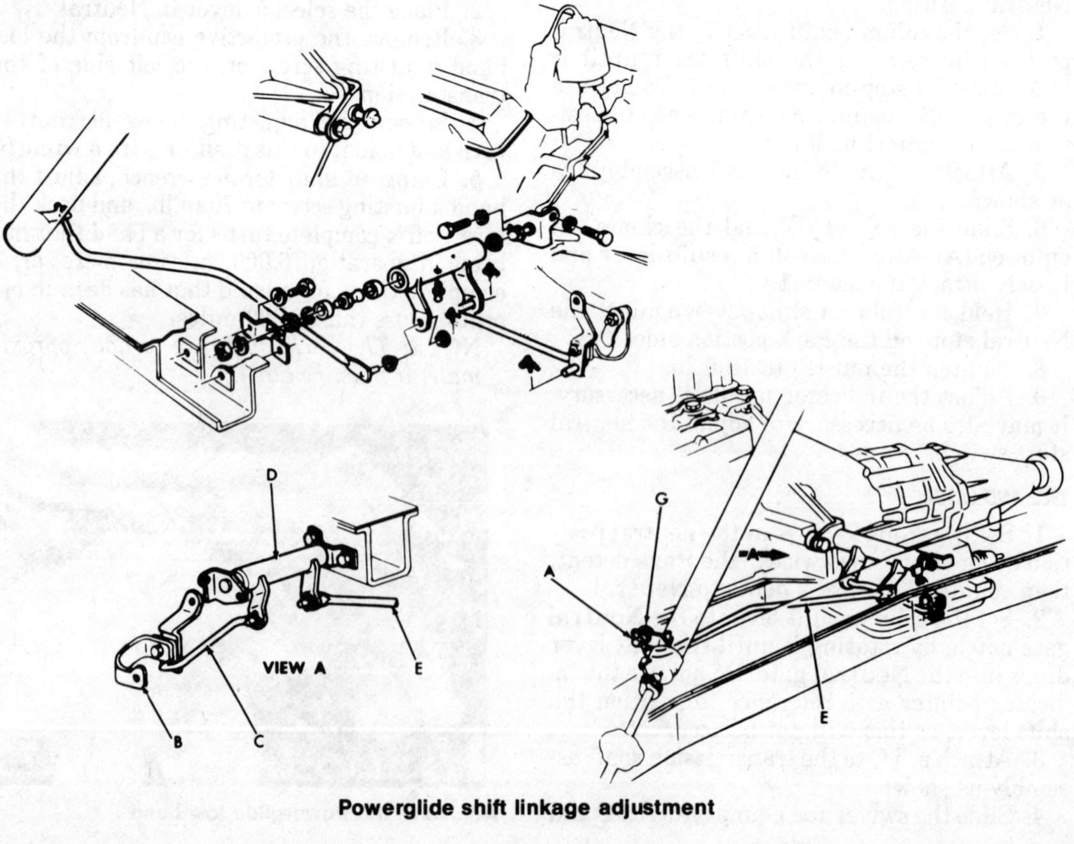

Powerglide shift linkage adjustment

1.6mm) off the lever stop and the transmission lever must be against the transmission internal stop.

1971 INLINE 6-CYLINDER

1. Remove the air cleaner.
2. Disconnect the throttle return spring.
3. Rotate the lever through the wide open throttle position and the throttle valve lever through the detent.
4. Hold the slot on the rod against the pin on the lever and adjust the swivel on the rod so that it freely enters the hold in the lever.
5. Hold the rod perpendicular to the pin on the lever and tighten the swivel nut. Connect the carburetor return spring.
6. Check the linkage for freedom of operation.

V8s

1. Remove the air cleaner.
2. Disconnect the accelerator linkage at the carburetor.
3. Disconnect the accelerator return spring and throttle valve rod return springs.
4. Pull the throttle valve rod forward until the transmission is through the detent. Open the carburetor to the wide open throttle position. The carburetor must reach the wide open throttle position at the same time that the ball stud contacts the end of the slot in the upper throttle valve rod.

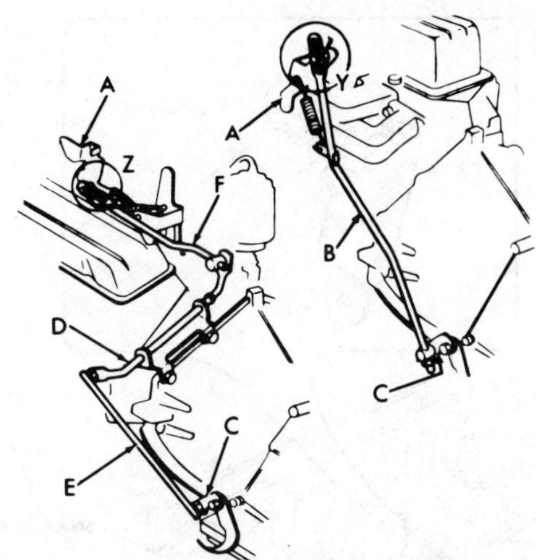

Powerglide downshift linkage adjustment

5. Adjust the swivel on the end of the upper throttle valve rod as per Step 4. The allowable tolerance is approximately $^{1}/_{32}$″ (0.79mm).
6. Connect and adjust the accelerator linkage.
7. Check for freedom of operation. Install the air cleaner.

Turbo Hydra-Matic 350

This cable runs from the carburetor linkage to the transmission. It regulates the throttle position at which a downshift occurs.

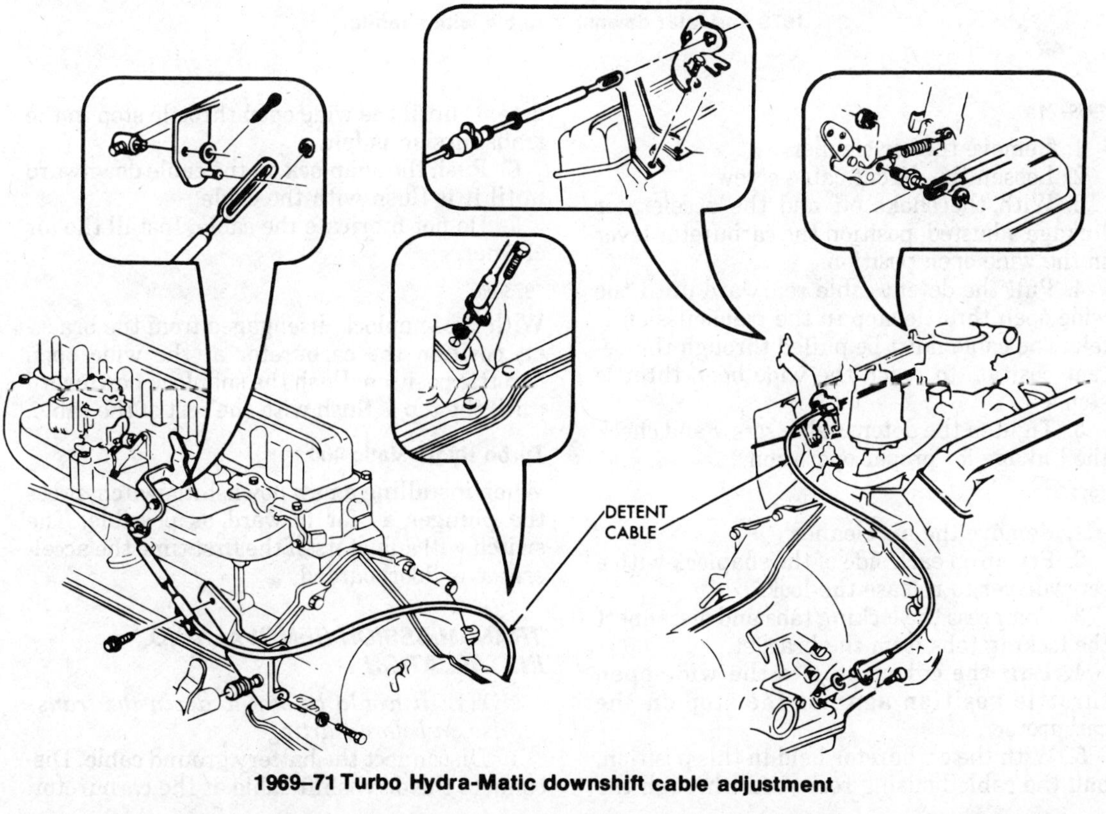

1969–71 Turbo Hydra-Matic downshift cable adjustment

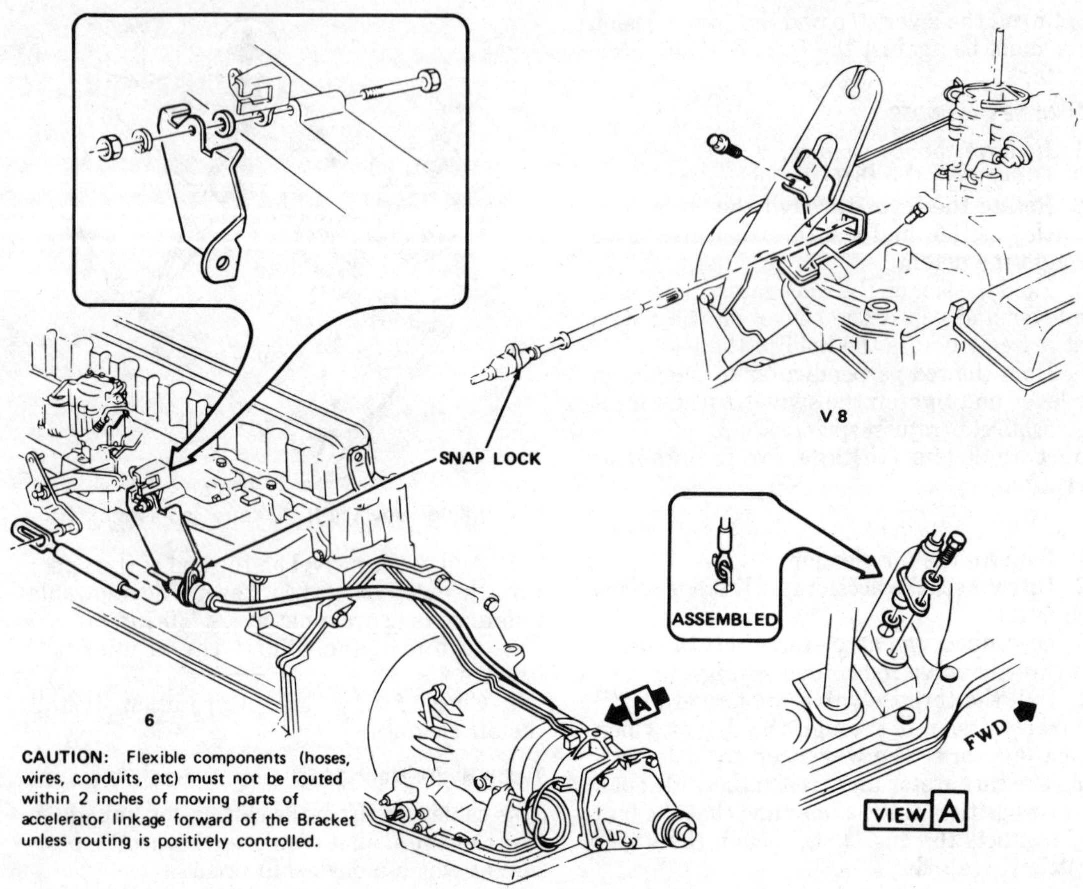

1973 and later downshift cable with snap-lock

1969–71

1. Remove the air cleaner.
2. Loosen the detent cable screw.
3. With the choke off and the accelerator linkage adjusted, position the carburetor lever in the wide open position.
4. Pull the detent cable rearward until the wide open throttle stop in the transmission is felt. The cable must be pulled through the detent position to reach the wide open throttle stop.
5. Tighten the detent cable screw and check the linkage for proper operation.

1972

1. Remove the air cleaner.
2. Pry up on each side of the snaplock with a screwdriver to release the lock.
3. Compress the locking tabs and disconnect the locking tabs from the bracket.
4. Pull the carburetor to the wide open throttle position against the stop on the carburetor.
5. With the carburetor held in this position, pull the cable housing rearward (through the detent) until the wide open throttle stop in the transmission is felt.
6. Push the snaplock on the cable downward until it is flush with the cable.
7. Do not lubricate the cable. Install the air cleaner.

1973–86

With the snaplock disengaged from the bracket, position the carburetor at the wide open throttle position. Push the snaplock downward until the top is flush with the rest of the cable.

Turbo Hydra-Matic 400

When installing a new downshift switch, press the plunger as far forward as possible. The switch will adjust itself the first time the accelerator is floorboarded.

TRANSMISSSION REMOVAL AND INSTALLATION

NOTE: *It would be best to drain the transmission before starting.*

1. Disconnect the battery ground cable. Disconnect the downshift cable at the carburetor.

2. Raise and support the truck.
3. Remove the driveshaft, after matchmarking its flange.
4. Disconnect the speedometer cable, downshift cable, vacuum modulator line, shift linkage, and fluid cooler lines at the transmission.
5. Support the transmission and unbolt the rear mount from the crossmember. Remove the crossmember.
6. Remove the converter underpan, matchmark the flywheel and converter, and remove the converter bolts.
7. Support the engine and lower the transmission slightly for access to the upper transmission to engine bolts.
8. Remove the transmission to engine bolts and pull the transmission back. Remove the filler tube. Rig up a strap or keep the front of the transmission up so the converter doesn't fall out.
9. Reverse the procedure for installation. Bolt the transmission to the engine first (35 ft.lb.), then the converter to the flywheel (35 ft.lb.). Make sure that the converter attaching lugs are flush and that the converter can turn freely before installing the bolts.

NOTE: *Lubricate the internal yoke splines at the transmission end of the driveshaft with lithium based grease. The grease should seep out through the vent hole.*

DRIVELINE

Tubular driveshafts are used on all models incorporating needle bearing U-joints. An internally splined sleeve at the forward end compensates for variation in distance between the rear axle and the transmission.

Long wheelbase models use a 2-piece driveshaft with a center support bearing. The front section is supported at the rear end by a rubber cushioned ball bearing mounted in a bracket attached to the frame crossmember. The ball bearing is permanently sealed and lubricated.

Driveshaft and U-Joints

REMOVAL AND INSTALLATION

1. Raise the vehicle and support it on jackstands. There is less chance of lubricant leakage from the rear of the transmission if the rear is raised.
2. Matchmark the driveshaft and rear pinion flange and both halves of 2-piece driveshaft. Remove the U-bolts or straps at the rear axle. Tape the bearing cups to the trunnions.
3. On models with 2-piece driveshaft, remove the bolts attaching the bearing support to the frame crossmember.

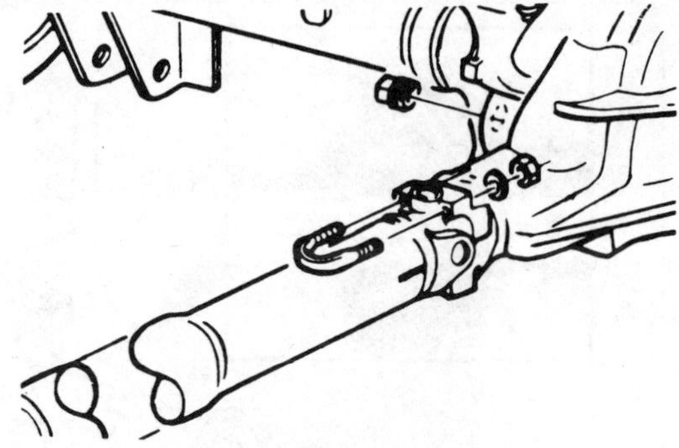

Rear driveshaft U-bolt attachment

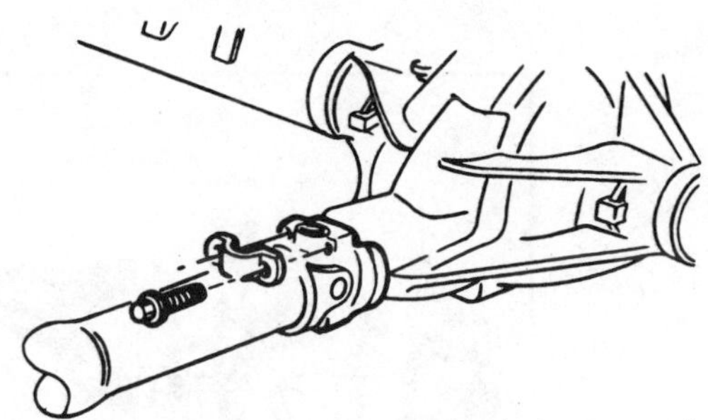

Rear driveshaft strap attachment

4. Slide the driveshaft forward and lower it. Slide the driveshaft toward the rear of the vehicle and disengage the splined sleeve from the output shaft of the transmission.
5. Remove the driveshaft from under the van.
6. Installation is the reverse of removal. Use the matchmarks made previously to help facilitate alignment. For models with 2-piece driveshaft, install the front half into the transmission and install the support to the crossmember. Rotate the shaft so that the front U-joint trunnions so that all are vertical. Rotate the rear shaft 4 splines to the left of the vehicle and connect the front and rear shaft. Some 2-piece driveshafts can only be assembled one way, in which case these instructions can be ignored. Attach the rear U-joint to the axle. On automatic transmission models, lubricate the internal yoke splines at the transmission end of the shaft with lithium base grease. The grease should seep out through the vent hole.

NOTE: *A thump in the rear driveshaft sometimes occurs when releasing the brakes after braking to a stop, especially on a downgrade. This is most common with automatic transmission. It is often caused by the driveshaft splines binding and can be cured by removing the driveshaft, inspecting the splines for rough spots or sharp edges, and carefully lubricating. A similar noise may also be caused*

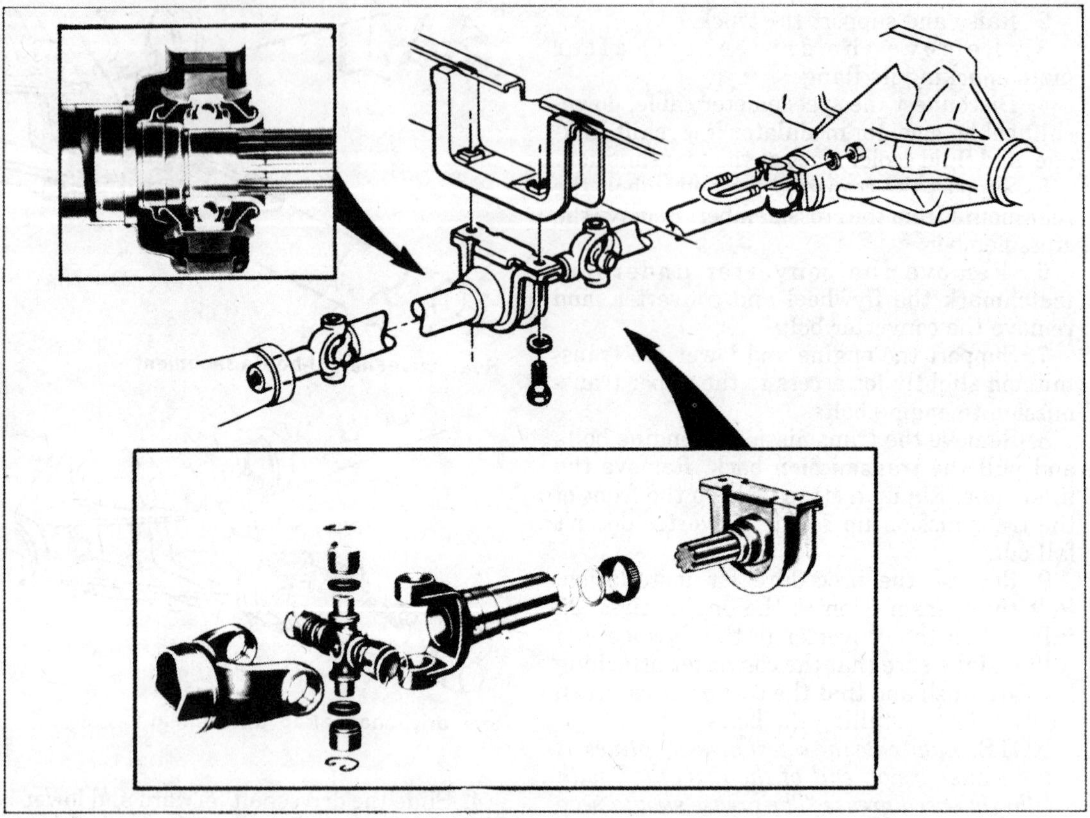

Typical two-piece driveshaft

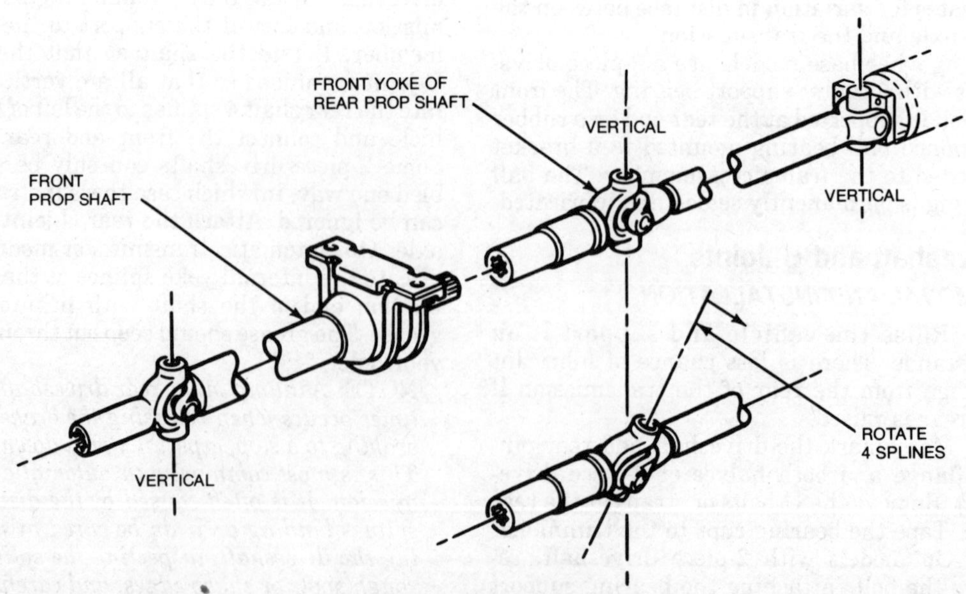

Two piece driveshaft alignment

by the clutch plates in Positraction (through 1973) limited slip rear axles binding. If this isn't caused by wear, it can be cured by draining and refilling the rear axle with the special lubricant and adding Positraction additive, both of which are available from dealers.

U-JOINT OVERHAUL

U-Joint is mechanic's jargon for universal joint. U-joints should not be confused with U-bolts, which are U-shaped bolts used to hold U-joints in place to the axle or transfer case.

There are two types of U-joints used in these trucks. The first is held together by wire snaprings in the yokes. The second type, first used in 1975, is held together with injection molded plastic retainer rings. This type cannot be reassembled, once disassembled. Repair kits are available, however.

Snapring Type

These U-joints may be found on all model years.

1. Remove the driveshaft(s) from the truck.

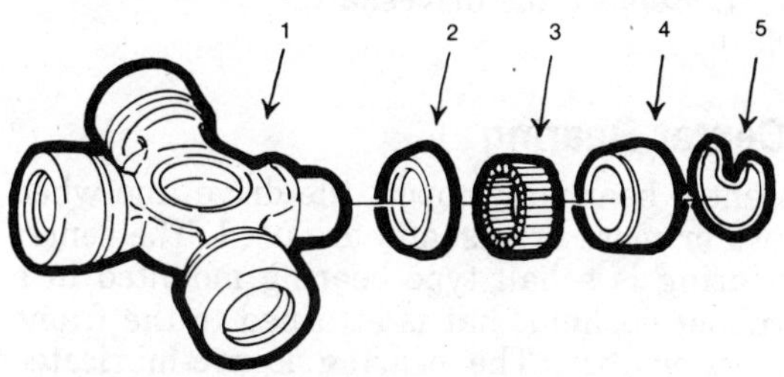

Snap ring type U-joint

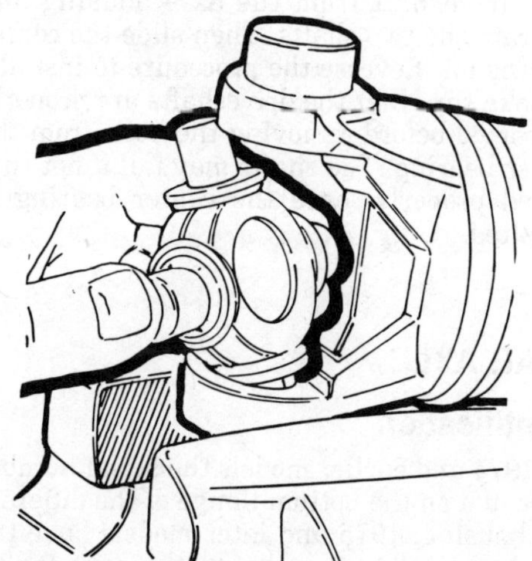

Installing the trunnion on the driveshaft yoke

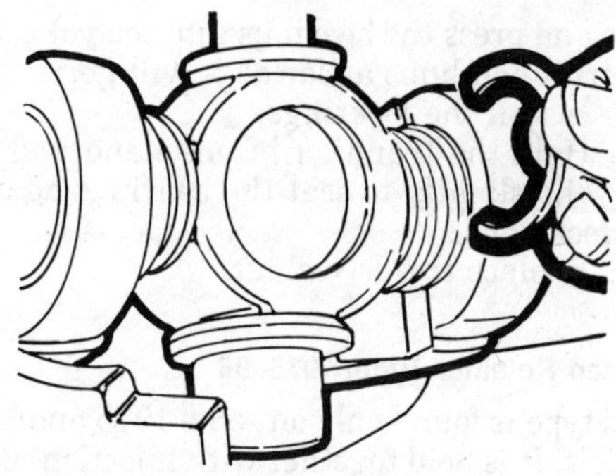

Installing the snap ring

2. Support the lockrings from the yoke and remove the lubrication fitting.
3. Support the yoke in a bench vise. Never clamp the driveshaft tube.
4. Use a socket to press against one trunnion bearing to press the opposite bearing from the yoke.
5. Grasp the cap and work it out.
6. Support the other side of the yoke and press the other bearing cap from the yoke and remove as in Steps 4 and 5.
7. Remove the trunnion from the driveshaft yoke.
8. If equipped with a sliding sleeve, remove the trunnion bearings from the sleeve yoke in the same manner as above. Remove the seal retainer from the end of the sleeve and pull the seal and washer from the retainer.
9. Disassemble the other U-joint. Clean and check the condition of all parts. You can buy U-joint repair kits to replace all the wearing parts.

To assemble the trunnion bearings:

10. Repack the bearings with grease and replace the trunnion dust seals after any operation that requires disassembly of the U-joint. Be sure that the lubricant reservoir at the end of the trunnion is full of lubricant. Fill the reservoirs with lubricant from the bottom.
11. Install the trunnion into the driveshaft

U-joint bearing cup removal with a vise

yoke and press the bearings into the yoke over the trunnion hubs as far as it will go.

12. Install the lockrings.

13. Hold the trunnion in one hand and tap the yoke slightly to seat the bearings against the lockrings.

14. Replace the driveshaft.

Molded Retainer Type, 1975–86

This type is found only on some 1975 and later models. It is held together with injection molded plastic rings.

NOTE: *Don't disassembly these joints unless you have a repair kit. The factory installed joints cannot be reassembled.*

1. Remove the driveshaft.

2. Support the dirveshaft in a horizontal position. Place the U-joint so that the lower ear of the shaft yoke is supported by a 1⅛" socket. Press the lower bearing cup of the yoke ear. This will shear the plastic retaining the lower bearing cup.

NOTE: *Never clamp the driveshaft tubing in a vise.*

3. If the bearing cup is not completely removed, lift the cross, insert a spacer and press the cup completely out.

4. Rotate the driveshaft, shear the opposite plastic retainer, and press the other bearing cup out in the same manner.

5. Remove the cross from the yoke. Production U-joints cannot be reassembled. There are no bearing retainer grooves in the cups. Discard all parts that were removed and substitute those in the overhaul kit.

6. Remove the sheared plastic bearing retainer from the yoke. Drive a small pin or punch through the injection holes to aid in removal.

7. If the other U-joint is to be serviced, remove the bearing cups from the slip yoke in the manner previously described.

8. Be sure that the seals are installed on the service bearing cups to hold the needle bearings in place for handling. Grease the bearings if they aren't pregreased.

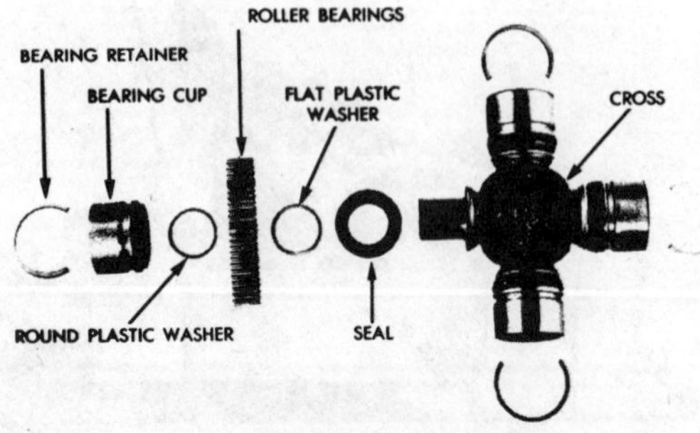

Molded retainer type U-joint repair kit

9. Install one bearing cup partway into one side of the yoke and turn this ear to the bottom.

10. Insert the cross into the yoke so that the trunnion seats freely in the bearing cup.

11. Install the opposite bearing cup partway. Be sure that both trunnions are started straight into the bearing cups.

12. Press against opposite bearing cups, working the cross constantly to be sure that it is free in the cups. If binding occurs, check the needle rollers to be sure that one needle has not become lodged under and end of the trunnion.

13. As soon as one bearing retainer groove is exposed, stop pressing and install the bearing retainer snapring.

14. Continue to press until the opposite bearing retainer can be installed. If difficulty installing the snaprings is encountered, rap the yoke with a hammer to spring the yoke ears slightly.

15. Assemble the other half of the U-joint in the same manner.

16. Check that the cross is free in the cups. If it is too tight, rap the yoke ears again to help seat the bearing retainers.

17. Replace the driveshaft.

Center Bearing

Center bearings support the drive line when two or more driveshafts are used. The center bearing is a ball type bearing mounted in a rubber cushion that is attached to the frame crossmember. The bearing is pre-lubricated and sealed by the manufacturer.

The center bearing is secured to the frame crossmember by two bolts, washers and nuts. Support the driveshafts properly and remove the bolts from the center bearing. Remove the rear driveshaft from the axle housing and seperate the two shafts. Then slide the center bearing off. Reverse the procedure to install.

Make sure that the driveshafts are properly supported before removing the bolts from the center bearing. The shafts may fall if not supported properly, once the center bearing is unbolted.

REAR AXLE

Identification

On 1974 and earlier models the serial number is located on the bottom flange of the differential housing. 1975 and later models have the serial number stamped into the axle shafts, near the differential housing.

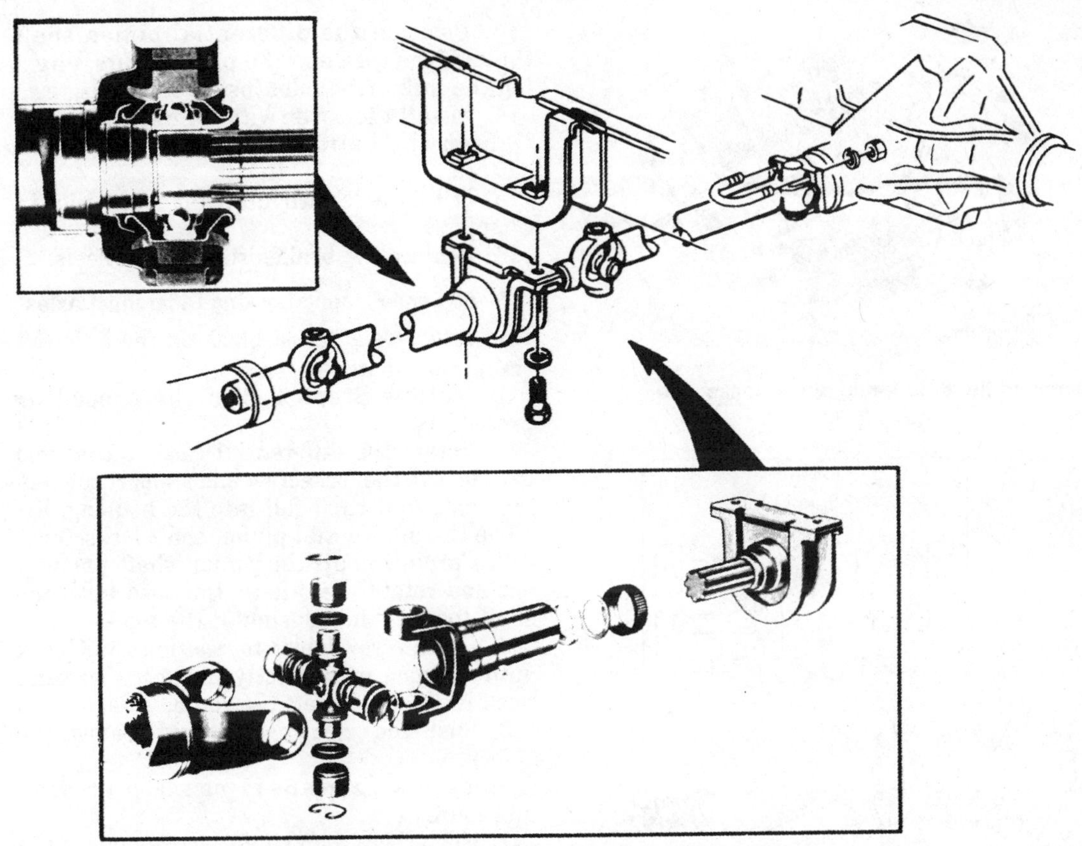

Driveshaft, U-joint and bearing support, 1971 and later

Determining Axle Ratio

Axle ratios offered in these trucks vary from a heavy duty ratio of 4.57:1 to an economy ratio of 2.73:1.

The axle ratio is obtained by dividing the number of teeth on the drive pinion gear into the larger number of teeth on the ring gear. It is always expressed as a proportion and is a simple expression of gear speed reduction and torque multiplication.

To find a unknown axle ratio, make a chalk mark on a tire and on the driveshaft. Move the truck ahead (or back) slowly for one tire rotation and have an observer note the number of driveshaft rotations. The number of driveshaft rotations if the axle ratio. You can get more accuracy by going more than one tire rotation and dividing the result by the number of tire rotations. This can also be done by jacking up both rear wheels and turning them by hand.

The axle ration is also identified by the axle serial number prefix on Chevrolet (GMC) axles. See Chapter 1 for serial number locations; the prefixes are listed in parts books. Dana axles usually have a tag under one of the cover bolts, giving either the ratio or the number of pinion ring gear teeth.

Axle Shaft, Bearing, and Seal

REMOVAL AND INSTALLATION

All Semi-Floating Axles Except 1974–86 Locking Differential

This procedure applies to all standard semi-floating rear axles and to those through 1973 with the optional Positraction limited slip differential.

1. Support the axle on jackstands.
2. Remove the wheels and brake drums.
3. Clean off the differential cover area, loosen the cover to drain the lubricant, and remove the cover.
4. Turn the differential until you can reach the differential pinion shaft lockscrew. Remove the lockscrew and the pinion shaft.
5. Push in on the axle end. Remove the C-lock from the inner (button) end of the shaft.
6. Remove the shaft, being careful of the oil seal.
7. You can pry the oil seal out of the housing

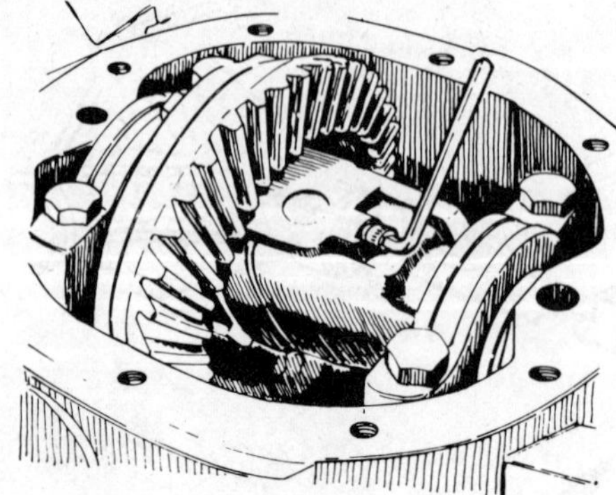

Removing the differential pinion lockscrew

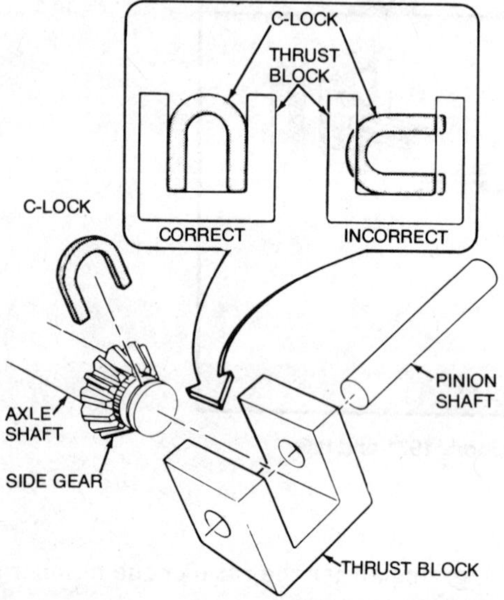

C-lock and thrust block installation—Eaton locking differential used in 1974 and later semi-floating axle

by placing the inner end of the axle shaft behind the steel case of the seal, then prying it out carefully.

8. A puller or a slide hammer is required to remove the bearing from the housing.

9. Pack the new or reused bearing with wheel bearing grease and lubricate the cavity between the seal lips with the same grease.

10. The bearing has to be driven into the housing. Don't use a drift, you might cock the bearing in its bore. Use a piece of pipe or a large socket instead. Drive only on the outer bearing race. In a similar manner, drive the seal in flush with the end of the tube.

11. Slide the shaft into place, turning it slowly until the splines are engaged with the differential. Be careful of the oil seal.

12. Install the C-lock on the inner axle end. Pull the shaft out so that the C-lock seats in the counterbore of the differential side gear.

13. Position the differential pinion shaft through the case and the pinion gears, aligning the lockscrew hole. Install the lockscrew.

14. Install the cover with a new gasket and tighten the bolts evenly in a criss-cross pattern.

15. Fill the axle with lubricant as specified in Chapter 1.

16. Replace the brake drums and wheels.

1974–86 Semi-Floating Locking Differential Axles

This axle uses a thrust block on the differential pinion shaft.

1. Follow Steps 1–3 of the preceding procedure.

2. Rotate the differential case so that you can remove the lockscrew and support the pinion shaft so it can't fall into the housing. Remove the differential pinion shaft lockscrew.

3. Carefully pull the pinion shaft partway out and rotate the differential case until the shaft touches the housing at the top.

4. Use a screwdriver to position the C-lock with its open end directly inward. You can't push in the axle shaft till you do this.

5. Push the axle shaft in and remove the C-lock.

6. Follow Steps 6–11 of the preceding procedure.

7. Keep the pinion shaft partway out of the differential case while installing the C-lock on the axle shaft. Put the C-lock on the axle shaft and carefully pull out on the axle shaft until the C-lock is clear of the thrust block.

8. Follow Steps 13–16 of the previous procedure.

Full-Floating Axles

The procedures are the same for locking and non-locking axles.

The best way to remove the bearings from the wheel hub is with an arbor press. Use of a press reduces the chances of damaging the bearing races, cocking the bearing in its bore, or scoring the hub walls. A local machine shop is probably equipped with the tools to remove and install bearings and seals. However, if one is not available, the hammer and drift method outlined can be used.

1. Support the axles on jackstands.

2. Remove the wheels.

3. Remove the bolts and lock washers that attach the axle shaft flange to the hub.

4. On 1971–72 trucks, install two ½″x13″ bolts in the threaded holes provided in the axle shaft flange. By turning these bolts alternately the axle shaft may be easily started and then removed from the housing.

5. On 1973 and later vans, rap on the flange with a soft faced hammer to loosen the shaft.

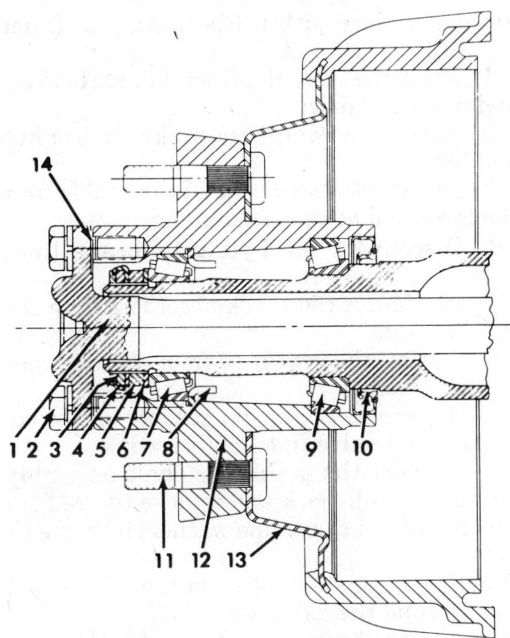

1. Axle shaft
2. Shaft-to-hub bolt
3. Locknut
4. Locknut retainer
5. Adjusting nut
6. Thrust washer
7. Hub outer bearing
8. Snap ring
9. Hub inner bearing
10. Oil seal
11. Wheel bolt
12. Hub assembly
13. Drum assembly
14. Gasket

Full-floating axle bearing and hub details

Grip the rib on the end of the flange with a pair of locking pliers and twist to start shaft removal. Remove the shaft from the axle tube.

6. The hub and drum assembly must be removed to remove the bearings and oil seals. You will need a large socket to remove and later adjust the bearing adjustment nut. There are also special tools available.

7. Disengage the tang of the locknut retainer from the slot or slat of the locknut, then remove the locknut from the housing tube.

8. Disengage the tang of the retainer from the slot or flat of the adjusting nut and remove the retainer from the housing tube.

9. Remove the adjusting nut from the housing tube.

10. Remove the thrust washer from the housing tube.

11. Pull the hub and drum straight off the axle housing.

12. Remove the oil seal and discard.

13. Use a hammer and a long drift to knock the inner bearing, cup, and oil seal from the hub assembly.

14. Remove the outer bearing snapring with a pair of pliers. It may be necessary to tap the bearing outer race away from the retaining ring slightly by tapping on the ring to remove the ring.

Removing the axle shaft—full floating axles

15. Drive the outer bearing from the hub with a hammer and drift.

16. To reinstall the bearings, place the outer bearing into the hub. The larger outside diameter of the bearing should face the outer end of the hub. Drive the bearing into the hub using a washer that will cover both the inner and outer races of the bearing. Place a socket on top of this washer, then drive the bearing into place with a series of light taps. If available, an arbor press should be used for this job.

17. Drive the bearing past the snapring groove, and install the snapring. Then, turning the hub assembly over, drive the bearing back against the snapring. Protect the bearing by placing a washer on top of it. You can use the thrust washer that fits between the bearing and the adjusting nut for the job.

18. Place the inner bearing into the hub. The thick edge should be toward the shoulder in the hub. Press the bearing into the hub until it seats against the shoulder, using a washer and socket as outlined earlier. Make certain that the bearing is not cocked and that it is fully seated on the shoulder.

19. Pack the cavity between the oil seal lips with the front wheel bearing grease specified in Chapter 9, and position it in the hub bore. Carefully press it into place on top of the inner bearing.

20. Pack the wheel bearings with grease, and lightly coat the inside diameter of the hub bearing contact surface and the outside diameter of the axle housing tube.

21. Make sure that the inner bearing, oil seal, axle housing oil deflector, and outer bearing are properly positioned. Install the hub and drum assembly on the axle housing, being careful so as not to damage the oil seal or dislocate other internal components.

22. Install the thrust washer so that the tang on the inside diameter of the washer is in the keyway on the axle housing.

23. Install the adjusting nut. Tighten to 50 ft.lb. while rotating the hub. Back off the nut and retighten to 35 ft.lb., then back off 1/4 turn.

24. Install the tanged retainer against the inner adjusting nut. Align the adjusting nut so that the short tang of the retainer will engage the nearest slot on the adjusting nut.

25. Install the outer locknut and tighten to 65 ft.lb. Bend the long tang of the retainer into the slot of the outer nut. This method of adjustment should provide 0.001–0.010″ (0.0254–0.254mm) end play.

26. Place a new gasket over the axle shaft and position the axle shaft in the housing so that the shaft splines enter the differential side gear. Position the gasket so that the holes are in alignment, and install the flange-to-hub attaching bolts. Torque to 90 ft.lb. through 1975, 115 ft.lb. for 1976 and later.

NOTE: *To prevent lubricant from leaking through the flange holes, apply a non-hardening sealer to the bolt threads. Use the sealer sparingly.*

27. Replace the wheels.

Axle Housing

REMOVAL AND INSTALLATION

Raise the vehicle on a hoist and support the axle assembly with a suitable lifting devise. For the 9¾″ (247.65mm) ring gear and the 10½″ (266.7mm) ring gear axles, raise the vehicle and place jackstands under the frame side rails for support.

1. Drain the lubricant from the axle housing and remove the driveshaft.
2. Remove the wheel, the brake drum or hub and the drum assembly.
3. Disconnect the parking brake cable from the lever and at the brake flange plate.
4. Disconnect the hydraulic brake lines from the connectors.
5. Disconnect the shock absorbers from the axle brackets.
6. Remove the vent hose from the axle vent fitting (if used).
7. Disconnect the height sensing and brake proportional valve linkage (if used).
8. Support the stabilizer shaft assembly with a hydraulic jack and remove (if used).
9. Remove the nuts and washers from the U-bolts.
10. Remove the U-bolts, spring plates and spacers from the axle assembly.
11. Lower the jack and remove the axle assembly.
12. Installation is the reverse of the removal procedure.

Suspension and Steering

7

FRONT SUSPENSION

Chevrolet and GMC vans from 1967–70 use an I-beam front axle with tapered leaf springs and a single shock absorber at each wheel. The I-beam is a conventional reverse Elliot type using solid kingpins and full floating steering knuckle bushing. The front wheel spindles are cast integral with the steering knuckles.

Vans from 1971 use an independent coil spring front suspension. This system consists of upper and lower control arms pivoting on bushings on shafts. which are attached to the crossmember. The control arms are attacked to the steering knuckle with ball joints and a coil spring is located between the lower control arm and the suspension crossmember.

A stabilizer (sway) bar is optional to minimize body lean and sway in curves. Heavy duty shock absorbers and springs have been optional on most models.

Springs

REMOVAL AND INSTALLATION

CAUTION: *The spring is under a great deal of tension! It's best to use a coil spring compressor when removing the spring. Mishandling the spring could cause it to fly out of its mounting, causing a great deal of personal damage!*

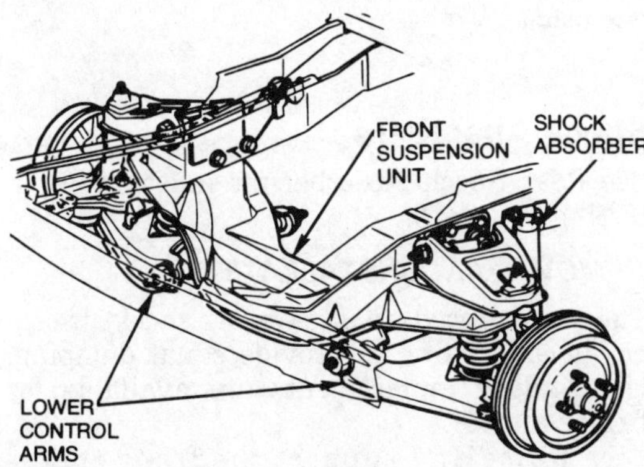

Independent front suspension

1967–70

1. Raise and support the van.
2. Support the axle with a floor jack so that the weight is taken off the spring.
3. Remove the spring-to-axle U-bolts.
4. Remove the front and rear spring eye bolts and remove the spring from the van.
5. Installation is the revers of removal. Position the spring so that the head of the center bolt is indexed with the axle spring seat. After the springs are attache, lower the van to the ground and bounce the front end up and down several times. Then torque the nuts and bolts as follows:
   - Leaf Spring U-bolt: 80 ft.lb.
   - Leaf Spring (front): 75 ft.lb.
   - Leaf Spring (rear): 50 ft.lb.

1971–86

1. Raise and support the van under the frame rails. The control arms should hang free.
2. Disconnect the shock absorber at the lower end and move it aside. Disconnect the stabilizer bar (if any) from the lower control arm.
3. Support the cross-shaft with a jack and install a spring compressor or chain the spring to the control arm as a safety precaution.
4. Raise and jack to remove the tension from the lower control arm cross-shaft and remove the 2 U-bolts securing the cross-shaft to the crossmember.

   NOTE: *The cross-shaft and lower control arms keeps the coil spring compressed. Use care when you lower the assembly.*
5. Slowly release the jack and lower the control arm until the spring can be removed. Be sure that all compression is relieved from the spring.

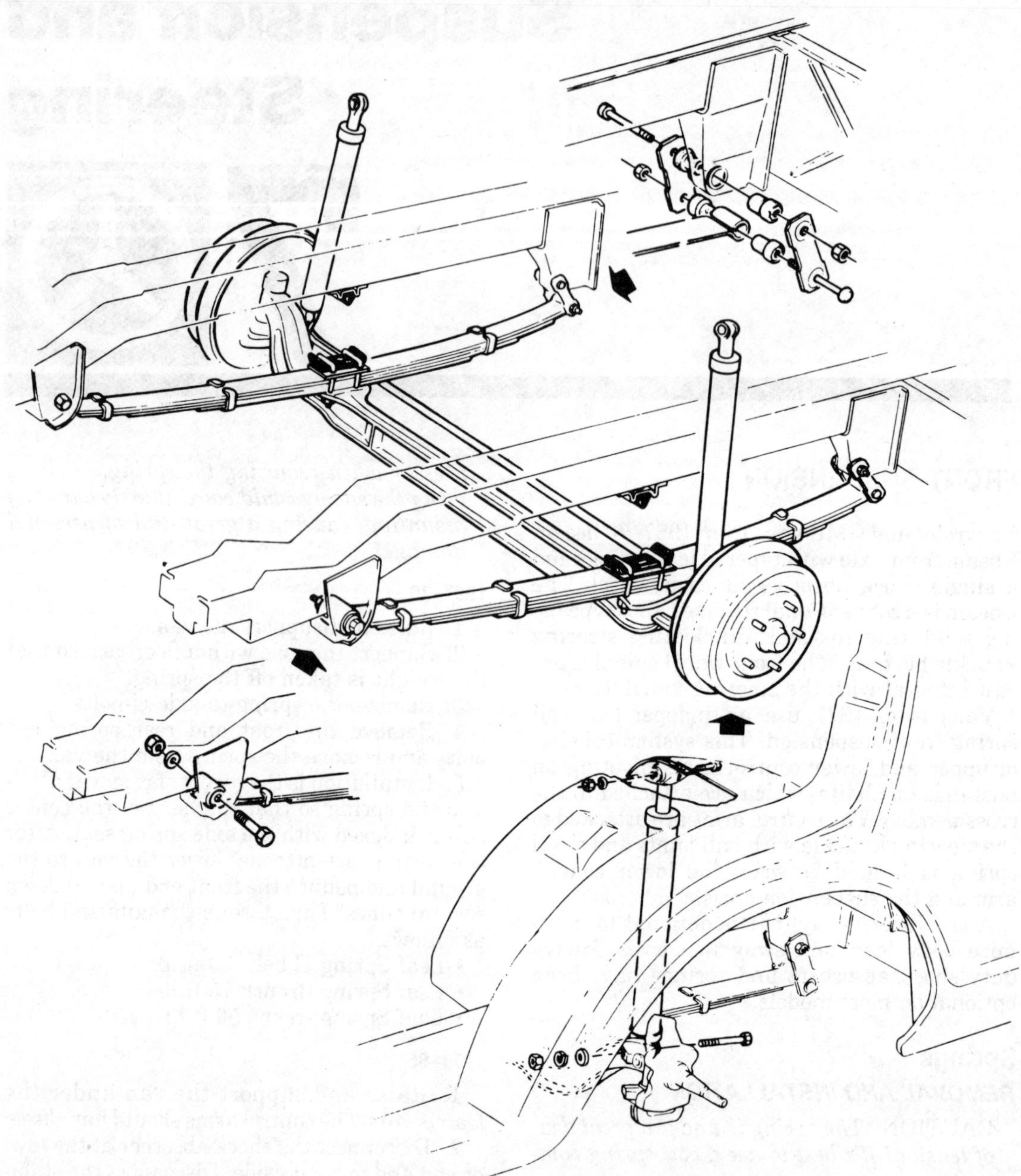

I-beam front suspension

6. Remove the spring.

7. To install, position the spring on the control arm and jack it into position. Use the spring compressor again as a precaution.

8. Position the control arm cross-shaft on the crossmember and install the U-bolts. Be sure that the front indexing hole in the cross-shaft is aligned with the crossmember attaching saddle stud.

9. Further installation is the reverse of removal. Have the front suspension alignment checked.

Shock Absorbers

See Rear Shock Absorber for information on testing.

REMOVAL AND INSTALLATION

The usual procedure is to replace shock absorbers in axle pairs, to provide equal damping. Heavy duty replacements are available for firmer control.

1. Raise and support the front end as necessary.

2. Remove the bolt and nut from the lower shock end.
3. Remove the upper bolt and nut.
4. Purge the new shock of air by extending it in its normal position and compressing it while inverted. Do this several times. It is normal for there to be more resistance to extension than to compression.
5. Install the shock absorber. Tighten the shock bolts to 75 ft.lb. except for the 1967–70 lower bolt; tighten these to 55 ft.lb.

INDEPENDENT FRONT SUSPENSION

Upper Control Arm

REMOVAL AND INSTALLATION

1. Raise and support the van on jackstands.
2. Support the lower control arm with a floor jack.
3. Remove the wheel and tire.
4. Remove the cotter pin from the upper control arm ball stud and loosen the stud nut until the bottom surface of the nut is slightly below the end of the stud.
5. Install a spring compressor on the coil spring for safety.
6. Loosen the upper control arm ball stud in the steering knuckle using a ball joint stud removal tool. Remove the nut from the ball stud and raise the upper arm to clear the steering knuckle. It may be necessary to remove the brake caliper and wire it to the frame to gain clearance. Do not allow the caliper to hang by the brake hose.
7. Remove the nuts securing the control arm shaft studs to the crossmember bracket and remove the control arm.
8. Tape the shims and spacers together and tag for proper reassembly.
9. Installation is the reverse of removal. Place the control arm in position and install the nuts. Before tightening the nuts, insert the caster and camber shims in the same order as when removed. Have the front end alignment checked, and as necessary adjusted.

Lower Control Arm

REMOVAL AND INSTALLATION

1. Raise and support the van on jackstands.
2. Remove the spring (see Spring Removal and Installation).
3. Support the inboard end of the control arm after spring removal.
4. Remove the cotter pin from the lower ball stud and loosen the nut.
5. Loosen the lower ball stud in the steering knuckle using a ball joint stud removal tool. When the stud is loose, remove the nut from the stud. It may be necessary to remove the brake caliper and wire it to the frame to gain clearance.
6. Remove the lower control arm.
7. Installation is the reverse of removal.

Ball Joints

INSPECTION

Excessive ball joint wear will usually show up as wear on the inside of the front tires. Don't jump to conclusions; front end misalignment can give the same symptom. The lower ball joint gets the most wear due to the distribution of suspension load. The wear limits given are the manufacturer's recommendation; they may not agree with your state's inspection law.

Upper

1. Raise and support the van so that the control arms hang free.
2. Remove the wheel.
3. Support the lower control arm with a jackstand and disconnect the upper ball stud from the steering knuckle.
4. On 1971 models, reinstall the nut on the ball stud and measure the torque required to rotate the stud. If it is not within 1–10 ft.lb., replace the joint.
5. On 1972 and later models, the upper ball joint is spring loaded in its socket. If it has any perceptible lateral shake or can be twisted in its socket, it should be replaced.
6. If there are no defects, connect the steering knuckle to the upper stud and torque the nut to 50 ft.lb. (90 ft.lb. for G-30 and 3500). Tighten the nut further to install the cotter pin but don't exceed 90 ft.lb. (130 for G-30 and 3500).

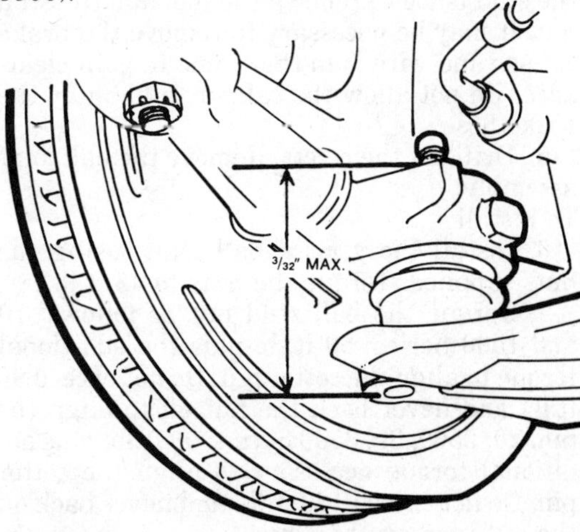

Checking the lower ball joint

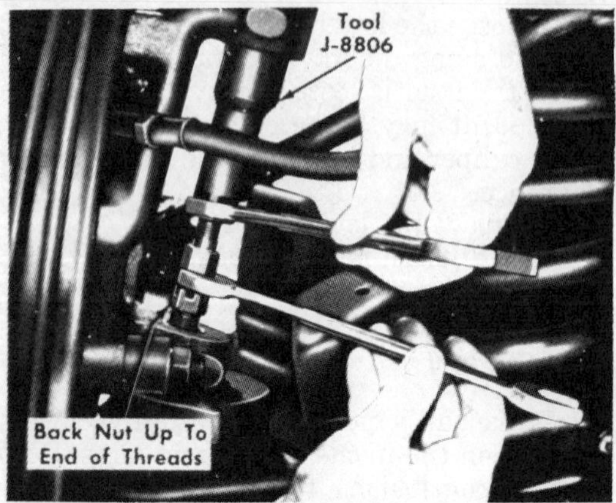

Loosening the lower ball joint stud

Lower

1. Support the weight of the control arm at the wheel hub.

2. Measure the distance between the tip of the ball joint stud and the grease fitting below the ball joint.

3. Move the support to the control arm and allow the hub and drum to hang free. Measure the distance again. If the variation between the 2 measurements exceeds $^{3}/_{32}$" (2.38mm) the ball joint should be replaced.

REMOVAL AND INSTALLATION

Upper

1. Raise and support the van.

2. Support the lower control arm with a floor jack.

3. Remove the cotter pin from the upper ball stud and loosen, buy do not remove, the stud nut.

4. Using a ball joint stud removal tool, loosen the ball stud in the steering knuckle. When the stud is loose, remove the tool and the stud nut. It may be necessary to remove the brake caliper and wire it to the frame to gain clearance. Do not allow the caliper to hang by the brake hose.

5. Drill out the rivets. Remove the ball joint assembly.

To install:

6. Install the service ball joint, using the nuts supplied. Torque the nuts to 45 ft.lb.

7. Torque the ball stud nut as follows: 10 and 1500 Series: 50 ft.lb. plus the additional torque to align the cotter pin. Do not exceed 90 ft.lb. and never back the nut off to align the pin. 20, 2500, 30, 3500 Series: 90 ft.lb. plus additional torque necessary to align the cotter pin. Do not exceed 130 ft.lb. and never back off the nut to align the pin.

8. Install a new cotter pin.

9. Install a new lube fitting and lubricate the new joint.

10. If removed, install the brake caliper.

11. Install the tire and lower the van.

Lower

1. Raise and support the van. Support the lower control arm with a floor jack.

2. Remove the tire and wheel.

3. Remove the lower stud cotter pin and loosen, buy do not remove, the stud nut.

4. Loosen the ball joint with a ball joint stud removal tool. It may be necessary to remove the brake caliper and wire it to the frame to gain enough clearance.

5. When the stud is loose, remove the tool and ball stud nut.

6. Install a spring compressor on the coil spring for safety.

7. Pull the brake disc and knuckle assembly up and off the ball stud and support the upper arm with a block of wood.

8. Remove the ball joint from the control arm with a ball joint tool. It must be pressed out.

To install:

9. Start the new ball joint into the control arm. Position the bleed vent in the rubber boot facing inward.

10. Seat the ball joint in the lower control arm. It must be pressed in.

11. Lower the upper arm and match the steering knuckle to the lower ball stud.

12. Install the brake caliper, if removed.

13. Install the ball stud nut and torque it to 80–100 ft.lb. plug the additional torque necessary to align the cotter pin hole. Do not exceed 130 ft.lb. or back the nut off the align the holes with the pin.

14. Install a new lube fitting and lubricate the new joint.

15. Install the tire and wheel.

16. Lower the van.

I-Beam Front Suspension

KINGPIN AND BUSHING REPLACEMENT

When these pivot parts wear out, the result is rapid wear on the inside of the front tires, shimmy, a clunking sound on bumps, and excessive steering play.

1. Raise and support the front axle. Remove the wheel and the brake drum.

2. Unbolt and remove the brake backing plate. Wire it up to prevent hose damage.

3. Detach the steering arm and tie rod, using a tie rod stud removal tool.

4. Remove the upper and lower kingpin dust caps. Remove the kingpin lockpin nut and lockpin from the axle.

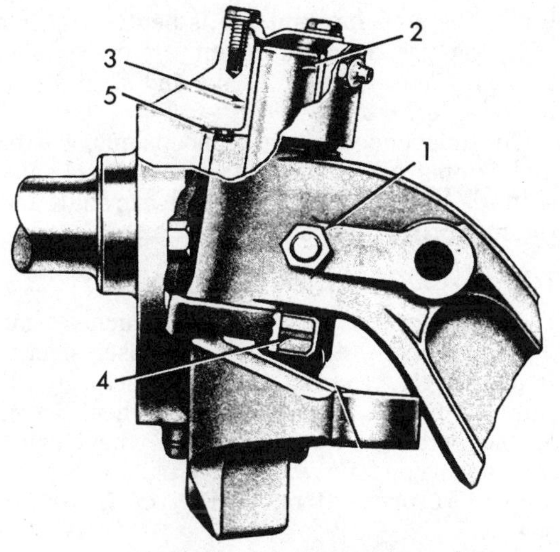

1. Lockpin 4. Thrust bearing
2. Kingpin 5. Seal
3. Bushing

Kingpin details, G-20 and 2500 shown

5. Tap the kingpin out from the bottom. Remove the steering knuckle from the axle, along with the shims and thrust washer.
6. Clean all parts. If there is excessive wear in the axle end, it can be machined to take an oversize kingpin. Clean up the bushing bores with emery cloth and wipe them clean. Lubricate the outside of the bushings and push them into the steering knuckle. Lubricate and place a new O-ring in the upper knuckle bore under the upper bushing on G-10 and 1500.
7. Place the steering knuckle and the original shims on the axle end. Be careful of the upper seal on the G-20 and 2500 axle.
8. Slide the new thrust washer assembly between the lower side of the axle and the steering knuckle. The thrust washer assembly is a bronze washer between tow steel washers, all encased in a dust shield. The G-20 and 2500 has an extra outer seal which must go over the thrust washer assembly.
9. Lubricate the kingpin and install it temporarily.
10. Raise the knuckle with a jack to take up all the clearance. Use feeler gauges to measure the clearance between the top of the axle and the steering knuckle. On G-10 and 1500, the clearance must be less than 0.005″ (0.127mm). On G-20 and 2500, it should be 0.003–0.008″ (0.0762–0.203mm). Add shims at the top to correct the clearance.
11. On final assembly, make sure the lockpin slot aligns with the hole. Install the lockpin and tighten the nut.
12. Install the kingpin dust caps with new gaskets.
13. Replace the brake backing plate, brake drum, and wheel. Replace the steering and tie rods.
14. Adjust the front wheel bearings and check the toe-in.

Front Wheel Bearings

REMOVAL, LUBRICATION, ADJUSTMENT AND INSTALLATION

Only front wheel bearings require periodic service. A premium high melting point grease meeting GM specification 6031-M must be used. Long fiber type greases must not be used. This service is recommended at the intervals in the Maintenance Intervals chart or whenever the van has been driven in water up to the hubs.

1. Remove the wheel and tire assembly, and the brake drum or brake caliper.
2. Remove the hub and disc as an assembly. Remove the caliper mounting bolts and insert a block between the brake pads as the caliper is removed. Remove the caliper and wire it out of the way. Do not allow the caliper to hang by the brake hose.
3. Pry out the grease cap, cotter pin, spindle nut, and washer, then remove the hub. Do not drop the wheel bearings.
4. Remove the outer roller bearing assembly from the hub. The inner bearing assembly will remain in the hub and may be removed after prying out the inner seal. Discard the seal.
5. Clean all parts in solvent (air dry) and check for excessive wear or damage.
6. Using a hammer and drift, remove the bearings caps from the hub. When installing new cups, make sure that they are not cocked and that they are fully seated against the hub shoulder.
7. Pack both wheel bearings using high melting point wheel bearing grease made for disc brakes. Ordinary grease will melt and ooze out, ruining the pads. Place a healthy globe of grease in the palm of one hand and force the edge of the bearing into it so that the grease fills the bearing. Do this until the wheel bearing is packed. Grease packing tools are available to make this job a lot less messy. There are also tools which make it possible to grease the inner bearing without removing it or the disc from the spindle.
8. Place the inner bearing in the hub and install a new inner seal, making sure that the seal flange faces the bearing cup.
9. Carefully install the wheel hub over the spindle.
10. Using you hands, firmly press the outer bearing into the hub. Install the spindle washer and nut.

11. To adjust the bearings through 1971 models, tighten the adjusting nut to 15 ft.lb. while rotating the hub. Back the nut off 1 flat ($^1/_6$ turn) and insert a new cotter pin. If the nut and spindle hole do not align, back the nut off slightly. There should be 0.001–0.008" (0.0254–0.203mm) end play in the bearing. This can be measured with a dial indicator, if you wish. Install the dust cap, wheel and tire.

12. To adjust the bearings on 1972 and later models, spin the wheel hub by hand and tighten the nut till it is just snug (12 ft.lb.). Back off the nut till it is loose, then tighten it finger tight. Loosen the nut until either hole in the spindle lines up with a slot in the nut and insert a new cotter pin. There should be 0.001–0.008" (0.0254–0.203mm) end play in the bearing through 1973, and 0.001–0.005" (0.0254–0.127mm) from 1974. This can be measured with a dial indicator, if you wish.

13. Replace the dust cap, wheel and tire.

Front End Alignment

Correct alignment of the front suspension is necessary to provide optimum tire life and for proper and safe handling of the vehicle.

CASTER AND CAMBER

Positive caster is the amount, in degrees, of the rearward tilt of the kingpin (I-beam axles) or of the steering knuckle (coil spring models). Camber is the amount, in degrees, of the outward tilt from the vertical of the front wheels.

On I-beams axles, the caster angle is adjusted by placing tapered shims between the axle spring seat and spring. To increase caster, place the thick end of the shim toward the rear of the van. To decrease caster, place the thick end of the shim toward the front of the van. If the camber is not correct, either the axle center or the steering knuckle is bent. In either case, repairs or replacement are necessary. Don't try this yourself. Leave any straightening of axles to a pro.

On independent front suspensions, caster and camber adjustments are made by placing shims between the upper control arm shaft and the mounting bracket.

TOE-IN ADJUSTMENT

Toe-in is the amount, measured in inches, that the centerlines of the wheels are closer together at the front than at the rear. Virtually all vehicles, except some with front wheel drive, are set with toe-in. Some front wheel drive cars, and some four wheel drive trucks, require toe-out to prevent excessive toe-in under power.

NOTE: *Some alignment specialists set toe-in to the lower specified limit on vehicles with radial tires. The reason is that radial tires have less drag, and therefore a lesser tendency to toe-out at speed. By the same reasoning, off-road tires would require the upper limit of toe-in.*

Toe-in must be checked after caster and camber have been adjusted, but it can be adjusted without disturbing the other two settings. You can make this adjustment without special equipment, if you make careful measurements. The adjustments is made at the tie rod sleeves. The wheels must be straight ahead.

1. Toe-in can be determined by measuring the distance between the centers of the tire treads, front and rear. If the tread pattern of your tires makes this impossible, you can measure between the edges of the wheel rims, but make sure to move the van forward and measure in a couple of places to avoid errors caused by bent rims or wheel runout.

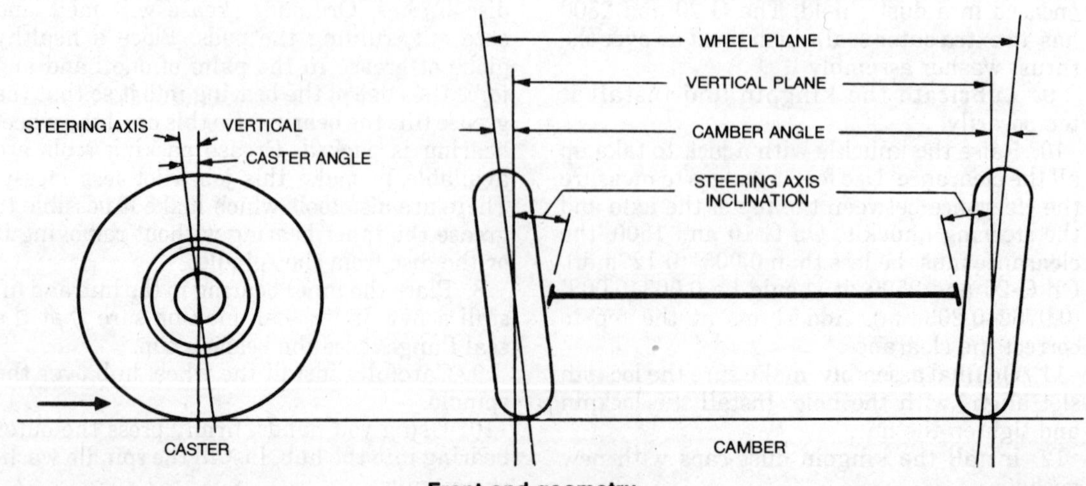

Front end geometry

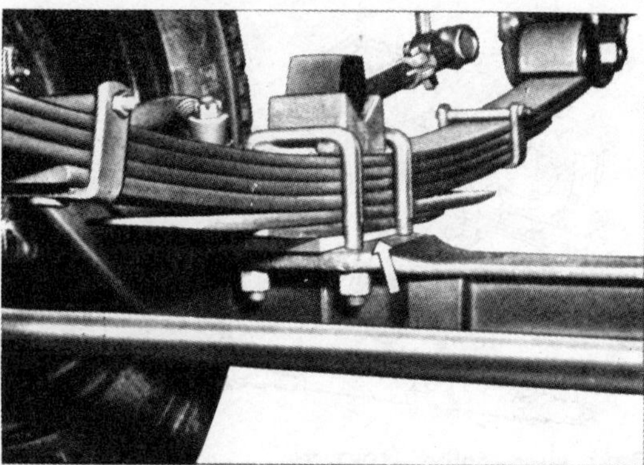

Caster shims—I-beam axle

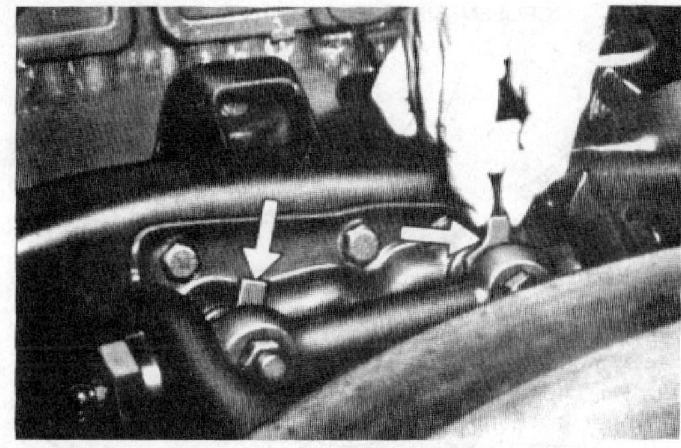

Caster-camber shims—independent front suspension

2. Loosen the clamp bolts on the tie rod sleeves.

3. Rotate the sleeves equally (in opposite directions) to obtain the correct measurement. If the sleeves are not adjusted equally, the steering wheel will be crooked.

NOTE: *If your steering wheel is already crooked, it can be straightened by turning the sleeves equally in the same direction.*

4. When the adjustment is complete, tighten the clamps.

STEERING AXIS INCLINATION

Steering axis inclination (coil spring models) or kingpin inclination (I-beam axles) is the tilt of the steering knuckle or the kingpin. If it is not within specifications, the steering knuckle is bent (coil spring models) and must be re-

Wheel Alignment Specifications

		Caster (deg)		Camber (deg)			
Year	Model	Range	Preferred Setting	Range	Preferred Setting	Toe-In (in.)	Steering Axis Inclination* (deg)
1967	All	2¼P–4¼P	3¼P	1¼P–1¾P	1½P	1/16–⅛ ①	7¼
1968	All	—	3¼P	—	1½P	3/32–3/16	7¼
1969–70	All	—	3¼P	½P–1½P	1P	3/32–3/16	7¼
1971	All	¼N–¼P	0	0–½P	¼P	⅛–¼	8½
1972	All	¼N–¼P	0	0–½P	¼P	3/16	8½
1973–80	All	②	②	0–½P	¼P	3/16	8½
1981–86	All	②	②	0–1P	½P	3/16	8½

—Not Available

*1967–70—Kingpin inclination

① Per wheel

② Measure the distance from the bump stop bracket to the frame. Read the caster angle from the chart below.

1973–80 Bumper stop bracket-to-frame (in.)			2½	2¾	3	3¼	3½	3¾	4	4¼	4½	4¾	5
Caster			2¼P	2P	1½P	1¼P	1P	¾P	½P	¼P	0	¼N	½N
1981–86 Bumper stop bracket-to-frame (in.)		1½	1¾	2	2¼	2½	2¾	3	3¼	3½	3¾	4	4¼
Caster	G10, 20	3½P	3⅓P	3⅒P	2 9/10P	2 7/10P	—	2⅖P	2⅕P	2⅒P	1 9/10P	1⅘P	1⅗P
	G30	2⅘P	2½P	2⅕P	1 9/10P	1⅗P	—	1P	7/10P	½P	⅕P	0	⅕N

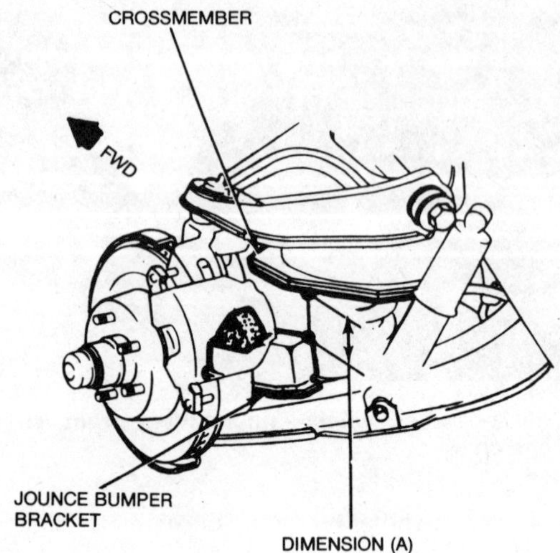

Bump stop bracket-to-frame measurement

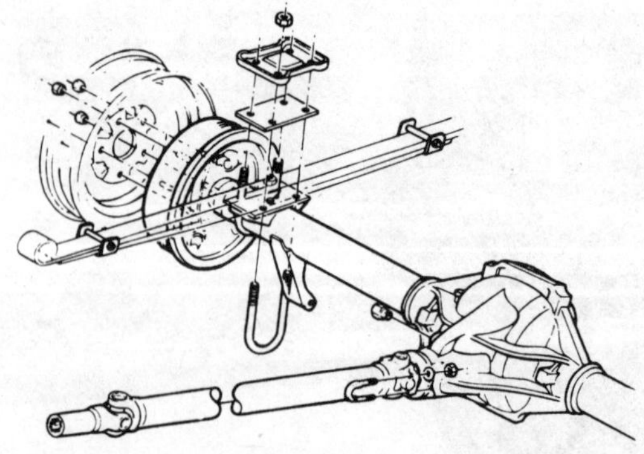
Rear suspension—1967–70

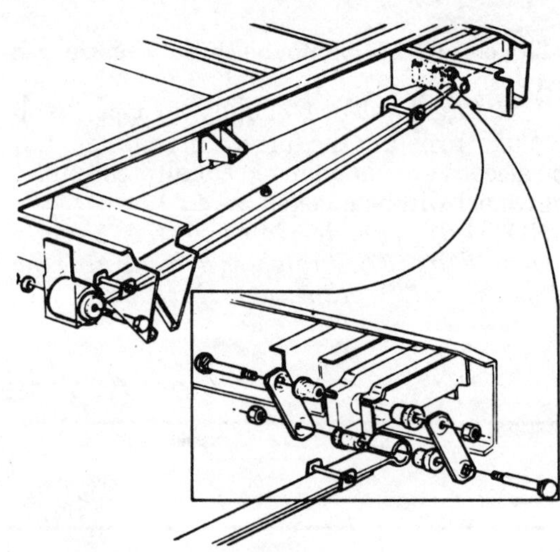
Rear spring shackle—1967–70

placed, or on I-beam axles, the axle center is bent and must be repaired or replaced. No means of adjustment is provided.

REAR SUSPENSION

These vans have leaf spring rear suspension. Staggered rear shock absorbers are used, starting 1971, to control axle hop on acceleration and braking. Heavy duty shock absorbers and springs have been available on most models.

Springs

REMOVAL AND INSTALLATION

1969–70

1. Raise and support the vehicle. Position the jackstands under the frame rails.
2. Support the axle with a floor jack so that the weight is taken off the springs.
3. Remove the spring-to-axle U-bolts, spacers and clamp plate.
4. Remove the front bolt from the spring eye and loosen the shackle to withdraw the lower shackle bolt.
5. Remove the spring from the van.
6. Installation is the reverse of removal. Position the spring so that the head of the center bolts is indexed in the axle spring seat. Be sure that the spring spacer is properly positioned. Tighten the U-bolt nuts and front spring bolt to 80 ft.lb. Tighten the shackle bolts to 50 ft.lb.

1971–86

1. Raise and support the van.
2. Support the axle so that the weight is taken off the springs.
3. Loosen, buy do not remove the spring-to-shackle retaining nut.
4. Remove the nut and bolt securing the shackle to the spring hanger.
5. Remove the nut and bolt securing the spring to the front hanger.
6. Remove the U-bolt retaining nuts and remove the U-bolts and spring plate.
7. Remove the spring.
8. Installation is the reverse of removal. Be sure that the spring is in position at both hangers. The shackle assembly must be attached to the rear spring eye before installing the shackle to the rear hanger. Tighten the U-bolt nuts to 120 ft.lb. (G-10, 1500, 20, and 2500) or 150 ft.lb. (G-30 and 3500). Torque the front eye bolt and rear shackle bolt to 135 ft.lb.

NOTE: *Aftermarket kits, consisting of longer axle U-bolts and blocks to be placed between the spring and axle, are available to adjust the rear side height. If this modification is carried to extremes, the front end caster angle and rear end stability will be affected.*

Shock Absorbers

The usual procedure for testing shock absorbers is to stand on the bumper at the end nearest the shock being tested and start the vehicle bouncing up and down. Step off; the vehicle should come to rest within one bounce cycle. The stiffness of the suspension on some models makes this rather difficult unless you are a very substantial individual indeed. Another good test is to drive the vehicle over a bumpy road. Bouncing over bumps is normal, the shock absorbers should stop the bouncing, after the bump is passed, within one or two cycles.

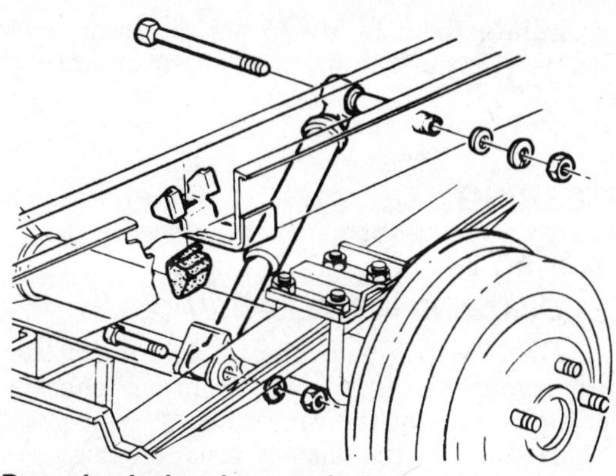

Rear shock absorber—typical

REMOVAL AND INSTALLATION

The usual procedure is to replace shock absorbers in axle pairs, to provide equal damping. Heavy duty replacements are available for firmer control. Air adjustable shock absorbers can be used to maintain a level rid with heavy loads or when towing.

1. Raise and support the van.
2. Support the rear axle with a floor jack.
3. If the van is equipped with air lift shocks, bleed the air from the lines and disconnect the line from the shock absorber.
4. Disconnect the shock absorber at the top by removing the nuts, washer and bolt.
5. Remove the nut, washer, and bolt from the bottom mount.
6. Remove the shock from the van.

NOTE: *Before installation, purge the new shock of air by repeatedly extending it in its normal position and compressing it while inverted. It is normal for there to be more resistance to extension than to compression.*

7. Installation if the reverse of removal. If the van is equipped with air lift shock absorb-

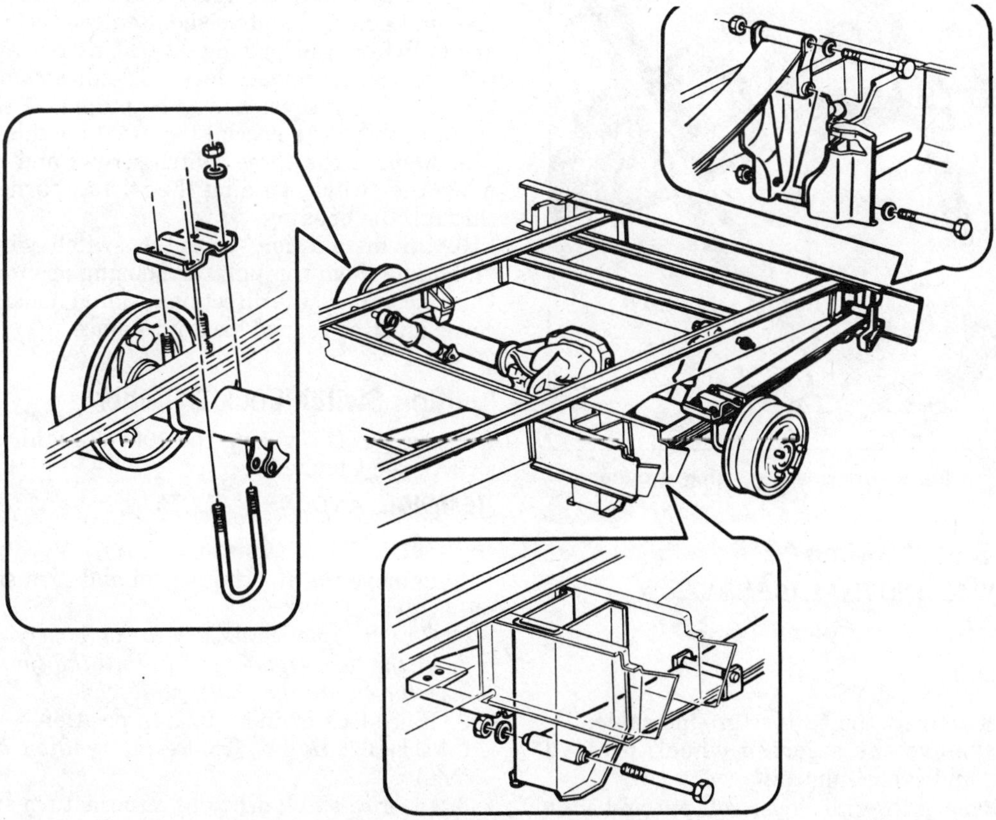

Rear spring—1971 and later

ers, inflate them to 10–15 psi minimum air pressure. Torque the shock absorber mounting nuts to 75 ft.lb.

STEERING

Steering Wheel

REMOVAL AND INSTALLATION

1. On 1967–70 models only, disconnect the turn signal wiring harness from the chassis wiring harness at the connector.
2. Disconnect the battery ground cable.
3. Remove the horn button, receiving cup, Belleville washer and bushing.
4. Mark the steering wheel-to-steering shaft relationship.
5. On 1975 and later models, remove the snapring from the steering shaft. Remove the nut and washer from the steering shaft.
6. Remove the steering wheel with a puller.
7. Installation is the reverse of removal. The turn signal control assembly must be in the Neutral position to prevent damaging the cancelling cam and control assembly.

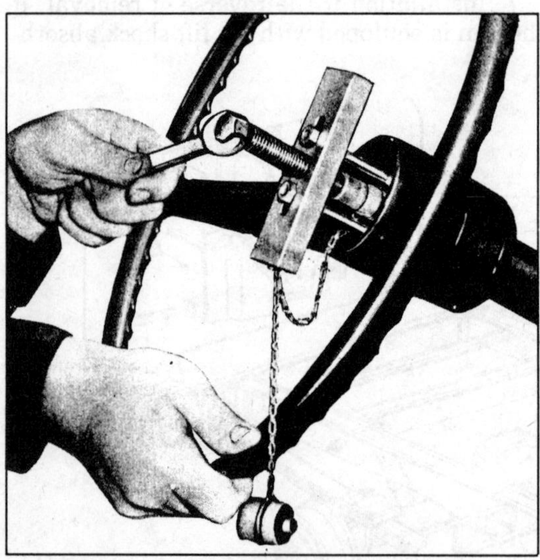

Removing the steering wheel using a puller

Turn Signal Switch

REMOVAL AND REPLACEMENT

1967–72

1. Disconnect the battery ground cable.
2. Remove the steering wheel, preload spring, and cancelling cam.
3. Remove the shift lever roll pin and shift lever (if applicable).
4. Remove the turn signal lever screw and the lever.
5. Push the hazard warning knob in. This must be done to avoid damaging the switch.
6. Disconnect the switch wires from the chassis harness located under the dash.
7. Remove the mast jacket upper bracket.
8. Remove the switch wiring cover from the column.
9. Unscrew the mounting screws and remove the switch, bearing housing, switch cover, and shift housing from the column.
10. Installation is the reverse or removal.

1973 and Later

1. Disconnect the battery ground cable. Remove the steering wheel.
2. Remove the switch cancelling spring and cam.
3. Remove the column to instrument panel trim plate, if any.
4. Disconnect the switch wiring harness at the half-moon connector.
5. Pry the wiring harness protector out of the column retaining slots.
6. Mark their locations, then remove each wire from the half-moon connector.
7. Remove the turn signal lever screw and the lever.
8. On tilt columns, remove the automatic transmission dial and needle. Remove the cap and bulb from the housing cover. Unscrew and remove the tilt release lever. The directional signal housing cover has to be pulled off the column; there is a special tool used for this.
9. Remove the three switch screws and remove the switch, guiding the wiring harness through the opening.
10. On installation, tape the switch wires and guide them through the housing opening. On tilt columns, the directional signal housing cover must be tapped back into place.

Ignition Switch/Lock Cylinder

For procedures covering the 1967–72 ignition switch, see Chapter 5.

REMOVAL AND INSTALLATION

1973–78

1. Remove the steering wheel and turn signal switch.

   NOTE: *It is not necessary to completely remove the turn signal switch. Pull the switch over the end of the shaft; no further.*
2. Place lock cylinder in Run position.

   CAUTION: *Do not remove the ignition key buzzer.*
3. Insert a small drift pin into the turn signal housing slot. Keeping the drift pin to the

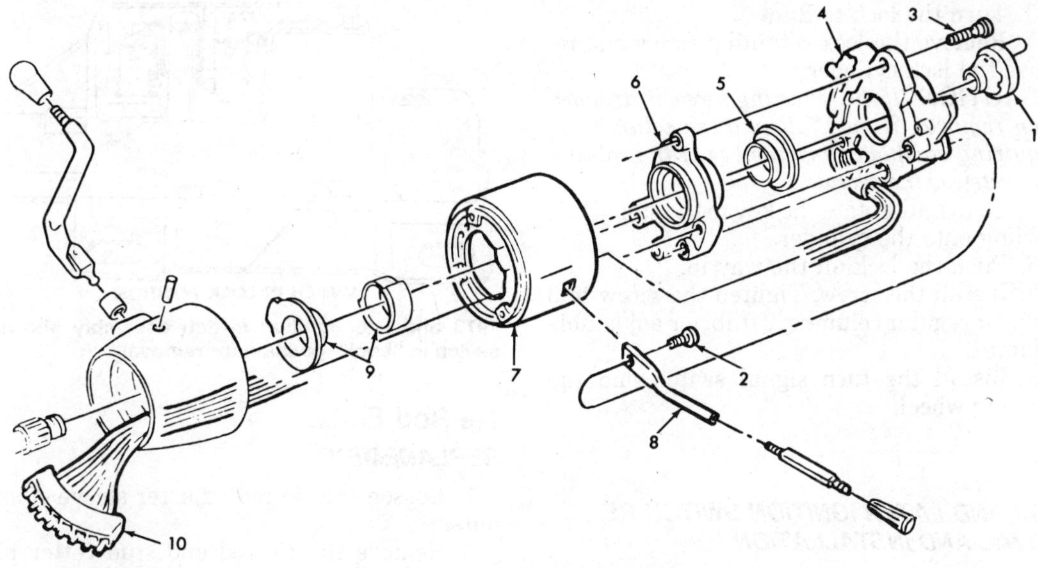

1. Cancelling cam
2. Directional lever retaining screw
3. Switch mounting screw
4. Switch
5. Upper bearing
6. Bearing support
7. Switch cover
8. Lever arm
9. Washer
10. Wiring connector

1967–72 turn signal switch details

right side of the slot, break the housing flash loose and depress the spring latch at the lower end of the lock cylinder. Remove the lock cylinder.

NOTE: *Considerable force may be necessary to break this casting flash, buy be careful not to damage any other parts. When ordering a new lock cylinder, specify a cylinder assembly. This will same assembling the cylinder, washer, sleeve and adapter.*

4. To install, hold the lock cylinder sleeve and rotate the knob clockwise against the stop. Insert the cylinder into the housing, aligning the key and keyway. Hold a 0.070" (1.778mm) drill between the lock bezel and housing. Rotate the cylinder counterclockwise, maintaining a light pressure until the drive section of the cylinder mates with the sector. Push in until the snapring pops into the grooves. Remove drill. Check cylinder operation.

CAUTION: *The drill prevents forcing the lock cylinder inward beyond its normal position. The buzzer switch and spring latch can hold the lock cylinder in too far. Complete disassembly of the upper bearing housing is necessary to release an improperly installed lock cylinder.*

1979 and Later

1. Remove the steering wheel.
2. Remove the turn signal switch. It is not necessary to completely remove the switch from the column. Pull the switch rearward far enough to slip it over the end of the shaft, but do not pull the harness out of the column.

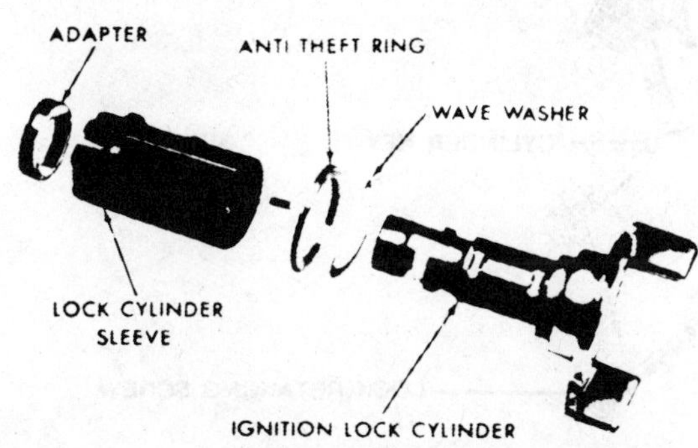

Ignition lock cylinder, 1973–78; later models similar

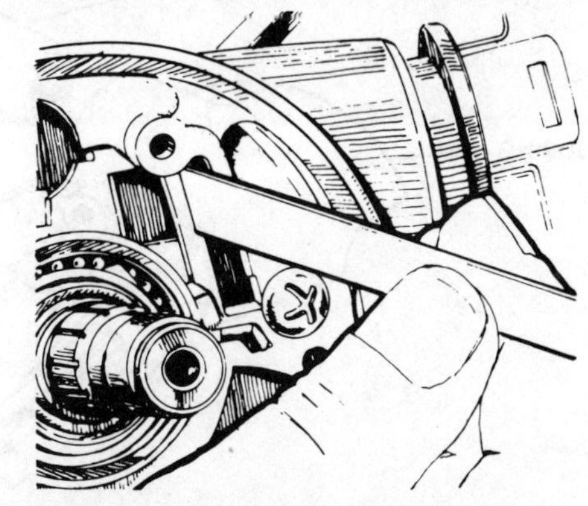

Ignition lock cylinder removal, 1973–78

3. Turn the lock to Run.
4. Remove the lock retaining screw and remove the lock cylinder.

CAUTION: *If the retaining screw is dropped on removal, it may fall into the column, requiring complete disassembly of the column to retrieve the screw.*

5. To install, rotate the key to the stop while holding onto the cylinder.
6. Push the lock all the way in.
7. Install the screw. Tighten the screw to 3 ft.lb. for regular columns, 2 ft.lb. for adjustable columns.
8. Install the turn signal switch and the steering wheel.

1973 AND LATER IGNITION SWITCH REMOVAL AND INSTALLATION

The switch is on the steering column, behind the instrument panel.

1. Lower the steering column, making sure that it is supported.

CAUTION: *Extreme care is necessary to prevent damage to the collapsible column.*

2. Make sure the switch is in the Lock position. If the lock cylinder is out, pull the switch rod up to the stop, then go down 1 detent.
3. Remove the two screws and the switch.
4. Before installation, make sure the switch is in the Lock position.
5. Install the switch using the original screws.

CAUTION: *Use of screws that are too long could prevent the column from collapsing on impact.*

6. Replace the column.

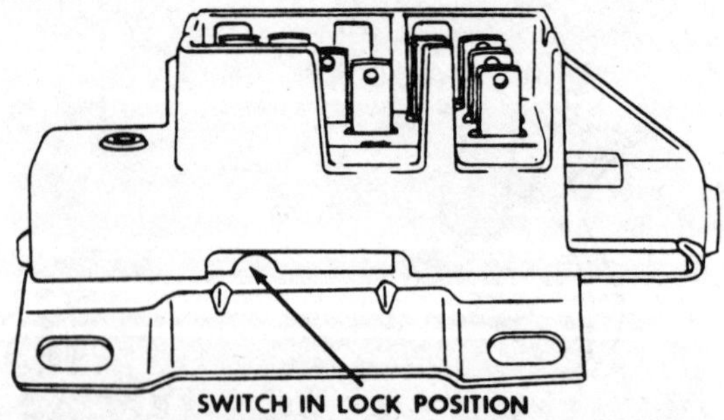

1973 and later ignition switch assembly showing switch in "Lock" position for removal

Tie Rod Ends

REPLACEMENT

1. Loosen the tie rod adjuster sleeve clamp nuts.
2. Remove the tie rod end stud cotter pin and nut.
3. You can use a tie rod end ball joint removal tool to loosen the stud, or you can loosen it by tapping on the steering arm with a hammer while using a heavy hammer as a backup.
4. Remove the inner stud in the same way.
5. Unscrew the tie rod end from the threaded sleeve. The threads may be left or right hand threads. Count the number of turns required to remove it.
6. To install, grease the threads and turn the new tie rod end in as many turns as were needed to remove it. This will give approximately correct toe-in. Tighten the clamp bolts.
7. Tighten the stud nuts and install new cotter pins. You may tighten the nut to align the cotter pin, buy don't loosen it.
8. Adjust the toe-in.

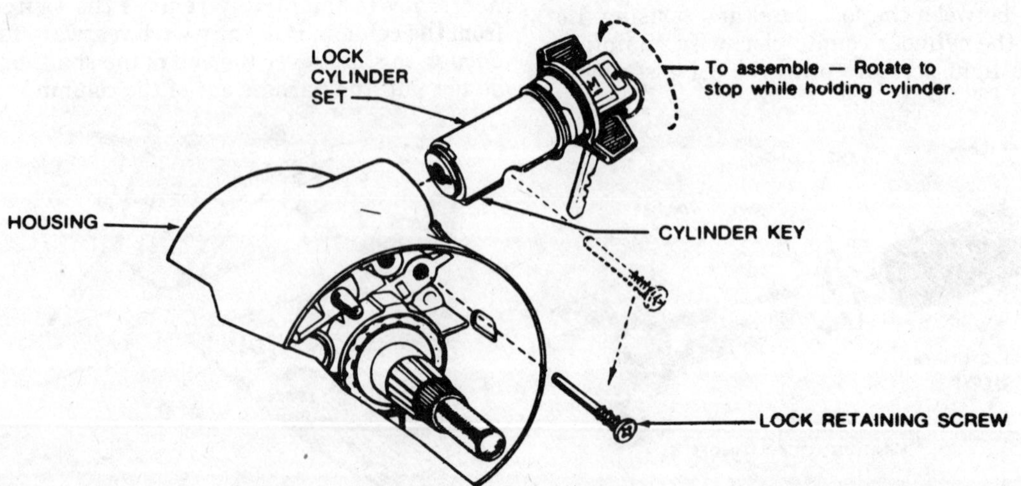

1979 and later ignition lock cylinder removal and installation

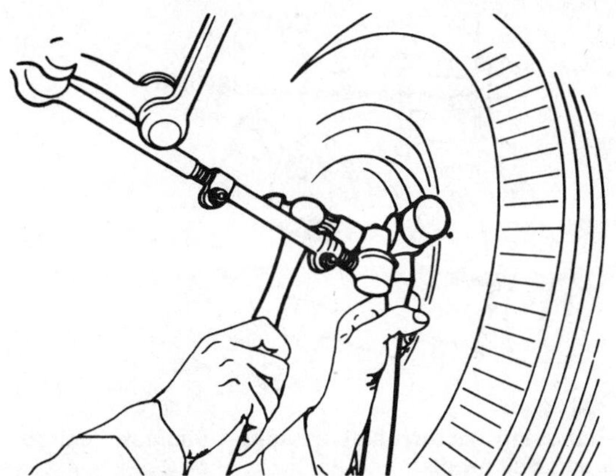

Freeing the tie-rod end; use another hammer as a backup

Manual Steering

ADJUSTMENT

Before any steering gear adjustments are made, it is recommended that the front end of the van be raised and a thorough inspection be made for stiffness or lost motion in the steering gear, steering linkage and front suspension. Worn or damaged parts should be replaced, since a satisfactory adjustment of the steering gear cannot be obtained if bent or badly worn parts exist.

It is also very important that the steering gear be properly aligned in the van. Misalignment of the gear places a stress on the steering worm shaft, therefore a proper adjustment is impossible. To align the steering gear, loosen the steering gear-to-frame mounting bolts to permit the gear to align itself. Check the steering gear to frame mounting seat. If there is a gap at any of the mounting bolts, proper alignment may be obtained by placing shims where excessive gap appears. Tighten the steering gear-to-frame bolts. Alignment of the gear in the van is very important and should be done carefully so that a satisfactory, trouble-free gear adjustment may be obtained.

The steering gear is of the recirculating ball nut type. the ball nut, mounted on the worm gear, is driven by means of steel balls which circulate in helical grooves in both the worm and nut. Ball return guides attached to the nut serve to recirculate the two sets of balls in the grooves. As the steering wheel is turned to the right, the ball nut moves upward. When the wheel is turned to the left, the ball nut moves downward.

The sector teeth on the pinion shaft and the ball nut are designed so that they fit the tightest when the steering wheel is straight ahead. This mesh action is adjusted by an adjusting screw which moves the pinion shaft endwise until the teeth mesh properly. The worm bearing adjuster provides proper preloading of the upper and lower bearings.

Before doing the adjustment procedures given below, ensure that the steering problem is not caused by faulty suspension components, bad front end alignment, etc. Then, proceed with the following adjustments.

STEERING WORM AND SECTOR ADJUSTMENT

1. Tighten the worm bearing adjuster plug until all end play has been removed, then loosen ¼ turn.
2. Use an $^{11}/_{16}$″ 12 point socket to carefully turn the wormshaft all the way into the right corner then turn back about ½ turn.
3. Tighten the adjuster plug until the proper thrust bearing preload is obtained (5–8 in.lb.). Tighten the adjuster plug locknut to 85 ft.lb.
4. Turn the wormshaft from one stop to the other counting the number of turns. Then turn the shaft back exactly half the number of turns to the center position.
5. Turn the lash (sector shaft) adjuster screw clockwise to remove all lash between the ball nut and sector teeth. Tighten the locknut to 25 ft.lb.
6. Using an $^{11}/_{16}$″ 12 point socket and an inch

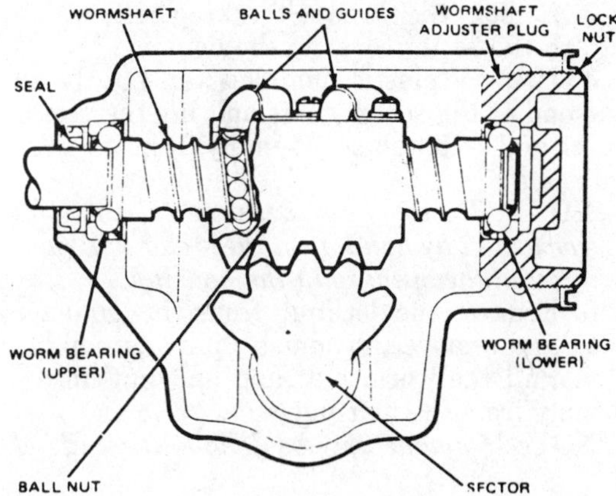

Cross section of Saginaw recirculating ball model.

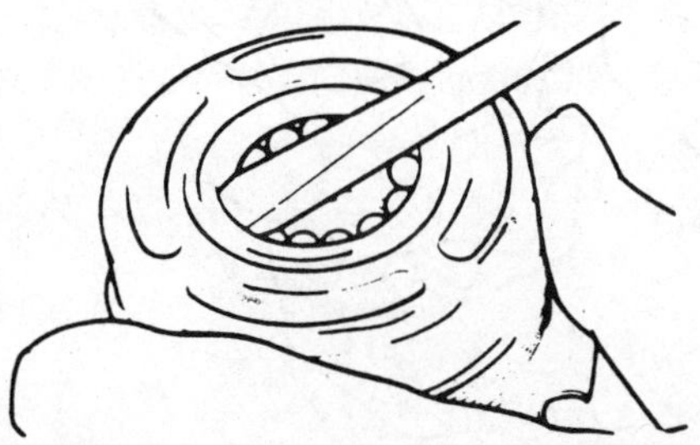

Removing the bearing retainer from the worm bearing adjuster—Saginaw recirculating ball model.

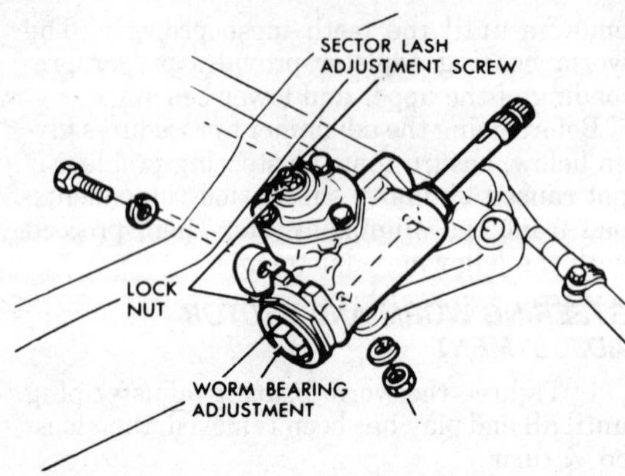

Steering Gear Adjustment Points-Typical

lb. torque wrench, observe the highest reading while the gear is turned through the center position. It should be 16 in.lb. or less.

7. If necessary repeat Steps 5 and 6.

Disassembly

1. Place the steering gear in a vise, clamping onto one of the mounting tabs. The wormshaft should be in a horizontal position.
2. Rotate the wormshaft from stop to stop and count the total number of turns. Turn back exactly halfway, placing the gear on center.
3. Remove the three self locking bolts which attach the sector cover to the housing.
4. Using a plastic hammer, tap lightly on the end of the sector shaft and lift the sector cover and sector shaft assembly from the gear housing.

NOTE: *It may be necessary to turn the wormshaft by hand until the sector will pass through the opening in the housing.*

5. Remove the locknut from the adjuster plug and remove the adjuster plug assembly.
6. Pull the wormshaft and ball nut an assembly from the housing.

NOTE: *Damage may be done to the ends of the ball guides if the ball nut is allowed to rotate to the end of the worm.*

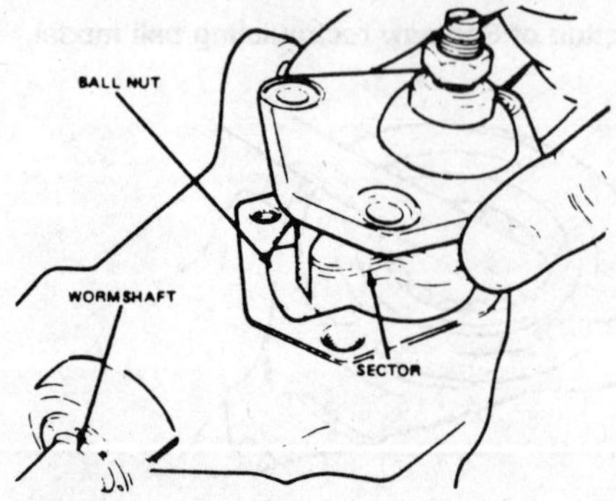

Removing sector shaft assembly—Saginaw recirculating ball model.

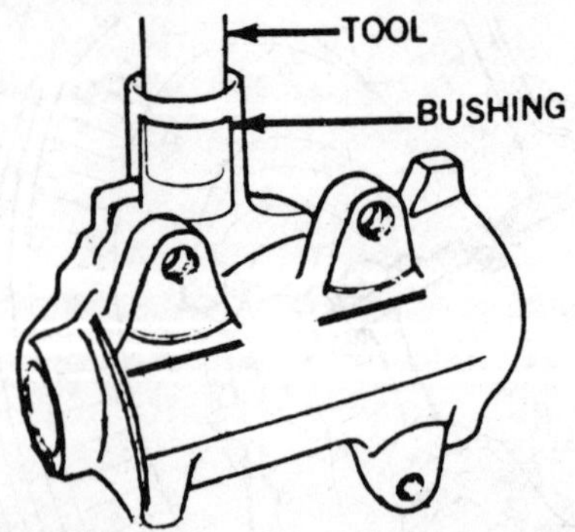

Removing sector shaft bushing—Saginaw recirculating ball model.

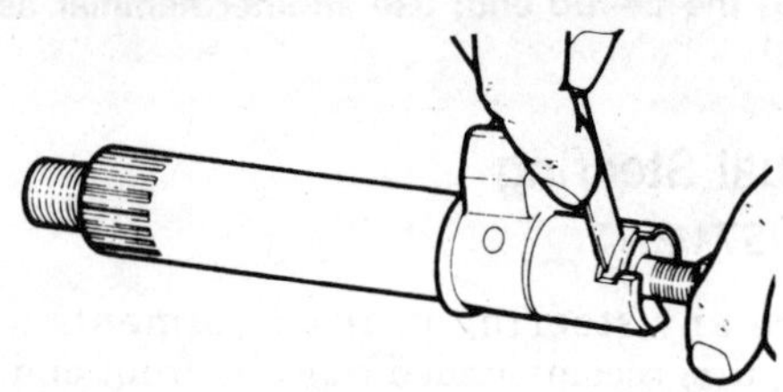

Checking lash adjuster end clearance —Saginaw recirculating ball model

7. Remove the worm shaft upper bearing from inside the gear housing.
8. Pry the wormshaft lower bearing retainer from the adjuster plug housing and remove the bearing.
9. Remove the locknut from the lash adjuster screw in the sector cover. Turn the lash adjuster screw clockwise and remove it from the sector cover. Slide the adjuster screw and shim out of the slot in the end of the sector shaft.
10. Pry out and discard both the sector shaft and wormshaft seals.

Inspection

1. Wash all parts in cleaning solvent and blow dry with an air hose.
2. Use a magnifying glass and inspect the bearings and bearing caps for signs of indentation, or chipping. Replace any parts that show signs of damage.
3. Check the fit of the sector shaft in the bushings in the sector cover and housing. If these bushings are worn, a new sector cover and bushing assembly or housing bushing should be installed.
4. Check steering gear wormshaft assembly for being bent or damaged.

SHAFT SEAL REPLACEMENT

1. Remove the old seal from the pump body.
2. Install the new seal by pressing the outer diameter of the seal with a suitable size socket.

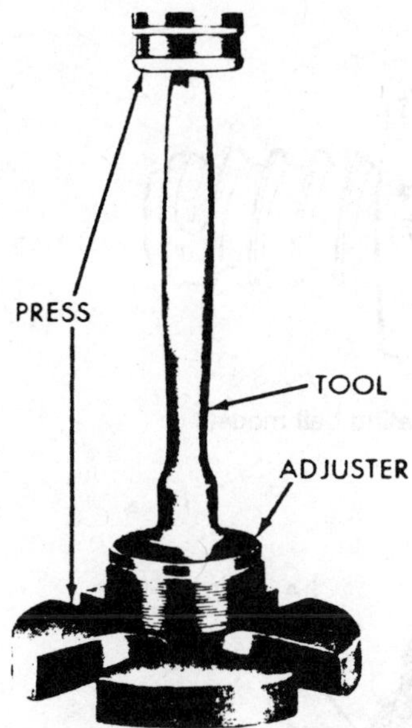

Installing the wormshaft upper bearing cup.

NOTE: *Make sure the socket is large enough to avoid damaging the external lip of the seal.*

SECTOR SHAFT BUSHING REPLACEMENT

1. Place the steering gear housing in an arbor press.
2. Press the sector shaft bushing from the housing.

NOTE: *Service bushings are bored to size and require no further reaming.*

SECTOR COVER BUSHING REPLACEMENT

The sector cover bushing is not serviced separately. The entire sector cover assembly including the bushing must be replaced as a unit.

BALL NUT SERVICE

If there is any indication of binding or tightness when the ball nut is rotated on the worm the unit should be disassembled, cleaned and inspected as follows:

Ball Nut Disassembly

1. Remove the screws and clamp retaining the ball guides in the ball nut. Pull the guides out of the ball nut.
2. Turn the ball nut upside down and rotate the wormshaft back and forth until all the balls have dropped out of the ball nut. The ball nut can now be pulled endwise off the worm.
3. Wash all parts in solvent and dry them with air. Use a magnifying glass and inspect the worm and nut grooves and the surface of all balls for signs of indentation. Check all ball guides for damage at the ends. Replace any damaged parts.

Ball Nut Assembly

1. Slip the ball nut over the worm with the ball guide holes up and the shallow end of the ball nut teeth to the left from the steering wheel position. Sight through the ball guide to align the grooves in the worm.
2. Place two ball guide halves together and insert them in the upper circuit in the ball nut. Place the two remaining guides together and insert them in the lower circuit.
3. Count out 25 balls and place them in a suitable container. This is the proper number of balls for one circuit.
4. Load the 25 balls into one of the guide holes while turning the wormshaft gradually away from that hole.
5. Fill the remaining ball circuit in the same manner.
6. Assemble the ball guide clamp to the ball nut and tighten the screws to 18–24 in.lb.
7. Check the assembly by rotating the ball nut on the worm to see that it moves freely.

NOTE: *Do not rotate the ball nut to the end of the worm threads as this may damage the ball guides.*

Assembly

1. Coat the threads of the adjuster plug, sector cover bolts and lash adjuster with a non-drying oil resistant sealing compound.

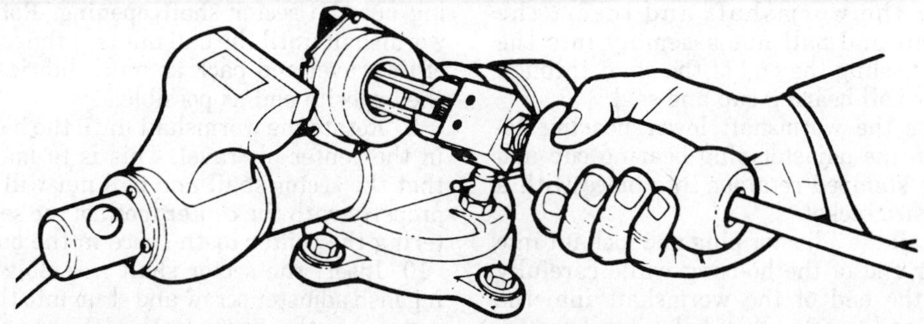

Removing worm shaft lower bearing cup from the adjuster plug—Saginaw recirculating ball model.

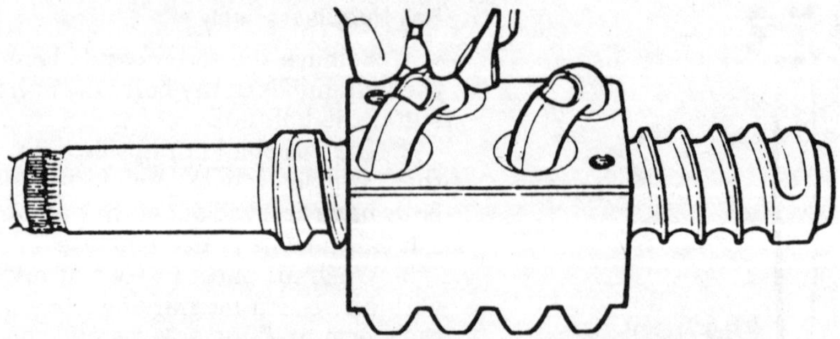
Filling the ball circuits—Saginaw recirculating ball model.

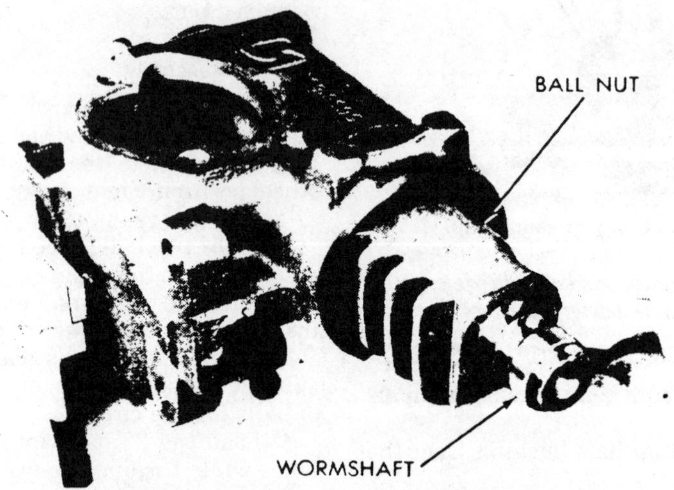

Removing the wormshaft and ballnut assembly.

NOTE: *Do not apply compound to the female threads. Use extreme care when applying compound to the bearing adjuster so that it does not come in contact with the wormshaft bearing.*

2. Place the steering gear housing in a vise with the wormshaft bore horizontal and the sector cover opening up.
3. Make sure that all seals, bushings and bearing cups are installed in the gear housing and that the ball nut is installed on the wormshaft.
4. Slip the wormshaft upper bearing assembly over the wormshaft and insert the wormshaft and ball nut assembly into the housing, feeding the end of the shaft through the upper ball bearing cup and seal.
5. Place the wormshaft lower bearing assembly in the adjuster plug bearing cup and press the stamped retainer into place with a suitable size socket.
6. Install the adjuster plug and locknut into the lower end of the housing while carefully guiding the end of the wormshaft into the bearing until nearly all end play has been removed from the wormshaft.
7. Position the lash adjuster including the shim in the slotted end of the sector shaft.

NOTE: *End clearance should not be greater than 0.002" (0.0508mm). If the end clearance is greater than 0.002" (0.0508mm), a shim package is available with thicknesses of 0.063" (1.6002mm), 0.065" (1.651mm), 0.067" (1.7018mm), 0.069 (1.7526mm).*

8. Lubricate the steering gear with 11 oz. (312g) of steering gear grease. Rotate the wormshaft until the ball nut is at the other end of its travel and then pack as much new lubricant into the housing as possible without losing out the sector shaft opening. Rotate the wormshaft until the ball nut is at the other end of its travel and pack as much lubricant into the opposite end as possible.
9. Rotate the wormshaft until the ball nut is in the center of travel. This is to make sure that the sector shaft and ball nut will engage properly with the center tooth of the sector entering the center tooth space in the ball nut.
10. Insert the sector shaft assembly including lash adjuster screw and shim into the housing so that the center tooth of the sector enters the center tooth space in the ball nut.

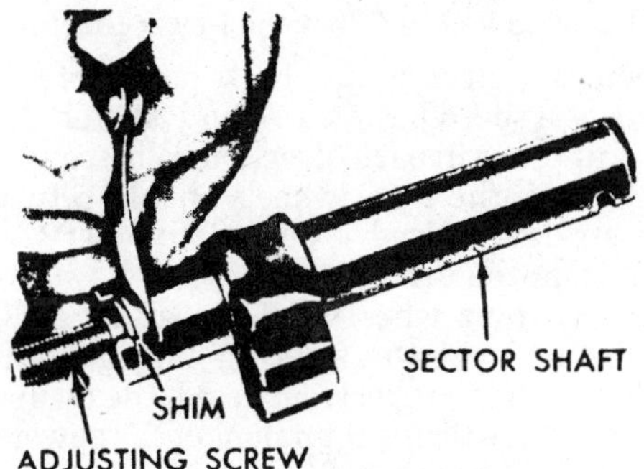

Measuring the sector shaft adjusting screw and clearance.

11. Pack the remaining portion of the lubricant into the housing and also place some in the sector cover bushing hole.

12. Place the sector cover gasket on the housing.

13. Install the sector cover onto the sector shaft by reaching through the sector cover with a screwdriver and turning the lash adjuster screw counterclockwise until the screw bottoms, then back the screw off ½ turn. Loosely install a new lock nut onto the adjuster screw.

14. Install and tighten the sector cover bolt to 30 ft.lb.

REMOVAL AND INSTALLATION

1. Set the front wheels in straight ahead position by driving vehicle a short distance on a flat surface.

2. Remove the flexible coupling to steering shaft flange bolts. Mark the relationship of the universal yoke to the wormshaft.

3. Mark the relationship of the Pitman arm to the Pitman shaft. Remove the Pitman shaft nut or Pitman arm pinch bolt and then remove the Pitman arm from the Pitman shaft, using puller J–6632.

4. Remove the steering gear to frame bolts and remove the gear assembly.

5. Remove the flexible coupling pinch bolt and remove the coupling from the steering gear wormshaft.

6. Install the flexible coupling onto the steering gear wormshaft, aligning the flat in the coupling with the flat on the shaft. Push the coupling onto the shaft until the wormshaft bottoms on the coupling reinforcement. Install the pinch bolt and torque to 24 ft.lb. The coupling bolt must pass through the shaft undercut.

7. Place the steering gear in position, guiding the coupling bolt into the steering shaft flange.

8. Install the steering gear to frame bolts and torque to 70 ft.lb.

9. If flexible coupling alignment pin plastic spacers were used, make sure they are bottomed on the pins, torque the flange bolt nuts to 25 ft.lb., and then remove the plastic spacers.

10. If flexible coupling alignment pin plastic spacers were not used, center the pins in the slots in the steering shaft flange and then install and torque the flange bolt nuts to 25 ft.lb.

11. Install the Pitman arm onto the Pitman shaft, lining up the marks made at removal. Install the Pitman shaft nut torque to 185 ft.lb.

Power Steering

The procedures for maintaining, adjusting, and repairing the power steering system and its components are to be done only after determining that the steering linkages and front suspension systems are correctly aligned and in good condition. All worn or damaged parts should be replaced before attempting to service the power steering system. After correcting any condition that could affect the power steering, do the preliminary test of the steering system components.

PRELIMINARY TESTS

Lubrication

Proper lubrication of the steering linkage and the front suspension components is very important for the proper operation of the steering systems of vans equipped with power steering. Most all power steering systems use the same lubricant in the steering gear box as in the power steering pump reservoir, and the fluid level is maintained at the pump reservoir.

With power cylinder assist power steering, the steering gear is of the standard mechanical type and the lubricating oil is self contained within the gear box and the level is maintained by the removal of a filler plug on the gear box housing. The control valve assembly is mounted on the gear box and is lubricated by power steering oil from the power steering pump reservoir, where the level is maintained.

Air Bleeding

Air bubbles in the power steering system must be removed from the fluid. Be sure the reservoir is filled to the proper level and the fluid is warmed up to operating temperature. Then, turn the steering wheel through its full travel three or four times until all the air bubbles are removed. Do not hold the steering wheel against its stops. Recheck the fluid level.

Fluid Level Check

1. Run the engine until the fluid is at the normal operating temperature. Then, turn the

steering wheel through its full travel three or four times, and shut off the engine.

2. Check the fluid level in the steering reservoir. If the fluid level is low, add enough fluid to raise the level to the Full mark on the dipstick or filler tube.

Pump Belt Check

Inspect the pump belt for cracks, glazing, or worn places. Using a belt tension gauge, check the belt tension for the proper range of adjustment. The amount of tension varies with the make of truck or van and the condition of the belt. New belts (those belts used less than 15 minutes) require a higher figure. The belt deflection method of adjustment may be used only if a belt tension gauge is not available. The belt should be adjusted for a deflection of ¼–⅜" (6.35–9.53mm).

Fluid Leaks

Check all possible leakage points (hoses, power steering pump, or steering gear) for loss of fluid. Turn engine on and rotate the steering wheel from stop to stop several times. Tighten all loose fittings and replace any defective lines or valve seats.

Turning Effort

Check the turning effort required to turn the steering wheel after aligning the front wheels and inflating the tires to the proper pressure.

1. With the vehicle on dry pavement and the front wheel straight ahead, set the parking brake and turn the engine on.

2. After a short warmup period for the engine, turn the steering wheel back and forth several times to warm the steering fluid.

3. Attach a spring scale to the steering wheel rim and measure the pull required to turn the steering wheel one complete revolution in each direction. The effort needed to turn the steering wheel should not exceed the limits specified.

NOTE: *This test may be done with the steering wheel removed and a torque wrench applied on the steering wheel nut.*

Power Steering Hose Inspection

Inspect both the input and output hoses of the power steering pump for worn spots, cracks, or signs of leakage. Replace hose if defective, being sure to reconnect the replacement hose properly. Many power steering hoses are identified as to where they are to be connected by special means, such as fittings that will only fit on the correct pump fitting, or hoses of special lengths.

Test Driving Van to Check the Power Steering

When test driving to check power steering, drive at a speed between 15 and 20 mph. Make several turns in each direction. When a turn is completed, the front wheels should return to the straight ahead position with very little help from the driver.

If the front wheels fail to return as they should and yet the steering linkage is free, well oiled and properly adjusted, the trouble is probably due to misalignment of the power cylinder or improper adjustment of the spool valve.

The power steering pump supplies all the power assist used in power steering systems of all designs. There are various designs of pumps used by the truck and van manufacturers but all pumps supply power to operate the steering systems with the least effort. All power steering pumps have a reservoir tank built onto the oil pump. These pumps are driven by belt turned by pulleys on the engine, normally on the front of the crankshaft.

During operation of the engine at idle speed, there is provision for the power steering pump to supply more fluid pressure. During driving speeds or when the van is moving straight ahead, less pressure is needed and the excess is relieved through a pressure relief and flow control valve. The pressure relief part of the valve is inside the flow control and is basically the same for all pumps. The flow control valve regulates, or controls, the constant flow of fluid from the pump as it varies with the demands of the steering gear. The pressure relief valve limits the hydraulic pressure built up when the steering gear is turned against its stops.

During pump disassembly, make sure all work is done on a clean surface. Clean the outside of the pump thoroughly and do not allow dirt of any kind to get inside. Do not immerse the shaft oil seal in solvent.

If replacing the rotor shaft seal, be extremely careful not to scratch sealing surfaces with tools.

REMOVAL AND INSTALLATION

1. Disconnect the hoses at the pump. When the hoses are disconnected, secure the ends in a raised position to prevent leakage. Cap the ends of the hoses to prevent the entrance of dirt.

2. Cap the pump fittings.

3. Loosen the bracket-to-pump mounting nuts.

4. Remove the pump drive belt.

5. Remove the bracket-to-pump bolts and remove the pump from the van.

6. Installation is the reverse of removal. Fill

the reservoir and bleed the pump by turning the pulley counterclockwise (as viewed from the front) until bubbles stop forming. Bleed the system as outlined following.

Bleeding the Hydraulic System

1. Fill the reservoir to the proper level and let the fluid remain undisturbed for at least 2 minutes.
2. Start the engine and run it for only about 2 seconds.
3. Add fluid as necessary.
4. Repeat Steps 1–3 until the level remains constant.
5. Raise the front of the vehicle so that the front wheels are off the ground. Set the parking brake and block both rear wheels front and rear. Manual transmissions should be in Neutral; automatic transmissions should be in Park.
6. Start the engine and run it at approximately 1500 rpm.
7. Turn the wheels (off the ground) to the right and left, lightly contacting the stops.
8. Add fluid as necessary.
9. Lower the vehicle and turn the wheels right and left on the ground.
10. Check the level and refill as necessary.
11. If the fluid is extremely foamy, let the van stand for a few minutes with the engine off and repeat the procedure. Check the belt tension and check for a bent or loose pulley. The pulley should not wobble with the engine running.
12. Check that no hoses are contacting any parts of the van, particularly sheet metal.
13. Check the oil level and refill as necessary. This step and the next are very important. When willing, follow Steps 1–10 above
14. Check for air in the fluid. Aerated fluid appears milky. If air is present, repeat the above operation. If it is obvious that the pump will not respond to bleeding after several attempts, a pressure test may be required.

The procedures for maintaining, adjusting, and repairing the power steering systems and components discussed in this chapter are to be done only after determining that the steering linkages and front suspension systems are correctly aligned and in good condition. All worn or damaged parts should be replaced before attempting to service the power steering system. After correcting any condition that could affect the power steering, do the preliminary tests of the steering system components.

PUMP OVERHAUL

The vane type power steering pump is used in Saginaw steering systems. Centrifugal force moves a number of vanes outward against the pump ring, causing a pumping action of the fluid to the control valve.

Disassembly

1. Clean the outside of the pump in a non-toxic solvent before disassembling.
2. Mount the pump in a vise, being careful not to squeeze the front hub too tight.
3. Remove the union and seal.
4. Remove the reservoir retaining studs and separate the reservoir from the housing.
5. Remove the mounting bolt and union O-rings.
6. Remove the filter and filter cage; discard the element.
7. Remove the end plate retaining ring by compressing the retaining ring and then prying it out with a removal tool. The retaining ring may be compressed by inserting a small punch in the ⅛″ (3mm) diameter hole in the housing and pushing in until the ring clears the groove.
8. Remove the end plate. The end plate is spring loaded and should rise above the housing level. If it is stuck inside the housing, a slight rocking or gentle tapping should free the plate.
9. Remove the shaft woodruff key and tap the end of the shaft gently to free the pressure plate, pump ring, rotor assembly, and thrust plate. Remove these parts as one unit.
10. Remove the end plate O-ring. Separate the pressure plate, pump ring, rotor assembly, and thrust plate.

Inspection

Clean all metal parts in a non-toxic solvent and inspect them as given below:

1. Check the flow control valve for free movement in the housing bore. If the valve is sticking, see if there is dirt or a rough spot in the bore.
2. Check the cap screw in the end of the flow control valve for looseness. Tighten if necessary being careful not to damage the machined surfaces.
3. Inspect the pressure plate and the pump plate surfaces for flatness and check that there are no cracks or scores in the parts. Do not mistake the normal wear marks for scoring.
4. Check the vanes in the rotor assembly for free movement and that they were installed with the radiused edge toward the pump ring.
5. If the flow control valve plunger is defective, install a new part. The valve is factory calibrated and supplied as a unit.
6. Check the driveshaft for worn splines, breaks, bushing material pick-up, etc.
7. Replace all rubber seals and O-rings removed from the pump.

8. Check the reservoir, studs, casting, etc. for burrs and other defects that would impair operation.

Assembly

1. Install a new shaft seal in the housing and insert the shaft at the hub end of housing, splined end entering mounting face side.
2. Install the thrust plate on the dowel pins with the ported side facing the rear of the pump housing.
3. Install the rotor on the pump shaft over the splined end. Be sure the rotor moves freely on the splines. Countersunk side must be toward the shaft.
4. Install the shaft retaining ring. Install the pump ring on the dowel pins with the rotation arrow toward the rear of the pump housing. Rotation is clockwise as seen from the pulley.
5. Install the vanes in the rotor slots with the radius edge towards the outside.
6. Lubricate the outside diameter and chamfer of the pressure plate with petroleum jelly so as not to damage the O-ring and install the plate on the dowel pins with the ported face toward the pump ring. Seat the pressure plate by placing a large socket on top of the plate and pushing down with the hand.
7. Install the pressure plate spring in the center groove of the plate.
8. Install the end plate O-ring. Lubricate the outside diameter and chamfer of the end plate with petroleum jelly so as not to damage the O-ring and install the end plate in the housing, using an arbor press. Install the end plate retaining ring while pump is in the arbor press. Be sure the ring is in the groove and the ring gap is positioned properly.
9. Install the flow control spring and plunger, hex head screw end in bore first. Install the filter cage, new filter stud seals and union seal.
10. Place the reservoir in the normal position and press down until the reservoir seats on the housing. Check the position of the stud seals and the union seal.
11. Install the studs, union, and driveshaft woodruff key. Support the shaft on the opposite side of the key when tapping the key into place.

Steering Trouble Diagnosis

Power Steering

Condition	Possible Cause	Correction
Intermittent or no power assist	1. Belt slipping and/or low fluid level. 2. Piston or rod binding in power cylinder. (Linkage type). 3. Sliding sleeve stuck in control valve. (Linkage type). 4. Improper pump operation.	1. Adjust or replace belt. Add fluid as necessary. 2. Repair or replace piston and rod. 3. Free-up or replace sleeve. 4. Refer to "Power Steering Pump."
Poor or no recovery from turns	1. Improper caster setting. 2. Steering gear adjustments too tight. 3. Improper spool nut adjustment. (Linkage type). 4. Valve spool installed backwards. (Linkage type). 5. Low tire pressure. 6. Tight steering linkage. 7. King pins frozen.	1. Adjust to specifications. 2. Adjust according to instructions. 3. Adjust according to instructions 4. Install valve spool correctly. 5. Inflate tires to recommended pressure. 6. Lubricate as necessary. 7. Lubricate as necessary.
Lack of effort (both turns)	1. Improper sector shaft adjustment. 2. Pressure plates on wrong side of reactions rings.	1. Adjust Sector Shaft. 2. Gear Recondition.
Lack of effort (left turn only)	1. Left turn reaction seal "O" ring worn, damaged or missing. 2. Left turn reaction oil passageway not drilled in housing or cylinder head. 3. Left turn reaction ring sticking in cylinder head.	1. Gear recondition. 2. Replace parts as required. 3. Replace parts as required
Lack of effort (right turn only)	1. Right turn U-shaped reaction seal worn, damaged, or missing. 2. Right turn reaction oil passageway not drilled in housing head, or ferrule pin. 3. Right turn reaction ring sticking in housing head.	1. Gear recondition. 2. Replace parts as required. 3. Replace parts as required.

Steering Trouble Diagnosis (cont.)

Power Steering

Condition	Possible Cause	Correction
Lack of assist (left turn only)	Left turn reaction seal "O" ring worn, damaged, or missing.	Gear recondition.
Lack of assist (right turn only)	1. Right turn U-shaped reaction seal worn, damaged, or missing. 2. Worm sealing ring (teflon) worm sleeve seal, ferrule pin "O" ring damaged or worn. 3. Excessive internal leakage thru piston end plug and/or side plugs.	1. Gear recondition. 2. Gear recondition. 3. Replace worm-piston assembly.
Lack of assist (both turns)	1. Low oil level in pump reservoir (usually accompanied by pump noise). 2. Loose pump belt. 3. Pump output low. 4. Engine idle too low. 5. Excessive internal leakage thru piston end plug and/or side plugs.	1. Fill to proper level. 2. Adjust belts. 3. Pressure test pump. 4. Adjust engine idle. 5. Replace worm-piston assembly.
Objectionable "hiss"	Noisy valve	Do not replace valve unless "hiss" is extremely objectionable. A replacement valve will also exhibit sight noise and is not always a cure for the objection.
Rattle or chuckle noise in steering gear	1. Gear loose on frame. 2. Steering linkages looseness. 3. Pressure hose touching other parts of truck. 4. Loose Pitman shaft over center adjustment. **NOTE:** A slight rattle may occur on turns because of increased clearance off the "high point". This is normal and clearance must not be reduced below specified limits to eliminate this slight rattle. 5. Loose Pitman arm.	1. Check gear mounting bolts. Torque bolts to specifications. 2. Check linkage pivot points for wear. Replace if necessary. 3. Adjust hose position. Do not bend tubing by hand. 4. Adjust 5. Torque Pitman arm pinch bolt.
Squawk noise in steering gear when turning or recovering from a turn	1. Dampener O-ring on valve spool cut. 2. Loose or worn valve.	1. Replace dampener O-Ring. 2. Replace valve.
Chirp noise in steering gear	Gear relief valve.	Replace relief valve.
Chirp noise in steering gear	Gear relief valve.	Replace relief valve.
Chirp noise in steering pump	Loose belt.	Adjust belt tension.
Belt Squeal (Particularly noticeable at full wheel travel and standstill parking)	Loose belt.	Adjust belt tension.
Growl noise in steering pump	Excessive back pressure in hoses or steering gear caused by restriction.	Locate restriction and correct. Replace part if necessary.
Growl noise in steering pump (particularly noticeable at standstill parking)	1. Scored pressure plates, thrust plate or rotor. 2. Extreme wear of cam ring.	1. Replace parts and flush system. 2. Replace parts.
Groan noise in steering pump	1. Low oil level. 2. Air in the oil. Poor pressure hose connection.	1. Fill reservoir to proper level. 2. Torque connector. Bleed system.
Rattle or knock noise in steering pump	Loose pump pulley nut.	Torque nut.

Steering Trouble Diagnosis (cont.)

Power Steering

Condition	Possible Cause	Correction
Rattle noise in steering pump	1. Vanes not installed properly. 2. Vanes sticking in rotor slots.	1. Install properly. 2. Repair or replace.
Swish noise in steering pump	Defective flow control valve.	Replace part.
Whine noise in steering pump	Pump shaft bearing scored.	Replace housing and shaft. Flush and bleed system.
Intermittent assist	1. Flow control valve sticking. 2. Slipping belt. 3. Low fluid level. 4. Low pump efficiency.	1. Pressure test pump and service as necessary. 2. Adjust belt. 3. Inspect and correct fluid level. 4. Pressure test pump and service as necessary.
No assist	1. Pump seizure. 2. Broken slipper spring(s). 3. Flow control bore plug ring not in place. 4. Flow control valve sticking.	1. Replace pump. 2. Recondition pump or replace as necessary. 3. Replace snap ring. Inspect groove for depth. 4. Pressure test pump and service as necessary.
No assist when parking only	1. Wrong pressure relief valve. 2. Broken "O" ring on flow control bore plug. 3. Loose pressure relief valve. 4. Low pump efficiency	1. Install proper relief valve. 2. Replace "O" ring. 3. Tighten valve. DO NOT ADJUST. 4. Pressure test pump and service as necessary.
Noisy pump	1. Low fluid level. 2. Belt noise. 3. Foreign material blocking pump housing oil inlet hole.	1. Inspect and correct fluid level. 2. Inspect for pulley alignment, paint or grease on pulley and correct. Adjust belt. 3. Remove reservoir, visually check inlet oil hole and service as necessary.
Pump vibration	1. Pump hose interference with sheet metal or brake lines. 2. Belt loose. 3. Pulley loose or out of round. 4. Crankshaft pulley loose or damaged. 5. Bracket pivot bolts loose.	1. Reroute hoses. 2. Adjust belt. 3. Replace pulley. 4. Replace crankshaft pulley. 5. If unable to tighten, replace bracket.
Pump leaks	1. Cap or filler neck leaks. 2. Reservoir-solder joints leak. 3. Reservoir "O" ring leaking. 4. Shaft seal leaking. 5. Loose rear bracket bolts. 6. Loose or faulty high pressure ferrule. 7. Rear bolt holes stripped or casting cracked.	1. Correct fluid level. 2. Resolder or replace reservoir as necessary. 3. Inspect sealing area of reservoir. Replace "O" ring or reservoir as necessary. 4. Replace seal. 5. Tighten bolts. 6. Tighten fitting to 24 foot-pounds or replace as necessary. 7. Repair, if possible, or replace pump.
Hard steering	1. Low or uneven tire pressure 2. Insufficient lubricant in the steering gear housing or in steering linkage. 3. Steering gear shaft adjusted too tight. 4. Improper caster or toe-in. 5. Steering column misaligned. 6. Loose, worn or broken pump belt. 7. Air in system. 8. Low fluid level in the pump reservoir.	1. Inflate the tires to recommended pressures. 2. Lubricate as necessary. 3. Adjust according to instructions. 4. Align the wheels. 5. See "Steering Gear Alignment." 6. Adjust or replace belt. 7. Bleed air from system. 8. Fill to correct level.

Steering Trouble Diagnosis (cont.)

Power Steering

Condition	Possible Cause	Correction
	9. Pump output pressure low.	9. See "Pressure Test."
	10. Leakage at power cylinder piston rings. (Linkage type).	10. Replace piston rings and repair as required.
	11. Binding or bent cylinder linkage. (Linkage type).	11. Replace or repair as required.
	12. Valve spool and/or sleeve sticking. (Linkage type).	12. Free-up or replace as required.

Brakes

BRAKE SYSTEM

All Chevrolet and GMC vans from 1967 are equipped with a split hydraulic braking system. The system is designed with separate systems for the front and rear brakes using a dual master cylinder with separate reservoirs. If a wheel cylinder or brake line should fail in either the front or the rear system, the van can still be stopped with reasonable control.

From 1967–70, vans were equipped with drum brakes front and rear. The front brakes are duo-servo anchor pin type which are self-adjusting. The rear brakes are of the same basic type.

Beginning 1971, vans were equipped with disc brakes at the front and drum brakes at the rear. The drum brakes are still of the duo-servo anchor pin self-adjusting type, while the front disc brakes are single piston sliding caliper types. The front disc brakes are inherently self-adjusting.

The parking brake is either hand or foot operated, but in any event, acts on the rear brakes.

Adjustment

FRONT OR REAR DRUM BRAKES

These brakes are equipped with self-adjusters and no manual adjustment is necessary, except when brake linings are replaced.

FRONT DISC BRAKES

These brakes are inherently self-adjusting and no adjustment is ever necessary or possible.

BRAKE PEDAL

The stop light switch provides for an automatic adjustment for the brake pedal when it is returned to its stop. With pedal in fully released position, the stop light switch plunger should be fully depressed against the pedal shank. Adjust the switch by moving in or out as necessary.

1. Make certain that the tubular clip is in brake pedal mounting bracket.
2. With brake pedal depressed, insert switch into tubular clip until switch body seats on clip. Audible clicks can be heard as the threaded portion of the switch is pushed through the clip toward the brake pedal.
3. Pull brake pedal fully rearward against pedal stop until audible clicking sounds can no longer be heard. Switch will be moved in tubular clip providing adjustment.
4. Release brake pedal and then repeat Step 3 to assure that no audible clicking sounds remain.

Master Cylinder

REMOVAL AND INSTALLATION

NOTE: *Clean any master cylinder parts in alcohol or brake fluid. Never use mineral based cleaning solvents such as gasoline, kerosene, carbon tetrachloride, acetone, or paint thinner as these will destroy rubber parts.*

CAUTION: *Do not allow brake fluid to spill*

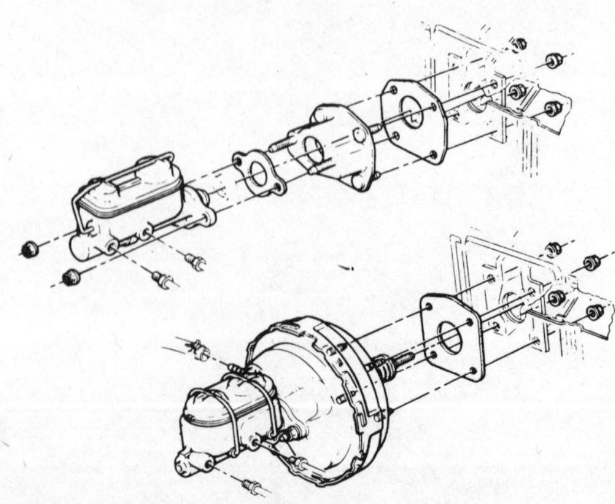

Master cylinder installation

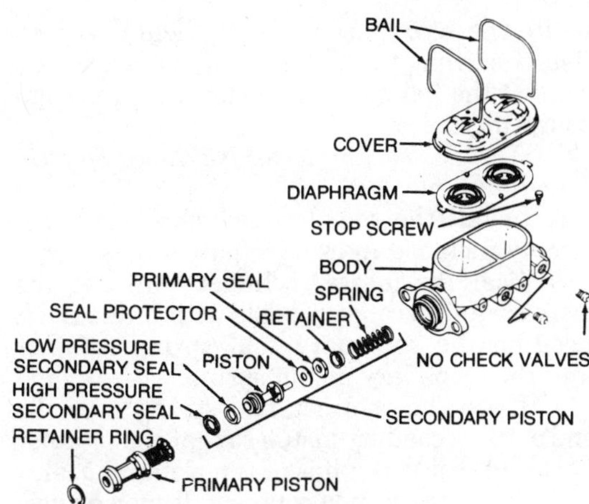

Exploded view of the typical master cylinder

on the vehicle's finish, it will remove the paint. Flush the area with water.

1. Using a clean cloth, wipe the master cylinder and its lines to remove excess dirt and then place cloths under the unit to absorb spilled fluid.
2. Remove the hydraulic lines from the master cylinder and plug the outlets to prevent the entrance of foreign material.
3. Disconnect the brake pushrod from the brake pedal on non-power brakes.
4. Remove the attaching bolts and remove the master cylinder from the firewall or the brake booster.

To install:

5. Connect the pushrod to the brake pedal with the pin and retainer.
6. Connect the brake lines and fill the master cylinder reservoirs to the proper levels.
7. Bleed the brake system as outlined in this Section.

OVERHAUL

In most years, there are 2 sources for master cylinders, Delco-Moraine and Bendix. The Bendix unit can readily be identified by the secondary stop bolt on the bottom, which is not present on the Delco-Moraine unit. Some early models use a Wagner unit which has the cover secured by a bolt. Master cylinders bearing identifying code letters should only be replaced with cylinders bearing the same code letters. Secondary pistons are also coded by rings or grooves on the shank or center section of the piston, and should only be replaced with pistons having the same code. The primary pistons also are of 2 types. One has a deep socket for the pushrod and the other has a very shallow socket. Be sure to replace pistons with identical parts. Failure to do this could result in a malfunction.

NOTE: *This procedure applies to all Delco*

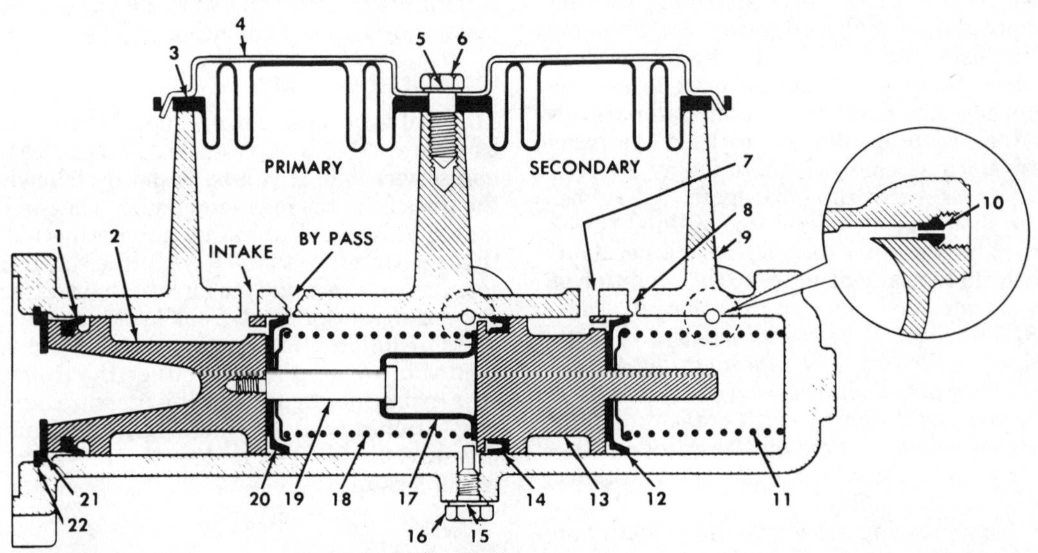

1. Primary piston seal cup
2. Primary piston
3. Cover seal
4. Reservoir housing
5. Gasket
6. Cover bolt
7. Intake port
8. By-pass port
9. Reservoir housing
10. Tube seat
11. Secondary piston return spring
12. Secondary piston pressure cup
13. Floating secondary piston
14. Secondary piston seal cup
15. Gasket
16. Stop bolt
17. Primary return spring retainer
18. Primarx return spring
19. Primary piston stop pin
20. Primary piston pressure cup
21. Stop plate
22. Retainer ring

Cross-section of the typical master cylinder

master cylinders, but not to the Bendix unit used on 1976 and later G-30 and 3500 motorhome models with the Hydro-Boost brake system.

1. Remove the secondary piston stop screw at the bottom of the master cylinder front reservoir.

2. Position the master cylinder in a vise covering the jaws with cloth to prevent damage. (Do not tighten the vise too tightly).

3. Remove the lockring from the inside of the piston bore. Once this is done, the primary piston assembly may be removed.

4. The secondary piston, piston spring, and the retainer may be removed by blowing compressed air through the stop screw hole. If compressed air is not available, the piston may be removed with a small piece of wire. Bend the wire ¼" (6.35mm) from the end to the edge of the secondary piston and pull it from the bore. The brass insert should not be removed unless it is being replaced.

5. Inspect the piston bore for corrosion or other obstructions. Make certain that the outer ports are clean and the fluid reservoirs are free of foreign matter. Check the by-pass and the compensating ports to see if they are clogged.

6. Remove the primary seal, seal protector, and secondary seals from the secondary piston.

Clean all parts in denatured alcohol or brake fluid. Use a soft brush to clean metal parts and compressed air to dry all parts. If corrosion is found inside the housing, either a crocus cloth or fine emery paper can be used to remove these deposits. Remember to wash all parts after this cleaning. Be sure to keep the parts clean until assembly. If there is any doubt of cleanliness, wash the part again. All rubber parts should be clean and free of fluid. Check each rubber part for cuts, nicks, or other damage. If there is any doubt as to the condition of any rubber part, it is best to replace it.

NOTE: *Since there are differences between master cylinders, it is important that the assemblies are identified correctly. There is a 2-letter metal stamp located at the end of the master cylinder. If the master cylinder is replaced, it must be replaced with a cylinder with the same markings.*

7. Install the new secondary piston assembly.

NOTE: *The seal which is nearest the flat end has its lips facing toward the flat end. On Delco units, the seal in the second groove has its lips facing toward the compensating holes of the secondary piston. On Bendix units, the seal is an O-ring.*

8. Install the new primary seal and seal protector over the end of the secondary piston opposite the secondary seals. It should be positioned so that the flat side of the seal seats against the flange of the piston with the compensating holes.

NOTE: *The seal protector isn't used on 1977 and later models.*

9. Install the complete primary piston assembly included in every repair kit.

10. Coat the master cylinder bore and the primary and secondary seals with brake fluid. Position the secondary seal spring retainer into the secondary piston spring.

11. Place the retainer and spring over the end of the secondary piston so that the retainer is placed inside the lips of the primary seal.

12. Seat the secondary piston. It may be necessary to manipulate the piston to get it to seat.

13. Position the master cylinder with the open end up and coat the primary and secondary seals on the primary piston with brake fluid. Push the primary piston into the bore of the master cylinder. Hold the piston and position the lockring.

14. Still holding the piston down, install and tighten the stop screw to torque of 25–40 in.lb.

15. Install the reservoir cover and also the cover on the master cylinder and its retaining clip.

16. Bleed the master cylinder of air by positioning it with the front slightly down, filling it with brake fluid, and working the primary piston until all the bubbles are gone.

Combination Valve

This valve is used on all models with disc brakes. It is non-adjustable and non-serviceable. It can be found by following the lines from the master cylinder. The combination valve itself contains a metering valve that restricts flow to the front brakes until the rear brakes overcome the force of their retracting springs to prevent front brake lockup, a pressure differential warning switch which activates a warning light if either the front or rear hydraulic circuit is losing pressure, and a proportioning valve which limits hydraulic pressure to the rear brakes to prevent rear wheel lockup.

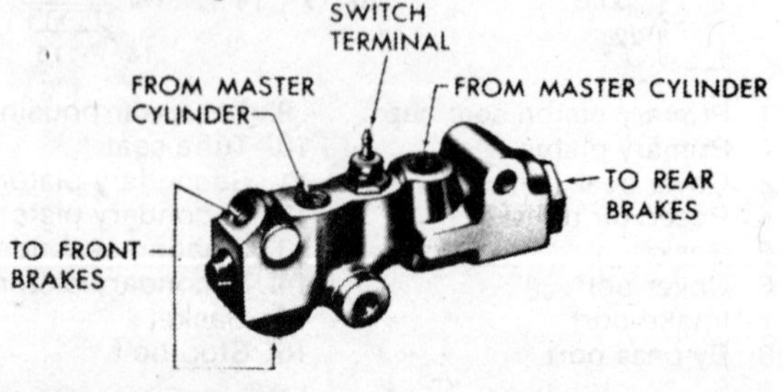

Combination valve

The pressure differential warning switch will reset itself automatically when the brakes are used after a malfunction causing the warning light to go on has been corrected.

When the brake hydraulic system is bled of air, the metering valve pin on the end of the combination valve must be hold in a slight amount to allow fluid flow to the front brakes.

CENTERING THE SWITCH

Whenever work on the brake system is done it is possible that the brake warning light will come on and refuse to go off when the work is finished. In this event, the switch must be centered.

1. Raise and support the truck.
2. Attach a bleeder hose to the rear brake bleed screw and immerse the other end of the hose in a jar of clean brake fluid.
3. Be sure that the master cylinder is full.
4. When bleeding the brakes, the pin in the end of the metering portion of the combination valve must be hold in the open position (with the tool described in the brake bleeding section installed under the pin mounting bolt). Be sure to tighten the bolt after removing the tool.
5. Turn the ignition key ON. Open the bleed screw while an assistant applies heavy pressure on the brake pedal. The warning lamp should light. Close the bleed screw before the helper releases the pedal.

To reset the switch, apply heavy pressure to the pedal. This will apply hydraulic pressure to the switch which will recenter it.

6. Repeat Step 5 for the front bleed screw.
7. Turn the ignition OFF and lower the truck.

NOTE: *If the warning lamp does not light during Step 5, the switch is defective and must be replaced.*

Bleeding the Brakes

The brake system must be bled when any brake line is disconnected or there is air in the system.

NOTE: *Never bleed a wheel cylinder when a drum is removed.*

1. Clean the master cylinder of excess dirt and remove the cylinder cover and the diaphragm.
2. Fill the master cylinder to the proper level. Check the fluid level periodically during the bleeding process, and replenish it as necessary. Do not allow the master cylinder to run dry, or you will have to start over.
3. Before opening any of the bleeder screws, you may want to give each one a shot of penetrating solvent. This reduces the possibility of breakage when they are unscrewed.

BLEEDER WRENCH

BLEEDER TUBE

TUBE MUST BE SUBMERGED IN BRAKE FLUID

Brake bleeding equipment

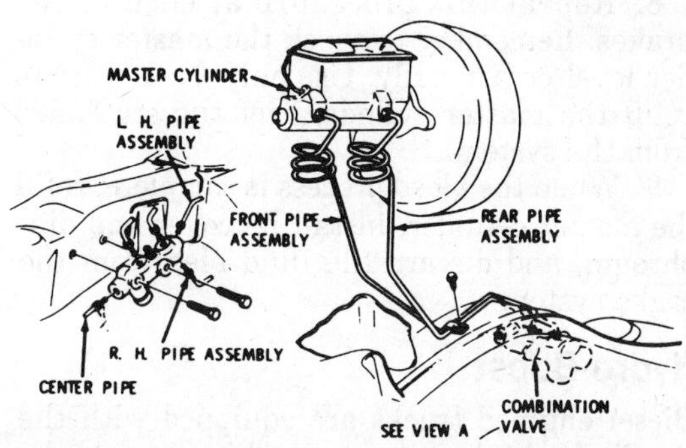

Combination valves are usually mounted blow the master cylinder on the frame rail. Clip or tape the metering pin "in" while bleeding the disc brakes

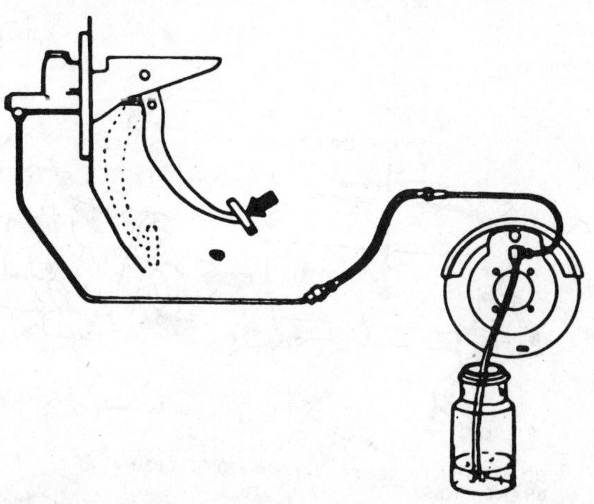

Have an assistant pump, then hold in the brake pedla while you bleed each wheel

4. Attach a length of vinyl hose to the bleeder screw of the brake to be bled. Insert the other end of the hose into a clear jar half full of brake fluid, so that the end of the hose is beneath the level of fluid. The correct sequence for bleeding is to work from the brake farthest from the master cylinder to the one closest; right rear, left rear, right front, left front.

5. The combination valve (all vehicles with disc brakes) must be held open during the bleeding process. A clip, tape, or other similar tool (or an assistant) will hold the metering pin in.

6. With power brakes, depress and release the brake pedal three or four times to exhaust any residual vacuum.

7. Have an assistant push down on the brake pedal. Open the bleeder valve slightly. As the pedal reaches the end of its travel, close the bleeder screw. Repeat this process until no air bubbles are visible in the expelled fluid.

NOTE: *Make sure your assistant presses the brake pedal to the floor slowly. Pressing too fast will cause air bubbles to form in the fluid.*

8. Repeat this procedure at each of the brakes. Remember to check the master cylinder level occasionally. Use only fresh fluid to refill the master cylinder, not the stuff bled from the system.

9. When the bleed process is complete, refill the master cylinder, install its cover and diaphragm, and discard the fluid bled from the brake system.

Hydro-Boost

Diesel engined trucks are equipped with the Bendix Hydro-boost system. This power brake booster obtains hydraulic pressure from the power steering pump, rather than vacuum pressure from the intake manifold as in most gasoline engine brake booster systems. Procedures from removing, overhauling, and replacing the master cylinder are the same as previously outlined. The master cylinder uses the same DOT 3 brake fluid recommended for other systems.

HYDRO-BOOST SYSTEM CHECKS

1. A defective Hydro-Boost cannot cause any of the following conditions:
   a. Noisy brakes
   b. Fading pedal
   c. Pulling brakes.

If any of these occur, check elsewhere in the brake system.

2. Check the fluid level in the master cylinder. It should be within ¼" (6.35mm) of the top. If is isn't add only DOT-3 or DOT-4 brake fluid until the correct level is reached.

3. Check the fluid level in the power steering pump. The engine should be at normal running temperature and stopped. The level should register on the pump dipstick. Add power steering fluid to bring the reservoir level up to the correct level. Low fluid level will result in both poor steering and stopping ability.

CAUTION: *The brake hydraulic system uses brake fluid only, while the power steering and Hydro-Boost systems use power steering fluid only. Don't mix the two.*

4. Check the power steering pump belt tension, and inspect all the power steering/Hydro-Boost hoses for kinks or leaks.

5. Check and adjust the engine idle speed, as necessary.

6. Check the power steering pump fluid for

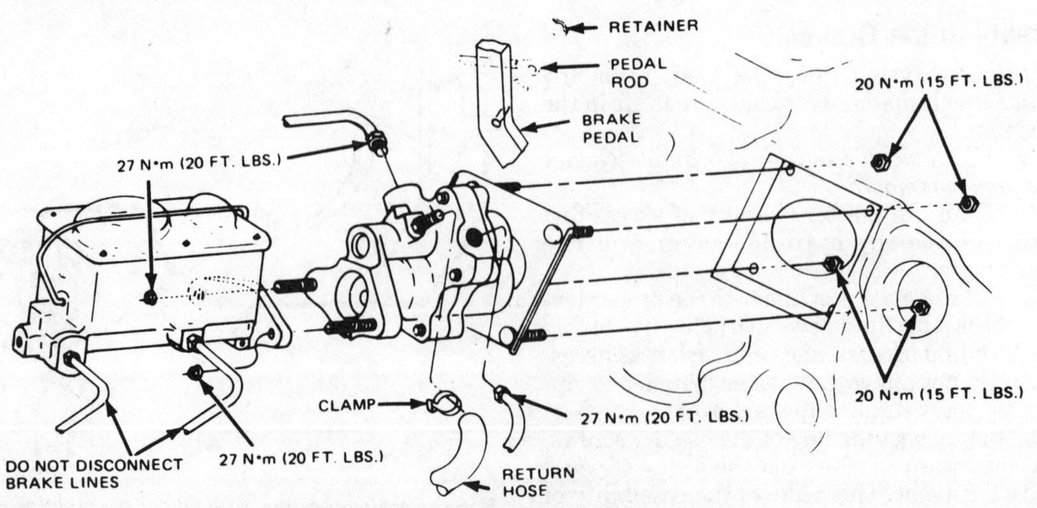

Removal and installation of Hydro-Booster

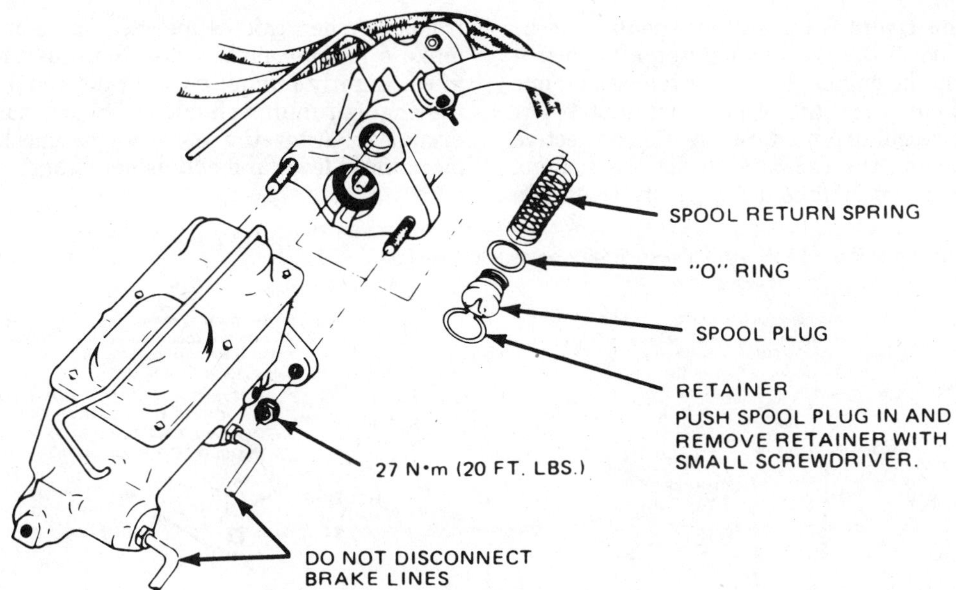

Removing Hydro-Boost spool valve and seal

bubbles. If air bubbles are present in the fluid, bleed the system:

a. Fill the power steering pump reservoir to specifications with the engine at normal operating temperature.

b. With the engine running, rotate the steering wheel through its normal travel 3 or 4 times, without holding the wheel against the stops.

c. Check the fluid level again.

7. If the problem still exists, go on to the Hydro-Boost test sections and troubleshooting chart.

HYDRO-BOOST TESTS

Functional Test

1. Check the brake system for leaks or low fluid level. Correct as necessary.
2. Place the transmission in Neutral and stop the engine. Apply the brakes 4 or 5 times to empty the accumulator.
3. Keep the pedal depressed with moderate (25–40 lbs.) pressure and start the engine.
4. The brake pedal should fall slightly and then push back up against your foot. If no movement is felt, the Hydro-Boost system is not working.

Accumulator Leak Test

1. Run the engine at normal idle. Turn the steering wheel against one of the stops; hold it there for no longer than 5 seconds. Center the steering wheel and stop the engine.
2. Keep applying the brakes until a hard pedal is obtained. There should be a minimum of 1 power assisted brake application when pedal pressure of 20–25 lbs. is applied.
3. Start the engine and allow it to idle. Rotate the steering wheel against the stop. Listen for a light hissing sound; this is the accumulator being charged. Center the steering wheel and stop the engine.
4. Wait one hour and apply the brakes without starting the engine. As in step 2, there should be at least 1 stop with power assist. If not, the accumulator is defective and must be replaced.

HYDRO-BOOST SYSTEM BLEEDING

The system should be bled whenever the booster is removed and installed.

1. Fill the power steering pump until the fluid level is at the base of the pump reservoir neck. Disconnect the battery lead from the distributor.

NOTE: *Remove the electrical lead to the fuel solenoid terminal on the injection pump before cranking the engine.*

2. Jack up the front of the car, turn the wheels all the way to the left, and crank the engine for a few seconds.
3. Check steering pump fluid level. If necessary, add fluid to the **Add** mark on the dipstick.
4. Lower the car, connect the battery lead, and start the engine. Check fluid level and add fluid to the **Add** mark is necessary. With the engine running, turn the wheels from side to side to bleed air from the system. Make sure that the fluid level stays above the internal pump casting.

5. The Hydro-Boost system should now be fully bled. If the fluid is foaming after bleeding, stop the engine, let the system set for one hour, then repeat the second part of Step 4.

The preceding procedures should be effective in removing the excess air from the system, however sometimes air may still remain trapped. When this happens the booster may make a gulping noise when the brake is applied. Lightly pumping the brake pedal with the engine running should cause this noise to disappear. After the noise stops, check the pump fluid level and add as necessary.

Remove And Install Spool Valve, Power Piston/Acuumulator And Seal.

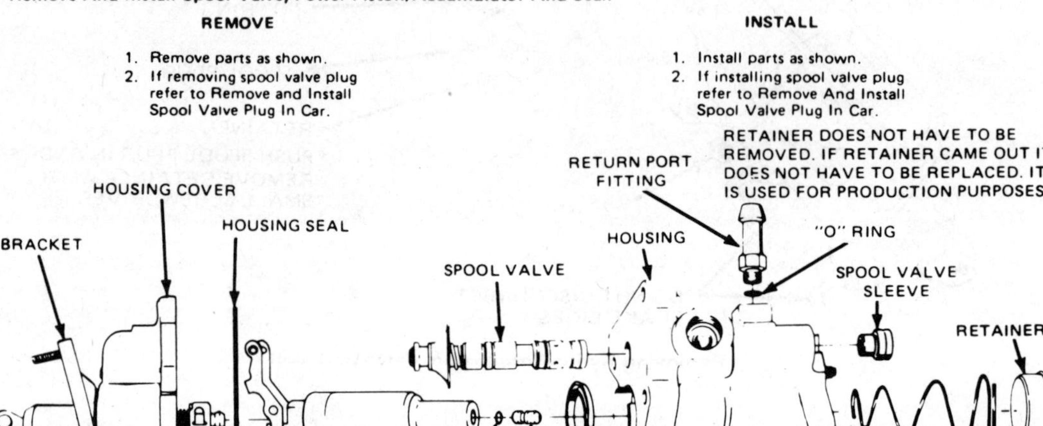

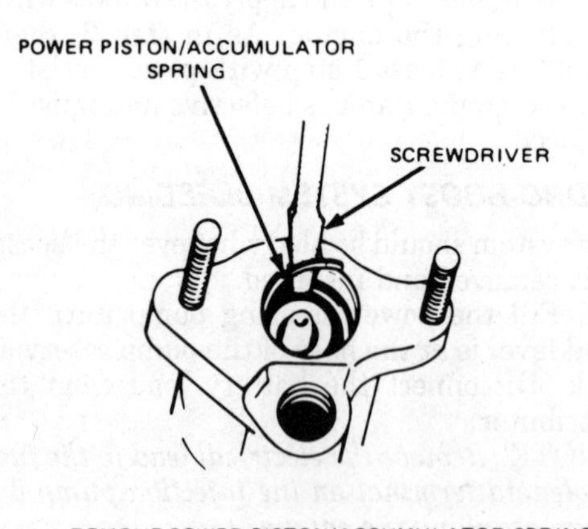

REMOVE POWER PISTON/ACCUMULATOR SPRING

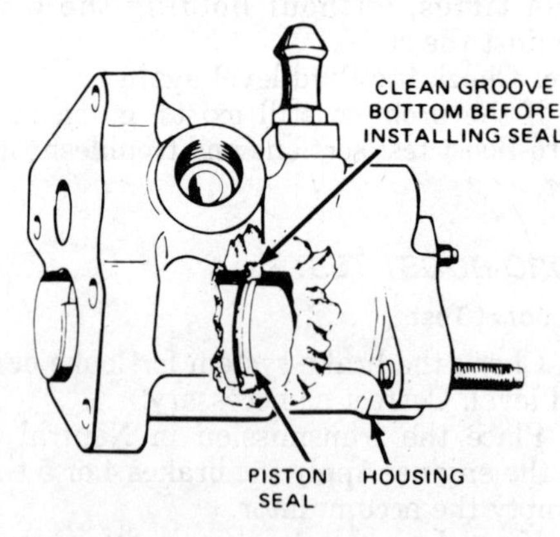

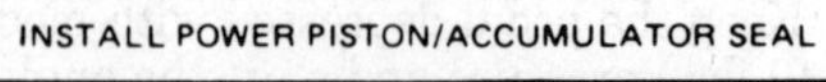
INSTALL POWER PISTON/ACCUMULATOR SEAL

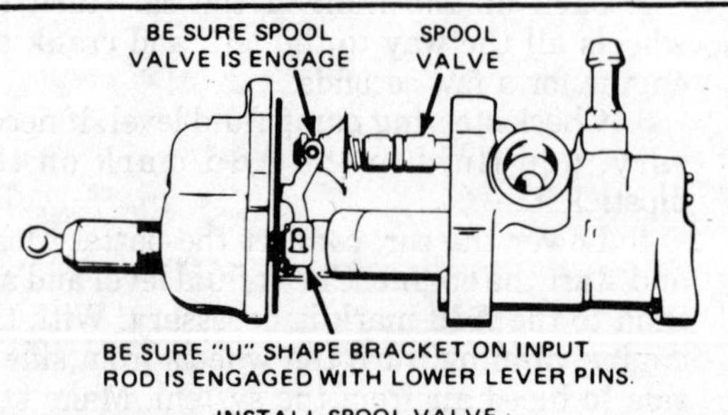

INSTALL SPOOL VALVE

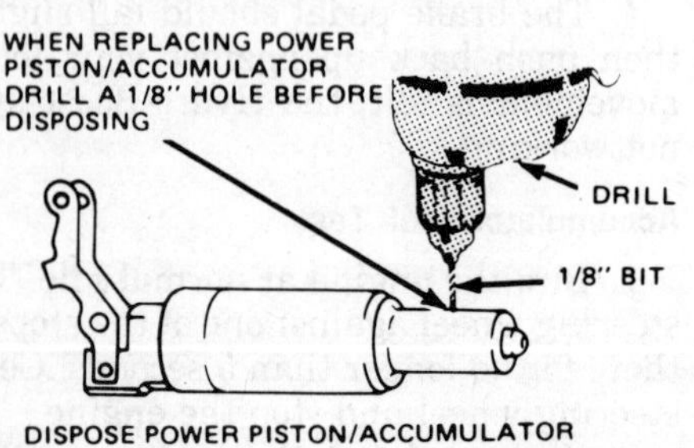

DISPOSE POWER PISTON/ACCUMULATOR

Hydro Boost overhaul

TROUBLESHOOTING THE HYDRO-BOOST SYSTEM

High Pedal and Steering Effort (Idle)

1. Loosen/broken power steering pump belt
2. Low power steering fluid level
3. Leaking hoses or fittings
4. Low idle speed
5. Hose restriction
6. Defective power steering pump

High Pedal Effort (Idle)

1. Binding pedal/linkage
2. Fluid contamination
3. Defective Hydro-Boost unit

Poor Pedal Return

1. Binding pedal linkage
2. Restricted booster return line
3. Internal return system restriction

Pedal Chatter/Pulsation

1. Power steering pump drive belt slipping
2. Low power steering fluid level
3. Defective power steering pump
4. Defective Hydro-Boost unit

Brakes Oversensitive

1. Binding linkage
2. Defective Hydro-Boost unit

Noise

1. Low power steering fluid level
2. Air in the power steering fluid
3. Loose power steering pump drive belt
4. Hose restrictions

OVERHAUL

GMC Hydro-Boost units may be rebuilt. Kits are available through auto parts jobbers and GMC/Chevrolet truck dealers.

NOTE: *Have a drain pan ready to catch and discard leaking fluid during disassembly.*

Use the accompanying illustrations to overhaul the Hydro-Boost system. If replacing the power piston/accumulator, dispose of the old one as shown.

SPOOL VALVE PLUG AND SEAL REMOVAL AND INSTALLATION

1. Turn the engine off and pump the brake pedal 4 or 5 times to deplete the accumulator inside the boost unit.
2. Remove the master cylinder from the boost unit with the brake lines attached. Fasten the master cylinder out of the way with tape or wire.
3. Push the spool valve plug in and use a small screwdriver to carefully remove the retaining ring.
4. Remove the spool valve plug and O-ring.
5. Installation is the reverse of removal. Bleed the system upon installation, following the above bleeding instructions.

HYDRO-BOOST UNIT REMOVAL AND INSTALLATION

CAUTION: *Power steering fluid and brake fluid cannot be mixed. If brake seals contact the steering fluid or steering seals contact the brake fluid, damage will result.*

1. Turn the engine off and pump the brake pedal 4 or 5 times to deplete the accumulator inside the unit.
2. Remove the two nuts from the master cylinder, and remove the cylinder keeping the brake lines attached. Secure the master cylinder out of the way.
3. Remove the three hydraulic lines from the booster.
4. Remove the booster unit from the firewall.
5. To install, reverse the removal procedure. Bleed the Hydro-Boost system.

FRONT DISC BRAKES

NOTE: *These procedures apply to Delco disc brake systems. They do not apply to the Bendix disc brakes used on G-30 and 3500 motorhomes, starting 1976.*

Brake Pads

INSPECTION

Support the front suspension or axle on jackstands and remove the wheels. Look in at the ends of the caliper to check the lining thickness of the outer pad. Look through the inspection hole in the top of the caliper to check the thickness of the inner pad. Minimum acceptable pad thickness is $\frac{1}{32}$" (0.79mm) from the rivet heads on original equipment riveted linings and ½" (12.7mm) lining thickness on bonded linings.

NOTE: *These manufacturer's specifications may not agree with your state inspection law.*

All original equipment pads are the riveted type; unless you want to remove the pads to measure the actual thickness from the rivet heads, you will have to make the limit for visual inspection $\frac{1}{16}$" (1.6mm) or more. The same applies if you don't know what kind of lining you have. 1974–86 original equipment pads and GM replacement pads have an integral wear sensor. This is a spring steel tab on the rear edge of the inner pad which produces a squeal by rubbing against the rotor to warn that the pads have reached their wear limit.

They do not squeal when the brakes are applied.

CAUTION: *The squeal will eventually stop if worn pads aren't replaced. Should this happen, replace the pads immediately to prevent expensive rotor (disc) damage.*

REPLACEMENT

The caliper has to be removed to replace the pads, so go on to that procedure. Skip steps 8–10, as there is no need to detach the brake line.

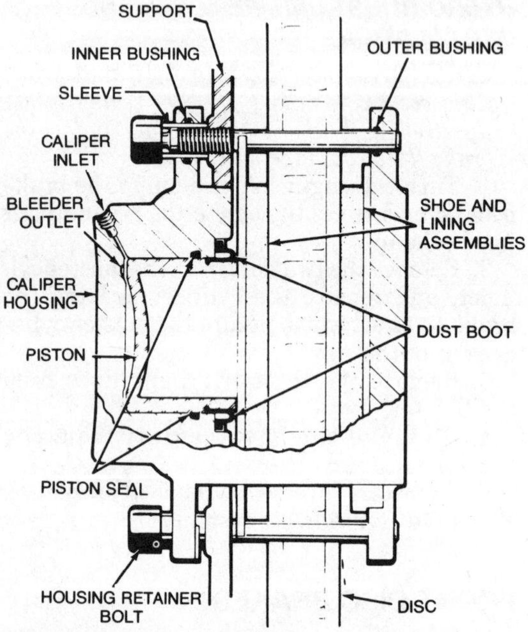

Disc and caliper components

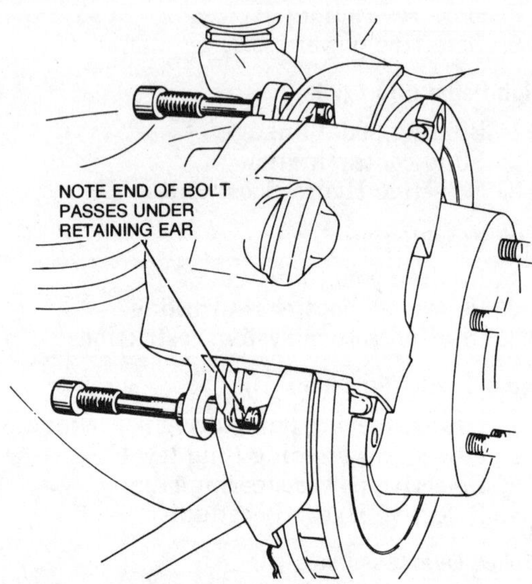

Caliper removal and installation

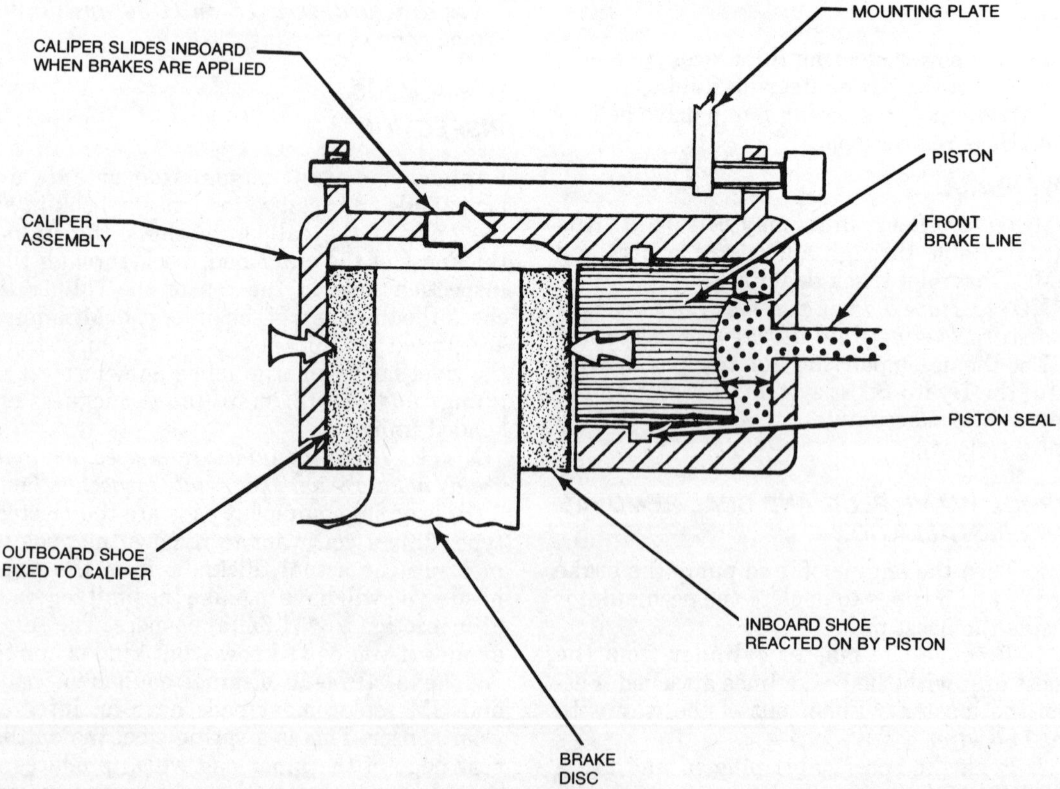

Disc brake operation

Caliper

REMOVAL AND INSTALLATION

1. Remove the cover on the master cylinder and siphon enough fluid out of the reservoirs to bring the level to ⅓ full. This step prevents spilling fluid when the piston is pushed back.

2. Raise and support the vehicle. Remove the front wheels and tires.

3. Push the brake piston back into its bore using a C-clamp to pull the caliper outward.

4. Remove the two bolts which hold the caliper and then lift the caliper off the disc.

CAUTION: *Do not let the caliper assembly hang by the brake hose.*

5. Remove the inboard and outboard shoe.

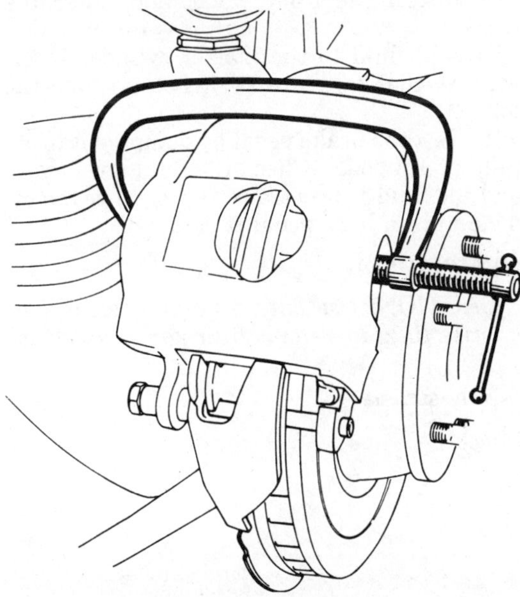

Pushing the piston back using a 7 in. C-clamp

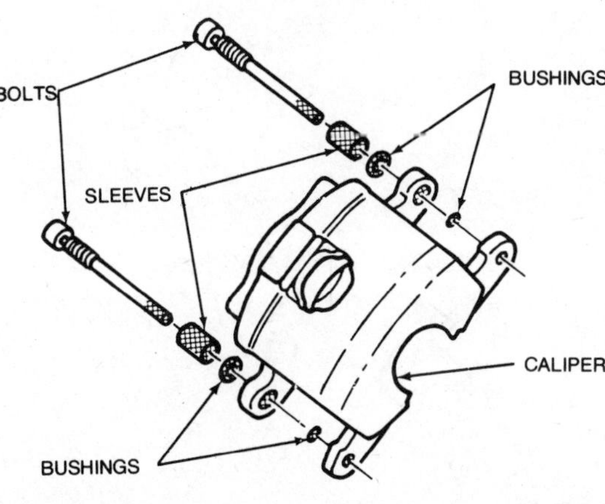

Caliper lubrication points

NOTE: *If the pads are to be reinstalled, mark them inside and outside.*

6. Remove the pad support spring from the piston.

7. Remove the two sleeves from the inside ears of the caliper and the 4 rubber bushings from the grooves in the caliper ears.

8. Remove the hose from the steel brake line and tape the fittings to prevent foreign material from entering the line or the hoses.

9. Remove the retainer from the hose fitting.

10. Remove the hose from the frame bracket and pull off the caliper with the hose attached.

NOTE: *Check the inside of the caliper for fluid leakage; if so, the caliper should be overhauled.*

CAUTION: *Do not use compressed air to clean the inside of the caliper as this may unseat the dust boot.*

11. Connect the brake line to start reinstallaiton. Lubricate the sleeves, rubber bushings, bushing grooves, and the end of the mounting bolts using silicone lubricant.

12. Install new bushing in the caliper ears along with new sleeves. The sleeve should be replaced so that the end toward the shoe is flush with the machined surface of the ear.

13. Position the support spring and the inner

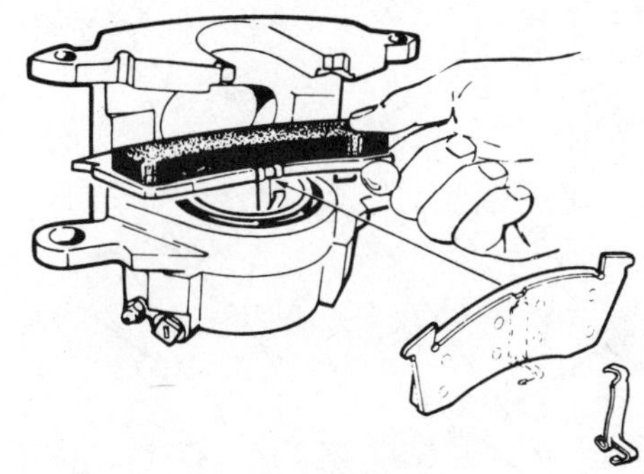

Support spring installation

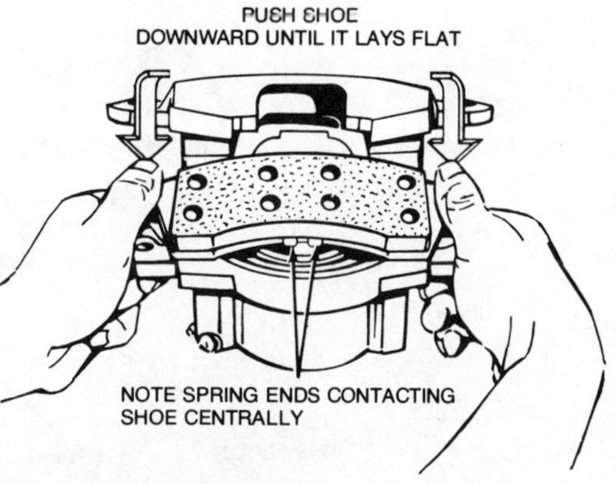

Inner brake pad installation

pad into the center cavity of the piston. The outboard pad has ears which are bent over to keep the pad in position while the inboard pad has ears on the top end which fit over the caliper retaining bolts. A spring which is inside the brake piston hold the bottom edge of the inboard pad.

14. Push down on the inner pad until it lays flat against the caliper. It is important to push the piston all the way into the caliper if new linings are installed or the caliper will not fit over the rotor.

15. Position the outboard pad with the ears of the pad over the caliper ears and the tab at the bottom engaged in the caliper cutout.

16. With the two pads in position, place the caliper over the brake disc and align the holes in the caliper with those of the mounting bracket.

CAUTION: *Make certain that the brake hose is not twisted or kinked.*

17. Install the mounting bracket bolts through the sleeves in the inboard caliper ears and through the mounting bracket, making sure that the ends of the bolts pass under the retaining ears on the inboard pad.

18. Tighten the mounting bolts to 35 ft.lb. Pump the brake pedal to seat the pad against the rotor. Don't do this unless both calipers are in place. Use a pair of channel lock pliers to

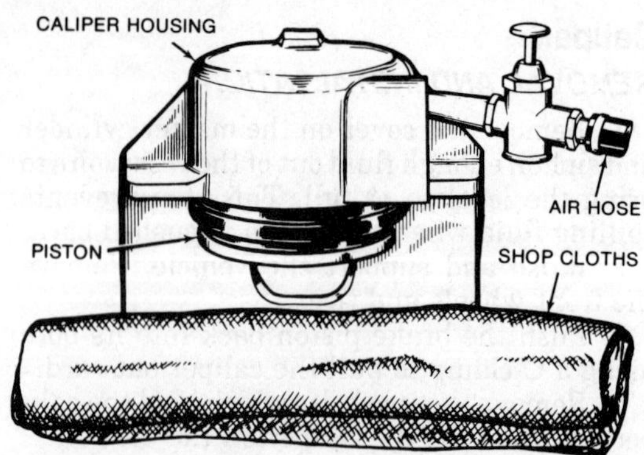

Removing the piston with compressed air

bend over the upper ears of the outer pad so it isn't loose.

19. Install the front wheel and lower the truck.

20. Add fluid to the master cylinder reservoirs so that they are ¼" (6.35mm) from the top.

21. Test the brake pedal by pumping it to obtain a hard pedal. Check the fluid level again and add fluid as necessary. Do not move the vehicle until a hard pedal is obtained.

OVERHAUL

CAUTION: *Use only denatured alcohol or brake fluid to clean caliper parts. Never use*

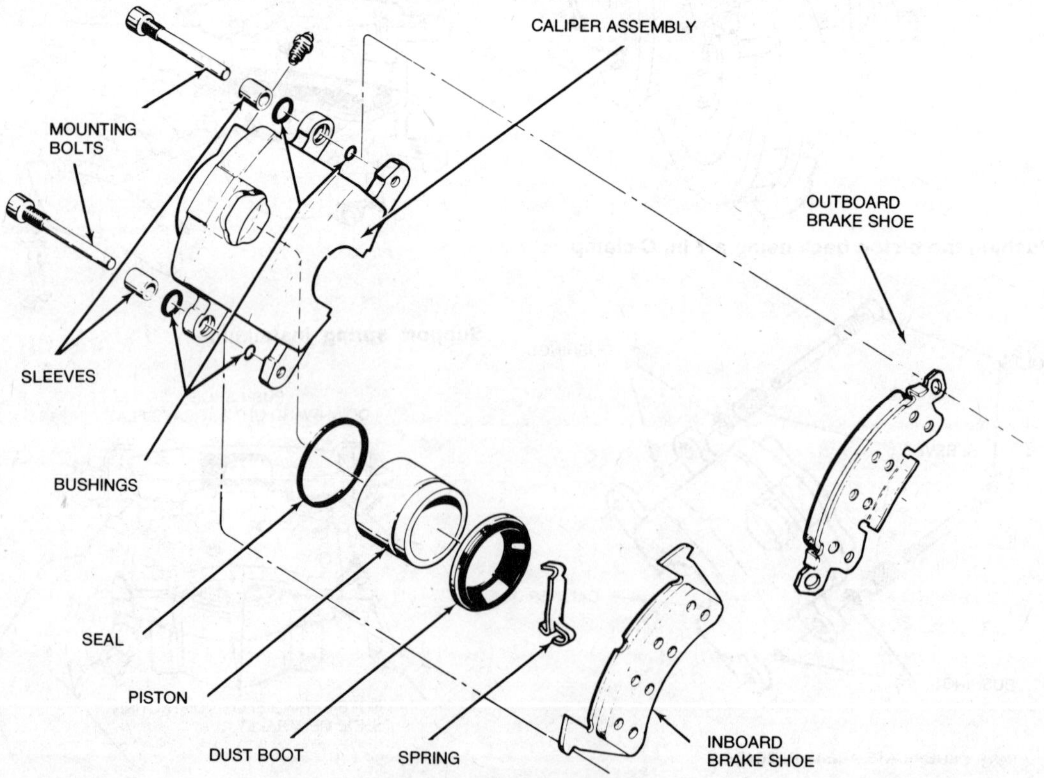

CALIPER ASSEMBLY
MOUNTING BOLTS
OUTBOARD BRAKE SHOE
SLEEVES
BUSHINGS
SEAL
PISTON
DUST BOOT
SPRING
INBOARD BRAKE SHOE

Caliper exploded view

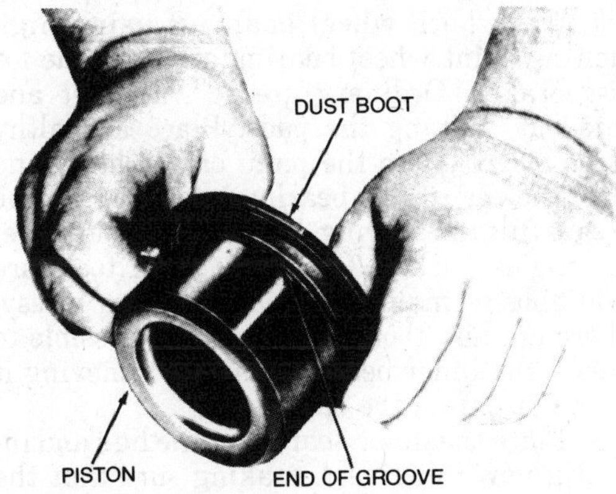

Piston boot installation

any mineral based cleaning solvents such as gasoline or kerosene as these solvents will deteriorate rubber parts.

1. Remove the caliper, clean it and place it on a clean and level work surface.
2. Remove the brake hose from the caliper and discard the copper gasket. Check the brake hose for cracks or deterioration. Replace the hose as necessary.
3. Drain the brake fluid from the caliper.
4. Pad the interior of the caliper with cloth and then apply compressed air to the caliper inlet hose.

CAUTION: *Do not place hands or fingers in front of the piston in an attempt to catch it. Use just enough air pressure to ease the piston out of the bore.*

5. Remove the piston dust boot by prying it out with a screwdriver. Use caution when performing this procedure.
6. Remove the piston seal from the caliper piston bore using a small piece of wood or plastic. DO NOT use any type of metal tool for this procedure.
7. Remove the bleeder valve from the caliper.

IMPORTANT: Dust boot, piston seal, rubber bushings, and sleeves are included in every rebuilding kit. These should be replaced at every caliper rebuild.

8. Clean all parts in the recommended solvent and dry them completely using compressed air if possible.

NOTE: *The use of shop air hoses may inject oil film into the assembly; use caution when using such hoses.*

9. Examine the mounting bolts for rust or corrosion. Replace them as necessary.
10. Examine the piston for scoring, nicks, or worn plating. If any of these conditions are present, replace them as necessary.

CAUTION: *Do not use any type of abrasive on the piston.*

11. Check the piston bore. Small defects can be removed with crocus cloth. If the bore cannot be cleaned in this manner, replace the caliper.
12. Lubricate the piston bore and the new piston seal with brake fluid. Place the seal in the caliper bore groove.
13. Lubricate the piston in the same manner and position the new boot into the groove in the piston so that the fold faces the open end of the piston.
14. Place the piston into the caliper bore using caution not to unseat the seal. Force the piston to the bottom of the bore.
15. Place the dust boot in the caliper counterbore and seat the boot. Make sure that the boot in positioned correctly and evenly.
16. Install the brake hose in the caliper inlet using a new copper gasket.

NOTE: *The hose must be positioned in the caliper locating gate to assure proper positioning of the caliper.*

17. Replace the bleeder screw.
18. Bleed the system.

Disc (Rotor)

REMOVAL AND INSTALLATION

1. Follow the procedures outlined for removing the caliper assembly.
2. Remove the bearing dust cap, cotter pin, center nut, and outer bearings.
3. Pull the rotor off the spindle and service it, as necessary.

To install the unit, reverse the removal procedure. Check the rotor before install it. Pack the inner and outer bearing to the proper specifications. (See Wheel Bearings).

The minimum wear thickness, 1.215" (30.861mm), is cast into each disc hub. This is a minimum wear dimension and not a refinish dimension. If the thickness of the disc after refinishing will be 1.230" (31.242mm) or less, it must be replaced. Refinishing is required whenever the disc surface shows scoring or se-

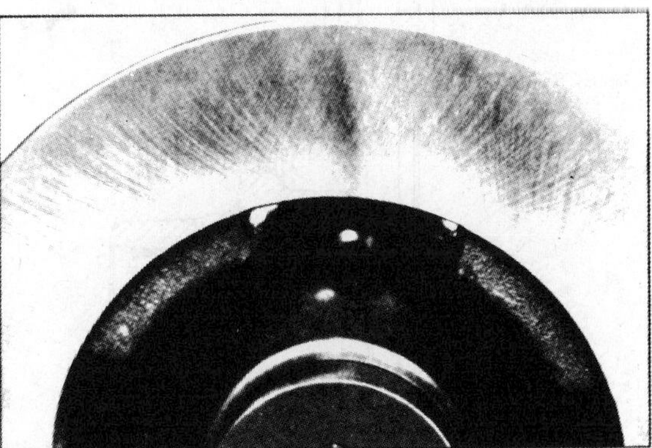

Disc finish

vere rust scale. Scoring not deeper than 0.015" (0.381mm) in depth can be corrected by refinishing.

NOTE: *Some discs have an anti-squeal groove. This should not be mistaken for scoring.*

Wheel Bearing Lubrication and Adjustment

Only front wheel bearings require periodic service. A premium high melting point grease meeting GM specification 6031-M must be used. Long fiber type greases must not be used. This service is recommended at the intervals in the Maintenance Intervals chart or whenever the van has been driven in water up to the hubs.

1. Remove the wheel and tire assembly, and the brake drum or brake caliper.
2. Remove the hub and disc as an assembly. Remove the caliper mounting bolts and insert a block between the brake pads as the caliper is removed. Remove the caliper and wire it out of the way. Do not allow the caliper to hang by the brake hose.
3. Pry out the grease cap, cotter pin, spindle nut, and washer, then remove the hub. Do not drop the wheel bearings.
4. Remove the outer roller bearing assembly from the hub. The inner bearing assembly will remain in the hub and may be removed after prying out the inner seal. Discard the seal.
5. Clean all parts in solvent (air dry) and check for excessive wear or damage.
6. Using a hammer and drift, remove the bearings caps from the hub. When installing new cups, make sure that they are not cocked and that they are fully seated against the hub shoulder.

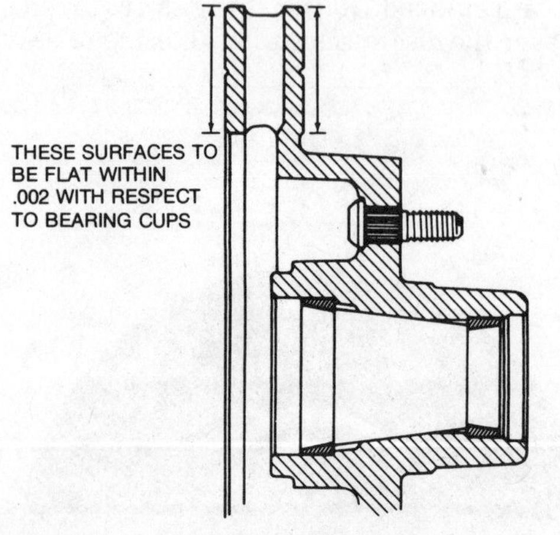

Surface flatness measurement

7. Pack both wheel bearings using high melting point wheel bearing grease made for disc brakes. Ordinary grease will melt and ooze out, ruining the pads. Place a healthy globe of grease in the palm of one hand and force the edge of the bearing into it so that the grease fills the bearing. Do this until the wheel bearing is packed. Grease packing tools are available to make this job a lot less messy. There are also tools which make it possible to grease the inner bearing without removing it or the disc from the spindle.
8. Place the inner bearing in the hub and install a new inner seal, making sure that the seal flange faces the bearing cup.
9. Carefully install the wheel hub over the spindle.
10. Using you hands, firmly press the outer bearing into the hub. Install the spindle washer and nut.
11. To adjust the bearings through 1971 models, tighten the adjusting nut to 15 ft.lb. while rotating the hub. Back the nut off 1 flat ($^1/_6$ turn) and insert a new cotter pin. If the nut and spindle hole do not align, back the nut off slightly. There should be 0.001–0.008" (0.0254–0.2032mm) end play in the bearing. This can be measured with a dial indicator, if you wish. Install the dust cap, wheel and tire.
12. To adjust the bearings on 1972 and later models, spin the wheel hub by hand and tighten the nut till it is just snug (12 ft.lb.). Back off the nut till it is loose, then tighten it finger tight. Loosen the nut until either hole in the spindle lines up with a slot in the nut and insert a new cotter pin. There should be 0.001–0.008" (0.0254–0.2032mm) end play in the bearing through 1973, and 0.001–0.005" (0.0254–0.127mm) from 1974. This can be measured with a dial indicator, if you wish.
13. Replace the dust cap, wheel and tire.

DRUM BRAKES

Drum

REMOVAL AND INSTALLATION

Drums can be removed by raising the vehicle, removing the wheel lugs and the tire, and pulling the drum from the brake assembly. If the brake drums have been scored from worn linings, the brake adjuster must be backed off so that the brake shoes will retract from the drum. To remove the drums from full floating rear axles, use Steps 1–11 of the Axle Shaft Removal and Installation procedure in Chapter 7. Full floating rear axles can readily be identified by the bearing housing protruding through the center of the wheel.

The adjuster can be backed off by inserting a brake adjusting tool through the access hole provided. In some cases the access hole is provided in the brake drum. A metal cover plate is over the hole. This may be removed by using a hammer and chisel.

NOTE: *Make sure all metal particles are removed from the brake drum before reassembly.*

To install, reverse the removal procedure.

CAUTION: *Do not blow the brake dust out of the drums with compressed air. Powdered asbestos has been found to be a cancer producing agent.*

INSPECTION

Lining

Remove the drum and inspect the lining thickness on both brake shoes. A front brake lining should be replaced if it is less than ⅛" (3mm) thick at the lowest point on the brake shoe. The wear limit for rear brake linings is $^1/_{16}$" (1.5875mm).

NOTE: *Brake shoes should always be replaced in axle sets. The wear specifications given may disagree with your state inspection rules.*

Drum

When the drum is removed, it should be inspected for cracks, scores, or other imperfections. These must be corrected before the drum is replaced.

CAUTION: *If the drum is found to be cracked, replace it. Do not attempt to service a cracked drum.*

Minor drum score marks can be removed with fine emery cloth. Heavy score marks must be removed by turning the drum. This is removing metal from the entire inner surface of the drum on a lathe in order to level the surface. Automotive machine shops and some large parts stores are equipped to perform this operation.

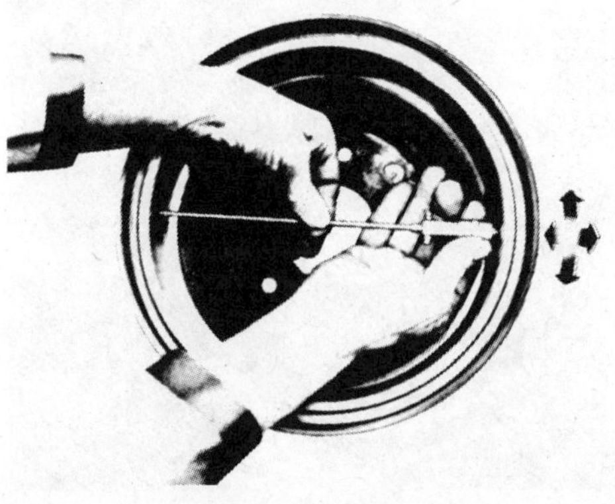

Measuring drum inside diameter

If the drum is not scored, it should be polished with fine emery cloth before replacement. If the drum is resurfaced, it should not be enlarged more than 0.060" (1.524mm).

NOTE: *Your state inspection law may disagree with this specification.*

It is advisable, while the drums are off, to check them for out-of-round. An inside micrometer is necessary for an exact measurement, therefore unless this tool is available, the drums should be taken to a machine shop to be checked. Any drum which is more than 0.006" (0.1524mm) out-of-round will result in an inaccurate brake adjustment and other problems, and should be refinished or replaced.

NOTE: *Make all measurements at right angles to each other and at the open and closed edges of the drum machined surface.*

Shoes

REMOVAL AND INSTALLATION

CAUTION: *Brake shoes contain asbestos, which has been determined to be a cancer causing agent. Never clean the brake surfaces with compressed air! Avoid inhaling any dust from any brake surface! When cleaning brake surfaces, use a commercially available brake cleaning fluid.*

1. Jack up and securely support the vehicle.
2. Loosen the parking brake equalizer enough to remove all tension on the brake cable (rear brakes only).
3. Remove the brake drums.

CAUTION: *The brake pedal must not be depressed while the drums are removed.*

4. Using a brake tool, remove the shoe springs. You can do this with ordinary tools, buy it isn't easy.
5. Remove the self-adjuster actuator spring.
6. Remove the link from the secondary shoe by pulling it from the anchor pin.
7. Remove the holddown pins. These are the brackets which run though the backing plate. They can be removed with a pair of pliers. Reach around the rear of the backing plate and hold the back of the pin. Turn the top of the pin retainer 45° with the plier. This will align the elongated tang with the slot in the retainer. Be careful, as the pin is spring loaded and may fly off when released. Use the same procedure for the other pin assembly.
8. Remove the adjuster actuator assembly.

NOTE: *Since the actuator, pivot, and override spring are considered an assembly it is not recommended that they be disassembled.*

9. Remove the shoes from the backing plate. Make sure that you have a secure grip on the assembly as the bottom spring will still exert pressure on the shoes. Slowly let the tops of the

shoes come together and the tension will decrease and the adjuster and spring may be removed.

NOTE: *If the linings are to be reused, mark them for identification.*

10. Remove the rear parking brake lever from the secondary shoe. Using a pair of plier,

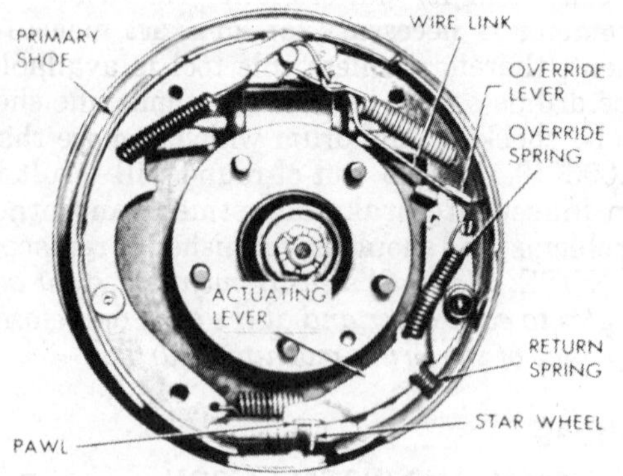

Self-adjusting brake

Unhooking the pull-back springs

Removing the hold-down springs

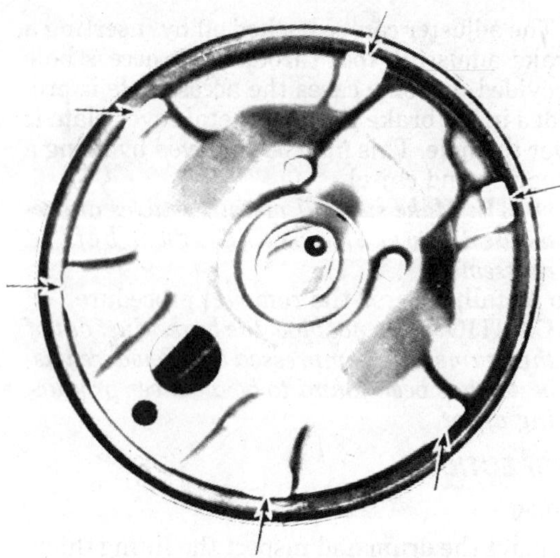

Backing plate lubrication areas

Checking the actuator mechanism

Aligning the drum

pull back on the spring which surrounds the cable. At the same time, remove the cable from the notch in the shoe bracket. Make sure that the spring does not snap back or injury may result.

11. Use a cloth to remove dirt from the brake drum. Check the drums for scoring and cracks. Have the drums checked for out-of-round and service the drums as necessary.

12. Check the wheel cylinders by carefully pulling the lower edges of the wheel cylinder boots away from the cylinders. If there is excessive leakage, the inside of the cylinder will be moist with fluid. If there is any leakage at all, a cylinder overhaul is in order. DO NOT delay, as a brake failure could result.

NOTE: *A small amount of fluid will be present to act as a lubricant for the wheel cylinder pistons.*

13. Check the flange plate, which is located around the axle, for leakage of differential lubricant. This condition cannot be overlooked as the lubricant will be absorbed into the brake linings and brake failure will result. Replace the seals as necessary. See Chapter 7 for details.

NOTE: *If new linings are being installed, check them against the old units for length and type.*

14. Check the new linings for imperfections.

CAUTION: *It is important to keep your hands free of dirt and grease when handling the brake shoes. Foreign matter will be absorbed into the linings and result in unpredictable braking.*

15. Lightly lubricate the parking brake and cable and the end of the parking brake lever where it enters the shoe. Use high temperature, waterproof, grease or special brake lube.

16. Install the parking brake lever into the secondary shoe with the attaching bolt, spring washer, lockwasher, and nut. It is important that the lever move freely before the shoe is attached. Move the assembly and check for proper action.

17. Lubricate the adjusting screw and make sure that it works freely. Sometimes the adjusting screw will not move due to lack of lubricant or dirt contamination and the brakes will not adjust. In this case, the adjuster should be disassembled, thoroughly cleaned, and lubricated before installation.

18. Connect the brake shoe spring to the bottom portion of both shoes. Make certain that the brake linings are installed in the correct manner, the primary and secondary shoe in the correct position. If you are not sure remove the other brake drum and check it.

19. Install the adjusting mechanism below the spring and separate the top of the shoes.

NOTE: *Make the following checks before installation:*

a. Be certain that the right hand thread adjusting screw is on the left hand side of the vehicle and the left hand screw is on the right hand side of the vehicle.

b. Make sure that the star adjuster is aligned with the adjusting hole.

c. The adjuster should be installed with the starwheel nearest the secondary shoe and the tension spring away from the adjusting mechanism;

d. If the original linings are being reused, put them back in their original locations.

20. Install the parking brake cable.

21. Position the primary shoe (the shoe with the short lining) first. Secure it with the holddown pin and with its spring by pushing the pin through the back of the backing plate and, while holding it with one hand, install the spring and the retainer using a pair of needlenose pliers. Install the adjuster actuator assembly.

22. Install the parking brake strut and the strut spring by pulling back the spring with pliers and engaging the end of the cable onto the brake strut and then releasing the spring.

23. Place the small metal guide plate over the anchor pin and position the self-adjuster wire cable eye.

CAUTION: *The wire should not be positioned with the conventional brake installation tool or damage will result. It should be positioned on the actuator assembly first and then placed over the anchor pin stud by hand with the adjuster assembly in full downward position.*

24. Install the actuator return spring. DO NOT pry the actuator lever to install the return spring. Position it using the end of a screwdriver or another suitable tool.

NOTE: *If the return springs are bent or in any way distorted, they should be replaced.*

25. Using the brake installation tool, place the brake return springs in position. Install the primary spring first over the anchor pin and then place the spring from the secondary show over the wire link end.

26. Pull the brake shoes away from the backing plate and apply a thin coat of high temperature, waterproof, grease or special brake lube in the brake shoe contact points.

CAUTION: *Only a small amount is necessary. Keep the lubricant away from the brake linings.*

27. Once the complete assembly has been installed, check the operation of the self-adjusting mechanism by moving the actuating lever by hand.

28. Adjust the brakes.

a. Turn the star adjuster until the drum slides over the brakes shoes with only a slight drag. Remove the drum:

b. Turn the adjuster back 1¼ turns.

c. Install the drum and wheel and lower the vehicle.

CAUTION: *Avoid overtightening the lug nuts to prevent damage to the brake disc or drum. Alloy wheels can also be cracked by overtightening. Use of a torque wrench is highly recommended.*

NOTE: *If the adjusting hole in the drum has been punched out, make certain that the insert has been removed from the inside of the drum. Install a rubber hole cover to keep dirt out of the brake assembly. Also, be sure that the drums are installed in the same position as they were when removed, with the locating tang in line with the locating hole in the axle shaft flange.*

d. Make the final adjustment by backing the vehicle and pumping the brakes until the self-adjusting mechanisms adjust to the proper level and the brake pedal reaches satisfactory height.

29. Adjust the parking brake. Details are given later.

Wheel Cylinders

REMOVAL

1. Raise and support the axle.
2. Remove the wheel and tire.
3. Back off the brake adjustment if necessary and remove the drum.
4. Disconnect and plug the brake line.
5. Remove the brake shoe pull-back springs.
6. Remove the screws securing the wheel cylinder to the backing plate. Later models have their wheel cylinders retained by a round retainer. To release the locking tabs, insert two awls (see illustration) into the access slots to bend the tabs back. Install the new retainer

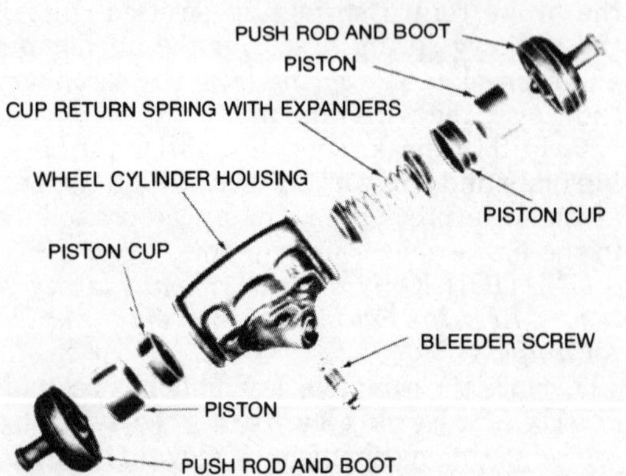

Exploded view of a wheel cylinder

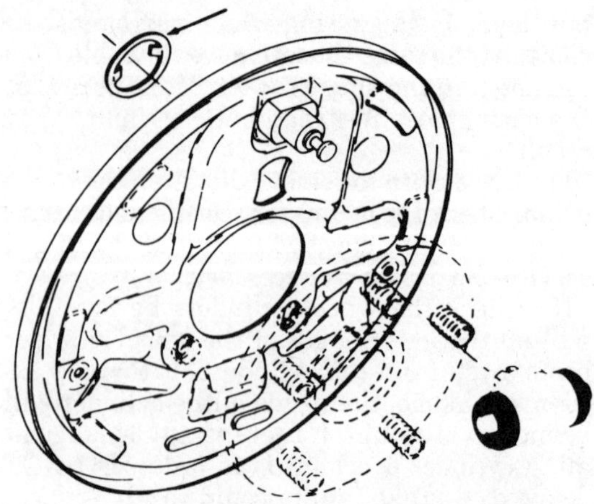

Later wheel cylindes are held in place by a retainer (arrow)

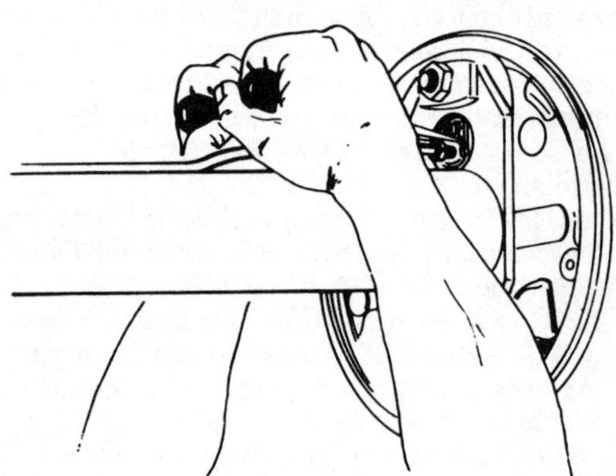

Bend back the tabs on the retainer using two awls simultaneously

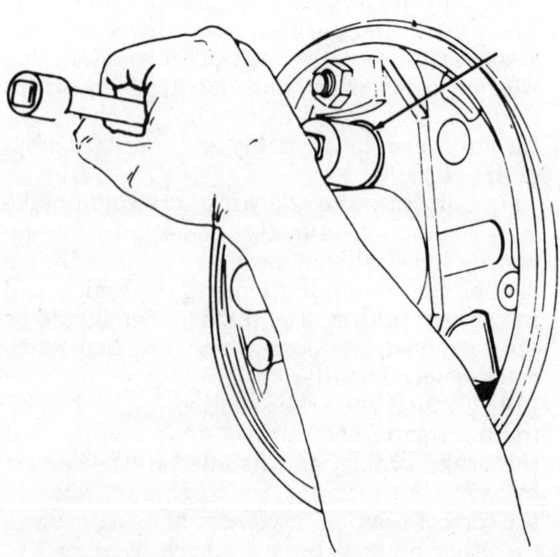

Install the new retainer over the wheel cylinder using 1⅛ in., 12-point socket and extension

over the wheel cylinder abutment using a 1⅛", 12 point socket and socket extension.

7. Disengage the wheel cylinder pushrods from the brake shoes and remove the wheel cylinder.

OVERHAUL

As with master cylinders, overhaul kits for wheel cylinders are readily available. When rebuidling and installing wheel cylinders, avoid getting any contaminants into the system. Always install clean, new high quality brake fluid. If dirty or improper fluid has been used, it will be necessary to drain the entire system, flush the system with proper brake fluid, replace all rubber components, refill, and bleed the system.

1. Remove the rubber boots from the cylinder ends with pliers. Discard the boots.
2. Remove and discard the pistons and cups.
3. Wash the cylinder and metal parts in denatured alcohol or clean brake fluid.

CAUTION: *Never use a mineral based solvent such as gasoline, kerosene, or paint thinner for cleaning purposes. These solvents will swell rubber components and quickly deteriorate them.*

4. Allow the parts to air dry or use compressed air. Do not use rags for cleaning since lint will remain in the cylinder bore.
5. Inspect the piston and replace it if it shows scratches.
6. Lubricate the cylinder bore and counterbore with clean brake fluid.
7. Install the rubber cups (flat side out) and then the pistons (flat side in).
8. Insert new boots into the counterbores by hand. Do not lubricate the boots.

INSTALLATION

Installation is the reverse of removal. Adjust the brakes and bleed the system.

Wheel Bearings

REMOVAL AND INSTALLATION, PACKING, ADJUSTMENT

This is covered earlier under Front Disc Brakes. Rear wheel bearings are covered in Chapter 7.

PARKING BRAKE

Cable

ADJUSTMENT

Before attempting parking brake adjustment, make sure that the rear brakes are fully adjusted by making several stops in reverse.

1. Raise and support the rear axle. Release the parking brake.
2. On 1967–70 models, apply the brake 2 notches. On 1971–75 models, apply the pedal 1 click, On 1976 and later models, apply the pedal 4 clicks.
3. Adjust the cable equalizer nut under the truck until a moderate drag can be felt when the rear wheels are turned forward.
4. Release the parking brake and check that there is no drag when the wheels are turned forward.

NOTE: *If the parking brake cable is replaced, prestretch it by applying the parking brake hard about three times before attempting adjustment.*

CABLE REPLACEMENT

Front Cable

1. Raise vehicle on hoist.
2. Remove adjusting nut from equalizer.
3. Remove retainer clip from rear portion of front cable at frame and from lever arm.
4. Disconnect front brake cable from parking brake pedal or lever assemblies. Remove

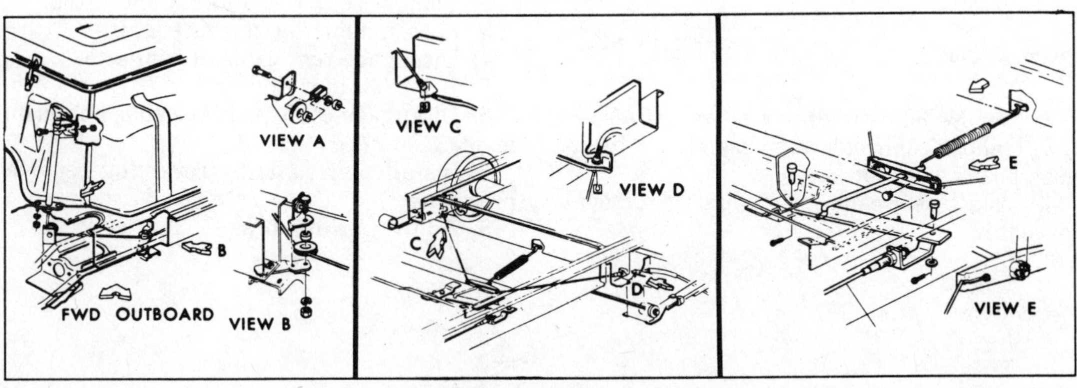

Parking brake linkage—1967–70

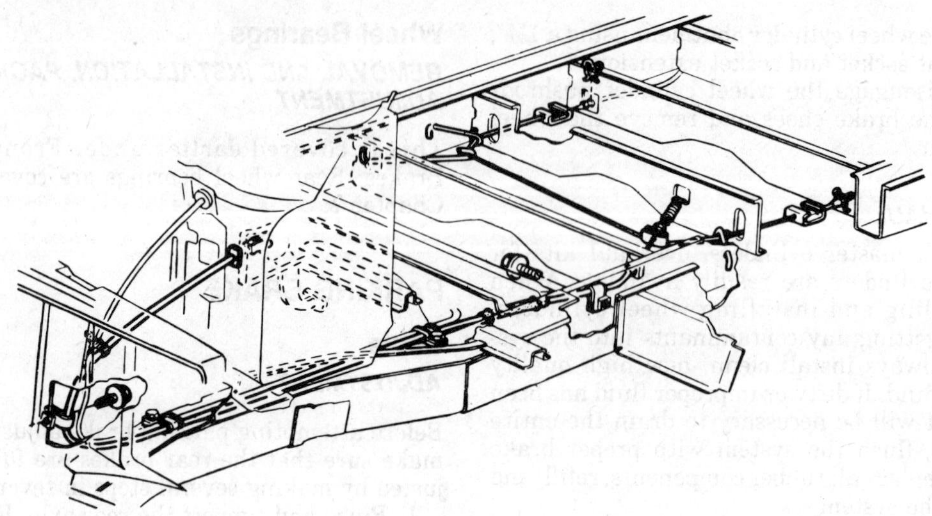

Parking brake linkage—1971–75

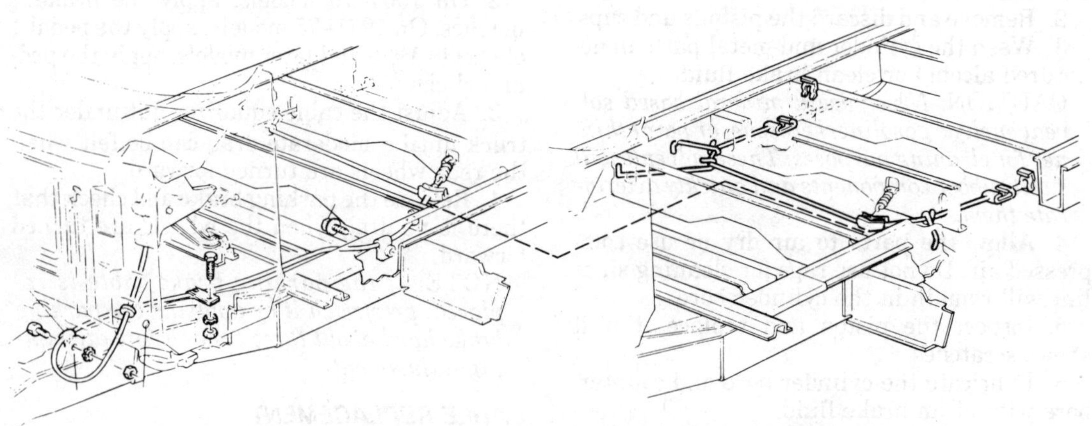

Parking brake linkage—1976 and later

front brake cable. On some models, it may assist installation of new cable if a heavy cord is tied to other end of cable in order to guide new cable through proper routing.

5. Install cable by reversing removal procedure.

6. Adjust parking brake.

Center Cable

1. Raise vehicle on hoist.
2. Remove adjusting nut from equalizer.
3. Unhook connector at each end and disengage hooks and guides.
4. Install new cable by reversing removal procedure.
5. Adjust parking brake.
6. Apply parking brake 3 times with heavy pressure and repeat adjustment.

Rear Cable

1. Raise vehicle on hoist.
2. Remove rear wheel and brake drum.
3. Loosen adjusting nut at equalizer.
4. Disengage rear cable at connector.
5. Bend retainer fingers.
6. Disengage cable at brake shoe operating lever.
7. Install new cable by reversing removal procedure.
8. Adjust parking brake.

Body and Trim

9

EXTERIOR

Front Doors

REMOVAL AND INSTALLATION

1. Remove the door trim pad and disconnect the electrical wiring harness from the door (if equipped).
2. Remove the kick panel (if equipped).
3. Remove the hinge bolt cover plate. Mark the position of the hinges on the door and the door pillar.
4. Support the door and remove the door frame to hinge bolts.
5. Remove the door from the vehicle.
6. Remove the hinge to door bolts and remove the hinges from the door.
7. Installation is the reverse of the removal procedure.

ADJUSTMENT

Special tool J-23457-A #50 Torx Wrench, or its equivalent is required to perform this procedure.

1. Remove the lock striker protector screw.
2. Remove the lock striker protector.
3. Remove the spring.
4. Remove the door striker using tool J-23457-A.

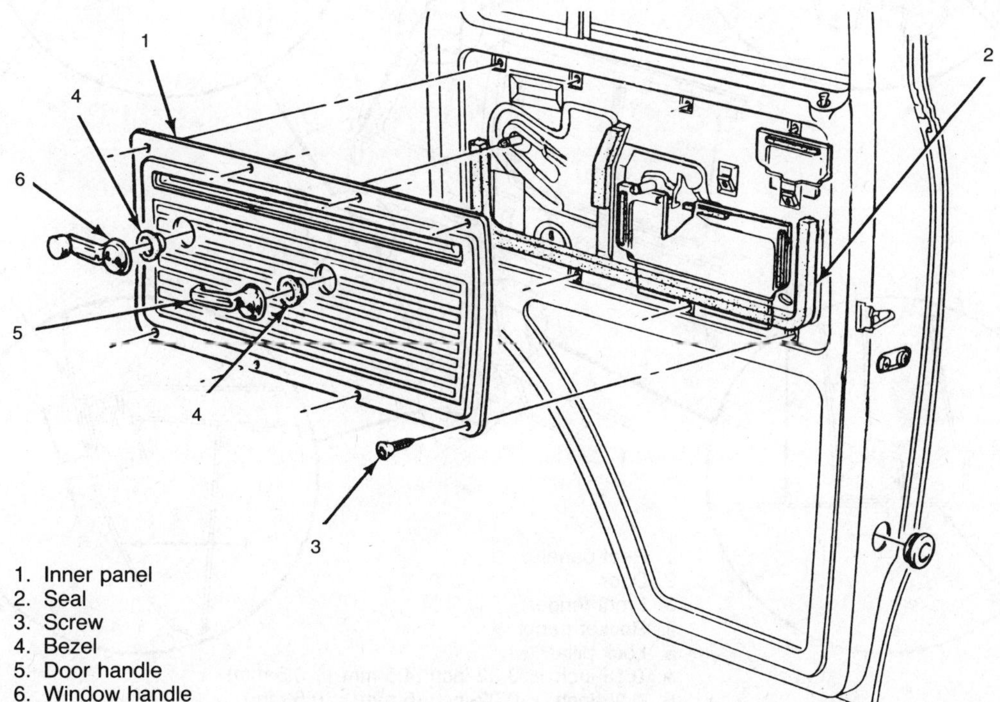

1. Inner panel
2. Seal
3. Screw
4. Bezel
5. Door handle
6. Window handle

Door trim inner panel

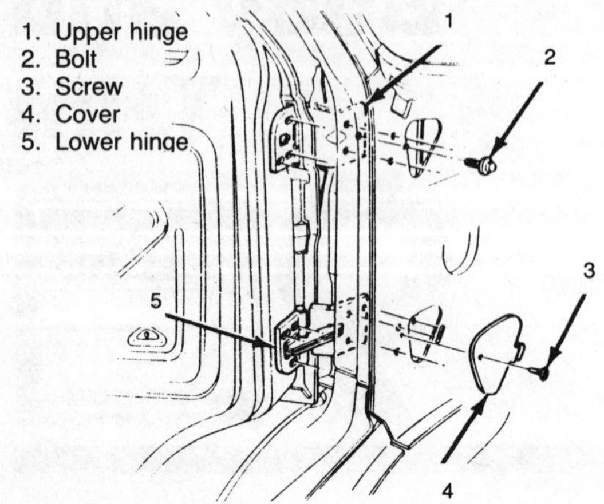

Door hinge components

5. Remove the spacer.
6. Remove the kick panel (if equipped).
7. Remove the hinge bolt cover screw.
8. Remove the hinge bolt cover.

Loosen the door hinge bolts as needed to adjust the door. Adjust the door up or down, forward or rearward, and in or out at the door hinges.

9. Adjust the door to obtain a gap of 0.18″ ± 0.02″ (4.6mm ± 0.51mm) between the front door and the roof panel.
10. The gap between the rocker panel and the front door at its base should be 0.25″ ± 0.02″ (6.35mm ± 0.51mm).
11. Adjust the door to obtain a gap of 0.18″ ± 0.02″ (4.6mm ± 0.51mm) between the doors rear edge and the rear door pillar.
12. The gap between the door's front edge

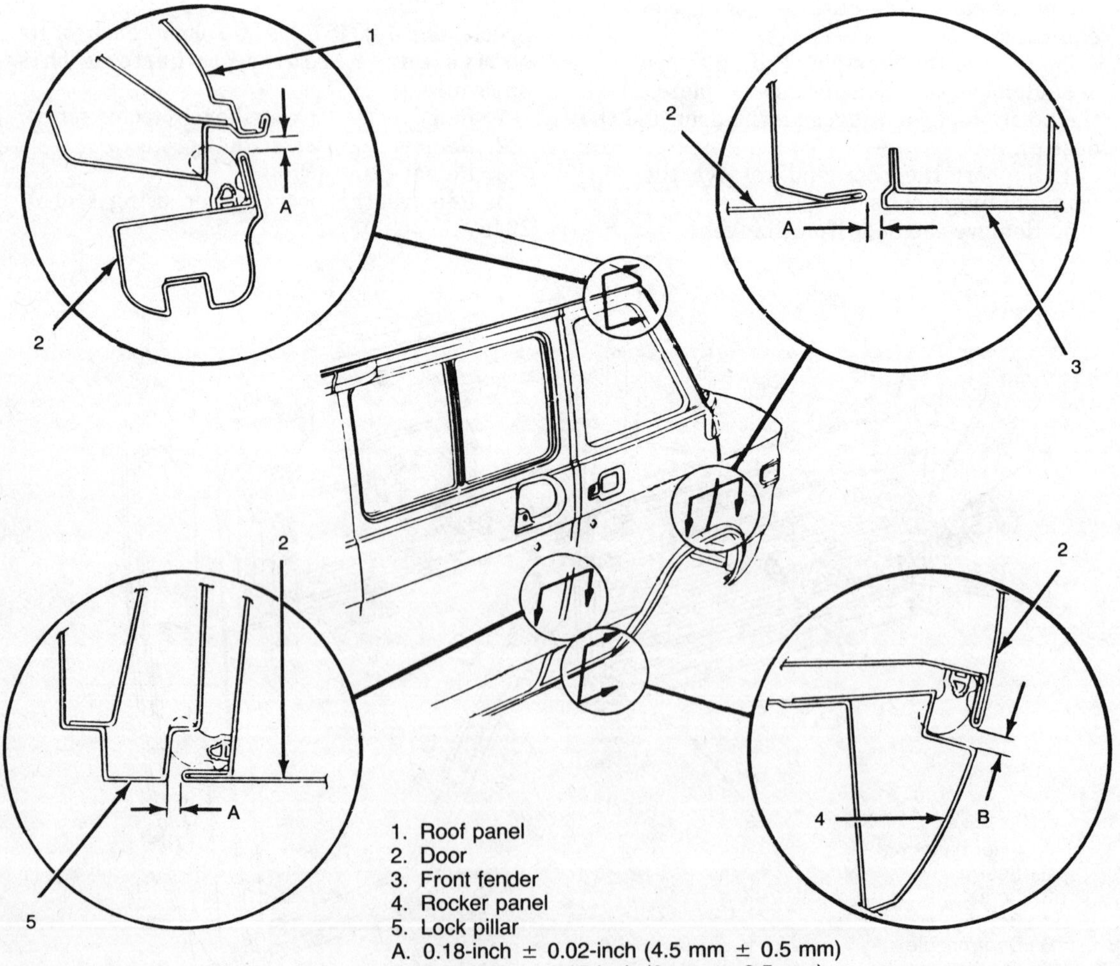

1. Roof panel
2. Door
3. Front fender
4. Rocker panel
5. Lock pillar

A. 0.18-inch ± 0.02-inch (4.5 mm ± 0.5 mm)
B. 0.25-inch ± 0.02-inch (6 mm ± 0.5 mm)

Door adjustments

and the rear edge of the fender should be 0.18″ ± 0.02″ (4.6mm ± 0.51mm).

13. Tighten the door hinge bolts that were loosened.

14. Reverse the removal procedure of the remaining component parts for installation.

Sliding Side Door

REMOVAL AND INSTALLATION

1. Remove the upper track cover and the hinge cover.
2. Open the door completely. Mark the position of the roller assembly on the door and remove the upper front roller assembly.
3. Remove the upper rear hinge retainer from the hinge.
4. Lift the upper rear hinge off of the track and remove the hinge.
5. Pivot the door away from the vehicle to disengage the rollers and lower the front roller from the track.
6. Remove the door from the vehicle.
7. Installation is the reverse of the removal procedure.

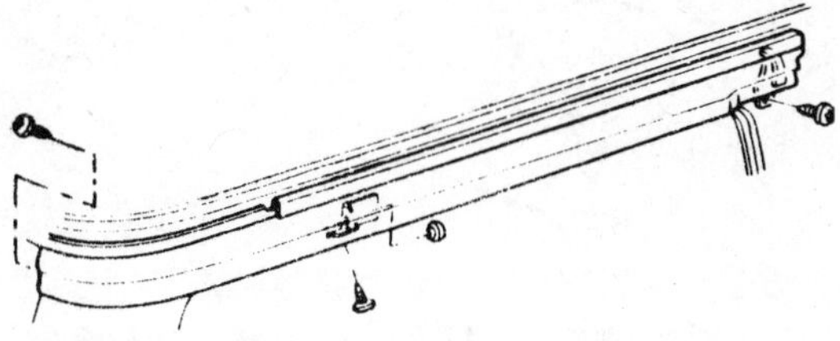

Upper track cover

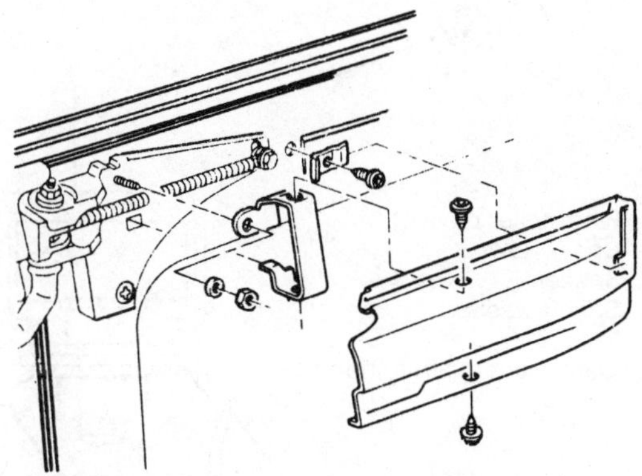

Upper hinge cover

ADJUSTMENTS

Up and Down

Special tool J-23457 #50 Torx Wrench, or its equivalent is required to perform this procedure.

1. Remove the upper rear hinge cover.
2. Remove the front lock striker.
3. Remove the rear lock striker using tool J-23457.
4. Remove the rear door wedge assembly.
5. Adjust the rear edge of the door to obtain a gap of 0.18″ ± 0.02″ (4.6mm ± 0.51mm) between the top of the door and the roof side rail.

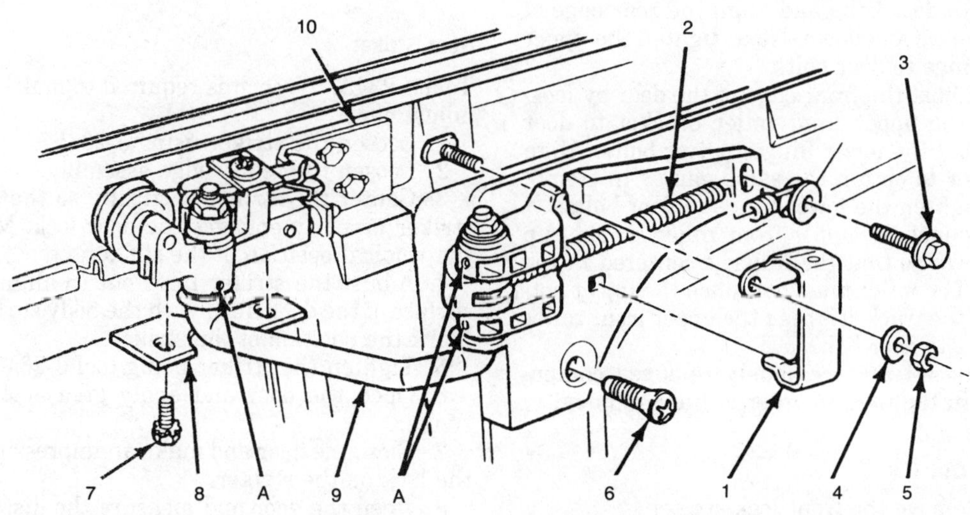

Upper rear hinge components

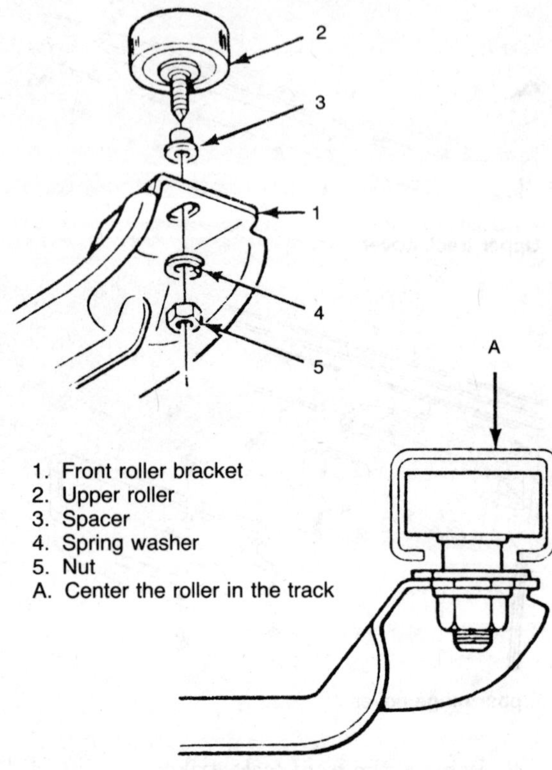

1. Front roller bracket
2. Upper roller
3. Spacer
4. Spring washer
5. Nut
A. Center the roller in the track

Upper front roller components

This adjustment should provide a gap of 0.25" ± 0.02" (6.35mm ± 0.51mm) between the bottom of the door and the rocker panel. To accomplish this adjustment, loosen the upper rear hinge to door bolts and align the rear edge of the door up and down. Next, tighten the upper rear hinge to door bolts.

6. Adjust the front edge of the door by loosening the upper front roller bracket to door bolts and the lower hinge to door bolts. Align the door to obtain the same gap as in step 5, then tighten the lower hinge to door bolts.

7. Adjust the upper front roller bracket up and down so that the roller is centered in the track. The roller must not touch the top or bottom of the track. Tighten the upper front roller bracket to door bolts.

8. Install the previously removed components in the reverse order of their removal.

In and Out

1. Remove the front lock striker.
2. Loosen the nut retaining the upper front roller to the upper roller bracket.
3. Loosen the lower front roller assembly to roller assembly bracket bolts.
4. Loosen the rear door lock striker.
5. Adjust the door in or out until the surface of the door is flush with the surface of the body.
6. Tighten the rear door lock striker.
7. Tighten the lower front roller assembly to roller assembly bracket bolts.
8. Tighten the nut retaining the upper front roller to the upper roller bracket.
9. Install the front lock striker.

Forward And Rearward

1. Mark the position of the front and rear latch strikers on the body pillars.
2. Remove the front and rear lock strikers.
3. Remove the upper front track cover.
4. Loosen the upper rear hinge striker.
5. Adjust the door forward or rearward to obtain a gap of 0.18" ± 0.02" (4.6mm ± 0.51mm) between the left and right door edge and the door pillars.
6. Tighten the upper rear hinge striker.
7. Install the upper front track cover.
8. Install the front and rear lock strikers at the position previously marked.

Front Striker

1. Loosen the front latch striker bolts.
2. Slide the door toward the striker.
3. The guide on the door must fit snugly into the rubber lined opening in the striker assembly.
4. Check that the latch fully engages the striker. Add or delete shims behind the striker to accomplish this adjustment.
5. Tighten the striker bolts.

Rear Striker

Tool J-23457 Wrench is required to make this adjustment.

1. Loosen the striker using J-23457.
2. Loosen the rear wedge assembly.
3. Center the striker vertically so that the striker properly engages the door lock. Mark the vertical position of the striker.
4. Adjust the striker in or out to align the surface of the door flush with the body surface. Mark the position of the striker.
5. Tighten the striker using tool J-23457.
6. Open the door and apply grease to the striker.
7. Close the door and make an impression of the lock on the striker.
8. Open the door and measure the distance from the rear of the striker head to the impression. The distance should be 0.20–0.30" (5.1–7.6mm).
9. Adjust the striker by adding or deleting shims. Align the striker to the previously made marks.
10. Tighten the striker using J-23457.

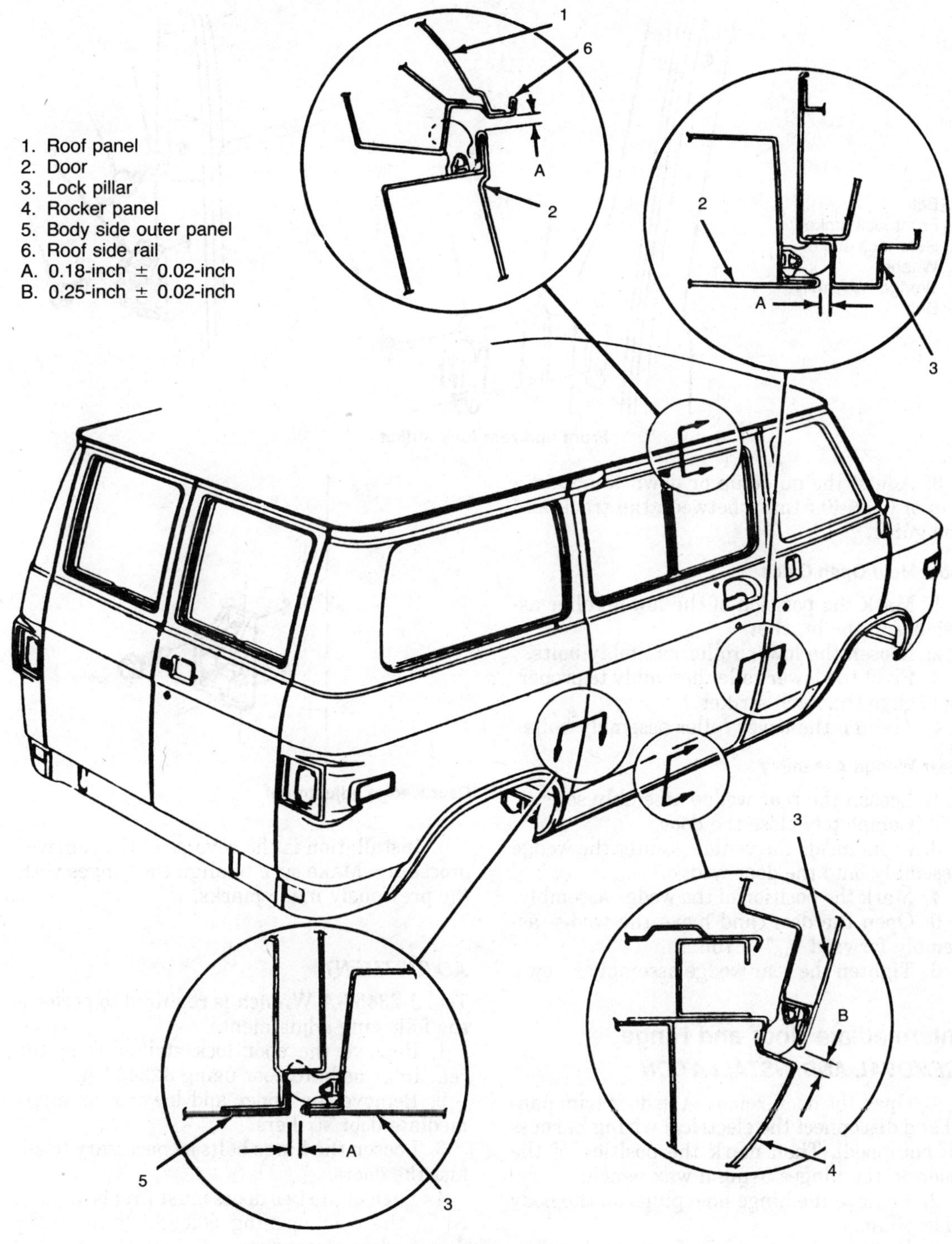

Door adjustments

Upper Rear Hinge

1. The lower hinge lever should have a gap of 0.10–0.16″ (2.54–4.06mm) between the outer edge of the lower hinge lever and the striker latch edge. This adjustment is made by adding an equal amount of shims between the guide block and the hinge assembly, and between the roller and the hinge assembly.

2. Adjust the striker up or down to obtain a gap of 0.06″ (1.5mm) between the lower edge of the striker plate and and the lower edge of the lower hinge lever.

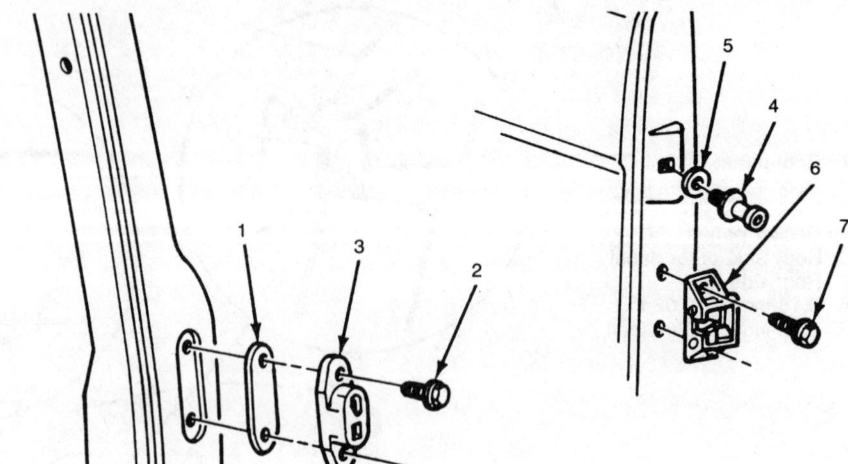

Front and rear lock striker

3. Adjust the guide up or down to obtain a gap of 0.02" (0.51mm) between the track and the guide.

Door Hold Open Catch

1. Mark the position of the lower roller assembly to the bracket.
2. Loosen the lower roller assembly bolts.
3. Pivot the lower roller assembly to properly engage the latch striker.
4. Tighten the lower roller assembly bolts.

Rear Wedge Assembly

1. Loosen the rear wedge assembly screws.
2. Completely close the door.
3. From inside the vehicle, center the wedge assembly onto the door wedge.
4. Mark the position of the wedge assembly.
5. Open the door, and move the wedge assembly forward $^3/_{16}$" (4.76mm).
6. Tighten the rear wedge assembly screws.

Intermediate Door and Hinge

REMOVAL AND INSTALLATION

1. Open the door, remove the door trim panel and disconnect the electrical wiring harness (if equipped). Then mark the position of the door on the hinges using a wax pencil.
2. Remove the hinge hole plugs on the body side pillar.
3. Remove the strap pin from the bracket, then remove the snapring from the pin, and pull the pin.
4. Support the door safely, and remove the hinge to body pillar bolts.
5. Remove the door from the vehicle.
6. Remove the hinge to door bolts.
7. Remove the hinges from the door.
8. Remove the retainers, seals, and grommets from the door or the hinges.

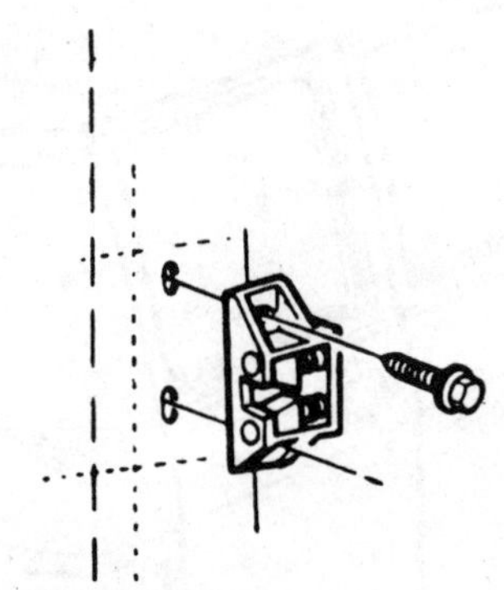
Rear wedge adjustment

9. Installation is the reverse of the removal procedure. Make sure to align the hinges with the previously made marks.

ADJUSTMENT

Tool J-23457-A Wrench is required to perform the following adjustments.

1. Remove the door lock striker from the rear intermediate door using J23457-A.
2. Remove the upper and lower rear intermediate door strikers.
3. Loosen the hinge bolts as necessary to adjust the doors.
4. Each of the two doors must first be adjusted in the door opening before adjusting the door to door clearance.
5. Adjust the door up and down, forward and rearward, and in and out, at the door hinges.
6. Adjust the door height so that there is a gap of 0.18" ± 0.020" (4.6mm ± 0.51mm) between the door and the roof panel.
7. Adjust the gap between the door and the rocker panel to 0.24" ± 0.020" (6.1mm ± 0.51mm).
8. Adjust the gap between the doors and the

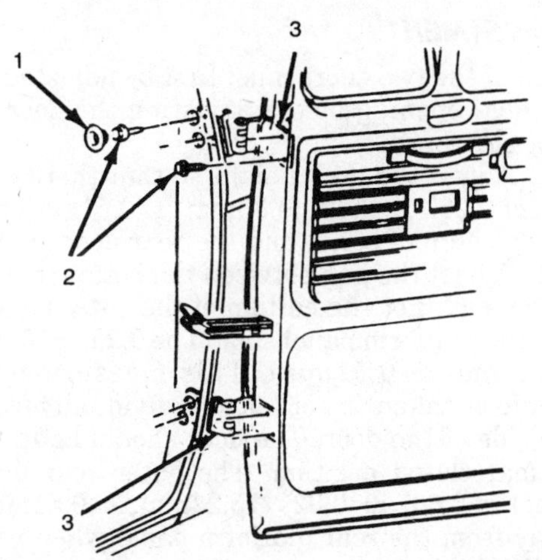

1. Cap
2. Bolt
3. Hinge
4. Grommet
5. Seal
6. Retainer

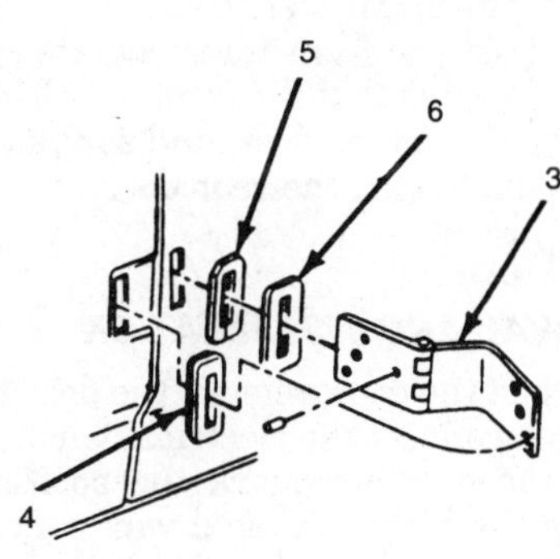

Door hinge components

body at the hinge pillars to 0.16″ ± 0.020″ (4.1mm ± 0.51mm).

9. Adjust the gap between the front and rear intermediate doors to 0.25″ ± 0.020″ (6.35mm ± 0.51mm).

10. Tighten the hinge bolts that were loosened.

11. Install the upper and lower rear intermediate door strikers to the body.

12. Install the door lock striker to the rear intermediate door using J-23457-A.

13. Adjust the upper and lower intermediate door striker to door clearance so that there is 0.172″ (4.37mm) between the striker and the

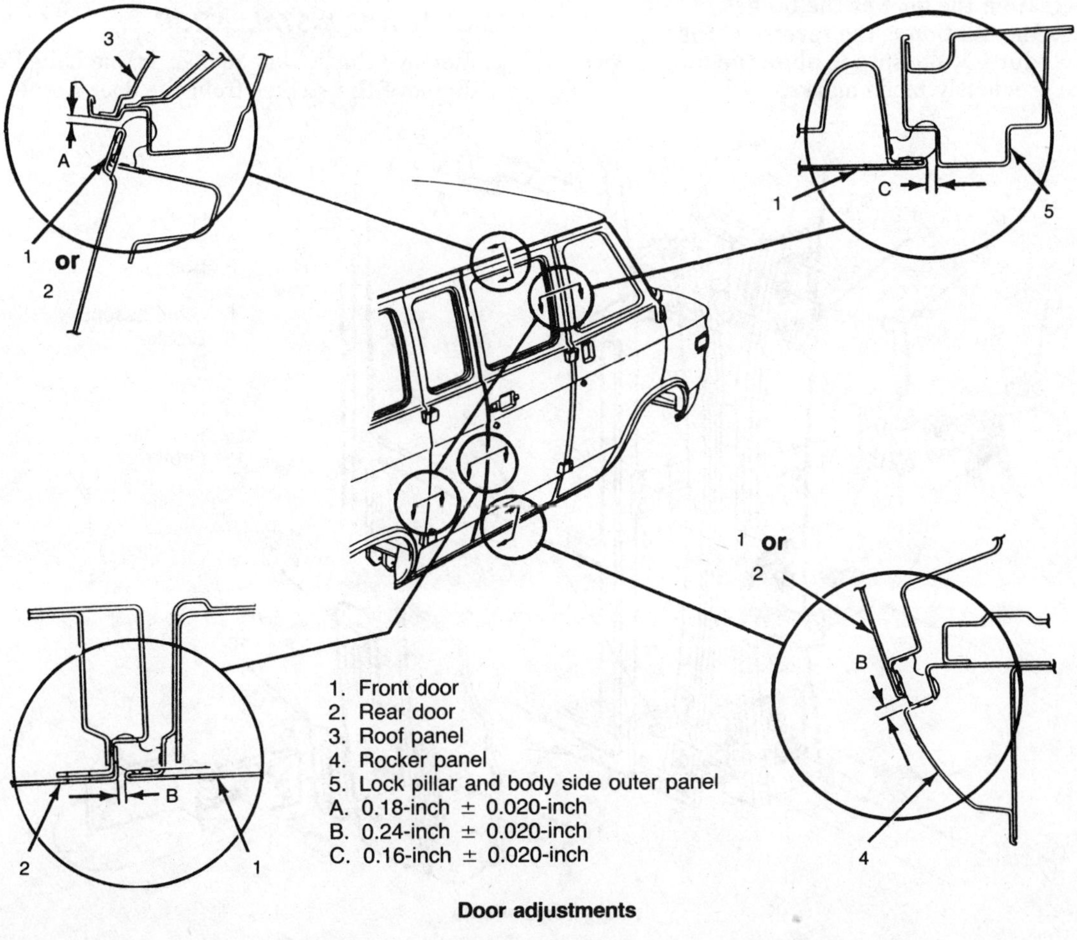

1. Front door
2. Rear door
3. Roof panel
4. Rocker panel
5. Lock pillar and body side outer panel

A. 0.18-inch ± 0.020-inch
B. 0.24-inch ± 0.020-inch
C. 0.16-inch ± 0.020-inch

Door adjustments

door latch when the door is in the secondary latch position. (The door is latched but not fully closed.) An $^{11}/_{16}''$ diameter drill bit may be used to gauge this clearance.

14. Adjust the front intermediate striker on the rear door so that the front door lock properly engages the rear door, and so that the front door is flush with the rear door.

Rear Door

REMOVAL AND INSTALLATION

1. Open the door, remove the door trim panel and disconnect the electrical wiring harness (if equipped). Then mark the position of the door on the hinges using a wax pencil.
2. Remove the hinge hole plugs on the body side pillar.
3. Remove the strap pin from the bracket, then remove the snapring from the pin, and pull the pin.
4. Support the door safely, and remove the hinge to body pillar bolts.
5. Remove the door from the vehicle.
6. Remove the hinge to door bolts.
7. Remove the hinges from the door.
8. Remove the retainers, seals, and grommets from the door or the hinges.
9. Installation is the reverse of the removal procedure. Make sure to align the hinges with the previously made marks.

ADJUSTMENT

Each of the two doors must first be adjusted in the door opening before adjusting the door to door clearance.

1. Adjust the door height so that there is a gap of 0.25″ ± 0.02″ (6.35mm ± 0.51mm) between the roof panel and the rear door panel.
2. Adjust the gap between the bottom of the door panel (not the bottom of the outer panel) and the platform panel should be 0.25″ ± 0.02″ (6.35mm ± 0.51mm). This measurement should be taken on each door individually from the side of the door. The door should be in its normal closed position. The outer rear door panel is 0.60″ ± 0.02″ (15.24mm ± 0.51mm) away from the rear platform panel when normally closed.
3. Adjust the rear door outer panel to the body side outer panel gap to 0.16″ ± 0.02″ (4.1mm ± 0.51mm).
4. The door to door clearance between the left and right outer door panels should be 0.25″ ± 0.02″ (6.35mm ± 0.51mm).

Rear Door Striker

REMOVAL AND INSTALLATION

1. Remove the striker to door frame bolts.
2. Remove the striker from the door frame.

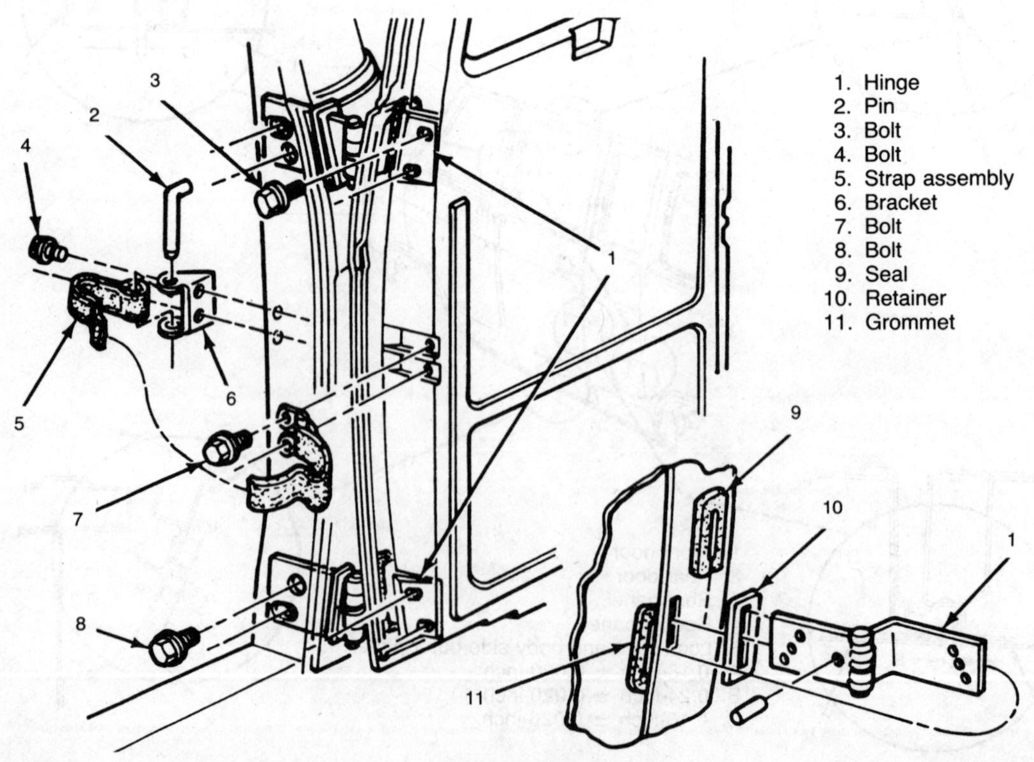

Hinge components

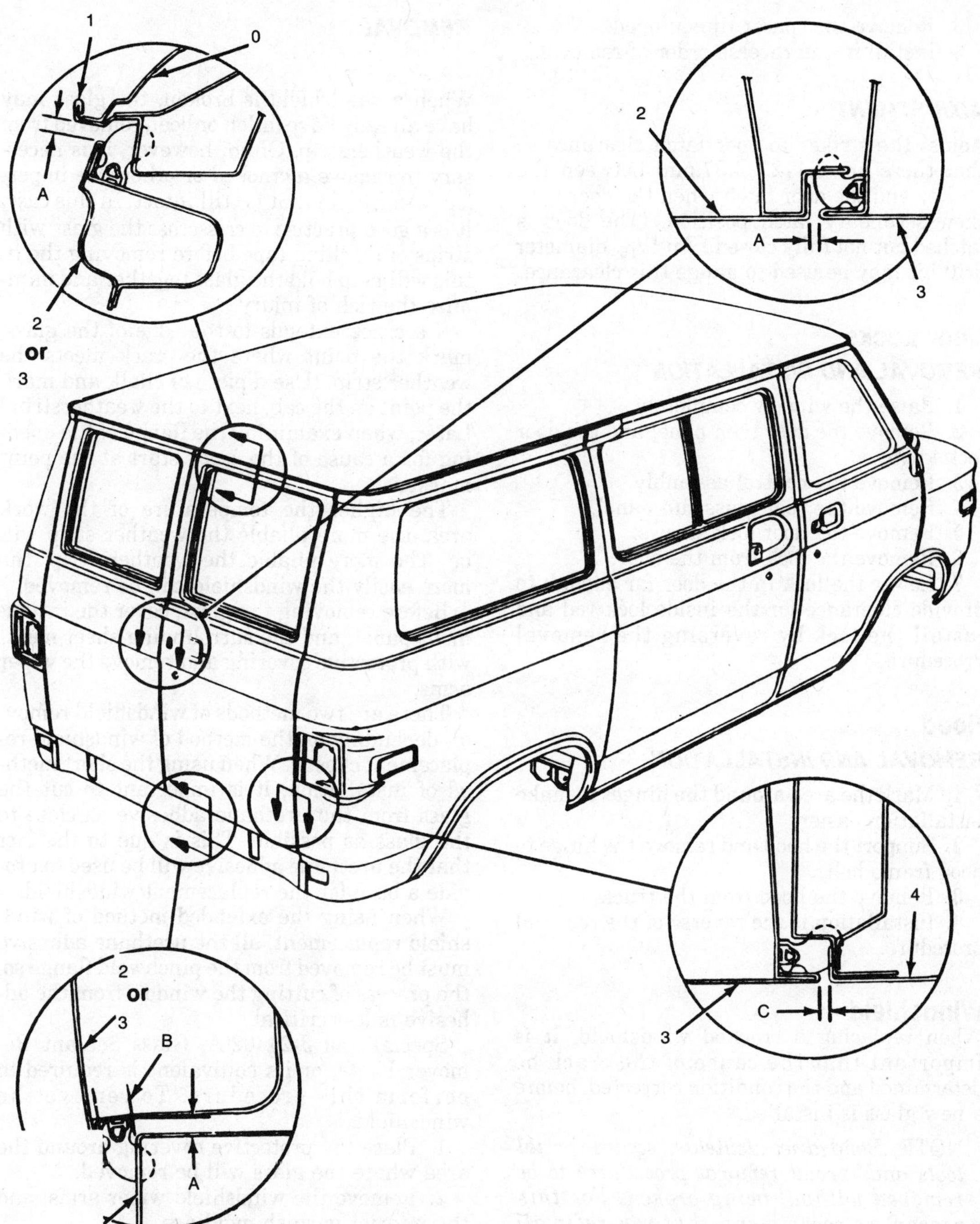

0. Roof panel
1. Roof side rail
2. Left door
3. Right door
4. Body side panel
5. Floor extension panel

A. 0.25-inch ± 0.020-inch
B. 0.60C-inch ± 0.020-inch
C. 0.16-inch ± 0.020-inch

Door adjustments

3. Remove the spacer (if equipped).
4. Install in the reverse order of removal.

ADJUSTMENT

Adjust the striker to door latch clearance so that there are 0.172" (4.37mm) between the striker and the door latch when the door is in thew secondary latch position. (The door is latched but not fully closed.) An $^{11}/_{16}$" diameter drill bit may be used to gauge this clearance.

Door Locks

REMOVAL AND INSTALLATION

1. Raise the window completely.
2. Remove the door trim panel and the door lock knob.
3. Remove the control assembly.
4. Remove the rear glass run panel.
5. Remove the door lock screws.
6. Remove the lock from the door.
7. Lower the lock in the door far enough to provide clearance for the inside lock rod and install the lock by reversing the removal procedure.

Hood

REMOVAL AND INSTALLATION

1. Mark the area around the hinges to make installation easier.
2. Support the hood and remove the hinge to hood frame bolts.
3. Remove the hood from the truck.
4. Installation is the reverse of the removal procedure.

Windshield

When replacing a cracked windshield, it is important that the cause of the crack be determined and the condition corrected, before a new glass is installed.

NOTE: *Bonded windshields require special tools and special removal procedures to be removed without being broken. For this reason we recommend that you refer all removal and installation to a qualified technician.*

CAUTION: *Always wear heavy gloves when handling glass to reduce the risk of injury.*

The cause of the crack may be an obstruction or a high spot somewhere around the flange of the opening; cracking may not occur until pressure from the high spot or obstruction becomes particularly high due to winds, extremes of temperature, or rough terrain.

Suggestions of what to look for are described later in this section under inspection.

REMOVAL

When a windshield is broken, the glass may have already have fallen or been removed from the weatherstrip. Often, however, it is necessary to remove a cracked or otherwise imperfect windshield that is still intact. In this case, it is a good practise to crisscross the glass with strips of masking tape before removing the it; this will help hold the glass together and minimize the risk of injury.

If a crack extends to the edge of the glass, mark the point where the crack meets the weather strip. (Use a piece of chalk and mark the point on the cab, next to the weatherstrip.) Later, when examining the flange of the opening for a cause of the crack start at the point marked.

The higher the temperature of the work area, the more pliable the weather strip will be. The more pliable the weather strip, the more easily the windshield can be removed.

Before removing the glass, cover the instrument panel, and the surrounding sheet metal with protective covering and remove the wiper arms.

There are two methods of windshield removal, depending on the method of windshield replacement chosen. When using the short method of installation, it is important to cut the glass from the urethane adhesive as close to the glass as possible. This is due to the fact that the urethane adhesive will be used to provide a base for the replacement windshield.

When using the extended method of windshield replacement, all the urethane adhesive must be removed from the pinchweld flange so, the process of cutting the window from the adhesive is less critical.

Special tool J-24402-A, Glass Sealant Remover Knife, or its equivalent is required to perform this procedure. To remove the windshield:

1. Place the protective covering around the area where the glass will be removed.
2. Remove the windshield wiper arms, and the interior garnish moldings.
3. Remove the exterior reveal moldings and the support support molding from the urethane adhesive by prying one end of the molding from the adhesive. Pull the free end of the molding away from the windshield or the pinchweld flange until the molding is completely free of the windshield.
4. Using J-24402-A cut the windshield from the urethane adhesive. If the short method of glass replacement is to be used, keep the knife as close to the glass as possible in order to leave a base for the replacement glass.

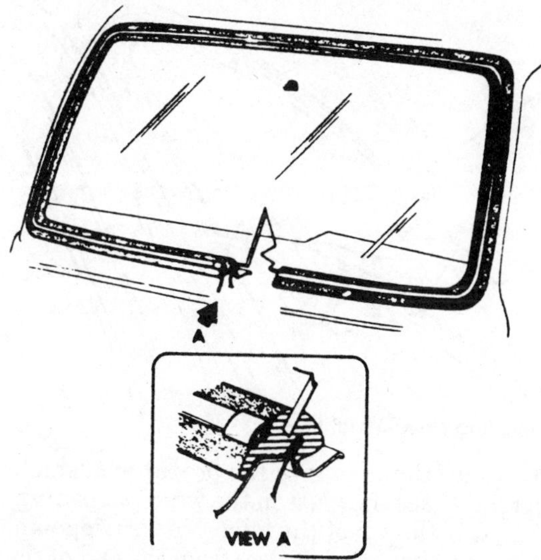

Typical windshield

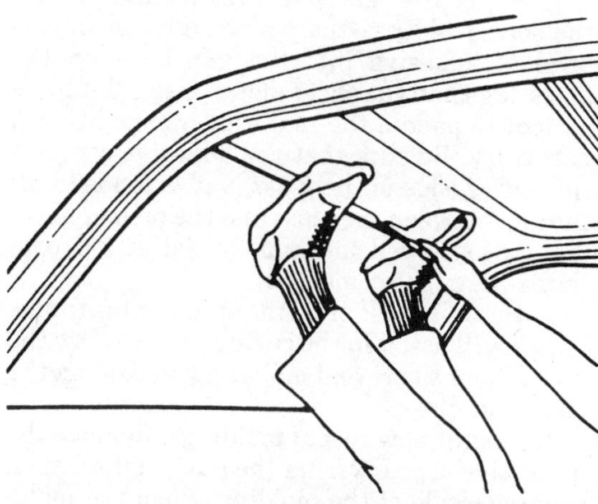
Applying pressure to windshield

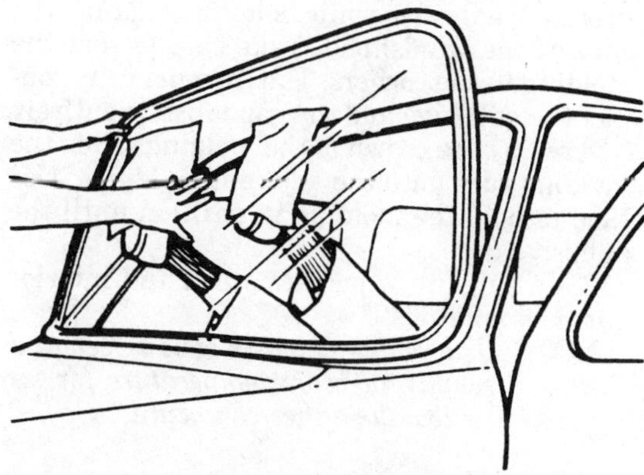
Removing windshield from opening

5. With the help of an assistant, remove the glass.

6. If the original glass is to be reinstalled, place it on a protected bench or a holding or holding fixture. Remove any remaining adhesive with a razor blade or a sharp scraper. Any remaining traces of adhesive material can be removed with denatured alcohol or lacqure thinner.

NOTE: *When cleaning windshield glass, avoid contacting the edge of the plastic laminate material (on the edge of the glass) with volatile cleaner. Contact may cause discoloration and deterioration of the plastic laminate. Do not use a petroleum based solvent such as gasoline or kerosene. The presence of oil will prevent the adhesion of new material.*

INSPECTION

An inspection of the windshield opening, the weather strip, and the glass may reveal the cause of a broken windshield. This can help prevent future breakage. If there is no apparent cause of breakage, the weatherstrip should be removed from the flange of the opening and the flange inspected. Look for high weld or solder spots, hardened spot welds sealer, or any other obstruction or irregularity in the flange. Check the weatherstrip for irregularities or obstructions in it.

Check the windshield to be installed to make sure that it does not have any chipped edges. Chipped edges can be ground off, restoring a smooth edge to the glass, and minimizing concentrations of pressure that cause breakage. Remove no more than necessary, in an effort to maintain the original shape of the glass and the proper clearance between it and the flange of the opening.

INSTALLATION METHODS

There are two methods used for windshield replacement. The short method described previously in the removal procedure is used when the urethane adhesive can be used as a base for the new glass. This method would be used in the case of a cracked glass, if, no other service needs to be done to the windshield frame such as sheet metal or repainting work.

The extended method should be used when work must be done to the windshield frame such as straightening or repairing sheet metal or repainting the windshield frame. In this method all of the urethane adhesive must be removed from the pinchweld flange.

INSTALLATION

To replace a urethane adhered windshield, GM adhesive service kit No. 9636067 contains some of the materials needed, and must be used to insure the original integrity of the windshield design. Materials in this kit include:

1. One tube of adhesive material.

2. One dispensing nozzle.
3. Steel music wire.
4. Rubber cleaner.
5. Rubber Primer.
6. Pinchweld primer.
7. Blackout primer.
8. Filler strip (for use on windshield installations for vehicles equipped with embedded windshield antenna).
9. Primer applicators.

Other materials are required for windshield installation which are not included in the service kit.

These include:

1. GM rubber lubricant No. 1051717.
2. Alcohol for cleaning the edge of the glass.
3. Adhesive dispensing gun J-24811 or its equivalent.
4. A commercial type razor knife.
5. Two rubber support spacers.

Extended Method

1. Clean all metal surrounding the windshield opening with a clean alcohol dampened cloth. Allow the alcohol to air dry.
2. Apply the pinchweld primer found in the service kit to the pinchweld area. Do not let any of the primer touch any of the exposed paint because damage to the finish may occur. Allow thirty minutes for the primer to dry.
3. Follow the steps listed under Short Method for the remainder of the procedure.

Short Method

1. Install the support molding onto the pinchweld flange from inside the vehicle. The joint of the molding should be located at the bottom center of the moulding.
2. Thoroughly clean the edge of the glass to which the adhesive material will be applied with a clean alcohol dampened cloth. Allow the alcohol to dry.
3. Apply the clear glass primer in the kit to the inner edge of the windshield from the edge of the glass inward 0.04″ (1.016mm). Apply the primer around the entire perimeter of the glass. Allow the primer to cure for thirty minutes.
4. Apply the blackout primer to the glass in the same area as the clear primer. Allow the blackout primer to dry to the touch.
5. Place two rubber blocks onto the base of the pinchweld flange. Place the blocks in line with the last screw on either side of the cowl grille cover.
6. With the aid of a helper, lift the glass into the opening. Center the glass in the opening, on top of the support molding.
7. Check the fit of the revel molding. If necessary remove the glass and cut away additional urethane to give the proper windshield height. Place the glass in the window opening.

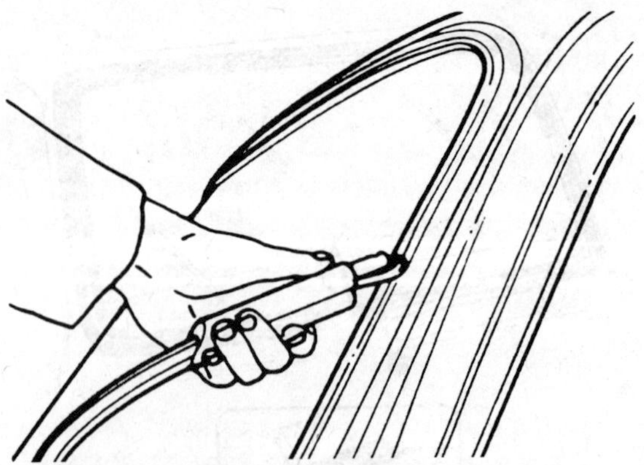

Installing Reveal molding

8. Cut the tip of the adhesive cartridge approximately $^{3}/_{16}$″ (4.76mm) from the end of the tip.
9. Apply the adhesive first in and around the spacer blocks. Apply a smooth continuous bead of adhesive into the gap between the glass edge and the sheet metal. Use a flat bladed tool to paddle the material into position if necessary. Be sure that the adhesive contacts the entire edge of the glass, and extends to fill the gap between the glass and the primer sheet metal (extended method) or solidified urethane base (short method).
10. Spray a mist of water onto the urethane. Water will assist in the curing process. Dry the area where the reveal molding will contact the body and glass.
11. Install new reveal moldings. Remove the protective tape covering the butyl adhesive on the underside of the molding. Push the molding caps onto each end of one of the reveal moldings. Press the lip of the molding into the urethane adhesive while holding it against the edge of the windshield. Take care to seat the molding in the corners. The lip must fully contact the adhesive and the gap must be entirely covered by the crown of the molding. Slide the molding caps onto the adjacent moldings. Use tape to hold the molding in position until the adhesive cures.
12. Install the wiper arms and the interior garnish moldings.

NOTE: *The vehicle should not be driven and should remain at room temperature for six hours to allow the adhesive to cure.*

INTERIOR

Door Panels

Special tool J-9886-01, Door Handle Clip Remover, is required to perform the following procedure.

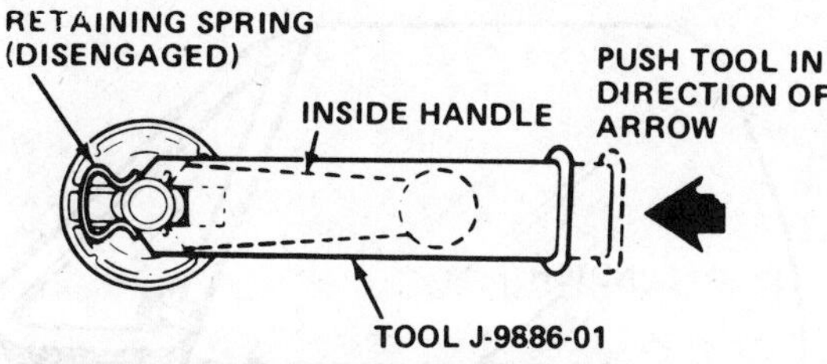

Clip Retained Inside Handle Removal

REMOVAL AND INSTALLATION

1. Remove the window regulator handle using tool J-9886-01.
2. Remove the window regulator handle bezel.
3. Remove the door lock assembly handle using J-9886-01.
4. Remove the control assembly handle bezel.
5. Remove the assist handle (if equipped).
6. Remove the arm rest (if equipped).
7. Remove the door trim outer panel screws and pull the panel away from the retainer.
8. Remove the door trim inner panel screws and remove the trim inner panel.
9. Installation is the reverse of the removal.

Door Vent/Window Run Channel Assembly

The door vent and the window run channel are one assembly. This assembly is fit into the front of the door frame.

REMOVAL AND INSTALLATION

1. Place the window in the lowered position and remove the door trim panel.
2. Remove the run channel molding. Pull the molding out of the vent assembly only.

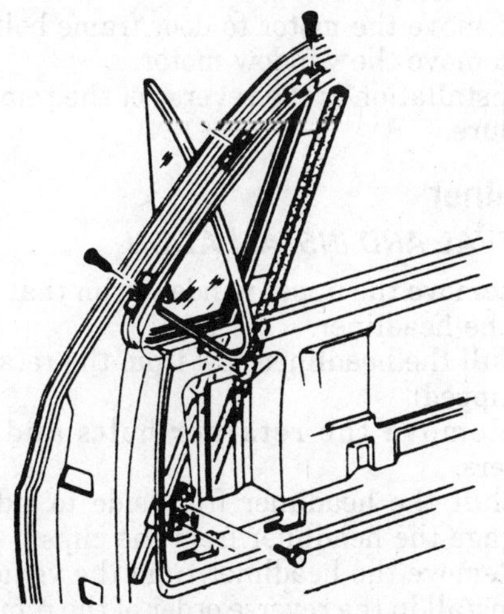
Door ventilator assembly

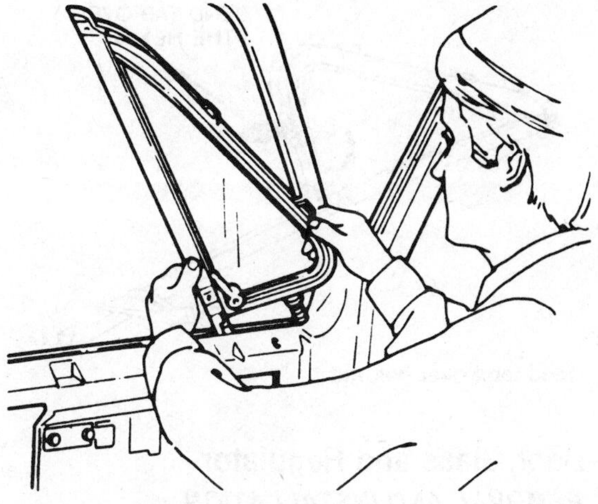
Removing ventilator assembly

3. Remove the door panel to run channel bolt.
4. Remove the door to ventilator screws.
5. Remove the door vent/window run channel assembly from the vehicle by pulling the top of the vent backwards away from the door frame. Then lift and rotate the assembly out of the door.
6. Installation is the reverse of the removal procedure.

ADJUSTMENT

1. Remove the door trim panel.
2. Bend the tabs on the adjustment nut away from the nut.
3. Adjust the vent by placing a wrench on the adjusting nut, and then turning the vent window to the proper tension.
4. Bend the tabs over the adjusting nut and install the door trim panel.

Adjusting tension

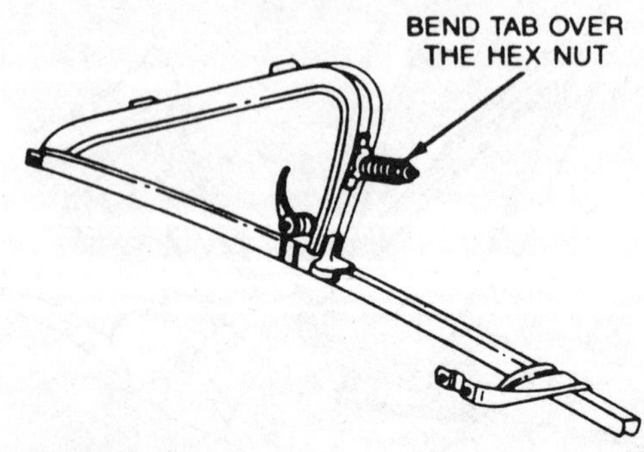

Bend tabs over hex nut

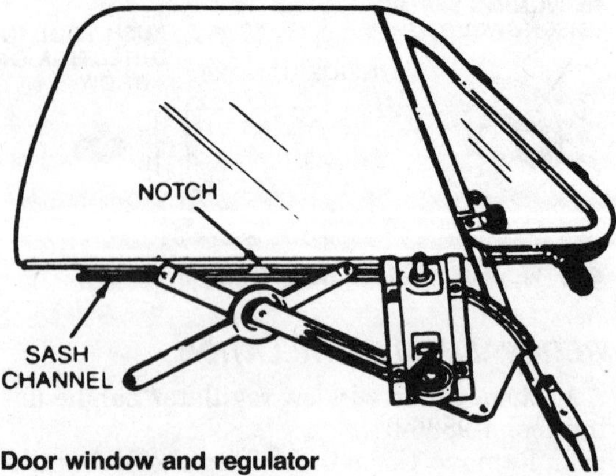

Door window and regulator

Door Glass and Regulator

REMOVAL AND INSTALLATION

CAUTION: *Always wear heavy gloves when handling glass to minimize the risk of injury.*

Door Glass

1. Lower the glass to the bottom of the door and remove the door trim panel.
2. Remove the door vent/window channel run assembly.

NOTE: *Mask or cover any sharp edges that could scratch the glass.*

3. Slide the glass forward until the front roller is in line with the notch in the sash channel.
4. Disengage the roller from the channel.
5. Push the window forward, then tilt it up until the rear roller is disengaged.
6. Place the window in a level position, and raise it straight up and out of the door.
7. Installation is the reverse of the removal procedure.

Regulator

1. Raise the window and tape the glass in the full up position using cloth body tape.

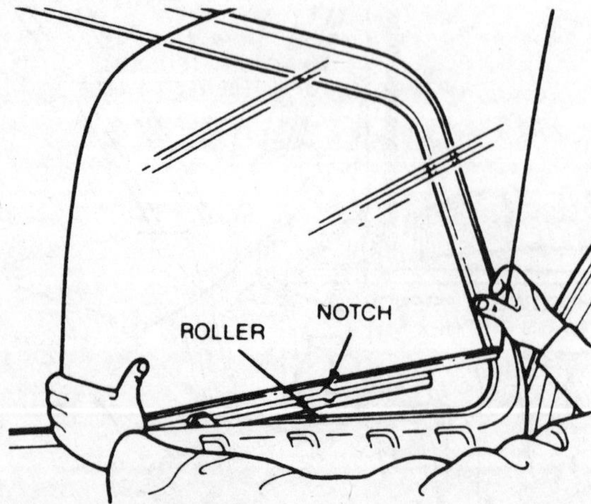

Removing door glass

2. Remove the door trim panel and the door panel to regulator bolts.
3. Slide the regulator rearward to disengage the rear roller from the sash channel. Then disengage the lower roller from the regulator rail.
4. Disengage the forward roller from the sash channel at the notch in the sash channel.
5. Collapse the regulator and remove it through the access hole in the door.
6. Lubricate the regulator and the sash channel and regulator rails with Lubriplate® or its equivalent.
7. Install the regulator in the reverse of the removal procedure.

Electric Window Motor

REMOVAL AND INSTALLATION

1. Disconnect the negative battery cable.
2. Remove the door panel as described in the above procedure.
3. Remove the window regulator for clearance (if necessary).
4. Disconnect the wiring connector to the window motor.
5. Remove the motor to door frame bolts.
6. Remove the window motor.
7. Installation is the reverse of the removal procedure.

Headliner

REMOVAL AND INSTALLATION

1. Remove the upper window trim that supports the headliner.
2. Pull the headliner bow from the retainer (if equipped).
3. Remove the retainer bolts and the retainers.
4. Shift the headliner from side to side to disengage the headliner from the clips.
5. Remove the headliner from the vehicle.
6. Install in the reverse order of the removal procedure.

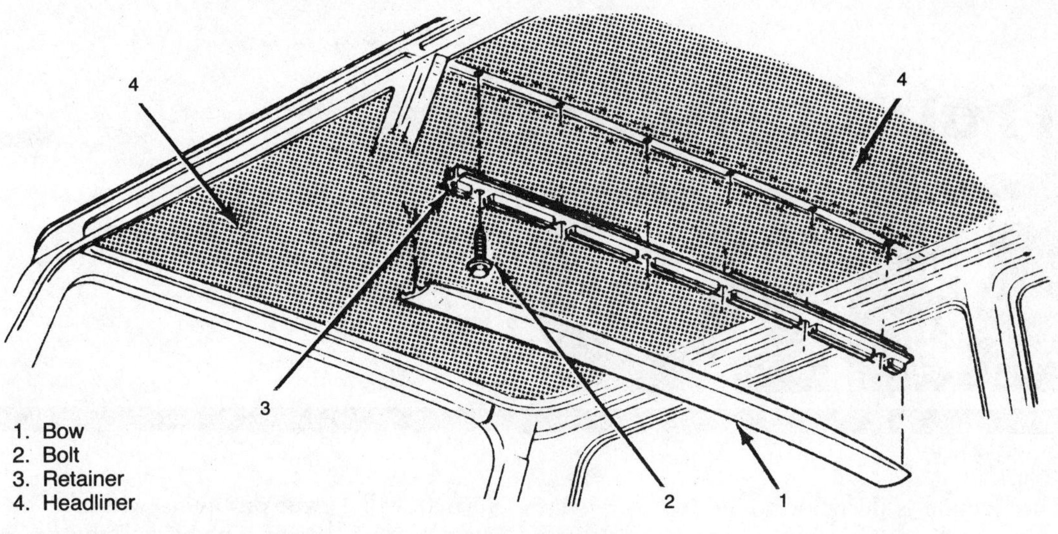

Headliner retainer

Troubleshooting

This section is designed to aid in the quick, accurate diagnosis of automotive problems. While automotive repairs can be made by many people, accurate troubleshooting is a rare skill for the amateur and professional alike.

In its simplest state, troubleshooting is an exercise in logic. It is essential to realize that an automobile is really composed of a series of systems. Some of these systems are interrelated; others are not. Automobiles operate within a framework of logical rules and physical laws, and the key to troubleshooting is a good understanding of all the automotive systems.

This section breaks the car or truck down into its component systems, allowing the problem to be isolated. The charts and diagnostic road maps list the most common problems and the most probable causes of trouble. Obviously it would be impossible to list every possible problem that could happen along with every possible cause, but it will locate MOST problems and eliminate a lot of unnecessary guesswork. The systematic format will locate problems within a given system, but, because many automotive systems are interrelated, the solution to your particular problem may be found in a number of systems on the car or truck.

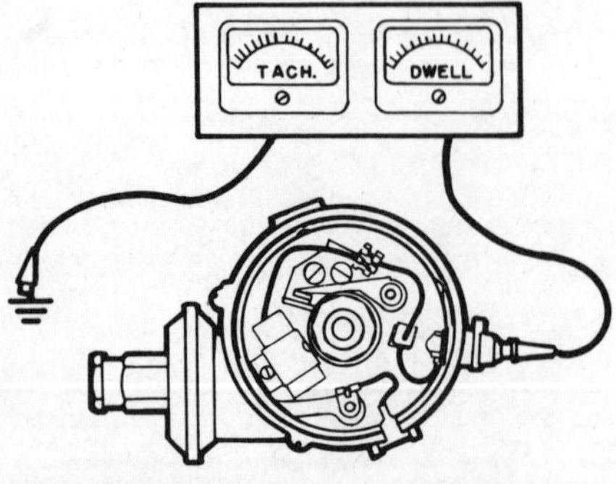

Tach-dwell hooked-up to distributor

USING THE TROUBLESHOOTING CHARTS

This book contains all of the specific information that the average do-it-yourself mechanic needs to repair and maintain his or her car or truck. The troubleshooting charts are designed to be used in conjunction with the specific procedures and information in the text. For instance, troubleshooting a point-type ignition system is fairly standard for all models, but you may be directed to the text to find procedures for troubleshooting an individual type of electronic ignition. You will also have to refer to the specification charts throughout the book for specifications applicable to your car or truck.

TOOLS AND EQUIPMENT

The tools illustrated in Chapter 1 (plus two more diagnostic pieces) will be adequate to troubleshoot most problems. The two other tools needed are a voltmeter and an ohmmeter. These can be purchased separately or in combination, known as a VOM meter.

In the event that other tools are required, they will be noted in the procedures.

Troubleshooting Engine Problems

See Chapters 2, 3, 4 for more information and service procedures.

Index to Systems

System	To Test	Group
Battery	Engine need not be running	1
Starting system	Engine need not be running	2
Primary electrical system	Engine need not be running	3
Secondary electrical system	Engine need not be running	4
Fuel system	Engine need not be running	5
Engine compression	Engine need not be running	6
Engine vacuum	Engine must be running	7
Secondary electrical system	Engine must be running	8
Valve train	Engine must be running	9
Exhaust system	Engine must be running	10
Cooling system	Engine must be running	11
Engine lubrication	Engine must be running	12

Index to Problems

Problem: Symptom	Begin at Specific Diagnosis, Number
Engine Won't Start:	
Starter doesn't turn	1.1, 2.1
Starter turns, engine doesn't	2.1
Starter turns engine very slowly	1.1, 2.4
Starter turns engine normally	3.1, 4.1
Starter turns engine very quickly	6.1
Engine fires intermittently	4.1
Engine fires consistently	5.1, 6.1
Engine Runs Poorly:	
Hard starting	3.1, 4.1, 5.1, 8.1
Rough idle	4.1, 5.1, 8.1
Stalling	3.1, 4.1, 5.1, 8.1
Engine dies at high speeds	4.1, 5.1
Hesitation (on acceleration from standing stop)	5.1, 8.1
Poor pickup	4.1, 5.1, 8.1
Lack of power	3.1, 4.1, 5.1, 8.1
Backfire through the carburetor	4.1, 8.1, 9.1
Backfire through the exhaust	4.1, 8.1, 9.1
Blue exhaust gases	6.1, 7.1
Black exhaust gases	5.1
Running on (after the ignition is shut off)	3.1, 8.1
Susceptible to moisture	4.1
Engine misfires under load	4.1, 7.1, 8.4, 9.1
Engine misfires at speed	4.1, 8.4
Engine misfires at idle	3.1, 4.1, 5.1, 7.1, 8.4

Sample Section

Test and Procedure	Results and Indications	Proceed to
4.1—Check for spark: Hold each spark plug wire approximately ¼″ from ground with gloves or a heavy, dry rag. Crank the engine and observe the spark.	→ If no spark is evident:	**4.2**
	→ If spark is good in some cases:	**4.3**
	→ If spark is good in all cases:	**4.6**

Specific Diagnosis

This section is arranged so that following each test, instructions are given to proceed to another, until a problem is diagnosed.

Section 1—Battery

Test and Procedure	Results and Indications	Proceed to
1.1—Inspect the battery visually for case condition (corrosion, cracks) and water level.	If case is cracked, replace battery:	**1.4**
	If the case is intact, remove corrosion with a solution of baking soda and water (**CAUTION:** ***do not get the solution into the battery***), and fill with water:	**1.2**

Inspect the battery case

Test and Procedure	Results and Indications	Proceed to
1.2—Check the battery cable connections: Insert a screwdriver between the battery post and the cable clamp. Turn the headlights on high beam, and observe them as the screwdriver is gently twisted to ensure good metal to metal contact.	If the lights brighten, remove and clean the clamp and post; coat the post with petroleum jelly, install and tighten the clamp:	**1.4**
	If no improvement is noted:	**1.3**

TESTING BATTERY CABLE CONNECTIONS USING A SCREWDRIVER

Test and Procedure	Results and Indications	Proceed to
1.3—Test the state of charge of the battery using an individual cell tester or hydrometer.	If indicated, charge the battery. **NOTE:** ***If no obvious reason exists for the low state of charge (i.e., battery age, prolonged storage), proceed to:***	**1.4**

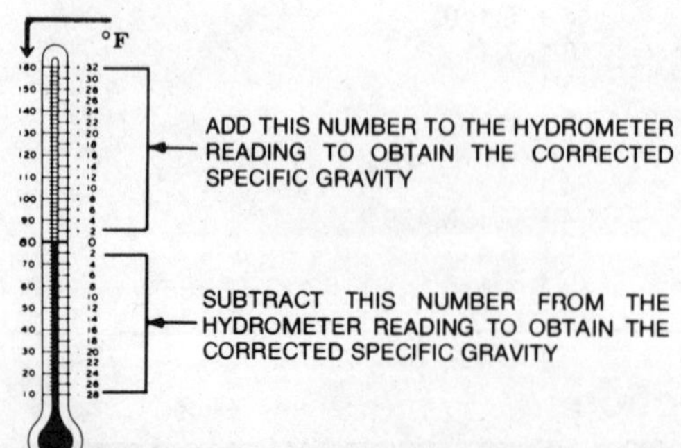

Specific Gravity (@ 80° F.)

Minimum	*Battery Charge*
1.260	100% Charged
1.230	75% Charged
1.200	50% Charged
1.170	25% Charged
1.140	Very Little Power Left
1.110	Completely Discharged

The effects of temperature on battery specific gravity (left) and amount of battery charge in relation to specific gravity (right)

Test and Procedure	Results and Indications	Proceed to
1.4—Visually inspect battery cables for cracking, bad connection to ground, or bad connection to starter.	If necessary, tighten connections or replace the cables:	**2.1**

Section 2—Starting System

See Chapter 3 for service procedures

Test and Procedure	Results and Indications	Proceed to
Note: Tests in Group 2 are performed with coil high tension lead disconnected to prevent accidental starting.		
2.1—Test the starter motor and solenoid: Connect a jumper from the battery post of the solenoid (or relay) to the starter post of the solenoid (or relay).	If starter turns the engine normally:	**2.2**
	If the starter buzzes, or turns the engine very slowly:	**2.4**
	If no response, replace the solenoid (or relay).	**3.1**
	If the starter turns, but the engine doesn't, ensure that the flywheel ring gear is intact. If the gear is undamaged, replace the starter drive.	**3.1**
2.2—Determine whether ignition override switches are functioning properly (clutch start switch, neutral safety switch), by connecting a jumper across the switch(es), and turning the ignition switch to "start".	If starter operates, adjust or replace switch:	**3.1**
	If the starter doesn't operate:	**2.3**
2.3—Check the ignition switch "start" position: Connect a 12V test lamp or voltmeter between the starter post of the solenoid (or relay) and ground. Turn the ignition switch to the "start" position, and jiggle the key.	If the lamp doesn't light or the meter needle doesn't move when the switch is turned, check the ignition switch for loose connections, cracked insulation, or broken wires. Repair or replace as necessary:	**3.1**
	If the lamp flickers or needle moves when the key is jiggled, replace the ignition switch.	**3.3**

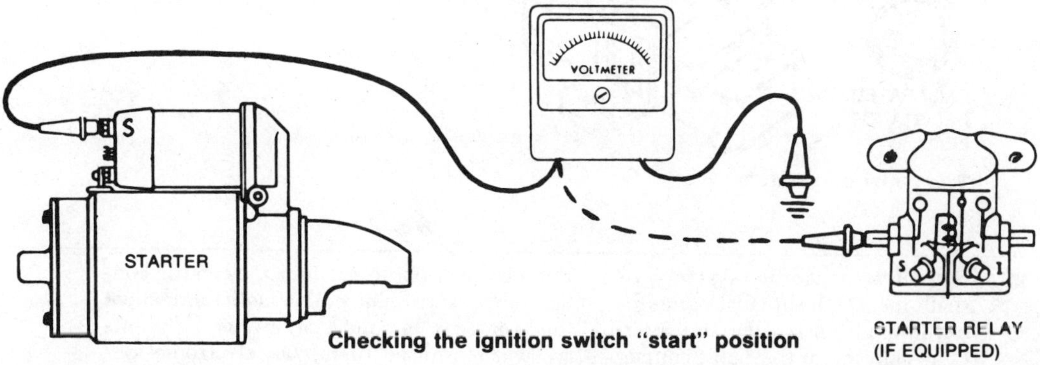

Checking the ignition switch "start" position

Test and Procedure	Results and Indications	Proceed to
2.4—Remove and bench test the starter, according to specifications in the engine electrical section.	If the starter does not meet specifications, repair or replace as needed:	**3.1**
	If the starter is operating properly:	**2.5**
2.5—Determine whether the engine can turn freely: Remove the spark plugs, and check for water in the cylinders. Check for water on the dipstick, or oil in the radiator. Attempt to turn the engine using an 18″ flex drive and socket on the crankshaft pulley nut or bolt.	If the engine will turn freely only with the spark plugs out, and hydrostatic lock (water in the cylinders) is ruled out, check valve timing:	**9.2**
	If engine will not turn freely, and it is known that the clutch and transmission are free, the engine must be disassembled for further evaluation:	**Chapter 3**

Section 3—Primary Electrical System

Test and Procedure	Results and Indications	Proceed to
3.1—Check the ignition switch "on" position: Connect a jumper wire between the distributor side of the coil and ground, and a 12V test lamp between the switch side of the coil and ground. Remove the high tension lead from the coil. Turn the ignition switch on and jiggle the key.	If the lamp lights:	3.2
	If the lamp flickers when the key is jiggled, replace the ignition switch:	3.3
	If the lamp doesn't light, check for loose or open connections. If none are found, remove the ignition switch and check for continuity. If the switch is faulty, replace it:	3.3

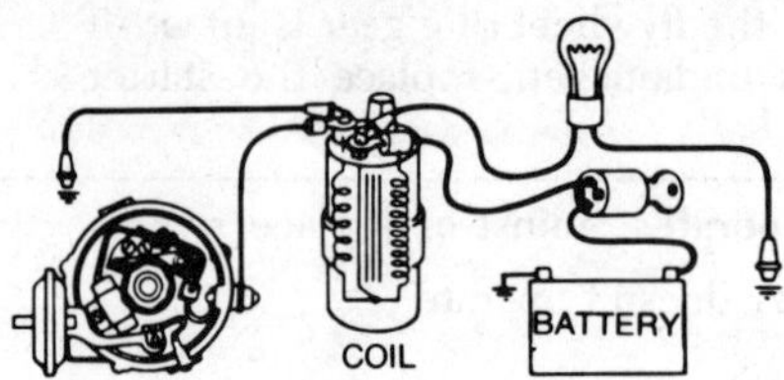

Checking the ignition switch "on" position

Test and Procedure	Results and Indications	Proceed to
3.2—Check the ballast resistor or resistance wire for an open circuit, using an ohmmeter. See Chapter 3 for specific tests.	Replace the resistor or resistance wire if the resistance is zero. **NOTE:** ***Some ignition systems have no ballast resistor.***	3.3

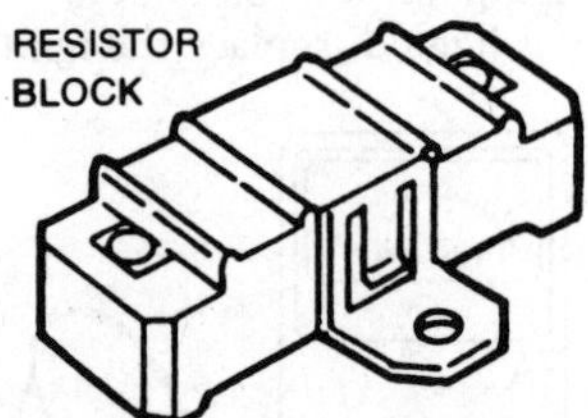

Two types of resistors

Test and Procedure	Results and Indications	Proceed to
3.3—On point-type ignition systems, visually inspect the breaker points for burning, pitting or excessive wear. Gray coloring of the point contact surfaces is normal. Rotate the crankshaft until the contact heel rests on a high point of the distributor cam and adjust the point gap to specifications. On electronic ignition models, remove the distributor cap and visually inspect the armature. Ensure that the armature pin is in place, and that the armature is on tight and rotates when the engine is cranked. Make sure there are no cracks, chips or rounded edges on the armature.	If the breaker points are intact, clean the contact surfaces with fine emery cloth, and adjust the point gap to specifications. If the points are worn, replace them. On electronic systems, replace any parts which appear defective. If condition persists:	3.4

Test and Procedure	Results and Indications	Proceed to
3.4—On point-type ignition systems, connect a dwell-meter between the distributor primary lead and ground. Crank the engine and observe the point dwell angle. On electronic ignition systems, conduct a stator (magnetic pickup assembly) test. See Chapter 3.	On point-type systems, adjust the dwell angle if necessary. **NOTE:** ***Increasing the point gap decreases the dwell angle and vice-versa.***	**3.6**
	If the dwell meter shows little or no reading;	**3.5**
	On electronic ignition systems, if the stator is bad, replace the stator. If the stator is good, proceed to the other tests in Chapter 3.	

CLOSE OPEN NORMAL DWELL

WIDE GAP SMALL DWELL INSUFFICIENT DWELL

NARROW GAP LARGE DWELL EXCESSIVE DWELL

Dwell is a function of point gap

Test and Procedure	Results and Indications	Proceed to
3.5—On the point-type ignition systems, check the condenser for short: connect an ohmmeter across the condenser body and the pigtail lead.	If any reading other than infinite is noted, replace the condenser	**3.6**

OHMMETER

Checking the condenser for short

Test and Procedure	Results and Indications	Proceed to
3.6—Test the coil primary resistance: On point-type ignition systems, connect an ohmmeter across the coil primary terminals, and read the resistance on the low scale. Note whether an external ballast resistor or resistance wire is used. On electronic ignition systems, test the coil primary resistance as in Chapter 3.	Point-type ignition coils utilizing ballast resistors or resistance wires should have approximately 1.0 ohms resistance. Coils with internal resistors should have approximately 4.0 ohms resistance. If values far from the above are noted, replace the coil.	**4.1**

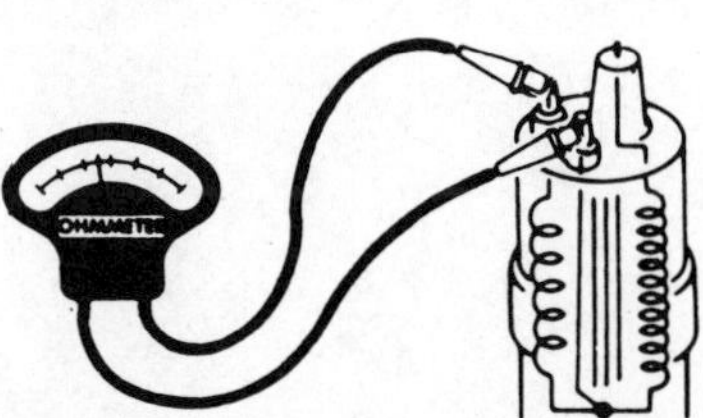

Check the coil primary resistance

Section 4—Secondary Electrical System

See Chapters 2–3 for service procedures

Test and Procedure	Results and Indications	Proceed to
4.1—Check for spark: Hold each spark plug wire approximately ¼″ from ground with gloves or a heavy, dry rag. Crank the engine, and observe the spark.	If no spark is evident:	**4.2**
	If spark is good in some cylinders:	**4.3**
	If spark is good in all cylinders:	**4.6**
Check for spark at the plugs		
4.2—Check for spark at the coil high tension lead: Remove the coil high tension lead from the distributor and position it approximately ¼″ from ground. Crank the engine and observe spark. **CAUTION:** ***This test should not be performed on engines equipped with electronic ignition.***	If the spark is good and consistent:	**4.3**
	If the spark is good but intermittent, test the primary electrical system starting at 3.3:	**3.3**
	If the spark is weak or non-existent, replace the coil high tension lead, clean and tighten all connections and retest. If no improvement is noted:	**4.4**
4.3—Visually inspect the distributor cap and rotor for burned or corroded contacts, cracks, carbon tracks, or moisture. Also check the fit of the rotor on the distributor shaft (where applicable).	If moisture is present, dry thoroughly, and retest per 4.1:	**4.1**
	If burned or excessively corroded contacts, cracks, or carbon tracks are noted, replace the defective part(s) and retest per 4.1:	**4.1**
	If the rotor and cap appear intact, or are only slightly corroded, clean the contacts thoroughly (including the cap towers and spark plug wire ends) and retest per 4.1:	
	If the spark is good in all cases:	**4.6**
	If the spark is poor in all cases:	**4.5**

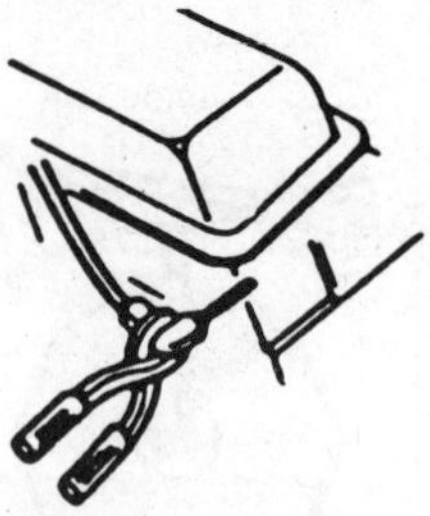

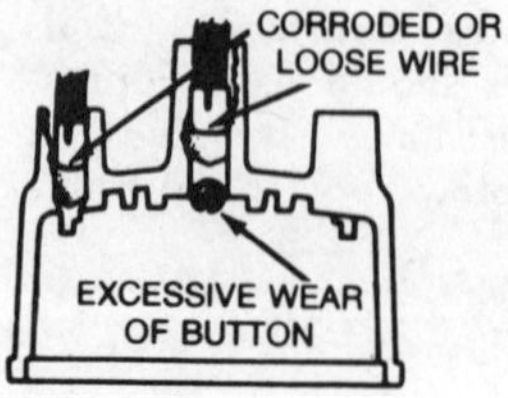

CORRODED OR LOOSE WIRE

EXCESSIVE WEAR OF BUTTON

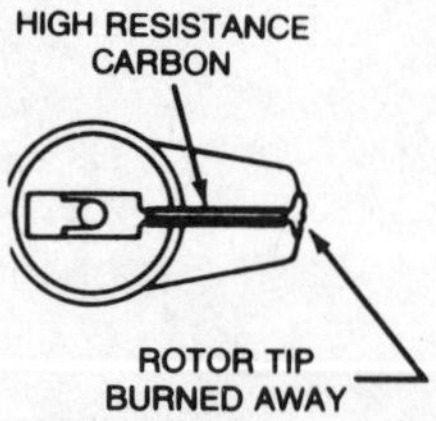

HIGH RESISTANCE CARBON

ROTOR TIP BURNED AWAY

Inspect the distributor cap and rotor

Test and Procedure	Results and Indications	Proceed to
4.4—Check the coil secondary resistance: On point-type systems connect an ohmmeter across the distributor side of the coil and the coil tower. Read the resistance on the high scale of the ohmmeter. On electronic ignition systems, see Chapter 3 for specific tests.	The resistance of a satisfactory coil should be between 4,000 and 10,000 ohms. If resistance is considerably higher (i.e., 40,000 ohms) replace the coil and retest per 4.1. **NOTE:** ***This does not apply to high performance coils.***	

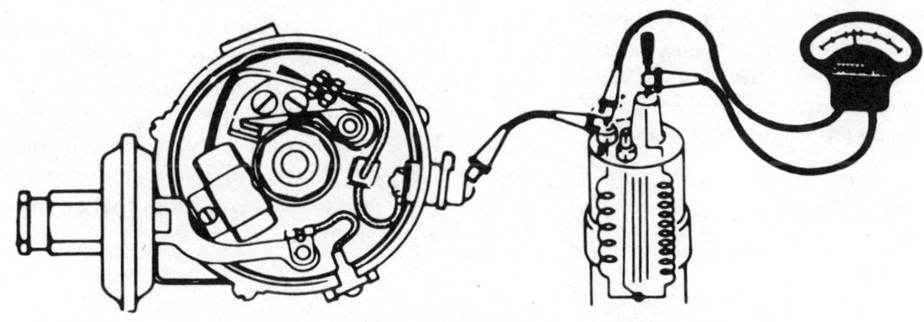

Testing the coil secondary resistance

Test and Procedure	Results and Indications	Proceed to
4.5—Visually inspect the spark plug wires for cracking or brittleness. Ensure that no two wires are positioned so as to cause induction firing (adjacent and parallel). Remove each wire, one by one, and check resistance with an ohmmeter.	Replace any cracked or brittle wires. If any of the wires are defective, replace the entire set. Replace any wires with excessive resistance (over 8000 Ω per foot for suppression wire), and separate any wires that might cause induction firing.	**4.6**

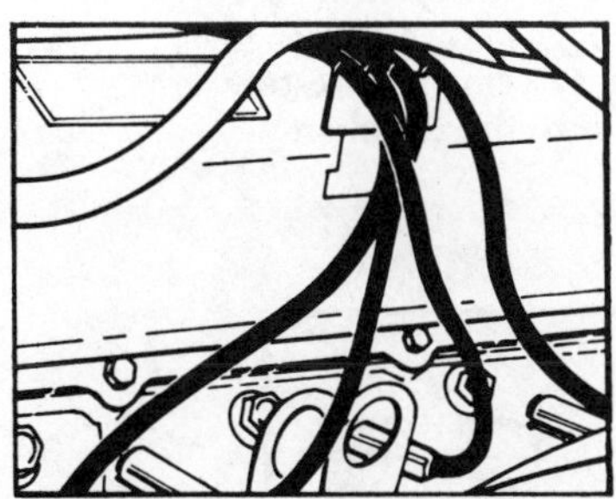

Misfiring can be the result of spark plug leads to adjacent, consecutively firing cylinders running parallel and too close together

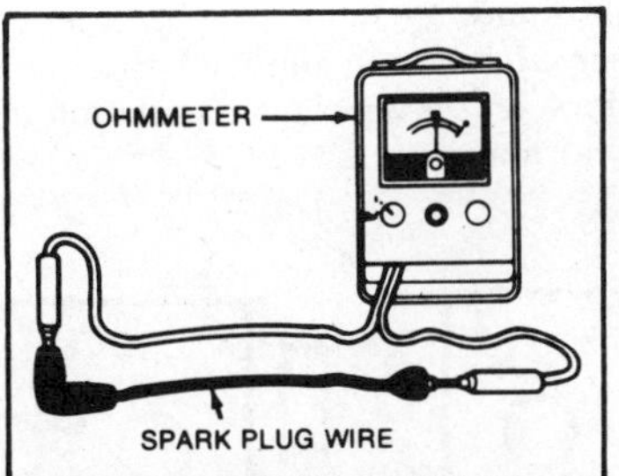

On point-type ignition systems, check the spark plug wires as shown. On electronic ignitions, do not remove the wire from the distributor cap terminal; instead, test through the cap

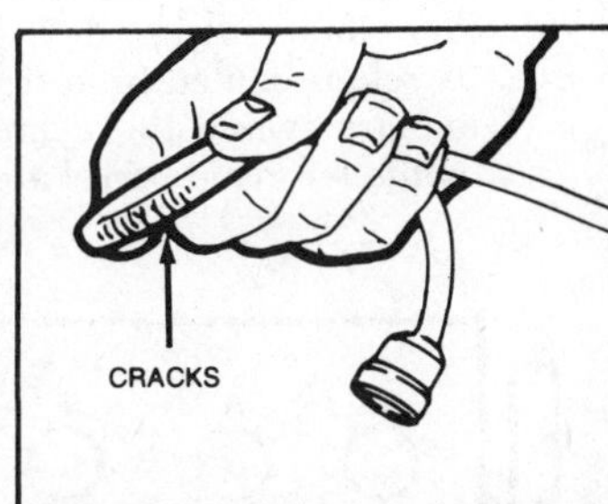

Spark plug wires can be checked visually by bending them in a loop over your finger. This will reveal any cracks, burned or broken insulation. Any wire with cracked insulation should be replaced

Test and Procedure	Results and Indications	Proceed to
4.6—Remove the spark plugs, noting the cylinders from which they were removed, and evaluate according to the color photos in the middle of this book.	See following.	**See following.**

Test and Procedure	Results and Indications	Proceed to
4.7—Examine the location of all the plugs.	The following diagrams illustrate some of the conditions that the location of plugs will reveal.	**4.8**

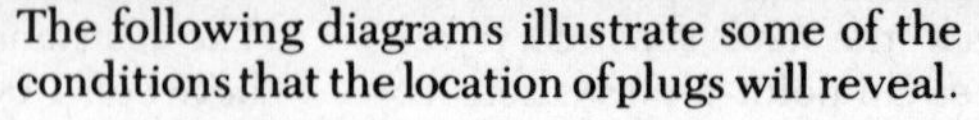

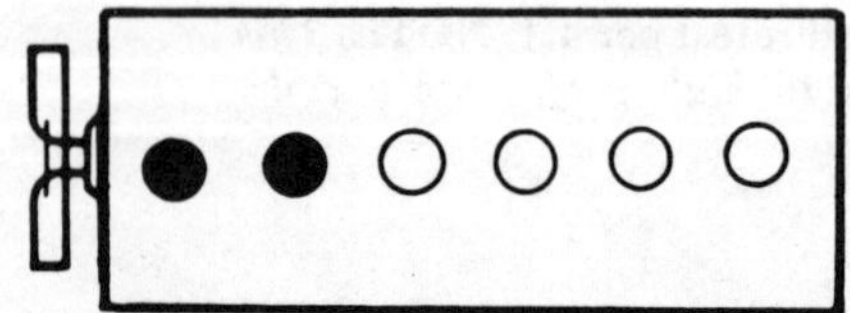

Two adjacent plugs are fouled in a 6-cylinder engine, 4-cylinder engine or either bank of a V-8. This is probably due to a blown head gasket between the two cylinders

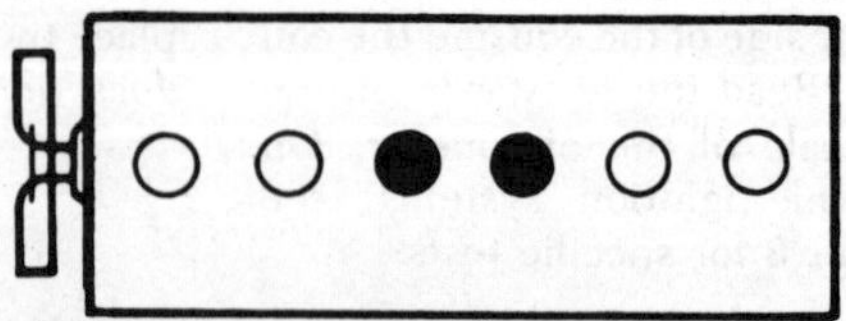

The two center plugs in a 6-cylinder engine are fouled. Raw fuel may be "boiled" out of the carburetor into the intake manifold after the engine is shut-off. Stop-start driving can also foul the center plugs, due to overly rich mixture. Proper float level, a new float needle and seat or use of an insulating spacer may help this problem

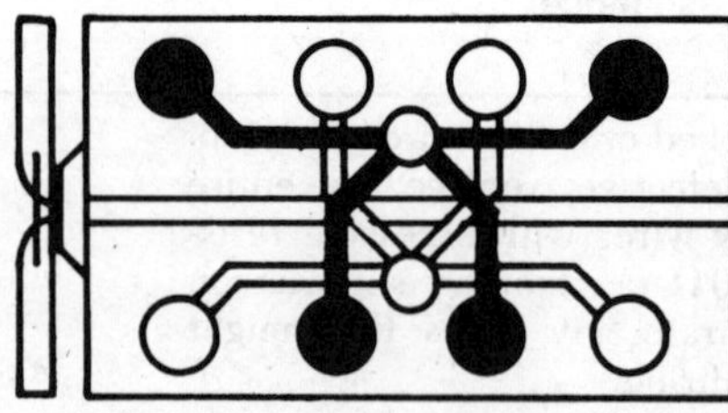

An unbalanced carburetor is indicated. Following the fuel flow on this particular design shows that the cylinders fed by the right-hand barrel are fouled from overly rich mixture, while the cylinders fed by the left-hand barrel are normal

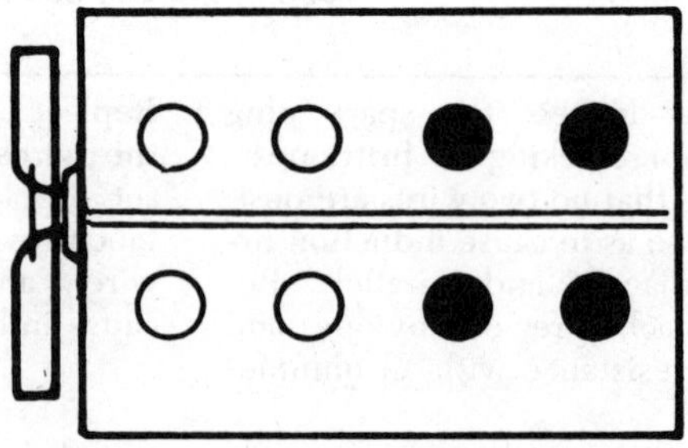

If the four rear plugs are overheated, a cooling system problem is suggested. A thorough cleaning of the cooling system may restore coolant circulation and cure the problem

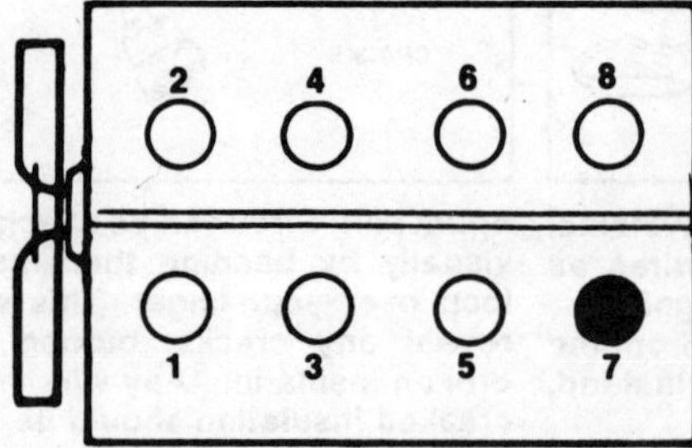

Finding one plug overheated may indicate an intake manifold leak near the affected cylinder. If the overheated plug is the second of two adjacent, consecutively firing plugs, it could be the result of ignition cross-firing. Separating the leads to these two plugs will eliminate cross-fire

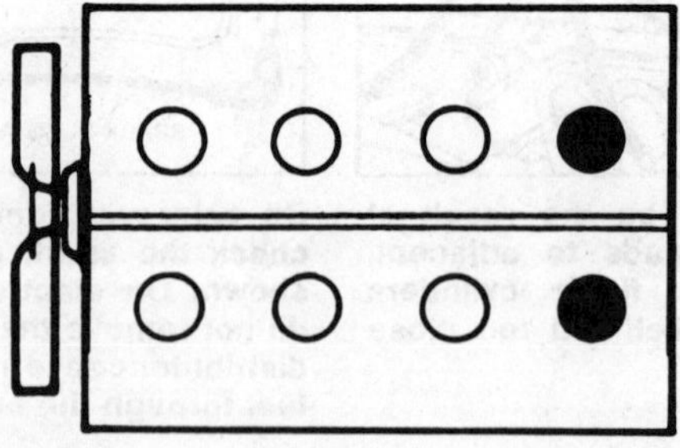

Occasionally, the two rear plugs in large, lightly used V-8's will become oil fouled. High oil consumption and smoky exhaust may also be noticed. It is probably due to plugged oil drain holes in the rear of the cylinder head, causing oil to be sucked in around the valve stems. This usually occurs in the rear cylinders first, because the engine slants that way

Test and Procedure	Results and Indications	Proceed to
4.8—Determine the static ignition timing. Using the crankshaft pulley timing marks as a guide, locate top dead center on the compression stroke of the number one cylinder.	The rotor should be pointing toward the No. 1 tower in the distributor cap, and, on electronic ignitions, the armature spoke for that cylinder should be lined up with the stator.	**4.8**
4.9—Check coil polarity: Connect a voltmeter negative lead to the coil high tension lead, and the positive lead to ground (**NOTE:** ***Reverse the hook-up for positive ground systems***). Crank the engine momentarily.	If the voltmeter reads up-scale, the polarity is correct:	**5.1**
	If the voltmeter reads down-scale, reverse the coil polarity (switch the primary leads):	**5.1**
	Checking coil polarity	

Section 5—Fuel System

See Chapter 4 for service procedures

Test and Procedure	Results and Indications	Proceed to
5.1—Determine that the air filter is functioning efficiently: Hold paper elements up to a strong light, and attempt to see light through the filter.	Clean permanent air filters in solvent (or manufacturer's recommendation), and allow to dry. Replace paper elements through which light cannot be seen:	**5.2**
5.2—Determine whether a flooding condition exists: Flooding is identified by a strong gasoline odor, and excessive gasoline present in the throttle bore(s) of the carburetor.	If flooding is not evident:	**5.3**
	If flooding is evident, permit the gasoline to dry for a few moments and restart.	
	If flooding doesn't recur:	**5.7**
	If flooding is persistent:	**5.5**
	If the engine floods repeatedly, check the choke butterfly flap	
5.3—Check that fuel is reaching the carburetor: Detach the fuel line at the carburetor inlet. Hold the end of the line in a cup (not styrofoam), and crank the engine.	If fuel flows smoothly:	**5.7**
	If fuel doesn't flow (**NOTE:** ***Make sure that there is fuel in the tank***), or flows erratically:	**5.4**

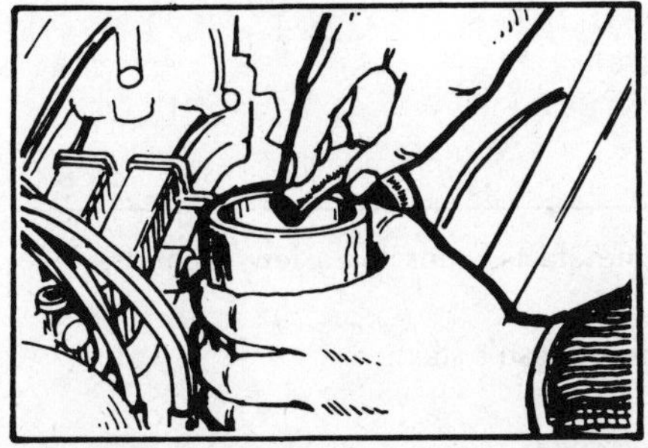

Check the fuel pump by disconnecting the output line (fuel pump-to-carburetor) at the carburetor and operating the starter briefly

Test and Procedure	*Results and Indications*	*Proceed to*
5.4—Test the fuel pump: Disconnect all fuel lines from the fuel pump. Hold a finger over the input fitting, crank the engine (with electric pump, turn the ignition or pump on); and feel for suction.	If suction is evident, blow out the fuel line to the tank with low pressure compressed air until bubbling is heard from the fuel filler neck. Also blow out the carburetor fuel line (both ends disconnected):	**5.7**
	If no suction is evident, replace or repair the fuel pump:	**5.7**
	NOTE: ***Repeated oil fouling of the spark plugs, or a no-start condition, could be the result of a ruptured vacuum booster pump diaphragm, through which oil or gasoline is being drawn into the intake manifold (where applicable).***	
5.5—Occasionally, small specks of dirt will clog the small jets and orifices in the carburetor. With the engine cold, hold a flat piece of wood or similar material over the carburetor, where possible, and crank the engine.	If the engine starts, but runs roughly the engine is probably not run enough.	
	If the engine won't start:	**5.9**
5.6—Check the needle and seat: Tap the carburetor in the area of the needle and seat.	If flooding stops, a gasoline additive (e.g., Gumout) will often cure the problem:	**5.7**
	If flooding continues, check the fuel pump for excessive pressure at the carburetor (according to specifications). If the pressure is normal, the needle and seat must be removed and checked, and/or the float level adjusted:	**5.7**
5.7—Test the accelerator pump by looking into the throttle bores while operating the throttle. 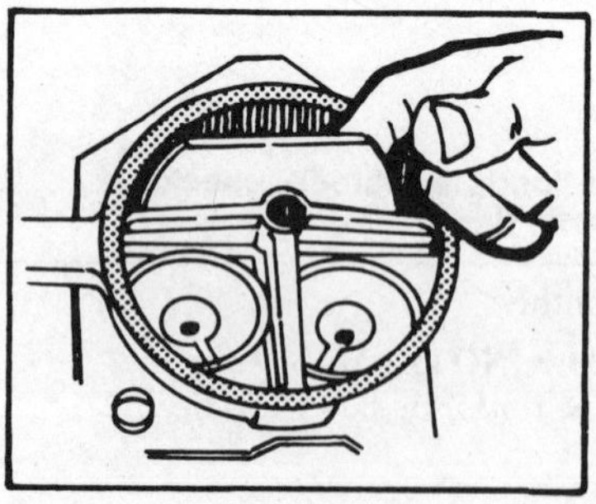	If the accelerator pump appears to be operating normally:	**5.8**
Check for gas at the carburetor by looking down the carburetor throat while someone moves the accelerator	If the accelerator pump is not operating, the pump must be reconditioned. Where possible, service the pump with the carburetor(s) installed on the engine. If necessary, remove the carburetor. Prior to removal:	**5.8**
5.8—Determine whether the carburetor main fuel system is functioning: Spray a commercial starting fluid into the carburetor while attempting to start the engine.	If the engine starts, runs for a few seconds, and dies:	**5.9**
	If the engine doesn't start:	**6.1**

Test and Procedure	Results and Indications	Proceed to
5.9—Uncommon fuel system malfunctions: See below:	If the problem is solved:	**6.1**
	If the problem remains, remove and recondition the carburetor.	

Condition	Indication	Test	Prevailing Weather Conditions	Remedy
Vapor lock	Engine will not restart shortly after running.	Cool the components of the fuel system until the engine starts. Vapor lock can be cured faster by draping a wet cloth over a mechanical fuel pump.	Hot to very hot	Ensure that the exhaust manifold heat control valve is operating. Check with the vehicle manufacturer for the recommended solution to vapor lock on the model in question.
Carburetor icing	Engine will not idle, stalls at low speeds.	Visually inspect the throttle plate area of the throttle bores for frost.	High humidity, 32–40° F.	Ensure that the exhaust manifold heat control valve is operating, and that the intake manifold heat riser is not blocked.
Water in the fuel	Engine sputters and stalls; may not start.	Pump a small amount of fuel into a glass jar. Allow to stand, and inspect for droplets or a layer of water.	High humidity, extreme temperature changes.	For droplets, use one or two cans of commercial gas line anti-freeze. For a layer of water, the tank must be drained, and the fuel lines blown out with compressed air.

Section 6—Engine Compression

See Chapter 3 for service procedures

Test and Procedure	Results and Indications	Proceed to
6.1—Test engine compression: Remove all spark plugs. Block the throttle wide open. Insert a compression gauge into a spark plug port, crank the engine to obtain the maximum reading, and record.	If compression is within limits on all cylinders:	**7.1**
	If gauge reading is extremely low on all cylinders:	**6.2**
	If gauge reading is low on one or two cylinders: (If gauge readings are identical and low on two or more adjacent cylinders, the head gasket must be replaced.)	**6.2**

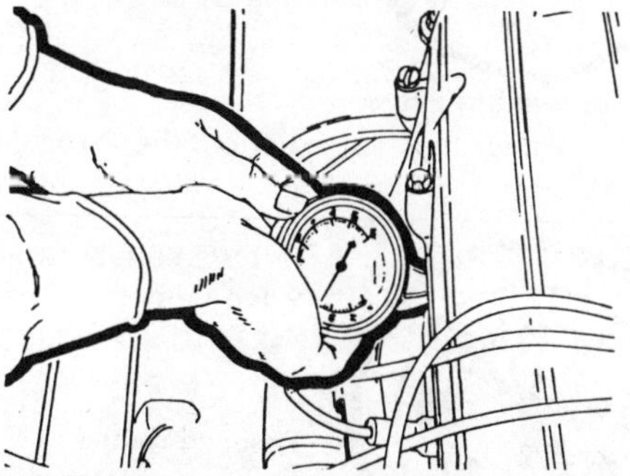

Checking compression

Test and Procedure	Results and Indications	Proceed to
6.2—Test engine compression (wet): Squirt approximately 30 cc. of engine oil into each cylinder, and retest per 6.1.	If the readings improve, worn or cracked rings or broken pistons are indicated:	**See Chapter 3**
	If the readings do not improve, burned or excessively carboned valves or a jumped timing chain are indicated: **NOTE:** ***A jumped timing chain is often indicated by difficult cranking.***	**7.1**

Section 7—Engine Vacuum

See Chapter 3 for service procedures

Test and Procedure	Results and Indications	Proceed to
7.1—Attach a vacuum gauge to the intake manifold beyond the throttle plate. Start the engine, and observe the action of the needle over the range of engine speeds.	See below.	**See below**

INDICATION: normal engine in good condition

Proceed to: 8.1

Normal engine

Gauge reading: steady, from 17–22 in./Hg.

INDICATION: sticking valves or ignition miss

Proceed to: 9.1, 8.3

Sticking valves

Gauge reading: intermittent fluctuation at idle

INDICATION: late ignition or valve timing, low compression, stuck throttle valve, leaking carburetor or manifold gasket

Proceed to: 6.1

Incorrect valve timing

Gauge reading: low (10–15 in./Hg) but steady

INDICATION: improper carburetor adjustment or minor intake leak.

Proceed to: 7.2

Carburetor requires adjustment

Gauge reading: drifting needle

INDICATION: ignition miss, blown cylinder head gasket, leaking valve or weak valve spring

Proceed to: 8.3, 6.1

Blown head gasket

Gauge reading: needle fluctuates as engine speed increases

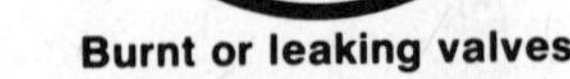

INDICATION: burnt valve or faulty valve clearance. Needle will fall when defective valve operates

Proceed to: 9.1

Burnt or leaking valves

Gauge reading: steady needle, but drops regularly

INDICATION: choked muffler, excessive back pressure in system

Proceed to: 10.1

Clogged exhaust system

Gauge reading: gradual drop in reading at idle

INDICATION: worn valve guides

Proceed to: 9.1

Worn valve guides

Gauge reading: needle vibrates excessively at idle, but steadies as engine speed increases

White pointer = steady gauge hand

Black pointer = fluctuating gauge hand

Test and Procedure	Results and Indications	Proceed to
7.2—Attach a vacuum gauge per 7.1, and test for an intake manifold leak. Squirt a small amount of oil around the intake manifold gaskets, carburetor gaskets, plugs and fittings. Observe the action of the vacuum gauge.	If the reading improves, replace the indicated gasket, or seal the indicated fitting or plug: If the reading remains low:	**8.1** **7.3**
7.3—Test all vacuum hoses and accessories for leaks as described in 7.2. Also check the carburetor body (dashpots, automatic choke mechanism, throttle shafts) for leaks in the same manner.	If the reading improves, service or replace the offending part(s): If the reading remains low:	**8.1** **6.1**

Section 8—Secondary Electrical System

See Chapter 2 for service procedures

Test and Procedure	Results and Indications	Proceed to
8.1—Remove the distributor cap and check to make sure that the rotor turns when the engine is cranked. Visually inspect the distributor components.	Clean, tighten or replace any components which appear defective.	**8.2**
8.2—Connect a timing light (per manufacturer's recommendation) and check the dynamic ignition timing. Disconnect and plug the vacuum hose(s) to the distributor if specified, start the engine, and observe the timing marks at the specified engine speed.	If the timing is not correct, adjust to specifications by rotating the distributor in the engine: (Advance timing by rotating distributor opposite normal direction of rotor rotation, retard timing by rotating distributor in same direction as rotor rotation.)	**8.3**
8.3—Check the operation of the distributor advance mechanism(s): To test the mechanical advance, disconnect the vacuum lines from the distributor advance unit and observe the timing marks with a timing light as the engine speed is increased from idle. If the mark moves smoothly, without hesitation, it may be assumed that the mechanical advance is functioning properly. To test vacuum advance and/or retard systems, alternately crimp and release the vacuum line, and observe the timing mark for movement. If movement is noted, the system is operating.	If the systems are functioning: If the systems are not functioning, remove the distributor, and test on a distributor tester:	**8.4** **8.4**
8.4—Locate an ignition miss: With the engine running, remove each spark plug wire, one at a time, until one is found that doesn't cause the engine to roughen and slow down.	When the missing cylinder is identified:	**4.1**

Section 9—Valve Train

See Chapter 3 for service procedures

Test and Procedure	Results and Indications	Proceed to
9.1—Evaluate the valve train: Remove the valve cover, and ensure that the valves are adjusted to specifications. A mechanic's stethoscope may be used to aid in the diagnosis of the valve train. By pushing the probe on or near push rods or rockers, valve noise often can be isolated. A timing light also may be used to diagnose valve problems. Connect the light according to manufacturer's recommendations, and start the engine. Vary the firing moment of the light by increasing the engine speed (and therefore the ignition advance), and moving the trigger from cylinder to cylinder. Observe the movement of each valve.	Sticking valves or erratic valve train motion can be observed with the timing light. The cylinder head must be disassembled for repairs.	**See Chapter 3**
9.2—Check the valve timing: Locate top dead center of the No. 1 piston, and install a degree wheel or tape on the crankshaft pulley or damper with zero corresponding to an index mark on the engine. Rotate the crankshaft in its direction of rotation, and observe the opening of the No. 1 cylinder intake valve. The opening should correspond with the correct mark on the degree wheel according to specifications.	If the timing is not correct, the timing cover must be removed for further investigation.	**See Chapter 3**

Section 10—Exhaust System

Test and Procedure	Results and Indications	Proceed to
10.1—Determine whether the exhaust manifold heat control valve is operating: Operate the valve by hand to determine whether it is free to move. If the valve is free, run the engine to operating temperature and observe the action of the valve, to ensure that it is opening.	If the valve sticks, spray it with a suitable solvent, open and close the valve to free it, and retest.	
	If the valve functions properly:	**10.2**
	If the valve does not free, or does not operate, replace the valve:	**10.2**
10.2—Ensure that there are no exhaust restrictions: Visually inspect the exhaust system for kinks, dents, or crushing. Also note that gases are flowing freely from the tailpipe at all engine speeds, indicating no restriction in the muffler or resonator.	Replace any damaged portion of the system:	**11.1**

Section 11—Cooling System

See Chapter 3 for service procedures

Test and Procedure	Results and Indications	Proceed to
11.1—Visually inspect the fan belt for glazing, cracks, and fraying, and replace if necessary. Tighten the belt so that the longest span has approximately ½″ play at its midpoint under thumb pressure (see Chapter 1).	Replace or tighten the fan belt as necessary: **Checking belt tension**	**11.2**
11.2—Check the fluid level of the cooling system.	If full or slightly low, fill as necessary:	**11.5**
	If extremely low:	**11.3**
11.3—Visually inspect the external portions of the cooling system (radiator, radiator hoses, thermostat elbow, water pump seals, heater hoses, etc.) for leaks. If none are found, pressurize the cooling system to 14–15 psi.	If cooling system holds the pressure:	**11.5**
	If cooling system loses pressure rapidly, reinspect external parts of the system for leaks under pressure. If none are found, check dipstick for coolant in crankcase. If no coolant is present, but pressure loss continues:	**11.4**
	If coolant is evident in crankcase, remove cylinder head(s), and check gasket(s). If gaskets are intact, block and cylinder head(s) should be checked for cracks or holes. If the gasket(s) is blown, replace, and purge the crankcase of coolant:	**12.6**
	NOTE: ***Occasionally, due to atmospheric and driving conditions, condensation of water can occur in the crankcase. This causes the oil to appear milky white. To remedy, run the engine until hot, and change the oil and oil filter.***	
11.4—Check for combustion leaks into the cooling system: Pressurize the cooling system as above. Start the engine, and observe the pressure gauge. If the needle fluctuates, remove each spark plug wire, one at a time, noting which cylinder(s) reduce or eliminate the fluctuation. **Pressurizing the cooling system**	Cylinders which reduce or eliminate the fluctuation, when the spark plug wire is removed, are leaking into the cooling system. Replace the head gasket on the affected cylinder bank(s).	

Test and Procedure	Results and Indications	Proceed to
11.5—Check the radiator pressure cap: Attach a radiator pressure tester to the radiator cap (wet the seal prior to installation). Quickly pump up the pressure, noting the point at which the cap releases.	If the cap releases within ± 1 psi of the specified rating, it is operating properly:	**11.6**
	If the cap releases at more than ± 1 psi of the specified rating, it should be replaced:	**11.6**

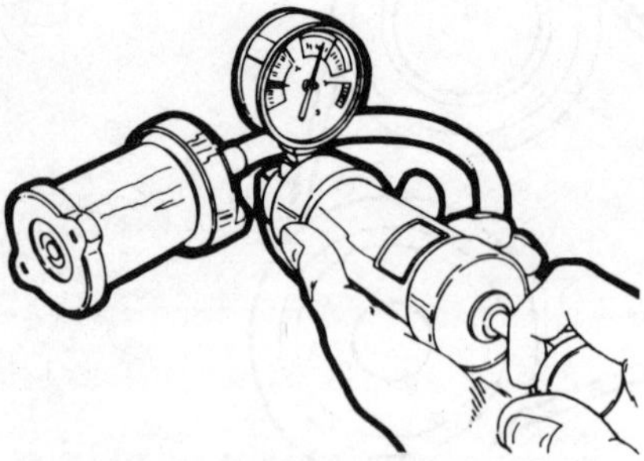

Checking radiator pressure cap

Test and Procedure	Results and Indications	Proceed to
11.6—Test the thermostat: Start the engine cold, remove the radiator cap, and insert a thermometer into the radiator. Allow the engine to idle. After a short while, there will be a sudden, rapid increase in coolant temperature. The temperature at which this sharp rise stops is the thermostat opening temperature.	If the thermostat opens at or about the specified temperature:	**11.7**
	If the temperature doesn't increase: (If the temperature increases slowly and gradually, replace the thermostat.)	**11.7**
11.7—Check the water pump: Remove the thermostat elbow and the thermostat, disconnect the coil high tension lead (to prevent starting), and crank the engine momentarily.	If coolant flows, replace the thermostat and retest per 11.6:	**11.6**
	If coolant doesn't flow, reverse flush the cooling system to alleviate any blockage that might exist. If system is not blocked, and coolant will not flow, replace the water pump.	

Section 12—Lubrication

See Chapter 3 for service procedures

Test and Procedure	Results and Indications	Proceed to
12.1—Check the oil pressure gauge or warning light: If the gauge shows low pressure, or the light is on for no obvious reason, remove the oil pressure sender. Install an accurate oil pressure gauge and run the engine momentarily.	If oil pressure builds normally, run engine for a few moments to determine that it is functioning normally, and replace the sender.	—
	If the pressure remains low:	**12.2**
	If the pressure surges:	**12.3**
	If the oil pressure is zero:	**12.3**
12.2—Visually inspect the oil: If the oil is watery or very thin, milky, or foamy, replace the oil and oil filter.	If the oil is normal:	**12.3**
	If after replacing oil the pressure remains low:	**12.3**
	If after replacing oil the pressure becomes normal:	—

Test and Procedure	Results and Indications	Proceed to
12.3—Inspect the oil pressure relief valve and spring, to ensure that it is not sticking or stuck. Remove and thoroughly clean the valve, spring, and the valve body.	If the oil pressure improves:	—
	If no improvement is noted:	**12.4**
12.4—Check to ensure that the oil pump is not cavitating (sucking air instead of oil): See that the crankcase is neither over nor underfull, and that the pickup in the sump is in the proper position and free from sludge.	Fill or drain the crankcase to the proper capacity, and clean the pickup screen in solvent if necessary. If no improvement is noted:	**12.5**
12.5—Inspect the oil pump drive and the oil pump:	If the pump drive or the oil pump appear to be defective, service as necessary and retest per 12.1:	**12.1**
	If the pump drive and pump appear to be operating normally, the engine should be disassembled to determine where blockage exists:	**See Chapter 3**
12.6—Purge the engine of ethylene glycol coolant: Completely drain the crankcase and the oil filter. Obtain a commercial butyl cellosolve base solvent, designated for this purpose, and follow the instructions precisely. Following this, install a new oil filter and refill the crankcase with the proper weight oil. The next oil and filter change should follow shortly thereafter (1000 miles).		

TROUBLESHOOTING EMISSION CONTROL SYSTEMS

See Chapter 4 for procedures applicable to individual emission control systems used on specific combinations of engine/transmission/model.

TROUBLESHOOTING THE CARBURETOR

See Chapter 4 for service procedures

Carburetor problems cannot be effectively isolated unless all other engine systems (particularly ignition and emission) are functioning properly and the engine is properly tuned.

Condition	Possible Cause
Engine cranks, but does not start	1. Improper starting procedure 2. No fuel in tank 3. Clogged fuel line or filter 4. Defective fuel pump 5. Choke valve not closing properly 6. Engine flooded 7. Choke valve not unloading 8. Throttle linkage not making full travel 9. Stuck needle or float 10. Leaking float needle or seat 11. Improper float adjustment
Engine stalls	1. Improperly adjusted idle speed or mixture **Engine hot** 2. Improperly adjusted dashpot 3. Defective or improperly adjusted solenoid 4. Incorrect fuel level in fuel bowl 5. Fuel pump pressure too high 6. Leaking float needle seat 7. Secondary throttle valve stuck open 8. Air or fuel leaks 9. Idle air bleeds plugged or missing 10. Idle passages plugged **Engine Cold** 11. Incorrectly adjusted choke 12. Improperly adjusted fast idle speed 13. Air leaks 14. Plugged idle or idle air passages 15. Stuck choke valve or binding linkage 16. Stuck secondary throttle valves 17. Engine flooding—high fuel level 18. Leaking or misaligned float
Engine hesitates on acceleration	1. Clogged fuel filter 2. Leaking fuel pump diaphragm 3. Low fuel pump pressure 4. Secondary throttle valves stuck, bent or misadjusted 5. Sticking or binding air valve 6. Defective accelerator pump 7. Vacuum leaks 8. Clogged air filter 9. Incorrect choke adjustment (engine cold)
Engine feels sluggish or flat on acceleration	1. Improperly adjusted idle speed or mixture 2. Clogged fuel filter 3. Defective accelerator pump 4. Dirty, plugged or incorrect main metering jets 5. Bent or sticking main metering rods 6. Sticking throttle valves 7. Stuck heat riser 8. Binding or stuck air valve 9. Dirty, plugged or incorrect secondary jets 10. Bent or sticking secondary metering rods. 11. Throttle body or manifold heat passages plugged 12. Improperly adjusted choke or choke vacuum break.
Carburetor floods	1. Defective fuel pump. Pressure too high. 2. Stuck choke valve 3. Dirty, worn or damaged float or needle valve/seat 4. Incorrect float/fuel level 5. Leaking float bowl

EASY STEP-BY-STEP TIPS FROM PROS

CHILTON'S AUTO BODY REPAIR TIPS

Tools and Materials • Step-by-Step Illustrated Procedures
How To Repair Dents, Scratches and Rust Holes
Spray Painting and Refinishing Tips

With a little practice, basic body repair procedures can be mastered by any do-it-yourself mechanic. The step-by-step repairs shown here can be applied to almost any type of auto body repair.

TOOLS & MATERIALS

You may already have basic tools, such as hammers and electric drills. Other tools unique to body repair — body hammers, grinding attachments, sanding blocks, dent puller, half-round plastic file and plastic spreaders — are relatively inexpensive and can be obtained wherever auto parts or auto body repair parts are sold. Portable air compressors and paint spray guns can be purchased or rented.

Auto Body Repair Kits

The best and most often used products are available to the do-it-yourselfer in kit form, from major manufacturers of auto body repair products. The same manufacturers also merchandise the individual products for use by pros.

Kits are available to make a wide variety of repairs, including holes, dents and scratches and fiberglass, and offer the advantage of buying the materials you'll need for the job. There is little waste or chance of materials going bad from not being used. Many kits may also contain basic body-working tools such as body files, sanding blocks and spreaders. Check the contents of the kit before buying your tools.

BODY REPAIR TIPS

Safety

Many of the products associated with auto body repair and refinishing contain toxic chemicals. Read all labels before opening containers and store them in a safe place and manner.

- Wear eye protection (safety goggles) when using power tools or when performing any operation that involves the removal of any type of material.
- Wear lung protection (disposable mask or respirator) when grinding, sanding or painting.

Sanding

1 Sand off paint before using a dent puller. When using a non-adhesive sanding disc, cover the back of the disc with an overlapping layer or two of masking tape and trim the edges. The disc will last considerably longer.

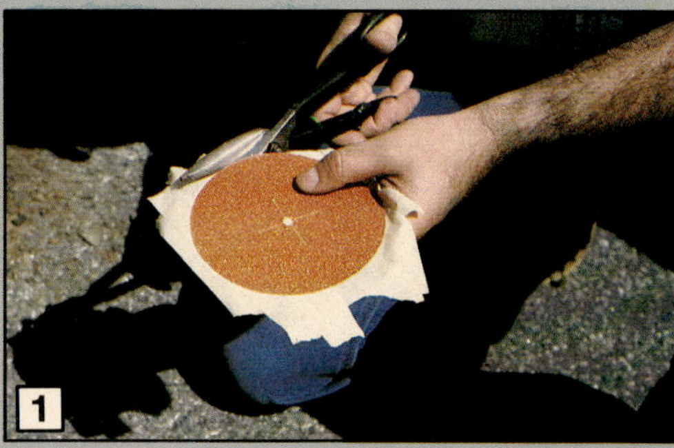
1

2 Use the circular motion of the sanding disc to grind *into* the edge of the repair. Grinding or sanding away from the jagged edge will only tear the sandpaper.

3 Use the palm of your hand flat on the panel to detect high and low spots. Do not use your fingertips. Slide your hand slowly back and forth.

3

WORKING WITH BODY FILLER

Mixing The Filler

Cleanliness and proper mixing and application are extremely important. Use a clean piece of plastic or glass or a disposable artist's palette to mix body filler.

1 Allow plenty of time and follow directions. No useful purpose will be served by adding more hardener to make it cure (set-up) faster. Less hardener means more curing time, but the mixture dries harder; more hardener means less curing time but a softer mixture.

2 Both the hardener and the filler should be thoroughly kneaded or stirred before mixing. Hardener should be a solid paste and dispense like thin toothpaste. Body filler should be smooth, and free of lumps or thick spots.

Getting the proper amount of hardener in the filler is the trickiest part of preparing the filler. Use the same amount of hardener in cold or warm weather. For contour filler (thick coats), a bead of hardener twice the diameter of the filler is about right. There's about a 15% margin on either side, but, if in doubt use less hardener.

3 Mix the body filler and hardener by wiping across the mixing surface, picking the mixture up and wiping it again. Colder weather requires longer mixing times. Do not mix in a circular motion; this will trap air bubbles which will become holes in the cured filler.

Applying The Filler

1 For best results, filler should not be applied over 1/4″ thick.

Apply the filler in several coats. Build it up to above the level of the repair surface so that it can be sanded or grated down.

The first coat of filler must be pressed on with a firm wiping motion.

Apply the filler in one direction only. Working the filler back and forth will either pull it off the metal or trap air bubbles.

REPAIRING DENTS

Before you start, take a few minutes to study the damaged area. Try to visualize the shape of the panel before it was damaged. If the damage is on the left fender, look at the right fender and use it as a guide. If there is access to the panel from behind, you can reshape it with a body hammer. If not, you'll have to use a dent puller. Go slowly and work the metal a little at a time. Get the panel as straight as possible before applying filler.

1 This dent is typical of one that can be pulled out or hammered out from behind. Remove the headlight cover, headlight assembly and turn signal housing.

2 Drill a series of holes ½ the size of the end of the dent puller along the stress line. Make some trial pulls and assess the results. If necessary, drill more holes and try again. Do not hurry.

3 If possible, use a body hammer and block to shape the metal back to its original contours. Get the metal back as close to its original shape as possible. Don't depend on body filler to fill dents.

4 Using an 80-grit grinding disc on an electric drill, grind the paint from the surrounding area down to bare metal. Use a new grinding pad to prevent heat buildup that will warp metal.

5 The area should look like this when you're finished grinding. Knock the drill holes in and tape over small openings to keep plastic filler out.

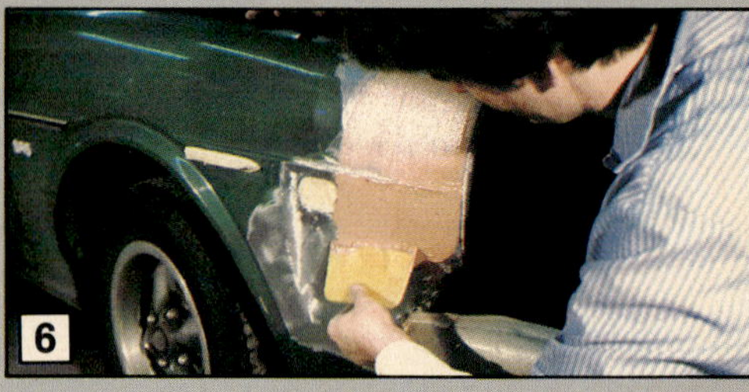

6 Mix the body filler (see Body Repair Tips). Spread the body filler evenly over the entire area (see Body Repair Tips). Be sure to cover the area completely.

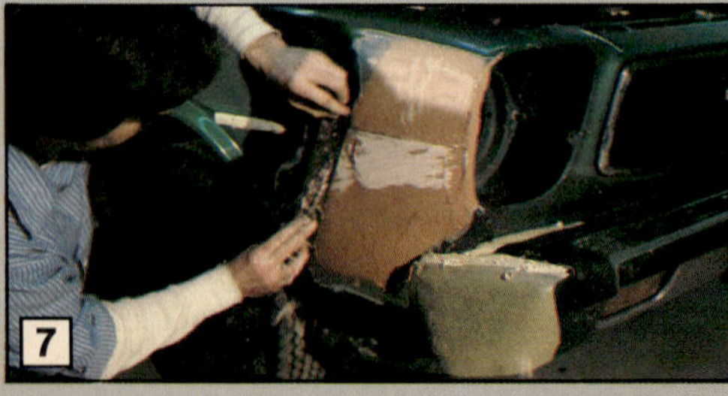

7 Let the body filler dry until the surface can just be scratched with your fingernail. Knock the high spots from the body filler with a body file ("Cheese-grater"). Check frequently with the palm of your hand for high and low spots.

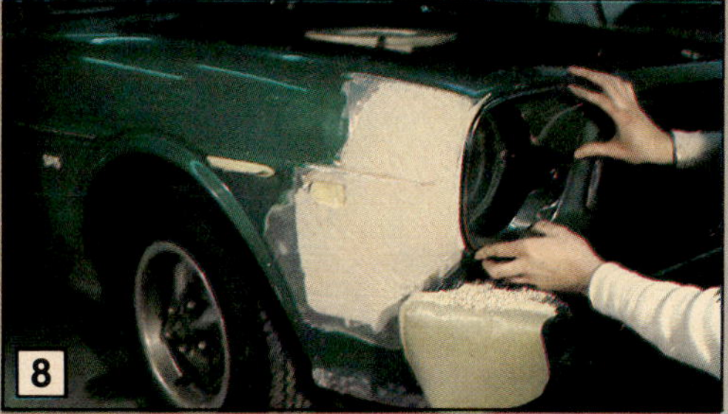

8 Check to be sure that trim pieces that will be installed later will fit exactly. Sand the area with 40-grit paper.

9 If you wind up with low spots, you may have to apply another layer of filler.

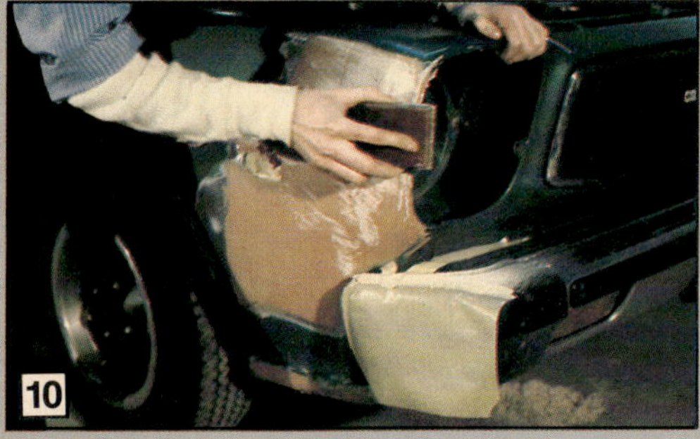

10 Knock the high spots off with 40-grit paper. When you are satisfied with the contours of the repair, apply a thin coat of filler to cover pin holes and scratches.

11 Block sand the area with 40-grit paper to a smooth finish. Pay particular attention to body lines and ridges that must be well-defined.

12 Sand the area with 400 paper and then finish with a scuff pad. The finished repair is ready for priming and painting (see Painting Tips).

Materials and photos courtesy of Ritt Jones Auto Body, Prospect Park, PA.

REPAIRING RUST HOLES

There are many ways to repair rust holes. The fiberglass cloth kit shown here is one of the most cost efficient for the owner because it provides a strong repair that resists cracking and moisture and is relatively easy to use. It can be used on large and small holes (with or without backing) and can be applied over contoured areas. Remember, however, that short of replacing an entire panel, no repair is a guarantee that the rust will not return.

1 Remove any trim that will be in the way. Clean away all loose debris. Cut away all the rusted metal. But be sure to leave enough metal to retain the contour or body shape.

2 Grind away all traces of rust with a 24-grit grinding disc. Be sure to grind back 3-4 inches from the edge of the hole down to bare metal and be sure all traces of paint, primer and rust are removed.

3 Block sand the area with 80 or 100 grit sandpaper to get a clear, shiny surface and feathered paint edge. Tap the edges of the hole inward with a ball peen hammer.

4 If you are going to use release film, cut a piece about 2-3″ larger than the area you have sanded. Place the film over the repair and mark the sanded area on the film. Avoid any unnecessary wrinkling of the film.

5 Cut 2 pieces of fiberglass matte to match the shape of the repair. One piece should be about 1″ smaller than the sanded area and the second piece should be 1″ smaller than the first. Mix enough filler and hardener to saturate the fiberglass material (see Body Repair Tips).

6 Lay the release sheet on a flat surface and spread an even layer of filler, large enough to cover the repair. Lay the smaller piece of fiberglass cloth in the center of the sheet and spread another layer of filler over the fiberglass cloth. Repeat the operation for the larger piece of cloth.

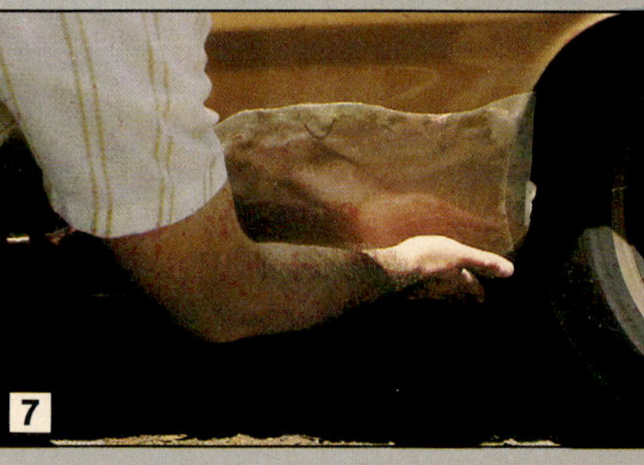

7 Place the repair material over the repair area, with the release film facing outward. Use a spreader and work from the center outward to smooth the material, following the body contours. Be sure to remove all air bubbles.

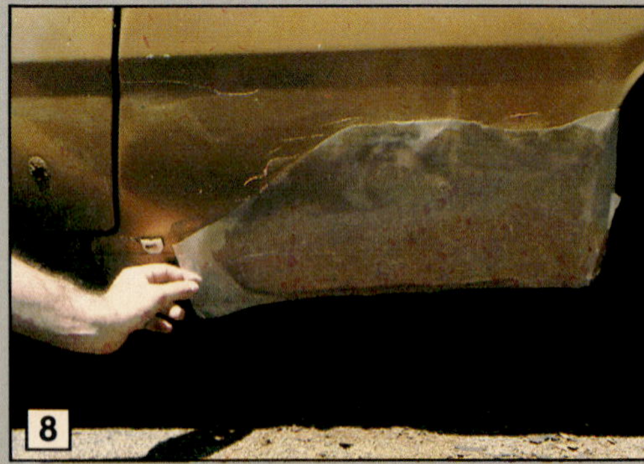

8 Wait until the repair has dried tack-free and peel off the release sheet. The ideal working temperature is 60°-90° F. Cooler or warmer temperatures or high humidity may require additional curing time. Wait longer, if in doubt.

9

9 Sand and feather-edge the entire area. The initial sanding can be done with a sanding disc on an electric drill if care is used. Finish the sanding with a block sander. Low spots can be filled with body filler; this may require several applications.

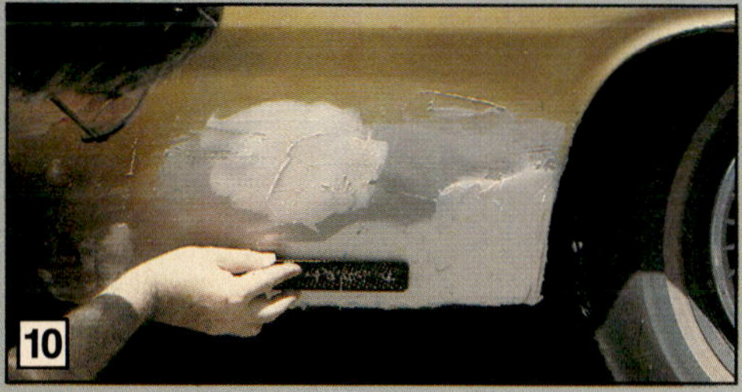
10

10 When the filler can just be scratched with a fingernail, knock the high spots down with a body file and smooth the entire area with 80-grit. Feather the filled areas into the surrounding areas.

11

11 When the area is sanded smooth, mix some topcoat and hardener and apply it directly with a spreader. This will give a smooth finish and prevent the glass matte from showing through the paint.

12

12 Block sand the topcoat smooth with finishing sandpaper (200 grit), and 400 grit. The repair is ready for masking, priming and painting (see Painting Tips).

Materials and photos courtesy Marson Corporation, Chelsea, Massachusetts

PAINTING TIPS

Preparation

1 SANDING — Use a 400 or 600 grit wet or dry sandpaper. Wet-sand the area with a 1/4 sheet of sandpaper soaked in clean water. Keep the paper wet while sanding. Sand the area until the repaired area tapers into the original finish.

2 CLEANING — Wash the area to be painted thoroughly with water and a clean rag. Rinse it thoroughly and wipe the surface dry until you're sure it's completely free of dirt, dust, fingerprints, wax, detergent or other foreign matter.

3 MASKING — Protect any areas you don't want to overspray by covering them with masking tape and newspaper. Be careful not get fingerprints on the area to be painted.

4 PRIMING — All exposed metal should be primed before painting. Primer protects the metal and provides an excellent surface for paint adhesion. When the primer is dry, wet-sand the area again with 600 grit wet-sandpaper. Clean the area again after sanding.

4

Painting Techniques

Paint applied from either a spray gun or a spray can (for small areas) will provide good results. Experiment on an old piece of metal to get the right combination before you begin painting.

SPRAYING VISCOSITY (SPRAY GUN ONLY) — Paint should be thinned to spraying viscosity according to the directions on the can. Use only the recommended thinner or reducer and the same amount of reduction regardless of temperature.

AIR PRESSURE (SPRAY GUN ONLY) — This is extremely important. Be sure you are using the proper recommended pressure.

TEMPERATURE — The surface to be painted should be approximately the same temperature as the surrounding air. Applying warm paint to a cold surface, or vice versa, will completely upset the paint characteristics.

THICKNESS — Spray with smooth strokes. In general, the thicker the coat of paint, the longer the drying time. Apply several thin coats about 30 seconds apart. The paint should remain wet long enough to flow out and no longer; heavier coats will only produce sags or wrinkles. Spray a light (fog) coat, followed by heavier color coats.

DISTANCE — The ideal spraying distance is 8″-12″ from the gun or can to the surface. Shorter distances will produce ripples, while greater distances will result in orange peel, dry film and poor color match and loss of material due to overspray.

OVERLAPPING — The gun or can should be kept at right angles to the surface at all times. Work to a wet edge at an even speed, using a 50% overlap and direct the center of the spray at the lower or nearest edge of the previous stroke.

RUBBING OUT (BLENDING) FRESH PAINT — Let the paint dry thoroughly. Runs or imperfections can be sanded out, primed and repainted.

Don't be in too big a hurry to remove the masking. This only produces paint ridges. When the finish has dried for at least a week, apply a small amount of fine grade rubbing compound with a clean, wet cloth. Use lots of water and blend the new paint with the surrounding area.

WRONG

Thin coat. Stroke too fast, not enough overlap, gun too far away.

CORRECT

Medium coat. Proper distance, good stroke, proper overlap.

WRONG

Heavy coat. Stroke too slow, too much overlap, gun too close.

Condition	Possible Cause
Engine idles roughly and stalls	1. Incorrect idle speed 2. Clogged fuel filter 3. Dirt in fuel system or carburetor 4. Loose carburetor screws or attaching bolts 5. Broken carburetor gaskets 6. Air leaks 7. Dirty carburetor 8. Worn idle mixture needles 9. Throttle valves stuck open 10. Incorrectly adjusted float or fuel level 11. Clogged air filter
Engine runs unevenly or surges	1. Defective fuel pump 2. Dirty or clogged fuel filter 3. Plugged, loose or incorrect main metering jets or rods 4. Air leaks 5. Bent or sticking main metering rods 6. Stuck power piston 7. Incorrect float adjustment 8. Incorrect idle speed or mixture 9. Dirty or plugged idle system passages 10. Hard, brittle or broken gaskets 11. Loose attaching or mounting screws 12. Stuck or misaligned secondary throttle valves
Poor fuel economy	1. Poor driving habits 2. Stuck choke valve 3. Binding choke linkage 4. Stuck heat riser 5. Incorrect idle mixture 6. Defective accelerator pump 7. Air leaks 8. Plugged, loose or incorrect main metering jets 9. Improperly adjusted float or fuel level 10. Bent, misaligned or fuel-clogged float 11. Leaking float needle seat 12. Fuel leak 13. Accelerator pump discharge ball not seating properly 14. Incorrect main jets
Engine lacks high speed performance or power	1. Incorrect throttle linkage adjustment 2. Stuck or binding power piston 3. Defective accelerator pump 4. Air leaks 5. Incorrect float setting or fuel level 6. Dirty, plugged, worn or incorrect main metering jets or rods 7. Binding or sticking air valve 8. Brittle or cracked gaskets 9. Bent, incorrect or improperly adjusted secondary metering rods 10. Clogged fuel filter 11. Clogged air filter 12. Defective fuel pump

TROUBLESHOOTING FUEL INJECTION PROBLEMS

Each fuel injection system has its own unique components and test procedures, for which it is impossible to generalize. Refer to Chapter 4 of this Repair & Tune-Up Guide for specific test and repair procedures, if the vehicle is equipped with fuel injection.

TROUBLESHOOTING ELECTRICAL PROBLEMS

See Chapter 5 for service procedures

For any electrical system to operate, it must make a complete circuit. This simply means that the power flow from the battery must make a complete circle. When an electrical component is operating, power flows from the battery to the component, passes through the component causing it to perform its function (lighting a light bulb), and then returns to the battery through the ground of the circuit. This ground is usually (but not always) the metal part of the car or truck on which the electrical component is mounted.

Perhaps the easiest way to visualize this is to think of connecting a light bulb with two wires attached to it to the battery. If one of the two wires attached to the light bulb were attached to the negative post of the battery and the other were attached to the positive post of the battery, you would have a complete circuit. Current from the battery would flow to the light bulb, causing it to light, and return to the negative post of the battery.

The normal automotive circuit differs from this simple example in two ways. First, instead of having a return wire from the bulb to the battery, the light bulb returns the current to the battery through the chassis of the vehicle. Since the negative battery cable is attached to the chassis and the chassis is made of electrically conductive metal, the chassis of the vehicle can serve as a ground wire to complete the circuit. Secondly, most automotive circuits contain switches to turn components on and off as required.

Every complete circuit from a power source must include a component which is using the power from the power source. If you were to disconnect the light bulb from the wires and touch the two wires together (don't do this) the power supply wire to the component would be grounded before the normal ground connection for the circuit.

Because grounding a wire from a power source makes a complete circuit—less the required component to use the power—this phenomenon is called a short circuit. Common causes are: broken insulation (exposing the metal wire to a metal part of the car or truck), or a shorted switch.

Some electrical components which require a large amount of current to operate also have a relay in their circuit. Since these circuits carry a large amount of current, the thickness of the wire in the circuit (gauge size) is also greater. If this large wire were connected from the component to the control switch on the instrument panel, and then back to the component, a voltage drop would occur in the circuit. To prevent this potential drop in voltage, an electromagnetic switch (relay) is used. The large wires in the circuit are connected from the battery to one side of the relay, and from the opposite side of the relay to the component. The relay is normally open, preventing current from passing through the circuit. An additional, smaller, wire is connected from the relay to the control switch for the circuit. When the control switch is turned on, it grounds the smaller wire from the relay and completes the circuit. This closes the relay and allows current to flow from the battery to the component. The horn, headlight, and starter circuits are three which use relays.

It is possible for larger surges of current to pass through the electrical system of your car or truck. If this surge of current were to reach an electrical component, it could burn it out. To prevent this, fuses, circuit breakers or fusible links are connected into the current supply wires of most of the major electrical systems. When an electrical current of excessive power passes through the component's fuse, the fuse blows out and breaks the circuit, saving the component from destruction.

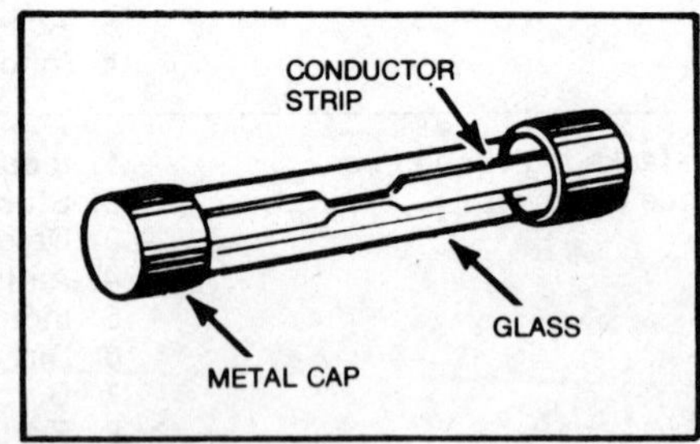

Typical automotive fuse

A circuit breaker is basically a self-repairing fuse. The circuit breaker opens the circuit the same way a fuse does. However, when either the short is removed from the circuit or the surge subsides, the circuit breaker resets itself and does not have to be replaced as a fuse does.

A fuse link is a wire that acts as a fuse. It is normally connected between the starter relay and the main wiring harness. This connection is usually under the hood. The fuse link (if installed) protects all the

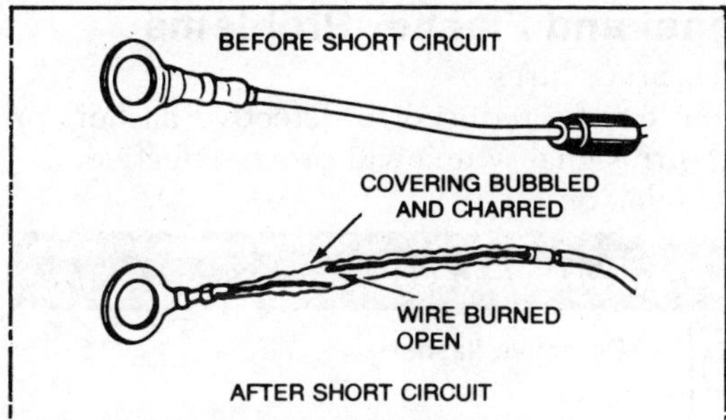

Most fusible links show a charred, melted insulation when they burn out

chassis electrical components, and is the probable cause of trouble when none of the electrical components function, unless the battery is disconnected or dead.

Electrical problems generally fall into one of three areas:

1. The component that is not functioning is not receiving current.
2. The component itself is not functioning.
3. The component is not properly grounded.

The electrical system can be checked with a test light and a jumper wire. A test light is a device that looks like a pointed screwdriver with a wire attached to it and has a light bulb in its handle. A jumper wire is a piece of insulated wire with an alligator clip attached to each end.

If a component is not working, you must follow a systematic plan to determine which of the three causes is the villain.

1. Turn on the switch that controls the inoperable component.
2. Disconnect the power supply wire from the component.
3. Attach the ground wire on the test light to a good metal ground.
4. Touch the probe end of the test light to the end of the power supply wire that was disconnected from the component. If the component is receiving current, the test light will go on.

NOTE: ***Some components work only when the ignition switch is turned on.***

If the test light does not go on, then the problem is in the circuit between the battery and the component. This includes all the switches, fuses, and relays in the system. Follow the wire that runs back to the battery. The problem is an open circuit between the battery and the component. If the fuse is blown and, when replaced, immediately blows again, there is a short circuit in the system which must be located and repaired. If there is a switch in the system, bypass it with a jumper wire. This is done by connecting one end of the jumper wire to the power supply wire into the switch and the other end of the jumper wire to the wire coming out of the switch. If the test light lights with the jumper wire installed, the switch or whatever was bypassed is defective.

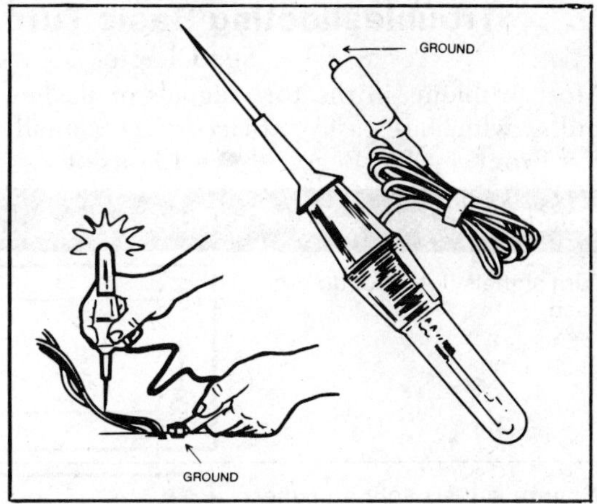

The test light will show the presence of current when touched to a hot wire and grounded at the other end

NOTE: ***Never substitute the jumper wire for the component, since it is required to use the power from the power source.***

5. If the bulb in the test light goes on, then the current is getting to the component that is not working. This eliminates the first of the three possible causes. Connect the power supply wire and connect a jumper wire from the component to a good metal ground. Do this with the switch which controls the component turned on, and also the ignition switch turned on if it is required for the component to work. If the component works with the jumper wire installed, then it has a bad ground. This is usually caused by the metal area on which the component mounts to the chassis being coated with some type of foreign matter.
6. If neither test located the source of the trouble, then the component itself is defective. Remember that for any electrical system to work, all connections must be clean and tight.

Troubleshooting Basic Turn Signal and Flasher Problems

See Chapter 5 for service procedures

Most problems in the turn signals or flasher system can be reduced to defective flashers or bulbs, which are easily replaced. Occasionally, the turn signal switch will prove defective.

F = Front R = Rear ● = Lights off ○ = Lights on

Condition		Possible Cause
Turn signals light, but do not flash	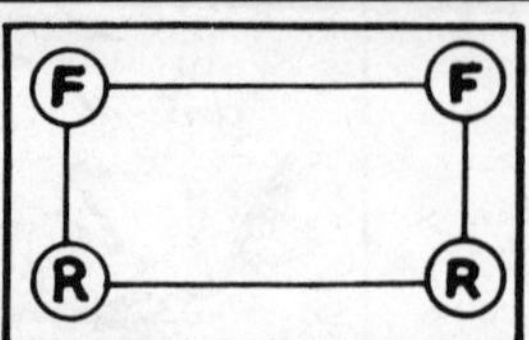	Defective flasher
No turn signals light on either side	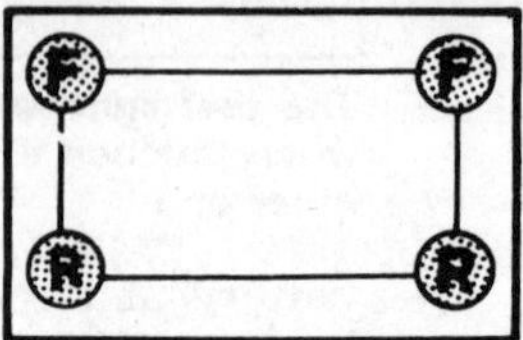	Blown fuse. Replace if defective. Defective flasher. Check by substitution. Open circuit, short circuit or poor ground.
Both turn signals on one side don't work	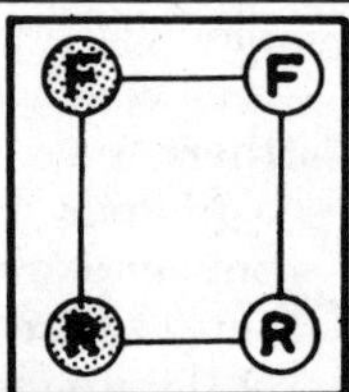	Bad bulbs. Bad ground in both (or either) housings.
One turn signal light on one side doesn't work	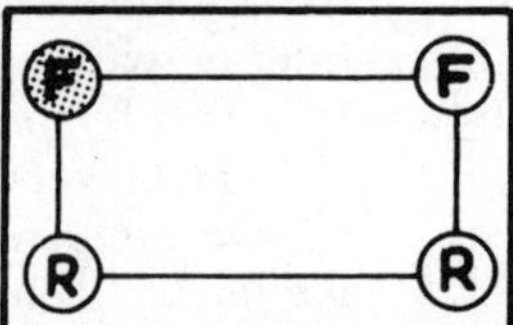	Defective bulb. Corrosion in socket. Clean contacts. Poor ground at socket.
Turn signal flashes too fast or too slowly	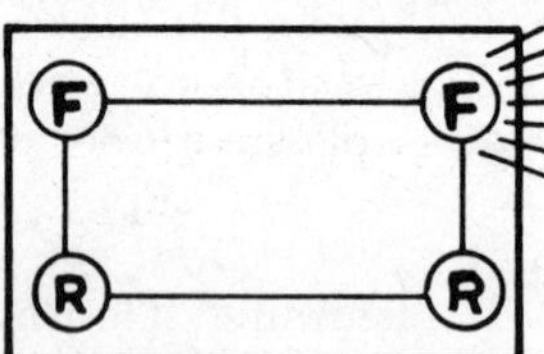	Check any bulb on the side flashing too fast. A heavy-duty bulb is probably installed in place of a regular bulb. Check the bulb flashing too slowly. A standard bulb was probably installed in place of a heavy-duty bulb. Loose connections or corrosion at the bulb socket.
Indicator lights don't work in either direction		Check if the turn signals are working. Check the dash indicator lights. Check the flasher by substitution.
One indicator light doesn't light		On systems with one dash indicator: See if the lights work on the same side. Often the filaments have been reversed in systems combining stoplights with taillights and turn signals. Check the flasher by substitution. On systems with two indicators: Check the bulbs on the same side. Check the indicator light bulb. Check the flasher by substitution.

Troubleshooting Lighting Problems

See Chapter 5 for service procedures

Condition	Possible Cause
One or more lights don't work, but others do	1. Defective bulb(s) 2. Blown fuse(s) 3. Dirty fuse clips or light sockets 4. Poor ground circuit
Lights burn out quickly	1. Incorrect voltage regulator setting or defective regulator 2. Poor battery/alternator connections
Lights go dim	1. Low/discharged battery 2. Alternator not charging 3. Corroded sockets or connections 4. Low voltage output
Lights flicker	1. Loose connection 2. Poor ground. (Run ground wire from light housing to frame) 3. Circuit breaker operating (short circuit)
Lights "flare"—Some flare is normal on acceleration—If excessive, see "Lights Burn Out Quickly"	High voltage setting
Lights glare—approaching drivers are blinded	1. Lights adjusted too high 2. Rear springs or shocks sagging 3. Rear tires soft

Troubleshooting Dash Gauge Problems

Most problems can be traced to a defective sending unit or faulty wiring. Occasionally, the gauge itself is at fault. See Chapter 5 for service procedures.

Condition	Possible Cause
COOLANT TEMPERATURE GAUGE	
Gauge reads erratically or not at all	1. Loose or dirty connections 2. Defective sending unit. 3. Defective gauge. To test a bi-metal gauge, remove the wire from the sending unit. Ground the wire for an instant. If the gauge registers, replace the sending unit. To test a magnetic gauge, disconnect the wire at the sending unit. With ignition ON gauge should register COLD. Ground the wire; gauge should register HOT.
AMMETER GAUGE—TURN HEADLIGHTS ON (DO NOT START ENGINE). NOTE REACTION	
Ammeter shows charge Ammeter shows discharge Ammeter does not move	1. Connections reversed on gauge 2. Ammeter is OK 3. Loose connections or faulty wiring 4. Defective gauge

Condition	Possible Cause
OIL PRESSURE GAUGE	
Gauge does not register or is inaccurate	1. On mechanical gauge, Bourdon tube may be bent or kinked. 2. Low oil pressure. Remove sending unit. Idle the engine briefly. If no oil flows from sending unit hole, problem is in engine. 3. Defective gauge. Remove the wire from the sending unit and ground it for an instant with the ignition ON. A good gauge will go to the top of the scale. 4. Defective wiring. Check the wiring to the gauge. If it's OK and the gauge doesn't register when grounded, replace the gauge. 5. Defective sending unit.
ALL GAUGES	
All gauges do not operate	1. Blown fuse 2. Defective instrument regulator
All gauges read low or erratically	3. Defective or dirty instrument voltage regulator
All gauges pegged	4. Loss of ground between instrument voltage regulator and frame 5. Defective instrument regulator
WARNING LIGHTS	
Light(s) do not come on when ignition is ON, but engine is not started	1. Defective bulb 2. Defective wire 3. Defective sending unit. Disconnect the wire from the sending unit and ground it. Replace the sending unit if the light comes on with the ignition ON.
Light comes on with engine running	4. Problem in individual system 5. Defective sending unit

Troubleshooting Clutch Problems

It is false economy to replace individual clutch components. The pressure plate, clutch plate and throwout bearing should be replaced as a set, and the flywheel face inspected, whenever the clutch is overhauled. See Chapter 6 for service procedures.

Condition	Possible Cause
Clutch chatter	1. Grease on driven plate (disc) facing 2. Binding clutch linkage or cable 3. Loose, damaged facings on driven plate (disc) 4. Engine mounts loose 5. Incorrect height adjustment of pressure plate release levers 6. Clutch housing or housing to transmission adapter misalignment 7. Loose driven plate hub
Clutch grabbing	1. Oil, grease on driven plate (disc) facing 2. Broken pressure plate 3. Warped or binding driven plate. Driven plate binding on clutch shaft
Clutch slips	1. Lack of lubrication in clutch linkage or cable (linkage or cable binds, causes incomplete engagement) 2. Incorrect pedal, or linkage adjustment 3. Broken pressure plate springs 4. Weak pressure plate springs 5. Grease on driven plate facings (disc)

Troubleshooting Clutch Problems (cont.)

Condition	*Possible Cause*
Incomplete clutch release	1. Incorrect pedal or linkage adjustment or linkage or cable binding 2. Incorrect height adjustment on pressure plate release levers 3. Loose, broken facings on driven plate (disc) 4. Bent, dished, warped driven plate caused by overheating
Grinding, whirring grating noise when pedal is depressed	1. Worn or defective throwout bearing 2. Starter drive teeth contacting flywheel ring gear teeth. Look for milled or polished teeth on ring gear.
Squeal, howl, trumpeting noise when pedal is being released (occurs during first inch to inch and one-half of pedal travel)	Pilot bushing worn or lack of lubricant. If bushing appears OK, polish bushing with emery cloth, soak lube wick in oil, lube bushing with oil, apply film of chassis grease to clutch shaft pilot hub, reassemble. NOTE: Bushing wear may be due to misalignment of clutch housing or housing to transmission adapter
Vibration or clutch pedal pulsation with clutch disengaged (pedal fully depressed)	1. Worn or defective engine transmission mounts 2. Flywheel run out. (Flywheel run out at face not to exceed 0.005") 3. Damaged or defective clutch components

Troubleshooting Manual Transmission Problems

See Chapter 6 for service procedures

Condition	*Possible Cause*
Transmission jumps out of gear	1. Misalignment of transmission case or clutch housing. 2. Worn pilot bearing in crankshaft. 3. Bent transmission shaft. 4. Worn high speed sliding gear. 5. Worn teeth or end-play in clutch shaft. 6. Insufficient spring tension on shifter rail plunger. 7. Bent or loose shifter fork. 8. Gears not engaging completely. 9. Loose or worn bearings on clutch shaft or mainshaft. 10. Worn gear teeth. 11. Worn or damaged detent balls.
Transmission sticks in gear	1. Clutch not releasing fully. 2. Burred or battered teeth on clutch shaft, or sliding sleeve. 3. Burred or battered transmission mainshaft. 4. Frozen synchronizing clutch. 5. Stuck shifter rail plunger. 6. Gearshift lever twisting and binding shifter rail. 7. Battered teeth on high speed sliding gear or on sleeve. 8. Improper lubrication, or lack of lubrication. 9. Corroded transmission parts. 10. Defective mainshaft pilot bearing. 11. Locked gear bearings will give same effect as stuck in gear.
Transmission gears will not synchronize	1. Binding pilot bearing on mainshaft, will synchronize in high gear only. 2. Clutch not releasing fully. 3. Detent spring weak or broken. 4. Weak or broken springs under balls in sliding gear sleeve. 5. Binding bearing on clutch shaft, or binding countershaft. 6. Binding pilot bearing in crankshaft. 7. Badly worn gear teeth. 8. Improper lubrication. 9. Constant mesh gear not turning freely on transmission mainshaft. Will synchronize in that gear only.

Condition	Possible Cause
Gears spinning when shifting into gear from neutral	1. Clutch not releasing fully. 2. In some cases an extremely light lubricant in transmission will cause gears to continue to spin for a short time after clutch is released. 3. Binding pilot bearing in crankshaft.
Transmission noisy in all gears	1. Insufficient lubricant, or improper lubricant. 2. Worn countergear bearings. 3. Worn or damaged main drive gear or countergear. 4. Damaged main drive gear or mainshaft bearings. 5. Worn or damaged countergear anti-lash plate.
Transmission noisy in neutral only	1. Damaged main drive gear bearing. 2. Damaged or loose mainshaft pilot bearing. 3. Worn or damaged countergear anti-lash plate. 4. Worn countergear bearings.
Transmission noisy in one gear only	1. Damaged or worn constant mesh gears. 2. Worn or damaged countergear bearings. 3. Damaged or worn synchronizer.
Transmission noisy in reverse only	1. Worn or damaged reverse idler gear or idler bushing. 2. Worn or damaged mainshaft reverse gear. 3. Worn or damaged reverse countergear. 4. Damaged shift mechanism.

TROUBLESHOOTING AUTOMATIC TRANSMISSION PROBLEMS

Keeping alert to changes in the operating characteristics of the transmission (changing shift points, noises, etc.) can prevent small problems from becoming large ones. If the problem cannot be traced to loose bolts, fluid level, misadjusted linkage, clogged filters or similar problems, you should probably seek professional service.

Transmission Fluid Indications

The appearance and odor of the transmission fluid can give valuable clues to the overall condition of the transmission. Always note the appearance of the fluid when you check the fluid level or change the fluid. Rub a small amount of fluid between your fingers to feel for grit and smell the fluid on the dipstick.

If the fluid appears:	It indicates:
Clear and red colored	Normal operation
Discolored (extremely dark red or brownish) or smells burned	Band or clutch pack failure, usually caused by an overheated transmission. Hauling very heavy loads with insufficient power or failure to change the fluid often result in overheating. Do not confuse this appearance with newer fluids that have a darker red color and a strong odor (though not a burned odor).
Foamy or aerated (light in color and full of bubbles)	1. The level is too high (gear train is churning oil) 2. An internal air leak (air is mixing with the fluid). Have the transmission checked professionally.
Solid residue in the fluid	Defective bands, clutch pack or bearings. Bits of band material or metal abrasives are ciinging to the dipstick. Have the transmission checked professionally.
Varnish coating on the dipstick	The transmission fluid is overheating

TROUBLESHOOTING DRIVE AXLE PROBLEMS

First, determine when the noise is most noticeable.

Drive Noise: Produced under vehicle acceleration.

Coast Noise: Produced while coasting with a closed throttle.

Float Noise: Occurs while maintaining constant speed (just enough to keep speed constant) on a level road.

External Noise Elimination

It is advisable to make a thorough road test to determine whether the noise originates in the rear axle or whether it originates from the tires, engine, transmission, wheel bearings or road surface. Noise originating from other places cannot be corrected by servicing the rear axle.

ROAD NOISE

Brick or rough surfaced concrete roads produce noises that seem to come from the rear axle. Road noise is usually identical in Drive or Coast and driving on a different type of road will tell whether the road is the problem.

TIRE NOISE

Tire noise can be mistaken as rear axle noise, even though the tires on the front are at fault. Snow tread and mud tread tires or tires worn unevenly will frequently cause vibrations which seem to originate elsewhere; *temporarily, and for test purposes only,* inflate the tires to 40–50 lbs. This will significantly alter the noise produced by the tires, but will not alter noise from the rear axle. Noises from the rear axle will normally cease at speeds below 30 mph on coast, while tire noise will continue at lower tone as speed is decreased. The rear axle noise will usually change from drive conditions to coast conditions, while tire noise will not. Do not forget to lower the tire pressure to normal after the test is complete.

ENGINE/TRANSMISSION NOISE

Determine at what speed the noise is most pronounced, then stop in a quiet place. With the transmission in Neutral, run the engine through speeds corresponding to road speeds where the noise was noticed. Noises produced with the vehicle standing still are coming from the engine or transmission.

FRONT WHEEL BEARINGS

Front wheel bearing noises, sometimes confused with rear axle noises, will not change when comparing drive and coast conditions. While holding the speed steady, lightly apply the footbrake. This will often cause wheel bearing noise to lessen, as some of the weight is taken off the bearing. Front wheel bearings are easily checked by jacking up the wheels and spinning the wheels. Shaking the wheels will also determine if the wheel bearings are excessively loose.

REAR AXLE NOISES

Eliminating other possible sources can narrow the cause to the rear axle, which normally produces noise from worn gears or bearings. Gear noises tend to peak in a narrow speed range, while bearing noises will usually vary in pitch with engine speeds.

Noise Diagnosis

The Noise Is:	Most Probably Produced By:
1. Identical under Drive or Coast	Road surface, tires or front wheel bearings
2. Different depending on road surface	Road surface or tires
3. Lower as speed is lowered	Tires
4. Similar when standing or moving	Engine or transmission
5. A vibration	Unbalanced tires, rear wheel bearing, unbalanced driveshaft or worn U-joint
6. A knock or click about every two tire revolutions	Rear wheel bearing
7. Most pronounced on turns	Damaged differential gears
8. A steady low-pitched whirring or scraping, starting at low speeds	Damaged or worn pinion bearing
9. A chattering vibration on turns	Wrong differential lubricant or worn clutch plates (limited slip rear axle)
10. Noticed only in Drive, Coast or Float conditions	Worn ring gear and/or pinion gear

Troubleshooting Steering & Suspension Problems

Condition	Possible Cause
Hard steering (wheel is hard to turn)	1. Improper tire pressure 2. Loose or glazed pump drive belt 3. Low or incorrect fluid 4. Loose, bent or poorly lubricated front end parts 5. Improper front end alignment (excessive caster) 6. Bind in steering column or linkage 7. Kinked hydraulic hose 8. Air in hydraulic system 9. Low pump output or leaks in system 10. Obstruction in lines 11. Pump valves sticking or out of adjustment 12. Incorrect wheel alignment
Loose steering (too much play in steering wheel)	1. Loose wheel bearings 2. Faulty shocks 3. Worn linkage or suspension components 4. Loose steering gear mounting or linkage points 5. Steering mechanism worn or improperly adjusted 6. Valve spool improperly adjusted 7. Worn ball joints, tie-rod ends, etc.
Veers or wanders (pulls to one side with hands off steering wheel)	1. Improper tire pressure 2. Improper front end alignment 3. Dragging or improperly adjusted brakes 4. Bent frame 5. Improper rear end alignment 6. Faulty shocks or springs 7. Loose or bent front end components 8. Play in Pitman arm 9. Steering gear mountings loose 10. Loose wheel bearings 11. Binding Pitman arm 12. Spool valve sticking or improperly adjusted 13. Worn ball joints
Wheel oscillation or vibration transmitted through steering wheel	1. Low or uneven tire pressure 2. Loose wheel bearings 3. Improper front end alignment 4. Bent spindle 5. Worn, bent or broken front end components 6. Tires out of round or out of balance 7. Excessive lateral runout in disc brake rotor 8. Loose or bent shock absorber or strut
Noises (see also "Troubleshooting Drive Axle Problems")	1. Loose belts 2. Low fluid, air in system 3. Foreign matter in system 4. Improper lubrication 5. Interference or chafing in linkage 6. Steering gear mountings loose 7. Incorrect adjustment or wear in gear box 8. Faulty valves or wear in pump 9. Kinked hydraulic lines 10. Worn wheel bearings
Poor return of steering	1. Over-inflated tires 2. Improperly aligned front end (excessive caster) 3. Binding in steering column 4. No lubrication in front end 5. Steering gear adjusted too tight
Uneven tire wear (see "How To Read Tire Wear")	1. Incorrect tire pressure 2. Improperly aligned front end 3. Tires out-of-balance 4. Bent or worn suspension parts

HOW TO READ TIRE WEAR

The way your tires wear is a good indicator of other parts of the suspension. Abnormal wear patterns are often caused by the need for simple tire maintenance, or for front end alignment.

Excessive wear at the center of the tread indicates that the air pressure in the tire is consistently too high. The tire is riding on the center of the tread and wearing it prematurely. Occasionally, this wear pattern can result from outrageously wide tires on narrow rims. The cure for this is to replace either the tires or the wheels.

This type of wear usually results from consistent under-inflation. When a tire is under-inflated, there is too much contact with the road by the outer treads, which wear prematurely. When this type of wear occurs, and the tire pressure is known to be consistently correct, a bent or worn steering component or the need for wheel alignment could be indicated.

Feathering is a condition when the edge of each tread rib develops a slightly rounded edge on one side and a sharp edge on the other. By running your hand over the tire, you can usually feel the sharper edges before you'll be able to see them. The most common causes of feathering are incorrect toe-in setting or deteriorated bushings in the front suspension.

When an inner or outer rib wears faster than the rest of the tire, the need for wheel alignment is indicated. There is excessive camber in the front suspension, causing the wheel to lean too much putting excessive load on one side of the tire. Misalignment could also be due to sagging springs, worn ball joints, or worn control arm bushings. Be sure the vehicle is loaded the way it's normally driven when you have the wheels aligned.

Cups or scalloped dips appearing around the edge of the tread almost always indicate worn (sometimes bent) suspension parts. Adjustment of wheel alignment alone will seldom cure the problem. Any worn component that connects the wheel to the suspension can cause this type of wear. Occasionally, wheels that are out of balance will wear like this, but wheel imbalance usually shows up as bald spots between the outside edges and center of the tread.

Second-rib wear is usually found only in radial tires, and appears where the steel belts end in relation to the tread. It can be kept to a minimum by paying careful attention to tire pressure and frequently rotating the tires. This is often considered normal wear but excessive amounts indicate that the tires are too wide for the wheels.

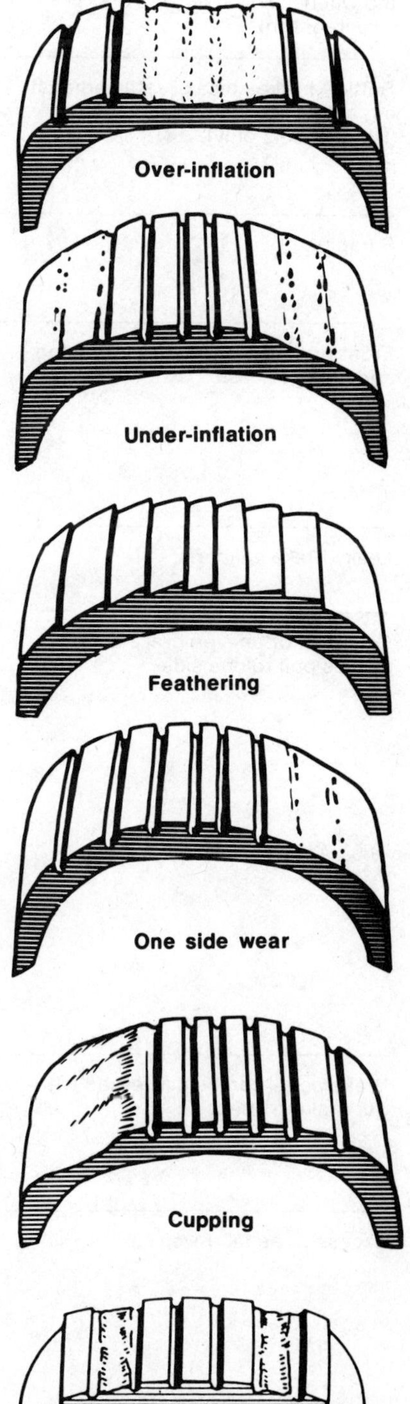

Troubleshooting Disc Brake Problems

Condition	Possible Cause
Noise—groan—brake noise emanating when slowly releasing brakes (creep-groan)	Not detrimental to function of disc brakes—no corrective action required. (This noise may be eliminated by slightly increasing or decreasing brake pedal efforts.)
Rattle—brake noise or rattle emanating at low speeds on rough roads, (front wheels only).	1. Shoe anti-rattle spring missing or not properly positioned. 2. Excessive clearance between shoe and caliper. 3. Soft or broken caliper seals. 4. Deformed or misaligned disc. 5. Loose caliper.
Scraping	1. Mounting bolts too long. 2. Loose wheel bearings. 3. Bent, loose, or misaligned splash shield.
Front brakes heat up during driving and fail to release	1. Operator riding brake pedal. 2. Stop light switch improperly adjusted. 3. Sticking pedal linkage. 4. Frozen or seized piston. 5. Residual pressure valve in master cylinder. 6. Power brake malfunction. 7. Proportioning valve malfunction.
Leaky brake caliper	1. Damaged or worn caliper piston seal. 2. Scores or corrosion on surface of cylinder bore.
Grabbing or uneven brake action—Brakes pull to one side	1. Causes listed under "Brakes Pull". 2. Power brake malfunction. 3. Low fluid level in master cylinder. 4. Air in hydraulic system. 5. Brake fluid, oil or grease on linings. 6. Unmatched linings. 7. Distorted brake pads. 8. Frozen or seized pistons. 9. Incorrect tire pressure. 10. Front end out of alignment. 11. Broken rear spring. 12. Brake caliper pistons sticking. 13. Restricted hose or line. 14. Caliper not in proper alignment to braking disc. 15. Stuck or malfunctioning metering valve. 16. Soft or broken caliper seals. 17. Loose caliper.
Brake pedal can be depressed without braking effect	1. Air in hydraulic system or improper bleeding procedure. 2. Leak past primary cup in master cylinder. 3. Leak in system. 4. Rear brakes out of adjustment. 5. Bleeder screw open.
Excessive pedal travel	1. Air, leak, or insufficient fluid in system or caliper. 2. Warped or excessively tapered shoe and lining assembly. 3. Excessive disc runout. 4. Rear brake adjustment required. 5. Loose wheel bearing adjustment. 6. Damaged caliper piston seal. 7. Improper brake fluid (boil). 8. Power brake malfunction. 9. Weak or soft hoses.

Troubleshooting Disc Brake Problems (cont.)

Condition	Possible Cause
Brake roughness or chatter (pedal pumping)	1. Excessive thickness variation of braking disc. 2. Excessive lateral runout of braking disc. 3. Rear brake drums out-of-round. 4. Excessive front bearing clearance.
Excessive pedal effort	1. Brake fluid, oil or grease on linings. 2. Incorrect lining. 3. Frozen or seized pistons. 4. Power brake malfunction. 5. Kinked or collapsed hose or line. 6. Stuck metering valve. 7. Scored caliper or master cylinder bore. 8. Seized caliper pistons.
Brake pedal fades (pedal travel increases with foot on brake)	1. Rough master cylinder or caliper bore. 2. Loose or broken hydraulic lines/connections. 3. Air in hydraulic system. 4. Fluid level low. 5. Weak or soft hoses. 6. Inferior quality brake shoes or fluid. 7. Worn master cylinder piston cups or seals.

Troubleshooting Drum Brakes

Condition	Possible Cause
Pedal goes to floor	1. Fluid low in reservoir. 2. Air in hydraulic system. 3. Improperly adjusted brake. 4. Leaking wheel cylinders. 5. Loose or broken brake lines. 6. Leaking or worn master cylinder. 7. Excessively worn brake lining.
Spongy brake pedal	1. Air in hydraulic system. 2. Improper brake fluid (low boiling point). 3. Excessively worn or cracked brake drums. 4. Broken pedal pivot bushing.
Brakes pulling	1. Contaminated lining. 2. Front end out of alignment. 3. Incorrect brake adjustment. 4. Unmatched brake lining. 5. Brake drums out of round. 6. Brake shoes distorted. 7. Restricted brake hose or line. 8. Broken rear spring. 9. Worn brake linings. 10. Uneven lining wear. 11. Glazed brake lining. 12. Excessive brake lining dust. 13. Heat spotted brake drums. 14. Weak brake return springs. 15. Faulty automatic adjusters. 16. Low or incorrect tire pressure.

Condition	Possible Cause
Squealing brakes	1. Glazed brake lining. 2. Saturated brake lining. 3. Weak or broken brake shoe retaining spring. 4. Broken or weak brake shoe return spring. 5. Incorrect brake lining. 6. Distorted brake shoes. 7. Bent support plate. 8. Dust in brakes or scored brake drums. 9. Linings worn below limit. 10. Uneven brake lining wear. 11. Heat spotted brake drums.
Chirping brakes	1. Out of round drum or eccentric axle flange pilot.
Dragging brakes	1. Incorrect wheel or parking brake adjustment. 2. Parking brakes engaged or improperly adjusted. 3. Weak or broken brake shoe return spring. 4. Brake pedal binding. 5. Master cylinder cup sticking. 6. Obstructed master cylinder relief port. 7. Saturated brake lining. 8. Bent or out of round brake drum. 9. Contaminated or improper brake fluid. 10. Sticking wheel cylinder pistons. 11. Driver riding brake pedal. 12. Defective proportioning valve. 13. Insufficient brake shoe lubricant.
Hard pedal	1. Brake booster inoperative. 2. Incorrect brake lining. 3. Restricted brake line or hose. 4. Frozen brake pedal linkage. 5. Stuck wheel cylinder. 6. Binding pedal linkage. 7. Faulty proportioning valve.
Wheel locks	1. Contaminated brake lining. 2. Loose or torn brake lining. 3. Wheel cylinder cups sticking. 4. Incorrect wheel bearing adjustment. 5. Faulty proportioning valve.
Brakes fade (high speed)	1. Incorrect lining. 2. Overheated brake drums. 3. Incorrect brake fluid (low boiling temperature). 4. Saturated brake lining. 5. Leak in hydraulic system. 6. Faulty automatic adjusters.
Pedal pulsates	1. Bent or out of round brake drum.
Brake chatter and shoe knock	1. Out of round brake drum. 2. Loose support plate. 3. Bent support plate. 4. Distorted brake shoes. 5. Machine grooves in contact face of brake drum (Shoe Knock). 6. Contaminated brake lining. 7. Missing or loose components. 8. Incorrect lining material. 9. Out-of-round brake drums. 10. Heat spotted or scored brake drums. 11. Out-of-balance wheels.

Troubleshooting Drum Brakes (cont.)

Condition	*Possible Cause*
Brakes do not self adjust	1. Adjuster screw frozen in thread. 2. Adjuster screw corroded at thrust washer. 3. Adjuster lever does not engage star wheel. 4. Adjuster installed on wrong wheel.
Brake light glows	1. Leak in the hydraulic system. 2. Air in the system. 3. Improperly adjusted master cylinder pushrod. 4. Uneven lining wear. 5. Failure to center combination valve or proportioning valve.

Mechanic's Data

General Conversion Table

Multiply By	To Convert	To	
	LENGTH		
2.54	Inches	Centimeters	.3937
25.4	Inches	Millimeters	.03937
30.48	Feet	Centimeters	.0328
.304	Feet	Meters	3.28
.914	Yards	Meters	1.094
1.609	Miles	Kilometers	.621
	VOLUME		
.473	Pints	Liters	2.11
.946	Quarts	Liters	1.06
3.785	Gallons	Liters	.264
.016	Cubic inches	Liters	61.02
16.39	Cubic inches	Cubic cms.	.061
28.3	Cubic feet	Liters	.0353
	MASS (Weight)		
28.35	Ounces	Grams	.035
.4536	Pounds	Kilograms	2.20
—	To obtain	From	Multiply by

Multiply By	To Convert	To	
	AREA		
.645	Square inches	Square cms.	.155
.836	Square yds.	Square meters	1.196
	FORCE		
4.448	Pounds	Newtons	.225
.138	Ft./lbs.	Kilogram/meters	7.23
1.36	Ft./lbs.	Newton-meters	.737
.112	In./lbs.	Newton-meters	8.844
	PRESSURE		
.068	Psi	Atmospheres	14.7
6.89	Psi	Kilopascals	.145
	OTHER		
1.104	Horsepower (DIN)	Horsepower (SAE)	.9861
.746	Horsepower (SAE)	Kilowatts (KW)	1.34
1.60	Mph	Km/h	.625
.425	Mpg	Km/1	2.35
—	To obtain	From	Multiply by

Tap Drill Sizes

National Coarse or U.S.S.

Screw & Tap Size	Threads Per Inch	Use Drill Number
No. 5	40	39
No. 6	32	36
No. 8	32	29
No. 10	24	25
No. 12	24	17
1/4	20	8
5/16	18	F
3/8	16	5/16
7/16	14	U
1/2	13	27/64
9/16	12	31/64
5/8	11	17/32
3/4	10	21/32
7/8	9	49/64

National Coarse or U.S.S.

Screw & Tap Size	Threads Per Inch	Use Drill Number
1	8	7/8
1 1/8	7	63/64
1 1/4	7	1 7/64
1 1/2	6	1 11/32

National Fine or S.A.E.

Screw & Tap Size	Threads Per Inch	Use Drill Number
No. 5	44	37
No. 6	40	33
No. 8	36	29
No. 10	32	21

National Fine or S.A.E.

Screw & Tap Size	Threads Per Inch	Use Drill Number
No. 12	28	15
1/4	28	3
6/16	24	1
3/8	24	Q
7/16	20	W
1/2	20	29/64
9/16	18	33/64
5/8	18	37/64
3/4	16	11/16
7/8	14	13/16
1 1/8	12	1 3/64
1 1/4	12	1 11/64
1 1/2	12	1 27/64

Drill Sizes In Decimal Equivalents

Inch	Decimal	Wire	mm	Inch	Decimal	Wire	mm	Inch	Decimal	Wire & Letter	mm	Inch	Decimal	Letter	mm	Inch	Decimal	mm
1/64	.0156		.39		.0730	49			.1614		4.1		.2717		6.9		.4331	11.0
	.0157		.4		.0748		1.9		.1654		4.2		.2720	I		7/16	.4375	11.11
	.0160	78			.0760	48			.1660	19			.2756		7.0		.4528	11.5
	.0165		.42		.0768		1.95		.1673		4.25		.2770	J		29/64	.4531	11.51
	.0173		.44	5/64	.0781		1.98		.1693		4.3		.2795		7.1	15/32	.4688	11.90
	.0177		.45		.0785	47			.1695	18			.2810	K			.4724	12.0
	.0180	77			.0787		2.0	11/64	.1719		4.36	9/32	.2812		7.14	31/64	.4844	12.30
	.0181		.46		.0807		2.05		.1730	17			.2835		7.2		.4921	12.5
	.0189		.48		.0810	46			.1732		4.4		.2854		7.25	1/2	.5000	12.70
	.0197		.5		.0820	45			.1770	16			.2874		7.3		.5118	13.0
	.0200	76			.0827		2.1		.1772		4.5		.2900	L		33/64	.5156	13.09
	.0210	75			.0846		2.15		.1800	15			.2913		7.4	17/32	.5312	13.49
	.0217		.55		.0860	44			.1811		4.6		.2950	M			.5315	13.5
	.0225	74			.0866		2.2		.1820	14			.2953		7.5	35/64	.5469	13.89
	.0236		.6		.0886		2.25		.1850	13		19/64	.2969		7.54		.5512	14.0
	.0240	73			.0890	43			.1850		4.7		.2992		7.6	9/16	.5625	14.28
	.0250	72			.0906		2.3		.1870		4.75		.3020	N			.5709	14.5
	.0256		.65		.0925		2.35	3/16	.1875		4.76		.3031		7.7	37/64	.5781	14.68
	.0260	71			.0935	42			.1890		4.8		.3051		7.75		.5906	15.0
	.0276		.7	3/32	.0938		2.38		.1890	12			.3071		7.8	19/32	.5938	15.08
	.0280	70			.0945		2.4		.1910	11			.3110		7.9	39/64	.6094	15.47
	.0292	69			.0960	41			.1929		4.9	5/16	.3125		7.93		.6102	15.5
	.0295		.75		.0965		2.45		.1935	10			.3150		8.0	5/8	.6250	15.87
	.0310	68			.0980	40			.1960	9			.3160	O			.6299	16.0
1/32	.0312		.79		.0981		2.5		.1969		5.0		.3189		8.1	41/64	.6406	16.27
	.0315		.8		.0995	39			.1990	8			.3228		8.2		.6496	16.5
	.0320	67			.1015	38			.2008		5.1		.3230	P		21/32	.6562	16.66
	.0330	66			.1024		2.6		.2010	7			.3248		8.25		.6693	17.0
	.0335		.85		.1040	37		13/64	.2031		5.16		.3268		8.3	43/64	.6719	17.06
	.0350	65			.1063		2.7		.2040	6		21/64	.3281		8.33	11/16	.6875	17.46
	.0354		.9		.1065	36			.2047		5.2		.3307		8.4		.6890	17.5
	.0360	64			.1083		2.75		.2055	5			.3320	Q		45/64	.7031	17.85
	.0370	63		7/64	.1094		2.77		.2067		5.25		.3346		8.5		.7087	18.0
	.0374		.95		.1100	35			.2087		5.3		.3386		8.6	23/32	.7188	18.25
	.0380	62			.1102		2.8		.2090	4			.3390	R			.7283	18.5
	.0390	61			.1110	34			.2126		5.4		.3425		8.7	47/64	.7344	18.65
	.0394		1.0		.1130	33			.2130	3		11/32	.3438		8.73		.7480	19.0
	.0400	60			.1142		2.9		.2165		5.5		.3445		8.75	3/4	.7500	19.05
	.0410	59			.1160	32		7/32	2188		5.55		.3465		8.8	49/64	.7656	19.44
	.0413		1.05		.1181		3.0		.2205		5.6		.3480	S			.7677	19.5
	.0420	58			.1200	31			.2210	2			.3504		8.9	25/32	.7812	19.84
	.0430	57			.1220		3.1		.2244		5.7		.3543		9.0		.7874	20.0
	.0433		1.1	1/8	.1250		3.17		.2264		5.75		.3580	T		51/64	.7969	20.24
	.0453		1.15		.1260		3.2		.2280	1			.3583		9.1		.8071	20.5
	.0465	56			.1280		3.25		.2283		5.8	23/64	.3594		9.12	13/16	.8125	20.63
3/64	.0469		1.19		.1285	30			.2323		5.9		.3622		9.2		.8268	21.0
	.0472		1.2		.1299		3.3		.2340	A			.3642		9.25	53/64	.8281	21.03
	.0492		1.25		.1339		3.4	15/64	.2344		5.95		.3661		9.3	27/32	.8438	21.43
	.0512		1.3		.1360	29			.2362		6.0		.3680	U			.8465	21.5
	.0520	55			.1378		3.5		.2380	B			.3701		9.4	55/64	.8594	21.82
	.0531		1.35		.1405	28			.2402		6.1		.3740		9.5		.8661	22.0
	.0550	54		9/64	.1406		3.57		.2420	C		3/8	.3750		9.52	7/8	.8750	22.22
	.0551		1.4		.1417		3.6		.2441		6.2		.3770	V			.8858	22.5
	.0571		1.45		.1440	27			.2460	D			.3780		9.6	57/64	.8906	22.62
	.0591		1.5		.1457		3.7		.2461		6.25		.3819		9.7		.9055	23.0
	.0595	53			.1470	26			.2480		6.3		.3839		9.75	29/32	.9062	23.01
	.0610		1.55		.1476		3.75	1/4	.2500	E	6.35		.3858		9.8	59/64	.9219	23.41
1/16	.0625		1.59		.1495	25			.2520		6.		.3860	W			.9252	23.5
	.0630		1.6		.1496		3.8		.2559		6.5		.3898		9.9	15/16	.9375	23.81
	.0635	52			.1520	24			.2570	F		25/64	.3906		9.92		.9449	24.0
	.0650		1.65		.1535		3.9		.2598		6.6		.3937		10.0	61/64	.9531	24.2
	.0669		1.7		.1540	23			.2610	G			.3970	X			.9646	24.5
	.0670	51		5/32	.1562		3.96		.2638		6.7		.4040	Y		31/64	.9688	24.6
	.0689		1.75		.1570	22		17/64	.2656		6.74	13/32	.4062		10.31		.9843	25.0
	.0700	50			.1575		4.0		.2657		6.75		.4130	Z		63/64	.9844	25.0
	.0709		1.8		.1590	21			.2660	H			.4134		10.5	1	1.0000	25.4
	.0728		1.85		.1610	20			.2677		6.8	27/64	.4219		10.71			

AIR/FUEL RATIO: The ratio of air to gasoline by weight in the fuel mixture drawn into the engine.

AIR INJECTION: One method of reducing harmful exhaust emissions by injecting air into each of the exhaust ports of an engine. The fresh air entering the hot exhaust manifold causes any remaining fuel to be burned before it can exit the tailpipe.

ALTERNATOR: A device used for converting mechanical energy into electrical energy.

AMMETER: An instrument, calibrated in amperes, used to measure the flow of an electrical current in a circuit. Ammeters are always connected in series with the circuit being tested.

AMPERE: The rate of flow of electrical current present when one volt of electrical pressure is applied against one ohm of electrical resistance.

ANALOG COMPUTER: Any microprocessor that uses similar (analogous) electrical signals to make its calculations.

ARMATURE: A laminated, soft iron core wrapped by a wire that converts electrical energy to mechanical energy as in a motor or relay. When rotated in a magnetic field, it changes mechanical energy into electrical energy as in a generator.

ATMOSPHERIC PRESSURE: The pressure on the Earth's surface caused by the weight of the air in the atmosphere. At sea level, this pressure is 14.7 psi at 32°F (101 kPa at 0°C).

ATOMIZATION: The breaking down of a liquid into a fine mist that can be suspended in air.

AXIAL PLAY: Movement parallel to a shaft or bearing bore.

BACKFIRE: The sudden combustion of gases in the intake or exhaust system that results in a loud explosion.

BACKLASH: The clearance or play between two parts, such as meshed gears.

BACKPRESSURE: Restrictions in the exhaust system that slow the exit of exhaust gases from the combustion chamber.

BAKELITE: A heat resistant, plastic insulator material commonly used in printed circuit boards and transistorized components.

BALL BEARING: A bearing made up of hardened inner and outer races between which hardened steel ball roll.

BALLAST RESISTOR: A resistor in the primary ignition circuit that lowers voltage after the engine is started to reduce wear on ignition components.

BEARING: A friction reducing, supportive device usually located between a stationary part and a moving part.

BIMETAL TEMPERATURE SENSOR: Any sensor or switch made of two dissimilar types of metal that bend when heated or cooled due to the different expansion rates of the alloys. These types of sensors usually function as an on/off switch.

BLOWBY: Combustion gases, composed of water vapor and unburned fuel, that leak past the piston rings into the crankcase during normal engine operation. These gases are removed by the PCV system to prevent the buildup of harmful acids in the crankcase.

BRAKE PAD: A brake shoe and lining assembly used with disc brakes.

BRAKE SHOE: The backing for the brake lining. The term is, however, usually applied to the assembly of the brake backing and lining.

BUSHING: A liner, usually removable, for a bearing; an anti-friction liner used in place of a bearing.

BYPASS: System used to bypass ballast resistor during engine cranking to increase voltage supplied to the coil.

CALIPER: A hydraulically activated device in a disc brake system, which is mounted straddling the brake rotor (disc). The caliper contains at least one piston and two brake pads. Hydraulic pressure on the piston(s) forces the pads against the rotor.

CAMSHAFT: A shaft in the engine on which are the lobes (cams) which operate the valves. The camshaft is driven by the crankshaft, via a belt, chain or gears, at one half the crankshaft speed.

CAPACITOR: A device which stores an electrical charge.

CARBON MONOXIDE (CO): a colorless, odorless gas given off as a normal byproduct of combustion. It is poisonous and extremely dangerous in confined areas, building up slowly to toxic levels without warning if adequate ventilation is not available.

CARBURETOR: A device, usually mounted on the intake manifold of an engine, which mixes the air and fuel in the proper proportion to allow even combustion.

CATALYTIC CONVERTER: A device installed in the exhaust system, like a muffler, that converts harmful byproducts of combustion into carbon dioxide and water vapor by means of a heat-producing chemical reaction.

CENTRIFUGAL ADVANCE: A mechanical method of advancing the spark timing by using flyweights in the distributor that react to centrifugal force generated by the distributor shaft rotation.

CHECK VALVE: Any one-way valve installed to permit the flow of air, fuel or vacuum in one direction only.

CHOKE: A device, usually a moveable valve, placed in the intake path of a carburetor to restrict the flow of air.

CIRCUIT: Any unbroken path through which an electrical current can flow. Also used to describe fuel flow in some instances.

CIRCUIT BREAKER: A switch which protects an electrical circuit from overload by opening the circuit when the current flow exceeds a predetermined level. Some circuit breakers must be reset manually, while other reset automatically

COIL (IGNITION): A transformer in the ignition circuit which steps of the voltage provided to the spark plugs.

COMBINATION MANIFOLD: An assembly which includes both the intake and exhaust manifolds in one casting.

COMBINATION VALVE: A device used in some fuel systems that routes fuel vapors to a charcoal storage canister instead of venting them into the atmosphere. The valve relieves fuel tank pressure and allows fresh air into the tank as fuel level drops to prevent a vapor lock situation.

COMPRESSION RATIO: The comparison of the total volume of the cylinder and combustion chamber with the piston at BDC and the piston at TDC.

CONDENSER: 1. An electrical device which acts to store an electrical charge, preventing voltage surges.

2. A radiator-like device in the air conditioning system in which refrigerant gas condenses into a liquid, giving off heat.

CONDUCTOR: Any material through which an electrical current can be transmitted easily.

CONTINUITY: Continuous or complete circuit. Can be checked with an ohmmeter.

COUNTERSHAFT: An intermediate shaft which is rotated by a mainshaft and transmits, in turn, that rotation to a working part.

CRANKCASE: The lower part of an engine in which the crankshaft and related parts operate.

CRANKSHAFT: The main driving shaft of an engine which receives reciprocating motion from the pistons and converts it to rotary motion.

CYLINDER: In an engine, the round hole in the engine block in which the piston(s) ride.

CYLINDER BLOCK: The main structural member of an engine in which is found the cylinders, crankshaft and other principal parts.

CYLINDER HEAD: The detachable portion of the engine, fastened, usually, to the top of the cylinder block, containing all or most of the combustion chambers. On overhead valve engines, it contains the valves and their operating parts. On overhead cam engines, it contains the camshaft as well.

DEAD CENTER: The extreme top or bottom of the piston stroke.

DETONATION: An unwanted explosion of the air fuel mixture in the combustion chamber caused by excess heat and compression, advanced timing, or an overly lean mixture. Also referred to as "ping".

DIAPHRAGM: A thin, flexible wall separating two cavities, such as in a vacuum advance unit.

DIESELING: A condition in which hot spots in the combustion chamber cause the engine to run on after the key is turned off.

DIFFERENTIAL: A geared assembly which allows the transmission of motion between drive axles, giving one axle the ability to turn faster than the other.

DIODE: An electrical device that will allow current to flow in one direction only.

DISC BRAKE: A hydraulic braking assembly consisting of a brake disc, or rotor, mounted on an axle, and a caliper assembly containing, usually two brake pads which are activated by hydraulic pressure. The pads are forced against the sides of the disc, creating friction which slows the vehicle.

DISTRIBUTOR: A mechanically driven device on an engine which is responsible for electrically firing the spark plug at a predetermined point of the piston stroke.

DOWEL PIN: A pin, inserted in mating holes in two different parts allowing those parts to maintain a fixed relationship.

DRUM BRAKE: A braking system which consists of two brake shoes and one or two wheel cylinders, mounted on a fixed backing plate, and a brake drum, mounted on an axle, which revolves around the assembly. Hydraulic action applied to the wheel cylinders forces the shoes outward against the drum, creating friction and slowing the vehicle.

DWELL: The rate, measured in degrees of shaft rotation, at which an electrical circuit cycles on and off.

ELECTRONIC CONTROL UNIT (ECU): Ignition module, module, amplifier or igniter. See Module for definition.

ELECTRONIC IGNITION: A system in which the timing and firing of the spark plugs is controlled by an electronic control unit, usually called a module. These systems have not points or condenser.

ENDPLAY: The measured amount of axial movement in a shaft.

ENGINE: A device that converts heat into mechanical energy.

EXHAUST MANIFOLD: A set of cast passages or pipes which conduct exhaust gases from the engine.

FEELER GAUGE: A blade, usually metal, of precisely predetermined thickness, used to measure the clearance between two parts. These blades usually are available in sets of assorted thicknesses.

F-Head: An engine configuration in which the intake valves are in the cylinder head, while the camshaft and exhaust valves are located in the cylinder block. The camshaft operates the intake valves via lifters and pushrods, while it operates the exhaust valves directly.

FIRING ORDER: The order in which combustion occurs in the cylinders of an engine. Also the order in which spark is distributed to the plugs by the distributor.

FLATHEAD: An engine configuration in which the camshaft and all the valves are located in the cylinder block.

FLOODING: The presence of too much fuel in the intake manifold and combustion chamber which prevents the air/fuel mixture from firing, thereby causing a no-start situation.

FLYWHEEL: A disc shaped part bolted to the rear end of the crankshaft. Around the outer perimeter is affixed the ring gear. The starter drive engages the ring gear, turning the flywheel, which rotates the crankshaft, imparting the initial starting motion to the engine.

FOOT POUND (ft.lb. or sometimes, ft. lbs.): The amount of energy or work needed to raise an item weighing one pound, a distance of one foot.

FUSE: A protective device in a circuit which prevents circuit overload by breaking the circuit when a specific amperage is present. The device is constructed around a strip or wire of a lower amperage rating than the circuit it is designed to protect. When an amperage higher than that stamped on the fuse is present in the circuit, the strip or wire melts, opening the circuit.

GEAR RATIO: The ratio between the number of teeth on meshing gears.

GENERATOR: A device which converts mechanical energy into electrical energy.

HEAT RANGE: The measure of a spark plug's ability to dissipate heat from its firing end. The higher the heat range, the hotter the plug fires.

HUB: The center part of a wheel or gear.

HYDROCARBON (HC): Any chemical compound made up of hydrogen and carbon. A major pollutant formed by the engine as a byproduct of combustion.

HYDROMETER: An instrument used to measure the specific gravity of a solution.

INCH POUND (in.lb. or sometimes, in. lbs.): One twelfth of a foot pound.

INDUCTION: A means of transferring electrical energy in the form of a magnetic field. Principle used in the ignition coil to increase voltage.

INJECTION PUMP: A device, usually mechanically operated, which meters and delivers fuel under pressure to the fuel injector.

INJECTOR: A device which receives metered fuel under relatively low pressure and is activated to inject the fuel into the engine under relatively high pressure at a predetermined time.

INPUT SHAFT: The shaft to which torque is applied, usually carrying the driving gear or gears.

INTAKE MANIFOLD: A casting of passages or pipes used to conduct air or a fuel/air mixture to the cylinders.

JOURNAL: The bearing surface within which a shaft operates.

KEY: A small block usually fitted in a notch between a shaft and a hub to prevent slippage of the two parts.

MANIFOLD: A casting of passages or set of pipes which connect the cylinders to an inlet or outlet source.

MANIFOLD VACUUM: Low pressure in an engine intake manifold formed just below the throttle plates. Manifold vacuum is highest at idle and drops under acceleration.

MASTER CYLINDER: The primary fluid pressurizing device in a hydraulic system. In automotive use, it is found in brake and hydraulic clutch systems and is pedal activated, either directly or, in a power brake system, through the power booster.

MODULE: Electronic control unit, amplifier or igniter of solid state or integrated design which controls the current flow in the ignition primary circuit based on input from the pick-up coil. When the module opens the primary circuit, the high secondary voltage is induced in the coil.

NEEDLE BEARING: A bearing which consists of a number (usually a large number) of long, thin rollers.

OHM: (Ω) The unit used to measure the resistance of conductor to electrical flow. One ohm is the amount of resistance that limits current flow to one ampere in a circuit with one volt of pressure.

OHMMETER: An instrument used for measuring the resistance, in ohms, in an electrical circuit.

OUTPUT SHAFT: The shaft which transmits torque from a device, such as a transmission.

OVERDRIVE: A gear assembly which produces more shaft revolutions than that transmitted to it.

OVERHEAD CAMSHAFT (OHC): An engine configuration in which the camshaft is mounted on top of the cylinder head and operates the valve either directly or by means of rocker arms.

OVERHEAD VALVE (OHV): An engine configuration in which all of the valves are located in the cylinder head and the camshaft is located in the cylinder block. The camshaft operates the valves via lifters and pushrods.

OXIDES OF NITROGEN (NOx): Chemical compounds of nitrogen produced as a byproduct of combustion. They combine with hydrocarbons to produce smog.

OXYGEN SENSOR: Used with the feedback system to sense the presence of oxygen in the exhaust gas and signal the computer which can reference the voltage signal to an air/fuel ratio.

PINION: The smaller of two meshing gears.

PISTON RING: An open ended ring which fits into a groove on the outer diameter of the piston. Its chief function is to form a seal between the piston and cylinder wall. Most automotive pistons have three rings: two for compression sealing; one for oil sealing.

PRELOAD: A predetermined load placed on a bearing during assembly or by adjustment.

PRIMARY CIRCUIT: Is the low voltage side of the ignition system which consists of the ignition switch, ballast resistor or resistance wire, bypass, coil, electronic control unit and pick-up coil as well as the connecting wires and harnesses.

PRESS FIT: The mating of two parts under pressure, due to the inner diameter of one being smaller than the outer diameter of the other, or vice versa; an interference fit.

RACE: The surface on the inner or outer ring of a bearing on which the balls, needles or rollers move.

REGULATOR: A device which maintains the amperage and/or voltage levels of a circuit at predetermined values.

RELAY: A switch which automatically opens and/or closes a circuit.

RESISTANCE: The opposition to the flow of current through a circuit or electrical device, and is measured in ohms. Resistance is equal to the voltage divided by the amperage.

RESISTOR: A device, usually made of wire, which offers a preset amount of resistance in an electrical circuit.

RING GEAR: The name given to a ring-shaped gear attached to a differential case, or affixed to a flywheel or as part a planetary gear set.

ROLLER BEARING: A bearing made up of hardened inner and outer races between which hardened steel rollers move.

ROTOR: 1. The disc-shaped part of a disc brake assembly, upon which the brake pads bear; also called, brake disc.

2. The device mounted atop the distributor shaft, which passes current to the distributor cap tower contacts.

SECONDARY CIRCUIT: The high voltage side of the ignition system, usually above 20,000 volts. The secondary includes the ignition coil, coil wire, distributor cap and rotor, spark plug wires and spark plugs.

SENDING UNIT: A mechanical, electrical, hydraulic or electromagnetic device which transmits information to a gauge.

SENSOR: Any device designed to measure engine operating conditions or ambient pressures and temperatures. Usually electronic in nature and designed to send a voltage signal to an on-board computer, some sensors may operate as a simple on/off switch or they may provide a variable voltage signal (like a potentiometer) as conditions or measured parameters change.

SHIM: Spacers of precise, predetermined thickness used between parts to establish a proper working relationship.

SLAVE CYLINDER: In automotive use, a device in the hydraulic clutch system which is activated by hydraulic force, disengaging the clutch.

SOLENOID: A coil used to produce a magnetic field, the effect of which is produce work.

SPARK PLUG: A device screwed into the combustion chamber of a spark ignition engine. The basic construction is a conductive core inside of a ceramic insulator, mounted in an outer conductive base. An electrical charge from the spark plug wire travels along the conductive core and jumps a preset air gap to a grounding point or points at the end of the conductive base. The resultant spark ignites the fuel/air mixture in the combustion chamber.

SPLINES: Ridges machined or cast onto the outer diameter of a shaft or inner diameter of a bore to enable parts to mate without rotation.

TACHOMETER: A device used to measure the rotary speed of an engine, shaft, gear, etc., usually in rotations per minute.

THERMOSTAT: A valve, located in the cooling system of an engine, which is closed when cold and opens gradually in response to engine heating, controlling the temperature of the coolant and rate of coolant flow.

TOP DEAD CENTER (TDC): The point at which the piston reaches the top of its travel on the compression stroke.

TORQUE: The twisting force applied to an object.

TORQUE CONVERTER: A turbine used to transmit power from a driving member to a driven member via hydraulic action, providing changes in drive ratio and torque. In automotive use, it links the driveplate at the rear of the engine to the automatic transmission.

TRANSDUCER: A device used to change a force into an electrical signal.

TRANSISTOR: A semi-conductor component which can be actuated by a small voltage to perform an electrical switching function.

TUNE-UP: A regular maintenance function, usually associated with the replacement and adjustment of parts and components in the electrical and fuel systems of a vehicle for the purpose of attaining optimum performance.

TURBOCHARGER: An exhaust driven pump which compresses intake air and forces it into the combustion chambers at higher than atmospheric pressures. The increased air pressure allows more fuel to be burned and results in increased horsepower being produced.

VACUUM ADVANCE: A device which advances the ignition timing in response to increased engine vacuum.

VACUUM GAUGE: An instrument used to measure the presence of vacuum in a chamber.

VALVE: A device which control the pressure, direction of flow or rate of flow of a liquid or gas.

VALVE CLEARANCE: The measured gap between the end of the valve stem and the rocker arm, cam lobe or follower that activates the valve.

VISCOSITY: The rating of a liquid's internal resistance to flow.

VOLTMETER: An instrument used for measuring electrical force in units called volts. Voltmeters are always connected parallel with the circuit being tested.

WHEEL CYLINDER: Found in the automotive drum brake assembly, it is a device, actuated by hydraulic pressure, which, through internal pistons, pushes the brake shoes outward against the drums.

A: Ampere

AC: Alternating current

A/C: Air conditioning

A-h: Ampere hour

AT: Automatic transmission

ATDC: After top dead center

μA: Microampere

bbl: Barrel

BDC: Bottom dead center

bhp: Brake horsepower

BTDC: Before top dead center

BTU: British thermal unit

C: Celsius (Centigrade)

CCA: Cold cranking amps

cd: Candela

cm^2: Square centimeter

cm^3, cc: Cubic centimeter

CO: Carbon monoxide

CO_2: Carbon dioxide

cu.in., in^3: Cubic inch

CV: Constant velocity

Cyl.: Cylinder

DC: Direct current

ECM: Electronic control module

EFE: Early fuel evaporation

EFI: Electronic fuel injection

EGR: Exhaust gas recirculation

Exh.: Exhaust

F: Fahrenheit

F: Farad

pF: Picofarad

μF: Microfarad

FI: Fuel injection

ft.lb., ft. lb., ft. lbs.: foot pound(s)

gal: Gallon

g: Gram

HC: Hydrocarbon

HEI: High energy ignition

HO: High output

hp: Horsepower

Hyd.: Hydraulic

Hz: Hertz

ID: Inside diameter

in.lb.; in. lb.; in. lbs: inch pound(s)

Int.: Intake

K: Kelvin

kg: Kilogram

kHz: Kilohertz

km: Kilometer

km/h: Kilometers per hour

kΩ: Kilohm

kPa: Kilopascal

kV: Kilovolt

kW: Kilowatt

l: Liter

l/s: Liters per second

m: Meter

mA: Milliampere

mg: Milligram

mHz: Megahertz

mm: Millimeter

mm^2: Square millimeter

m^3: Cubic meter

MΩ: Megohm

m/s: Meters per second

MT: Manual transmission

mV: Millivolt

μm: Micrometer

N: Newton

N-m: Newton meter

NOx: Nitrous oxide

OD: Outside diameter

OHC: Over head camshaft

OHV: Over head valve

Ω: Ohm

PCV: Positive crankcase ventilation

psi: Pounds per square inch

pts: Pints

qts: Quarts

rpm: Rotations per minute

rps: Rotations per second

R-12: A refrigerant gas (Freon)

SAE: Society of Automotive Engineers

SO_2: Sulfur dioxide

T: Ton

t: Megagram

TBI: Throttle Body Injection

TPS: Throttle Position Sensor

V: 1. Volt; 2. Venturi

μV: Microvolt

W: Watt

∝: Infinity

‹: Less than

›: Greater than

Index

Chilton's Repair & Tune-Up Guides

The Complete line covers domestic cars, imports, trucks, vans, RV's and 4-wheel drive vehicles.

RTUG Title	Part No.
AMC 1975-82 Covers all U.S. and Canadian models	7199
Aspen/Volare 1976-80 Covers all U.S. and Canadian models	6637
Audi 1970-73 Covers all U.S. and Canadian models.	5902
Audi 4000/5000 1978-81 Covers all U.S. and Canadian models including turbocharged and diesel engines	7028
Barracuda/Challenger 1965-72 Covers all U.S. and Canadian models	5807
Blazer/Jimmy 1969-82 Covers all U.S. and Canadian 2- and 4-wheel drive models, including diesel engines	6931
BMW 1970-82 Covers U.S. and Canadian models	6844
Buick/Olds/Pontiac 1975-85 Covers all U.S. and Canadian full size rear wheel drive models	7308
Cadillac 1967-84 Covers all U.S. and Canadian rear wheel drive models	7462
Camaro 1967-81 Covers all U.S. and Canadian models	6735
Camaro 1982-85 Covers all U.S. and Canadian models	7317
Capri 1970-77 Covers all U.S. and Canadian models	6695
Caravan/Voyager 1984-85 Covers all U.S. and Canadian models	7482
Century/Regal 1975-85 Covers all U.S. and Canadian rear wheel drive models, including turbocharged engines	7307
Champ/Arrow/Sapporo 1978-83 Covers all U.S. and Canadian models	7041
Chevette/1000 1976-86 Covers all U.S. and Canadian models	6836
Chevrolet 1968-85 Covers all U.S. and Canadian models	7135
Chevrolet 1968-79 Spanish	7082
Chevrolet/GMC Pick-Ups 1970-82 Spanish	7468
Chevrolet/GMC Pick-Ups and Suburban 1970-86 Covers all U.S. and Canadian 1/2, 3/4 and 1 ton models, including 4-wheel drive and diesel engines	6936
Chevrolet LUV 1972-81 Covers all U.S. and Canadian models	6815
Chevrolet Mid-Size 1964-86 Covers all U.S. and Canadian models of 1964-77 Chevelle, Malibu and Malibu SS; 1974-77 Laguna; 1978-85 Malibu; 1970-86 Monte Carlo; 1964-84 El Camino, including diesel engines	6840
Chevrolet Nova 1986 Covers all U.S. and Canadian models	7658
Chevy/GMC Vans 1967-84 Covers all U.S. and Canadian models of 1/2, 3/4, and 1 ton vans, cutaways, and motor home chassis, including diesel engines	6930
Chevy S-10 Blazer/GMC S-15 Jimmy 1982-85 Covers all U.S. and Canadian models	7383
Chevy S-10/GMC S-15 Pick-Ups 1982-85 Covers all U.S. and Canadian models	7310
Chevy II/Nova 1962-79 Covers all U.S. and Canadian models	6841
Chrysler K- and E-Car 1981-85 Covers all U.S. and Canadian front wheel drive models	7163
Colt/Challenger/Vista/Conquest 1971-85 Covers all U.S. and Canadian models	7037
Corolla/Carina/Tercel/Starlet 1970-85 Covers all U.S. and Canadian models	7036
Corona/Cressida/Crown/Mk.II/Camry/Van 1970-84 Covers all U.S. and Canadian models	7044

RTUG Title	Part No.
Corvair 1960-69 Covers all U.S. and Canadian models	6691
Corvette 1953-62 Covers all U.S. and Canadian models	6576
Corvette 1963-84 Covers all U.S. and Canadian models	6843
Cutlass 1970-85 Covers all U.S. and Canadian models	6933
Dart/Demon 1968-76 Covers all U.S. and Canadian models	6324
Datsun 1961-72 Covers all U.S. and Canadian models of Nissan Patrol; 1500, 1600 and 2000 sports cars; Pick-Ups; 410, 411, 510, 1200 and 240Z	5790
Datsun 1973-80 Spanish	7083
Datsun/Nissan F-10, 310, Stanza, Pulsar 1977-86 Covers all U.S. and Canadian models	7196
Datsun/Nissan Pick-Ups 1970-84 Covers all U.S and Canadian models	6816
Datsun/Nissan Z & ZX 1970-86 Covers all U.S. and Canadian models	6932
Datsun/Nissan 1200, 210, Sentra 1973-86 Covers all U.S. and Canadian models	7197
Datsun/Nissan 200SX, 510, 610, 710, 810, Maxima 1973-84 Covers all U.S. and Canadian models	7170
Dodge 1968-77 Covers all U.S. and Canadian models	6554
Dodge Charger 1967-70 Covers all U.S. and Canadian models	6486
Dodge/Plymouth Trucks 1967-84 Covers all 1/2, 3/4, and 1 ton 2- and 4-wheel drive U.S. and Canadian models, including diesel engines	7459
Dodge/Plymouth Vans 1967-84 Covers all 1/2, 3/4, and 1 ton U.S. and Canadian models of vans, cutaways and motor home chassis	6934
D-50/Arrow Pick-Up 1979-81 Covers all U.S. and Canadian models	7032
Fairlane/Torino 1962-75 Covers all U.S. and Canadian models	6320
Fairmont/Zephyr 1978-83 Covers all U.S. and Canadian models	6965
Fiat 1969-81 Covers all U.S. and Canadian models	7042
Fiesta 1978-80 Covers all U.S. and Canadian models	6846
Firebird 1967-81 Covers all U.S. and Canadian models	5996
Firebird 1982-85 Covers all U.S. and Canadian models	7345
Ford 1968-79 Spanish	7084
Ford Bronco 1966-83 Covers all U.S. and Canadian models	7140
Ford Bronco II 1984 Covers all U.S. and Canadian models	7408
Ford Courier 1972-82 Covers all U.S. and Canadian models	6983
Ford/Mercury Front Wheel Drive 1981-85 Covers all U.S. and Canadian models Escort, EXP, Tempo, Lynx, LN-7 and Topaz	7055
Ford/Mercury/Lincoln 1968-85 Covers all U.S. and Canadian models of FORD Country Sedan, Country Squire, Crown Victoria, Custom, Custom 500, Galaxie 500, LTD through 1982, Ranch Wagon, and XL; MERCURY Colony Park, Commuter, Marquis through 1982, Gran Marquis, Monterey and Park Lane; LINCOLN Continental and Towne Car	6842
Ford/Mercury/Lincoln Mid-Size 1971-85 Covers all U.S. and Canadian models of FORD Elite, 1983-85 LTD, 1977-79 LTD II, Ranchero, Torino, Gran Torino, 1977-85 Thunderbird; MERCURY 1972-85 Cougar,	6696

continued on next page

RTUG Title	Part No.
1983-85 Marquis, Montego, 1980-85 XR-7; LINCOLN 1982-85 Continental, 1984-85 Mark VII, 1978-80 Versailles	
Ford Pick-Ups 1965-86 Covers all $^1/_2$, $^3/_4$ and 1 ton, 2- and 4-wheel drive U.S. and Canadian pick-up, chassis cab and camper models, including diesel engines	6913
Ford Pick-Ups 1965-82 Spanish	7469
Ford Ranger 1983-84 Covers all U.S. and Canadian models	7338
Ford Vans 1961-86 Covers all U.S. and Canadian $^1/_2$, $^3/_4$ and 1 ton van and cutaway chassis models, including diesel engines	6849
GM A-Body 1982-85 Covers all front wheel drive U.S. and Canadian models of BUICK Century, CHEVROLET Celebrity, OLDSMOBILE Cutlass Ciera and PONTIAC 6000	7309
GM C-Body 1985 Covers all front wheel drive U.S. and Canadian models of BUICK Electra Park Avenue and Electra T-Type, CADILLAC Fleetwood and deVille, OLDSMOBILE 98 Regency and Regency Brougham	7587
GM J-Car 1982-85 Covers all U.S. and Canadian models of BUICK Skyhawk, CHEVROLET Cavalier, CADILLAC Cimarron, OLDSMOBILE Firenza and PONTIAC 2000 and Sunbird	7059
GM N-Body 1985-86 Covers all U.S. and Canadian models of front wheel drive BUICK Somerset and Skylark, OLDSMOBILE Calais, and PONTIAC Grand Am	7657
GM X-Body 1980-85 Covers all U.S. and Canadian models of BUICK Skylark, CHEVROLET Citation, OLDSMOBILE Omega and PONTIAC Phoenix	7049
GM Subcompact 1971-80 Covers all U.S. and Canadian models of BUICK Skyhawk (1975-80), CHEVROLET Vega and Monza, OLDSMOBILE Starfire, and PONTIAC Astre and 1975-80 Sunbird	6935
Granada/Monarch 1975-82 Covers all U.S. and Canadian models	6937
Honda 1973-84 Covers all U.S. and Canadian models	6980
International Scout 1967-73 Covers all U.S. and Canadian models	5912
Jeep 1945-87 Covers all U.S. and Canadian CJ-2A, CJ-3A, CJ-3B, CJ-5, CJ-6, CJ-7, Scrambler and Wrangler models	6817
Jeep Wagoneer, Commando, Cherokee, Truck 1957-86 Covers all U.S. and Canadian models of Wagoneer, Cherokee, Grand Wagoneer, Jeepster, Jeepster Commando, J-100, J-200, J-300, J-10, J20, FC-150 and FC-170	6739
Laser/Daytona 1984-85 Covers all U.S. and Canadian models	7563
Maverick/Comet 1970-77 Covers all U.S. and Canadian models	6634
Mazda 1971-84 Covers all U.S. and Canadian models of RX-2, RX-3, RX-4, 808, 1300, 1600, Cosmo, GLC and 626	6981
Mazda Pick-Ups 1972-86 Covers all U.S. and Canadian models	7659
Mercedes-Benz 1959-70 Covers all U.S. and Canadian models	6065
Mereceds-Benz 1968-73 Covers all U.S. and Canadian models	5907
Mercedes-Benz 1974-84 Covers all U.S. and Canadian models	6809
Mitsubishi, Cordia, Tredia, Starion, Galant 1983-85 Covers all U.S. and Canadian models	7583
MG 1961-81 Covers all U.S. and Canadian models	6780
Mustang/Capri/Merkur 1979-85 Covers all U.S. and Canadian models	6963
Mustang/Cougar 1965-73 Covers all U.S. and Canadian models	6542
Mustang II 1974-78 Covers all U.S. and Canadian models	6812
Omni/Horizon/Rampage 1978-84 Covers all U.S. and Canadian models of DODGE omni, Miser, 024, Charger 2.2; PLYMOUTH Horizon, Miser, TC3, TC3 Tourismo; Rampage	6845
Opel 1971-75 Covers all U.S. and Canadian models	6575
Peugeot 1970-74 Covers all U.S. and Canadian models	5982
Pinto/Bobcat 1971-80 Covers all U.S. and Canadian models	7027
Plymouth 1968-76 Covers all U.S. and Canadian models	6552
Pontiac Fiero 1984-85 Covers all U.S. and Canadian models	7571
Pontiac Mid-Size 1974-83 Covers all U.S. and Canadian models of Ventura, Grand Am, LeMans, Grand LeMans, GTO, Phoenix, and Grand Prix	7346
Porsche 924/928 1976-81 Covers all U.S. and Canadian models	7048
Renault 1975-85 Covers all U.S. and Canadian models	7165
Roadrunner/Satellite/Belvedere/GTX 1968-73 Covers all U.S. and Canadian models	5821
RX-7 1979-81 Covers all U.S. and Canadian models	7031
SAAB 99 1969-75 Covers all U.S. and Canadian models	5988
SAAB 900 1979-85 Covers all U.S. and Canadian models	7572
Snowmobiles 1976-80 Covers Arctic Cat, John Deere, Kawasaki, Polaris, Ski-Doo and Yamaha	6978
Subaru 1970-84 Covers all U.S. and Canadian models	6982
Tempest/GTO/LeMans 1968-73 Covers all U.S. and Canadian models	5905
Toyota 1966-70 Covers all U.S. and Canadian models of Corona, MkII, Corolla, Crown, Land Cruiser, Stout and Hi-Lux	5795
Toyota 1970-79 Spanish	7467
Toyota Celica/Supra 1971-85 Covers all U.S. and Canadian models	7043
Toyota Trucks 1970-85 Covers all U.S. and Canadian models of pick-ups, Land Cruiser and 4Runner	7035
Valiant/Duster 1968-76 Covers all U.S. and Canadian models	6326
Volvo 1956-69 Covers all U.S. and Canadian models	6529
Volvo 1970-83 Covers all U.S. and Canadian models	7040
VW Front Wheel Drive 1974-85 Covers all U.S. and Canadian models	6962
VW 1949-71 Covers all U.S. and Canadian models	5796
VW 1970-79 Spanish	7081
VW 1970-81 Covers all U.S. and Canadian Beetles, Karmann Ghia, Fastback, Squareback, Vans, 411 and 412	6837

Chilton's Repair & Tune-Up Guides are available at your local retailer or by mailing a check or money order for **$13.95** plus **$3.25** to cover postage and handling to:

Chilton Book Company
Dept. DM
Radnor, PA 19089

NOTE: When ordering be sure to include your name & address, book part No. & title.